Bodies, Borders, Believers

Bodies, Borders, Believers

Ancient Texts and Present Conversations

Essays in Honour of Turid Karlsen Seim on Her 70th Birthday

Edited by
Anne Hege Grung,
Marianne Bjelland Kartzow,
and Anna Rebecca Solevåg

James Clarke & Co

James Clarke & Co
P.O. Box 60
Cambridge
CB1 2NT
United Kingdom

www.jamesclarke.co
publishing@jamesclarke.co

ISBN: 978 0 227 17596 5

British Library Cataloguing in Publication Data
A record is available from the British Library

First published by James Clarke & Co, 2016

Copyright © Marianne Bjelland Kartzow,
Anna Rebecca Solevåg, and Anne Hege Grung, 2016

Published by arrangement
with Pickwick Publications

Contents

PART 4–Patterns of Ambiguity

Acknowledgments

THIS VOLUME IS AN expression of appreciation and gratitude to Turid Karlsen Seim.

As she is celebrating her seventieth birthday she can look back on an outstanding career, where she has made a significant impact through her engagement in ecumenical encounters, as a professor of Theology and New Testament studies and as the Head of Department at the Norwegian Institute in Rome. She was the first woman to receive a doctoral degree in theology from a Norwegian university, the first female professor in New Testament studies in Norway, and until recently the only woman to serve as Dean at the Faculty of Theology at the University of Oslo.

What she has achieved remains an inspiration, particularly to the generation of women academics who have followed. The three editors of this volume are in a particular position of gratitude as her former doctoral students. Seim's special gift for critically reading texts, detailed and thoroughly, has been a great advantage to us.

We would like to thank Svein Helge Birkeflet, Academic Librarian at the theological library at the University of Oslo, for collecting Turid Karlsen Seim's publications in the bibliography at the end of this volume.

This book was made possible with the generous support of several institutions and organizations. We want in particular to thank the Faculty of Theology and the Faculty of Humanities at the University of Oslo, The Church of Norway, and The Norwegian Women's Theologian Association (NKTF) for economical contributions. The editors are also grateful to the three institutions at which they work for seeing the value of this book project. The wonderful staff at the publishing house Wipf and Stock, Pickwick Publications, also deserve thanks for professional and qualified cooperation. Last but not least, we want to thank all the authors for engaging in scholarship corresponding to the broad interests of Turid Karlsen Seim. All articles in this volume are fully the responsibility of each author.

Anne Hege Grung, Marianne Bjelland Kartzow,
and Anna Rebecca Solevåg

Oslo/Stavanger, December 2014

Contributors

David L. Balch, Professor of New Testament, Pacific Lutheran Theological Seminary, California Lutheran University, Graduate Theological Union, Berkeley

André Birmelé, Professor at the Institute for Ecumenical Research (Lutheran World Federation), Strasbourg

Kari Elisabeth Børresen, Senior Professor (Emerita), Theological Gender Studies, Faculty of Theology, University of Oslo.

Adela Yarbro Collins, Buckingham Professor of New Testament Criticism and Interpretation at the Yale University Divinity School

John J. Collins, Holmes Professor of Old Testament, Yale University

Stephanie Dietrich, Professor of Theology and Diaconal Studies at Diakonhjemmet University College, Oslo

Line Cecilie Engh, Postdoctoral Research Fellow at the Department of Philosophy, Classics, History of Art and Ideas, The Norwegian Institute in Rome, University of Oslo

Ingvild Sælid Gilhus, Professor of Religion, University of Bergen

Anne Hege Grung, Associate Professor in Practical Theology, the Practical-Theological Seminary, Oslo

Contributors

David Hellholm, Professor Emeritus, Faculty of Theology, University of Oslo

Marianne Bjelland Kartzow, Professor of New Testament Studies, Faculty of Theology, University of Oslo

Karen L. King, Hollis Professor of Divinity, The Divinity School, Harvard University

Ursula King, FRSA, Professor Emerita of Theology and Religious Studies and Senior Research Fellow, Institute for Advanced Studies, University of Bristol

Outi Lehtipuu, Academy Research Fellow, University of Helsinki

Hugo Lundhaug, Professor of Biblical Reception and Early Christian Literature at the Faculty of Theology, University of Oslo

Margaret Y. MacDonald, Dean of Arts, Saint Mary's University, Halifax, Nova Scotia

Antti Marjanen, Professor of Gnostic Studies, University of Helsinki

Halvor Moxnes, Professor Emeritus, Faculty of Theology, University of Oslo

Katariina Mustakallio, Dean of the School of Language, Translation and Literary Studies, University of Tampere

Anna Rebecca Solevåg, Associate Professor, School of Mission and Theology, Stavanger

Per Sigurd Tveitevåg Styve, Postdoctoral Research Fellow, Department of Arts and Media Studies, Norwegian University of Science and Technology, Trondheim

Olav Fykse Tveit, General Secretary, World Council of Churches

Introduction

"The double message nurtures a dangerous remembrance."

—TURID KARLSEN SEIM,
THE DOUBLE MESSAGE, p. 260

CONCLUDING HER GROUNDBREAKING BOOK on patterns of gender in Luke-Acts, this sentence may also summarize what Turid Karlsen Seim has initiated and contributed to a variety of fields and discourses for more than forty years. In international ecumenical work, as professor of Theology and New Testament Studies, and as Head of Department at the Norwegian Institute in Rome, she has looked critically for double messages hidden in ancient texts or revealed in present conversations. She has contributed with creative and innovative thinking, based on her exceptional gift of reading, ancient texts, or theological documents alike. Seim is herself a pioneer in her interdisciplinary and border-crossing movements, but also as the first woman to receive a doctoral degree in theology from a Norwegian university (in 1990). In this volume colleagues, former students, and friends honor her work and engage with some of the themes central to her scholarship.

This book, titled *Bodies, Borders, Believers,* represents a broad spectrum of issues. Contributors from different contexts with interest in text, history, and contemporary communities, all relate in one way or another to Seim's broad research interests. Among the contributors many scholarly traditions, theoretical orientations and methodological approaches are represented, making this book an interdisciplinary and border-crossing endeavor in itself. This cross-disciplinary collection includes biblical scholars, ecumenical theologians, archeologists, classicists, art historians, and church historians, working side by side to probe the past and its receptions in the present.

There are several reasons why **bodies** matter. In this book, concepts and ideas about bodies as they appear in ancient texts and as they exist in our world as concrete human beings are put under scrutiny. A variety of theories and methods are used in order to emphasize the importance of a critical perspective on the body. To pay attention to birth and lifegiving processes, gender and sexuality, enslaved bodies, life stages, bodily transformations, and metamorphoses reveals how complex human life is and always has been. In what way can we relate to the body? How can we use the body to think with? What kinds of bodies have been and are worth remembering? Is there any continuity between bodies of the past and bodies of the present and, if so, what about the future? To play with Seim's words: How may we reveal the double messages? How may we nurture a dangerous remembrance? How may we probe the complexities of human life?

Borders are there to organize and categorize reality, but they can also be crossed. They may change and many are surprisingly flexible. The distinction between life and not-life is not always fixed in ancient texts, where resurrection, transformation, and immortality disturb the order of such categories. Death is not always the opposite of life, especially if eschatology or metamorphosis is at the center of attention. There are also borders in human life, stable or flexible, between the different life stages, between childhood and adulthood, between being a boy and becoming a man, between children and parents. And there are borders between different groups, such as slave and free, men and women, "Greek and Jew," although the power to uphold them can be contested and negotiated. Some borders can be blurred or porous, for example between religious groups, ethnicities, or traditions, and representatives or members of such groups can meet in dialogue and constructive encounters—or in open conflict. Some transitions have rituals to help the person and its surroundings negotiate and give meaning to change, such as the Christian practice of baptism. To cross borders can be a way of opposing or protesting against status quo. To move between worlds culturally, mentally, or geographically can open up new spaces, but it can also be destabilizing and even threatening. To cross borders has been characteristic of Seim's career. She has crossed borders between research areas, traveled between countries, and challenged and defied norms related to gender and academic leadership.

A central way to categorize those who belong to a religious tradition, in particular the Christian communities, is to call them **believers**. But what do they believe and how are their lives influenced by what they believe? How do such believers relate to each other, how do they agree or disagree, how do they navigate each other's worlds when they do not share values or visions? How do believers from different faiths and religions relate to each other, in particular the three traditions that share the destiny of being called "children of Abraham"?

The early Christian believers, from whom texts in different languages, genres, and shapes have survived, most certainly represented a rather diverse group, concerning background, social status, and the way they interpreted the role of Christ. But these Christ-believers produced documents that are considered canonical in many parts of the world today. Moreover, they are important texts not only as religious foundation but also as cultural memory. The ecumenical dialogue in which Seim has participated for many years represents one important place where these complex processes are discussed and strategies of coexistence and community are explored.

We have divided the various contributions in this volume into four parts. The first part is called *Visions across Time and Space*. Karen L. King contributes with a comparative study of Philo of Alexandria and a contemporary Korean-American Presbyterian Church and examines how they use, however differently, sex-gender strategies to represent and negotiate group boundaries. Outi Lehtipuu's article "No Sex in Heaven—Nor on Earth?" follows, in which the early Christian discourse on resurrection and asceticism is contextualized and scrutinized, with Luke 20:27–38 as the point of departure. Hugo Lundhaug writes about the body of God and the corpus of historiography, related to the anthropomorphic controversy. Stories about Eve have changed as the myth traveled across time and space. Antti Marjanen looks at how the Eve tradition from Genesis is reworked in the *Apocryphon of John*. The ethereal substance of light in early renaissance paintings is the theme of Per Sigurd Tveitevåg Styve's contribution. He shows how the context of medieval optics provided art theorists and artists with a concept of light.

The second part, *Life Stages and Transformations* opens with an article about the transience of ethnic categories. John J. Collins reads the ancient novel *Joseph and Aseneth* as a story about a foreign woman who is transformed into a proper Jewish wife. The transformative idea of resurrection is the focus of Ingvild Sælid Gilhus's article on the apologetic text *Octavius* by Minucius Felix. She discusses the conceptions of animals, human beings, and superhuman beings and their relation to change and permanence. Margaret Y. MacDonald discusses the role of education, socialization, and parenting in early Christian discourse related to Roman ideas about the family, with a special view to Ephesians. Marriage and birth are life stages that together with the concept of slavery were used as salvation metaphors in early Christianity. Anna Rebecca Solevåg asks in what way these salvation metaphors shaped early Christian ideas about slavery, marriage, and birth. Line Cecilie Engh's article is an example of the versatile potential inherent in biblical texts. Engh discusses how Ephesians 5 was used in pro-papal propaganda in the later Middle Ages.

The third part, *Contested Dynamics of Community,* starts with an article by Adela Yabro Collins, who examines ancient texts on female prophecy. Another female religious role is studied by Katariina Mustakallio. She shows how the special identity of the Vestal Virgins of Rome was created by means of rituals, legal and sacral privileges, and obligations and how their social bonds and emotional ties with their original families were regarded. Kari Elisabeth Børresen explores the Roman Catholic teachings on priesthood related to men and women in an *imago Dei* perspective, and relates this to the ecumenical challenge of women priests. Ecumenical dialogue is the focus in the remaining articles in this section. André Birmelé presents development and prospects in the dialogue between Catholics and Lutherans. Olav Fykse Tveit discusses the unity of the church in the light of WCC's general assembly 2014 in Busan. Stephanie Dietrich's contribution focuses on the discussion of the church's identity as a diaconal church and how this should be mirrored in church structures.

The last part, *Patterns of Ambiguity,* deals with texts and contexts in which complex categories like sexuality, gender, and ethnicity are addressed. These categories are often ambiguous, contested, and under constant negotiation. Halvor Moxnes builds on Seim's thesis from *The Double Message* and asks about the place of men and masculinities in Luke's Gospel. David L. Balch compares two Greco-Roman mother-and-son pairs in his article and finds patterns of similarity as well as difference. He reads Luke's portrayal of Jesus and Mary in light of Dionysius of Halicarnassus's portrayal of the Roman warrior Coriolanus and his mother, Veturia. Ursula King lifts up how religious traditions can contribute to the making of peace and how they can confront seeds of violence. Marianne Bjelland Kartzow uses present discussion on reproductive health, infertility, and surrogacy and theories of intersectionality to ask some new questions to various texts dealing with the slave girl Hagar, in particular in Paul's Letter to the Galatians 4:21–31. David Hellholm rereads Rom 1:21–32 and discusses the role of same-sex relations related to the "heathens" Paul is constructing. In the final contribution of this volume Anne Hege Grung presents Muslim and Christian women's readings of sacred texts, looking for strategies and models to deal with complex texts and complex contexts.

All of these articles show the contributors' interest in engaging with Turid Karlsen Seim and her many areas of scholarship. Her outstanding career remains an inspiration. As several of the authors in this volume express, she is valued as colleague, teacher, and mentor. We believe that to continue the conversation, from the past to the present and into the future, and to engage with the "dangerous remembrance" of bodies, borders, and believers is the best way to honor Turid Karlsen Seim.

We would like to end this introduction where we started: with *The Double Message*. Published more than twenty years ago, it still offers an important perspective on Luke-Acts. According to Seim, although Luke is unique in mentioning several women, in particular in the Gospel but also in Acts, there is a certain ideology telling them to be silent and stay out of leadership. It is not merely a question of whether Luke is good or bad news for women; said with the nuanced and complex analytical reasoning that always has characterized Seim's way of reading and interpreting:

> In his narrative Luke manages the extraordinary feat of preserving strong traditions about women and attributing a positive function to them, while at the same time harbouring an ironic dimension that reveals the reasons for the masculine preferences in Acts presentation of the organization of the Christian group, of the public missionary activity and legal defence before the authorities. (p. 259)

Yet, this double message still nurtures a dangerous remembrance.

In honor of Turid Karlsen Seim on her seventieth birthday,
and with the hope that the conversation may continue.

PART I

Visions across Time and Space

1

Comparative Study of Gendered Strategies to Represent the Sacrality of the Group

Philo of Alexandria and a Korean-American Presbyterian Church

Karen L. King

Throughout her distinguished academic career, Turid Karlsen Seim has focused on issues of women and religion. In doing this work, she crossed many borders and boundaries, professionally and geographically, opening up innovative new spaces of inquiry in the field of New Testament Studies and operating on an international scope. This comparative study of sex-gender strategies that are used to represent and negotiate group boundaries is dedicated to her in gratitude for her friendship and appreciation for her leadership in the field.

Introduction

Frequently social tensions that arise in contemporary pluralistic societies appear to concern issues about gender, women's roles, or sexual ethics. Dress, driving, same-sex marriage, child brides, genital cutting, contraception, and abortion come quickly to mind among others. Many of these are at times linked with particular religious groups, either by a group's self-representation or in popular imagination and rhetoric. Although they receive media attention almost solely when sparking conflict, sociologists note that encounters between groups in pluralistic settings can lead to instabilities that potentially also engender innovative negotiation, both within the group and in relation to outsiders. In this essay, I want to ask what might be learned about sites of conflict and negotiation by inquiring comparatively about how religious-ethnic groups deploy sex-gender strategies to construct group boundaries. The study will focus on comparing Philo of Alexandria and Korean-American Presbyterians in Chicago.

My analysis draws heavily on the comparative method described by David Frankfurter.[1] Four of his points are particularly helpful. The first is that "comparison is the very foundation of *generalization*, which historians do habitually, with every second-order term they use or system they observe."[2] Such terms include *inter alia* "ethnicity," "gender," and "religion." Each of these can be considered to be a "second-order, heuristic category of classification that implies applicability to a particular spectrum of like data."[3] From this perspective, it is clear that choosing which cases are relevant for the topic at hand already implies involvement in comparative work. My initial choice of cases implicitly assumed a complex, second-order pattern of social analysis that focuses selectively on certain aspects of human social life and not others. I chose Philo and Korean-American Presbyterians for comparison because differences as well as similarities loom large from the outset. Both are "foreign" minority groups (Jews and Korean Christians) in religiously and ethnically plural societies (ancient Alexandria and contemporary Chicago) with historical and immediate relations to "imperial" powers (Greece/Rome and China/US). And yet they appear in contexts that are widely divergent in many obvious respects, including time, geographical location, and culture.

A second point concerns the status of second-order terms and patterns. As Frankfurter writes, "We do not, of course, delude ourselves with the impression that the patterns exist apart from their *heuristic* function in making sense of religion in context or that they grasp in any way the totality of content or experience. They simply aid us in making sense of phenomena and in bringing our observations to new situations."[4] Frankfurter's point emphasizes that such heuristic, posited patterns are subject to reconsideration and rectification. Indeed reflexive critique of the categories and pattern is crucial both to the method and to the goal of the comparison. What does

---

1. Frankfurter, "Comparison."
2. Ibid., 85.
3. Ibid.
4. Ibid., 88.

comparison of Philo and Korean-American Presbyterians help us to see that we do not by looking at each case in isolation?

Third, Frankfurter notes that the frequently stated concern that one cannot control the necessary data across widely dispersed fields misses the point: "(I)t is not infinitely broad expertise that is required to invite a comparison but a sense of what it is one is trying to describe, to form, to clarify."[5] This formulation is an invitation to consider the goals of the project. In this study, my initial interest was in using comparison to help deepen my understanding of how sex-gender discourses function in group self-definition, the limits and possibilities.

Finally, as a procedural method, Frankfurter suggests beginning exploration "*not* with the question, 'what is this datum *like*?' but rather by asking, 'Of what phenomenon or system in religion might the datum be an *example*?'" He emphasizes that "one uses the pattern not as a static grid to force on the data but as (a) a gauge of *difference* among cases across history while also a principle for *relating* those cases . . . ; (b) a hypothetical *dynamic system* in which a text or archeological datum makes sense *pending additional data*; and (c) a means of bringing an historical artifact—text, object, event—into broader conversation with humanistic inquiry, not as an amusing anecdote or exotic anomaly but as a critically described *case* of some revealingly human phenomenon."[6] This procedure gives a central place to my initial assumption that the data under examination are examples of an operative pattern in which gender ideologies that mark religious-ethnic boundaries and work rhetorically and performatively to establish identities are themselves unstable. It is this way of framing the pattern that opens the question of what happens when those ideologies are overtly called into question.[7]

Part of the comparative project includes attention to the modern frameworks of analysis, both those of the modern studies on which I rely and certain assumptions of my own framework. In the discussion of the two cases that follow I draw on a number of contemporary scholars, but rely in particular upon the work of Maren Niehoff for Philo and Kelly Chong for Korean-Americans. Both take up Frederik Barth's anthropological, circumstantialist framework in which ethnicity is not treated as a fixed, primordial,

---

5. Ibid., 92.

6. Ibid., 98.

7. Much happens of course "under the radar," so to speak. Many changes are not brought to overt speech, in part an effect of where attention is directed ("don't look here"; "this cannot be spoken"). The strategy of silence (and silencing) can be one of the most effective modes of negotiation, as well as of maintaining the status quo, but here I will consider only sites of overt tension.

and essentialized characteristic identifying an homogeneous group, but rather ethnicity is understood to be shaped strategically in particular contexts in interaction with others. In my framework, the relation of religion and sex-gender discourses to this dynamic is not predetermined, but appears differentially depending upon particular aims as well as constraining and enabling conditions. Essentializing representations of ethnicity, religion, or sex-gender norms are treated as rhetorical and discursive constructions mobilized toward certain aims but producing multiple effects. Both Philo and Korean-Americans naturalize (constructed) categories of sex-gender and rhetorically value morality in terms of performative deviation from a normative gender script, but, as we will see, each is negotiating particular circumstances in which their categories and valuations are being contested in certain limited regards.[8] Similarly, although Philo and Korean-Americans use the terms "*Iudaios*" and "Christian" respectively as if their meanings were fixed, each is deeply implicated in projects of defining and negotiating what it means to be Jewish or Christian, respectively. I use the term "religion" to discuss these projects, but with the caveat that this term, too, is a second-order heuristic category with a complex history in modernity.[9]

Let's turn now to consider each of the two cases separately before returning to comparison. While the brief and highly selective exposition of these cases certainly does not do justice to their full complexities, my hope is that it will provide a mapping of the territory which will allow certain broader points of comparison to appear.

Philo of Alexandria

Philo (c. 20 BCE—50 CE) was a Greek-speaking Jew living in Alexandria, in the Roman province of Egypt. He came from a wealthy and distinguished family, and authored a relatively large corpus of philosophically sophisticated literature treating special topics and books of Scripture (LXX).[10] Later in life, he acted as the leader of a Jewish delegation to the Roman emperor Caligula following the widespread violence against Jews that broke out in Alexandria in 38 CE. Two of his treatises deal with the strained situation of the Jews of Alexandria under Roman rule (*Legatio ad Gaius* and *In Flaccum*). Although scholars are not entirely certain about the precise legal

8. For a performative treatment of sex-gender, see especially Butler, *Undoing Gender*.

9. For an incisive sketch of that history, see Smith, "Religion, Religions, Religious."

10. See Barclay, *Jews in the Mediterranean Diaspora*, 158–80.

status of Jews under Ptolemaic or Roman rule, the sources seem to indicate, as Barclay argues, that under the previous Greek, Ptolemaic regime, the Jews in Alexandria had been recognized as "privileged residents," not aliens, a status far above that of other non-resident aliens as well as Egyptians. In particular, their right to practice their "ancestral laws" was ensured. In 38 CE, however, the Roman governor Flaccus dissolved these privileges, and it is in the aftermath of this change of status, as well as the anti-Jewish violence, that Philo wrote the two treatises.[11] Maren Niehoff argues that, in these latter treatises in particular, it is possible to read Philo's attempts to negotiate an esteemed position for Jews within the Roman world, and Egypt in particular.

In what follows I rely in particular on her illuminating monograph, *Philo on Jewish Identity and Culture*. There she offers an analysis of "the ways in which Philo constructed Jewish identity and culture in first-century Alexandria."[12] Her book draws heavily on patterns of ethnic grouping developed by the Norwegian anthropologist, Fredrik Barth, in which the focus is on the processes of generating and maintaining ethnic groups, and on ethnic boundaries and boundary maintenance.[13] Niehoff's use of his framework results in a variety of results useful for our topic of religion, gender, identity, and boundaries. I limit myself to those areas that fit this topical interest, stressing that gender is only one site among others in Philo's strategic, rhetorical construction of Jewish identity.

A major strength of Niehoff's analysis is to show how Philo aims to negotiate the place of Jews in the context of Roman Egypt. As she concludes: "The way in which he [Philo] constructed Jewish descent, significant Others and distinctly Jewish values are interpreted in light of contemporary Roman concerns."[14] She also emphasizes that Philo is neither representative of Jewish diaspora nor is his the only voice or position. Often he appears to be formulating his position directly against those of other Jews, as well as in response to the views of non-Jews, including Egyptians and Romans. While he is highly literate in Greek culture, Niehoff stresses that his views "have to be appreciated not only vis-à-vis Greek culture, but also in relation to the discourse among Romans, Egyptians and other Jews of various political colours."[15] In short, with Philo we find ourselves engaging with the positionality of an elite male member of a minority group in a multi-religious,

---

11. See ibid., 48–71; see also Modrzejewski, *The Jews of Egypt*, 161–83.

12. Niehoff, *Philo*, 1.

13. See Barth, Introduction, esp. 199.

14. Niehoff, *Philo*, 9; see also 6–9.

15. Ibid., 13.

imperial context in which certain tensions are evident. Some concern disagreements among Alexandrian Jews over various perspectives and practices in relation to their wider environment.[16] Others are framed in reaction to disparagement of distinctive Jewish practices (like circumcision) or the violence against Jews under Flaccus, including setting up images of the emperor Gaius Caligula in Alexandrian synagogues, and later Jewish retaliation during the reign of Claudius.[17]

Much of Philo's writing concerning Jewish identity can be read as attempts to negotiate these tensions, and certain gendered positions arguably belong to this larger enterprise. We will discuss three: the role of maternal descent in establishing Jewish identity; gender strategies in setting boundaries (esp. of Egyptians as the Other); and portraying the superiority of Jewish religiously-based sexual mores to position Jews as superior to other groups.

Maternal descent in Judaism first appears in the Roman imperial period.[18] Niehoff notes how Philo's early and innovative treatment of this topic coincides with Roman policy that rigorously distinguished ethnic groups (Romans, Greeks, Alexandrian citizens, Jews, Metropolitans, and Egyptians) in terms of social class and taxed each at a different rate.[19] The status of mothers played a determinative role in assigning status to offspring.[20] Niehoff argues that Philo's emphasis on Jewish maternal descent was articulated in this context: "He asserted the superior standing of the Jews by constructing their descent in a way which conformed to Roman perspectives and policies."[21] Philo's main focus was therefore not on purity, but on the civil status of the mother,[22] and he reinterpreted Biblical stories to fit this new social reality.[23] In his hands, foreign women married to important Biblical figures (such as Hagar, Zilpah, Bilhah, and Tamar) were transformed into exemplary Jewish matriarchs.[24] Niehoff concludes, "As an upper-class citizen, he (Philo) emphatically asserted the high social status and proper Jewishness of the Biblical matriarchs. He accepted neither slaves

---

16. See Barclay, *Jews in the Mediterranean Diaspora*, 103–228.

17. See the discussion of ibid., 55–60.

18. See Cohen, *The Beginning of Jewishness*, 263–307. Cohen also notes the gendered character of conversion history and practice (306–7)—another relevant topic for gender, religion, and border-crossings.

19. Niehoff, *Philo*, 20.

20. Ibid., 21.

21. Ibid., 22.

22. Ibid., 17–18.

23. For a general discussion of this phenomenon, see Gruen, *Heritage and Hellenism*.

24. See Niehoff, *Philo*, 23–33.

nor foreigners in the pedigree of the Jews."[25] Philo's exclusion of slaves and foreigners from Jewish pedigree is in line with Roman practice that placed such groups at the lowest levels of social status.

Moreover, Niehoff points to Barth's argument that in a multi-ethnic society where boundary-crossing contact is "pervasive and unavoidable," the construction of a strong Other is a rhetorically crucial foundation for tightening a group's boundaries.[26] She notes that Philo is most clearly engaging in this kind of boundary work in portraying low-status Egyptians as the feminized Other over against his positive portrait of masculine Jews. His rhetoric is, however, more complex in relating Jews to Greeks and Romans. Philo painted these relations as complementary, while yet portraying Jews as superior to Greeks (who had learned much from Moses), and ultimately even to Romans, although he aligned Jews most closely with the latter.[27] As Niehoff shows, however, not all Jews in Alexandria would have accepted Philo's positionality, and Philo tends to portray Jews who cross his stringent boundaries too far as deserters.[28]

One strategy among others in Philo's arsenal is the claim of superior piety and values, including strict sexual mores.[29] He claims that Jewish women, unlike other women in their urban environment, are exemplary in their modesty and are entirely segregated. He also charges that the Egyptians engage in licentiousness and incestuous marriages; the Greeks, in homoerotic relations. Even the Roman general Mark Antony, he suggests, could be overcome by the wiles of Cleopatra and thus become feminized and un-Roman, but the Jewish patriarch Joseph in contrast refused Potiphar's wife and displayed Jewish zeal for continence, piety, and masculine self-control. In general, however, Philo aligns Jewish sexual and family values with those of the Romans.

Mary Rose D'Angelo fills out and extends Niehoff's portrait focusing more precisely on the gendered aspects of Philo's connection of Jewish piety to Roman family values. She argues that:

> Philo's creative apologetic response . . . does not reproduce Roman law or the moral propaganda that accompanied it, but represents the moral demands of Judaism as meeting, and indeed exceeding, those of the imperial order. He thus assures both the Jews of Alexandria and their Roman masters that Jewish sexual

25. Ibid., 32.

26. See ibid., 45; Barth, Introduction, 198–99.

27. See Niehoff, *Philo*, 45–74.

28. See ibid., 46

29. See ibid., 75–110, esp. 95–105.

> probity, marital chastity and familial devotion are of such a high standard that the Jewish tradition can instruct the empire and its subjects in the piety, restraint and manliness that enable rule of the world.[30]

She points out one additional element that will be useful to comparison below. In Philo's interpretive hands, the fifth commandment to honor parents is broadened to include patron-client and ruler-subject relations as part of the Mosaic legislation. In this way, D'Angelo suggests, Philo is able to formulate Jewish piety "in response to the gendered protocols of imperial family values."[31] She concludes that Philo refers to the fifth commandment to argue that Jewish devotion to the one God and to Mosaic legislation are what "makes the Jews the most moral and law-abiding, the most family-oriented and responsible of the emperors' subjects."[32]

The interpretive adaptation of Scripture to negotiate the situation of Alexandrian Jews as a criticized minority group in Roman Egypt is striking, but no less so than Philo's strategies of group boundary setting in relation to Roman legal, civic, and discursive norms of sex, family, and masculinity. In defending and promoting the status of Alexandrian Jews, Philo adopted and adapted Roman ideology that valorized obedient subordination to Roman rule, reinscribed Roman social, gender, and ethnic hierarchies, and hardened civic identity around the ethnic status of mothers. These reinscriptions involved to some extent rewriting the story of Hebrew slaves in Egypt and shifting the ethnic identity of important matriarchs, while simultaneously portraying a denigrated Egyptian Other against which Jewish superiority could be highlighted. It is hard not to conclude that, in the context of the violence against Jews in Alexandria, Philo perceived what was at stake in the status of Jews in Alexandria to be no less than their safety and even survival under Roman rule. Indeed only decades later, Jewish revolts in the eastern Mediterranean resulted in the nearly complete destruction of the Jewish community in Alexandria.[33] Philo's works survived only through Christian mediation.[34]

---

30. D'Angelo, "Gender and Geopolitics," 64–65; see also esp. 75–81, 88.

31. Ibid., 75.

32. Ibid., 74.

33. See Barclay, *Jews in the Mediterranean Diaspora*, 78–81; Modrzejewski, *The Jews of Egypt*, 198–205.

34. See Runia, *Philo in Early Christian Literature*.

Korean–American Presbyterians

The history of Korean-American Christians is tied to both US missions in Korea and US immigration policy. The first Protestant missionaries in Korean were US citizens: Horace Allen (a Presbyterian physician in 1884), Horace Underwood (Presbyterian, 1885), and Rev. and Mrs. Henry Appenzeller (Methodists, also 1885). By the early twentieth century groups of Protestant missionaries and churches in Korea were working together to found hospitals and universities. Because of these efforts, Korean Christians have played strong roles in education and medicine in the modern period. In addition, the persecution of Christians during Japanese occupation gave Christians a reputation for supporting Korean nationalism and contributed to their prominence after Korean independence. The presence of the US military during and following the Korean War also worked to solidify ties between Korea and the US.[35]

US immigration policy, however, tells its own story. While a few persons immigrated already in the late nineteenth century and prominent individuals were educated in the US, larger numbers of Koreans arrived only with shifts in US immigration policy, first in 1952 (especially for spouses of military servicemen) and then more rapidly in 1965 when quotas for Asians were abolished. Koreans have been in the top five countries of origin for immigration since 1975. Between 70–80% of Korean-Americans identify as Christian, with the largest denomination being the PCUSA.[36]

In this essay, I want to focus briefly on two scenarios: Kelly Chong's sociological study of second-generation Korean Americans at two ethnic churches in Chicago in 1995 (Presbyterian Church USA and Methodist), and the 2010 General Assembly of the PCUSA.

Chong's study offers evidence contrary to the assimilationist paradigm of US immigration, which postulates that second-generations reject "native" religion and ethnicity in favor of the American "melting pot." Instead, her study documents the vitality of second generation Korean Americans' robust ethnic church affiliation. She argues that "when an ethnic group is faced with a strong sense of social marginalization believed to arise from its racial status, the ethnic church can play a dominant role in the group's quest for identity and a sense of belonging."[37] From her analysis, she concludes that the Korean ethnic church supports a defensive and exclusive identity in two key ways: "first, through a general institutional transmission

35. See Kim, *History of Christianity in Korea*; Moffatt, *The Christians of Korea*.

36. See Chong, "What It Means to Be Christian," 260; Lee, "From the Coercive to the Liberative," 76–84.

37. Chong, "What It Means to Be Christian," 259; see also 262, 268.

of Korean culture and second, by the way a set of core traditional Korean values are legitimized and sacralized through the identification with conservative Christian morality and worldview."[38] Her method is ethnographic, as a participant-observer and conducting interviews. The theoretical framework engages sociological work on immigration and especially ethnicity,[39] but she, too draws on Frederik Barth's work.[40]

Chong's study lets us see the ways in which the tension between the desire to maintain ethnic identity and the pressure to assimilate exerted by mainstream denominational structures[41] is productive in adaptively negotiating the intersecting boundaries of religion, ethnicity, and gender.[42] As in Niehoff's study of Philo, she found appeal to a superior sexual morality to be a part of the group's self-construction. Strategies involved advocating proper male/female distinctions in dress styles, segregating men and women,[43] forbidding pre-marital sex, and emphasizing hierarchical relations of respect and obedience toward parents, elders, and men generally. While noting that Korean Americans affirm the same family and sexual values and conduct as other conservative American Christians, Chong states that gender and age-based hierarchies reflect particularly Korean (Confucian) values. In this way, identifying themselves and their values as Christian worked to "sacralize" Korean social values. As interviewees put it: "The more you believe in God, the more Korean you tend to be," and "You have to become Korean to become Christian."[44] Chong found that eliding Korean and Christian identity served to justify other kinds of conduct aimed at facilitating strong ethnic group boundaries and bonding, such as intragroup marriage.

At the same time, emphasis upon these values allowed members to consider their practice of Christianity superior to that of (other) Americans. One example is in the way that Biblical interpretation of the fifth commandment to honor parents is used both to reinforce Korean age and

38. Ibid., 259.

39. See ibid., 262–66. For another approach focused on transnationalism and religion, see Levitt, *God Needs No Passport.*

40. See Chong, "What It Means to Be Christian," 269, where she notes his point that "basic value orientations" are crucial to setting group boundaries."

41. See Lee, "Fruits and Challenge," a study of Protestant Korean Christians in the US which provides an illuminating discussion of this issue.

42. A problem for me in her framework is what seems to be a sharp and uninterrogated distinction between religion and ethnicity (see esp. Chong, "What It Means To Be Christian," 265), but it is clearly one shared by her informants who speak overtly about the troubled relation between being Christian and being Korean.

43. Bible classes, for example, are "strictly gender-segregated" (ibid., 274).

44. See ibid., 273.

gender-related family hierarchies and reciprocally to mark the superiority of Korean Christianity over white American social values and practices. Chong also points more broadly to "visceral critiques of American society which seem to crop up ubiquitously in sermons." She concludes: "In this fusion of Christian and Korean worldviews, the rationale for boundary maintenance becomes one of conservative morality, which is articulated in its critique against the 'moral decay' of society, including sexual immorality, extreme individualism, relativism, and lack of family values and discipline."[45] Here we might point again to Barth's point that self-definition requires an Other. Sex-gender strategies ("conservative morality") thus aimed to strengthen inner-group ties and to offer a positive valuation of Korean identity in the context of white racism.

Such strategies, however, are not without their own complexities. For example, within the Korean ethnic church, intergenerational tensions over gender roles occur that intersect with broader tensions in the US over racial/ethnic diversity, sexuality (esp. pre-marital and same-sex relations), and women's roles in religion and society. Chong notes that, particularly among younger and second-generation Korean Christians, push-back occurs against a variety of practices and attitudes, such as the views that women are supposed to be submissive and accept a top-down administration and decision-making process; girls are not supposed to be friendly with boys; and widows are encouraged not to remarry but to be devoted and chaste to their deceased husband and his family.[46] Ambivalence is felt not only in tensions with the values of the wider society but in the fact that the Korean ethnic church "serves a classic 'double function': as an apology and legitimation for the status quo, but also as a means of empowerment, protest, and liberation for the socially subordinate group."[47] Chong argues that the high valuation attached to female submission sharpened the ambivalence felt especially by women members.

An example of this ambivalence was on full display at the 2010 General Assembly of the PCUSA, held in Minneapolis, MN. Participants in this annual meeting were asked to consider an "overture" to establish a non-geographical Korean language presbytery within the Synod of the South Atlantic. In the discussion of this overture (G-04.08), three second-generation, Korean-American women clergy spoke against it.[48] In a later account of the

45. Ibid., 279.

46. Ibid., 277.

47. Ibid., 282.

48. In the same assembly, it can be noted, Korean American Presbyterians actively opposed the ordination of same-sex persons (see "Korean Congregations Issue Plea to Support Amendment O," *The Layman Online*, at http://www.layman.org/news7ebb/

event, one of the women, Theresa Cho, elaborated her reasoning, saying that:

> just as Korean-speaking pastors and elders find it challenging to participate in presbyteries that are primarily English-speaking, women have difficulty participating in Korean-language presbyteries, because their voices traditionally are not honored and respected. Our contention was that Korean women are most likely to have a voice when they are able to speak with the whole body of the church rather than only within the Korean community. A Korean American presbytery would create an insular environment and promote male-only leadership.[49]

The assembly supported the women clergy and voted 514–125 against the overture. In the aftermath, however, the three women clergy were harassed and told they were betraying their race/ethnic group. Theresa Cho, for example, was charged by male Korean pastors with pursuing her own agenda to gain personal power at the expense of the Korean group. In my view, this reaction works less to reveal Rev. Cho's motives than it does to expose the fragility of the "double function" strategy which attempts to empower Koreans in the context of white racism in the US by justifying women's subordination.

In an on-line essay posted on the Website of the Presbyterian Mission Agency, Mary Paik, a senior pastor in the PCUSA, reflected on these events in terms of her own experience within the Korean-American church across more than three decades.[50] Her comments thoughtfully lay out the complexity of the issues involved: power struggles within the PCUSA; difficulties of Korean-speaking parishioners within a largely English-speaking denomination; shifting American values of gender and sexual equality in (ordained) leadership and marriage, including controversies over same-sex relations; white racism, including struggles about "inclusivity" and "racial justice"; and generational change and conflict. This complexity makes it quite clear that the sacralizing of sex-gender norms as a strategy for strengthening ethnic boundary-setting, such that gender, ethnicity and religion are aggregated in group self-definition, will always be partial, fragmentary, and unstable. This instability can be perceived as unsettling but it offers the potential for alternative constructive performances. I think, for example, of Sang Chang, a Korean New Testament scholar, ordained Presbyterian minister, and former president of Ewha University, who is now the President of the World

[accessed May 29, 2014]).

49. Cho, "Room to Speak," 13.

50. See Paik, "A Reflection."

Council of Churches from Asia. The exemplary public leadership of this Korean Presbyterian woman on the global stage offers its own argument for implementing new intersections of ethnicity, religion, and gender in the US as well.

Comparison

One of the things that struck me most forcefully in reflecting on these two cases was how similar are the sex-gender strategies used by Philo and Korean-American Presbyterians. In both cases, sex-gender discourse is used:

- to define and police religious-ethnic identity and boundaries in terms of superior heteronormative morality and masculinity;
- to define the character of (ideal) inner-group bonds in terms of hierarchical relations of obedience, duty, and respect among members defined by sex-gender status and norms;
- and to police individuals' sexual and gendered behaviors.

While these similarities are produced in part by the heuristic framework of analysis, that is, the second-order terms and pattern that selectively highlighted certain elements, they are nonetheless striking given the distance between the two cases in time, geography, and culture. The similarities do become more muted and dissipated when differences are considered—not least in ancient versus modern sex-gender discourses, notions of race/ethnicity, and political organization (empire and nation state), among others.

Differences appear by looking at the specific contexts in which the sex-gender strategies are deployed. For Philo, the context is the imperial Roman lowering of the status of Alexandrian Jews relative to other ethnic groups (Greeks and Egyptians), as well as the violence against Jews that broke out in 38 CE. For Korean-Americans Christians, the context is immigration of a minority ethnic group into the USA, a democratic but white racist nation state where Christianity is highly valorized. In both contexts, groups are ranked on a scale that rhetorically correlates social status with conformity to established (or perceived) norms of ethics and morality, thus enabling gendered strategies of empowerment. In this context, one of Philo's arguments is that Jews should be ranked higher due to their superior continence and masculinity, and their ethnic privileges restored and protected, while Korean-American Presbyterians assert the superiority of their strict gender/age hierarchies and heterosexual family relations, and, partially on that basis, claim an appropriate position of prestige and respect within the PCUSA.

Comparison illuminates how similar strategies serve these contextually differing aims. Three examples will serve as illustrations:

- Both Philo and Korean-American ministers appeal to Scripture to attest their exemplary piety. Each cites the fifth commandment to honor parents in order to emphasize the gender subordination of female to male, children to parents. They do so, however, in service of different aims. According to Niehoff, Philo appeals to the commandment to align Jews with broader Roman social structures—not just the ancient patriarchal family, but patron-client and imperial ruler-subject relations. The Korean-Americans Chong studied, on the other hand, appeal to it to distinguish themselves from other types of American parent-child relations and to intensify conformity to strictly hierarchical norms of gender and age within the Korean church group.

- Both Philo and the leadership of the Chicago Korean Presbyterian Church also argue for segregation of women and female chastity as markers of group superiority. But for Philo, this behavior is represented as conforming to and surpassing Roman values and practices, while for the Korean Church, it is contrasted with deficient mainstream US American values and practices.

- Finally, both assume distinct sex-gendered roles of male and female in a variety of realms including family, education, space, and leadership (although the specifics of each of these differ), and they define "deviant" sexual behaviors as those belonging to inferior "Others" (e.g., incest, adultery, same-sex relations—again not understood precisely the same way). Yet while both appeal to sacred texts and sacralizing discourse to mark sex-gender values as specifically Jewish or Christian, Philo is attempting to use this discourse to align himself with Roman (imperial) "family values," while Korean-Americans are using it to distinguish themselves from "American decadence."

What comparison clearly shows in these examples is that any particular sex-gender strategy is not predictably tied to a particular aim, but can be deployed to do a wide variety of work socially and politically.

It might seem, however, that the strategies are aimed in different directions. Philo's argument appears to be set over against religious others (Romans, Greeks, Egyptians), while the Chicago church's argument is an intra-religious (Presbyterian) matter. Yet Philo is implicitly defining what it means to be Jewish even as the Chicago church is defining what it means to be properly Christian, and both are deploying discourses of strict female chastity and subordination, as well as rejection of same-sex relations, to mark group superiority in pluralistic contexts.[51] That is, no matter where the strategies are immediately and consciously aimed, setting borders has reciprocal (and perhaps unintended) implications for determining who are insiders as well as for positioning a group within the broader, socially plural context.

Not only aims, but outcomes can be considered. The ultimate failure of Philo's negotiation of the complexities of being Jewish in the pluralistic social context of Roman Alexandria raises questions about possible outcomes of Korean-American Presbyterians' negotiation of US society. While Philo may have had some, perhaps even considerable, influence in his own day, subsequent Jewish revolts resulted in the destruction of the Alexandrian Jewish community under Roman rule,[52] and in the long term it was the rabbis whose strategies of group self-definition would come to dominate Jewish practice. Might this history suggest relativizing the sex-gender strategies of Korean-American church leaders in light of powerful factors such as patterns of immigration, shifts in US racial demographics, or the effectiveness of civil rights legislation? Might the increasing percentage of Koreans in the PCUSA lead to appropriation of Korean values of gender and age hierarchies within that denomination, or might the rhetorical linkage of those values to Korean ethnicity undermine a broader impact among non-Korean-Americans? Or might something else entirely occur? It is not possible to say, not least because such strategies have multiple, often unpredicted effects. In the case of the Chicago church, the appeal to strict sexual mores and segregation, especially for women, puts pressure on members to conform to group-distinctive behaviors, but the effects varied: some were drawn to deepen ties with the church further into the group, while others, especially Korean youth, became alienated. We can imagine similarly multiple responses to Philo's attempts to define Jewish identity in terms of normative Roman and Jewish sex-gender mores, given the evidence of varied and divergent practices by Jews in Alexandria and Egypt more broadly.[53] Indeed Philo's nephew serves as one example of the possibilities and limits for advancement for elite Jews within the Roman imperial system.[54]

51. The requirement of in-group marriage would be an additional arena of tension and contention.

52. See Modrzejewski, *The Jews of Egypt*, 161–83, 198–205; Barclay, *Jews in Mediterranean Diaspora*, 48–81.

53. See, for example, Barclay, *Jews in the Mediterranean Diaspora*, 103–228. Although his framework of analysis, which evaluates practices according to "levels of assimilation," is problematic, his study offers fascinating evidence of a variety of behaviors and attitudes among Egyptian Jews.

54. See Modrzejewski, *The Jews of Egypt*, 185–90.

Comparison does caution against assuming that Korean-American sex-gender strategies will be effective at strengthening a positive ethnic group identity in the US in the long term.

One "crack" already became apparent in the challenge of Korean-American woman ministers to the establishment of Korean-language presbyteries in which their roles would potentially be diminished. The success of their challenge within the PCUSA suggests that much depends on the broader social context. In the US, debates over women's roles, constructions of masculinity, and GLBTQ sexualities destabilize strategies that sacralize sex-gender norms of heterosexual-reproductive marriage and male dominance. In this climate, deploying a conservative sex-gender discourse based on gender and age hierarchies makes Korean-American Christians' assertions of superiority on sex-gender grounds vulnerable, as is seen when second-generation Korean-Americans question women's subordination, the exclusion of younger members from decision-making, or (less frequently) the disparagement of GLBTQ sexualities. Moreover, insofar as gender and age subordination and the emphasis on natal family (including heterosexual marriage and reproduction) are specified as ethnically Korean values, resistance to them implies a critique of the linkage of ethnicity to religion (i.e., of tying being Korean to being truly Christian). As we saw with the women pastors who challenged the establishment of a Korean-language presbytery, challenging women's subordination within the church could be perceived not only as contrary to Christian teaching on gender roles but as a breach of ethnic loyalty. What does this imply about how gender, ethnicity, and religion are related? Comparison again is helpful.

Arguable, the rhetoric of both Philo and some Korean-American Presbyterian ministers naturalizes gender (i.e., certain constructed and performative sex-gender norms). With regard to ethnicity and religion, however, difference appears. In Philo's construction of being Jewish, no terms distinguishing religion from ethnicity are operating,[55] while in the Chicago Church case, the categories of "Christian" (religion) and "Korean"

---

55. Scholars generally agree that the term "religion" is a modern Western concept arising and functioning within certain discourse. But Burrus notes that "one might also say that it is in late antiquity that something *like* a mapping of religious identity first emerges, as a complex effect of both Roman imperialism and the rise of Christianity, each of which profoundly unsettles proper links between ethnicity, locality and cult, thus giving rise to discursive strategies of ethical-religious subjectification partly disembedded from race or place" ("Mapping as Metamorphosis," 9). Burrus then asks: "Is religious discourse then mapped in antiquity as a competition among cultural claimants of masculine perfection? Alternatively, is it mapped as an irruption of ambivalently subversive or counterhegemonic genders to which empire paradoxically gives rise?" (10) She answers both questions in the affirmative.

(ethnicity/race) are treated as separable domains, and their relationship is a topic of overt reflection and dispute. Indeed what is under dispute is precisely the apparent strategy of the some Korean-American Presbyterian ministers to attempt, as Philo does,[56] to aggregate sex-gender practices, ethnic identity, and religious sacrality (i.e., obedience respectively to Mosaic legislation or Scripture). That is, they aggregate being Korean, being Christian, and observing certain sex-gender values and practices into the rhetorically constructed bundle of proper Presbyterian identity. The potential in modernity to disaggregate religion, ethnicity, and gender, however, implies that challenge to any one category exposes not only the instabilities of each, but opens fractures and cracks in their posited alignment. The wide availability of such distinctions in modern social discourse (and not just in academic analysis) makes disaggregation easier than for Philo. It is such disaggregation that potentially leads to greater instabilities, increased need for negotiation, and possibilities for new modes of performing race, sexuality, and sacrality. It is perhaps ironic that the invention of the categories of "religion, religions, religious" has come to offer potentials most certainly unforeseen by those who invented and deployed them for quite different ends.

Concluding Reflections

The similarities of the sex-gender strategies of Philo and Korean-American Christians demonstrate the perdurance of hetero-normative sex-gender strategies to empower minority ethnic and religious minority groups. As I noted at the beginning of this essay, however, the instabilities in group strategies and encounters as well as shifts in performative contexts can also lead to innovative negotiation. Indeed any pattern used to analyze how sex-gender strategies are deployed to define group boundaries needs to have room for potential opposition, resistance, and negotiation, as well as alternative strategies for adaptation to varying social-material-political conditions. The complexity of forces at play in the contemporary world offer many possibilities. Among these, the possibility for the discursive disaggregation of sex-gender from religion and ethnicity may suggest particularly rich possibilities.

　　In the end, the hope for me is that the religious tradition I share in common with Koreans and with these fellow Americans may (continue to) work to provide a space for fully realizing democratic values of respect for

56. See the discussion of Buell, *"Why This New Race?,"* regarding both the discursive stability and the possibilities for ethnic mutability in Mediterranean antiquity.

people, young and old, of all sexualities and racial-ethnic groups, as well as for activism in securing protection from violence and discrimination. In this hope, I take inspiration in looking to Turid Karlsen Seim, whose life and work have been in the service of just such goals.

Bibliography

Barclay, John M. G. *Jews of the Mediterranean Diaspora from Alexander to Trajan (323 BCE—117 CE)*. Berkeley: University of California Press, 1996.

Barth, Fredrik. Introduction to *Ethnic Groups and Boundaries* (1969). Reprinted in *Process and Form in Social Life: Selected Esays of Fredrik Barth*, 1:198–227. London: Routledge, 1981.

Buell, Denise Kimber. *"Why This New Race?" Ethnic Reasoning in Early Christianity*. New York: Columbia University Press, 2005.

Burrus, Virginia. "Mapping as Metamorphosis: Initial Reflection on Gender and Ancient Religious Discourses." In *Mapping Gender in Ancient Religious Discourses*, edited by Todd Penner and Caroline Vander Stichele, 1–10. Biblical Interpretation 84. Atlanta: SBL, 2007.

Butler, Judith. *Undoing Gender*. New York: Routledge, 2004.

Cho, Teresa. "Room to Speak: Korean-American Women in the PCUSA." *Christian Century* 127.24 (2010) 13.

Chong, Kelly H. "What It Means to Be Christian: The Role of Religion in the Construction of Ethnic Identity and Boundary among Second-Generation Korean Americans." *Sociology of Religion* 59 (1998) 259–86.

Cohen, Shaye J. D. *The Beginnings of Jewishness: Boundaries, Varieties, Uncertainties*. Berkeley: University of California Press, 1999.

D'Angelo, Mary Rose. "Gender and Geopolitics in the Work of Philo of Alexandria: Jewish Piety and Imperial Family Values." In *Mapping Gender in Ancient Religious Discourses*, edited by Todd Penner and Caroline Vander Stichele, 63–88. Biblical Interpretation Series 84. Atlanta: SBL, 2007.

Frankfurter, David. "Comparison and the Study of Religion in Late Antiquity." In *Comparer en histoire des religions antiques: Controverses et propositions*, edited by Claude Calame and Bruce Lincoln, 83–98. Liège, Belgium: Presses Universitaires de Liège, 2012.

Gruen, Erich S. *Heritage and Hellenism: The Reinvention of Jewish Tradition*. Berkeley, CA: University of California Press, 1998.

Kim, In Soo. *History of Christianity in Korea*. Seoul: Qumran, 2011.

Lee, Timothy S. "From the Coercive to the Liberative: Asian and Latino Immigrants and Christianity in the United States." In *American Christianities: A History of Dominance and Diversity*, edited by Catherine A. Brekus and W. Clark Gilpin, 76–101. Chapel Hill: University of North Carolina Press, 2011.

———. "Fruits and Challenges of Adhesively Skeletonizing a Church Community: Korean Americans in the Presbyterian Church (U.S.A.)." Lecture, Harvard University, October 16, 2013.

Levitt, Peggy. *God Needs No Passport: Immigrants and the Changing American Landscape*. London: New Press, 2007.

Modrzejewski, Joseph Mélèze. *The Jews of Egypt from Ramses II to Emperor Hadrian.* Princeton: Princeton University Press, 1995.

Moffett, Samuel Hugh. *The Christians of Korea.* New York: Friendship, 1962.

Niehoff, Maren. *Philo on Jewish Identity and Culture.* TSAF 86. Tübingen: Mohr Siebeck, 2001.

Paik, Mary. "A Reflection." Website of the Presbyterian Mission Agency, October 2010. www.presbyterianmission.org/ministries/theologyandworhip/relfction-mary-paik/.

Runia, David T. *Philo in Early Christian Literature: A Survey.* Compendia Rerum Iudaicarum ad Novum Testamentum III/3. Assen: Van Gorcum, 1993.

Smith, Jonathan Z. "Religion, Religions, Religious." In *Critical Terms for Religious Studies*, edited by Mark C. Taylor, 269–84. Chicago: University of Chicago Press, 1998.

2

No Sex in Heaven–Nor on Earth?

Luke 20:27–38 as a Proof-Text in Early Christian Discourses on Resurrection and Asceticism

OUTI LEHTIPUU

ACCORDING TO ALL THREE Synoptic Gospels, Jesus engages in a controversy with the Sadducees over the resurrection of the dead.[1] The story has puzzled scholars and other readers of the Bible alike. In her monograph *The Double Message: Patterns of Gender in Luke–Acts* and subsequent articles, Turid Karlsen Seim has offered a persuasive reading of Luke's version of the debate demonstrating that the Lukan Jesus promotes celibacy as a sign of an anticipatory participation in the resurrection. Those who "neither marry nor are given in marriage" are like angels (ἰσάγγελοι) and cannot die. The passage became important for several early Christian writers in their discussions on resurrection and on celibacy. In this essay, I analyze some early interpretations of the passage as a token of my gratitude to all that I have learned from Turid and her scholarship.

In the narrative, some Sadducees who "say that there is no resurrection, or angel, or spirit"[2] try to trip Jesus up by asking him whose wife a woman who has married seven brothers, one after another, will be at the resurrection. Jesus escapes the trap by denying any marriage after resurrection: "For when they rise from the dead, they neither marry nor are given

---

1. Mark 12:18–27; Matt 22:23–33; Luke 20:27–38.

2. Cf. Acts 23:8. All biblical passages are according to the *New Revised Standard Version*, copyright 1989, 1995 by the Division of Christian Education of the National Council of the Churches of Christ in the United States of America, if not otherwise noted.

in marriage, but are like angels in heaven." He then confirms the reality of resurrection by quoting the story of Moses and the burning bush: "And concerning the dead being raised, have you not read in the book of Moses, in the story about the bush, how God said to him, 'I am the God of Abraham, and the God of Isaac, and the God of Jacob'? He is not God of the dead, but of the living."

Jesus' answer contains several peculiarities. If Jesus wants to demonstrate the reality of resurrection, why does he appeal to the example of the patriarchs? In what sense can they be a proof of God being "God of the living"—were they not dead both at the time of Moses and at the time of Jesus, until the resurrection on the last day? The incongruity is even stronger in Luke's version of the story, for he has made an addition: "He is not the God of the dead, but of the living, for all live to him."[3] The present tense of the verb ζάω implies that the patriarchs are alive—have they, then, already been raised from the dead? The phrase "all live to him" has a close counterpart in 4 Maccabees, a writing that does not speak about resurrection but about immortality (ἀθανασία) and that links "living to God" both to the patriarchs long gone and the contemporary faithful: "they believe that they, like our patriarchs Abraham and Isaac and Jacob, do not die to God, but live to God"[4] and "those who die for the sake of God live to God as do Abraham and Isaac and Jacob and all the patriarchs."[5]

It may be asked, however, whether the tension is only ostensible, or whether it is based on the presupposition that "resurrection" is something other than "immortality." This has been the traditional view in scholarship where the "Hebrew" concept of the resurrection of the body and the "Greek" concept of the immortality of the soul have been sharply contrasted and taken to be mutually exclusive.[6] Early Jewish and Christian belief, it has been claimed, cherishes a monistic understanding of the human being where body and soul make up a unified whole. Greek thinking, in contrast, is believed to promote strict dualism of body and soul. The evidence does not support such a clear-cut dichotomy, for both ideas and different kinds of combinations of them exist side by side in early Jewish sources and the many Greco-Roman polytheistic cults and mythological stories were no less

3. This is a literal translation of the Greek πάντες γὰρ αὐτῷ ζῶσιν. The *NRSV*'s rendering of the phrase is "to him all of them are alive."

4. ζῶσιν τῷ θεῷ; 4 Macc 7:19.

5. ζῶσιν τῷ θεῷ; 4 Macc 16:25.

6. A classic example of this is Cullman, "Immortality of the Soul or Resurrection of the Dead," 9–35.

diverse. The traditional stance has been thoroughly refuted[7] but echoes of it still frequently appear in the scholarly literature.[8]

The Lukan version of the resurrection debate shows how, instead of representing clearly distinguishable alternatives, the concepts were often blurred and conflated. Jesus gives the Sadducees a "double answer";[9] the dead are raised and the patriarchs are alive. The logic of Jesus' argument in v. 38 requires that the patriarchs have been alive all along. Their resurrection means their postmortem exaltation to heaven where they already participate in spiritual and immortal heavenly life.[10] "Resurrection is being recast as immortality," as Turid has phrased it.[11]

There is more to Luke's reshaping of Jesus' answer. Whereas Mark—and Matthew who follows Mark closely in this passage—makes a temporal distinction between life now, when people marry and (be)get children, and life after resurrection, when they neither marry nor are given in marriage but are like angels in heaven, Luke puts less emphasis on the chronological dichotomy. According to Turid's reading, while Luke's Jesus does not totally abandon the temporal categories, his accent is on spatiality and on transfer from an earthly to a heavenly sphere.[12] This means that the distinction in Luke's version is not so much between now and then but between two groups of people: "children of this age" and "children of the resurrection."[13] These are concurrent groups that are not differentiated by time but by ethical characteristics.[14] Those who are considered "worthy of a place in that age and in the resurrection from the dead" show their belonging to this group by not marrying; that is, by choosing celibacy. They have become like angels and can no longer die.[15] Through their ascetically inclined lifestyle they already participate in the resurrection and "live to God" like the patriarchs.[16]

---

7. Nickelsburg, *Resurrection, Immortality, and Eternal Life*, 219–23.

8. For a recent example, see Segal, *Life after Death*, 533–35.

9. Fitzmyer, *Luke*, 1301.

10. McDannell and Lang, *Heaven*, 26–27.

11. Seim, "In Heaven as on Earth," 28.

12. Seim, *Double Message*, 215–17; "Children of the Resurrection," 119–20; "In Heaven as on Earth," 23.

13. Luke 20:34, 36. Seim, *Double Message*, 216–17.

14. Cf. the juxtaposition of "children of this age" and "children of light" in Luke 16:8. In this passage, it is clear that Jesus refers to two coexisting but morally different groups of people.

15. The connection between celibacy and immortality shows that there is a link between marriage and death: marriage and procreation are needed in order to overcome death by gaining afterlife through progeny. Seim, *Double Message*, 219.

16. There are several other early Jewish and Christian texts, such as *Joseph and*

Angelic Beings and the Resurrection of the Flesh

The question of how Jesus' answer to the Sadducees should be interpreted became a topic of a heated debate early on. During the formative centuries of Christianity, the resurrection of the dead—one of the most controversial issues—was often used as a test or touchstone for belonging: in several texts only those who understand resurrection in the same way as the author are counted as authentic Christians.[17] Often the question evolved into a dispute concerning the resurrection of the flesh: would resurrection entail the recovery of the earthly body or not? Jesus' words about the resurrected ones as angels offered an important proof-text for those Christians who rejected the belief in the resurrection of the flesh. It is noteworthy that they did not necessarily refute a bodily resurrection—but for them the resurrection body would undergo a complete transformation and be made of another substance than the imperfect and weak earthly flesh. The defenders of the resurrection of the flesh did not deny that there would be some change; the resurrection body would be a perfected body, no longer subject to sin, weakness, and corruption. However, they insisted that it would still be the same body of flesh and blood.

There were several reasons why some Christians found the idea of the resurrection of the flesh untenable. In a writing entitled *On the Resurrection* that was formerly ascribed to Justin Martyr (and whose anonymous author is therefore called Pseudo-Justin) three sets of reasons are given. First, the resurrection of the flesh is impossible (ἀδύνατον), since that which is corrupt and disassembled cannot be restored to the same state in which it was previously. Second, it is useless (ἀσύμφορον), for who would want back the weak flesh that causes humans to sin. If the flesh will rise, its deficiencies will also rise with it. Third, either the body will rise in its entirety, with all its members and body parts, or it will rise only in part. If the latter is the case, God's power is manifestly imperfect since he cannot make the whole body rise. The former alternative, however, is strange and out of place (ἄτοπον), since there is no need for all body members after the resurrection. Had not Jesus said "they will be like angels" and being angel-like denotes life without sexual intercourse and eating? Why, then, would the risen body include sexual and alimentary organs?[18]

Aseneth or Philo's idealizing description of the Therapeutae in *De vita contemplativa* that link immortality with a certain lifestyle; see Dunderberg, *Beyond Gnosticism*, 39–42.

17. I discuss the topic in detail in my book *The Debate over the Resurrection of the Dead: Constructing Early Christian Identity*.

18. Pseudo-Justin, *On the Resurrection* 2.

For Pseudo-Justin, an ardent promoter of the resurrection of the flesh, this is an inferior opinion (χείρων) and the arguments used only mislead the faithful ones. Both this and the fact that his opponents use Jesus' words as their proof show that these deniers of the physical resurrection are other Christians. Strikingly, their arguments are very similar to the ones that Celsus, the most famous second-century critic of Christianity, brings forward.[19] This indicates that there were no clear borderlines, on the one side Christians defending the resurrection of the flesh and on the other side non-Christians ridiculing it, but the boundaries crisscrossed and often ran between diversely thinking Christian groups. For example, Origen, Celsus' Christian partner-in-dialogue, did not attack Celsus' reasoning against resurrection, but rather complained that he had not understood the true Christian position. It is only the "simpler believers" who maintain that the earthly flesh will rise again. In his reading of Jesus' debate with the Sadducees, Origen takes "being like angels" to mean that at the resurrection the human body will be transformed into a celestial spiritual body that is of a much finer and higher substance than the earthly body.[20]

In his counterargument, Pseudo-Justin creates an alternative exegesis of Jesus' words. He does not reject the reasoning of his opponents as such; he agrees that there is no sex or eating in heaven. However, the rival interpretation goes wrong when it maintains that this logically leads to the conclusion that there is no bodily resurrection.[21] At the resurrection, sexual organs will remain intact but they will not be used for the same functions as on earth. The basic function of the womb is to become pregnant and that of the "masculine part" (μόριον ἀνδρικόν) to beget. However, neither function is necessary: there are barren women who do not become pregnant even though they have a womb and others, both women and men, who abstain from sexual intercourse and still have their sexual organs.[22] To strengthen his argument, the writer even refers to the animal world; mules have sexual organs but they do not bear or beget. If having sexual organs does not unavoidably lead to sexual intercourse in this world, it will certainly not do so in the world to come.

19. See Origen, *Against Celsus* 5.14.

20. Origen, *On First Principles* 2.2.2. This passage, as most of the work, is only preserved in Rufinus's Latin translation, which is not a literal one. Thus, it is not entirely certain whether it corresponds to what Origen wrote in the original Greek.

21. Pseudo-Justin, *On the Resurrection* 3.

22. Cf. Tertullian, *On the Resurrection* 61.6–7: "We also, as we are able, give the mouth release from food, and even abstain from sexual intercourse. How many voluntary eunuchs are there, how many virgins wedded to Christ, how many barren of both sexes equipped with genitals that bear no fruit."

All in all, the writer has a negative attitude toward sexual intercourse. He praises Jesus for not falling to the "desires of the flesh" and values the virgin birth which "destroyed begetting by lawless desire." In his life, Jesus showed that sexual intercourse can be abolished; even though he otherwise submitted himself to a fully human life and had to eat, drink, and clothe himself, he did not have sex. This, in Pseudo-Justin's view, shows that sexual intercourse is not a necessity like the others. The logic of this line of thought for bodily resurrection is not completely clear. Pseudo-Justin draws an analogy between this life and the life to come. If the redundancy of sexual intercourse in this life implies that it is not necessary in the world to come, does not the necessity of food, drink, and clothing for the earthly flesh imply their inevitability for the resurrected flesh as well? According to a strong tradition, however, angels did not eat[23]—how could those who will be like angels in heaven need food or drink? In his counterargument, however, Pseudo-Justin does not address the question of eating but restricts his discussion to sex.

Another early defender of the resurrection of the flesh was Tertullian of Carthage. He faced similar challenges as Pseudo-Justin when interpreting Jesus' words about angels and solved them much in a similar fashion but went even further in elaborating a counterexegesis. In his treatise which is also known by the name *On the Resurrection*, Tertullian reminds his readers that those who asked Jesus about the woman of seven husbands at the resurrection were Sadducees, who were known for refuting the resurrection of both the body and the soul. In his answer, the Lord affirmed the resurrection of both parts: the scriptures openly preach resurrection and God certainly has the power to raise the dead. The Sadducees, who do not believe in the resurrection, show ignorance of the scriptures and disbelief in the power of God, he claims,[24] as do all those who understand Jesus' words

---

23. The Jewish tradition knew many stories where angels appear in human guise and seem to be eating but this proves to be an illusion. For example, in Tobit, when the archangel Raphael discloses his true identity, he explains that "although you were watching me, I really did not eat or drink anything—but what you saw was a vision" (Tob 12:19). Similarly, in the *Testament of Abraham*, the archangel Michael is one of the three men who visit Abraham in the oaks of Mamre. Abraham invites the visitors to dine with him and Michael needs advice from God. He says: "Lord, all the heavenly spirits are incorporeal, and they neither eat nor drink. Now he has set before me a table with an abundance of all the good things which are earthly and perishable. And now, Lord, what shall I do? How shall I escape his notice while I am sitting at one table with him?" The Lord answers: "Go down to him and do not be concerned about this. For when you are seated with him I shall send upon you an all-devouring spirit, and, from your hands and through your mouth, it will consume everything which is on the table" (*TAbr* 4:9–10; trans. Sanders in *OTP*).

24. Tertullian, *On the Resurrection* 36. Cf. Mark 12:24.

as proof of a non-bodily resurrection. What the Lord says is: "they will not marry"—he does not say "they will not be raised." They will certainly be raised but they will be transformed "into an angelic state by that garment of incorruptibility" (*in statum angelicum per indumentum illud incorrupt-ibilitatis*). Since their substance has changed, they do not marry and they do not die—yet they are raised in a fleshly substance. Tertullian turns the reasoning of his rivals upside down and states that the whole question of the Sadducees about the prospective heavenly marriage of the woman implies that they will be raised bodily—without a body with all its members capable to marry, the whole question would be senseless.

Tertullian also emphasizes that the body will be raised in its entirety. His rivals ridicule such a view by asking what mouth, teeth, throat, gullet, intestines, and stomach would serve when eating and drinking have ceased. And why would there be a need for the reproductive organs, when there is no marriage and no procreation?[25] Tertullian counters these contradictions with arguments similar to those of Pseudo-Justin; the members have one set of functions in this life and another set in the future life. "When life itself has been delivered from necessities the members also will be delivered from their functions: but they will not for that reason be unnecessary."[26] First of all, it is necessary that all body parts will remain since they will also be judged. Secondly, there are many other functions for them. For example, the most important function for teeth is not eating but praising God, as the example of Adam shows. "Adam pronounced names for the animals before he plucked of the tree: he was a prophet before he was an eater."[27] Other important functions for the teeth consist in helping in articulation and adorning the mouth.

Similarly, the different apertures of the "lower parts" of men and women (*inferna in viro et in femina*) are not needed for copulation only but also for health so that "the excreta may be filtered" and the function of the womb is not only to gather the male seed but to control the excess of blood "which the less energetic sex has not the strength to throw off."[28] These functions may be in line with ancient medical understanding, but Tertullian's reasoning faces the same problem as those of Pseudo-Justin above: if angels, and those like them, do not eat, do they then need to defecate?

25. Tertullian, *On the Resurrection* 60.2–3.

26. Ibid., 60.5. Translation here and elsewhere follows that of Evans in *Tertullian's Treatise on the Resurrection*.

27. Ibid., 61.1.

28. Ibid., 61.3.

In a further passage of the same treatise,[29] Tertullian develops another line of argument. When Jesus speaks of the "children of the resurrection" he says that they will be *like* angels—not that they will be angels. He refers to the story of the three men visiting Abraham in Mamre, who were widely believed to have been angels.[30] According to Tertullian, the story shows that angels can be like human beings. Even though they do not lose their angelic substance and have no human flesh, they eat, drink and have their feet washed. If angels, who are spiritual beings, can be treated as if they had human flesh, why would human beings—who are of flesh—not be able to partake in heavenly life, "being, under their angelic clothing, no more tied to the usages of the flesh than the angels then, under human clothing, were tied to the usages of the spirit?"[31]

In another writing aimed against Marcion's understanding of the resurrection of Christ, however, Tertullian gives a different reading of the Genesis passage. Marcion, who claimed that the visible world was created by a lower God, did not accept the physical resurrection of Christ but maintained rather that the disciples saw the spirit of the resurrected Christ and that his fleshly form was only apparent.[32] This was similar to the appearance of the angels to Abraham and Lot. Tertullian rejects this interpretation and affirms that the angels were of "veritable and complete human substance."[33] He adds ironically that perhaps Marcion's God, who has never produced any flesh, would not have been able to provide the angels with a fleshly body. In contrast, "my God who reshaped into the quality we know, that flesh which he had taken up out of clay . . . was no less able out of any material whatsoever to construct flesh for angels as well."[34] Tertullian even refers to Jesus' debate with the Sadducees but without countering Marcion's interpretation of it: "And truly, if your god promises to humans some time the true substance of angels—They will, he says, be as the angels—why should not my God too have granted to angels the true human substance, from wheresoever he may have taken it?"[35]

Debates over the meaning of Jesus' words to the Sadducees continued in later centuries. An early fourth-century example is offered in the

---

29. Ibid., 62.

30. Genesis 18; cf. n23 above.

31. Tertullian, *On the Resurrection* 62.3.

32. Cf. Luke 24:39.

33. Tertullian, *Against Marcion* 3.9.2. Translation here and elsewhere by Evans (with slight modifications).

34. Ibid., 3.9.3.

35. Ibid., 3.9.4.

Discourse on the Resurrection by Methodius, the bishop of Olympos. The text is cast into a dialogue with a certain Aglaophon, but it is directed against the alleged views of Origen. The text has survived only in parts, preserved in later writings.[36] Methodius' reasoning follows along lines similar to his predecessors but he develops them further. He draws arguments in favor of the resurrection of the flesh from the heavenly hierarchy, from the goodness of creation, and from the metaphorical nature of Jesus' words.

Methodius shares Tertullian's viewpoint and explains that Jesus speaks of the resurrected ones as being like angels but he does not identify them with angels.[37] Angels are only one class of immortals; in addition to them, there are rulers (ἄρχοντες) and powers (ἐξουσίαι) and all of them have "different species, bodies and varieties." A creature of one class cannot be changed into another kind; angels cannot become powers for each class of beings has its own place and order. Thus, human nature will not be changed into an angelic one but only resemble it. When God created humans He intended them to be humans, not angels. Proposing that humans become angels at the resurrection implies that the creation of humans was a mistake. Either God had originally wished to make an angel but was too weak to accomplish it, or his creation was bad and he repented of it. Both ideas would be blasphemous.

In Methodius' view, being like angels at the resurrection does not denote resurrection without flesh but life without marriage. Resurrection life will be angelic life in the sense that it will resemble life in paradise in honor and glory. Instead of marriage-feasts and other festivities, the resurrected ones will be in the presence of Christ and praise him with the angels. Yet there is gradation between the "children of the resurrection" and angels. Just as it is possible to say of the moon on a bright night that it "shines like the sun" without meaning that it is the sun, it can similarly be said of the resurrected ones that they are like angels even though they are not transformed into angels. Lastly, Methodius makes a terminological point. Raising up cannot mean the resurrection of the soul only, because only the one that has fallen can be raised up. It is the body that dies and is laid down into the grave, while the soul remains immortal. Thus, those who say that there is no resurrection of the flesh, deny any kind of resurrection. Jesus talked about the raising of the dead which cannot be anything other than raising their flesh into a new life.

---

36. A largish portion is preserved in Epiphanius's *Panarion* 64.12–62, and another fragment in Photius's *Bibliotheca* 234.

37. Cf. Epiphanius, *Panarion* 64.41.3—43.8.

Jerome, another ardent opponent of Origen, writing at the end of the fourth century, agrees; human beings also remain human at the resurrection. In his letter to Theodora which he wrote to console her after the death of her husband, Jerome explains that the words "they neither marry nor are given in marriage but are like the angels in heaven" do not mean that the "natural and real" body would be taken away. Instead, it indicates what kind of a glory is awaiting. The resurrected ones will not cease to be human and the difference of sex will also remain. "The apostle Paul will still be Paul, Mary will still be Mary."[38] The physical differences between sexes, however, do not necessitate marriage. Jerome refers to the marriage of Theodora and her late husband as a sister/brother relationship where they voluntarily abstained from sexual intercourse. If this was possible in the corruptible world, how much more in the incorruptible one![39]

In another of his letters, written to Eustochium to console her after the death of her mother Paula, Jerome comes back to the question of the resurrection of the flesh and sexual distinction. He recalls an event when Paula was encountered by a teacher who opposed the belief in the resurrection of the flesh and who tried to prove his point by questions such as whether in the next world there will be a distinction of sexes. If yes, will there not also be marriage and procreation? If no, will the bodies not be transformed into something other than what they are in this world? Jerome's answer to this dilemma is that the bodies will remain the same, which includes sexual distinction. "If the woman shall not rise again as a woman nor the man as a man, there will be no resurrection of the body for the body is made up of sex and members."[40] As a proof of this Jerome refers to Jesus' controversy with the Sadducees. Their whole discussion is about marriage. This implies that both parties knew that the distinction of sex will remain in resurrection. "For no one says of things which have no capacity for marriage such as a stick or a stone that they neither marry nor are given in marriage; but this may well be said of those who while they can marry yet abstain from doing so by their own virtue and by the grace of Christ." Abstaining from sex means participation in the life of angels and in their bliss. Already in this world all holy men and virgins lead an angelic life when they stay continent. Yet, their human nature is not changed, not on earth and not in heaven, for what the Lord promises is a likeness to the angels, not becoming them.

As these examples show, Jesus' comparison of resurrectional to angelic life compelled the defenders of the resurrection of the flesh to walk a thin

---

38. Jerome, *Letter 75 (To Theodora)* 2.

39. Cf. 1 Cor 15:53.

40. Jerome, *Letter 108 (To Eustochium)* 23 (trans. Freemantle).

line in order to reconcile their belief with Jesus' words. A popular way of doing this was to allow for the theoretical possibility of marriage and children in the future world but to emphasize the voluntary abstinence from them in an angelic manner. Many writers appealed to the example of virgins and others who chose celibacy in this world. For some, celibacy became a sign of the future life, an ideal way of life that would lead into eternal life and bliss.

Virgins Are Already Beginning to Be Angels

One of the central characteristics of early Christian way of life was the ideal of ascetic renunciation.[41] Several influential authors produced exhortations to virginity,[42] addressed primarily to women.[43] Not infrequently they linked virginity with resurrection by referring to Jesus' debate with the Sadducees. The link between celibacy and resurrection took several forms. First, those who led a life of an ascetic were seen to be already partaking in the angelic life of resurrection. Second, future resurrection and judgment served as reminders of the importance of the modest ascetic lifestyle. Third, those who strove to maintain their virginity were promised the better rewards in the future resurrection life.

An illuminating example of this is offered by Cyprian of Carthage in his treatise, *On the Dress of Virgins*, written in the first half of the third century. In his instructions to virgins about chastity and a modest life he often refers to resurrection. He promises to those who hold fast to virginity that chastity brings an immense advantage both for this life and especially for the future life.[44] First, virgins will not experience any sorrows and pain associated with child bearing and they do not have to submit to their husbands.[45] Second, since they do not marry or are given to marriage they are counted worthy of resurrection. Jesus' words, "they are like angels and are children of God, being children of the resurrection,"[46] mean participation in the future life already in this life:

41. Brown, *Body and Society,* 33–64; Clark, *Reading Renunciation*, 14–42; Lehtipuu, "Example of Thecla," 361–69.

42. E.g., Cyprian, *On the Dress of Virgins*; Novatian, *In Praise of Purity*; Methodius, *Symposium (on Virginity)*; John Chrysostom, *On Virginity*; Gregory of Nyssa, *On Virginity*.

43. Castelli, "Virginity and Its Meaning for Women's Sexuality," 76–86.

44. Cyprian, *On the Dress of Virgins* 22.

45. Both were common *topoi* in early Christian discourses on virginity; Lehtipuu, "Example of Thecla," 361–62.

46. Cyprian seems to quote the Lukan passage by heart and writes: "they are equal to the angels of God, being children of the resurrection" (*On the Dress of Virgins* 22).

What we shall be, already you have begun to be. The glory of the resurrection you already have in this world; you pass through the world without the pollution of the world; while you remain chaste and virgins, you are equal to the angels of God.[47]

According to Cyprian, virgins are already participating in the process of becoming angels. This requires perseverance in modesty, not seeking "necklaces and clothing as adornments, but right conduct" and setting one's mind on God and heaven, instead of the "lust of the flesh" and earth. Cyprian warns those who are tempted by the flesh and want to adorn themselves outwardly. Using cosmetics or otherwise altering outward appearance may mean that God will not recognize His image at judgment:

Are you not afraid . . . that when the day of resurrection comes, your Maker may not recognize you again, and may turn you away when you come to His rewards and promises, and may exclude you . . . and say: This is not my work, nor is this our image. You have defiled [the] skin with a lying cosmetics, you have changed [the] hair with an adulterous color, your face is violently taken possession of by a lie, your figure is corrupted, your countenance is another's. You cannot see God, since your eyes are not those which God made but which the devil has infected. Him you have followed; the red and painted eyes of the serpent have you imitated; adorned like your enemy, with him you shall likewise burn.[48]

Even though the virginal life is already participation in the angelic life, temptations lurk and succumbing to them means an absolute fall. For those who endure, however, Cyprian promises the best rewards: "But when He says that in His Father's house there are many mansions,[49] He points to the homes of a better habitation. Those better dwellings you are seeking; by cutting away the desires of the flesh you are obtaining the reward of a greater grace in heaven."[50] All who have been sanctified by baptism, have put off the old nature[51] and will be saved, but "the greater sanctity and truth of the second birth belong to you who no longer have any desires of the flesh and of the body."

Several other thinkers linked virginity, participation in the resurrection, and special rewards in the afterlife in a manner similar to Cyprian.

47. Cyprian, *On the Dress of Virgins* 22. Translation here and elsewhere by Keenan.

48. Ibid. 17.

49. Cf. John 14:2.

50. Cyprian, *On the Dress of Virgins* 23.

51. Cf. Eph 4:22.

Gregory of Nyssa, writing in the late fourth-century Cappadocia viewed sexuality as a secondary means of survival, which only appeared after Adam's fall. Marriage and childbirth did not belong to God's original plan but became necessary to enable humankind to produce offspring and thus to conquer death.[52] In his treatise *On the Making of Humanity*, Gregory reasons that the resurrection means the restoration of humankind to its original, paradisiacal state where there will be no marriage and procreation. Life before the fall resembled the life of angels and Jesus' words to the Sadducees reveal that the final condition of humans will again be angelic.[53] Gregory also penned a treatise *On Virginity* where he claims that a peculiar characteristic of angelic nature is that angels are free of marriage (ἀπηλλάχθαι τοῦ γάμου). Being angel-like requires that one imitates the purity of angels by renouncing marriage here and now and thus takes part of the blessings of the future life.[54]

Another prolific late fourth-century writer, John Chrysostom, thinks along similar lines in his treatise *On Virginity*. According to him, virgins come as close to being angels as is possible for humans who, by nature, are inferior to heavenly beings. Virgins resemble angels in two respects. First, like angels they "neither marry nor are given in marriage" and, second, they continuously stand before God and serve him.[55] Living in this world, virgins are unable to ascend to heaven as angels do, since their flesh holds them back. However, they already receive heavenly consolation and magnificent blessing knowing what awaits them.

For these writers, sexual abstinence means participating in the heavenly life already on earth. Resurrection becomes a process that starts in this life and that finds its fulfillment in heaven where the best places are reserved for those who voluntarily give up the pleasures of this world. In the rhetoric of the promoters of virginity, purity of body and soul which is seen in the renouncing of sexual intercourse and in modest behavior makes virgins almost equal to angels. Novatian, the third-century writer who was known for his rigorist ideas and whose followers called themselves the pure ones (καθαροί), went even further. He claimed that virgins will actually be superior to angels for they, unlike angels, have flesh against which they must struggle to gain mastery. "What is virginity, if not a magnificent contemplation of the afterlife?," he exclaims.[56]

---

52. Brown, *Body and Society*, 294–97.

53. Gregory of Nyssa, *On the Making of Humanity* 17.2.

54. Gregory of Nyssa, *On Virginity* 14.4.

55. John Chrysostom, *On Virginity* 11.1.

56. Novatian, *On Praise of Purity* 7.3 (trans. DeSimon).

Monogamy as a Happy Medium between Excessive Asceticism and Immorality

The "higher calling" of virginity, although praised by many early theologians, was not an option for all. Most Christians did get married and raised children—a new Christian generation.[57] Moreover, celibacy was not always an individual choice; especially with the development of monasticism it was often the parents who decided which one(s) of their children would become an ascetic.[58] The sources describing the life of early ascetics are mostly confined to exceptional individuals, such as Anthony of Egypt, and, especially in the case of women, to elite point-of-view. What was possible for upper class ladies such as Macrina or Olympias, was not necessarily an option for women of lower classes.[59] Many ascetically inclined early Christian writers also valued marriage as a proper way of life for "ordinary" Christians. However, for those who wanted to strive for perfection, sexual abstinence remained the standard ideal.

Clement of Alexandria is one of the writers who values marriage and procreation. He wants to strike a happy medium between two extremes, both of which he finds unreasonable. On the one hand, he disapproves of rigorous sexual asceticism; on the other hand, he condemns all promiscuous behavior.[60] In his view, both "celibacy and marriage have their distinctive services of the Lord"[61] and although he does not refuse voluntary celibacy, he regards monogamous marriage as the better choice.[62] This conviction guides his reading of the Sadducean controversy, too. Jesus' answer does not mean rejection of marriage as such but it confirms that after the resurrection, there will be no physical desire.[63] In another passage, Clement points out that the words "they do not marry and are not given in marriage" only refer to life after resurrection.[64] Marriage is part of human life on earth, just like eating is. He appeals to the words of the Apostle Paul who declared, "Food is for the stomach and the stomach for food, and God will put an end

---

57. Osiek and MacDonald, *Woman's Place*, 4–6; Brown, *Body and Society*, 138.

58. Vuolanto, "Choosing Asceticism," 288–91.

59. Cf. Brown, *Body and Society*, 6. "Only the privileged or the eccentric few could enjoy the freedom to do what they pleased with their sexual drives."

60. Buell, "Ambiguous Legacy," 46–47.

61. *Stromateis* 3.12.79.5.

62. Brown, *Body and Society*, 122–39. Clement reinforces his argument by maintaining that even Paul was married, *Stromateis* 3.6.53.1.

63. *Stromateis* 3.12.87.1–2.

64. Ibid., 3.6.47.3.

to both."[65] Even though it is true that in the world to come, there will be no sex and no food, both of them belong to this life. Those who think that they have already attained the state of resurrection and for this reason repudiate marriage should consequently also stop eating and drinking.[66]

Clement particularly attacks those Christians who abolish marriage altogether and who claim that marriage, established by the devil, is fornication.[67] They justify their claim by appealing to the example of the Lord who did not marry. Such reasoning is, from Clement's viewpoint, pure arrogance and he complains that these deniers of marriage boast that their understanding of the gospel is profounder than anyone else's. Clement counters their argument by maintaining that Christ was a special case who cannot be imitated. First, he had his own bride, the church. Second, he was not an ordinary man who needed a partner; as God's son he was immortal and thus had no obligation to produce children. Third, in several passages Christ speaks about marriage as belonging to normal human life.[68] In another context, becoming equal to angels is for Clement also the ideal goal of a believer. However, it is the spiritually advanced Christian, the true "gnostic" (γνωστικός) who has proceeded along the path of perfection from faith to gnosis.[69] This ideal Christian lifestyle did include adhering to certain moral values but renouncing marriage was not one of them.[70]

Another writer whose texts both contain approval of celibacy and monogamous marriage is Clement's contemporary Tertullian. On the one hand, he praises those who have "preferred to be wedded to God" and to stay celibate. By so doing, they have done away with their covetous desire and have declared themselves as "children of that age" and made themselves fit to enter Paradise.[71] On the other hand, a total abolition of marriage is heretical. Tertullian approves of monogamy as the moderate stance between immorality and extreme abstinence.[72] He particularly fights against second

---

65. 1 Cor 6:13.

66. *Stromateis* 3.6.48.1.

67. Ibid., 3.6.49.1–6.

68. Clement appeals to such passages as Matt 19:6 ("Let no one separate what God has joined together"); Luke 17:26–28 ("Just as it was in the days of Noah, so too it will be in the days of the Son of Man. They were . . . marrying and being given in marriage . . . just as it was in the days of Lot: they were . . . planting and building"); and Luke 21:23 ("There will be great distress for those who are pregnant and to those who are nursing infants in those days!").

69. *Stromateis* 7.10.58.4–5.

70. Brown, *Body and Society*, 133–38.

71. Tertullian, *On Exhortation to Chastity* 13.4.

72. Tertullian, *On Monogamy* 1.1.

marriage which he deems to be fornication. Believers need to commit themselves to their only spouse even after his or her death since at the resurrection they will be raised together and are liable for one another to account
for their actions.[73] Tertullian hastens to refute a possible counterargument;
if in the age to come "they neither marry nor are given in marriage but are
equal to angels," does this not mean that the spouses will not be bound to
each other at the resurrection? No, says Tertullian. Even though there will
not be any conjugal relations in the "better condition" (*in meliorem statum*),
the spiritual relationship will remain. If we did not recognize ourselves or
our near ones and did not remember our life on earth, how could we praise
God to all eternity?[74]

Conclusion: Angelic Life, Resurrection, and Sexual Abstinence

Luke's version of Jesus' controversy with the Sadducees over resurrection
combines the ideas of resurrection, likeness to the angels, and celibacy in
a unique way which made it one of the favorite proof-texts of many later
ascetics, as Turid Karlsen Seim herself has noticed.[75] She refers to an article of Sebastian Brock who has analyzed how the passage was read among
early Syrian Christians.[76] In this essay, I have illustrated that the ascetic
understanding of the story was popular also among Greek and Latin writers. Participation in the resurrection was deemed possible already in this life
for those who "neither marry nor are given in marriage" and, thus, lead an
angel-like existence.

The passage was also one of the favorite proof-texts of those Christians
who understood resurrection in spiritual terms as not including the earthly
flesh. In their view, Jesus' words proved that the resurrected ones will be
transformed into an angel-like state which was qualified by characteristics
not possible for beings of flesh and blood. Moreover, they maintained that
the abolition of marriage in the life to come denoted that the earthly body
with all its members, including sexual organs, would not be raised. What

---

73. Ibid., 10.7–8.

74. Cf. Tertullian's other treatise, *To His Wife* 1.1.4–5, where he similarly refers to
Jesus' debate with the Sadducees and claims that, after resurrection, there will be no
returning to marriage and, thus, no "carnal jealousy" (*de carnis zelo*) because believers
will be transferred to an angelic quality and holiness. This, however, does not mean that
they are allowed to remarry after the death of their spouses.

75. Seim, *Double Message*, 214.

76. Brock, "Early Syrian Asceticism," 1–19.

need would there be for all body parts when the life of angels would not involve sex or food?

Neither reading—the one denying the resurrection of the flesh and the other promoting total sexual abstinence—went unchallenged. Those who accepted marriage interpreted Jesus' words to mean that the conjugal relationship belonged to this life and would cease after resurrection. They brought forth other passages to strengthen their case where Jesus speaks about marriage approvingly. Similarly, those who believed in the resurrection of the flesh built elaborate exegeses of the passage to counter the ideas they were opposing. They remarked that Jesus speaks of being like angels but he does not identify the resurrected ones with angels.

To all these Christians, it was important to show that they had scriptural proof for their views. Thus, in their meaning making of biblical texts they used reading strategies that did not challenge their beliefs but validated them. They were not ready for compromises—there might have been several ways to understand a text but only one of them was genuine. To the present-day reader, their interpretations at times appear far-fetched and fanciful. To the early Christian commentators, however, they—and only they—remained faithful to the apostolic tradition.

Bibliography

Brock, Sebastian P. "Early Syrian Asceticism." *Numen* 20 (1973) 1–19.

Brown, Peter. *The Body and Society: Men, Women, and Sexual Renunciation in Early Christianity.* Lectures on the History of Religions 13. New York: Columbia University Press, 1988.

Buell, Denise K. "Ambiguous Legacy: A Feminist Commentary on Clement of Alexandria's Works." In *A Feminist Companion to Patristic Literature*, edited by Amy-Jill Levine with Maria Mayo Robbins, 26–55. Feminist Companions to the New Testament and Early Christian Writings 12. London: T. & T. Clark, 2008.

Castelli, Elizabeth A. "Virginity and Its Meaning for Women's Sexuality in Early Christianity." In *A Feminist Companion to Patristic Literature*, edited by Amy-Jill Levine with Maria Mayo Robbins, 72–100. Feminist Companions to the New Testament and Early Christian Writings 12. London: T. & T. Clark, 2008.

Clark, Elizabeth A. *Reading Renunciation: Asceticism and Scripture in Early Christianity.* Princeton: Princeton University Press, 1999.

Cullmann, Oscar. "Immortality of the Soul or Resurrection of the Dead." In *Immortality and Resurrection*, edited by Krister Stendahl, 9–35. New York: Macmillan, 1965.

Dunderberg, Ismo. *Beyond Gnosticism: Myth, Lifestyle, and Society in the School of Valentinus.* New York: Columbia University Press, 2008.

Evans, Ernst. *Tertullian's Treatise on the Resurrection.* London: SPCK, 1960.

Fitzmyer, Joseph A. *The Gospel according to Luke: Introduction, Translation and Notes.* AB 28B. Garden City, NY: Doubleday, 1985.

Lehtipuu, Outi. "The Example of Thecla and the Example(s) of Paul: Disputing Women's Role in Early Christianity." In *Women and Gender in Ancient Religions: Interdisciplinary Approaches*, edited by Stephen Ahearne-Kroll et al., 338–67. Wissenschaftliche Untersuchungen zum Neuen Testament 263. Tübingen: Mohr Siebeck, 2010.

———. *Debates over the Resurrection of the Dead: Constructing Early Christian Identity*. Oxford: Oxford University Press, 2015.

McDannell, Colleen, and Bernhard Lang. *Heaven: A History*. New Haven: Yale University Press, 1988.

Nickelsburg, George W. E. *Resurrection, Immortality, and Eternal Life in Intertestamental Judaism and Early Christianity*. Exp. ed. Cambridge: Harvard University Press, 2006.

Osiek, Carolyn, and Margaret Y. MacDonald, with Janet H. Tulloch. *A Woman's Place: House Churches in Earliest Christianity*. Minneapolis: Fortress, 2006.

Segal, Alan F. *Life after Death: A History of the Afterlife in the Religions of the West*. New York: Doubleday, 2004.

Seim, Turid Karlsen. *The Double Message: Patterns of Gender in Luke–Acts*. Nashville: Abingdon, 1994.

———. "Children of the Resurrection: Perspectives on Angelic Asceticism in Luke–Acts." In *Asceticism and the New Testament*, edited by Leif E. Vaage and Vincent L. Wimbush, 115–26. New York: Routledge, 1999.

———. "In Heaven as on Earth? Resurrection, Body, Gender and Heavenly Rehearsals in Luke–Acts." In *Christian and Islamic Gender Models in Formative Traditions*, edited by Kari Elisabeth Børresen, 17–41. Studi e Testi Tardo Antichi 2. Rome: Herder, 2004.

Vuolanto, Ville. "Choosing Asceticism: Children and Parents, Vows and Conflicts." In *Children in Late Ancient Christianity*, edited by Cornelia B. Horn and Robert R. Phenix, 255–91. Studien und Texte zu Antike und Christentum 58. Tübingen: Mohr Siebeck, 2009.

3

The Body of God and the Corpus of Historiography

The *Life of Aphou of Pemdje* and the Anthropomorphite Controversy[1]

HUGO LUNDHAUG

IN A LETTER WRITTEN to bishop Calosirius in Middle Egypt, archbishop Cyril of Alexandria says he has been told that there are monks in the bishop's area who go around saying that since "divine Scripture says that man was created in God's image we ought to believe that the Godhead has human shape or form."[2] According to Cyril, this is "utterly witless and capable of making those who choose to think it incur the charge of most extreme blasphemy. Man is unquestionably in God's image, but the likeness is not a bodily one for God is incorporeal."[3]

Indeed, what does it mean that man was created in the image of God, as Gen 1:26 tells us? What does this account of creation tell us about the human constitution, and what does it tell us about God? Is it not logical that the inference can be drawn in both directions, that not only does man resemble God, but also that God resembles man? And what does such resemblance entail—in either case? These are indeed questions that have been up

---

1. It is an honor to contribute to this *Festschrift* for Turdi Karlsen Seim, to whom I owe a debt of gratitude, not least for including me in her research projects *Body and Processes of Life in Antiquity (LOKA)* (2003–2006), and *Metamorphoses: Resurrection, Taxonomies and Transformative Practices in Early Christianity* at the Centre for Advanced Study (CAS) in Oslo, both of which were highly challenging and fruitful.

2. Cyril of Alexandria, *Letter to Calosirius* (Wickham, *Select Letters*, 214–15).

3. Ibid. On the image of God in Cyril's thought, see, e.g., Burghardt, *Image of God*.

for debate at various points throughout the history of the Christian church. Around the turn of the fifth century in Egypt the question was the center of what is usually referred to as the Anthropomorphite controversy. This was during Cyril's predecessor Theophilus' time as archbishop of Alexandria, and the question regarding the image of God was also a rather more pressing matter for Theophilus than it was for Cyril. It is nevertheless noteworthy that, also in Cyril's case, the erroneous notions concerning the image of God are associated specifically with monks.

The so-called Anthropomorphite controversy is described in several ancient sources, both from within and outside Egypt, and, not surprisingly, they are not all in agreement. In the present article I will take a closer look at these differences and assess the value of one of these texts in particular as a source for the history of the conflict. The text in question is a Coptic account of the life of an otherwise scarcely attested monk contemporary with Theophilus.

The *Life of Aphou of Pemdje*

The anonymous hagiographical account of the *Life of Aphou of Pemdje*[4] details the monastic and ecclesiastical career of Aphou, who is supposed to have lived in the late fourth and early fifth centuries as an anchorite outside of the city of Pemdje (Oxyrhynchus), where he was later appointed bishop by Theophilus. The text is known from a single papyrus manuscript deriving from Thinis in Upper Egypt, which is now kept in the Egyptian Museum in Turin.[5] The manuscript is one of eighteen seventh- to eighth-century codices that all derive from the same ancient collection.[6] The text follows Aphou from the time when he put aside his clothes and went off into the desert to live as an anchorite, and relates how he lived a simple life for many years together with the local antelopes, only coming into the city of Pemdje, in secret, once a year to hear the reading of the annual festal letter from the archbishop of Alexandria.[7]

4. Clavis Coptica 0407.

5. The Coptic text has been published by Rossi, *Tre Manoscritti Copti*, 5–22. It is preserved in manuscript GIOV.AC. On the Coptic papyrus codices from Thinis, now kept in Turin, see esp. Orlandi, "Les papyrus coptes"; Orlandi, "Turin Coptic Papyri." German translation can be found in Bumazhnov, *Der Mensch*, 219–28; Norwegian translation in Lundhaug, *Koptiske skrifter*, 223–35.

6. Orlandi, "Turin Coptic Papyri," 526–27. Apart from this text, Aphou is known only from short references in the *Apophthegmata Patrum* and the Coptic hagiographical account of the *Life of Paul of Tamma* (see Bumazhnov, *Der Mensch*, 140–42).

7. A festal letter was sent every year by the archbishop of Alexandria to the churches

One such occasion, in 399, is described as an important turning point in his life, for it led him to travel to Alexandria to speak with the archbishop in person. He was in fact persuaded to go to Alexandria by no less than an angel, having that year been shocked by the heretical nature of what he heard when the festal letter was read aloud. Rather than go back to his friends the antelopes in the wilderness, he thus decided to seek out the archbishop instead. The letter he heard was of course Theophilus' famous 14th *Festal Letter* of 399, which sparked the Anthropomorphite controversy. What Theophilus had written there, which provoked Aphou's trip to Alexandria, was, as the *Life of Aphou* presents it, that the image borne by human beings is not in God's image.

When he arrives in Alexandria, Aphou sits patiently outside Theophilus' door for three days before he is given an audience. We will return to Aphou's conversation with the archbishop once we have taken a look at how other sources describe Theophilus' 14th *Festal Letter* and the athropomorphite controversy that ensued.

The Accounts of Socrates Scolasticus, Sozomen, and John Cassian

Unfortunately Theophilus *Festal Letter* of that year has not been preserved to us, so we cannot know exactly how it was phrased, but we have accounts of its contents, and especially its consequences, from the fifth-century writers Socrates Scolasticus, Sozomen, and John Cassian.[8] These accounts make it clear that the letter landed Theophilus in serious trouble. According to these sources, the letter was not received favorably by the monks across Egypt when it was read in the monasteries.[9] The monks were in fact so enraged by it that many of them gathered in Alexandria to lynch the archbishop, whom they felt to be guilty of heresy.[10] According to Socrates Scolasticus,

---

and monasteries around Egypt to make known the time of the Easter celebrations, but it was also an important venue for theological discourse and for the archbishop to make known his views on important matters of theology (see, e.g., Brakke, "Canon Formation"; John Cassian, *Conferences* 10.2).

8. Quotations of their works follow the NPNF translations unless otherwise stated.

9. Davis, *Early Coptic Papacy*, 66–67; Clark, *Origenist Controversy*, 44–51.

10. Socrates, *Ecclesiastical History* 6.7; Sozomen, *Ecclesiastical History* 8.11; cf. Griggs, *Early Egyptian Christianity*, 187; Golitzin "Demons Suggest," 13. On Socrates and Sozomen, see, e.g., Woods, "Late Antique Historiography," 361–62; Treadgold, *Early Byzantine Historians*, 134–55; Leppin, "Church Historians."

who wrote sometime between 438 and 443,[11] most monks were originally in agreement with Theophilus that God was without body and form, but many of those Socrates describes as the simpler monks were of the opinion that God indeed had both a body and human form.[12] Sozomen, however, who wrote ca. 443,[13] states that most of the monks of Egypt held that God was anthropomorphic.[14]

Confronted by the mob of angry monks in Alexandria, Theophilus appears to have gotten cold feet and quickly, and drastically, changed his position. According to the accounts of Socrates and Sozomen he is even supposed to have addressed the mob, stating that looking at the monks was like looking at the face of God.[15] He then started an extensive campaign against those whose theology he had previously supported on the issue of God's image, as expressed in the 14th *Festal Letter*. These were monks inspired by the writings and theology of Origen, including most prominently the so-called "tall brothers," who held the view that God was bodiless and without form.[16] In the following years Theophilus strongly attacked the teachings of Origen and his followers on many points of doctrine, as can be seen in the festal letters of 401, 402, and 404.[17]

Theophilus thus appears to have completely switched sides and turned upon his former friends, but what was it about his festal letter of 399 that made such an impression on the Egyptian monks? John Cassian, writing in in the 420s,[18] tells the story of how the letter was received by the pious old monk Sarapion.[19] For Sarapion it was impossible to accept Theophilus' denial of God's human form. Indeed, this notion appeared to Sarapion to be a completely new innovation that was not in accordance with Scripture. Indeed, he found it especially objectionable in light of Gen 1:26, where God states "Let us make Man in our image, after our likeness." Although

11. Chesnut *First Christian Histories*, 167.

12. Sokrates, *Ecclesiastical History* 6.7.

13. Chesnut *First Christian Histories*, 199.

14. Sozomen, *Ecclesiastical History* 8.11.

15. Sokrates, *Ecclesiastical History* 6.7; Sozomen, *Ecclesiastical History* 8.11.

16. Sokrates, *Ecclesiastical History* 6.7; Sozomen, *Ecclesiastical History* 8.12; Evelyn-White, *Monasteries*, 132–44.

17. These letters are preserved in Jerome's Latin translation (English translation in Russell, *Theophilus of Alexandria*, 101–59). *Festal Letter* 16 of 401 is also partly preserved in Shenoute's Coptic translation, quoted almost in full in Shenoute's *I Am Amazed* (see Cristea, *Schenute von Atripe*, 231–40 [Coptic and Latin], 279–304 [German translation]).

18. Skeb, "Johannes Cassian," 336.

19. Cassian, *Conferences* 10.3.

Sarapion is eventually persuaded to change his views on the matter, he then has problems when he tries to pray to God and can no longer picture him for his inner eye. In tears he thus exclaims, according to Cassian, "They have taken away my God from me!"[20]

John Cassian, Socrates Scholasticus, and Sozomen all explain the "simple" monks' problems accepting God's lack of a human image by their simplemindedness and lack of education. The educated, thinking monks, however, agreed with Theophilus' stance as it was presented in the festal letter of 399. It is not surprising that these writers, who all held "Origenist" sympathies, describe the events and questions in this way, but it is important to take their own positions on this matter into account when evaluating the value of their descriptions as historical sources. There is certainly no doubt where their sympathies lie, and they all have a negative view of Theophilus' actions. Thus, their portrayal of Theophilus' supporters and opponents, as well as of the core issues of the controversy, are not completely reliable. But do we have any alternative?

Aphou's Conversation with Theophilus

This brings us back to the *Life of Ahpou of Pemdje* and the dialogue between its protagonist and Theophilus in Alexandria. The conversation between the two is related in detail,[21] and is fascinating reading when compared to the way the conflict between Theophilus and the Anthropomorphite monks is described by Cassian, Socrates, and Sozomen.

Once Aphou is given the opportunity to speak with Theophilus, he opens the conversation by asking Theophilus to read the festal letter to him as he originally wrote it, for Aphou doubts that Theophilus could in fact have written the letter in the form in which he had heard it. Perhaps the scribe who copied the version he had heard had made a mistake, for Theophilus could hardly have been the author of the heretical notions he had heard concerning the image of God? When Theophilus obliges and reads the letter to him, however, Aphou realizes that its heretical contents are indeed the same. Aphou is disgusted, throws himself to the ground, and exclaims: "All men are created in the image of God!" This does not initially impress Theophilus, who answers by asking Aphou if he really thinks that a lame or a blind person could be said to possess God's image, not to mention an Ethiopian. Aphou replies by referring to Scripture, accusing Theophilus of contradicting Gen 1:26. Theophilus, however, disagrees. In his opinion,

20. Ibid.

21. *Life of Aphou of Pemdje*, 7–13.

nobody but Adam was in created in the image of God. All the descendants of Adam, on the other hand, did not possess this image. It would simply be impossible to contemplate common human beings, with all their faults and diseases, having the image of God. Aphou presses on, however, and in addition to Scripture he now also refers to established ritual practice, and utilizes the common strategy of associative anti-Judaism.[22] Referring to John 6:41, he implies that Theophilus is just like the Jews who would not understand Jesus' statement that he was the bread from heaven, and moves on from this to connect the issue of the image of God to the dogma of the real presence of the body and blood of Christ in the Eucharist, insinuating that Theophilus must then also doubt this important tenet. Just like it is necessary to believe that the elements of the Eucharist are truly the body and blood of Christ, argues Aphou, it is likewise necessary to believe that human beings have the image of God.

Aphou then explains his position by means of an analogy:[23] The relationship between the image of God and human beings is "like a king who will order a picture to be painted, and everyone subsequently agrees that it is the image of the king, although they know at the same time that it is a piece of wood with paint."[24] Human deficiencies and frailties in relation to the image of God are simply to be regarded in the same way as the relationship between the painted image of the king and the king himself. Moreover, since people do consider the painting to be an image of the king, and even worship it, even though it does not have any spirit, how much more is it not the case that human beings, who possess the Holy Spirit, are in the image of God?[25]

Not surprisingly, since this conversation is related in the *Life of Aphou*, Theophilus is convinced by this argument and is in awe of Aphou's wisdom: "Truly, the knowledge is with those who pray alone in silence. For as for us, the thoughts of our heart are confusing, so that we through ignorance err like this."[26] Theophilus even wants this wise monk to stay with him in Alexandria, and pleads with him not to return to the desert. The call of the wilderness is too strong, however, and Aphou returns, heading back to the antelopes, leaving behind a sad archbishop.[27]

---

22. On associative anti-Judaism, see, e.g., Brakke, "Jewish Flesh."

23. *Life of Aphou of Pemdje*, 14–15.

24. Ibid., 14.

25. Ibid., 15.

26. Ibid., 16.

27. Ibid., 18–19.

The *Life of Aphou of Pemdje* as an Historical Source

Now, the pertinent quesitons are: How can we use the *Life of Aphou of Pemdje* as a source? What is it a source of? Can we use it to correct the other sources for the Anthropomorphite controversy or to give us an alternative perspective on what happened in 399?[28] Can it tell us anything about the motivations behind Theophilus' apparent change of heart?

The Contradictions between the Accounts

First we have to ask if it is at all possible to consolidate the account given in the *Life of Aphou* with those given by Socrates, Sozomen, and John Cassian. Considering the differences in theological stance between the sources sympathetic to the "Origenists" and the *Life of Aphou* it is certainly only to be expected that the accounts differ, but can all the differences be explained on such grounds? There are indeed some glaring contradictions between the account found in the *Life of Aphou* and the others. In fact, when we place the stories side by side, hardly any of the details match up.

All the sources agree that the question of the image of God was central to the controversy, but while Socrates, Sozomen, and Cassian describe the question as whether or not God could be said to have a body and human form, the *Life of Aphou* presents it as a question of whether human beings can be said to possess God's image. So, while similar, the questions are certainly not the same. Is God like man or is man like God? There are also major differences between the sources in how the conflict is described, and the contexts in which the descriptions are placed. Cassian, for instance, discusses the issue in connection with practices of prayer, a theme that was close to his heart.[29] Should one picture God for one's inner eye when praying, or should prayer rather be imageless? Cassian is clear in pronouncing Sarapion, who felt the need to picture God in human form, to have been ignorant and misinformed, stating that Sarapions "grievous error" was most likely caused by "the craft of most vile demons."[30]

In Cassian's story, the simple monk Sarapion had difficulty praying without imagining God in human form. In the *Life of Aphou*, on the other hand, prayer is not an issue at all, and neither is the topic of picturing God

---

28. This has been argued by, e.g., Gould, "Image of God."

29. Stewart, *Cassian the Monk*; Driver, *John Cassian*. Ledegang, "Anthropomorphites and Origenists," argues that disagreement over prayer was at the heart of the controversy itself.

30. Cassian, *Conferences* 10.4.

in human form discussed. In the *Life of Aphou* it is Eucharistic theology and biblical exegesis that are at stake. According to Aphou, Theophilus spoke against Gen 1:26 and John 6 in his festal letter. Moreover, Aphou argues that neither the incarnation nor the Eucharist would make any sense if human beings did not possess the image of God. This would not least jeopardize the efficacy of the Eucharist, which for Aphou is clearly dependent on the real presence of the body and blood of Christ in the elements. In summary, the way the controversy is described in the *Life of Aphou* is very different from the other sources. The question is not whether God has human shape or form, but whether man possesses God's image.[31]

Moreover, the context surrounding Theophilus' change of heart is fundamentally different in the *Life of Aphou*. While the sources sympathetic to the "Origenist" position describes his change of allegiance as a matter of succumbing to the pressure created by a mob of angry monks descending on his residence in Alexandria threatening to kill him,[32] in the *Life of Aphou* it is the lone, humble monk who goes to Alexandria, patiently waits for several days to see him, and then convinces him by means of theological arguments. No mob of angry monks are mentioned here. In fact, Theophilus even asks Aphou why he comes alone! The impression we get of the controversy and its main players is thus radically different. Theophilus, for instance, emerges in a far better light in the *Life of Aphou* than in the other sources. He realizes his earlier mistake after having been convinced on theological grounds by a pious and saintly monk of great knowledge. In this account, Theophilus is thus not a turncoat and a villain, but a rather a good guy. He is in fact the model of a good Christian who is convinced by theological arguments made by a holy man. Even though later in the story he hunts down and captures Aphou in order to make him bishop of Pemdje (in 402), he does so for a good cause, and because he had been so impressed by the monk when he came to Alexandria.[33] Moreover, the opponents of the "Origenist" position, here represented by Aphou, are not presented as ignorant, simple monks unable to understand advanced theology, but rather as being well-versed in Scripture, liturgy, and tradition. Moreover, Aphou does not in any way stress God's human form—in fact he even describes God's glory as impossible to behold due to its incredible light.[34] And crucially, his allegory of the painting of the king does not only highlight the likeness between human

31. Cf. Golitzin "Demons Suggest"; "Vision of God"; Clark, *Origenist Controversy*.

32. Socrates, *Ecclesiastical History* 6.7; Sozomen, *Ecclesiastical History* 8.11.

33. *Life of Aphou of Pemdje*, 19–24.

34. Ibid., 13–14.

beings and God, but also the differences.[35] Moreover, it is also conspicuous that neither Origen nor "Origenists" are mentioned at all in the *Life of Aphou*. In short, Aphou is by no means a stereotypical representative of the Anthropomorphite position.

The *Life of Aphou* not only presents Aphou himself as a holy man, who, reluctantly and only after having been persuaded by an angel, goes to Alexandria and lectures to the archbishop, and later reluctantly ends up as bishop, having been forcefully captured by Theophilus, but it also presents Theophilus in a good light. Not only is he presented as a good guy by letting himself be persuaded by the arguments of the hero of the story, but also by showing his admiration for Aphou, a pure ascetic and monk, by making him bishop of the important city of Pemdje, no small concession to the power and influence of monasticism in Egypt. At the same time Aphou has to bow to Theophilus' authority and accept ordination, thus emphasizing the archbishop's authority. Aphou did not, of course, want such ecclesiastical power, but once ordained he became a model bishop.[36]

The *Life of Aphou*'s account of the events of 399 is not only different from those of Cassian, Socrates, and Sozomen, but it is also conspicuously close to Theophilus' own later explanation of the controversy as being in essence a theological conflict, a question of orthodoxy and heresy, rather than one that was primarily about power and church politics. The opposite description is of course what we get in Cassian, Socrates, and Sozomen, who all present Theophilus' anti-Origenist campaign as a struggle driven by a power hungry and opportunistic archbishop, who is described as a turncoat. In fact, Theophilus' changed position on the question of God's image, which in these sources is presented in a negative light, is given a decidedly positive spin in the *Life of Aphou*. Moreover, the consequences of Theophilus' change of mind are radically different. On the basis of what we know from Socrates and Sozomen, it resulted in the persecution of monks of an "Origenist" persuasion, but in the *Life of Aphou* we hear nothing of the sort. There, Theophilus simply writes a new letter to congregations of Egypt, distancing himself from the problematic formulations of the 14th *Festal Letter*.[37]

Scholars have been divided on the question of Theophilus' motivations in the Origenist (and Anthropomorphite) controversy. Was he motivated primarily by political or theological reasons? Before scholars started taking the *Life of Aphou* into consideration, most highlighted his political

35. Ibid., 14–15.
36. Ibid., 24–31.
37. Ibid., 16.

motivations.[38] After the *Life of Aphou* was included in the discussion, however, several scholars have placed more weight on the theological aspects of the controversy.[39] While the latter group of scholars may rightly point to the fact that the *Life of Aphou* gives us an interesting alternative perspective on the question of the image of God, I would argue that the fact that the church political context of the turn of the fifth century is completely ignored in the *Life of Aphou* would tend to render it problematic to use it to shed additional light on that controversy. The fact that the *Life of Aphou* makes it seem like Aphou was the only one who reacted against Theophilus' festal letter, and the only one who went to speak to him about it, certainly does not lend much credibility to its version of the events.

Similarly problematic is the fact that the text does not mention Origen, Origenists, or Origenism at all. This is especially strange in light of Socrates' and Sozomen's accounts, where the monks demand of Theophilus that he ban the works of Origen. In the *Life of Aphou* the entire question of the image of God seems to take place in a vacuum, involving just Theophilus and Aphou and no one else. Moreover, Theophilus' change of heart only has theologial consequences, besides the fact that it ultimately causes him to ordain Aphou as bishop of Pemdje. In the *Life of Aphou* the function of the whole controversy over the image of God is as a story demonstrating Aphou's knowledge and piety, and as the reason why Theophilus made him bishop of Pemdje. It is the major turning point in Aphou's career, eventually turning him into a model bishop of a major town, from his previous career as a model, if unknown, anchorite. It is worth noting in this context that Theophilus' capture and forceful institution of Aphou as bishop has an interesting parallel in Socrates' account. We hear from Socrates how Theophilus, before the events of 399, made Dioscorus, one of the "Origenist" "tall brothers," bishop of Hermopolis "against his will, having forcibly drawn him from his retreat."[40] The way Theophilus makes Aphou bishop of Pemdje thus becomes a mirror image of his institution of Dioscorus as bishop of Hermopolis before he fell out with the "Origenists."[41]

Some scholars have nevertheless argued that it is the *Life of Aphou* that gives us the best account of the doctrinal contents of the Anthropomorphite

---

38. See, e.g., Tillemont, *Mémoires*; Schiwietz, *Das morgenländische Mönchtum*; Sheridan, "Modern Historiography," 2004. For this view, see also, e.g., Ledegang, "Anthropomorphites and Origenists."

39. See, e.g., Florovsky, "Anthropomorphites"; Florovsky, "Theophilus of Alexandria"; Clark, *Origenist Controversy*; Golitzin, "Demons Suggest"; "Vision of God."

40. Socrates, *Ecclesiastical History* 6.7.

41. This parallel is also noted by Florovsky, "Theophilus of Alexandria," 127.

controversy,[42] others that it gives us a valuable alternative perspective. Graham Gould, for instance, while noting that the *Life of Aphou* "touches the major incidents in the accounts of Socrates and Cassian at no point," still argues that "it surely deserves serious consideration as a third source for the controversy."[43] In his opinion, the text "preserves a genuine recollection from within monastic circles of what doctrinal questions were believed to have been raised by Theophilus' letter,"[44] and constitute "the best account of the doctrinal point of the controversy."[45] While Gould's assessment would seem like an overstatement, it is difficult to disagree with Elizabeth Clark's cautious observation that the *Life of Aphou* "shows the *kinds* of Scriptural and theological justifications that could be given for the Anthropomorphite position."[46] However, while it does show us some arguments that may have been made, there are no other indications that they were in fact made. As for Golitzin's argument that the *Life of Aphou* gives us evidence of the persistence of an ancient tradition about the luminous body of God and the throne of Glory,[47] it lacks the necessary demonstration of parallels close enough to the text and contents of the *Life of Aphou* to be persuasive.

In summary, the *Life of Aphou* is a hagiographical story, and Aphou's encounter with Theophilus is an important part of it, but there is not much to connect Aphou as a person or his perspective on the major theological question of the Anthropomorphite controversy to the actual events of 399. Although Gould urges us not to "dismiss the evidence of the *Life of Aphou* simply because it is of uncertain provenance, or because it belongs to the allegedly unhistorical genre of hagiography,"[48] these issues taken together with the many glaring contradictions in the accounts should certainly caution us against placing too much weight upon this text in our reconstructions of the Anthropomorphite controversy.

42. See, e.g., Gould, "Image of God."

43. Ibid., 550. For similar views, see, e.g., Drioton, "La Discusion"; Florovsky, "Theophilus of Alexandria"; Clark, *Origenist Controversy*; Golitzin, "Vision of God"; DelCogliano, "Situating Sarapion's Sorrow."

44. Gould, "Image of God," 550.

45. Ibid.

46. Clark, "Origenist Controversy," 52n54; emphasis original.

47. Golitzin, "Vision of God."

48. Gould, "Image of God," 552.

Other Contexts

If we therefore conclude that the *Life of Aphou* is of dubious value as a source for the events around the turn of the fifth century, this does not mean that it is without use as an historical source. What we may use it for, however, is as a source for the situation at a later stage of the history of the Coptic Church, and of what was then considered ideal monastic and ecclesiastical practices. While the date of authorship of the *Life of Aphou* is very difficult to determine,[49] I would argue that this text may tell us more about ecclesiastical and monastic ideals closer to the time our preserved manuscript was produced and used, in the seventh or eighth century,[50] than to the time of the Anthropomorphite controversy. As with most Coptic texts, it is difficult to backdate the *Life of Aphou* with confidence from the time when the codex that preserves it was made, since we must be aware of the high degree of fluidity of such hagiographical texts. As with other medieval textual traditions in the vernacular, texts like these were often rewritten and adapted to fit the contexts in which they were copied,[51] and we cannot know to what degree the preserved text of the *Life of Aphou* has undergone such changes from the time it was originally authored to our preserved copy.[52]

While it is difficult to say much about the context of the original authorship of the text, we can say something about its current codicological context. In Codex AC from the Thinis manuscript hoard, the *Life of Aphou* is found after two (probably pseudepigraphical) sermons on John the Baptist, and is followed by the *Didascalia Apostolorum* and the *Martyrdom of Herai*. We thus see how the Eucharistic discussion in the *Life of Aphou* and its descriptions of Aphou's conduct as bishop go well together with the *Didascalia*, while as a hagiography it works well together with the *Martyrdom of Herai*.[53] The function of the *Life of Aphou* as providing a model for imitation is thus strengthened by its placement in the codex together with these other texts.

Codices like these were commonly used in the liturgy and were publically recited.[54] This was not least the case in the monasteries, where Coptic

---

49. Bumazhnov (*Der Mensch*, 139) argues for a probable date of authorship in the late fifth century. Orlandi ("Theophilus," 101) simply states that its early origin "is not to be disputed."

50. Orlandi, "Turin Coptic Papyri," 526–27.

51. Cf. Cerquiglini, *In Praise of the Variant*; Zumthor, *Toward a Medieval Poetics*.

52. Indeed, considering the textual transmission of traditions such as these it is highly problematic to operate with the concept of a single author at all.

53. Cf. Harvey, "Martyr Passions and Hagiography."

54. Emmel "Coptic Literature," 94; cf. Sheridan, "Rhetorical Structure," 29.

texts were produced, edited, and transmitted as parts of liturgical books.[55] There are thus good reasons to consider the implications of the use of the *Life of Aphou* in such a context. Those who listened to the *Life of Aphou* in the monastery or church where manuscript GIOV.AC was used were presented with an ideal picture of the monastic life, ecclesiastical practice, and leadership, in matters of economy as well as liturgy, by means of the example of Aphou. They would hear about the time of prayer, practices of Scriptural memorization, and instruction on how to dress correctly for the Eucharist. There is little doubt that Aphou is presented as an example to imitate, for monks, priests, bishops, and lay people alike.

The text also shows us how the Bible could be interpreted with a view towards ritual practice. We see, for instance, how the text interprets Gen 1:26 in light of the Eucharist. For the *Life of Aphou*, it is necessary that the image of God can be understood concretely in terms of the real presence of the body and blood of Christ in the Eucharistic elements. The efficacy of the ritual depends on it. At the same time we also see in the *Life of Aphou* how such a concrete understanding of the image of God guides its portrayal of the significance of Aphou's ascetic practice in the early parts of the story, before his travels to Alexandria.

The Agenda of the *Life of Aphou*

What is the agenda of the *Life of Aphou*? What does the text set out to do? While some have argued that the text is free of the polemics of the Greek and Latin sources, and thus more reliable,[56] the text is certainly not without an agenda of its own. Seeing as the *Life of Aphou* even has Theophilus himeself extolling the virtues and wisdom of the monks, it is not without reason that Tito Orlandi has concluded that the text "is plainly a monastic creation."[57] The text clearly describes Aphou as the ideal monk. In addition, however, it also presents him as the ideal bishop, when he, after not inconsiderable pressure, accepts the appointment. Although Elizabeth Clark has commented that the *Life of Aphou* "seems designed rather to serve to elevate the role of the bishop of Pemdje vis-à-vis the archbishop of Alexandria,"[58] it seems to me the authority of the archbishop is in fact not denigrated, but rather affirmed by the way Theophilus is portrayed in this text. At the same time the *Life of Aphou* also underlines a positive relationship between

55. Müller, "Die alte koptische Predigt."

56. See Drioton, "La Discussion"; DelCogliano, "Situating Sarapion's Sorrow," 381.

57. Orlandi, "Theophilus of Alexandria," 101.

58. Clark, "Origenist Controversy," 52n54.

the archbishop of Alexandria and the Egyptian monks, presenting the pure ascetic as a guarantor of proper ecclesiastical practice. Looking at the *Life of Aphou* as a whole, rather than simply at the encounter with Theophilus and the discussion concerning the image of God, Dimitrij Bumazhnov concludes that the text's main focus is on the tensions between the spiritual freedom of the monks and their connection to the church.[59] While Bumazhnov is on the right track in basing his analysis on the text as a whole, rather than focusing only on its central dialogue, it seems to me that the way in which the text treats the relationship between Aphou and Theophilus, and later between Aphou and his congregation in Pemdje, while it certainly highlights the spiritual superiority of the pure, saintly ascetic over against his ecclesiastical superior, it also places great emphasis on the importance of harmony and cooperation between the monk and the church, and even stresses the monk's duty towards the latter. While spiritually superior to Theophilus, Aphou is organizationally subordinated to him and defers to his authority.

Conclusion

The *Life of Aphou* is a highly interesting Coptic hagiography with strong sympathies for both the Alexandrian archepiscopate and monastic spirituality. It stresses theology, biblical interpretation, the pious ascetic life, and sound ecclesiastical practice. As an historical source it must, however, be regarded as of dubious value for the period which it purports to describe, while giving us valuable insight into the ascetic and ecclesiastical ideals current in Egypt at a later date. Since texts like these were inherently fluid, being rewritten to various extents as they were transmitted by various people in shifting contexts over time, it is necessary to take this fluidity fully into account when we evaluate such texts as historical sources. Indeed, the inherent instability of textual transmission in a manuscript culture is even reflected on by the text itself, when it relates that Aphou was predisposed to believe that the objectionable contents of the *Festal Letter* of 399 did not go back to Theophilus himself, but was added later by a scribe.[60]

---

59. Bumazhnov, *Der Mensch*, 218.

60. This article has been written under the aegis of project NEWCONT (New Contexts for Old Texts: Unorthodox Texts and Monastic Manuscript Culture in Fourth- and Fifth-Century Egypt) at the University of Oslo. The project is funded by the European Research Council (ERC) under the European Community's Seventh Framework Programme (FP7/2007–2013) / ERC Grant agreement no 283741.

Bibliography

Brakke, David. "Canon Formation and Social Conflict in Fourth-Century Egypt: Athanasius of Alexandria's Thirty-Ninth *Festal Letter*." *Harvard Theological Review* 87 (1994) 395–419.

———. "Jewish Flesh and Christian Spirit in Athanasius of Alexandria." *Journal of Early Christian Studies* 9 (2001) 453–81.

Bumazhnov, Dimitrij. *Der Mensch als Gottes Bild im christlichen Ägypten: Studien zu Gen 1,26 in zwei koptischen Quellen des. 4.-5. Jahrhunderts*. Studien und Texte zu Antike und Christentum 34. Tübingen: Mohr Siebeck, 2006.

Burghardt, Walter J. *The Image of God in Man according to Cyril of Alexandria*. Woodstock, MD: Woodstock College Press, 1957.

Cerquiglini, Bernard. *In Praise of the Variant: A Critical History of Philology*. Translated by Betsy Wing. Parallax: Re-Visions of Culture and Society. Baltimore: Johns Hopkins University Press, 1999.

Chesnut, Glenn F. *The First Christian Histories: Eusebius, Socrates, Sozomen, Theodoret, and Evagrius*. Paris: Beauchesne, 1977.

Clark, Elizabeth A. *The Origenist Controversy: The Cultural Construction of an Early Christian Debate*. Princeton: Princeton University Press, 1992.

Cristea, Hans-Joachim. *Schenute von Atripe: Contra Origenistas: Edition des koptischen Textes mit annotierter Übersetzung und Indizes einschließlich einer Übersetzung des 16. Osterfestbriefs des Theophilus in der Fassung des Hieronymus (ep. 96)*. Studien und Texte zu Antike und Christentum 60. Tübingen: Mohr Siebeck, 2011.

Davis, Stephen J. *The Early Coptic Papacy: The Egyptian Church and Its Leadership in Late Antiquity*. The Popes of Egypt 1. Cairo: American University in Cairo Press, 2004.

DelCogliano, Mark. "Situating Sarapion's Sorrow: The Anthropomorphite Controversy and the Historical and Theological Context of Cassian's Tenth Conference on Pure Prayer." *Cistercian Studies Quarterly* 38 (2003) 377–421.

Drioton, Etienne. "La Discussion d'un moine Anthropomorphite Audien avec le patriarche Théophile d'Alexandrie en l'année 399." *Revue de l'Orient Chrétien* 10 (1915–1917) 93–100, 113–28.

Driver, Steven D. *John Cassian and the Reading of Egyptian Monastic Culture*. Medieval History and Culture 8. New York: Routledge, 2002.

Emmel, Stephen. "Coptic Literature in the Byzantine and Early Islamic World." In *Egypt in the Byzantine World, 300–700*, edited by Roger S. Bagnall, 83–102. Cambridge: Cambridge University Press, 2007.

Evelyn-White, Hugh G., *The Monasteries of the Wâdi 'n Natrûn. Part II: The History of the Monasteries of Nitria and of Scetis*. New York: Metropolitan Museum of Art, 1932.

Florovsky, Georges. "The Anthropomorphites in the Egyptian Desert." In *Aspects of Church History*, 89–96, 289. Collected Works of Georges Florovsky 4. Belmont, MA: Nordland, 1975.

———. "Theophilus of Alexandria and Apa Aphou of Pemdje: The Anthropomorphites in the Egyptian Desert, Part II." In *Aspects of Church History*, 97–129, 290–96. Collected Works of Georges Florovsky 4. Belmont, MA: Nordland, 1975.

Golitzin, Alexander, "'The Demons Suggest an Illusion of God's Glory in a Form': Controversy over the Divine Body and Vision of Glory in Some Late Fourth, Early Fifth Century Monastic Literature." *Studia Monastica* 44 (2002) 13–43.

Golitzin, Alexander, "The Vision of God and the Form of Glory: More Reflections on the Anthropomorphite Controversy of AD 399." In *Abba: The Tradition of Orthodoxy in the West: Festschrift for Bishop Kallistos (Ware) of Diokleia*, edited by John Behr et al., 273–97. Crestwood, NY: St. Vladimir's Seminary Press, 2003.

Gould, Graham. "The Image of God and the Anthropomorphite Controversy in Fourth Century Monasticism." In *Origeniana Quinta: Papers of the 5th International Origen Congress, Boston College, 14–18 August 1989*, edited by Robert J. Daly, 549–57. BETL 105. Leuven: Peeters, 1992.

Griggs, C. Wilfred. *Early Egyptian Christianity From Its Origins to 451 CE*. Brill's Scholars List. Leiden: Brill, 1990.

Harvey, Susan Ashbrook. "Martyr Passions and Hagiography." In *The Oxford Handbook of Early Christian Studies*, edited by Susan Ashbrook Harvey and D. G. Hunter, 603–27. Oxford: Oxford University Press, 2008.

Ledegang, Fred. "Anthropomorphites and Origenists in Egypt at the End of the Fourth Century." In *Origeniana Septima: Origenes in den Auseinandersetzungen des 4. Jahrhunderts*, edited by W. A. Bienert and U. Kühneweg 375–79. BETL 137. Leuven: Peeters, 1999.

Leppin, Hartmut. "The Church Historians (I): Socrates, Sozomenus, and Theodoretus." In *Greek and Roman Historiography in Late Antiquity: Fourth to Sixth Century A.D.*, edited by Gabriele Marasco, 219–54. Leiden: Brill, 2003.

Lundhaug, Hugo. *Koptiske skrifter*. Verdens Hellige Skrifter. Oslo: De norske bokklubbene, 2012.

Müller, Caspar Detlef Gustav. "Die alte koptische Predigt: Versuch eines Überblicks." PhD diss., Ruprecht-Karl-Universität, Heidelberg, 1954.

Orlandi, Tito. "Les papyrus coptes du musée égyptien de Turin." *Le Muséon* 87.1–2 (1974) 115–27.

———. "Theophilus of Alexandria in Coptic Literature." *Studia Patristica* 16 (1985) 100–104.

———. "The Turin Coptic Papyri." *Augustinianum* 53 (2013) 501–30.

Rossi, Francesco. *Trascrizione di Tre Manoscritti Copti del Museo Egizio di Torino*. Memorie della Reale academia delle scienze di Torino II/37. Torino: Loescher, 1885.

Russell, Norman. *Theophilus of Alexandria*. Early Church Fathers. London: Routledge, 2007.

Schiwietz, Stephan. *Das morgenländische Mönchtum: Erster Band: Das Ascetentum der drei ersten christlichen Jahrhunderte und das egyptische Mönchtum im vierten Jahrhundert*. Mainz: Kirchheim, 1904.

Sheridan, Mark. "The Modern Historiography of Early Egyptian Monasticism." In *Il monachesimo tra eredità e aperture: Atti del simposio "Testi e temi nella tradizione del monachesimo cristiano" per il 500 anniversario dell'Istituto Monastico di Sant' Anselmo, Roma, 28 maggio—10 giugno 2002*, edited by Maciej Bielawski and Daniël Hombergen, 197–220. SA 140, Analecta Monastica 8. Rome: Centro Studi S. Anselmo, 2004.

———. "Rhetorical Structure in Coptic Sermons." In *The World of Early Egyptian Christianity: Language, Literature, and Social Context*, edited by James E. Goehring and Janet A. Timbie, 25–48. CUA Studies in Early Christianity. Washington, DC: Catholic University of America Press, 2007.

Skeb, M. "Johannes Cassian." In *Lexicon der antiken christlichen Literatur*, edited by S. Döpp and W. Geerlings, 335–36. Freiburg: Herder, 1998.

Stewart, Columba. *Cassian the Monk.* Oxford: Oxford University Press, 1998.

Tillemont, Lenain de. *Mémoires pour servir à l'histoire ecclésiastique des six premiers siècles, justifies par les citations des auteurs originaux, avec une chronologie, où l'on fait un abrégé de l'histoire ecclésiastique et profane et des notes pour éclaircir les difficultéz des faits et de la chronologie. Tome onziéme.* Paris: Robustel, 1706.

Treadgold, Warren. *The Early Byzantine Historians.* New York: Palgrave Macmillan, 2010.

Wickham, Lionel R. *Cyril of Alexandria: Select Letters.* Oxford: Clarendon, 1983.

Woods, David, "Late Antique Historiography: A Brief History of Time." In *A Companion to Late Antiquity*, edited by Philip Rousseau, 357–71. Blackwell Companions to the Ancient World. Malden, MA: Blackwell, 2009.

Zumthor, Paul. *Toward a Medieval Poetics.* Minneapolis: University of Minnesota Press, 1992.

4

Rewritten Eve Traditions in the *Apocryphon of John*

Antti Marjanen

The first four chapters of Genesis constitute one of the most important parts of the Bible, insofar as they have triggered the imaginations of later Jewish and Christian writers in the form of new interpretations. It is especially the so-called Sethian texts[1] that have drawn their inspiration from these chapters while presenting their views of the origin of the material world and that of human beings. Most of the studies dealing with the use of these chapters in Sethian texts focus on the figure of Adam. The purpose of the present article is somewhat different. I will explore how those parts of the first four chapters of Genesis dealing with the figure of Eve have been employed and rewritten, and show what kind of interpretive strategies these new readings serve in one of the most important Sethian texts, the *Apocryphon of John*.[2] It has been preserved in four different manuscripts:

1. For a brief but excellent introduction of Sethianism and Sethian writings, see Williams, "Sethianism," 32–63. Rather than speaking only of Sethian writings and mythology, Rasimus, *Paradise Reconsidered in Gnostic Mythmaking*, 9–62, has distinguished between three related mythologies—Barbeloite, Sethite, and Ophite—which together form what he calls the Classic Gnostic mythology. According to Rasimus, the *Apocryphon of John* should be seen as a text where all the three related mythologies come together, thus representing a prime example of the Classic Gnostic theology with a specifically Christian brand. Rasimus's refined categories are in many ways helpful; yet, whether the *Apocryphon of John* should be called Sethian or Classic Gnostic is very much a matter of taste. For the sake of convenience, I here retain the traditional designation "Sethian."

2. It is a pleasure to write this contribution to a volume that is dedicated to my colleague and friend, Prof. Turid Karlsen Seim, whom I learned to know when we were both "young Nordic scholars" in a conference on the western coast of Sweden in the early 1980s. Since then we have met and cooperated on various occasions, one of the most memorable being when Turid invited me to participate in the research project

three among the Nag Hammadi Codices (NHC), of which two represent a long version (Codex II; Codex IV) and one a short version (Codex III), and one in the Berlin Codex providing a parallel to the short version of the NHC III (BG = Codex Berolinensis Gnosticus 8502).[3]

The Creation of Eve

In their description of the appearance of Eve, the long and short versions of the *Apocryphon of John* contain both similarities and differences when compared with the narrative of Genesis.[4] It is also worth noting that the two extant versions of the *Apocryphon of John* do not present a uniform view of the Eve traditions but interpret and utilize them in different ways.

Both versions of the *Apocryphon of John* agree with Gen 2:22 and insist that Eve was created by the Creator God (II 22.36—23.4; III 29.19–24; BG 59.12–19). Yet the two versions of the *Apocryphon of John* differ in three respects in their interpretation from the account of Genesis. First, the Creator God is not identical with the highest God but is Yaldabaoth, the imperfect product of Sophia, the last female aeon of the realm of the highest God. She produces Yaldabaoth in her desire to create something like herself, without the consent of the highest God, the invisible Spirit, and her own male partner (II 9.28–30; III 14.13–23; BG 36.20—37.6). Yaldabaoth is a Sethian caricature of the Jewish God, Yahweh.

The second difference between Genesis and both versions of the *Apocryphon of John* is that the latter texts emphasize that Eve was *not* formed from Adam's rib. In the long version of Codex II and the short version of BG, Yaldabaoth created her from the power of Adam (II 22.36–23.1; BG 59.12–15),[5] which he had received from his mother Sophia and had acci-

---

"Metamorphoses: Resurrection, Taxonomies, and Transformative Practices in Early Christianity," which she led in 2006–2007. I had the chance to become a fellow of the Centre for Advanced Study at the Norwegian Academy of Science and Letters and to spend a five-week research period in Oslo in the spring of 2007.

3. The text edition of these versions of the *Apocryphon of John* used in this study is that of Waldstein and Wisse, *The Apocryphon of John*. Citations to the Nag Hammadi texts refer to codex, page, and line; citations to the Berlin Codex (BG) refer to page and line. Since the version in the fourth codex of the Nag Hammadi Library is rather fragmentary I refer to it only in those cases where it clearly disagrees with the version of codex II and is sufficiently preserved to draw reliable conclusions.

4. Other Nag Hammadi passages in which Eve appears and to some of which I occasionally refer include *Hyp. Arch.* 89.3—92.3; *Orig. World* 112.25—121.27; *Gos. Phil.* 60.34—61.12; 68.22–26; 70.9–22; *Exeg. Soul* 133.1–6; *Melch.* 9–10; *Testim. Truth* 45.23—47.14; cf. also *Gos. Judas* 52.14—53.4.

5. In II 22.36—23.1 it is emphasized that Yaldabaoth took a part of the power,

dentally given to Adam while breathing his spirit into his psychical body[6] (II 19.25–32; BG 51.12–17; III 24.4–12). In the short version of Codex III the kind of material Yaldabaoth uses for the creation of Eve is not explained.[7] There it simply says that Yaldabaoth made a new female form in order to bring the power out of Adam (III 29.18–20).

Unlike NHC III, both the long and the BG text appear to emphasize that Eve is not solely Yaldabaoth's product, but rather that she has her origin in the spiritual power which Sophia first gave to Yaldabaoth and then Yaldabaoth only inadvertently passed on to Adam. Yet even NHC III seems to imply that Eve, despite being Yaldabaoth's creation, is not without spiritual quality. After Adam wakes up from his trance, during which Yaldabaoth has created Eve, and sees her, he recognizes her as "his fellow-essence (*tefsunousia*) who is like him" (III 29.4). Thus, in both versions of the *Apocryphon of John*, although both Adam and Eve are products of Yaldabaoth, their formation does not corroborate the normal primeval pattern of generation dominant in the creative processes described in the *Apocryphon of John*, according to which "like follows like."[8] Adam and Eve are not only psychical or bestial beings like their Creator Yaldabaoth, but they come to possess spiritual essences as well. In the case of Adam this is due to the interference of the divine realm in Yaldabaoth's creative activity by making Yaldabaoth impart spiritual power unknowingly to Adam. In the case of Eve this is a result of Yaldabaoth's conscious strategy to use Adam's spiritual power in producing her.

The third difference between Genesis and both versions of the *Apocryphon of John* has to do with Yaldabaoth's motive in creating Eve. Whereas in Genesis Eve is created by Yahweh in order to provide Adam with a helper (Gen 2:18 [LXX]: *boēthos*), in both versions of the *Apocryphon of John* the purpose of creating Eve is to mold a human prison so that Yaldabaoth might grab hold of "enlightened Insight"[9] (*epinoia ᵉnouoein*).[10] Enlightened Insight has been sent by the highest God to be Adam's helper, to protect Adam

---

while BG 59.12–15 states that Yaldabaoth "wanted to bring the power out of Adam in order to make a figure once again, (this time) with a female form."

6. The psychical (and material) body was all the authorities of Yaldabaoth were able to create (II 15.5–6; 19.3–6).

7. Logan, *Gnostic Truth and Christian Heresy*, 193, insists that both short versions have this view, but in fact BG agrees with the long version.

8. For this principle of generation, see King, *The Secret Revelation of John*, 94.

9. The translation is derived from Meyer, "The Apocryphon of John," 107–32.

10. As Logan, *Gnostic Truth and Christian Heresy*, 193–94, has pointed out, the same motive for creating earthly Eve seems to underlie Irenaeus's description of the Ophite myth (*Adv. haer.* 1.30.7) and *Hyp. Arch.* 89.3–11.

from Yaldabaoth and his powers, and to restore Adam—or better his divine self, the power blown into him by Yaldabaoth in connection with his creation—to the pleroma, the realm of the highest God; for this purpose, she hid herself in Adam (II 20.14–28; III 25.6–23; BG 53.4—54.4).

The creation of Eve thus serves Yaldabaoth's attempt to fight the divine realm of light in its rescue operation. The physical body of Eve is meant to constitute a new dwelling place for enlightened Insight, a place of confinement, in which Yaldabaoth can hold enlightened Insight under his control. It remains unclear why the earthly Eve is seen as a better "prison" for enlightened Insight than Adam, in whom she already is. Does the text want to suggest that a woman is a greater obstacle to the activities of a spiritual power than a man? Or does the way the narrative of Genesis describes the creation of Eve simply determine how the role of Eve is depicted in the *Apocryphon of John*? No certain answer can be given. Nevertheless, the fact that Yaldabaoth and his powers are not able to fetter enlightened Insight within the earthly Eve, as our next chapter will show, suggests that the use of a fixed literary tradition is a most likely reason for making Yaldabaoth exploit Eve as an instrument to get enlightened Insight under his control.

With the introduction of the figure of enlightened Insight, the use of the Eve tradition from Genesis takes a new turn in the *Apocryphon of John*. Some of the characteristics Genesis ascribes to Eve are attached to this figure from the divine realm of the highest God. Hence, the character of Eve as she appears in Genesis is actually split in two, as my earlier treatment of enlightened Insight has already suggested and as we are going to see even more clearly in the next chapter of this essay.

Enlightened Insight or the Spiritual Eve

The fact that Eve is seen as the helper of Adam in Genesis (2:18, 20) is not completely overlooked by the authors of the *Apocryphon of John*, but this characteristic is removed from the presentation of earthly Eve, and instead it is attributed to enlightened Insight, a figure belonging to the realm of light, a kind of spiritual Eve (II 20.14–17; III 25.6–10; BG 53.4–9).[11] That this is really a reshaping of the Eve tradition of Genesis is indicated by the fact that enlightened Insight is not only called a helper for Adam but also "Life ($z\bar{o}\bar{e}$)" (II 20.19; III 25.11; BG 53.10) in accordance with the description of Eve in Gen 3:20 (LXX). Yet the way the helping function and the "life" character of enlightened Insight are understood differs remarkably from the way they are perceived in Genesis.

---

11. Cf. heavenly Adam and Seth in II 8.28—9.14; III 12.24—13.19; BG 34.19—36.2.

The task of enlightened Insight is to help Adam "by restoring him to his perfection (*plērōma*), by teaching him about the descent of his seed[12] and by teaching him about the way of ascent, which is the (same) way he came down" (II 20.20–24; cf. III 25.13–17; BG 53.12–18). Enlightened Insight is thus supposed to give Adam the *gnōsis* he needs in order to return to the realm of light. Hence, enlightened Insight, the spiritual Eve, has a role as a savior. That it is not only Adam personally who is the target of her salvific action but all the Gnostics is underlined by the fact that, according to both versions of the *Apocryphon of John*, the object of her activity is described with a collective term "creation" (*ktisis*; II 20.19; *sōnt*; BG 53.11). In this sense enlightened Insight has a more positive role in the *Apocryphon of John* than she has in the *Hypostasis of the Archons* of the Nag Hammadi Library, another Sethian text. In the *Hypostasis of the Archons* enlightened Insight[13] certainly makes Adam alive in connection with his creation (89.11–17), and she also appears to Adam and Eve in the form of a serpent instructing them to eat from the tree of the knowledge of evil and good (89.31—90.12). Yet, all this does not grant Adam and Eve salvific knowledge, but it only makes them aware of everything they lack (90.13—91.11). In fact, in that text it remains unclear whether Adam and Eve can partake of salvation at all. In addition, the role of the conveyer of the salvific message is not given to enlightened Insight but to the true human,[14] the offspring of Eve's daughter, Norea (*Hyp. Arch.* 96.19—97.9).

The role of the spiritual Eve, enlightened Insight, as a savior figure is underscored in the long version of the *Apocryphon of John* by the fact that she is also identified with Sophia, that is, "Life" or the Mother of the Living (II 23.20–25). While speaking about the appearance of enlightened Insight to Adam the text emphasizes that it is actually Sophia herself who has now descended in the figure of enlightened Insight to rectify her earlier mistake that took place in connection with the creation of Yaldabaoth. She has come down in order that the living might taste "perfect knowledge" (II 23.26).[15]

12. Codex III and BG read here "defect" (*hysterēma*) instead of "seed" (*sperma*); both terms refer to the divine element Sophia gave to Yaldabaoth and Yaldabaoth blew into Adam in order to make him arise. It needs to be restored to the pleroma to make it perfect.

13. The *Hypostasis of the Archons* does not use the title "enlightened Insight," though it speaks about the "spiritual woman," but they are identical figures.

14. "The true human" refers to a future revealer of the salvific message, most probably to Jesus.

15. As noted by Barc and Funk, *Le Livre des secrets de Jean. Recension bréve*, 294, the short version only speaks about "the Mother's (Sophia's) *sunzugos*" who will be sent forth to rectify her deficiency (III 30.10–12; BG 60.12–14). This reference seems to presuppose an appearance of Jesus, the seed of the Mother-Father (III 39.10–13; BG

The Rape of Eve

The most significant new feature that the *Apocryphon of John* introduces in its portrait of Eve, compared with Genesis 1–4, is that she is raped by Yaldabaoth, the Creator. This incident is described in all the four versions even though the long and short versions of the *Apocryphon of John* disagree on the details (II 24.8–17; IV 37.17–29; BG 62.3–10; III 31.6–12). According to the long version the actual target of Yaldabaoth's violent behavior is enlightened Insight who has appeared in Eve who stands next to Adam. The long version does not provide any explicit explanation for Yaldabaoth's action. Based on the context, one can assume that Yaldabaoth simply tries to do some damage to the realm of light by attempting to rape its messenger. Nevertheless, just before Yaldabaoth undertakes his impudent deed, enlightened Insight is assisted by Providence to leave Eve and to save herself and the realm of light from the attack of the lower world. In a way, the text provides "a docetic tack."[16] Thus the text strongly underlines the impossibility of evil influence on the affairs of the realm of light.

Neither of the short versions of the *Apocryphon of John* introduces enlightened Insight into the rape scene. The direct target of Yaldabaoth's shameless act in this version of the text is the earthly Eve. The fact that Yaldabaoth's action is motivated by his desire "to raise offspring from her (= the earthly Eve)" (BG 62.6–7)[17] corroborates the idea that the purpose of the rape is not intended to interfere with the pleromatic world. In both versions of the *Apocryphon of John* the rape scene only serves to indicate that the two first sons of Eve (Cain and Abel, who actually are Eloim and Yave, the two biblical names of the Jewish God) are the rulers of the tomb, i.e., the material world or body (II 24.32–34; BG 63.9–12; III 32.3–6). When Seth, the ancestor of the Sethian Gnostics in the *Apocryphon of John*, is born, he is not a product of the earthly Eve. Rather, as we will see, Adam is producing him together with "the likeness of his own foreknowledge"[18] (II 24.35–36) or "his *ousia*"

75.10–13). Yet III 39.18–21 (cf. BG 76.1–5) suggests that the Mother (= Sophia) had already come to the world another time to rectify her deficiency, which seems to imply a tradition similar to that of II 23.20–25.

16. So Perkins, "Sophia as Goddess," 110.

17. King, *The Secret Revelation of John*, 66, translates: "to sow a seed in her." The meaning of King's translation remains obscure and is also somewhat surprising in light of BG 74.3–4, which employs the same expression as BG 62.6–7 and speaks about the angels of Yaldabaoth who want to have a sexual intercourse with the daughters of men so that they might "raise offspring from them" (this is also King's translation in that passage [p. 76]).

18. Gr. *prognōsis* is the title that is used of Barbelo in II 9.28. Her likeness is most probably enlightened Insight. *tefousia* stands in BG 60.4 for enlightened Insight

(BG 63.13), i.e., enlightened Insight or the spiritual Eve,[19] who again appears on the scene after the episode of the rape of the earthly Eve.

Not only does the motif of rape appear in the *Apocryphon of John* among the Nag Hammadi texts; it also occurs in the Sethian *Hypostasis of the Archons* (89.17–31) and in *On the Origin of the World* (116.11—117.15). Unlike in the *Apocryphon of John*, in these latter texts it is not Yaldabaoth who perpetrates the rape but his archons. The motive behind the rape is also different. In the *Hypostasis of the Archons* the archons simply yield to their lusts, while in *On the Origin of the World* the purpose of the rape is to make the spiritual Eve impure and therefore unable to return to the realm of light as well as to beget children who will serve the archons. The latter text clearly represents a later and more developed form of the motive. Yet it is a commonality to all three texts as well as to both versions of the *Apocryphon of John* that the spiritual Eve, who is the target of the attack of the archons, escapes and it is the earthly Eve who is raped. Yaldabaoth and his powers are not permitted to exercise any direct influence on the pleromatic world. The function of the earthly Eve seems to be that of a substitute for the spiritual Eve who can free herself from an unpleasant event. Nevertheless, the fact that the pleromatic world remains untouched by the brutal attack of the evil powers in all three writings by no means minimizes the indefensibility of the act. Rape was and is a powerful means to subordinate and humiliate women. The fact that neither of the versions of the *Apocryphon of John* presents any moral condemnation of the act is very unfortunate.[20]

The major consequence of the rape of Eve in both versions of the *Apocryphon of John* is the introduction of sexual intercourse into the material world. In both cases, it is seen as an evil work of the chief archon. As Karen King has pointed out, there is nevertheless an interesting difference between the descriptions of the two versions.[21]

While in the long version, sexual desire is located in Eve,[22] in BG the desire for offspring is placed in Adam. The difference between the two versions becomes even more conspicuous when one realizes that in both versions the desire for sexual intercourse is clearly seen in negative terms while

---

(epinoia).

19. So also Barc and Funk, *Le Livre des secrets de Jean. Recension bréve*, 302n206; Turner, *Sethian Gnosticism and the Platonic Tradition*, 233.

20. In *On the Origin of the World* the act of rape by the powers of Yaldabaoth is regarded as a wicked and foul act (117.4–6). In the *Hypostasis of the Archons* it is stated that by raping Eve the Archons "condemned themselves" (89.29–30).

21. King, "Sophia and Christ in the *Apocryphon of John*," 170–71.

22. The long version of the *Apocryphon of John* follows Gen 3:16.

the desire for offspring has soteriological value.[23] In both versions the fact that Adam came to know[24] the spiritual Eve (II 24.35—25.1; BG 63.12–14) led to the birth of Seth, the ancestor of a Gnostic race, through whom the saving knowledge was conveyed to future generations. The fact that the long version of the *Apocryphon of John* explicitly attributes sexual desire to woman, who thus "draws man down into the filth of fleshly intercourse,"[25] tends to lead to the devaluation of the feminine.

One last question remains concerning the rape of Eve. Since this motif is so prominent in two important Sethian writings, the *Apocryphon of John* and the *Hypostasis of the Archons*, as well as in *On the Origin of the World*, which is also in many ways related to Sethian thinking,[26] one is compelled to ask whether the notion of the rape of Eve has its origin among Sethians. Is it possible that the Jewish seduction motif connected with the serpent's effort to tempt Eve, which readily has sexual undertones, has evolved into an explicit rape of Eve tradition among Sethian writers?[27] This is not impossible, but there is one early Christian text which seems to contain a rape of Eve motif and which is hardly dependent on the above-mentioned Sethian texts. According to the *Protevangelium of James*, Joseph the carpenter finds Mary pregnant when he returns home from his building projects. When Joseph describes his experience he compares it to that of Adam who "was praying when the serpent came and found Eve alone, deceived her, and corrupted (*emianen*) her" (13:5).[28] In its context the verb *miainō* clearly has a connotation of rape. Still, there is nothing in the text which would suggest that it would be dependent on any of the Nag Hammadi texts we have discussed above. The most likely explanation is that it presupposes a common tradition with them. This tradition of the rape of Eve has provided the authors of the three Nag Hammadi texts with the possibility of creating an aetiology for sexual procreation (*Apocryphon of John*) or lust (*Hypostasis of the Archons*) or even the birth of non-Gnostic people (*On the Origin of the World*).

23. To be sure, the short version of Codex III in the Nag Hammadi Library describes Adam's act of knowing the spiritual Eve as that of "lawlessness"; cf. King, "Sophia and Christ in the *Apocryphon of John*," 107.

24. This is of course a euphemism for sexual intercourse.

25. King, "Sophia and Christ in the *Apocryphon of John*," 171.

26. Rasimus, *Paradise Reconsidered in Gnostic Mythmaking*, 62, regards *On the Origin of the World* as a representative of Ophite mythology, which, according to him, is one of the three components constituting what he calls Classic Gnostic mythology, an alternative term to Sethian Gnosticism.

27. For these traditions, see Stroumsa, *Another Seed*, 38–53.

28. The translation derives from Hock, *The Infancy Gospels of James and Thomas*, 55–57.

Eve's Children

If the rape of Eve was a completely new addition to the cluster of Eve traditions in Genesis 1–4, the story of the children of Eve builds more closely on
the material found in Genesis, although in various Nag Hammadi texts, including the *Apocryphon of John*, these traditions are remarkably reworked.
We have already mentioned how the authors of the *Apocryphon of John* want
the readers to perceive the figures of Cain and Abel. He is, however, not
interested in the story of fratricide at all. The first brothers are not to be seen
as humans—therefore the murder of Abel by Cain is not important—but
they function as code names for the two main characteristics of the Jewish
God, justice and injustice.[29] They also control the four classical elements of
the material world: fire, wind, water, and earth (*Ap. John* II 24.15–25) and
are thus Yaldabaoth's important assistants.

The third child of Eve, Seth, who also in Genesis attracts some attention (Gen 4:25–26; 5:3), is one of the key figures in the *Apocryphon of
John*. In Genesis he is the replacement of his two older brothers, Abel who
was murdered by Cain, and Cain "who went away from the presence of the
Lord" (Gen 4:16); Seth thus becomes the new ancestor of humankind. In the
Apocryphon of John Seth has an even more important role to play although
his name is not mentioned very many times. Not only is he a spiritual ancestor of future Sethian Gnostics, but like Adam and the spiritual Eve, he also
has a dwelling in the pleromatic world which is located in the eternal realm
of one of the luminaries, Oroiael (*Ap. John* II 9.11–14). His offspring are
stationed in the realm just below him. When Seth takes his place in the material world he appears as Adam's son but the earthly Eve is not his mother;
rather, he is a result of the fact that Adam "came to know"[30] his counterpart,
i.e., enlightened Insight or the spiritual Eve. This means that Seth is not an
ordinary human but through his mother he is connected with the realm of
light. In addition, Seth's mother sends her spirit, which is a copy (*antitupos*)
of what is in the pleromatic world, to him and to his offspring who are going
to dwell in the material world (*Ap. John* II 24.34—25.7). Moreover, Seth is
a copy (*eine*) of the Son of Man, the Autogenes, the third member of the

---

29. In II 24.17–20 Eloim stands for justice and Yave for injustice, whereas in IV
37.30—38.6 Eloim stands for injustice and Yave for justice.

30. The expression derives from the terminology of Gen 4:25 and is a euphemism
for sexual intercourse. Yet, the use of this euphemism probably suggests that the expression does not refer to the same impure sexual intercourse that is condemned as an act
of Yaldabaoth in the text (*Ap. John* II 24.26–27), but to a special act of procreation that
leads to the birth of the Sethian race.

divine trinity (II 14.15; 25.1), which consists of the Invisible Spirit, Barbelo, and the Autogenes.[31]

Concluding Remarks

The authors of the two versions of the *Apocryphon of John* utilize many of the Eve-traditions of Genesis in their presentations of the origin of the material world and the anthropogony. Yet it is equally clear that they rewrite practically all the details of the Eve-traditions to serve their own purposes. The most significant rewriting has to do with the split of Eve into two figures: the earthly Eve and the spiritual Eve or enlightened Insight. With this operation, the author can employ Eve to counter the attacks which the material world and its powers, mainly Yaldabaoth the Creator God, aim at the realm of light. These attacks culminate when Yaldabaoth rapes Eve. Since Yaldabaoth's action is directed at the earthly Eve only, no direct harm is done to the realm of light. Yet Yaldabaoth's action seems to have one fatal consequence as far as the material world and humankind is concerned. Yaldabaoth plants sexual desire in men and women. This is seen as a destructive fate for humankind. According to the long version of the *Apocryphon of John* it is especially women who are susceptible to sexual temptations. In this way the text clearly devalues the ability of women to reach the spiritual standard the text holds desirable. The long version of the *Apocryphon of John* thus maintains those cultural notions of its time which held that women were less capable of controlling their behavior, especially in the area of sexuality. At the same time, the text also defined ascetic ideals in such a way that procreation was seen as a repulsive activity encouraged by Yaldabaoth (II 24.29–32). To be sure, it is not fully clear whether or not the Sethian race is allowed to procreate, since their progenitor, Seth, also has its origin in sexual intercourse between Adam and the spiritual Eve (II 24.34—25.2).

Since Eve is split into two figures in both versions of the text it also gives the authors possibilities to grant her various roles. As enlightened Insight or as the spiritual Eve she assumes a salvific role. Furthermore, this salvific role is connected with Eve's role as a helper (*boēthos*). When the "auxiliary" task is depicted it is presented as the role of a teacher or as that of one who restores a person (= Adam) to his fullness (*Ap. John* II 20.19–24).

---

31. In Christian Sethian texts, such as the *Apocryphon of John*, the Autogenes seems to be a Christ figure; for this, see Turner, *Sethian Gnosticism and the Platonic Tradition*, 286.

In an interesting twist the categories seem to be redefined: a helper gains a key role in the plan of salvation.

Bibliography

Barc, Bernard, and Wolf–Peter Funk. *Le Livre des secrets de Jean. Recension bréve (NH III,1 et BG,2).* Bibliothèque copte de Nag Hammadi, section "Textes" 35. Leuven: Peeters, 2012.

Hock, Ronald F. *The Infancy Gospels of James and Thomas.* Santa Rosa, CA: Polebridge, 1995.

King, Karen L. *The Secret Revelation of John.* Cambridge: Harvard University Press, 2006.

———. "Sophia and Christ in the *Apocryphon of John.*" In *Images of the Feminine in Gnosticism,* edited by Karen L. King, 158–76. Studies in Antiquity and Christianity. Philadelphia: Fortress, 1988.

Logan, Alastair H. B. *Gnostic Truth and Christian Heresy: A Study in the History of Gnosticism.* London: T. & T. Clark, 2004.

Meyer, Marvin. "The Apocryphon of John." In *The Nag Hammadi Scriptures,* edited by Marvin Meyer, 107–32. New York: HarperCollins, 2007.

Perkins, Pheme. "Sophia as Goddess in the Nag Hammadi Codices." In *Images of the Feminine in Gnosticism,* edited by Karen L. King, 96–112. Studies in Antiquity and Christianity. Philadelphia: Fortress, 1988.

Rasimus, Tuomas. *Paradise Reconsidered in Gnostic Mythmaking: Rethinking Sethianism in Light of the Ophite Evidence.* NHMS 68. Leiden: Brill, 2009.

Stroumsa, Gedaliahu A. G. *Another Seed: Studies in Gnostic Mythology.* NHS 24. Leiden: Brill, 1984.

Turner, John D. *Sethian Gnosticism and the Platonic Tradition.* Bibliothèque copte de Nag Hammadi, section "Études" 6. Leuven: Peeters, 2001.

Waldstein, Michael, and Frederick Wisse. *The Apocryphon of John: Synopsis of Nag Hammadi Codices II,1; III,1; and IV,1 with BG 8502,2.* NHMS 33. Leiden: Brill, 1995.

Williams, Michael A. "Sethianism." In *A Companion to Second-Century Christian "Heretics,"* edited by Antti Marjanen and Petri Luomanen, 32–63. Supplements to Vigiliae Christianae 76. Leiden: Brill, 2005.

———— 5 ————

Sub luce videantur

The Time of Light in Early Renaissance Painting

PER SIGURD TVEITEVÅG STYVE

> Tutte le cose le quali si uegono da essere compreso nel tempo. La
> cosa visibile non è fatto se non nel tempo della trasportatione
> della assis radiale sopra la cosa veduta.
>
> —LORENZO GHIBERTI, *I COMMENTARII*

Introduction

ART HISTORIANS HAVE LONG debated the apparent paradox, that while the development of pictorial depth in the late fourteenth century permitted complex narratives, with a number of events depicted within the same spatial location, the prevalence of this method in the fifteenth century seems progressively inconsistent with the rationalization of the pictorial space.[1]

1. The article was carried out when I was a post-doctorate at Kunsthistorisches Institute in Florenze, Max-Planck. I would like to thank the members of the research group on light in the painting of the early modern period Dir. Prof. Alessandro Nova, Dr. Hana Grüendler, and Dr. Rodolfo Maffeis, for many fruitful discussions on the topic. I also want to thank Prof. Victor Plathe Tschudi for valuable comments on the article, and Dir. Prof. Turid Karlsen Seim at the Norwegian Institute in Rome for many instructive discussions on the more general issue concerning historical conditions for the concept of time.

The reason for this is that the mathematical method of central perspective fixates the gaze of the beholder in a geometrically defined point on the surface, a *punctum unicus*, which by immobilizing the eye seemingly privileges depiction of a singular moment, thus radically limiting the horizon of narrative possibilities first opened up by the invention of pictorial space.[2] However, fifteenth century treatises on art do not reflect an understanding of the perspectival constructed image as restricted to depiction of a frozen moment. The discourse on pictorial composition (*compositio*) and narration (*narratio*) revolves, rather, around the ability of the painted *storia* (or *istoria*, the alternative Italian translation of the Latin *historia*) to move emotionally "the mind of the beholder" by depicting the events as if "unfolding before our eyes."[3] Renaissance authors frequently discuss the events and persons of the *storia* in temporal terms as "moving freely" in all directions within the pictorial space: performing, speaking and interacting with each other and with the beholder.[4]

Significantly, nor did the prevailing artistic practice of representing more than one event in time pose any art theoretical problem;[5] on the contrary, painterly perspective probed into issues concerning ideas of temporality. Artists, indeed, were well aware that painterly perspective, *perspectiva artificialis*, through the application of Euclidian geometry, was founded on medieval visual theory, *perspectiva communis* or *naturalis*, where the act of seeing was regarded a temporal process; the very word *perspectiva* still primarily referred to the science of the transmission of light rays. Put differently, while the geometry of perspective concerned the construction of a coordinative system in which one could denote the diminishing of all objects in space by drawing orthogonal lines from one or several vanishing points to the bottom edge, on a fundamental level painterly perspective concerned the imitation of operating principles of vision (*visio*). As Sven Dupré and others have pointed out, the artistic geometrical *technique* was only the more limited domain of drawing in perspective;[6] in harmony with

---

2. For a summary of the debate on continuous narrative, see Lew Andrews, "Structuring Time," 287–313; Andrews, *Story and Space*.

3. On the meaning of "historia" in Leon Battista Alberti's *De Pictura* and its Italian translations into *storia* and *istoria* in the early theory of painting, see esp. Grafton, "Historia," 199–223. On the humanistic vocabulary in descriptions of painting in the renaissance in general and its basis in ancient rhetorical theory, see esp. Baxandall, *Giotto and the Orators*.

4. See Greenstein, "Mantegna," 217–42.

5. It was not formulated as a problem until the mid-sixteenth century through the impact of Aristotle's Poetics on the theory of painting. See esp. Velli, *Le immagini e il tempo*.

6. Dupré, "The Historiography," 34–61.

medieval theories on vision, perspective in fifteenth-century treatises on painting is described as light rays manifesting themselves in a number of pyramids connecting every point of the surface with the eye. The process of seeing is thus regarded as a continuous transmission of images from the object to the eye, and by revealing the shape of forms and their relationships in space only over time, light in renaissance theories on painting appropriates a crucial function of mediating between space and time. In this article, I am less concerned with the geometry of perspective and optics as a general science in the late medieval and early modern period, both representing fields of research on their own, and more with how the context of medieval optics provided art theorists and artists with a concept of light that added a temporal dimension to *perspectiva artificialis*. The article consists of two parts. In the first part, I will discuss the significance of the temporal dimension in the understanding of light and the act of seeing in the early treatises on painting. I argue that the importance of the concept of light in optics provided a theoretical framework for an understanding of the "mimetic transparency" of the image as a temporal as well as spatial construct. In the second part, I will turn to the experimentation with different perspectival solutions in the period's artistic practice. Furthermore, by analyzing the relationship between these solutions and the depicted *storia*, I hope to demonstrate how the renaissance concept of light structures and combines space and time in painting, permitting, rather than putting an end to, the practice of representing numerous time-units within the same perspectival constructed space.

Alberti and the Temporal Dimension of Light Rays in the Early Theory of Painting

In pre-modern optics, the act of seeing is without exception discussed as a process that unfolds in time even though, to quote Alhacen, "time itself might be imperceptible because of the speed with which air receives the forms of light," a problem that Leonardo later on was to probe in his studies of movement.[7] Sight-lines were generally identified with rays of light, *radii*

---

7. In the context of dynamics, Leonardo discusses the time and movement of all things in nature, including perception: "I moti sono di nature, de' quali il primo è detto temporale, perché sol s'imaccia del movimento del tempo, e questo abbraccia in sé tutti li altri. Il secondo è della vita delle cose. Terzo è detto mentale, e questo sta ne' corpi animati. *Quarto è quello delle spezie delle cose, che si spargon per l'aria per linie rette; questo pare non essere sottoposto al tempo, perché è fatto in tempo indivisibile, e quella cosa che colla mente non si po dividere, non si trova infra noi.*" Leonardo, Il Codex, 543v/203v; my italics.

or *specie*, transmitting the images either directly, by reflection or by refraction, before they are received into the eye through a complex transition from pure sensation to cognition.[8] When Arab and late medieval optical theories at the beginning of the 15th century were put into wide circulation, translated, and commented upon, as they proved relevant for a range of new fields of knowledge,[9] art theorists and intellectually ambitious artists also turned to this corpus of texts in order to comprehend the empirical basis for *perspectiva artificialis*.[10] They thus inherited a concept of light that was inextricable from notions of vision (*visio*) as a fundamentally temporal process in the receiving of images continuously emanating from objects in nature.

In *Della Pittura* (1436), Leon Battista Alberti made painters not trained in Latin familiar with these optical concepts. By applying Euclidian geometry, he formulated a recipe to reconstruct the visual pyramid of the medieval optics, and showed how knowledge on the behaviour of light rays forms the basis in constructing a convincing illusion (fig. 5.1).

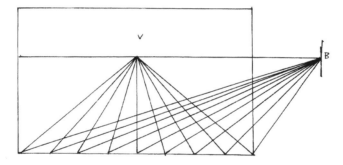

Figure 5.1. Reconstruction of Albertian one-point perspective (V=Vanishing point, B=Beholder) by Eldbjørg Styve.

8. In the context of Alberti, see esp. Greenstein, "Om Alberi's," 683–86.

9. See: Lindberg, "Lines," 66–83; Lindberg, *John Pecham*, 29ff; Smith, "Alhacen's," lxxxiii–lxxxix. The importance of Biagio Pelacani (Biagio da Parma) for the dissemination of the medieval optics in the early fifteenth century and its impact on the construction of *perspectiva artificialis* is well known. Between 1377 and 1411, he lectured on the sciences of optics at Padova and Florence. His *Quaestiones perspectivae*, 1390, had at the time become authoritative, and Paolo Toscanelli is said to have brought a copy of it when he came to Florence from Padua in 1424. See for instance: Parronchi, "Le fonti," 3–32; Thorndike, *A History of Magic*, 72.

10. Especially *De Aspectibus* by Alhacen (Aarab Abu Ali` al Hasan ibn al Haytham, 965–1040), and the various works by the "Perspectivists" at the turn of the thirteenth century, such as Witelo's *Optics* (*Perspectiva*), Roger Bacon's *On Rays* (*De radiis*), and John Peckham's *General Optics* (*Perspectiva communis*), had a profound impact on the early theory of painting. See: Vescovini, *Le teorie*, 367–483. On the distinction between the *perspectiva naturalis* or *perspctiva communis*, as a science of optics, and the *perspectiva artificialis*, as construction of pictorial space, see Domenique, *L'hypothèse d'Oxford*, 16–23.

At the beginning of his discussion "On the reception of light," Alberti makes it clear that he is not concerned with the question of whether these rays come from the object or from the eye, a question that had been permeated with theological significance since the thirteenth century, especially in the scholastic debate on spiritual vision.[11] What interests him, rather, is how light rays, which propagate themselves in a number of straight lines, "depart from the surface of the plane for the eye fill the pyramid . . . with the colours and brilliant lights with which the surface gleams." When describing the geometry of perspective, he explicates how these rays of light furthermore link the eye to all points in an observed continuum:

> For these same rays, stretched between the eye and the surface come together very quickly by their own force and by a certain marvellous subtlety, penetrating the air and thin and clear objects, they strike against something dense and opaque, where they strike with a point and adhere to the mark they make . . . The rays, gathered together within the eye, are like a stalk; the eye is like a bud which extends its shoots rapidly and in straight line to the plane opposite.[12]

For Alberti, then, the fact that *perspectiva artificialis* presupposes a fixed point of viewing does not pose any theoretical problem in regard to the alteration caused by the time involved in vision.[13] On the contrary, through the adaption of medieval optics, the conceptual rationale of the theories of painterly perspective, from Alberti to Piero, and from Leonardo to Lomazzo, implied crucial notions of a temporal dimension.[14] One important source in this respect was Bacon's *Perspectiva* in which he states that: "The multiplication of light [lucis multiplicationem] in the perceptual process is a successive and temporal alteration [esse alterationem successivam et temporale]."[15] Bacon, and the "Perspectivists" in general, conceive of

11. Alberti, *On Painting*, 46.

12. Ibid. I have made minor alterations to the translation.

13. Leonardo is the first to discuss at length the problem of the movement of the eye in relation to perspective drawing. The literature on Leonardo's optical writings is extensive. On Leonardo's dissatisfaction with the strictly geometrical descriptions of light and vision in optics and treatises on perspective where the eye is thought of as a fixed point, see Ackerman, "Leonardo's," 97–151.

14. On these art theorists' writings on light in general, see Barasch, *Light and Color*. Lomazzo divides his study of perspective in three parts of which one is on light. See Lomazzo, *Trattato*, 211. On Leonardo's optical sources, see Kemp, "'Il Concetto," 120–21. On Leonardo's optics and notions of time in perception, see esp. Fehrenbach, "Der ozillierende Blick," 522–44.

15. Quoted from Lindberg, *Theories of Vision*, 147.

these light rays as lines, as opposed to singular points. Discussing Aristotle's *Physics*, Bacon elaborates on this relationship:

> Moreover as an instant is to time, so is a point to a line. There-
> fore, by permutation, as an instant is to a point, so is time to a
> line. But the traversal of a point occurs in an instant; therefore,
> traversal of every line occurs in time. Therefore, a species tra-
> versing a linear space, however small, will traverse it in time.
> Prior and posterior in space are the cause of prior and poste-
> rior in the traversal of space and in duration . . . but prior and
> posterior in duration do not exist without time since they (the
> species) cannot exist in an instant . . . it is impossible for an
> instant to exist without time, just as it is for a point to exist with-
> out a line. Therefore, the remaining possibility is that light is
> multiplied in time, and likewise every species of a visible thing
> and of the eye.[16]

Even though time itself is not something that can be sensed by sight, Bacon concludes, for vision sensible time is required.[17] John Pecham, another
oft-cited authority by the early renaissance art theorists, similarly asserts
that: "certification of a visible object is achieved only in a period of time
by the passage of the axis of the pyramidal radiation over it."[18] Renaissance
art theorists at the beginning of the century adapted these general notions
regarding how visual rays travelling in straight lines determine the observation and description of vision. When, for example, Lorenzo Ghiberti discusses the time of light in perception in *I Commentarii*, he virtually repeats
Pecham's ideas, concluding that: "all things to be seen is seen in time."[19]

The debate on the relationship between the point and the line provided
the necessary means to explicate light's role in the geometry of painterly
perspective as a relationship between moment and duration. Nicholas of
Cusa, who wrote a treatise on light (*De dato patris luminum*, 1446) in order
to explore God's relationship to the intellect and creation, even compares

16. "Item sicut se habet instans ad tempus, sic punctus ad lineam. Ergo permutatim,
sicut se habet instans ad punctum, sic tempus ad lineam. Sed pertransitus puncti est in
instant; ergo emnis line pertransitus est in tempore. Igtur species pertransiens spatium
lineare quantumcunque parvum pertransibit in tempore . . . Sed impossibile est instans
esse sine tempore, sicut nec punctum sine linea. Relinquitur ignitur quod lux multi-
plicatur in tempore, et omnis species rei visibilis et visus similiter. Sed tamen non in
tempore sensibili et perceptibili a visu." Quoted from Lindberg, *Roger Bacon*, 136, 138.

17. Lindberg, *Roger Bacon*, 132.

18. *Perspectiva communis*, pt. I, prop. 53. Quoted from Lindberg, *John Pecham*, 135.
The importance of Pecham's treatise caused it to be revised by Fazio Cardano, most
likely published in Milan in 1492.

19. Ghiberti, *Der Dritte*, 228.

the drawing of a line in "one's mind" (in developing an argument) with the painter's drawing of an actual line as a temporal process of unfolding. He explains how the point is always in line, and how "the line unfolds (*explicatio*) the enfolding (*complicatio*) of the point"; likewise, the present instant, which is comparable to the point, unfolds in time "because nothing is found in time but the present instant." Cusa concludes that motion, therefore, is unfolded rest.[20] Alberti, who most likely met Nicholas of Cusa on several occasions, describes in comparable terms how the visual rays that form the basis of linear perspective measure quantity just as we orient ourselves in space with a compass:[21]

> All space on the surface that is between any two points on the outline is called a quantity. The eye measures these quantities with the visual rays as with a pair of compass. In every surface there is as many quantities as there are spaces between point and point. Height from top to bottom, width from left to right, breadth from near to far and whatever other dimension or measure which is made by sight makes use of the extrinsic rays . . . This is why it is usually said that vision occurs by means of a triangle whose base is the quantity seen and whose sides are those same rays which are stretched to the eye from extreme points of that quantity.[22]

Having established this, Alberti goes on to elucidate the nature of what he terms median rays:

> Median rays, that multitude in the pyramid [which lie] within the extrinsic rays, remains to be treated. These behave, in a manner of speaking, like the chameleon . . . Since these rays carry both the colours and lights on the surface from where they touch it up to the eye, they should be found lighted and coloured in a definite way wherever they are broken.[23]

Alberti here talks of light rays in the visual pyramid, which carry images through the air into the very room of the beholder. The easy shift from theoretical inferences about the nature of light in relation to the point and the

---

20. See, for instance, Bellitto et al., *Introducing Nicholas of Cusa*, 382–88. On the significance and meaning of the point and line in Alberti's *Della Pittura*, see Greenstein, "On Alberti's," 683–86.

21. On Alberti and Cusa, see Harries, "On the Power," 105–27; Santinello, *Leon Battista Alberti*, 265–96.

22. Alberti, *On Painting*, 46–47.

23. Ibid., 48. Regarding Alberti's distinction between "median rays," "extrinsic rays," and "centric rays," see Ackerman, "Alberti's," 59–97; Barasch, *Light and Color*, 69–71.

line to the realm of practical advice to the painter suggests (as Pier Lomazzo also insists on a century later) that artistic practice must be grounded on a comprehension of optics: How light emanates from a source and reflects "as it touches it [the objects seen in the painting] to the eye."[24] The renaissance concept of the picture as a cross-section of the visual pyramid thus becomes very concrete and dynamic: As we look through a window (*finestra aperta*) or veil (*velo*), rays of light continuously penetrate the surface toward the eye of the beholder.

Alhacen's *De Aspectibus* is crucial for this understanding of the image as conditioned by the temporal process of vision; the book had a considerable impact on the 15th century theory of painting, not least through Biagio da Pelacani's comments and Guerruccio di Cione Federighi's early translation of the text into Italian.[25] His explanation of the aperture of the eye and the process of vision indeed frames general ideas of light in the early theory of painting as formulated, for example, by Alberti and Ghiberti. Art theorists were therefore unquestionably highly attentive to the substantial part of the book that Alhacen devotes to a discussion on the time of movement of light rays:

> If the air receives the light in successive intervals, then light can only reach the body facing the aperture by moving, but motion will only occur in time. On the other hand, if the air as a whole receives the light all at once, the light's reaching the air after it was not there will happen only in time, even though it may be imperceptible . . . Thus, the instant, or point in time, at which the light reaches the air inside the aperture, or a portion of that air, is different from the instant at which the initial portion of the aperture is opened. And between each of these two instants there is an interval of time. Therefore, light passes from the air outside the aperture to the air inside the aperture only over time . . .[26]

This basic notion that the line expressing a quantity is linked to the time of the act of vision prevailed in the artistic discourse on light throughout

24. Lomazzo, *Trattato*, I, 392.

25. See, for instance, Vescovini, "Il problema," 349–87. According to Vescovini, Ghiberti most likely read the popular version of Alhazen's *De Aspectibus*; see Vescovini, "Contributo," 17–45. On Biagio Pelacani and Alhacen, see Vescovini, "Biagion-Pelacani"; Barocelli, "Per Biagio," 21–36.

26. Alhacen concludes in terms of a Nietzschean apology about the senses being too coarsely tuned to take notice of the time-span involved: "But the sense lacks a means of perceiving this time because it is so short and because the sense lacks adequate precision, being too weak to perceive whatever is exceptionally small. Thus, with respect to the sense, this time-interval amounts to an instant." Smith, *Alhazen's Theory*, 446–47.

the renaissance; at the turn of the century Leonardo, for instance, states in comparable terms that, "a line is made by the movement of a point; a surface is made by the movement of a line which travels in straight lines; the point in time is to be compared to an instant, and the line represents time with a length."[27] The eyes' direct relationship to the moving images nature ema-nates—before the images are transposed into the brain, causing additional image-movements—and the artists' transformation of these simulacra into physical objects (on the surface) became indeed a powerful argument in Leonardos *Paragone* of images cognitive primacy over words.[28]

Early renaissance artists were therefore aware of the fact that by codifying optical rules in their perspective constructions, they provided the pictures with a temporal dimension and thus developed formulas of "liv-ing images." Perspectival construction thus allowed for and even privileged representations of a number of events within a single image. What in par-ticular concerns us here is the emphasis on the temporal dimension in the comprehension of the image through the application of optics, viz. how and to what extent it conditioned the perception and construction of pictorial space as materialization of vision. In what follows, therefore, I will turn to the artistic experimentation with different perspectival systems in the first half of the fifteenth century, which forms the visual part of the discourse on the temporal dimension of light.

Sight Lines in Early *Quattrocento* Painting: The Problem of Plural Distance Points

Although art historians and historians of science seem to agree that the use of multiple perspectival points in drawings, paintings and reliefs in the early fifteenth century reflect some of the crucial problems in the artistic recep-tion of the newly acquired knowledge of optics, they differ in explanatory

---

27 Leonardo, *Arundel*, Codex 263, fol. 190v. Here quoted from: Kemp, *Leonardo da Vinci*, 250. On Leonardo in this context, see also Feherenbach, "Der ozillierende Blick," 522–44. Leonardo could already have been familiar with the theories of light rays in his youth when he worked together with Andrea del Verrocchio who, according to Vasari, studied optics and geometry, and was regarded a "prospettivo," meaning both a master in perspective representation and the science of optics. See Vasari, *Le Vite*, III, 375ff. On Leonardo and Andrea del Verrochio, see Barasch, *Light and Color*, 48–50. On the scientific milieu of Verrochio's workshop, see Olschki, *Literatur der Technik*, 270; Chastel, *Art et humanism*, 190.

28. See Frank Fehrenbach, "Blick der Engel," 169–206. On Leonardo's interest in dynamics in general, see the important study Fehrenbach, *Licht und Wasser*.

categories and concepts.[29] Alessandro Parronchi claims, for instance, that Ghiberti's use of plural perspective points on some of the panels of the Doors of Paradise on the Baptistery in Florence is a response to the optical issue of the "double image," viz. the problem caused by the fact that we have two eyes receiving the visual rays separately.[30] Opposed to Parronchi's interpretation, Martin Kemp has argued, more convincingly, that the distance between the converging points in pictures from this period usually is too great to be a response to the minor differences caused by the distance between the eyes.[31] According to him, the problem of plural distance points in many cases is more likely an answer to the optical notion of the movement of the eye, i.e. the disjunction in time which ruptures a momentary vision as we shift the focus from one place on the surface to another.

Earlier depictions of receding lines in checkerboard pavements and ceilings, such as Pietro Lorenzetti's *The Birth of Mary* on the altarpiece from the Cathedral of Siena (1342), may have paved the way for this tradition long before optics was related to the theory of painting. According to Hans Belting, artists in the fourteenth century tried to imitate symbolically the paths that light travels between physical objects and the eye. They did this, "by depicting floor tiles or- most easily- ceiling beams . . . thereby rendering visible the distances and angles of vision that had played a central role in the earlier Arab theory of optics."[32] As both Biagio Pelacani and Alberti testify, these invisible rays were regarded as instruments of vision, not physical entities; and in constructing space artists struggled to imitate these rays on the basis of their knowledge of *perspectiva communis*. Filarete, a student of Alberti, provides perhaps the most explicit evidence for this when he says that, "orthogonal lines to the principal point are analogous ("asimilitudine")

29. See for instance the discussion between Robert Klein and Samuel Edgerton. In an instructive article on the mathematical principle of Pomponius Gauricus, Robert Klein shows that artists of the early renaissance experimented with a variety of perspectival systems, and that the geometrically defined one-point perspective was only one of several solutions. In a polemic with Klein, Edgerton argues that the artistic practice of plural perspectival points and the one-point geometrical perspective were not incongruent logical systems; the former, rather, was but a step in the evolution of the latter into a general principle of pictorial construction. See Klein, "Pomponius Gauricus," 211–30; Edgerton Jr., "Alberti's Perspective," 367–78.

30. Parronchi, "Le Misure," 18–48. An alternative interpretation is offered by Bloom, "Lorenzo Ghiberti's Space," 164–69. Whether the bifocal construction of space was a forerunner, alternative or founding practice in relation to the Albertian and Brunelleschian one-point perspective is debated. See Klein, "Pomponius Gauricus"; Parronchi, "Il 'punctum,'" 58–72; Edgerton Jr., "Alberti's Perspective."

31. Kemp, *The Science of Art*, 39.

32. Belting, *Florence & Bagdad*, 136.

to visual rays."[33] In harmony with this understanding, artists from the first decades of the fifteenth century constructed space with plural distance points in order to lead the eye over the surface from one motif to another. Remarkably, in a number of paintings, drawings, and reliefs multiple vanishing points also correspond with the different moments in the narrative, thus relating the perception of various spaces to particular time-units.[34]

An interesting example is Lorenzo Ghiberti's *Story of Jacob and Esau*, c. 1435, on the east door of the Baptistery in Florence. In order to visualize a movement from the first event placed at the centre to the next one at the upper far right, he totally disregards a central-point perspective in favour of a bifocal system (Fig. 5.2). The shift in the axis of viewing, that changes the angle of exposure of visual rays, thus links to the passage of narrative time from the first to the second event.

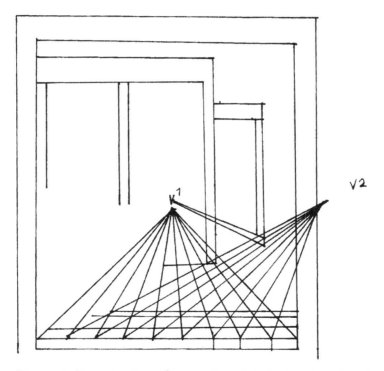

Figure 5.2. Reconstruction of perspective of Ghiberti's *Story of Jacob and Esau* (V1= Vanishing point of first event, V2= Vanishing point of second event) by Eldbjørg Styve.

33. Filarete, *Filarete's Treatise*, 22.177v.
34. Kemp, *The Science*, 35–39.

In the third book of *I Commentarii* Ghiberti explains the process of how vision grasps movements of objects only in time: "Like point in a line vision comprehends movement through the comprehension of a moving thing that is seen in two different positions at two different times between which is a sensible duration."[35] Ghiberti's writings on light are indeed in great part a compilation of Arab and late medieval authorities on optics; and in the cited paragraph, he seems to follow Alhacen closely, in particular *De Aspectibus*.[36] Having described the principles of moving rays in *De Aspectibus*, Alhacen goes on to discuss in detail how the perception of objects moving from one point to another necessarily involves time:

> Now sight perceives the motion of a visible object only by perceiving the visible object in two different locations or according to two different spatial dispositions. But the location or spatial disposition of a visible object changes only over time. Thus, when sight perceives a visible object in two different places or according to two different spatial dispositions, this will occur only at two different instants. But between any two different instants there is some time-interval. Thus, sight only perceives motion over time. [37]

Ghiberti shared his concern about perspective embodying temporality with other artists. In his famous bronze relief of the *Feast of Herod* (1423–7) on the font in the Baptistery of the Siena Cathedral, his contemporary Donatello similarly arranges the two separate episodes in time using two individual points of convergence (Fig. 5.3).

35. Ghiberti, *I Commentarii*, 104. Regarding the impact of Arab and late medieval optics on Ghiberti's concept of light, see esp. Vescovini, *Le teorie*, 367–425; Ghiberti, *Der Dritte*, xiii–xcvii, ci.

36. Ghiberti, *Der Dritte*, 570–73.

37. Smith, *Alhazen's Theory*, 498–99. Alhazen regarded vision a three-stage process that necessarily involved a time-span. See esp. Sabra, "Sensation," 160–85.

Figure 5.3. Donatello, Feast of Herod, c. 1427, bronze relief, 60 x 60 cm, baptistery of the Siena Cathedral, Italy. Photo Credit: Scala/Art Resource, NY.

While the receding orthogonal sight-lines in the extreme foreground meet approximately in the centre of the plane unifying the event in the foreground (the feast of Herod), the event depicted in the far background (the martyrdom of Saint John the Baptist) is subject to a second vanishing point placed a little above the one in the centre (Fig. 5.4). Hence, the slight shift in the angle of viewing, from the upper converging point to the lower, correlates with the disjunction in narrative time, which in turn creates the impression that the history unfolds in a spatiotemporal movement towards us, from the background to the foreground.

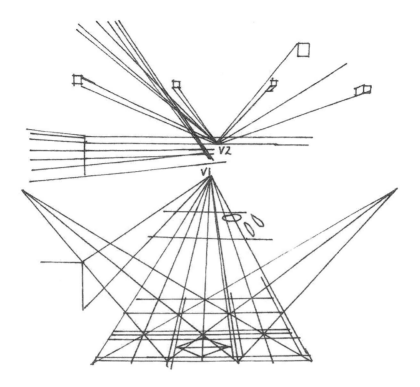

Figure 5.4. Reconstruction of perspective of Donatello's Feast of Herod (V₁= Lower vanishing point, V₂= Top vanishing point) by Eldbjørg Styve.

Though there is no textual evidence for Donatello's knowledge of optics comparable to that of Ghiberti, the important fact is that both participated in an artistic and intellectual milieu where ideas on optics and light formed an essential part of the discourse on visual representation.[38] The one-point

38. On the significance of Biagio Pelacani's comment on Pecham's optics in *Questioni di perspectiva* on the early *Quattrocento* art theory, see Vescovini, *Studi*, 243; Vescovini, "BiagionPelacani"; Barocelli, "Per Biagio," 21–36. On Pelacani and Brunelleschi, see Parronchi, "Le fonti." A manuscript of Pelanani's treatise is available at Biblioteca Laurenziana, Florence, Plut. 18–29. The text is published in Vescovini, "Le Questioni," 163–243. Antonino Pierozzo, who probably knew Pelacani's writings, is also a key figure in this respect. He was prior at the convent of San Marco from 1439 and later Archbishop of Florence, and frequently used optical terms in his sermons and writings. His treatise on the similarity between divine light and earthly light, *De duodecim proprietatibus divinae gratiae ad similitudinem lucis materialis*, is published. See *Sancti Antonini Summa*, 461–68. Edgerton Jr. has convincingly argued that Antonino's teachings possibly had significant impact on the experimentation with light effects by such

linear perspective did not establish a general principle for construction of space until much later; in the first half of the fifteenth century it was only one of several perspective systems.[39] The potential of plural perspective was therefore in many cases considered more important than the coherency of a unified space, having the advantage of taking the mobility of the eye and the movement of the sight lines into account as much as possible.

Significant in this respect is also Gentile da Fabriano's use of multiple perspectives (even though not mathematically correct) in the Adoration-scene of the Strozzi-Altarpiece, c. 1423 (Fig. 5.5). The painting depicts four episodes, starting with three scenes of the journey of the magi from where they first met to the city of Jerusalem and to Bethlehem. The events are portrayed in miniature in the background within three separate lunettes, conceived in gothic style, framing the alter-piece at the top. Continuing from their departure from the city of Bethlehem depicted in the right lunette the retinue arrives at the stable, the Adoration of the Christ Child scene, represented in the main pictorial field below. They are placed in the foreground, the size of the figures in the retinue being considerably larger. Like Ghiberti and Donatello, Gentile da Fabriano uses individual vanishing points as an organizing principle, one in each of the three separate lunettes, unifying the time and the place of the three particular events. What generates the impression that the various events at the same time are connected as points in a line is the shared landscape that relates the episodes to each other and to the main event in the pictorial field below.

---

artists Fra Filippo Lippi and Fra Angelico. See: Edgerton Jr., *The Mirror*, 30–43; Edgerton Jr., "How Shall This Be?," 45–53. On Antonino's writings on painters, see Gilbert, "The Archbishop," 75–87.

39. In the art critical tradition of the late sixteenth-century perspective is often used in plural, *prospettive*. Giorgio Vasari, discussing the life of the early quattrocento artists, praises them for "depicting objects in different perspectives" in the same picture. However, "perspective" is also used in the broadest sense of the term, as for instance, "putting things in perspective" or "a good painting being full of perspectives," which rather points to several perspectival methods and to the variety of semiotic levels of the term. See Elkins, "Renaissance," 209–30.

Figure 5.5. Gentile da Fabriano, Strozzi-Altarpiece (Adoration of the Magi), c. 1423, tempera on panel, 203 x 282 cm, Uffizi, Florence. Photo Credit: Alfredo Dagli Orti / The Art Archive at Art Resource, NY. Image availiable in color at: http://www.artres.com/C.aspx?VP3=ViewBox&VB ID=2UN3658N1RDWK&VBIDL=&SMLS=1&RW=1349&RH=610

In addition, the temporal distinctions and the passage of time are inge-niously accentuated by an alteration of the direction of the depicted light as well as the position and the size of the light-source (the Star of Bethlehem) from one episode to the other.[40] Consequently, the journey of the magi seems to progress in time and space; they move from left to right in the upper part of the altar-piece, and hence towards us to the Adoration-scene in the foreground.

40. On the temporal dimension of the represented natural light in the painting, see Brock, "La lumière," 227–48.

Being aware of Paolo Uccello's well-documented knowledge of how to construct a mathematically correct central perspective to unify the pictorial space, art historians have been puzzled by the fact that Uccello in many cases preferred alternative perspectival solutions. An illustrating example is the *Deluge*, c. 1448, formerly in Sta. Maria Novella in Florence (Fig. 5.6), already mentioned by Giorgio Vasari.[41] In *Le vite dei più eccellenti pittori, scultori e architetti*, Vasari indeed praises Uccello for the bifocal perspectival system used in this painting, but, interestingly, he also criticizes him for being obsessively concerned with correlating the perspective with the narrative, running the risk of sacrificing the naturalism and beauty of the *istoria*. According to him, "Uccello did not know other delight than to investigate certain difficulties, no, problems of perspective, which although they were fanciful and beautiful, yet hindered him so greatly in the painting of figures, that the older he grew the worse he did them."[42] In harmony with two individual vanishing points *The Deluge* shows the Ark of Noah twice, first when the earth is flooded, depicted on the left side, and then when the water subsided, and the saving of the few, to the right, thus structuring the two episodes analogous to the time involved in the movement of the eyes from the one point to the other.[43] Rather than placing the two vanishing points on the same horizontal line with sufficiently distance to clearly distinguish between the time-units in the narrative, they are placed in such a way that the orthogonal lines from the bottom edge cross each other at the upper part of the surface.[44] The short distance between the two vanishing points in the *Deluge*, one slightly above the other, thus generates the impression of a

41. See also Uccello's Urbino panel of the Profanation of the Host and the saving of the Host, where two separate vanishing points distinguish two events, the attempt to destroy the Host to the far left and the soldiers attacking in order to save the Host portrayed to the far right. The first panel has a clear central perspective, yet the orthogonal and traversal lines in the left part of the panel do not follow the central converging point, but are determined by the vanishing point of the adjacent scene. Consequently, the two converging points directs the gaze in accordance with the narrative from the first to the second scene. On the panel, see Goukovskj, "A Representation," 170–77; Parronchi, *Studi*, 296–312, 468–548.

42. Vasari, *Vite*, II, 210, 297.

43. For a reconstruction of the perspectival construction, see Battisti, "Il faut," figs. 14, 15.

44. See for instance the arrangement of the two events represented in Francesco d'Antonio's *The Healing of the Lunatic Boy and The Blood Money*, where an overarching architectural framework situates them within the same architectural location. The space between the two time-units thus defines a timespan that directs the eyes in harmony with the temporal unfolding of the narrative. The painting has been variously attributed to Masaccio, Andrea di Giusto, and Francesco d'Antonio. See Shell, "Andrea d'Antonio," 465–69.

correspondingly short time-span. In this way the narrow canal in between the two representations of the Ark of Noah, where a number of persons are depicted drowning, visualizes the dramatic moments from the climax of the flooding to the water subsiding.

Figure 5.6. Paolo Uccello, The Flood, c. 1448, Fresco, 215 x 510 cm, Green Cloister, Santa Maria Novella, Florence. Photo Credit: Alinari / Art Resource, NY. Image available in color at: http://www.artres.com/C.asp x?VP3=ViewBox&VBID=2UN3658N1RSJU&VBIDL=&SMLS=1&RW=1 366&RH=610

At the turn of the fifteenth century, beginning with Piero della Francesca's *De prospectiva pingendi*, written sometime between 1460 and 1482, the art of perspective became increasingly extracted from the science of optics and, as Robert Klein has pointed to, correspondingly more closely tied to Platonizing and Pythagorizing mathematics. Until this point, however, the dynamics of vision was a main issue and concern among intellectually ambitious artists active in cultural centres, such as Florence.[45] By choosing multiple perspectives they did this at the expense of a space unified by a one-point perspective to provide the image with a temporal dimension. Based on their newly acquired knowledge of light's behaviour and role in the act of seeing, plural vanishing points not only allowed for depictions of a variety of time-units, but in harmony with alterations of exposure of

45. Klein, "Pomponius Gauricus," 213.

light-rays in the movement of the eyes from one point of focus to another, thus articulating in material form the very process of vision.

Concluding Remarks

In this article, I have pointed out some historical conditions for the concept of the image in the fifteenth century. In contrast to modern experiences with the photographic image, renaissance art theorists and artists did not conceive of painterly perspective as a mere mathematical abstraction of vision, nor did they think of the image as a frozen moment. Imitating the path of rays in a pyramidal construction in accordance with optical theory, the understanding of the image as "mimetic transparency," first formulated by Alberti, aimed at deceiving the eye by taking into account the temporal dimension in the act of seeing. The discussions on narrative (*istoria*) also testify to such an understanding. That the rationalization of space reduces the narrative possibilities by only allowing for depiction of one event was evidently remote from the period's artistic comprehension of and interests in *perspectiva artificialis*. As Baxandall has pointed to, the mere realistic depiction of acting figures had only a limited significance in the renaissance ideal of *imitatio della natura*; on a basic level, as *imitatio del vero*, artists sought to imitate the operating principles of vision—how pictures, reproducing nature, continuously emanate images—in order to create living images echoing the three-dimensional world on a two-dimensional surface.[46] Accordingly, vision (*visio*) in the fifteenth century was increasingly understood in this double sense, as both the images seen and the actual process of seeing. The concept of light thus gained an important role also for the general understanding of the relationship between the eye and image; optics, rather than stabilizing the gaze, provided artists with a theoretical legacy for depicting a number of succeeding events in order to generate an impression that they unfold before our eyes, and by objectifying the very mechanisms of vision, to absorb the beholder into the painting's narrative structure.

Bibliography

Ackerman, James S. *Distance Points. Essays in Theory and Renaissance Art and Architecture*. Cambridge, MA: MIT Press, 1991.
Alberti, Leon Battista. *On Painting*. Translated by John R. Spencer. New Haven: Yale University Press, 1966.

46. On the meaning of *imitatio della natura* as *imitation del vero* in the early fifteenth century, see Baxandall, *Painting*, 118.

Andrews, Lew. "Structuring Time and Space in Renaissance Narratives." In *Figura e racconta: Narrazione letteraria e narrazione figurativa in Italia dall'Antichità al primo Rinascimento; atti del convegno di studi, Losanna, 25–26 novembre 2005,* edited by Marco Praloran et al., 287–313. Florence: SISMEL Ed. del Galluzzo, 2009.

———. *Story and Space in Renaissance Art: The Rebirth of Continuous Narrative.* Cambridge: Cambridge University Press, 1998.

Barasch, Moshe. *Light and Color in the Italian Renaissance Theory of Art.* New York: New York University Press, 1978.

Battisti, Eugenio. "Il faut périr en perspective. Relazioni conclusivi." In *La Prospettiva Rinascimentale, Atti del Convegno internazionale di studi tenutosi al Castello Sforzesco, Civiche Raccolte d'Arte di Milano, dall'11 al 15 ottobre del 1977,* edited by Marisa Dalai Emiliani, 349–71. Florence: Centro Di, 1980.

Barocelli, Francesco. "Per Biagio Pelacani." In *Filosofia, scienza e astrologia,* edited by Federico Vescovini et al., 21–36. Padova: Il Poligrafo, 1992.

Baxandall, Michael. *Painting and Experience in the 15th Century Italy: A Primer in the Social History of Pictorial Style.* Oxford: Oxford University Press, 1988.

———. *Giotto and the Orators: Humanist Observers of Painting in Italy and the Discovery of Pictorial Composition.* Oxford: Clarendon, 1988.

Bellitto, Christopher M., et al. *Introducing Nicholas of Cusa: A Guide to a Renaissance Man.* New York: Paulist, 2004.

Belting, Hans. *Florence & Bagdad: Renaissance Art and Arab Science.* Translated by Deborah L. Schneider. 2008. Reprint, Cambridge, MA: Belknap, 2011.

Bergdolt, Klaus. *Der Dritte kommentar Lorenzo Ghibertis.* Translated with an introduction by Klaus Bergdolt. Weinham: VCH, Acta Humaniora, 1988.

Bloom, Kathry. "Lorenzo Ghiberti's Space in Relief: Theory and Method." *Art Bulletin* 51 (1969) 164–69.

Brock, Maurice. "La lumière de l'étoile dans la "Pala Strozzi" de Gentile da Fabriano (1423)." In *Du visible à l'intelligible lumière et ténèbres de l'Antiquité à la Renaissance,* edited by Christian Trottmann et al., 227–48. Paris: Champion, 2004.

Chastel, André. *Art et humanisme à Florence au temps de Laurent le Magnifique, Etudes sur la Renaissance et l'humanisme platonicien.* Paris: Presses universitaires de France, 1961.

Creighton, Gilbert. "The Archbishop and the Painters of Florence, 1450." *Art Bulletin* 41 (1959) 75–87.

Da Vinci, Leonardo. *Il Codice Atlantico di Leonardo da Vinci nella Biblioteca Ambrosiana di Milano.* Transcription by A. Marinoni. 12 vols. Riprint Reale Accademia dei Lincei. Florence: Giunti, 1973–80.

Domenique, Raynaud. *L'hypothèse d'Oxford. Essai sur les origins de la perspective.* Paris: Presses Univ. de France, 1998.

Dupré, Sven, "The Historiography of Perspective and Reflexy-const in Netherlandish Art." *Nederlands kunsthistorisch jaarboek* 61 (2011) 34–61.

Edgerton, Samuel Y., Jr. *The Mirror, the Window, and the Telescope: How Renaissance Linear Perspective Changed our Vision of the Universe.* Ithaca, NY: Cornell University, 2009.

———. "How Shall This Be?' Reflections on Filippo Lippi's 'Annunciation' in London, Part II." *Artibus et Historiae* 16 (1987) 45–53.

————. "Alberti's Perspective: A New Discovery and a New Evaluation." *The Art Bulletin 48* (1966) 367–78.

Elkins, James. *The Poetics of Perspective*. Ithaca, NY: Cornell University Press, 1994.

————. "Renaissance perspectives." *Journal of the History of Ideas* 2 (1992) 209–30.

Feherenbach, Frank. "Der ozillierende Blick. Sfumato und die Optik des späten Leonardo." *Zeitschrift für Kunstgeschichte* 65 (2002) 522–44.

————. "Blick der Engel und Lebendige Kraft: Bildzeit, Sprachzeit und Naturzeit bei Leonardo." In *Leonardo da Vinci: Natur im Übergang. Beiträge zu Wissenschaft, Kunst und Technik*, edited by Frank Fehrenbach, 169–206. Munich: Fink, 2002.

————. *Licht und Wasser. Zur Dynamik naturphilosophischer Leitbilder im Werk Leonardo da Vincis*. Tübingen: Wasmuth, 1997.

Filarete, *Filarete's Treatise on Architecture: Being the Treatise by Antonio Di Piero Averlino, Known as Filarete*. Translated with an introduction and notes by John R. Spencer. New Haven: Yale University Press, 1965.

Ghiberti, Lorenzo. *I Commentarii*. Edited by Ottavio Morisani. Naples: Ricciardi, 1947.

Goukovskj, M. A. "A Representation of the Profanation of the Host: A Puzzling Painting in the Hermitage and Its Possible Author." *Art Bulletin* 51 (1969) 170–73.

Grafton, Anthony. "*Historia* and *istoria*. Alberti's terminology in context." In *The Renaissance. Italy and Abroad*, edited by John J. Martin, 199–223. London: Routledge, 2003.

Greenstein, Jack M. "Mantegna, Leonardo and the times of painting." *Word & Image: A Journal of Verbal/Visual Enquiry* 15 (1999) 217–42.

————. "On Alberti's "Sign": Vision and Composition in Quattrocento Painting." *Art Bulletin* 79 (1997) 683–86.

Harries, Karsten. "On the Power and Poverty of Perspective. Cusanus and Alberti." In *Cusanus: The Legacy of Learned Ignorance*, edited by Peter J. Casarella, 105–27. Washington, DC: Catholic University of America Press, 2006.

Kemp, Martin. *The Science of Art. Optical Themes in Western Art from Brunelleschi to Seurat*. New Haven: Yale University Press, 1990.

————. *Leonardo da Vinci. The Marvelous Works of Nature and Man*. Cambridge: Harvard University Press, 1981.

————. "Il Concetto dell'Anima in Leonardo's Early Skull Studies." *Journal of the Warburg and Courtauld Institutes* 34 (1971) 115–34.

Klein, Robert. "Pomponius Gauricus on Perspective." *Art Bulletin* 43 (1963) 211–30.

Edgerton, Samuel Y., Jr. "Alberti's Perspective: A New Discovery and a New Evaluation." *Art Bulletin 48* (1966) 367–78.

Lindberg, David C. "Lines of Influence in the Thirteenth Century Optics: Bacon, Witelo, and Pecham." *Speculum* 46 (1971) 66–83.

————. *Roger Bacon and the Origins of Perspectiva in the Middle Ages: A Critical Edition and English Translation of Bacon's Perspectiva with Introduction and Notes*. Oxford: Oxford University Press, 1996.

————. *Theories of Vision from Al-Kindi to Kepler*. University of Chicago History of Science and Medicine. Chicago: University of Chicago Press, 1976.

Lindberg, David C., trans. *John Pecham and the Science of Optics: Perspectiva communis*. Madison: University of Wisconsin Press, 1970.

Lomazzo, Giovanni Paolo. *Trattato del l'arte della pittura, scultura, ed archittetura*. Milan: 1585.

Olschki, Leonardo. *Literatur der Technik und der angewandten Wissenschaften vom Mittelalter bis zur Renaissance.* Heidelberg: Winter, 1919.

Parronchi, Alessandro. *Studi sulla "dolce" prospettiva.* Milan: Martello, 1964.

———. "Il 'punctum dolens' della 'costruzione legittima.'" *Paragone* 145 (1962) 58–72.

———. "Le Misure dell'occhio' secondo il Ghiberti." *Paragone* 133 (1961) 18–48.

———. "Le fonti di Paolo Uccello." *Paragone* 89 (1957) 3–33.

Pierozzo, Antonino. *Sancti Antonini Summa Theologica.* Verona, 1740, fascimile edition. Graz, Austria: 1959, vol. titulus 8, cap. 1, cols. 461–68.

Sabra, A. I. "Sensation and Inference in Alhazen's Theory of Vision." In *Studies in Perception: Interrelations in the History of Philosophy and Science*, edited by Peter K. Machamer and Robert G. Turnbull, 160–85. Columbus: Ohio State University Press, 1978.

Santinello, Giovanni. "Nicolo Cusanus e Leon Battista Alberti: Pensieri sul bello e sull'arte." In *Leon Battista Alberti. Una Visione Estetica del Mondo e della vita*, 265–96. Florence: Sansoni, 1962.

Shell, Curtis. "Andrea d'Antonio and Masaccio." *Art Bulletin* 47 (1965) 465–69.

Smith, A. Mark. *Alhazen's Theory of Visual Perception. A Critical Edition, with English Translation and Commentary, of the First Three Books of Alhacen's De Aspectibus, the Medieval Latin Version of Ibn al-Haytham's Kitab al-Manazir.* Vol. 2. Translated by A. Mark Smith. Philadelphia: American Philosophical Society, 2001.

Thorndike, Lynn. *A History of Magic and Experimental Science.* New York: Columbia University Press, 1934.

Vasari, Giorgio. *Le vite de' più eccellenti architetti, pittori, et scultori italiani, da Cimabue insino a' tempi nostri.* Edited by Lorenzo Torrentino. Florence, 1550.

Velli, Silvia Tomasi. *Le immagini e il tempo: narrazione visiva, storia e allegoria tra Cinque e Seicento.* Scuola Normale Superiore, Pisa: Studi. Pisa: Normale, 2007.

Vescovini, Graziella Federici. *Le teorie della luce e della visione ottica dal IX al XV secolo: studi sulla prospettiva medievale e altri saggi.* Perugia: Morlacchi, 2006.

———. "Il problema delle fonti ottiche medievali del Commentario terzo di Lorenzo Ghiberti." In *Lorenzo Ghiberti nel suo tempo: Atti del Convegno Internazionale di Studi, Firenze 18–21 Ottobre, vol. 2, 1978*, 349–87. Florence: Olschki, 1980.

———. "Biagio Pelacani a Firenze, Alhazen e la prospettiva del Brunelleschi." In *Filippo Brunelleschi, la sua opera e il suo tempo (Atti del Convegno Internazionale di Studi Brunelleschiani, Firenze, 16–22 ottobre 1977)*, 1:333–48. Florence: Olschki, 1980.

———. "Contributo per la storia della fortuna di Alhacen in Italia: il volgarizzamento del Ms. Vat. 4595 e il 'commentario terzo' del Ghiberti." *Rinascimento* 2, no. 5 (1965) 17–45.

———. *Studi sulla prospettiva medievale.* Torino: Giappichelli, 1965.

———. "Le Questioni di perspectiva di Biagio Pelacani." *Rinascimento* 1 (1961) 163–243.

PART II

Life Stages and Transformations

6

The Transformation of Aseneth

JOHN J. COLLINS

SCHOLARLY VIEWS OF THE nature and role of religion in the ancient world have undergone considerable revision in recent years, to the point where some question whether we can speak of religion as a distinct phenomenon at all.[1] The practices and beliefs that have traditionally been labeled as "religion" are seen as constituent parts of the ethnic identity of specific peoples, rather than as a free-standing system of thought and practice accessible in principle to anyone. In the case of Judaism, this view has had the corollary that the word *Ioudaios* should be translated as "Judean" rather than "Jew." This argument has been made most forcefully by Steve Mason. Mason offers a fairly standard view of ethnicity: "Each *ethnos* had its distinctive nature or character (*physis, ethos*), expressed in unique ancestral traditions (*ta patria*), which typically reflected a shared (if fictive) ancestry (*syggeneia*); each had its charter stories (*mythoi*), customs, norms, conventions, mores, laws (*nomoi, ethe, nomima*), and political arrangements or constitution (*politeia*)."[2] He goes on to add that "an ancient *ethnos* normally had a national cult . . . involving priests, temples, and animal sacrifice. This cannot be isolated from the *ethnos* itself, since temples, priesthood and cultic practices were part and parcel of a people's founding stories, traditions, and civic structures."[3] Consequently, he argues that "there was no category of 'Judaism' in the Graeco-Roman World, no 'religion' too, and that the *Ioudaioi* were understood until late antiquity as an ethnic group comparable to other ethnic groups, with their distinctive laws, traditions, customs, and God. They were

---

1. See especially Nongbri, *Before Religion*.
2. Mason, "Jews, Judaeans, Judaizing, Judaism," 484.
3. Ibid.

indeed Judaeans."[4] Conversion entailed "a decisive shift from one *ethnos* to another."[5] Mason translates *Ioudaioi* as Judeans by analogy with other ethnic groups in antiquity (Romans, Idumeans). What we might regard as religious beliefs and practices were integral to ethnic identity.[6]

Other scholars, however, argue that while religion was normally bound up with ethnic identity, a distinction could be made, and was made specifically in the case of Judaism. Shaye Cohen argues that prior to the Maccabean revolt, the word *Ioudaios*, and its Hebrew and Aramaic equivalents "always and everywhere mean 'Judaean,' and not 'Jew,'" in the sense that they refer to an *ethnos* rather than a religion.[7] Thereafter, Judaism was an "ethno-religion"; "for most *Ioudaioi* in antiquity, the ethnic definition was supplemented, not replaced by the religious definition. Jewishness became an ethno-religious identity."[8] It is this shift that makes conversion possible. It was now possible to be a "Jew" by virtue of beliefs and practices, regardless of descent and kinship. A *Ioudaios* was now "someone who worships the God whose temple is in Jerusalem and who follows the way of life of the Jews."[9]

Cohen's view finds some support in the writings of the Egyptian Jewish Diaspora. Aristobulus, writing in Alexandria in the middle of the second century BCE, spoke of Judaism as a philosophical school, abstracting from its historical and local embodiment in the land of Israel: "All philosophers," he wrote, "agree that it is necessary to hold devout convictions about God, something which our school prescribes particularly well."[10] Yet neither Cohen nor anyone else would deny that in most cases religion and ethnicity went hand in hand.

4. Mason, "Jews, Judaeans, Judaizing, Judaism," 457. For a similar perspective, see Esler, "Judean Ethnic Identity in Josephus' Against Apion," 73–91; Boyarin, "Rethinking Jewish Christianity," 7–36.

5. Mason, "Jews, Judaeans, Judaizing, Judaism," 508

6. Ethnic identity is, of course, no less contested a concept than religion. See Hutchinson and Smith, eds., *Ethnicity*; and especially Barth, "Ethnic Groups and Boundaries," in Hutchinson and Smith, eds., *Ethnicity*, 75–83 (= Barth, ed., *Ethnic Groups and Boundaries*, 10–19).

7. Cohen, *The Beginnings of Judaism*, 104.

8. Ibid., 137.

9. Ibid., 78–79

10. Aristobulus fragment four in Eusebius, *Praeparatio Evangelica* 13.12. See Holladay, *Fragments from Hellenistic Jewish Authors Vol III. Aristobulus*, 175.

Joseph and Aseneth

Some light may be cast on this debate by considering the most elaborate story of conversion to the worship of the God of Israel that has come down to us from Antiquity. This is the story generally known as *Joseph and Aseneth,* although the title varies in the ancient manuscripts.[11] The story has been a subject of controversy in recent years. The textual history is exceptionally complicated. The earliest manuscript evidence is a Syriac translation from the sixth century CE.[12] The text exists in both short and long recensions.[13] Most scholars have accepted the arguments of Christoph Burchard, supplemented now by those of Uta B. Fink,[14] that the short recension is secondary, but a few scholars still defend its priority.[15] It is not the case that either recension preserves the original text in its pristine state. Some manuscripts omit scenes and others embellish them.[16] There is, however, a consistent story line and much of the imagery is found in both recensions.

In part because of the lateness of the textual witnesses, there is ongoing debate as to whether the composition should be regarded as Jewish or Christian. The original editor, Pierre Battifol, regarded it as Christian,[17] but the great majority of scholars have taken it as Jewish. The possibility of Christian provenance has been raised again vigorously by Ross Kraemer and Rivka Nir,[18] but it remains a minority position.[19] If the original work is Jewish, it is almost certainly earlier than the Diaspora revolt of 115–118 CE. Since it presupposes the Septuagint, it can hardly be earlier than the first century BCE. Egypt is by far the most likely place of origin.[20]

For purposes of the present essay I rely on Burchard's edition of the long recension, as revised by Fink,[21] and use his English translation as the

---

11. Vogel, "Einführung in die Schrift," in Reinmuth, ed., *Joseph und Aseneth,* 5.

12. See Kraemer, *When Aseneth Met Joseph,* 225.

13. For the short recension, see Philonenko, *Joseph et Aséneth*; for the long recension, Burchard, *Joseph und Aseneth.*

14. Fink, "Textkritische Situation," in Reinmuth, ed., *Joseph und Aseneth,* 33–53.

15. Standhartinger, *Das Frauenbild im Judentum der hellenistischen Zeit,* 219–55; Kraemer, *When Aseneth Met Joseph,* 9, 50–88.

16. Ahearne-Kroll, "Joseph and Aseneth," 827.

17. Battifol, "Le Livre de la Prière d'Aseneth," 1–115.

18. Kraemer, *When Aseneth Met Joseph,* 245–85; Nir, *Joseph and Aseneth.*

19. See my essay, "Joseph and Aseneth: Jewish or Christian?," 97–112. Davila, *The Provenance of the Pseudepigrapha,* 190–95, is indecisive.

20. See Zangenberg, "Joseph und Aseneths Ägypten," 159–86.

21. Fink, "Joseph und Aseneth" (Text: Uta Barbara Fink; Übersetzung: Eckart Reinmuth), in Reinmuth, ed. *Joseph und Aseneth,* 56–137.

basis for citations.[22] I presuppose arguments I have offered elsewhere for the Jewish provenance of the story, granting the possibility of some Christian embellishments (such as the cross that is drawn on the honeycomb in 16:17),[23] and I assume a date in the late Ptolemaic or early Roman period, with a preference for the former.[24] The issue on which I wish to focus is the manner in which Aseneth is transformed in the course of the story. The main outline of that transformation is common to all the textual traditions.

A Story of Conversion

Joseph and Aseneth has two episodes that are distinct but by no means unrelated. The first of these, in chapters 1–21, explains how the marriage of Aseneth to Joseph came about. The second, in chapters 21–29, recounts the story of ensuing conflict with Pharaoh's sons, in which Joseph's brothers are divided. The transformation of Aseneth is mainly recounted in the first episode, but the second one also sheds light on the end state of her transformation.

The first episode has an obvious jumping off point in the Joseph story in Genesis. According to Gen 41:45, Pharaoh gave Joseph Aseneth daughter of Potipher, priest of On (later Heliopolis) as wife. For interpreters of the Hellenistic and Roman periods, this brief notice posed a problem: "How did Joseph, an Israelite, marry an Egyptian woman, who was the daughter of an Egyptian priest, particularly in light of numerous biblical prohibitions against such marriages."[25] The story resolves this problem by explaining that Aseneth underwent a conversion experience, abandoned idolatry, and came to worship the God of Israel. The story, then, is at once a romance or love-story, which has much in common with Hellenistic romances that became popular from the first century BCE onwards,[26] and a story of religious conversion. The second episode does not arise from an obvious problem in the biblical text, but it explains how Joseph rather than Pharaoh's son became ruler of Egypt. It would be reductionistic, however, to say that either

22. Burchard, "Joseph and Aseneth," 177–247.

23. The case for Christian interpolations was argued especially by Holtz, "Christliche Interpolationen in 'Joseph und Aseneth,'" 482–97, but his suggestions have not found much acceptance. See the comments of Sänger, "Brot des Lebens."

24. Collins, "Joseph and Aseneth. Jewish or Christian?"

25. Kraemer, *When Aseneth Met Joseph*, 20.

26. Wills, *The Jewish Novel*, 170–84; Hezser, "'Joseph and Aseneth,'"1–40; Johnson, *Historical Fictions and Hellenistic Jewish Identity*, 108–20; Ahearne-Kroll, "Joseph and Aseneth and Jewish Identity," 88–42.

episode exists primarily to resolve an exegetical problem. The biblical text provides a starting point, but the story goes on to address issues that are not adumbrated in Genesis at all.

The first episode, recounting the romance of Joseph and Aseneth, lends itself to comparison with anthropological accounts of rites of passage and initiation, specifically with Arnold van Gennep's three stage pattern of separation, liminality and aggregation.[27] The first part of the story sets the stage by describing Aseneth as she was before her encounter with Joseph, and their initial mutual rejection. The second part describes Aseneth in the liminal state of repentance, at the end of which she has a mystical encounter with an angel. This enables her re-emergence for a new encounter with Joseph, culminating in their marriage. The implications of her marriage for her integration into a new community are developed in the second episode of the story. Aseneth, however, is not a member of a group undergoing a ritual, and indeed she cannot be said to go through a ritual at all. Her experience is peculiar to her individual status. She initially enjoys a higher status than would be typical for women in the Hellenistic world.[28] Her period of repentance is liminal in the sense that she is "betwixt and between" two social orders. Her liminal phase, however, does not involve solidarity or "communitas" with common humanity stripped of hierarchy, such as postulated by Victor Turner for the liminal stage of the ritual process.[29] Her transformation is not a matter of initiation into a higher phase of a continuous social order, but rather involves a breach with one social order and integration into another one that is quite different. The analogy with rites of passage in tribal societies studied by anthropologists, then, is limited. She experiences a radical conversion, which is aptly described in the text as a passage from death to life, with the implication that her initial condition was a state of "death" even before she repudiated it.[30]

27. Van Gennep, *The Rites of Passage*, esp. 1–11; Douglas, "Liminality and Conversion in Joseph and Aseneth," 31–42; Wetz, *Eros und Bekehrung*, 60–68.

28. Lincoln, *Emerging from the Chrysalis*, 103, argues that "women cannot be truly said to be a part of the social hierarchy, or to have any significant independent status. Never having such status, they cannot be deprived of it, and one is forced to conclude either that there can be no liminal state for women or that women exist always in a liminal state." This argument loses its force in the case of the aristocratic Aseneth.

29. Turner, *The Ritual Process*, 96–97.

30. Chesnutt, *From Death to Life*; Inowlocki, *Des idoles mortes et muettes au dieu vivant*.

Aseneth's Initial State

At the beginning of the story, Aseneth is described as a virgin of eighteen years and very beautiful. Her beauty, however, is unlike that of the Egyptians, but in all respects like that of Hebrew women, a detail that points to Jewish rather than Christian authorship. She is said, however, to be boastful and arrogant and devoted to the worship of innumerable Egyptian deities. When her father tells her about Joseph, she responds with disdain, dismissing him as an alien and a fugitive and a shepherd's son. When she sees him, however, she is struck with remorse, for he appears to her "like the sun from heaven on its chariot" and she recognizes that he is a "son of God." The recognition scene is reminiscent of some eschatological judgment scenes—e.g. in the Similitudes of Enoch when the wicked see "that Son of Man" whom they did not believe existed (1 *Enoch* 62), or the Wisdom of Solomon, chapter 5, where the wicked see that the righteous are vindicated.[31] In this case, however, Aseneth has time to repent.

Her repentance is not triggered only by the recognition of Joseph's quasi-divine status, but also by the sting of rejection. Joseph disdains Egyptian women, and has been warned by his father to guard against the strange woman. Even when he is assured that Aseneth will not molest him, and he agrees to welcome her as a sister, he still refuses to kiss her, for "it is not fitting for a man who worships God, who will bless with his mouth the living God and eat blessed bread of life and drink a blessed cup of immortality and anoint himself with blessed ointment of incorruptibility to kiss a strange woman who will bless with her mouth dead and dumb idols and eat from their table bread of strangulation and drink from their libation a cup of insidiousness and anoint herself with ointment of destruction" (8:5–7). He softens the blow, however, by praying to the Lord to bless her and "make her alive again by your life, and let her eat your bread of life and drink your cup of blessing and number her among your people that you have chosen before all (things) came into being, and let her enter your rest which you have prepared for your chosen ones and live in your eternal life for ever (and) ever" (8:9). Aseneth retires in confusion.

The initial mutual dislike of the future lovers is a stock theme in romances, ancient and modern. Here it is overlain with other connotations. Aseneth initially despises Joseph as a foreigner, and one of lowly status besides. Joseph has general contempt for Egyptian women, but his objection to Aseneth is more specific: he refuses to associate with idolators. It is an abomination to him to eat with Egyptians, and he refuses to do so, even

---

31. Nickelsburg, *Resurrection, Immortality and Eternal Life*, 67–118.

when he is a guest in an Egyptian home. This mutual disdain is bound up with perceptions of ethnicity, but the critique of idolatry introduces a criterion that is traditionally termed "religious."

The initial characterization of the protagonists might suggest a rather antagonistic relationship between Hebrews and Egyptians, and John Barclay has gone so far as to claim that Joseph and Aseneth as a whole is an instance of "cultural antagonism."[32] Joseph's view of the Egyptian gods, and indeed the view espoused by the narrator, would seem to leave little room for mutual respect. Remarkably enough, Pentephres, father of Aseneth, even though he is an Egyptian priest, shows nothing but admiration for Joseph. But in any case, mutual antagonism is the starting point of the story, not its culmination. One might argue that the purpose of the narrative is to show how this antagonism may be overcome.[33]

The antagonistic ways of life are spelled out clearly by Joseph, in terms of food, drink and ointment. One side eats the bread of life, drinks the cup of immortality and uses the ointment of incorruptibility. The other eats food that has been strangled, drinks insidious libations and uses the ointment of destruction. There has been endless debate as to whether the reference here is to specific cultic activities.[34] On the one hand the mention of the table of idols and of libations evokes pagan sacrificial meals, although the "ointment of destruction" is puzzling. The positive formula occurs six times in the long recension, three times including the ointment,[35] three times omitting it.[36] (In the short recension, the triadic formula occurs twice and the dyadic formula once).[37] The variation has been taken as evidence that it was not a fixed cultic formula.[38] In any case, the sequence that has anointing after eating and drinking is very odd. Analogies with ritualized meals among the Qumran covenanters, Therapeutae or early Christians, break down on the mention of anointing. On the contrary, "grain, wine and oil" are viewed as staples of life as early as the Book of Hosea (Hos 2:8). Randall Chestnut has argued persuasively that "in various ancient Jewish sources, oil ranks with food and drink as those items deemed most vulnerable to pagan defilement, and conversely, if used properly, as representative items to express a

---

32. Barclay, *Jews in the Mediterranean Diaspora*, 204–16.

33. See Brooke, "Joseph, Aseneth, and Lévi-Strauss."

34. Chesnutt, *From Death to Life*, 128–37; Sänger, *Antikes Judentum und die Mysterien*, 167–74; Sänger, "Brot des Lebens."

35. 8:5; 15:5; 16:16.

36. 8:9; 19:5; 21:21.

37. Triadic in 8:5; 15:4; dyadic in 8:11. See Chesnutt, *From Death to Life*, 129.

38. So Sänger, "Brot des Lebens."

distinctive Jewish identity."[39] If the reference is to a ritual meal, it is to one that is not otherwise attested. It seems safer to conclude that the contrast is between two ways of life. Sacrificial meals are characteristic of the pagan way, but in the case of the Jewish (or Judean) way, the point is simply to underline the importance of commensality.

Joseph and Aseneth, however, does not speak of the bread of commensality, but of the bread of life and the cup of immortality. Analogies with the Gospel of John come to mind, but the hope of immortality is well attested in Hellenistic Judaism. The assumption here is that the Jewish/Judean way of life leads to eternal life, while the worship of idols leads to death. The transformation of Aseneth is two-fold. On the one hand, it involves integration into a social community, as indicated by the emphasis on commensality. On the other hand, it qualifies her for eternal life. The dual goals of the transformation are explicit in Joseph's prayer for Aseneth in 8:9: number her among your people, and let her enter into your rest and live in your eternal life.

Aseneth's Repentance

Aseneth now goes into seclusion and engages in repentance and mortification that mark the complete repudiation of her former life. She throws away her finery and puts on a black robe of mourning. She also throws out her idols. She throws her food to strange dogs, lest her own dogs be contaminated by food sacrificed to idols. In the prayer that follows, she also claims that her mother and father have repudiated her because she destroyed their gods (11:5; 12:12). There is no indication of such repudiation in the actual narrative; on the contrary, her parents rejoice in her marriage to Joseph. The prayer here seems to draw on a traditional motif, which was probably grounded in the experience of many proselytes. Philo praises proselytes who abandon "their kinsfolk by blood, their country, their customs, and the temples and the images of their gods, and the tributes and honors paid to them."[40] It is apparent that to become a proselyte to Judaism had social and ethnic implications in the Hellenistic world.

The formula for escaping from Aseneth's current condition is to confess her sins and pray for God's mercy. We find a similar formula in the Prayer of Nabonidus from Qumran and in Daniel chapter 4, each of which recounts how an idolator turned to the worship of the true God.[41] Aseneth,

---

39. Chesnutt, "Perceptions of Oil in Early Judaism," 113.

40. Philo, *Virt.* 102; Cohen, *The Beginnings of Jewishness*, 157

41. Collins, "The Prayer of Nabonidus," 83–93; Collins, *Daniel*, 208–34.

however, will not only change her devotional practices but join a new family, or ethnos.

Aseneth's Acceptance

There is no public ritual to mark Aseneth's transition to Judaism, other than the marriage itself. A man would presumably have been circumcised.[42] Proselyte baptism is not attested in Judaism until the second century CE.[43] The fact that Aseneth does not undergo baptism weighs heavily against the suggestion that the book is of Christian origin.

Instead, she has a mystical encounter with an angel. The angelophany seems to be modeled on the apparition of the angel in Daniel 10.[44] It is not the result of adjuration; Aseneth neither compels nor expects the angel to appear.[45] Neither is it the result of a ritual. The angel introduces himself as the "chief of the house of the Lord and commander of the whole host of the Most High" (14:8). In appearance, he is "in every respect similar to Joseph."

The angel informs Aseneth that her repentance has been accepted by God. As a result her name has been written in the book of the living in heaven, and will not be erased forever (15:4). Henceforth, "you will be renewed and formed anew and made alive again, and you will eat blessed bread of life and drink a blessed cup of immortality, and anoint yourself with blessed ointment of incorruptibility." She is given a new name, "City of Refuge," "because in you many nations will take refuge in the Lord Most High."

She is not, however, given bread to eat or a cup to drink. The bread, cup and ointment evidently do not refer to a special initiatory meal, but to the ongoing practice to which she will be introduced. Instead, the angel gives her to eat from a mysterious honeycomb which appears miraculously in her store room. The symbolism of the honeycomb has been much disputed.[46] On the one hand, it recalls the manna in the Exodus story. On the other, it may be associated with the goddess Neith, whose symbols included the bee. Its significance in this story is stated explicitly: "for this comb is

---

42. Kartzow, *Destabilizing the Margins*, 59–69, suggests that Aseneth's body is marked by her extraordinary virginity, but this is a premise for conversion, rather than something that marks her transition.

43. See the thorough discussion by Chesnutt, *From Death to Life*, 152–84.

44. Ahearne-Kroll, "The Portrayal of Aseneth in Joseph and Aseneth," 39–58.

45. Contra Kraemer, *When Aseneth Met Joseph*, 89–109. See the comments of Brooke, "Men and Women as Angels in Joseph and Aseneth," 174–75.

46. See Collins, *Between Aseneth and Jerusalem*, 235, and the literature there cited. Also Humphreys, "On Bees and Best Guesses"; and Portier-Young, "Sweet Mercy Metropolis." Portier-Young argues that the honey symbolizes mercy.

(full of) the spirit of life. And the bees of the paradise of delight have made this from the dew of the roses of life that are in the paradise of God. And all the angels of God eat of it and all the chosen of God and all the sons of the Most High, because this is a comb of life, and everyone who eats of it will not die for ever (and) ever" (16:14). Aseneth can now partake of the food of the angels. Like Joseph, whose appearance is angelomorphic, she has made the transition to a higher life.[47]

Her transformation, however, is not a private experience for herself alone. Two details in the encounter with the angel point to its broader social significance. One is her new name, "City of Refuge," which is said to mean that she will be a refuge for Gentiles who attach themselves to the Most High God in the name of repentance (15:7).[48] This would seem to imply that Aseneth is a paradigmatic proselyte, whose example provides a supportive precedent for others who abandon idolatry. We may infer that proselytes needed support. On the one hand, they were likely to be repudiated by their own people; on the other, not all Judeans were receptive to them. The example of Aseneth, however, showed that proselytes had divine approval and could overcome any opposition that they might encounter.

The possibility of opposition is also hinted at in the second detail, an enigmatic passage about bees that arise from the honeycomb and encircle Aseneth. These, we are told, were "white as snow, and their wings like purple and like violet and like scarlet and like gold-woven linen cloaks, and golden diadems were on their heads, and they had sharp stings, and they would not injure anyone" (16:18). Yet in the following paragraph we are told that when the bees flew away to heaven, "those who wanted to injure Aseneth fell to the ground and died," although they were subsequently resurrected. The symbolism is obscure, but it seems to indicate that Aseneth is now surrounded by a community that has the ability to use force but is basically peaceful and supportive. It does, nonetheless, include people who might wish to harm Aseneth, but these will be dealt with by divine power. On this reading, this mysterious episode foreshadows the story of Joseph's brothers in the final part of the book, where the reception of Aseneth in the Judean community is addressed more directly.[49]

47. On the role of angelomorphism in the story see especially Brooke, "Men and Women as Angels."

48. Portier-Young, "Sweet Mercy Metropolis," 135–8.

49. Bohak, *Joseph and Aseneth and the Jewish Temple in Heliopolis*, 11, has argued that the colors of the bees corresponds to those of the priestly garments in Exod 28:4–5, and that the bees are therefore a symbolic representation of Jewish priests, specifically the Oniad priest at Leontopolis. The symbolism is unclear, however, and the interpretation remains uncertain.

Aseneth had already changed out of her robe of mourning when the angel appeared to her, and put on a new linen robe. After his departure she changes into a wedding robe, with a golden crown. When she leans over to wash her face she sees that "it was like the sun and her eyes (were) like a rising morning star, and her cheeks like the fields of the Most High" (18:9). The person responsible for her nourishment (*tropheus*) discerns that "the Lord God of heaven has chosen you as a bride for his firstborn son, Joseph." She has already taken on the likeness of her future husband.

The Wedding

The second encounter of Joseph and Aseneth is free of the suspicions and misunderstandings of their first meeting. The angel has also spoken to Joseph. Joseph kisses Aseneth and imparts to her the spirits of life, wisdom, and truth (19:11). Their union is celebrated by the Pharaoh, who affirms that Joseph is the firstborn son of God. No mention is made of separate tables for Hebrews and Egyptians at the marriage feast. The cultural antagonism portrayed at the beginning of the story has disappeared.

Families and Conflicts

The second major episode in *Joseph and Aseneth* deals with the acceptance of Aseneth in the family of Jacob. Aseneth wants to meet Jacob, "because your father Israel is like a father to me and (a) god" (22:3). He receives her with open arms.

Her reception by Jacob's family is not without tensions, however. Pharaoh's son, the jilted suitor of Aseneth, seeks to kill Pharaoh and kidnap Aseneth. He seeks the help of Levi and Simeon but is rejected. but the sons of Jacob's maidservants, Dan and Gad, Naphtali and Asher, are envious, and hostile to Joseph and Aseneth. The plot against Pharaoh fails, and Naphtali and Asher have second thoughts. The other brothers and Pharaoh's son ambush Aseneth, but Levi and the other brothers come to the rescue. Aseneth persuades them not to return evil for evil, but to leave their punishment to the Lord, for they are, after all, brothers (28:14).[50] Moreover, Levi tries to save the life of Pharaoh's son who was wounded in battle, reasoning that "if he lives, he will be our friend after this, and his father Pharaoh will be like our

---

50. On the theme of non-retaliation in Hellenistic Jewish sources, see Zerbe, *Non-Retaliation in Early Jewish and New Testament Texts.*

father" (29:4). The son dies, but Joseph succeeds to the throne until Pharaoh's younger son comes of age (somewhat belatedly, forty eight years later).

The final episode makes clear the communal, ethnic, dimension of Aseneth's conversion.[51] She is absorbed into a new family through her marriage to Joseph, even if she is not initially welcomed by everyone. It should be noted, however, that Joseph speaks of Pharaoh as "like our father." There are also familial bonds between the Hebrews and the Egyptians. The emphasis is on reconciliation, not cultural antagonism. Intermarriage is possible, even if it presents difficulties. It remains true, of course, that such reconciliation is possible only on Jewish terms. Intermarriage is only possible with those who renounce idolatry and worship the God of Israel. But the tone of the narrative is affirmative nonetheless. As Erich Gruen put it: "the fable plainly promotes concord between the communities," even while "it asserts the superiority of Jewish traditions and morality."[52]

While the story cannot be read as a simple political allegory, the last episode inevitably brings to mind the warrior-priests of the Jewish community at Leontopolis.[53] It imagines a situation when Judeans in Egypt were a military force to be reckoned with, as they were until the end of Ptolemaic rule. Josephus claims that in the mid-second century BCE "Ptolemy Philometor and his consort Cleopatra entrusted the whole of their realm to Jews, and placed their entire army under the command of Jewish generals, Onias and Dositheus" (Ag Ap 2.49). Even if the claim is exaggerated, it still reflects a time when Judeans enjoyed military prominence in Egypt. The episode in *Joseph and Aseneth* is far more intelligible in a Jewish than in a Christian context, and suggests a date in the century before rather than after the turn of the era.[54] In this context, the story is at pains to emphasize the loyalty of the Israelites, under the priestly leadership of Levi. Indeed, their loyalty is greater than that of Pharaoh's own son—a claim that does not seem unreasonable in view of the internecine strife of the late Ptolemaic era. It is also at pains to claim that the sons of Jacob use their military ability sparingly as a matter of last recourse, and pose no threat to Pharaonic (Ptolemaic?) rule.

51. The ethnic character of that to which Aseneth converts is emphasized by Barclay, *Jews in the Mediterranean Diaspora*, 213–14.

52. Gruen, *Heritage and Hellenism*, 96.

53. See especially Bohak, *Joseph and Aseneth*. He summarizes the history of the Oniad temple on 19–40.

54. So also Hacham, "Joseph and Aseneth."

Conclusion

It is clear then that conversion as envisioned by *Joseph and Aseneth* had an essential ethnic component. It entailed aggregation to a different ethnic group, with all the tensions that involved. In that sense, it vindicates the argument of Mason and others that to be a Judean meant first of all to belong to a people whose ancestral homeland was in Judea, even if one joined that people by conversion.

But it is equally true that the conversion of Aseneth involves a spiritual transformation that is traditionally described as "religious." Her transformation is defined first of all by the repudiation of idolatry and acceptance of the God of Israel. She is not only gathered to the chosen people; she also gains access to eternal life, and is given to eat the food of angels. Indeed she is transformed already in this life to the angel-like state that Joseph also enjoys. We need not infer that all proselytes, or all Judeans, were thought to be like angels. Joseph and Aseneth are exceptional characters, specially favored by, and close to, God. Joseph is repeatedly said to be God's firstborn son. But then we should remember that in Exod 4:22 it is Israel who is declared to be God's firstborn son. Joseph may be an idealized representative of Israel, but he is a representative nonetheless, and Aseneth likewise is an idealized proselyte. Israel, in *Joseph and Aseneth*, is an ethnic group, but an ethnic group with heightened spiritual significance. In Shaye Cohen's terminology, it is an "ethnoreligion," whose distinctive character lies not only in shared descent and traditional customs but also in a spiritual dimension that finds expression in the angelomorphic character of its leading representatives.[55]

Bibliography

Ahearne-Kroll, Patricia. "Joseph and Aseneth and Jewish Identity in Greco-Roman Egypt." PhD diss., University of Chicago, 2005.

Ahearne-Kroll, Patricia. "The Portrayal of Aseneth in Joseph and Aseneth. Women's Religious Experience in Antiquity and the Limitations of Ancient Narratives." In *Women and Gender in Ancient Religions: Interdisciplinary Approaches,* edited by Stephen P. Ahearne-Kroll, Paul A. Holloway, and James A. Kelhoffer, 39–58. Tübingen: Mohr Siebeck, 2010.

Ahearne-Kroll, Patricia. "Joseph and Aseneth." In *The Eerdmans Dictionary of Early Judaism,* edited by John J. Collins and Daniel C. Harlow, 826–28. Grand Rapids: Eerdmans 2010.

Barclay, John M. G. *Jews in the Mediterranean Diaspora: From Alexander to Trajan (323 BCE—117 CE).* Edinburgh: T. & T. Clark, 1996.

55. It is a pleasure to dedicate this essay to Turid Karlsen Seim, in memory of her hospitality in Oslo in May–June 2007, in connection with the *Metamorphoses* project.

Barth, Frederik, "Ethnic Groups and Boundaries." In *Ethnicity*, edited by John Hutchinson and Anthony D. Smith, 75–83. Oxford: Oxford University Press, 1996. (= Barth, ed., *Ethnic Groups and Boundaries*, 10–19 [Boston: Little, Brown, 1969].)

Battifol, Pierre. "Le Livre de la Prière d'Aseneth." In *Studia Patristica: Études d'ancienne literature chrétienne*, 1–115. Paris: Leroux, 1889–90.

Bohak, Gideon. *Joseph and Aseneth and the Jewish Temple in Heliopolis*. SBLEJL 10. Atlanta: Scholars, 1996.

Boyarin, Daniel. "Rethinking Jewish Christianity: An Argument for Dismantling a Dubious Category (to which is Appended a Correction of my *Border Lines*)." *JQR* 99 (2009) 7–36.

Brooke, George J. "Joseph, Aseneth, and Lévi-Strauss." In *Narrativity in Biblical and Related Texts*, edited by George J. Brooke and J.-D. Kaestli, 185–200. BETL 149. Leuven: Peeters, 2000.

———. "Men and Women as Angels in Joseph and Aseneth." *JSP* 14 (2005) 159–77.

Burchard, Christoph. "Joseph and Aseneth." In *Old Testament Pseudepigrapha*, edited by James H. Charlesworth, 2:177–247. Garden City, NY: Doubleday, 1985.

Burchard, Christoph. *Joseph und Aseneth*. PVTG 5. Leiden: Brill, 2003.

Chesnutt, Randall D. *From Death to Life: Conversion in Joseph and Aseneth*. JSPSup 16. Sheffield: Sheffield Academic, 1995.

Chesnutt, Randall D. "Perceptions of Oil in Early Judaism and the Meal Formula in Joseph and Aseneth." *JSP* 14 (2005) 113–32.

Cohen, Shaye J. D. *The Beginnings of Jewishness: Boundaries, Varieties, Uncertainties*. Berkeley: University of California Press, 1999.

Collins, John J. *Between Athens and Jerusalem*. 2nd ed. Grand Rapids: Eerdmans, 2000.

———. *Daniel: A Commentary on the Book of Daniel*. Hermeneia. Minneapolis: Fortress, 1993.

———. "Joseph and Aseneth: Jewish or Christian?" *JSP* 14(2005) 97–112. Reprint, John J. Collins, *Jewish Cult and Hellenistic Culture*, 112–27. JSJSup 100. Leiden: Brill, 2005.

———. "The Prayer of Nabonidus." In *Qumran Cave 4. XVII*, edited by George J. Brooke et al., 83–93. DJD 22. Oxford: Clarendon, 1996.

Davila, James R. *The Provenance of the Pseudepigrapha: Jewish, Christian, or Other?* JSJSup 105. Leiden Brill, 2005.

Douglas, Rees Conrad. "Liminality and Conversion in Joseph and Aseneth." *JSP* 3 (1988) 31–42.

Esler, Philip F. "Judean Ethnic Identity in Josephus' Against Apion." In *A Wandering Galilean: Essays in Honour of Seán Freyne*, edited by Zuleika Rodgers with Margaret Daly-Denton and Anne Fitzpatrick McKinley, 73–91. JSJSup 132. Leiden: Brill, 2009.

Fink, Uta B. "Joseph und Aseneth" (Text: Uta Barbara Fink; Übersetzung: Eckart Reinmuth). In *Joseph und Aseneth*, edited by Eckart Reinmuth, 56–137. Sapere 15. Tübingen: Mohr Siebeck, 2009.

———. "Textkritische Situation." In *Joseph und Aseneth*, edited by Eckart Reinmuth,33–53. Sapere 15. Tübingen: Mohr Siebeck, 2009.

Gennep, A. van. *The Rites of Passage*. Translated by Monika B. Vizedom and Gabrielle L. Caffe. Chicago: University of Chicago Press, 1960.

Gruen, Erich S. *Heritage and Hellenism: The Reinvention of Jewish Tradition*. Berkeley: University of California Press, 1998.

Hacham, Noah. "Joseph and Aseneth: Loyalty, Traitors, Antiquity and Diaspora Identity." *JSP* 22 (2012) 63–67.

Hezser, Catherine. "'Joseph and Aseneth' in the Context of Ancient Greek Novels." *Frankfurter judäistische Beiträge* 24 (1997) 1–40.

Holladay, Carl. *Fragments from Hellenistic Jewish Authors*. Vol 3, *Aristobulus*. Atlanta: SBL, 1995.

Holst, Traugott. "Christliche Interpolationen in 'Joseph und Aseneth.'" *NTS* 14 (1967/68) 482–97.

Humphreys, Edith M. "On Bees and Best Guesses: The Problem of Sitz im Leben from Internal Evidence, as Illusrated by Joseph and Aseneth." *Currents in Research: Biblical Studies* 7 (1999) 223–36.

Hutchinson, John, and Anthony D. Smith, eds. *Ethnicity*. Oxford: Oxford University Press, 1996.

Inowlocki, Sabrina. *Des idoles mortes et muettes au dieu vivant: Joseph, Aseneth, et le fils de Pharaon dans un roman du judaisme hellénisé*. Turnhout: Brepols, 2002.

Johnson, Sara Raup. *Historical Fictions and Hellenistic Jewish Identity: Third Maccabees in Its Cultural Context*. Berkeley: University of California, 2004.

Kartzow, Marianne Bjelland. *Destabilizing the Margins: An Intersectional Approach to Early Christian Memory*. Eugene OR: Pickwick, 2012.

Kraemer, Ross Shepard. *When Aseneth Met Joseph: A Late Antique Tale of the Biblical Patriarch and His Egyptian Wife Reconsidered*. New York: Oxford University Press, 1998.

Lincoln, Bruce. *Emerging from the Chrysalis: Studies in Rituals of Women's Initiation*. Cambridge: Harvard University Press, 1981.

Mason, Steve. "Jews, Judaeans, Judaizing, Judaism: Problems of Categorization in Ancient History." *JSJ* 38 (2007) 457–512.

Nickelsburg, George W. E., *Resurrection, Immortality and Eternal Life in Intertestamental Judaism*. Expanded ed. Harvard Theological Studies 56. Cambridge: Harvard University Press, 2006.

Nir, Rivka. *Joseph and Aseneth. A Christian Book*. Sheffield: Sheffield Phoenix, 2012.

Nongbri, Brent. *Before Religion. A History of a Modern Concept*. New Haven: Yale University Press, 2013.

Philonenko, Marc. *Joseph et Aséneth. Introduction, texte critique, traduction et notes*. SPB 13. Leiden: Brill 1968.

Portier-Young, Anathea. "Sweet Mercy Metropolis: Interpreting Aseneth's Honeycomb." *JSP* 14 (2005) 133–57.

Reinmuth, Eckart, ed. *Joseph und Aseneth*. Sapere 15. Tübingen: Mohr Siebeck, 2009.

Sänger, Dieter. *Antikes Judentum und die Mysterien Religionsgeschichtliche Untersuchungen zu Joseph und Aseneth*. WUNT 2/5. Tübingen: Mohr Siebeck, 1980.

———. "'Brot des Lebens, Kelch der Unsterblichkeit.' Vom Nutzen des Essens in Joseph und Aseneth." In *Sacred Meal, Communal Meal, Table Fellowship, and the Eucharist I: Old Testament, Early Judaism, New Testament*, edited by David Hellholm and Dieter Sänger. Tübingen: Mohr Siebeck, forthcoming.

Standhartinger, Angela. *Das Frauenbild im Judentum der hellenistischen Zeit: Ein Beitrag anhand von "Joseph und Aseneth."* AGJU 26. Leiden: Brill, 1995.

Turner, Victor. *The Ritual Process: Structure and Anti-Structure*. Chicago: Aldine, 1969.

Vogel, Manuel. "Einführung in die Schrift." In *Joseph und Aseneth*, edited by Eckart Reinmuth, 3–53. Sapere 15. Tübingen: Mohr Siebeck, 2009.

Wetz, Christian. *Eros und Bekehrung. Anthropologische und religionsgeschichtliche Untersuchungen zu "Joseph und Aseneth."* Novum Testamentum et Orbis Antiquus / Studien zur Umwelt des Neuen Testaments 87. Göttingen: Vandenhoeck & Ruprecht, 2010.

Wills, Lawrence M. *The Jewish Novel in the Ancient World.* Ithaca, NY: Cornell University Press, 1995.

Zangenberg, Jürgen K. "Joseph und Aseneths Ägypten. Oder: Von der Domestikation einer 'gefährlichen' Kultur." In *Joseph und Aseneth*, edited by Eckart Reinmuth, 159–86. Sapere 15. Tübingen: Mohr Siebeck, 2009.

Zerbe, Gordon M. *Non-Retaliation in Early Jewish and New Testament Texts: Ethical Themes in Social Contexts.* JSPSup 13. Sheffield: Sheffield Academic, 1993.

7

"The Springtime of the Body"

Resurrection in Minucius Felix's *Octavius*[1]

INGVILD SÆLID GILHUS

Religio versus superstitio

THREE FRIENDS STROLLING ALONG the shore of Ostia, so "that the fresh sea
breeze might invigorate our limbs, and that the yielding sand might give
the delightful sensation of subsidence at each footstep" (2,4). The timeless
image of effortless living shifts when Caecilius notices a statue of Serapis,
"and as is the superstitious habit of the vulgar—put his hand to his mouth
and blew it a kiss" (2,4). His ritual gesture makes the Christian Octavius
reproach the third in the party, Marcus Minucius Felix, because he did not
stop his friend, "when you know that the shame of his error redounds no
less to your discredit than to his" (3,1). A discussion follows to settle which
is the true religion.[2]

Octavius is a Christian apologetic text and a dialogue cast in Cicero-
nian style between the Christian Octavius and the Pagan Caecilius and with
the Christian Minucius Felix, the author, as the arbiter (4,6). *Octavius* is also
a memory text, praising him who has given the text its name and whom
the readers are given the impression is dead.[3] It is further a conversion

1. The English quotations from *Octavius* are from Minucius Felix with an English
translation by Gerald H. Rendall.

2. The discussion is set up as a formal philosophical controversy, Carver, "A note
on," 355–57.

3. There is a discussion whether Octavius is imagined as dead or alive when the
dialogue was written. The tendency is to see him as dead and that the text was written
"in part to enshrine the memory of a departed (i.e., deceased) friend." (Clarke, *The*

109

text, because the persuasive speech of Octavius, makes Caecilius convert to Christianity: "If he has been victorious over me, I too have had my triumph over error" (40,1).[4]

At the centre of *Octavius* is the debate about true religion (*religio*) versus superstition (*superstitio*).[5] There is no surprise that Christianity comes out as the winner, a main intention with the speech of Caecilius, we suspect, is that it shall be easy for Octavius to refute. What is surprising, however, is that the content of Christianity is reduced to a minimum, a fact, which has frequently been stressed.[6] According to Simon Price, "there is little on the Bible, little Christology, nothing about the Holy Spirit or the emerging doctrine of the Trinity; little on the Redemption (only Judgement); nothing about the Church, its ministry, sacraments, and other practices."[7] Price suggests that the reason for this was that only things that especially interested Pagan readers were discussed and that the context for the discussion was the persecutions. Crucial points are the nature of the Christian god and the resurrection.[8] According to Jean Beaujeu, the *credo* of *Octavius* is reduced to a confession of God the creator, the resurrection and eternal life, the rest is passed in silence.[9]

Caecilius, speaks up for Paganism and does it in a rather caricatured way: Caecilius "is the only philosophical or at least philosophically inspired position in late antiquity I am aware of which reasonably straightforwardly corresponds to our conception of polytheism," says Michael Frede.[10] Frede elaborates on this point and claims that Caecilius "does believe in and worship many traditional gods, in part precisely because his scepticism, however mitigated it may be, prevents him from committing himself to a more theoretical, more speculative conception of matters divine. In this he is completely unrepresentative of the attitude of philosophers in late antiquity, but, I suspect, also of the general attitude of the educated elite at least in the East."[11]

Octavius,164). I share this view.

4. The texts starts with a reference to Caecilius who *ad ueram religionem reformauit. Reformo*, meaning "reshaped" or "transformed," designates Caecilius' conversion to Christianity.

5. Dale Martin discusses the historical development of the concept of superstition in his book, *Inventing Superstition*.

6. Schubert, "Minucius Felix," 813–15

7. Price, "Latin Christian Apologetics," 123. Price refers to Minucius Felix together with Tertullian and Cyprian.

8. Ibid., 123–24.

9. Beaujeu, *Minucius Felix*, xvii.

10. Frede, "Monotheism," 43.

11. Ibid., 43.

Octavius, who promotes the monotheistic position, is in line with what the majority of philosophers in late antiquity taught.[12] Frede does "not see any way in which the Christians are in a position to claim that they believe in one God, whereas the pagan philosophers believe in many gods."[13]

In a way Octavius usurps a traditional monotheistically inclined philosophical position, presents it as a Christian position, and refutes a caricatured version of traditional Graeco-Roman religion. The first point is in line with what Minucius Felix' mouthpiece Octavius says after he has presented "the opinions of almost all philosophers of any marked distinction," that one might suppose, "either that Christians of today are philosophers, or that philosophers of old were already Christians" (20,1). What *Octavius* does defend, however, which Pagan philosophers and intellectuals did not share with Christianity, is the notion of resurrection.[14] This is a crucial notion in the text and part of a general process of elevating humans at the cost of other biological as well as supra-biological entities. The general process is not restricted to Christianity in antiquity, but it got a specific Christian formulation in the interplay between the exaltation of a supreme god; the idea of a human being, who transcends the human/divine divide, *i.e.* Jesus; and the belief in human resurrection modelled on the resurrection of Jesus.

Octavius was written at the end of the second or the first half of the third century and has been a popular object of research since it was rediscovered in 1560,[15] focussing on origin of motifs, textual loans, allusions, and dependence on other texts.[16] This article takes another approach and follows up some of the questions in Turid Karlsen Seim's research project at the Centre of Advanced Studies in Oslo:[17] "What were the frameworks within which transformative ideas such as resurrection and also experiences of having become "a new being" were shaped? . . . How did taxonomic patterns, that is constructions of an ordered design of the created world, accommodate or challenge transformative movements?"[18]

12. Ibid., 55.

13. Frede, "Monotheism," 60.

14. As Dag Øistein Endsjø has shown, the idea of resurrection also appeared among Pagans, but the idea was universalized in Christianity (Endsjø, *Greek Resurrection*, 211–17).

15. Kytzler, *M. Minucius Felix*, 11.

16. Especially the relationship between *Octavius* and Tertullian's *Apologeticus* has been debated. (Cf. Beaujeu, *Minucius Felix*, LIV–LXVII; Schubert, "Minucius Felix," 807, 820–23; Price, "Latin Christian Apologetics," 112, note 17.

17. *Metamorphoses: Resurrection, Taxonomies and Transformative Practices in Early Christianity* at the Centre for Advanced Study, 2006/2007

18. Seim and Økland, "Introduction," 1.

The special theme of this article is Minucius' use of biological and supra-biological categories, which means humans, animals and plants on the one hand, and gods, spirits and demons on the other. The juggling with these categories was part of an effort to create a Christian identity. In what follows, I discuss the conceptions of animals in *Octavius*, proceed to super-human beings and then ask: How does Minucius discuss Christian identity and status by means of biological and supra-biological categories? How do these categories relate to change and permanence? What does the notion of resurrection imply in this text?

Better than Animals

In *Octavius*, animals appear both as a general contrast to humans and to create specific effects. Animals are good to think with, but equally important, also to trigger emotional responses. Their function in *Octavius* is to put people in their place, alternatively to show the working of divine providence.

Caecilius includes animals in two of his accusations against the Christians. He claims that Christians worship the head of an ass (9,3), and that they initiate their sexual orgies when a dog, tied to a lampstand, is thrown a morsel of meat and begins to run after it so that the light is blown out (9,6–7).[19] Both species—the ass and the dog—are closely connected to sexual promiscuity and sexual slander, which was stock in trade in the accusations against Christians—at least when these accusations are referred to in Christian texts.[20] The accusation of worshipping the head of an ass is countered by Octavius, who says that the Pagans worship Epona, the popular horse goddess of the Celts, hybrid deities, as well as Apis and crocodiles in Egypt (28,7). In the effort trying not to be stuck with the beasts, Caecilius gets the worst of it, because Octavius refers to facts, Caecilius to fiction and rumours: Epona was a popular god in the Roman Empire, the Egyptians had a special relationship to divine animals, but the Christians did not worship the head of an ass. The text conveys that deities in the form of animals or animal hybrids are *superstitio* and a base version of religion.[21]

In Octavius' monologue, the special position of humans in the universe is described in a traditional way by making a contrast between the earthbound gaze of animals, which is fixed on their food, in contrast to the

19. Cf. Tertullian, *Apol.* 7,1; 8,7.

20. Cf. Knust, *Abandoned to Lust*, 104f.; Hargis, *Against the Christians*, 1–16.

21. Religion is used in two ways in this article, as an emic concept, which is how it is used in *Octavius* (*religio*), and as an etic concept where both *religio* and *superstitio* are included.

erect position and heavenward gaze of humans, endowed with speech and reason, and which enables humans to "recognize, perceive and imitate God" (17,2).[22] This contrast is part of the wise ordering of the cosmos and the providence of the universe. One example is the special protective equipment which each species of animals has: "some armed with horns, some fenced with teeth, and shod with hoofs, or barbed with stings, or kept immune by swiftness of foot or soaring wing" (17,10). The human form with its erect poise and upward look is held up as a contrast to animals and presented as the peak of creation. In line with the human/animal contrast, one could read Caecilius' criticism of Christians, that they should not be prying into the regions of the sky, because it is "enough for the ignorant and uncultured, the rude and boorish, to look at what is under their nose" (12,7) as a way to associate them with animals.

The ordering of societies of animals is further an argument for monotheism as naturally given: "Look where you will; bees have but one king, flocks one leader, cattle one monarch of the herd. Can you suppose that in heaven the supreme power is divided . . ." (18, 7). Minucius Felix uses a *minore ad majus* argumentation when he describes how mice, swallows, kites and spiders gnaw images of gods, perch and settle on statues and images of gods and spin webs across their faces: "How much truer the judgement which the dumb animals pass instinctively upon those gods of yours!" (22,6). Exactly because animals are on a lower and qualitatively different level than human, they are used as a shaming device to put humans in their place and show true religion opposed to superstition (cf. also 36,5).

In line with Aristotle's thinking, the species in *Octavius* are fixed, and there is no opening up for the existence of hybrids. Minucius, through his mouthpiece Octavius, makes fun of Greek composite mythological entities such as Scylla, Chimaera and Centaurs (20,3), the Egyptian dog-headed god Anubis—the Cynocephalus (23,1), human beings who, according to myths and fables, change into birds and beasts (20,4) and the idea attributed to Pythagoras and Plato that the souls of men pass into sheep, birds and beasts (34,7). No transformations take place across the animal/human divide—either when it comes to hybrids or to metamorphosis and reincarnation in animal shapes.[23] The boundary between animals and humans is

---

22. For Greek, Roman and Christian authors who refer to the upright position of humans, see Sorabji, *Animal Minds*, 92 n. 114.

23. Metamorphoses had from Hellenistic times been a way to accentuate the characteristics of a person. This notion is also present in the idea of reincarnation, where, in a similar way, people become what they do—a gluttonous man in this life may turn into a pig in the next.

impenetrable—humans do not become animals, and animals never turn into humans. As opposed to humans, animals lack divine archetypes.

Two of the institutions of animals in the empire, the arena and the animal sacrifice, are mentioned. Opposition against traditional sacrifices plays only a minor role in the text. It is referred to when the Graeco-Roman gods are treated as unclean spirits or demons: They produce diseases, but may also cure them, "when glutted with the reek of altars or with victim beasts, they may loosen the tightened bonds and claim to have effected a cure" (27,2).

Wild beasts in the arenas were sometimes used to punish and kill Christians in a *damnatio ad bestias* (37,5). In *Octavius,* Minucius applies a language of triumph and victory to describe the suffering and death of martyrs (37,1–3). In line with how Christ and sacrificial language connected to him is absent in *Octavius* (see below), Minucius does not compare the victims of martyrdom with sacrifices, which was otherwise common.[24] Instead he compares the wealthy and mighty, who are raised high and then punished by god with the sacrificial victims: "They are like victims fattened for sacrifice, and garlanded for execution" (37,7). Traditional animal sacrifices are here seen as punishment.

Minucius points out that Pagans eat the meat from wild beasts, which have died in the arenas, "fresh glutted with blood and gorged with the limbs and entrails of men" (30,6). And then he adds a curious comment: "For us it is not permissible either to see or to hear of human slaughter; we have such a shrinking from human blood that at our meals we avoid the blood of animals used for food" (30,6). Information that Christians do not eat blood has its parallel in other Christian texts.[25] It is obvious to see it in consonance with the biblical prohibition against eating the blood of animals and the idea that the life or soul was thought to be in the blood.[26] Since it is impossible to distinguish between animal blood and human blood, this lack of distinction points at a basic sameness between humans and animals in a text which otherwise presupposes that there is a fundamental difference.[27]

24. The punishment of the damnation is mainly described in Christian texts from the second and the beginning of the third century, that is roughly the same time as *Octavius* was written. In these texts the martyrs are frequently described in a sacramental and sacrificial language. See Gilhus, *Animals,* 195–200.

25. Tert. *Apol.* 9,13; Clem *Paed.* 3.3.25.2, see Clarke, *The Octavius,* 337 n. 508.

26. Gen 9:3–4; Lev 17:10–14; Acts 15:28–29.

27 An alternative to seeing the similarity between human and animal blood, is to see the difference between types of meat, á la Paul and the Stoics. In 1 Cor 15: 39, Paul points out: "Not all flesh is alike, but there is a flesh for human beings, another for animals, another for birds, and another for fish."

In *Octavius* humans and animals are not united by soul, but divided by reason.[28] In line with Stoic thinking, Minucius' view is that animals belong to a different category than humans and this categorical difference determines what he writes about them—humans are rational, animals are irrational. This is in line with how animals were usually treated in philosophical and theological texts of a Christian or Stoic provenance.[29] Similar to the Stoic tradition, the universe of Minucius Felix exists *hominum causa*, "for the sake of humans" (32,2).[30]

Better than Gods, Spirits and Demons

If animals are good to think with, so are supra-biological entities. In *Octavius* both categories are put to work. Supra-biological entities have several functions, among others to illuminate the position of humans in the world and their relationship to each other. Several varieties of superhuman beings appear—spirits, gods, demons as well as a transcendent god. There is a purposeful attempt to make a shift in the ontological hierarchy of real and imagined creatures of the universe, and most of the imagined creatures are re-evaluated and moved down in the ontological hierarchy. This downward movement is brought about by means of change of status and place, for instance when gods are seen as dead humans or turned into demons.

Caecilius speaks about gods (*deos*) (6,2), deities (*numen*) (6,2), manes (*manes*) (6,2) and immortal gods (8,1), but says that Christians "spit upon the gods" (8,4), which means that they treat them as evil spirits. Octavius defends a philosophically stamped monotheism, which was part of the Graeco-Roman elite culture.[31] The traditional gods are, according to a euhemeristic view, seen as deified humans (21,3, cf. 23). In line with this view, Minucius criticises their changeability and anthropomorphic character (22) and their being part of cycles of birth, procreation and death (24). Gods change, grow old, bear children and humans even celebrate these changes. Characteristic for Minucius' theological views is that the border between gods and humans has become weak, and his euhemeristic explanation contributes to degrade the gods.

When Octavius will "try to get to the true source of error and perversity, which lies behind the thick darkness, expose its roots, and let in the light of day," he transforms gods and deities into unclean spirits and demons

28. Cf. Gilhus, *Animals*, 37–63.

29. Cf. Sorabji, *Animal Minds*, 195–207.

30. Cf. Clarke, *The Octavius*, 344.

31. Cf. 19, see Frede, "Monotheism."

(26,8–9). These impure spirits and demons lurk beneath statues (27,1). They are everywhere, stand behind all sorts of miseries and calamities and even slip into people's minds. Demons are the source of Pagan slander against Christians (28,6).

In line with Christian, as well as with elite Pagan thinking, the chief category of superhuman beings, God, is moved to a transcendent position. Parallel to the relocation of the superhuman, humans are moved to a higher level in the universe than they were before. Octavius makes a division between humans and humans, those that have chosen Christianity, which are better *en bloc* than everyone else, "if we Christians are compared with you, although in some cases our training falls short of yours, yet we shall be found on a much higher level than you" (*multo tamen vobis melioeres deprehendemur*) (35,5) and non-Christians. This does not mean, however, that resurrection is reserved for Christians; non-Christians will rise again to be tortured forever in hell.[32] This implies that all humans are on the same level in the ontological hierarchy, but a sharp moral division determines their different lot in the hereafter.

It is striking that resurrection happens independent of the Christian/non-Christian divide, but there is a systematic logic in the view that all human beings will be revived after death. There is in this text a devaluation of superhuman beings (gods, spirits, demons), and a fundamental divide between animals and humans. Both the degrading of superhuman beings and the sharp human/animal divide contribute to make human beings stand out as the most special creatures of the world, natural born survivors of biology and death.

There is however, an anomaly in this neat worldview. The anomaly is the status of vegetative life. Plants are at the bottom of the "Great Chain of Being,"[33] but in Minucius' universe and in other second and third century Christian texts as well, plants have qualities that make them metaphorically, but sometimes also literally, apt to outgrow their humble place and be associated with humans. We will return to the function and meaning of plants below.

32. The view has a parallel in Rev 20:11–15.

33. There is continuity in the cosmos, but no evolution, from plants, to animals and from animals to humans. They are all part of what can be called "the Great Chain of Being," even of an extended chain because in *Octavius* supra-biological entities are also included (cf. Lakoff and Turner, *More than Cool*, 166ff). The Great Chain of Being is a cultural model, which is implicit in ancient cultures. The Extended Great Chain concerns the relationship of humans to gods, society and the universe (cf. Lakoff and Turner, *More than Cool*, 167 and 208–13).

Change and Permanence

Both Octavius and Caecilius agree that Christians hold the idea of a final conflagration, an idea, which was also shared by several of the philosophical schools (34,1–4). The conflagration is the final and total change in which everything will perish (11,1–3; 34,1–4). Against this cataclysm stands human resurrection and eternal life.

There are, nevertheless, also ideas of permanence in Minucius' text as well. Its use of memory is important—*Octavius* is presented as a memory-text: "I pondered and reflected over memories (*memori*) of my good and trusty comrade, Octavius . . . I seemed somehow reliving in the past, rather than recalling to memory things over and done; so vividly did his image, though withdrawn from the eyes, remain imprinted on my heart and inmost sense" (1,1–2). Commentators have, as already mentioned, discussed whether the book presents memories of real persons or whether it is about imaginary persons and events.[34] We will not go into this debate, only stress that Minucius stages plot and themes as if the events that he describes have happened.

In addition to staging memories as a source of permanence, there are descriptions of timeless moments, for instance when Minucius presents the small children, "trying to form broken words, in the pretty prattle which the broken efforts of a stumbling tongue render still sweeter," (2,1); the sea walking—"and that the yielding sand might give the delightful sensation of subsidence at each footsteps" (2,4); and the *epostrakismos*, "we saw a party of boys competing eagerly in their game of throwing sherds into the sea" (3,5). These actions are universal, speak to readers across centuries and illustrate the eternity of specific moments. They create a longing for that which has gone, but at the same time exist forever in line with Ibsen: "Eternally owned is but what's lost."[35] These eternal memories and moments are universally shared human experiences. In Roman literature, they are literary topics as well,[36] which also contributes to make them vehicles of permanence.

The most special type of permanence in *Octavius* is the idea of resurrection. The text presents eternal life, dependent on the resurrection of the body, as the hallmark of Christianity. Since resurrection is an answer to the problem of death, this answer is given a special relevance because the text that bears his name presupposes that Octavius is dead and that the text is written in memory of him (cf. note 3). In *Octavius* the resurrection of

---

34. Cf. Hasenhütl, *Die Heidenrede*, 20–27; 73–74.

35. Ibsen, *Brand*, Act 4.

36. Clarke, *The Octavius*, 170; 179.

humans is *not*, as already mentioned, connected to the resurrection of Jesus, which is never referred to and therefore never used as a model of human resurrection.

Jesus is referred to by Caecilius, who says that the object of veneration of the Christians is "a malefactor put to death for his crimes, and wood of the death-dealing cross" (9,4). Octavius counters this and says, "you go very far wide of the truth, in supposing that a criminal deserved or that a mortal man had the right to be believed in as God" (29,2). Clarke points out that this is "a remarkable avoidance of any mention of the Incarnation . . . Indeed so anxious is M.F. to avoid admitting such a difficult doctrine that he gives the appearance of denying it."[37] Perhaps M.F. does deny the incarnation? Octavius explicitly denies that the Christians have set their hope in a mortal man (29,3) and he denies any adoration of the cross—both beliefs are instead saddled on the Pagans (29,2–8).

The absence of Jesus and the denial of his significance have troubled the commentators. It has been argued that the reason why Jesus is not mentioned is because learning about him belongs to the advanced stages of Christian doctrine. But we do not really know that, we know nothing about what lies behind the text and about the type of Minucius' Christian affiliation—though he obviously has one.[38] There is reason to believe that the intended readers of *Octavius* were Pagans, which means that the text was written as an exoteric treatise.[39] The Pagan readers were presented with a version of Christianity where Jesus in the main was absent. This means that human resurrection, at least to the Pagan readers, was not mediated by the god/man Jesus. Thus resurrection was not rooted in a paradigmatic act of salvation, which probably contributed to resurrection in this text being cast more like a natural continuation of human life.

Resurrection

Resurrection is in the main treated in two chapters in *Octavius*. In the first, Caecilius attacks the idea (11), in the second Octavius defends it (34). Caecilius raises standard and crucial objections against resurrection and asks if it is with bodies or without bodies, and if it is the body that rises, what body is it that rises, the same body or a new body? (11,7). And Caecilius adds that there is no proof that resurrection ever happened (11,8). He also makes a contrast between the atoms and cyclic worldview of Philosophy (5.8) where

---

37. Clarke, *The Octavius*, 327.

38. Cf. Schubert, "Minucius Felix," 812.

39. Price, "Latin Christian," 105; 111–12; Hasenhütl, *Die Heidenrede*, 144–45.

the individuals are lost, but the species continue, which is an alternative view on the relationship between change and permanence.

Caecilius' questions do not receive very profound answers by Octavius—we are far from the ingenious and enigmatic elaborations of Paul,[40] and the treatment of resurrection in Irenaeus' *Adversus haereses* and Tertullian's *De resurrectione carnis*, partly dependent on Paul.[41] If Minucius' views are discussed in the research literature there is a tendency to treat them together with the other treatises on resurrection in the late second and early third century.[42]

Octavius presents four arguments in favour of resurrection. The first is that the philosophers agree that something persists after death. In this case it is the soul, and reincarnation is set up as a parallel and contrast (34,6ff.). But while Minucius puts forward this argument to show a shared belief in continuity after death, he disagrees with its actual content. He refutes that souls alone continue after death and he refutes reincarnation (34,6), especially in animals (34,7). Belief in reincarnation is clearly seen as a non-compatible alternative to resurrection. Reincarnation expresses permanence in the form of eternal change and movement, while resurrection in *Octavius* expresses permanence as lack of change. Even the bodies that are burnt in eternal fire will never be consumed.

The following three arguments are specifically in support of the resurrection of the body. The first of the three is that God may reshape a human being from nothingness, and Minucius draws a parallel to birth (34,9). The second argument is that God preserves the elements of the dead body (34,10). This argument either contradicts the former or qualifies it.[43] The two arguments about fragmentation are followed by a sentence about the Christian preference for earth-burials and a passage where resurrection is made credible by means of parallels in nature:[44] "The sun dips down and is born again; the stars sink and return; the flowers fall and renew their life; shrubs age and then break into leaf; seeds must decay in order to renew their

40. Engberg-Pedersen, "Complete and Incomplete"; Lehtipuu, "Flesh and Blood"; and Seim, "The Resurrected Body."

41. Lehtipuu, "Flesh and Blood."

42. Minucius Felix is only mentioned briefly in Gunnar af Hällström's *Carnis Resurrectio*, which concentrates on Ps.Justin, Athenagoras and Tertullian. He is not treated in Turid Karlsen Seim and Jorunn Økland, eds., *Metamorphoses: Resurrection, Body, and Transformative Practices in Early Christianity*. Caroline Walker Bynum discusses *Octavius* in *The Resurrection of the Body in Western Christianity, 200–1336*, in close connection to the late second-century and early third-century debate.

43. Cf. Beaujeu, *Minucius Felix*, 151.

44. Cf. also Tertullian, *Apol.* 48,7–9.

life" (34,11). This argument seems to be the most important, because it is the last and the most elaborate, presenting several suggestive examples. The peak in the passage is the comparison of "the body in the grave" with trees in winter, "they conceal their greenness under a show of dryness. Why press that in raw winter it should revive and return to life? We must wait too for the springtime of the body" (34,11–12). In this passage resurrection is made into a natural thing. The terms used for how "all nature suggests a future resurrection" (*resurrectionem futuram omnis natura medietur*) are *nasco* (to be born), *redeo* (to come back), *revivisco* (come to life again), *frondesco* (to shoot, put on leaves), *reviresco* (to grow green, become young), *revivisco et redeo* (revive and return (to life)). The comparisons are on the whole to vegetative life and natural phenomena. This is not original in Minucius Felix; much of the early literature applied this type of naturalistic images, frequently dependent on Paul's metaphors of seeds and first fruits.[45]

According to Caroline Walker Bynum, "Minucius uses natural analogies to justify the idea that the specific material components of the body subsists after death."[46] Bynum points out that the words for destruction in *Octavius* are "eating," "consuming" and "digesting" (*nutrire, consumare, pascere*).[47] These are the things that the human body triumphs over.[48] The bits and pieces of the human body are reassembled after death.[49] According to Bynum, Minucius "sees the resurrected body merely as the reassemblage of bits or parts" and she connects this view to the importance and challenge of martyrdom in the period when Octavius and the other treatises on resurrection were written.[50] I modify this view by stressing that Minucius presents at least two views of resurrection—a reassembling of fragments on the one hand and continuity and renewal on the other. He ends with the second view and with metaphorical language of seasons, days and plants to describe renewal and continuity. I would rather see this last view in connection with how *Octavius* is staged as being in memory of a dear and idealized friend. I further point out that the view of resurrection as continuity is in line with how this text describes Octavius and with its use of memories.

When plants are used metaphorically to describe resurrection, a question is what characteristics are mapped from plants (the source domain) to resurrection (the target-domain). In an ascetic setting, plants presumed

45. Bynum, *The Resurrection*, 23–24; Lehtipuu, "Flesh and Blood."

46. Bynum, *The Resurrection*, 35.

47. Ibid., 35.

48. Ibid.

49. Ibid., 38.

50. Ibid.

lack of sexual life and their not being nourished by eating made them into ideal illustrations of the ascetic life.[51] This, however, seems not to be an important part of their mapping in *Octavius* where the issue is resurrection. In the frequently used conceptual metaphor, PEOPLE ARE PLANTS, plants describe a human life cycle, which inevitably ends with withering and decline. When plants are used to describe resurrection, however, the main point seems rather to be their continuity and revival in the earth, where, hidden from view, a metamorphosis finally happens. If humans are like plants, they will not perish in the earth after death, like animals do, but experience a new spring.[52]

Where do metaphors stop and reality take over?[53] This is a difficult question, which is probably best solved by pointing to blurred boundaries. In the case of dead bodies, they were not thought of as plants, but all the same, as having crucial characteristics in common with them. When bodies are buried in the ground, reality seems to creep up on metaphors. Inhumation contra cremation is a theme raised by Caecilius and countered by Octavius, the theme even pops up in the middle of his argumentation about resurrection. Although Minucius by means of Octavius denies that there is a strong ideological reason why Christians prefer inhumation, it is necessary to question this view. If the ruling metaphorical context of Christian funerals is fragmentation, a funeral pyre is as well suited as inhumation. However, if the stress is on vegetative life and its continuation from summer through winter to a new summer, the inhumation practice is more in line with this thinking in which the seed is in the earth and will eventually sprout again. Here the body can more straightforwardly be regarded as a seed or a plant.

Plants in Graeco-Roman culture were used as wreaths, for instance connected to burials, inhumation, sarcophaguses and sepulchres. According to Minucius, the Christians neither adorned themselves nor their graves with wreaths (12,6). They were reserved for non-Christian funerals.[54] Chapter 38 returns to the subject of garlands for the dead. Why is this subject so important? One thing is that lack of garlands marked Christian funerals as distinct from Pagan. But in addition, they pertain more directly to Christian interpretations of death and resurrection. When Minucius urges

51. Gilhus, "Why is it better."

52. One mythcal beast, which was frequently used to describe resurrection, was the phoenix.

53. There were discussions about the relationship between animals and humans, cf. Gilhus, *Animals*, as well as discussions about the borders between animals and plants (see Sorabji, *Animal Minds*, 97–104). Manichaeism is one example of a religion where the conception of these borders was redefined.

54. Clarke, *The Octavius*, 238–39.

not to bind "a garland that withers" (38,4), an implication is that a withering garland sends the wrong signal, because the goal is to receive a garland from God "of flowers that blossom forever" (38,4). In this case actual plants are changed for supra-biological versions of them.

The two views on resurrection in the text, reassembling of fragments contra continuity and revival, reflect two views on resurrection. The first is more directly dependent on the intervention of God and probably connected to martyrdom, as has been suggested.[55] The second presents resurrection more like a natural development of dead bodies and describes it by means of vegetative life. This view has a special relevance in relation to Octavius' position in the text and to the text being in memory of him.

Conclusion

In the Graeco-Roman world, metamorphoses implied that it was possible to transform from higher to lower levels, from humans to animals. Animals did not change into humans,[56] and humans did not become gods. In the centuries when Christianity developed from the ideas and practices of small groups to a religion of the empire, general cultural processes were at work where humans distanced themselves from animals and approached closer to the divine. The Stoics fixed the borders between humans and animals so that they became impenetrable, a view that dominates *Octavius* and most Christian texts.

Octavius takes part in a degrading of superhuman beings (gods, spirits, demons) in order to make space for humans to rise above these beings, and to establish a transcendent conception of god. The euhemeristic view of the gods, which Minucius adheres to, teaches that it was possible for humans to become divine. This view blurs the boundaries between gods and humans, by degrading gods and elevating humans.

In Christianity, metamorphoses no longer happen from humans to animals, but from an earthly and biological human being to a supra-biological entity. Jesus does not play a significant role in *Octavius*, and resurrection is described both as an assembling of fragments and as a natural process and the second stage in the lives of all humans. According to the last description, the resurrected human being becomes in some ways curiously similar to a plant.

---

55. Bynum, *The Resurrection*, 43–51.
56. Gilhus, *Animals*, 82; cf. also Czachesz, "Metamorphosis and Mind."

Bibliography

Beaujeu, Jean. *Minucius Felix, Octavius: Texte établi et traduit.* Paris: Belles lettres, 1964.

Bynum, Caroline Walker. *The Resurrection of the Body in Western Christianity, 200–1336.* New York: Columbia University Press, 1995.

Carver, G. L. "A Note on Minucius Felix, *Octavius* 4.4." *Phoenix* 28 (1974) 355–57.

Clarke, Graeme W. *The Octavius of Marcus Minucius Felix.* Translated and annotated by G. W. Clarke. New York: Newman, 1974.

Czachesz, István. "Metamorphosis and Mind: Cognitive Explorations of the Grotesque in Early Christian Literature." In *Metamorphoses: Resurrection, Body, and Transformative Practices in Early Christianity,* edited by Turid Karlsen Seim and Jorunn Økland, 207–30. Ekstasis 1. Berlin: de Gruyter, 2009.

Endsjø, Dag Øistein. *Greek Resurrection Beliefs and the Success of Christianity.* London: Palgrave Macmillian, 2009.

Engberg-Pedersen, Troels. "Complete and Incomplete Transformation in Paul—a Philosophical Reading of Paul on Body and Spirit." In *Metamorphoses: Resurrection, Body, and Transformative Practices in Early Christianity,* edited by Turid Karlsen Seim and Jorunn Økland, 123–46. Ekstasis 1. Berlin: de Gruyter, 2009.

Frede, Michael. "Monotheism and Pagan Philosophy in Later Antiquity." In *Pagan Monotheism in Late Antiquity,* edited by Polymnia Athanassiadi and Michael Frede, 41–67. Oxford: Oxford University Press, 1999.

Gilhus, Ingvild Sælid. *Animals, Gods and Humans: Changing Attitudes to Greek, Roman and Early Christian Ideas.* London: Routledge, 2006.

———. "Why Is It Better to Be a Plant than an Animal? Cognitive Poetics and Ascetic Ideals in the Book of Thomas the Contender (NHC II,7)." In *Chasing Down Religion: In the Sights of History and the Cognitive Sciences. Essays in Honour of Luther H. Martin,* edited by Panayotis Pachis and Donald Wiebe, 115–33. Thessaloniki: Barbounakis, 2010.

Hällström, Gunnar af. *Carnis resurrectio: The Interpretation of a Credal Formula.* Commentationes humanarum litterarum 86. Helsinki: Societas scientiarum Fennica, 1988.

Hargis, Jeffrey W. *Against the Christians: The Rise of Early Christian Polemic.* Patristic Studies 1. New York: Lang, 1999.

Hasenhütl, Franz. *Die Heidenrede im "Octavius" des Minucius Felix als Brennpunkt antichristlicher Apologetik.* Theologie 89. Münster: Lit, 2008.

Knust, Jennifer Wright. *Abandoned to Lust: Sexual Slander and Ancient Christianity.* New York: Columbia University Press, 2006.

Kytzler, Bernhard. *M. Minucius Felix. Latenisch-Deutsch.* Darmstadt: Wissencahftliche Buchgesellschaft, 1991.

Lakoff, George, and Mark Turner. *More than Cool Reason: A Field Guide to Poetic Metaphor.* Chicago: University of Chicago Press, 1989.

Lehtipuu, Outiu. "'Flesh and Blood Cannot Inherit the Kingdom of God': The Transformation of the Flesh in the Early Christian Debates." In *Metamorphoses: Resurrection, Body, and Transformative Practices in Early Christianity,* edited by Turid Karlsen Seim and Jorunn Økland, 147–68. Ekstasis 1. Berlin: de Gruyter, 2009.

Martin, Dale. *Inventing Superstition: From the Hippocratics to the Christians.* Cambridge: Harvard University Press, 2004.

Minucius Felix. *Octavius*. In *Tertullian, Apology, de Sepctaculis, Minucius Felix, Octavius*. Translated by T. R. Glover and G. H. Rendall. LCL 250. Cambridge: Harvard University Press, 1984.

Price, Simon. "Latin Christian Apologetics: Minucius Felix, Tertullian, and Cyprian." In *Apologetics in the Roman Empire: Pagan, Jews, and Christians*, edited by Mark Edwards, Martin Goodman, and Simon Price, in association with Christopher Rowland, 105–29. Oxford: Oxford University Press, 1999.

Schubert, Christoph. "Minucius Felix." In *Reallexikon für Antike und Christentum* 24:804–27. Stuttgart: Hiersemann, 2011.

Seim, Turid Karlsen. "The Resurrected Body in Luke–Acts: The Significance of Space." In *Metamorphoses: Resurrection, Body, and Transformative Practices in Early Christianity*, edited by Turid Karlsen Seim and Jorunn Økland, 19–39. Ekstasis 1. Berlin: de Gruyter.

Seim, Turid Karlsen, and Jorunn Økland. "Introduction." In *Metamorphoses: Resurrection, Body, and Transformative Practices in Early Christianity*, edited by Turid Karlsen Seim and Jorunn Økland, 1–18. Ekstasis 1. Berlin: de Gruyter, 2009.

Seim, Turid Karlsen, and Jorunn Økland, eds. *Metamorphoses: Resurrection, Body, and Transformative Practices in Early Christianity*. Ekstasis 1. Berlin: de Gruyter, 2009.

Sorabji, Richard. *Animal Minds and Human Morals: the Origins of the Western Debate*. Ithaca, NY: Cornell University Press, 1993.

8

Like Father Like Son

Reassessing Constructions of Fatherhood
in Ephesians in Light of Cultural Interests
in Family Continuity

MARGARET Y. MACDONALD

FEMINIST ANALYSIS OF THE household codes has tended to emphasize the prescriptive as opposed to descriptive quality of the discourse.[1] Specifically with respect to women's actual lives and gender roles, feminist scholars have warned that New Testament instructions calling for hierarchy in the household ruled by a male head should not be understood as descriptions of reality. In addition, in examining texts like Eph 5:22–33, scholars have identified constructions of gender that often stand in complex, and even tangential and oppositional relationships to the community of believers to which prescriptions are addressed. [2] The purpose of this essay is to draw upon these insights with respect to the role of fathers. It will be argued that fatherhood is a central concept in Ephesians despite the brevity of the exhortations in Eph 6:1–4. Moreover, notwithstanding first appearances,

1. On feminist analysis and the household codes see MacDonald, "Beyond the Topos of Household Management," 74–79.

2. Here the work of Turid Karlsen Seim has been influential. See Seim, "A Superior Minority," 167–81; "Interfacing House and Church," 53–69. In the latter study, for example, she offers the following insight about Eph 5:21–33: "The husband's headship is qualified by the requirement that it be Christ-like in that it mirrors Christ's caring love. Christ's paradigmatic love is self-giving, but it is undoubtedly also a hierarchical expression and exercise of power. A conventional patriarchal construction of power is thereby maintained and restrained at the same time" (56). On this topic see also Osiek and MacDonald, *A Woman's Place*, 118–43.

Ephesians does not offer a straightforward reinforcement of patriarchy, but uses concepts of parenting to define leadership and to anchor theological concepts of God and community identity.

Fathers, Demography, and Parenting in the Roman World

There has been little attention paid to the child-parent exhortations in the household codes of Colossians and Ephesians for the brief exhortations (Col 3:20–21; Eph 6:1–4) at first glance appear to contain nothing novel or re-velatory. It is not surprising that Eph 6:4 focuses specifically on the author-ity of fathers over their children for ideological and legal statements gave fathers ultimate authority over their children even if the extent to which this was applied in real life remains a matter of debate among scholars. Extreme assertions of authority were balanced, however, with calls for moderation in the exercise of discipline. Following the example of Colossians, but with slightly different terminology, Ephesians instructs fathers not to provoke their children. While it may reflect more moderate attitudes, this teaching in no way reflects a novel or countercultural approach.[3]

One comes closer to awareness of a distinct perspective in consid-ering what is different about Ephesians in comparison with Colossians. Even a cursory comparison reveals a significantly longer treatment of the child-parent relationship in Ephesians, with an explicit emphasis on the educational role of fathers (Eph 6:4). The concern to reinforce the role of believing fathers as educators of children is one of many indications in the Ephesian household code of the infusion of Christian ideals and concepts into the traditional treatment of familial relationships, typical of discussions of household management in the Roman world. While it is not as obvious as the metaphorical exploration of marriage as an indicator of the connection between Christ and the church, the call to fathers to raise their children in "the discipline and instruction of the Lord" points to the same tendency: imagining and re-imagining family relations in terms of the mission and identity of the *ekklēsia*.

Subtle indications of "Christianization," as well as pointers to complex family circumstances, can be detected in the exhortations to children in Eph 6:1–3 where both parents are in view. In contrast to Colossians, Ephesians does not speak of children obeying their parents "in all things," but rather simply calls children to obey their parents "in the Lord." It is important to

---

3. See, for example, Pseudo-Plutarch, *Lib. ed.* (*Mor.* 8F); Ps.-Phoc. 207.

think carefully about what it might mean to obey parents "in the Lord," and not jump to the conclusion that obedience to biological parents or even step-parents is mainly in view. [4] Obedience to parents is clearly prized as the citation from the Decalogue concerning the honor due to parents makes clear. But the language of commitment to the Lord identifies an ultimate priority that may well involve an implicit acknowledgement of the kind of disobedience that might result from a child joining a church group without the permission of his or her father who is not "in the Lord." The notion that children might need to disobey their parents in unusual situations was not unknown in the Roman world. Musonius Rufus, for example, entertained the possibility that in certain circumstances a child might actually disobey a father, especially in the interests of philosophy.[5] New Testament scholars have frequently drawn attention to evidence of wives who chose to join church groups without their husbands (1 Pet 3:1–2) and ultimately in defiance of their religious authority in the household; but the children of such marriages must not be forgotten (1 Cor 7:14) and the possibility must be grappled with that children made their way into church groups without the permission of parents. It is important to take into consideration scholarship on the domestic/work world of the first believers and on the nature of household spaces; this scholarship highlights the potential for children to enter church groups via the networks created by childcare, play, and even chance encounters in workshops and crowded urban streets in a Mediterranean environment.[6]

The centrality of fatherhood in Ephesians needs to be evaluated in light of the realities of family constituency and pseudo-parenting in the Roman world. As is the case with all of the NT household codes, the precise delineation of categories is misleading. For the purposes of this essay, it is especially important to remember that slaves were both fathers (as well as mothers) and children, in addition to being slaves subject to masters. Slaves could be the biological children of their owners and it has even been suggested that

4. It should be noted that "in the Lord" (*en kyriō*) may not have been part of the original text as it is absent several early manuscript witnesses. However, on balance, the longer reading is preferred. For evaluation of the evidence, see MacDonald, *Colossians and Ephesians*, 332.

5. See discussion in Balla, *The Child-Parent Relationship*, 74–75. It is interesting here to consider the testimony of Epictetus who, like the author of Colossians, recommends that children obey their parents "in everything," but at the same time cautions that the philosopher's commitment to the "good" should represent the top priority (*Diatr.* 2.10.7). See Balla, *The Child-Parent Relationship*, 175.

6. Here the work on early Christian families and households has been especially influencial. See Moxnes, *Constructing Early Christian Families*; Osiek and Balch, *Families in the New Testament World*; Osiek and MacDonald, *A Woman's Place*.

the sexual use of slaves by masters was the most common source of house-hold slaves.[7] Despite the lack of legal recognition of slave marriages, families, paternity, or patrimony, it is clear from inscriptions on commemorations erected by freed persons that slaves freely employed family terminology to refer to their relationships and aspired to familial continuity and stability.[8] Overlapping identities meant that the messages encoded in these ethical teachings could also be overlapping and even conflicting. Among a multi-tude of scenarios we might consider is the slave father who was exhorted to bring up his children in the discipline and instruction of the Lord (Eph 6:4), when he was also bidden to obey his earthly master (6:5) who might well be against encouraging the household slaves to follow Christ. We should not be too quick to assume that freeborn believing fathers represented the majority of fathers in these early communities.[9]

An understanding of the broad-reaching phenomenon of pseudo-parenting also raises numerous questions about the instructions to children and fathers in Eph 6:1–4. Pseudo-parenting took many forms in the Roman world. Sometimes the phenomenon crossed or tested the boundaries of the slave-master relationship. Although it was rare, sometimes slave children were reared with the expectation that they would eventually share in the educational and inheritance benefits (cf. Col 3:24) of the freeborn children of the household.[10] Sometimes slave children were raised as "favorites" for the delight of their masters; but pseudo-parenting efforts in such circum-stances sometimes turned into sexual abuse.[11]

Especially when considering the presence and influence of fathers in church communities, however, it is important to keep demographic realities in mind. In thinking about the individual family units which formed part of early church communities, it crucial to remember that it is estimated that approximately 25 percent would have lost their fathers by the age of ten. Sur-rogate fathers of various kinds were commonplace. Dislocation of parents and children resulted from death and divorce, and children were fostered by side kin, older siblings, or even adopted into other families. In speaking about flexible care arrangements in the Roman world Ann-Cathrin Harders

7. This has been debated, but see Scheidel, "The Demographic Background," 31–40.

8. On the multiple identities of slaves based especially on inscriptional evidence, see, for example, Martin, "Slave Families."

9. This question is especially relevant in the case of the Colossian community where the slave presence is of obvious concern (Col 3:22—4:1).

10. See discussion of inscriptional evidence in Rawson, *Children and Childhood in the Roman World*, 259–61.

11. On the phenomenon of favorites or *delicia* children, see Laes, "*Delicia*-Children Revisited."

has aptly described the situation as one of "patchwork" families.[12] The legal authority of the father (*pater familias*) or male head of household did not always define reality in the case of widowhood or divorce. In practice, mothers appealed to natal kin for assistance and paternal influence was exercised by dominant surrogate fathers such as maternal uncles, step-fathers, or, especially in the case of well-to-do widows, the single mothers themselves.[13] Such social realities suggest that there were well established patterns of surrogate fatherhood in the Roman world that could be reworked into opportunities for community leadership in house-church environments; it is vital to question the identity and role of fathers in Eph 6:4 and to be open to various possibilities beyond a biological father in a nuclear family grouping. The implications of gender constructions become even more difficult to determine when one recalls the possibility of single mothers acting as surrogate fathers; women continue to be named without male counterparts in the disputed letters of Paul, including Nympha who has a church in her house (Col 4:15–16), and Eunice and Lois, with their formative influence on Timothy (2 Tim 1:5).

All of this means that the reference to the children belonging to believing fathers should not be taken too literally. There is much in the societal practices of the day to suggest that paternal authority and protection in church groups could extend over children and slave children who in reality belonged to non-believers or were orphaned or abandoned. Building upon existing cultural patterns and reflecting conventional values does not mean, however, that dominant values were not questioned. In particular, a focus on the role of the father as educator in Ephesians leads to identification of a challenge to the status quo with respect to criteria for membership tied to a father's role in ensuring family continuity. Despite some documented exceptions, the pervasive trend was for freeborn and slave children, who were often raised by the same slave care-givers, to be separated by a cultural chasm in adulthood. Such a divide could be anticipated in the treatment of the children of the house by the *pater familias*. It is instructive to consider the case made by Seneca for the indulgence of household slaves: while the *pater familias* must meter out the most severe discipline (or in Seneca's words, be a severe and demanding maestro of virtue) with his own sons, he can be free to indulge household slaves, paying little attention to their education and even taking delight in their vices.[14] In contrast, as will be ar-

12. As indeed Harders has done in "Roman Patchwork Families," 53.

13. Ibid.

14. See especially Seneca, *de providentia* 1.5–6, as discussed by Mencacci, "*Modestia vs licencia*," 223–25.

gued below, such disregard based on lineage seems absent from Ephesians, with indications of an alternate ideology defining familial bonds. Ephesians contains a challenge to traditional notions of paternity and entitlement.

Fathers as Educators

Ephesians 6:4 exhorts fathers to raise their children "in the discipline (*paideia*) and instruction (*nouthesia*) of the Lord." This is the first instance in early Christian literature of an explicit directive to impart a body of instruction with Christian content to children in a household/ house-church setting.[15] Colossians 3:20–21 addresses children and fathers directly in manner that establishes their importance in the community and, in sociological terms, represents an effort to socialize these groups. But in Ephesians socialization includes a deliberate attempt to educate—directives are framed with an eye to future, the incorporation of the next generation via education.[16]

The special responsibility of fathers for the religious education of children is well attested in Jewish and Greco-Roman courses. Scripture highlights the role of fathers in passing down traditions: "Listen, children, to a father's instruction and be attentive, that you may gain insight; for I give you good precepts: do not forsake my teaching" (Prov 4:1–2; cf. 4:1–4, NRSV). Likewise, fathers played a key role in protecting and disseminating religious knowledge in the Roman world. Often conveyed orally, knowledge of rites associated with the ancestor's traditions, was passed down from father to son, generation to generation.[17] Sons were expected to accompany and observe fathers in performances of various sacrifices tied to civic duty.[18] Fathers were to safeguard continuity and cultivate a child's memory. There is no question that women played an important role in the education of young children (2 Tim 1:5) and of adolescent girls into adults (Tit 2:3–5). In *reality*, they may often have been much more influential teachers than our sources would lead us to believe. Yet, on an ideological level, the education of sons by their fathers receives unmistakable pride of place. Plutarch describes how "Cato the Elder took care of his son's education himself when he could have employed one of the best tutors of his time. He taught him

15. See Barclay, "The Family as the Bearer of Religion," 77.

16. For interpretation of the differences between Colossians and Ephesians from a social-constructionist position, see especially MacDonald, "Parenting, Surrogate Parenting and Teaching."

17. Prescendi, "Children and Transmission of Religious Knowledge," 73–75, citing especially Ovid, *Fast.* 5.431–32; [Pseudo]-Plutarch, *Mor.* 9E; *Lib. ed.*

18. Ibid., 78, citing Xenophon, *Anab.* 5.6.29.

literature, law, and gymnastics. He also wrote a history book 'in big letters so that his son would have the means to learn about the ancient traditions of his country at home.'"[19]

As can be sensed in Plutarch's description, the father-son relationship was at the heart of family identity in the Roman world. Public perception of this relationship mattered and the public frequently deemed the father as the living image (*imago, effigies*) of his father. This designation was based not so much on physical appearances, but socialization within the family (what we might call "airs") and the attribution of identity by others. In order to guarantee the perpetuation of family traditions, the imitation of the father by the son (*imatatio patri*) was essential; such imitation enabled the participation of the son in the continuum of family identity that stretched backward in time, allowing the young man to live up to the memory of his ancestors.[20] Addressing sons directly, the stoic philosopher Epictetus expressed such sentiments boldly in warning of the obligations for obedience that flow from the fundamental relationship between fathers and sons:

> Now bear in mind that you are a son. What is the profession of this character? To treat everything that is his own as belonging to his father, to be obedient to him in all things, never to speak ill of him to anyone else, nor to say or do anything that will harm him, to give way to him in everything and yield to him in precedence, helping him as far as is within his power.[21]

Deference to a father's authority and allegiance to him in every respect defined the essence of the son's character.

The notion of fathers molding the characters of their sons presupposes educational influence that moderns might describe as both knowledge-based and practical. This combination is reflected also in Eph 6:4 containing reference to instruction (*nouthesia*) and discipline or training (*paideia*). The latter term is particularly significant for it encompasses broad concepts of education, including that which might more closely resemble formation than teaching in any narrow intellectual sense. While in Ephesians it is applied to the teaching of children, the term does not only refer to the upbringing of a child in the strict sense, but also ongoing formation that begins in childhood and extents into adulthood. It is instructive to consider Josephus' use of the concept in laying out the two schemes of education or

19. Prescendi, "Children and Transmission of Religious Knowledge," 77; citing Plutarch, *Cato* 20. For the emphasis placed on the education of sons, see also Harders, "Roman Patchwork Families," 49–59.

20. On these dynamics, see Harders, "Roman Patchwork Families," 52.

21. Epictetus, *Diatr.* 2.10.7 (trans. Oldfather, LCL).

training (*paideia*) (by precept and by practical exercising of the character) which are combined in Jewish teaching of the Law:

> Our legislator, on the other hand, took great care to combine both systems. He did not leave practical training in morals inarticulate; nor did he permit the letter of the law to remain inoperative. Starting from the very beginning with the food of which we partake from infancy and the private life of the home, he left nothing, however insignificant, to the discretion and caprice of the individual. What meats a man should abstain from, and what he may enjoy; with what persons he should associate; what period should be devoted respectively to strenuous labor and to rest.[22]

While it is less explicit, the approach taken to education by the author of 2 Timothy also seems to build upon Jewish notions of formation throughout the life course. In recalling the formation of Timothy, 2 Tim 3:15 describes his education from infancy (*brephos*) in the sacred writings (*hiera grammata*).[23] References Scripture (*graphē*) and discipline or training (*paideia*) occur in a second text where there is a clear emphasis on teaching; training (*paideia*) in righteousness is the purpose of Scripture (2 Tim 3:16–17), along with teaching (*didascalia*), reproof (*elegmos*) and correction (*epanorthōsis*). The focus in this case is more directly on the instruction of adults, but the teaching of children is by no means ruled out. In fact, one detects in this text a similar interest in the combination of precepts and the practical application thereof which Josephus identifies as a hallmark of the teaching of the Law.[24]

On the basis of such comparisons, it seems clear that the reference to fathers in Eph 6:4 is intended to encourage the same type of practical instruction which calls for leadership on the part of fathers (they should not provokes their children to anger) that extends into their old age and invites reverence and obedience from their children. In addition, such practical

---

22. Josephus, *C. Ap.* 2.173–74 (trans. Thackeray, LCL). On the two schemes, see also *Against Apion* 2.171–72. On the teaching of the Law throughout the life-course see discussion of the Dead Sea Scrolls by Wassen in "On the Education of Children."

23. This term was widely employed by Greek-speaking Jews to refer to the Scriptures. See Johnson, *The First and Second Letters to Timothy*, 419.

24. Such links between the conceptual and the practical also can be found in the Greco-Roman world. The saving role of education draws its origins from "Hellenistic moral philosophy" (Dio Chrysostom, *Or.* 32.15–16; *Alex.*). See Fiore, *Pastoral Epistles*, 22. From roughly the same era, comes *1 Clement*'s notion of the instruction of children, which involves "discipline (or training; (*paideias*) that is in Christ," *1 Clem* 21.8–9 (trans. Ehrman, LCL).

instruction is rooted in scriptural traditions and tied to theological concepts about God. This is one of several indications of a re-definition of family in Ephesians that operates in conjunction with an apologetic presentation of parenting.

Parenting and Apology

The ideological convergence between the NT household codes and ancient treatments of household management, highlighting conventional features of family structure, have very frequently led to theories concerning the apologetic function of the codes. Scholars have detected attempts to quiet criticism from the outside society in the traditional family posturing.[25] The slave-master and marital relationships have figured prominently in such theorizing, but virtually no attention has been paid to the role of the child-parent and father-child exhortations. Notwithstanding this tendency to neglect parenting, the ideological importance of the role of fathers in preparing the next generation invites one to reconsider some of the works that have been compared to New Testament texts in building arguments concerning the apologetic intent of such texts.

In his apologetic discourse in *Against Apion*, Flavius Josephus emphasized values associated with the firm authority of the *pater familias* that were viewed as crucial to the grounding children in tradition. According to Josephus, Jews living under the Law were as under a father and master (*hupo patri toutō kai despotē*; cf. Gal 3:24).[26] The household head of the Jewish family was not only responsible for order in the family, but metered out disciple for disobedience matching the scope of discipline which was the prerogative of the Roman *pater familias*.[27] Such a comparison and appeals to concepts like *eusebeia* to describe the piety of the Jews resonate with Josephus' apologetic intent; *eusebeia* is a concept typically linked with devotion to matters of state and family, especially the obedience of children.[28] The education children in Jewish traditions is so important as to be identified as a priority: "Above all we pride ourselves on the education of our children, and regard

25. On apology as a theory for understanding the function of household codes, see MacDonald, "The Topos of Household Management," 73–74.

26. Josephus, *C. Ap.* 2.174.

27. Ibid., 2.217 According to Reinhartz and Shier, Josephus's comments reflect familiarity with the Roman concept of *patria potestas*, which gave the *pater familias* absolute (life and death) authority over the members of his household, especially his children. See Reinhartz and Shier, "Josephus on Children and Childhood," 370.

28. Josephus, *C. Ap.* 2.181.

as the most essential task in life the observance of our laws and of the pious practices (*eusebeian*), based thereupon, which we have inherited."[29] According to Josephus' ideal family vision, children should be taught to read and rooted in the traditions of the forefathers, involving deeds to be imitated and laws to be absorbed.[30]

While the apologetic overtones are not always as apparent as in the text cited above, in other places Josephus stresses the authority of parents in a manner that invites comparison with Roman ideals. Commenting on the case of the rebellious son in Deut 21:18–21, Josephus reports what the parents would have said to the son while disciplining him. The most serious consequences are introduced only as a last resort:

> In cases in which young men disdain their parents and do not grant them honor—whether because of shame or lack of understanding—demeaning them, let the parents first of all warn them with words, for they are autonomous judges over their sons, saying that they came together with each other not for the sake of pleasure, nor of increasing their wealth by placing in common what the two of them had, but in order that they might have children who would tend them in their old age and who would have from them whatever they needed: "When you were born, we raised you with joy, and giving the greatest thanks to God we reared you with devotion, sparing nothing of what seemed to be useful for your well-being and education in the best things. Now, however, for it was necessary to grant pardon for the failings of youth, you have sufficiently disregarded honor toward us. Change to the more reasonable way, considering that God is also annoyed with those who commit outrage against parents, because He Himself is also the father of the whole human race."[31]

There are many aspects of Josephus' comments that invite comparison to Eph 6:1–4. The reference to a failure to grant parents honor calls to mind the instruction honor parents in Eph 6:2 which is rooted in the command from the Decalogue (LXX Exod 20:12; Deut 5:16). The command to honor parents is a frequent theme Hellenistic Jewish literature; as in the text cited

---

29. Ibid., 1.60 (trans. Thackeray, LCL).

30. Ibid., 2.204. For more extensive discussion of the role of children in Josephus's apologetic discourse, with parallel texts from Philo of Alexandria, see MacDonald, "A Place of Belonging," 267–88.

31. Josephus, *Ant.* 4.260–63. See *Jewish Antiquities*. Trans and ed. Feldman. Ongoing reverence for parents was a moral ideal that Romans shared with Jews in the ancient world. See for example Seneca, *Ben.* 3.38.2.

above, we find sanctions for the divine authority of parents and allusions to the consequences positive and negative associated with obedience and disobedience.[32] Josephus' comments along with many other texts from the Roman era make it clear that direction to honor parents included the expectation on the part of parents that they would be cared for in their old age. Honoring parents meant bestowing honor upon them for the whole of their lives.[33]

Josephus' use of the fatherhood of God (the father of the whole human race) as justification for the anger of God directed towards human sons invites examination of how similar theological constructions of the fatherhood of God in Eph 3:14–15 (see further below) might be related to family life in church groups. It is important to consider how allegiance to God the Father was related to adherence to leaders whose fatherhood (including pseudo-fatherhood) was viewed as threatening in the neighborhoods where early Christian groups developed. The highly polemical comments of the second-century pagan critic Celsus have often been examined in light family structures in the Roman world; the place of women and slaves in the diatribe has frequently been noted. But if we approach the text with a focus on the father's responsibility for the education of children and his role as a guarantor of family memory and continuity, references to subordinate members of the household as the target group for early Christian evangelization efforts gain even more significance.

Celsus criticized the early Christians for usurping of the educational authority of the *pater familias* over his children and his influence in the selection of appropriate teachers. In Celsus's presentation the base of operations was the house (no doubt including the house church) and the shop where many slaves worked. Children accompanied by "stupid" women were exposed to a curriculum based on nonsense taught by disreputable Christian teachers.[34] According to Celsus, early Christian groups violated the almost sacred bond between father and son with gatherings seemed intent on winning over adolescent boys; they created the very antitheses of an assembly

---

32. On the divine authority of parents, see Philo, *Decal.* 107. On the blessings that accompany obedience to parents see Sir 3:1–8. For the mortal consequences that follow disobedience of one's parents, see Josephus, *C. Ap.*, 2.217, citing Deut 21:18–21.

33. See especially Exod 21:15, 17; Prov 19:26; 20:20; 28:24; Mark 7:9–13; Matt 15:4–6. New Testament scholars have debated whether Eph 6:1–3 is directed at young or adult children. But in an ancient context this distinction is essentially moot. It is a mistake to envisage rigid endpoints for childhood and rigid demarcations between grown and young children in the Roman world. On this topic, see especially Rawson, *Children and Childhood in Roman Italy*, 142–45.

34. See Origen, *Cels.* 3.55; see also 3.44.

of honorable and intelligent men.[35] It is against such a background that one should evaluate the exhortation to fathers to bring up their children in the discipline and instruction of the Lord. With curricular interests in Scripture and early Christian tradition, the fathers of Ephesians were honing the membership of the children in the community of the saints (cf. Eph 1:2, 18; 3:8; 4:12).[36] But from a Roman perspective, this type of participation would violate the traditional familial sanctity.

The Fatherhood of God and the Allegiance of the Community

The role of fathers in fostering a distinctive (and in many respects problematic identity) in the Roman world is visible in Jewish texts from the same era as Ephesians.[37] Although it is just now being recognized, the Dead Sea Scrolls contain fascinating material concerning the education of children presented within the framework of the life course and exploring the connection between fatherhood and the capacity to teach.[38] In many ways, in their approach to teaching of children, the Dead Sea Scrolls simply build upon the Hebrew Bible (cf. Deut 6:6–7).[39] With an emphasis on distinct identity which has much in common with the perspective of the Dead Sea Scrolls, Ephesians values the socialization of children drawing upon scriptural traditions.[40] Ephesians 6:1–3 appeals to Deut 5:16 with its promise of wellbeing and long life to children who honor their parents (cf. Deut 6:2–3). Ephesians calls upon traditional scriptural notions of family and generational continuity to define the interaction between parents and children in the

35. See Origen, *Cels.* 3.50. On how Celsus's discourse presents Christianity as violating the ideals of masculinity, see Osiek and MacDonald, *A Woman's Place*, 134–35.

36. On the frequent use of the term saints (the holy ones) in Ephesians, see MacDonald, *Colossians and Ephesians*, 191.

37. Examples from Josephus's thought have been discussed above.

38. The two documents that provide rare evidence concerning the education of children in the late Second Temple period are the Rule of the Congregation (1QSa) and the Damascus Document (CD). These documents have been examined thoroughly in relation to this theme by Cecilia Wassen who also considers various translation and textual issues. See Wassen, "On the Education of Children."

39. While the immediate context of the proclamation is the important annual Renewal of the Covenant ceremony, 1QSa 1:4–8 reveals expectations of the teaching of the laws throughout the life course. Like the covenantal ceremony described in Deut 31:10–13, the presence of the children is significant (Deut 31:12, 13). Ibid., 351–52.

40. On Ephesians and Qumran, see especially Perkins, *Ephesians*. For a much more detailed comparison the perspectives on children and education found in Ephesians and the Qumran literature, see MacDonald, *The Power of Children*.

house-church community. The fulfilment of commandments and instruction of children (Eph 6:4) becomes a means of articulating the parameters of the community which is lived out day by day. But when the role of father is opened up to include surrogate fathers, as is suggested above, this type of commitment to the Lord emerges as less of a straightforward act of preserving tradition and more of a re-definition of family and reorientation of ultimate commitments.

While it cannot be examined in detail here, the presentation of the Examiner in the Damascus Document develops an association between the leadership role of the teacher and fatherhood in a way that is very suggestive from understanding the context of Ephesians. In a very fragmentary text which forms part of "the rule for the Examiner of the camp" (CD 13:7–19), there is a very brief reference to the role of the Examiner in instructing children where he is told to demonstrate kindness and to avoid wrathful anger (4Q266 9 iii 6–9/CD 13:17–20).[41] The same type of instruction is found in the preceding passages which bring out the metaphorical association between fathers and teachers (CD 13:9) and where the examiner is to teach the whole congregation ("the many") and is to "pity them as a father does his children." Emphasis on moderation and gentleness is also found in Ephesians' warning to fathers to not provoke their children to anger (Eph 6:4; Col 3:21).

Once again calling for comparison to Eph 6:4, with its emphasis on instruction and discipline of children ultimately leading to adulthood, the Damascus Document presents the role of the Examiner in the initiation of the children of adult members: "And all who have entered the covenant for all of Israel as an eternal statute shall let their children, who have reached (the age) to cross over into those who are enrolled, take the oath of the covenant (CD 15:5–6)."[42] The broader context here is the role of the Examiner in teaching and examining components having to do with living according to the laws (cf. CD 15:5–15). The "oath of the covenant" appears to include the promise to live according to the correct interpretation of the laws. The approach with respect to children seems to be a type of perfecting of what the children have learned until this point within the community and within the context of their own families; the children will now take on full responsibility for living according to the received knowledge of the laws.[43]

---

41. For Hebrew text and discussion of various textual and translation issues, see Wassen, "On the Education of Children in the Dead Sea Scrolls," 356.

42. For Hebrew text and discussion of various textual and translation issues, see ibid.

43. Ibid., 357–58.

Comparison of Ephesians to material from the Dead Sea Scrolls alerts one to how household and community teaching under the guidance of father figures can operate in tandem. The familial language embedded in the theological constructions, along with the references to community structures and learning, need to be considered in order to grasp the full significance of the children-father exhortations in Eph 6:1–4. Several key texts should be examined, beginning with Eph 4:1–16. The nature of the emphasis on the role of teacher in this text reveals an underlying notion of building upon grounding in the family by community teachers. In describing Christ's role in the giving of gifts, the author of Ephesians brings together several leadership roles with teaching and/or preaching components: the apostles, the prophets, the evangelists, the pastors, and the teachers (4:11).[44] While it is impossible to distinguish precisely between the functions, one gains a better sense of their impact within the community by paying attention to the interweaving of family and education metaphors.

While the family connotations are rarely recognized, according to Eph 4:13, the ultimate goal of the work of the teacher-preachers is arrival at maturity, to the measure of the full stature of Christ. The Greek text expresses maturity as mature manhood (*eis andra teleion*; cf. Col 1:28 [*anēr*]). The obvious connection between an expression of Christian perfection and gender ideology calls for comment. As explained above, the mature man in the Roman world is one who emulates his father, becomes the image of his father and thereby preserves the continuity of the family. The idea is to measure up to the Son of God, specifically expressed in almost educational terms as knowledge of the Son of God (Eph 4:13). Despite the indisputable presence of conventional ideals about male perfection which underlie Eph 4:13, the verse is framed with indications that the whole community of males and females is capable of such perfection and maturity. Once again employing family metaphors, there is a contrast drawn with the immaturity of children generally who are vulnerable to being led astray (Eph 4:14; cf. 1 Cor 14:20). There is no doubt that the whole community of men and women is in view even if inclusivity is expressed in terms of potentially exclusively male, Christ-like perfection (cf. Eph 2:15). Mature manhood is a corporate entity essentially equated with the built-up body of Christ (Eph 5:12) and stands in contrast to children who are easily led astray by the changing winds of false teaching. The role of the teacher is to share life-giving knowledge with both male and female children as they progress to become men and women

---

44. On the significance of these terms and their relationship to the leadership structures of the community underlying Ephesians, see MacDonald, *Colossians and Ephesians*, 249–50, 291–92, 299; MacDonald, *The Pauline Churches*, 132–33; Horrell, "Leadership Patterns."

of the full stature of Christ. This is knowledge that cannot be fully grasped in childhood, calling to mind the emphasis on initiation and transition in the Dead Sea Scrolls.[45]

Knowledge is a key theme in Ephesians (cf. Eph 1:9, 17; 3:4–5, 16–19; 4:13, 18–19), and the acquisition of knowledge is fundamental to the formation of identity. It is particularly striking that Eph 4:20 conveys transformation from the state of unbelief to the life believers as that of having "learned Christ," followed by a recollection of the teaching that the recipients received (Eph 4:21–24). "Learned Christ" refers to learning traditions about Christ (cf. Acts 5:42; Col 1:6–7); the following verse tells of "hearing of him" and "having been taught in him, as truth is in Jesus."[46] The significance of the name of Jesus alone (the only such reference in Ephesians) is not clear; it may constitute a stylistic variation of the expression "in Christ" or it may point to the teachings of the historical Jesus.[47] But in either case, some type of prior instruction about Christ is presumed. In keeping with our exploration of the relationship between family structures and a community where teachers and instruction are clearly valued, it is important to remember that for many recipients such prior instruction would have been received from the fathers (and mothers) in the community (Eph 6:4). With an inclusive vision of who may be counted as a "learner," Ephesians propounds of a vision of a type of ongoing spiritual progression, with awareness of the vastness of the love of Christ that transforms the universe (3:17, 10) and of the fullness of God (Eph 3:19). Childhood and adulthood are both shaped by teaching and learning with the goal of maturity and the course is now set for a new type of continuity from generation to generation. Such transformation is due to the power of God. Whereas in previous generations insight into the mystery of Christ was not made known (Eph 3:5), a new reality is celebrated in the only doxology in the New Testament which refers to generations (*genea*): "to him be glory in the church to Christ and in Christ Jesus to all generations, forever and ever" (Eph 3:23).

There is a definite connection between the reference to generations in Eph 3:23 and the manner in which the dominion of God the Father is described in Eph 3:15. He is the Father "from whom every family in heaven and on earth takes his name." The recipients are being comforted by an

45. The terminology of Eph 4:13–14 has sometimes led commentators to suggest that the author of Ephesians is responding to Gnostic false teaching, but the terminology can be accounted for in other ways. See discussion in MacDonald, *Colossians and Ephesians*, 294.

46. The issues of grammar and translation for Eph 5:21 are subject to a few different interpretations. See MacDonald, *Colossians and Ephesians*, 303–4.

47. Ibid.

identity that has been fully transformed; they belong to a family that transcends the earthly world. But to grasp the full force of what is being asserted
one must remember that family memory and insolubility were one of the
most important components of Greco-Roman culture. [48] The mention of
a family name is by no means incidental for it was key to perceptions of
survival and continuity of reputation.[49] The Greek play on words in Eph
3:15, which is obscured by English translations, makes it clear that this
community of believers, united in a new family, *does* have a family name
with a reputation beyond dispute. Believers belong to the *patria* (family) of
the Father (*pater*). In the Roman world, it was children (legitimate heirs),
who propagated continuity and lineage in the Roman world.[50] Believers
now belonged to a spiritual family which did not require the continuity of
legitimate heirs.[51] Traditional values do shape exhortations to some extent,
however, for there is a type of continuity proclaimed in the presentation of
the *ekklēsia* as a family community which will extend into the future for
generations. Ephesians is also concerned with the education of children
(Eph 6:4) by their fathers, acknowledging the need for the socialization of
the next generation. But this community has loosened the requirements for
lineage and expanded definitions of fatherhood, both in its theological symbolism and in the practical structures of its daily operations.

Further evidence of a transformed identity can be found in the unusual manner in which the life of believers is described in Eph 5:1. Rather,
than employing the more usual expression of "imitators of Christ," believers
are called to be imitators of God as beloved children—the only use of such
an expression in the New Testament. In light of the previous discussion of
the importance of the importance children (especially sons) imitating their
fathers in the Roman, the call to imitate the Father should be understood as
a reinforcement of a new identity. The Father exercises his authority over all,
leads all, unites all, and parents all families—human or angelic (cf. Eph 1:2,
3, 17; 2:18; 3:14–15; 4:6; 5:20; 6:23). The fatherhood of God is one of many
ways that Ephesians emphasizes universality and unity. In this case such
emphasis communicates important messages about access to fatherhood for
members of *ekklēsia*. Openness to all children and all parents defies many

---

48. See Ville Vuolanto, "Children and the Memory of Parents," 174.

49. Ibid., 176.

50. Ibid., 174.

51. This becomes even more explicit in later early Christian literature dealing with
asceticism. See ibid., 181.

dominant views concerning patrimony and inheritance that were viewed as central to carrying on family and individual identity and traditions.[52]

Conclusion

An examination of fatherhood in Ephesians, as it is expressed both practically and symbolically, reveals both points of contact with dominant cultural values and social structures concerning family continuity and lineage and some elements of resistance to these same structures and values. Comparison to Jewish evidence brings out an interest in ongoing educational practices within the communal house-church setting that build upon household-based initiatives. Teachers acted like pseudo-fathers imparting scriptural traditions potentially at odds with the traditional instructions that should be imparted from father to son among the Gentiles.

The presentation of children belonging to believing fathers in Eph 6:4 should not be understood in a narrow sense. Widely accepted practices of pseudo-parenting in the Roman world prepared the way for redefinitions of parenting. Paternal authority and protection in church groups could extend over children and slave children who in reality belonged to non-believers or were orphaned or abandoned.

There are many questions that arise about how concepts of fatherhood in Ephesians should be understood both in terms of lives of women (what of the mothers?) and in terms of constructions of gender (how does the bride of Christ imagery fit with the presentation of fatherhood of God?). On the basis of the above analysis, however, it is clear that Ephesians propounds an inclusive vision of who may be counted as a "learner" and there is no particular emphasis on sons as legitimate heirs preserving family traditions. Instead, there are several indications in Ephesians of a redefined concept of the *ekklēsia* as a family whose name draws its origins from God the Father (Eph 3:14–15). This new family has transformed its requirements for membership/lineage and expanded its definitions of fatherhood, both in its theological symbolism and in the practical structures of its daily operations.

---

52. Ibid., 183. For links between the fatherhood of God and the family life of the community see *1 Clem.* 22–23. In highlighting some social dimensions of fatherhood of God language in Ephesians, I am grateful to Jerry Sumney for his paper presentation, "Filial Language in Ephesians," SBL Meeting, Baltimore, November 2013.

Bibliography

Balla, P. *The Child-Parent Relationship in the New Testament and Its Environment.* WUNT 155. Tübingen: Mohr Siebeck, 2003.

Barclay, John M. G. "The Family as the Bearer of Religion in Judaism and Early Christianity." In *Constructing Early Christian Families: Family as Social Reality and Metaphor*, edited by Halvor Moxnes, 66–80. London: Routledge, 1997.

Feldman, Louis H. *Jewish Antiquities.* Leiden: Brill, 2004.

Fiore, B. *The Pastoral Epistles.* Sacra Pagina 12. Collegeville, MN: Liturgical, 2007.

Harders, Ann-Catherin. "Roman Patchwork Families: Surrogate Parenting, Socialization, and the Shaping of Tradition." In *Children, Memory, and Family Identity in Roman Culture*, edited by Véronique Dasen and Thomas Späth, 49–72. Oxford: Oxford University Press, 2010.

Horrell, D. G. "Leadership Patterns and the Development of Ideology in Early Christianity." In *Social Scientific Approaches to New Testament Interpretation*, 309–38. Edinburgh: T. & T. Clark, 1999.

Johnson, Luke Timothy. *The First and Second Letters to Timothy.* AB 35A. New York: Doubleday, 2001.

Laes, Christian. *Children in the Roman Empire: Outsiders within.* Cambridge: Cambridge University Press, 2011.

———. "*Delicia*-Children Revisited: The Evidence of Statius' Silvae." In *Children, Memory, and Family Identity in Roman Culture*, edited by Véronique Dasen and Thomas Späth, 245–72. Oxford: Oxford University Press, 2010.

MacDonald, Margaret Y. "Beyond Identification of the Topos of Household Management: Reading the Household Codes in Light of Recent Methodologies and Theoretical Perspectives in the Study of the New Testament." *NTS* 57 (2010) 74–79.

———. *Colossians and Ephesians.* Sacra Pagina 17. Collegeville, MN: Liturgical, 2000.

———. *Early Christian Women and Pagan Opinion: The Power of the Hysterical Woman.* Cambridge: Cambridge University Press, 1996.

———. "Parenting, Surrogate Parenting and Teaching: Reading the Household Codes as Sources for Understanding Socialization and Education in Early Christian Communities." In *Theologische und soziologische Perspektiven auf früheristliche Lebenswelten*, edited by Dorothee Dettinger and Christof Landmesser, 85–102. Leipzig: Evangelische, 2014.

———. *The Pauline Churches: A Socio-historical Study of the Institutionalization in the Pauline and Deutero-Pauline Writings.* SNTSMS 60. Cambridge: Cambridge University Press, 1988.

———. *The Power of Children: Constructing Early Christian Families in the Greco-Roman World.* Waco, TX: Baylor University Press, 2014.

Martin, D. B. "Slave Families and Slaves in Families." In *Early Christian Families in Context: An Interdisciplinary Dialogue*, edited by David L. Balch and Carolyn Osiek, 207–30. Grand Rapids: Eerdmans, 2003.

Mencacci, Francesca. "*Modestia* vs. *licentia*: Seneca on Childhood and Status in the Roman Family." In *Children, Memory, and Family Identity in Roman Culture*, edited by Véronique Dasen and Thomas Späth, 223–44. Oxford: Oxford University Press, 2010.

Moxnes, Halvor, ed. *Constructing Early Christian Families: Family as Social Reality and Metaphor.* London: Routledge, 1997.

Osiek, Carolyn, and David L. Balch. *Families in the New Testament World: Households and House Churches.* Family, Religion, Culture. Louisville: Westminster John Knox, 1997.

Osiek, Carolyn, and Margaret Y. MacDonald (with Janet H. Tulloch). *A Woman's Place: House Churches in Earliest Christianity.* Minneapolis: Fortress, 2006.

Perkins, Pheme. *Ephesians.* Abingdon New Testament Commentaries. Nashville: Abingdon, 1997.

Prescendi, Francesca. "Children and the Transmission of Religious Knowledge." In *Children, Memory, and Family Identity in Roman Culture*, edited by Véronique Dasen and Thomas Späth, 73–93. Oxford: Oxford University Press, 2010.

Rawson, Beryl. *Children and Childhood in Roman Italy.* Oxford: Oxford University Press, 2003.

Reinhartz, Adele, and Kim Shier. "Josephus on Children and Childhood." *Studies in Religion* 41 (2012) 364–75.

Scheidel, W. "The Demographic Background." In *Growing up Fatherless in Antiquity*, edited by S. R. Huebner and D. M. Razan, 31–40. Cambridge: Cambridge University Press, 2009.

Seim, Turid Karlsen. "Interfacing House and Church: Converting Household Codes to Church Order." In *Text, Image, and Christians in the Graeco-Roman World: A Festschrift in Honor of David Lee Balch*, edited by Aliou Cissé Niang and Carolyn Osiek, 53–86. Princeton Theological Monograph Series 176. Eugene, OR: Pickwick Publications, 2012.

———. "A Superior Minority: The Problem of Men's Headship in Ephesians 5." In *Mighty Minorities? Minorities in Early Christianity—Positions and Strategies: Essays in Honor of Jacob Jervell on His 70th birthday, 21 May 1995*, edited by David Hellholm, Halvor Moxnes, and Turid Karlsen Seim, 167–71. Oslo: Scandinavian University Press, 1995.

Vuolanto, Ville. "Children and the Memory of Parents in the Late Roman World." In *Children, Memory, and Family Identity in Roman Culture*, edited by Véronique Dasen and Thomas Späth, 173–92. Oxford: Oxford University Press, 2010.

Wassen, Cecilia. "On the Education of Children in the Dead Sea Scrolls." *Studies in Religion* 41 (2012) 350–63.

———— 9 ————

Salvation as Slavery, Marriage and Birth

Does the Metaphor Matter?

ANNA REBECCA SOLEVÅG

Slaves, obey your earthly masters with fear and trembling, in singleness of heart, as you obey Christ; not only while being watched, and in order to please them, but as slaves of Christ, doing the will of God from the heart.[1]

—EPH 6:5-6

Then the Kingdom of the heavens shall be likened to ten virgins. They took their torches and went out to meet the bridegroom.[2]

—MATT 25:1

Jesus answered, "Very truly, I tell you, no one can enter the kingdom of God without being born of water and Spirit. What is born of the flesh is flesh, and what is born of the Spirit is spirit. Do not be astonished that I said to you, "You must be born from above."

—JOHN 3:5-7

1. Unless otherwise noted, English bible translations are taken from NRSV.
2. My translation.

144

Introduction

IN EARLY CHRISTIAN TEXTS, there are many different images used to depict the concept of salvation. To mention only a few, salvation is described as becoming a child (Mark 10:13–16), becoming male (*Gos. Thom.* 114), winning a fight or athletic contest and receiving the crown of victory (e.g., 1 Cor 9:24–27; 1 Tim 6:12), resting (Matt 11:28–29; Rev 14:13), feeding (e.g., John 6:32–35) and putting on new clothing (e.g., Eph 4:22–24; *Acts Thom.* 111–114). Salvation is an abstract theological concept that has different nuances in different texts. It usually contains the aspect of rescue from a negative worldly condition, somewhat realized in the present life of the believer. Eternal life after death also emerges as an important element.[3] When different images are used to describe salvation, is this mere ornamentation, or do the metaphors shape the meaning of the concept? In other words, what difference does the metaphor make?

In this essay I will focus on three central salvation metaphors from the New Testament: the metaphors of slavery, marriage and birth. The imagery of *slavery* as salvation can be found in Paul's letters (e.g., Rom 6:22; 1 Cor 7:22), as well as in the parables of Jesus found in the gospels (e.g., Matt 18:23–35; Luk 12:35–48). Drawing on imagery from the Song of Songs, the metaphor of *marriage* to Christ is evident in the two wedding parables from the gospels; the parable of the Wise and Foolish Virgins (Matt 25:1–13) and the Wedding Banquet for the King's Son (Matt 22:1–14). Paul uses the metaphor when he says to the Corinthian community in 2 Cor 11:2, "I promised you in marriage to one husband, to present you as a chaste virgin to Christ." In Eph 5:22–33, the pseudo-Pauline author also compares marriage and the relationship between husband and wife to the relationship between Christ and the church. The most well known example of soteriological *birthing* imagery is arguably Jesus' words to Nicodemus in John 3, that "no one can see the kingdom of God without being born from above" (John 3:3). Salvation as birthing is prevalent in 1 John (e.g., 1 John 3:8–10; 4:7–10) and also appears in Titus and 1 Peter, where "rebirth" seems to be connected with baptism (Tit 3:5; 1 Pet 1:3; 23).

The conceptualization of salvation as slavery, marriage and birth appears in texts that came to be considered canonical and thus have had a long and influential reception history. These metaphors relied on a social reality of institutionalized slavery, patriarchal marriage and gendered ideas about men and women's role in conception and childbearing. This essay will explore this connection between social reality and metaphor. I will examine

---

3. Slusser, "Salvation," 102–25.

the kyriarchal (see definition below) framework of these images and some of their metaphorical and literal uses in early Christian texts. It is my contention that the metaphors matter. The particular soteriological imagery of slavery, marriage and birth made a profound impact on Christian theology and shaped family life for centuries to come.

The Kyriarchal Structure of Greco-Roman Society

In this essay, I will use intersectionality as a framework to structure and make sense of early Christian salvation metaphors. Intersectionality is an interdisciplinary approach at the crossroads of feminist, gender, anti-racist, postcolonial and class sensitive modes of analysis. An intersectional approach tries to identify how different vectors of domination and oppression function together, while remembering that categories sometimes overlap and that identities are complex.[4]

With a view to intersectional analysis of early Christian texts, Elisabeth Schüssler Fiorenza has coined the term *kyriarchy* and puts it forward as a useful model for interpretation. She defines the term as such: "Derived from the Greek term lord, this coinage underscores that domination is not simply a matter of patriarchal, gender-based dualism but of more comprehensive, interlocking, hierarchically ordered structures of discrimination."[5] By employing this term, Schüssler Fiorenza shows how important the role of the *kyrios/paterfamilias* is for understanding the intersecting power structures of antiquity. Following Schüssler Fiorenza's model, I argue that within the kyriarchal structure of Greco-Roman society, the groups of the household are the quintessential categories for an intersectional analysis. The *kyrios* of the household held authority over wife, slaves and children, and thus the most important differentials are those of gender (male/female), status (slave/free) and age (adult/child)/generation (parent/offspring). According to Aristotle, these three relationships together constituted household management (*oikonomia*) and represented the microcosm of society.[6] Hence, the Emperor was configured as a *paterfamilias* for all of his subordinates, "the ultimate father and lord, the *pater patriae*."[7]

The three soteriological metaphors that I will explore, slavery, marriage and birth, are each closely connected to one of the three relationships that organize the kyriarchal household: the owner-slave relationship, the

4. Kartzow, *Destabilizing the Margins*, 10.

5. Schüssler Fiorenza, *Rhetoric and Ethic*, ix.

6. Aristotle, *Pol.* 1253b.

7. Schüssler Fiorenza, *The Power of the Word*, 152.

husband-wife relationship and the parent-child relationship. In a kyriarchal society, childbearing, marriage and slavery are closely intertwined. Kyriarchy is the common matrix and the concepts cannot be understood separately. For example, the institution of slavery regulated who was deemed free and thus fit to legitimately marry, and since marriage was for the purpose of procreation, childbirth in a legitimate marriage had completely different implications than childbirth by a slave. Sheila Murnaghan and Sandra R. Joshel have pointed out that to the ancient Greeks and Romans, "gender and slavery are not independent phenomena that operate in parallel ways, but intersecting variables in a process . . . whereby women and slaves are assimilated only to be distinguished, compared but never quite identified."[8] An intersectional approach helps us to keep this close connection in mind, and perhaps to ask new questions of the texts: When a text speaks of marriage, what does it implicitly say about slavery? When a text speaks about slavery, what does it implicitly say about childbearing, and so on?[9]

Metaphors Matter

The study of metaphor goes back to ancient Greece, where Plato and Aristotle, among others, brooded about its meaning and proper use. Aristotle was particularly interested in how metaphors recognized similarity and analogy.[10] Thus, according to Eva Feder Kittay, Aristotle recognized that metaphor is "a conceptual tool of much power." In their seminal book, *Metaphors we live by*, George Lakoff and Mark Johnson argue that metaphors are among our principal vehicles of meaning and that they play a central role in the construction of social and political reality.[11] More than rhetorical flourish or poetic creativity, metaphors are integral to the way we think.[12] Specifically, conceptual metaphors function as powerful cognitive tools that enable readers or listeners to think about abstract and difficult theological concepts in terms of more concrete and familiar ideas and imagery.[13] Different conceptual metaphors are often used to highlight various aspects of a given concept.[14]

8. Joshel and Murnaghan, "Introduction: Differential Equations," 3.

9. See Kartzow, "Asking the Other Question."

10. Kittay, *Metaphor*, 2–3.

11. Lakoff and Johnson, *Metaphors We Live By*, 159.

12. Ibid., 3–4.

13. Lundhaug, *Images of Rebirth*, 27.

14. Ibid., 27.

It is important to note that early Christian texts employ the metaphors of childbearing, slavery and marriage in a discursive context in which literal slavery, marriage and childbearing are integral parts of everyday life. It is not only the metaphorical side of slavery, marriage and childbearing that we encounter in the New Testament; we find numerous references to these social realities. For example, we read about slaves in the gospel narratives, because they were a natural component of the social fabric of first century Palestine. Similarly, we find advice on the treatment of slaves, as well as guidance on how slaves should behave, in the epistles of the New Testament. The letter to Philemon is in its entirety devoted to the issue of what to do with the (runaway?) slave Onesimus. When it comes to marriage, both Jesus, Paul and the other letter writers offer advice as well. Childbearing is a less prominent theme, but we nevertheless find it in the birth narratives of Jesus and in the curious soteriology of 1 Tim 2:15, which states that women "will be saved through childbearing."[15] In early Christian texts, then, we read about both literal and metaphorical childbearing, slavery and marriage. In this essay, I will take particular interest in the mutual interplay between theological metaphor and social reality. What shape does the social context give the theological metaphor, and how did the theologized concept shape kyriarchal family organization?

Salvation as Slavery

In the Roman Empire, slave ownership was an indispensable component of the economy and slaves were thus an inextricable aspect of the social reality. Aristotle called the slave an "animate piece of property" (ὁ δοῦλος κτῆμα, τι ἔμψυχον, *Pol,* 1253b)[16] and, as Jennifer Glancy has noted, slaves were often referred to as bodies (σώματα), indicating the slave's instrumental function as a mere extension of the owner's body.[17] Such bodies were exempt of honor, they were bought and sold and they were vulnerable to abuse, physical punishment and sexual exploitation. It was an important characteristic of the slave in contrast to the free male that he or she could not control the boundaries of his or her own body.[18] A slave was either male or female, but the categories of man (ἀνήρ/*vir*) and woman (γυνή/*mulier*) were—in Greek as well as Latin—connected to honor, and thus conceptually incompatible

15. For a discussion of this passage as part of early Christian childbearing discourse, see Solevåg, *Birthing Salvation.*

16. My translation; Greek retreived from TLG.

17. Glancy, *Slavery in Early Christianity,* 10–11.

18. Ibid., 12, 25.

with the status of a slave. Female slaves were especially vulnerable to sexual violence and abuse and their labor was often reproductive. Even if they could not produce legitimate heirs, female slaves' reproductive capacity was useful, since they could regenerate the slave population and thus contribute to the increased wealth of the owner.[19]

An important source of early Christian slavery imagery is, as already noted, Paul. Although Paul was a free man, he sometimes draws on slavery imagery to describe himself (e.g., 1 Cor 9:19). He designates himself as a slave of Christ, Δοῦλος Χριστοῦ Ἰησοῦ, at the beginning of several of his letters (see, e.g., Rom 1:1; Phil 1:1; Gal 1:10). Glancy has pointed out that Paul uses a number of tropes of slavery and freedom.[20] Some of his metaphors engage overarching narratives of enslavement, sale and manumission, but not all of his uses are commensurate with each other. Sometimes he stresses the freedom of the saved condition, other times he stresses the enslavement of the believer to God. Salvation is not only described as slavery, but also as freedom and release from enslavement, as adoption and thus becoming legitimate children and heirs (e.g., Rom 8:14–17; Galatians 4). In Rom 6:16ff, Paul uses the imagery of slavery to sin. The paradoxical condition of every believer is that s/he is both slave and free: "But now that you have been freed from sin and enslaved to God, the advantage you get is sanctification. The end is eternal life" (Rom 6:22). In Paul's metaphorical usage of slavery discourse, to be saved is to live as free (from sin) and enslaved (to God). In a comment on this passage, Elisabeth Castelli makes two points that are interesting for our purposes. Firstly, she argues that the ways in which Paul's audience first heard and experienced these statements probably depended on their social location. This metaphor of bondage must have held different resonances for slave owners, who had not experienced the bodily suffering and profound social dislocation of slavery, than for the slave members of Christian communities.[21] Secondly, Castelli points out that even though this passage is clearly not ultimately about slavery, "it depends on the reality of slavery to convey its meanings and therefore reinscribes the relation of slavery."[22]

The metaphor of slavery was also used to draw out the meaning of salvation in the gospels. Several parables about the Kingdom of God/Heaven draw on slavery imagery, and particularly on the difference between good

19. For a discussion of the reproductive labor of slaves, see Solevåg, *Birthing Salvation*, 51–54.

20. For this and the following quotations, see Glancy, *Slavery in Early Christianity*, 99.

21. Castelli, "Romans," 294.

22. Ibid.

and bad slaves, in order to extol the reward for believers (salvation and eternal bliss) and the punishment for misbehavior (eternal suffering). In the parable of the Unmerciful Servant in Matt 18:23–35, God is cast as a slave owner. He is portrayed as a kind master who forgives his slave his debt, but also as a harsh one who punishes the slave for not showing the same mercy to his fellow slave as the owner had shown him:

> Then his lord summoned him and said to him, "You wicked slave! I forgave you all that debt because you pleaded with me. Should you not have had mercy on your fellow slave, as I had mercy on you?" And in anger his lord handed him over to be tortured [παρέδωκεν αὐτὸν τοῖς βασανισταῖς] until he would pay his entire debt. So my heavenly Father will also do to every one of you, if you do not forgive your brother or sister from your heart. (Matt 18:32–35)

Glancy has noted that in the parables of Jesus, slaves' bodies are vulnerable to abuse—they are often beaten and even killed.[23] In this parable, the slave is handed over to torturers (βασανισταί). The background for this image may have been wealthy estate owners who would have had detention centers for recalcitrant slaves.[24]

"Blessed are those slaves whom the master finds alert when he comes; truly I tell you, he will fasten his belt and have them sit down to eat, and he will come and serve them," says Jesus in Luke 12:37. The believer who is prepared for the Son of Man's return from heaven is likened to the vigilant servant who patiently awaits his master's arrival. Eternal punishment is also likened to the just torture of misbehaving slaves in this parable (Luk 12:46). These are but two of the many parables that draw on the imagery of slavery to cast God as *kyrios*, as ruler and slave-owner, and to cast believers as his slaves (see, e.g., Matt 13:24–30; Mark 12:1–12; Luke 17:7–10).

Paul and the parables' metaphorical use of the concept of slavery is intricately connected with the social reality of slavery in the Greco-Roman world. The brutality and violence in the parables reflect the harsh reality of slave life in antiquity. This metaphorical usage also draws on negative stereotyping of slave behavior. Slaves are cast in Greco-Roman discourse as morally inferior beings, prone to steal, lie, and behave promiscuously.[25] In the parables discussed above, the underlying assumption is that slaves are naturally disposed to misbehave when the master is absent. Paul's image of slavery under sin links the idea of naturally bad slave morality with the

23. Glancy, *Slavery in Early Christianity*, 103.

24. Βασανιστής, BDAG.

25. Bradley, *Slavery and Society at Rome*, 123.

notion of sin. The exceptional "good slave" is the slave whose innermost self is completely conformed to the master's will.[26]

As noted above, Paul also confronts the issue of slavery as a lived experience within the communities to whom he writes. In 1 Cor 7:20–25, Paul gives words of advice to both free and slave members of the Corinthian community and recommends that each remain "in the condition in which you were called" (7:20). In this passage, metaphorical and literal aspects of slavery are combined. Slave believers are called "the Lord's freedmen" [ἀπελεύθερος κυρίου] and free believers are "Christ's slaves" (7:22). The interpretation of this passage is disputed. Is Paul encouraging slaves to become free or to remain in slavery? The ambiguity particularly hinges on the understanding of the phrase μᾶλλον χρῆσαι in verse 21. Should the one who was called as a slave "better make use of" his/her opportunity to become free or his/her current position as slave?[27] But perhaps some of the difficulty also derives from the profound interlocking of literal and metaphorical slavery in the passage. Paul's phrasing blurs the boundaries between slave and free here, as it does in Gal 3:26–28 when he claims that the distinctions between Jew and gentile, slave and free, male and female do not exist among believers because they are all sons of God (3:26). Slaves are sons, just as women are men and Gentiles are Jews. The question that arises from both passages is whether this is meant to be interpreted as socially disruptive speech or whether Paul is being intentionally vague.[28] I am inclined to think that Paul is negotiating the potentially counter-kyriarchal message in the early Christian kerygma of "we are all one in Christ Jesus." By upgrading the terminology and claiming that "in Christ," slaves are simultaneously free, women are men and pagans are Jews, he gives an egalitarian discursive veneer to his otherwise conservative social stance.

Harsher and more clear-cut advice is given to slaves in the household codes of Colossians, Ephesians and the Pastorals. Instructions to slaves in the Pastorals (1 Tim 6:1–2; Tit 2:9–10) are not tied into metaphorical imagery of slavery.[29] In Col 3: 22–25 and Eph 6:5–8, however, slaves are urged to

---

26. Harrill, *Slaves in the New Testament*, 23–24.

27. See, e.g., Conzelmann et al., *1 Corinthians*, 127; Schüssler Fiorenza, *In Memory of Her*, 219.

28. The scholarly dispute about how to understand the Letter to Philemon may be another indication about Paul's vagueness when it comes to slavery. Is he arguing for the manumission of a runaway slave? Or returning a dispatched slave he has borrowed to his rightful owner? See discussions in, e.g., Harrill, *Slaves in the New Testament*, 6–16; Glancy, *Slavery in Early Christianity*, 91–92.

29. In these letters, however, the "household of God," modeled on the kyriarchal Greco-Roman household, is the primary metaphor for the Christian community.

surrender themselves to their owners as they submit themselves to Christ and thereby create an analogy between the will of the slaveholder and the will of Christ, the ultimate *kyrios*. In Colossians, fear of the Lord (φοβούμενοι τὸν κύριον, 3:22) who punishes the wrongdoer (3:25) is instilled. In Ephesians, slaves are called "slaves of Christ" (δοῦλοι Χριστοῦ, 6:6), mimicking Pauline usage, but also developing it. Here, it is not the free who are slaves of Christ, but the slaves themselves who are doubly so. Both *Haustafeln* invoke the heavenly Lord who watches even when earthly masters are absent (Col 3:22; Eph 6:6).

Instructions to slaves with metaphorical overtones can also be found in 1 Pet 2:18–21. In contrast to Colossians and Ephesians, 1 Peter draws a connection between slaves and Christ, rather than slaveholders and Christ.[30] The author compares slaves' endurance of unjust beatings to Christ's suffering on the cross (1 Pet 2:21). According to Glancy, "The equation between the violated bodies of slaves and the tortured body of Jesus, which underlies the advice of 1 Peter, invites Christians to align themselves not with slaveholders but with slaves."[31] Nevertheless, the message is not socially subversive, but uses Christian ethics to teach slaves to be submissive and accept unjust beatings.

As we have seen from these textual examples, early Christian slavery discourse employs both metaphorical and literal components of slavery with various social and theological outcomes. With the exception of 1 Peter, the metaphorical usage reinscribes slavery and gives the social institution theological weight.

Salvation as Marriage to Christ

The legal and social institution of marriage gave rise to a range of metaphors in early Christianity, and not only soteriologial ones. Here, I will only concern myself with the metaphor that likens salvation to marriage with Christ.

The nuptial imagery of the Song of Songs and Psalm 45 form the background for New Testament references to Christ as bridegroom/husband (e.g., Matt 9:15//Mark 2:19–20//Luke 5:34–35; John 3:29–30; 2 Cor 11:2;

---

30. In the *Martyrdom of Perpetua and Felicitas*, the slave woman Felicitas is likened to Christ in her suffering, and so is Blandina in the *Letter of the Churches of Lyons and Vienne*, another martyrdom story. These images depend on the fact of Jesus' crucifixion—a degrading form of death preserved for slaves and criminals in the Roman empire—but perhaps also draw on the description in Phil 2:7 of Jesus taking the form of a slave as he becomes a human being.

31. Glancy, *Slavery in Early Christianity*, 150.

Rev 19:6–9).[32] The Matthean parables about the royal wedding feast (Matt 22:1–14//Luke 14:16–24)[33] and the ten virgins (Matt 25:1–13)[34] liken the Kingdom of Heaven to a wedding and establish Christ as eschatological bridegroom.[35] The bride, however, is strangely absent from both parables. These parables play on the liminality of the wedding to cast salvation as an eschatological event—the transitional moment of consummation. Salvation is compared to a heavenly wedding feast that comes unannounced and thus calls for vigilance.

In Matt 22:1–14, many of those invited to the wedding refuse to come, causing the king to cast his circle of invitees ever wider. The violent treatment of those who refuse the invitation (22:7) or show up improperly dressed (22:13) stands in stark contrast to the exuberance and joy of the wedding feast (22:4). In Matt 25:1–13, there is a similar focus on the differentiation between those who deserve to enter the feast with the bridegroom (the five wise virgins) and those who—futilely pounding on the door—have only themselves to blame for being excluded (the foolish virgins). As noted, there is no explicit bride or wife in these parables, only servants and virgins. The theme of vigilance and good behavior overlaps with the slave parables discussed above. God is the king and master who has the power to both throw extravagant parties for those whom he chooses to invite and to punish and exclude those who misbehave.

In 2 Cor 11:2–3, Paul draws on the marriage metaphor. Here, the bride, the chaste virgin being promised to Christ, is quite explicitly the believing community, the Corinthians. Paul, the father of the Christ-believers at Corinth, fears for the bride's "virginity." He is afraid that the community has been deceived by other apostles. Paul compares them to Eve, who was deceived by the serpent. However, the imagery from the Hebrew Bible of the fornicating wife, Israel, who cheats on YHWH also seems to resonate here (see, e.g., Hosea 1–3; Jeremiah 3; Ezekiel 16; 23; and the Jezebel cycle in 1

---

32. The Wedding at Cana (John 2:1–11) could perhaps also be included in this list.

33. The Lukan parallel does not identify the party as a wedding feast (γάμος), but as a banquet (δεῖπνον μέγα, Luk 14:16). The host in Luke is not a king, but a householder (οἰκοδεσπότης, Luk 14:21).

34. There are no direct synoptic parallels to this parable, but Luke includes a parable involving male slaves vigilantly waiting for their master to come home from a wedding feast (Luke 12:35–38). For Luke's masculinization of the parable, see Seim, *The Double Message*, 81.

35. Luz, *Matthew 21–28*, 234–35.

King 21 and 2 King 9).[36] The imagery reflects kyriarchal sexual ethics, in which the virginity of the bride is of prime importance.[37]

The most well known use of the marriage metaphor is perhaps Eph 5:22–27, and it should be noted that in this letter it is closely connected to the relations between real husbands and real wives. According to this passage, the mystery of salvation can be compared to the union of husband and wife. Just as a husband cares for his wife, the savior redeems the church (7:23). The husband-wife imagery is combined with body imagery to explicate the relationship: as the head rules the body, thus rules Christ over his church (and saves her) and the husband rules over his wife (and loves her). Earthly marriage mimics a heavenly, mysterious pattern (7:32). The passage is part of the Ephesian household code, in which wives are ordered to submit to their husbands; they must live out this metaphor in their marriages. As Turid Karlsen Seim has pointed out, the patriarchal marriage pattern is here justified christologically.[38] Again, we see the close relation between social reality and metaphor. In this case the metaphor gives added weight to the instructions about female subordination and male headship. It sanctions kyriarchal prerogative and power both within marriage and within the *ekklesia*. Seim has argued that Ephesians struggles to negotiate an early Christian ethos of "mutual submission" (cf. Eph 5:21: "Be subject to one another out of reverence for Christ").[39] The major purpose of the Ephesian household code is, according to Seim, to explore an understanding of domination that does not violate the ideal of mutual submission and that is found "theologically acceptable provided that it is exercised according to the paradigm of Christ's love for his church."[40] The social maneuvering is similar to what I argued above concerning Paul's use of slavery metaphors: the Ephesian household code seems to negotiate a potentially egalitarian ethos, but in an ultimately conservative direction.

However, this is not the only way that the marriage metaphor functioned in early Christianity. It was also used in the discourse of sexual continence. Elisabeth Clark has noted that "the metaphor of 'celibate Bridegroom' enabled Christians simultaneously to valorize the institution of marriage while lauding (in a titillating manner) sexual continence."[41] The imagery

36. For the use of the imagery of fornication for religious infidelity, both in the Hebrew Bible and in early Christian literature, see Streete, *The Strange Woman*.

37. Cf. Joseph, who wants to break off the engagement with Mary for fear that she has become "damaged goods," Matt 1:18–25.

38. Seim, "Interfacing House and Church," 56.

39. Seim, "A Superior Minority?," esp. 174–77.

40. Ibid., 177, 80.

41. Clark, "The Celibate Bridegroom and His Virginal Brides," 1.

of Christ as bridegroom to the chaste believer held together 'marriage' and 'celibacy' ideologies in a creative tension and ensured that even a virgin was *someone's* wife.[42] In two texts from the late second and early third centuries, the *Martyrdom of Perpetua and Felicitas* and the *Acts of Andrew*, we also find this imagery of marriage to Christ. Perpetua is called "matrona Christi," the wife of Christ (18.2), as she enters the arena to fight the wild beasts.[43] In the *Acts of Andrew*, the Christian convert Maximilla is called to renounce sexual relations with her husband.[44] Simultaneously, Christ is called Maximilla's inner husband (ἔσω ἀνδρί, 16). Both these texts devalue marriage—the *Martyrdom of Perpetua and Felicitas* for the sake of martyrdom, the *Acts of Andrew* for the sake of sexual renunciation—but concurrently reconstitute it by relying upon it metaphorically.[45] These are two early examples of what would become a very popular usage of the metaphor, as Christianity turned gradually more ascetic in Late Antiquity.[46]

Salvation as Birth

In early Christian discourse, the imagery of birth was used in several different ways. Seim has shown how birthing imagery was used in apocalyptic discourse in Second Temple Judaism and the New Testament to denote the pain and affliction of the believing community, but also the eschatological transition from adversity to joy.[47] Paul draws on childbearing imagery to express his own birthing and nourishing role in relation to the communities he had founded (e.g., 1 Cor 4:15; Gal 4:19). However, to expound the idea of God's parentage and the inheritance God has in store for his heirs (i.e. salvation), Paul combines childbearing imagery with metaphor of adoption (Rom 8:12–23).[48] In this passage from Romans, salvation is simultaneously adoption and childbearing. It is, however, not God, but "creation" and "we ourselves" who are "groaning in labor pains" [συστενάζει καὶ συνωδίνει] and awaiting "the redemption of our bodies" (8:22–23).

42. Ibid., 2, 9.

43. The text in its original Latin and a translation may be found in Musurillo, *The Acts of the Christian Martyrs*, 106–31.

44. The text in its original Greek and a translation may be found in MacDonald, *The Acts of Andrew and the Acts of Andrew and Matthias in the City of the Cannibals*.

45. Solevåg, *Birthing Salvation*, 251.

46. See, e.g., Brown, *The Body and Society*, 259–60; Clark, *Reading Renunciation*, 360; Clark, "The Celibate Bridegroom and His Virginal Brides."

47. Seim, "Smerte og forløsning," esp. 88–92.

48. Seim, "Motherhood and the Making of Fathers in Antiquity," 107.

In the New Testament, the soteriological use of birthing imagery is most prevalent in the Johannine literature, where it seems to be less connected to a baptismal setting than in the two other New Testament texts that cast believers as reborn children of God (Tit 3:5; 1 Pet 1:3, 23).[49] In the Gospel of John and the First letter of John, birthing imagery is an important component of both Christology and soteriology. The verb γεννάω[50] with God as the agent recurs in both the gospel (e.g., 1:13; 3:3; 8:41) and in 1 John (e.g., 2:29; 3:9; 4:7; 5:1). The use of γεννάω in this way is a unique feature compared to other New Testament writings.[51] In the gospel, the special relationship between God the father, and his son, Jesus Christ, derives from Jesus' status as μονογενής, only-begotten (John 1:14; 18). Jesus is unique as the *son* of God, but believers are still the *children* of God (John 1:12), and they become so through a special birthing process. All who receive the son as the *logos* are "born, not of blood or of the will of the flesh or of the will of man, but of God [ἐκ θεοῦ ἐγεννήθησαν]" (John 1:13). They are born from above (ἄνωθεν, John 3:3; 7), of water and spirit (John 3:5).

Following Adele Reinhartz, Seim has argued that John draws on ancient understandings of conception and genetics, and more specifically the Aristotelian notion of *epigenesis,* to develop his idea of birth from a heavenly father.[52] Aristotle's embryological theory claims that it is only the male that contributes form, and thus *logos* and *pneuma*, in conception.[53] The female contributes only matter: the mother is the fertile soil, the breeding ground for the fully formed, life-giving seed of the father. Aristotle argued against the Hippocratics, who believed that both males and females contributed with seed at conception, a position that Galen also supported.[54] Seim states that John uses this embryological theory to construct an omnipotent, male, birthing God and, moreover, that the mother of Jesus "does not matter because matter is what she provides."[55] Her point is that a birthing God does not necessarily possess feminine or maternal qualities. I agree with Seim—in John, God's birthing rather represents "male completion and omnipotence."[56]

---

49. Lieu, *The Theology of the Johannine Epistles*, 34, 38. See also Seim's discussion of baptismal language in John in Seim, "Baptismal Reflections in the Fourth Gospel."

50. Γεννάω: beget; become the father of; bear (of women), BDAG.

51. Seim, "Motherhood and the Making of Fathers in Antiquity," 107.

52. Seim, "Descent and Divine Paternity in the Gospel of John."

53. Reinhartz, "And the Word Was Begotten," 88–89.

54. Solevåg, *Birthing Salvation*, 72.

55. Seim, "Descent and Divine Paternity in the Gospel of John," 375.

56. Ibid.

Similar to their portrayal in John's gospel, believers in 1 John are born of God the father. They cannot sin, it is claimed, because God's seed (σπέρμα) dwells in them (1 John 3:9). The children of God are here juxtaposed with "the children of the devil" (τὰ τέκνα τοῦ διαβόλου, 1 John 3:10). According to Judith Lieu, this static quality of no possibility to sin, and the starkly developed dualism between the children of God and the children of the devil (1 John 3:7–10), differs from the Gospel of John, where "this birth is an option laid before the individual which demands a response."[57] The generative language of God's seed imparted in the believer seems nevertheless to resonate with the gospel's discourse and may imply that the notion of *epigenesis* also informed the theology of this letter writer.

In 1 Pet 1:3 and 1:23, the believers are reborn from God (ἀναγεννάω). Their birth is of imperishable seed (σπορά ἀφθάρτου). The term used here is not σπέρμα, the common word for human semen that is used in 1 John 3:9, but σπορά, the term used for plant seeds and thus, vegetative generation. The term is perhaps used to create a bridge to the following quote from Isa 40:6–8: "All flesh is like grass." However, the likeness between human/animal and plant regeneration is also quite clear in Aristotles' *epigenesis* theory, in that the woman acts as "fertile soil" for the generative seed/semen. The divine element in 1 Peter, the "imperishable seed," is thus clearly male, as in the Johannine literature. In 1 Peter, the writer continues to draw on the imagery of birth from God, the Father, when he refers to the believers as newborn infants (βρέφος) who should long for spiritual milk so that they can grow into salvation (1 Pet 2:2). The strong emphasis on baptism in 1 Pet 3:18–22, in which baptism is conceived of as salvation through water (1 Pet 3:20–21), makes it likely that rebirth from God in this letter's theology occurs during baptism.[58]

In the Pastorals, childbearing imagery is developed in several interesting way. Childbearing is quite literally woman's way to salvation, according to 1 Tim 2:15.[59] The childbearing discourse in the Pastorals is primarily concerned with real women bearing real children (see, e.g., 1 Tim 2:9–15; 5:14: Tit 2:3–5). In Tit 3:3–7, however, childbearing imagery is employed metaphorically to speak about salvation. Interestingly, it draws together several images from the kyriarchal matrix:

> For we ourselves were once foolish, disobedient, led astray, **slaves** to various passions and pleasures, passing our days in malice and envy, despicable, hating one another. But when the

57. Lieu, *The Theology of the Johannine Epistles*, 37.

58. Moxnes, "Because of 'The Name of Christ,'" 609.

59. As I argue in Solevåg, *Birthing Salvation*, esp. 112–35.

> goodness and loving kindness of God our Savior appeared, he
> saved us, not because of any works of righteousness that we had
> done, but according to his mercy, through the ***water of rebirth***
> [λουτροῦ παλιγγενεσίας] and renewal by the Holy Spirit. This
> Spirit he poured out on us richly through Jesus Christ our Sav-
> ior, so that, having been justified by his grace, we might become
> ***heirs*** according to the hope of eternal life. (Tit 3:3–7)

The imagery in this passage draws on Paul's notion of "enslavement to sin"
and is dependent upon the Greco-Roman assumption about slaves' bad
morality. The letter argues that "the water of rebirth" has changed the believers' situation from slavery into one of heredity, of inclusion into a family as son and heir. The ritual alluded to as "the water of rebirth [λουτροῦ
παλιγγενεσίας]" (Tit 3:5) is presented as a sign of the future possibility of
eternal life. If this is a reference to baptism, as is commonly assumed,[60] it is
an example of the early Christian notion of baptism as a second birth.[61] As
in Rom 8, the imagery of birth is used here, along with images of manumission and adoption. The baptismal birth is a transition to the state of being
legitimate children. In the Greco-Roman world, there was a huge difference
between the childbearing of a free, married woman and that of a slave (a
difference that Paul draws on in Gal 4:1–7). A wife gave birth to a legitimate
heir, a slave woman to a piece of property that could be sold or dispensed
with as the owner pleased. This passage draws on the kind of birthing the
free, married woman does, the one that produces a legitimate child. Slavery is referred to as a previous state in this passage, and there is negative
stereotyping of slave behavior as foolish and disobedient. Yet, slavery was
not a previous state, but a present condition for some of the recipients of
this letter, as we now from the Household Code in Tit 2:9–10. Again, we see
how images of slavery, marriage and childbearing are connected to the kyriarchal matrix. Speaking of baptism as (re-)birth, the author simultaneously
draws on ideas connected to slavery, inheritance and adoption.

This imagery of birth gradually became an important paradigm for
the understanding of baptism in early Christianity.[62] From the middle of
the second century onwards, baptism was understood as generation from
mother church, thus reinstating a female element in the divine birthing
process.[63] The water in the baptismal rite could, then, refer to the amniotic

60. Vegge, "Baptismal Phrases in the Deuteropauline Epistles," 553–57; Fiore, *The
Pastoral Epistles*, 219–20; Dibelius and Conzelmann, *The Pastoral Epistles*, 148–50.

61. Vegge, "Baptismal Phrases in the Deuteropauline Epistles," 556.

62. Miles, *Carnal Knowing*, 35–36; Räisänen, *The Rise of Christian Beliefs*, 188. See
also Ysebaert, *Greek Baptismal Terminology*, 130–54.

63. Jensen, "*Mater Ecclesia* and *Fons Aeterna*," 139.

fluid, the life-giving water of the womb that flows forth at birth. But, as Seim discusses, lifegiving 'water' in antiquity could just as easily be interpreted as the watery fluid that carried the lifegiving seed: semen.[64]

Conclusion

In this essay I have scrutinized three metaphors of salvation—the slavery metaphor, the marriage metaphor and the childbearing metaphor—and their close relationship with the kyriarchal structure of the Greco-Roman family. All these metaphors draw on the same social figure, *the paterfamilias/kyrios*, to represent God as simultaneously slave master, bridegroom/husband and (birthing) father. Salvation in these contexts means holding the inferior position in a relationship to this figure, as a devoted, overachieving slave who receives favors beyond her/his status; as a bride anticipating the consummation of the wedding night or a wife dutifully submitting to patriarchal authority; and finally, as a fetus in the process of being born by the heavenly father, whose parentage has entirely usurped that of the female.

Although the metaphors may seem to be distinct, they are interrelated in many ways. In the parables, virgins wait, just as slaves do, in anticipation for the Lord and bridegroom to return; the good receive their reward, the bad, eternal punishment. In Paul's rhetoric, sonship and slavery are intricately connected; at times, one becomes the other, at other times he tries to keep them apart. Childbearing imagery overlaps with slavery imagery in Rom 8:18–22, as well as in Tit 3:3–7 by way of adoption and inheritance as a metaphorical link. As soteriological metaphors that all derive from the same kyriarchal matrix, we should expect that when one is used, the others, too, can be easily invoked.

There is a certain flexibility in these metaphors. The metaphors work differently depending on the text and can be used for different purposes. Sometimes, social reality and metaphor reinforce each other. For example, in Ephesians both wives and slaves are ordered to submit to the householder and their submission is Christologically justified. In other texts, however, the metaphor is employed when the literal level is devalued, as we saw in the repurposing of childbearing in contexts of asceticism and martyrdom. The marriage metaphor, similarly, has been used to devalue marriage. Finally, in 1 Peter, slavery discourse allows for identification between the divine and the slave rather than the divine and the slaveholder.

Despite this flexibility, the widespread early Christian use of these kyriarchal metaphors had profound effects towards a preservation of kyriarchal

---

64. Seim, "Motherhood and the Making of Fathers in Antiquity," 115–16.

structures in family and church. The choice of kyriarchal imagery more often than not reinscribed hierarchy and gave it added theological weight.[65] Having been preserved and canonized in the New Testament, these metaphors have had an impact throughout the history of Christianity.[66]

The choice of metaphors, then, mattered. It profoundly shaped people's understanding of salvation as well as people's understanding of the proper organization of church and home. These images continue to have effects today. We can find evidence of the metaphorical connection between salvation and slavery, marriage and childbearing in our sad legacy of slavery, in discussions over gay marriage and even, as Marianne Bjelland Kartzow argues in this volume, in current debates about reproductive technology. What do we do with this troublesome legacy from the New Testament? Remembrance, critique and creativity may be three useful key words. I would like to end with a quotation from *The Double Message*. Although Seim is specifically referring to Luke's ambiguous message concerning women, I also find it fitting for the conclusion of this discussion:

> It is precisely in the remembrance of this past story that the key to critical insight and to a new evaluation and a new understanding is to be found. *Remembrance unmasks critically and it also creatively opens up people's eyes.*[67]

65. At certain points in the textual material I have discussed, it seems like the sources are concerned with a divine "reality" with similar structures to the worldly, rather than just metaphor. Seim argues that this is the case concerning the generational language in the gospel of John. Seim, "Motherhood and the Making of Fathers in Antiquity," 107. Similarly, Reinhartz argues that the Johannine understanding of the relationship between God and Jesus was that "Jesus was quite literally begotten by God." In my opinion, it is also valuable to examine the headship/marriage metaphor in Eph 5:21–33 from this perspective.

66. Line Cecilie Engh's article in this volume shows how the marriage metaphor in Eph 5 was used in twelfth-century debates about the authority of the pope.

67. My emphasis. Seim, *The Double Message: Patterns of Gender in Luke–Acts*, 260. With thanks and gratitude to a formidable Doktormutter.

Bibliography

Bradley, Keith R. *Slavery and Society at Rome*. Key Themes in Ancient History. Cambridge: Cambridge University Press, 1994.

Brown, Peter. *The Body and Society. Men, Women and Sexual Renunciation in Early Christianity*. Lectures on the History of Religions. New York: Colombia University Press, 1988.

Clark, Elizabeth A. "The Celibate Bridegroom and His Virginal Brides: Metaphor and the Marriage of Jesus in Early Christian Ascetic Exegesis." *Church History* 77 (2008) 1–25.

———. *Reading Renunciation. Asceticism and Scripture in Early Christianity*. Princeton: Princeton University Press, 1999.

———. "Romans." In *Searching the Scriptures*, edited by Elisabeth Schüssler Fiorenza, 2:272–300. London: SCM, 1994.

Conzelmann, Hans. *1 Corinthians: A Commentary on the First Epistle to the Corinthians*. Translated by James Leitch. Hermeneia. Philadelphia: Fortress, 1975.

Dibelius, Martin, and Hans Conzelmann. *The Pastoral Epistles: A Commentary on the Pastoral Epistles*. Translated by Philip Buttolph and Adela Yarbro. Hermeneia. Philadelphia: Fortress, 1972.

Fiore, Benjamin. *The Pastoral Epistles: First Timothy, Second Timothy, Titus*. Sacra Pagina. Collegeville, MN: Liturgical, 2007.

Glancy, Jennifer A. *Slavery in Early Christianity*. Oxford: Oxford University Press, 2002.

Harrill, James Albert. *Slaves in the New Testament: Literary, Social, and Moral Dimensions*. Minneapolis: Fortress, 2006.

Jensen, Robin. "*Mater Ecclesia* and *Fons Aeterna*: The Church and Her Womb in Ancient Christian Tradition." In *A Feminist Companion to Patristic Literature*, edited by Amy-Jill Levine with Maria Mayo Robbins, 137–55. London: T&T Clark, 2008.

Joshel, Sandra R., and Sheila Murnaghan. "Introduction: Differential Equations." In *Women and Slaves in Greco-Roman Culture: Differential Equations*, edited by Sandra R. Joshel and Sheila Murnaghan, 1–21. London: Routledge, 1998.

Kartzow, Marianne Bjelland. "'Asking the Other Question': An Intersectional Approach to Galatians 3:28 and the Colossian Household Code." *Biblical Interpretation* 18 (2010) 364–89.

———. *Destabilizing the Margins: An Intersectional Approach to Early Christian Memory*. Eugene, OR: Pickwick Publications, 2012.

Kittay, Eva Feder. *Metaphor. Its Cognitive Force and Linguistic Structure*. Oxford: Clarendon, 1987.

Lakoff, George, and Mark Johnson. *Metaphors We Live By*. Chicago: University of Chicago Press, 1980.

Lieu, Judith. *The Theology of the Johannine Epistles*. New Testament Theology. Cambridge: Cambridge University Press, 1991.

Lundhaug, Hugo. *Images of Rebirth: Cognitive Poetics and Transformational Soteriology in the Gospel of Philip and the Exegesis on the Soul*. Nag Hammadi and Manichaean Studies 73. Leiden: Brill, 2010.

Luz, Ulrich. *Matthew 21–28: A Commentary*. Translated by James E. Crouch. Hermeneia. Minneapolis: Fortress, 2005.

MacDonald, Dennis R. *The Acts of Andrew and the Acts of Andrew and Matthias in the City of the Cannibals*. Texts and Translations 33. Atlanta: Scholars, 1990.

"The Martyrdom of Perpetua and Felicitas." In *The Acts of the Christian Martyrs*, edited by Herbert Musurillo, 106–31. Oxford: Clarendon, 1972.

Miles, Margaret R. *Carnal Knowing: Female Nakedness and Religious Meaning in the Christian West*. Boston: Beacon, 1989.

Moxnes, Halvor. "Because of 'The Name of Christ': Baptism and the Location of Identity in 1 Peter." In *Ablution, Initiation, and Baptism: Late Antiquity, Early Judaism, and Early Christianity*, edited by David Hellholm et al., 605–28. BZNW 176. Berlin: de Gruyter, 2011.

Reinhartz, Adele. "'And the Word Was Begotten': Divine *epigenesis* in the Gospel of John." *Semeia* 85 (1999) 83–103.

Räisänen, Heikki. *The Rise of Christian Beliefs: The Thought World of Early Christians*. Minneapolis: Fortress, 2010.

Schüssler Fiorenza, Elisabeth. *In Memory of Her: A Feminist Theological Reconstruction of Christian Origins*. 2nd ed. New York: SCM, 1994.

———. "Introduction: Exploring the Intersections of Race, Gender, Status, and Ethnicity in Early Christian Studies." In *Prejudice and Christian Beginnings: Investigating Race, Gender, and Ethnicity in Early Christian Studies*, edited by Elisabeth Schüssler Fiorenza and Laura Salah Nasrallah, 1–23. Minneapolis: Fortress, 2009.

———. *The Power of the Word: Scripture and the Rhetoric of Empire*. Minneapolis: Fortress, 2007.

———. *Rhetoric and Ethic: The Politics of Biblical Studies*. Minneapolis: Fortress, 1999.

Seim, Turid Karlsen. "Baptismal Reflections in the Fourth Gospel." In *Ablution, Initiation and Baptism: Late Antiquity, Early Judaism, and Early Christianity*, edited by David Hellholm et al., 717–34. BZNW 176/1. Berlin: de Gruyter, 2011.

———. "Descent and Divine Paternity in the Gospel of John: Does the Mother Matter?" *NTS* 51 (2005) 361–75.

———. *The Double Message: Patterns of Gender in Luke–Acts*. Translated by Brian McNeil. Edinburgh: T&T Clark, 1994.

———. "Interfacing House and Church: Converting Household Codes to Church Order." In *Text, Image, and Christians in the Graeco-Roman World: A Festschrift in Honor of David Lee Balch*, edited by Aliou Cissé Niang and Carolyn Osiek. Princeton Theological Monograph Series 176. Eugene, OR: Pickwick, 2011.

———. "Motherhood and the Making of Fathers in Antiquity: Contextualizing Genetics in the Gospel of John." In *Women and Gender in Ancient Religions: Interdisciplinary Approaches*, edited by Stephen P. Ahearne-Kroll, Paul A. Holloway, and James A. Kelhoffer. WUNT 263. Tübingen: Mohr Siebeck, 2010.

———. "Smerte og forløsning: Nytestamentlige fødselsbilder i spenningen mellom virkelighet og ritualisert utopi." *Norsk teologisk tidsskrift* 91 (1990) 85–99.

———. "A Superior Minority? The Problem of Men's Headship in Ephesians 5." In *Mighty Minorities? Minorities in Early Christianity—Positions and Strategies*, edited by David Hellholm, Halvor Moxnes, and Turid Karlsen Seim, 167–81. Oslo: Scandinavian University Press, 1995.

Solevåg, Anna Rebecca. *Birthing Salvation: Gender and Class in Early Christian Childbearing Discourse*. Biblical Interpretation Series 121. Leiden: Brill, 2013.

Slusser, Michael. "Salvation." In *Encyclopedia of Early Christianity*. 2nd ed. New York: Garland, 1999.

Streete, Gail Corrington. *The Strange Woman: Power and Sex in the Bible*. Louisville: Westminster John Knox, 1997.

Vegge, Tor. "Baptismal Phrases in the Deuteropauline Epistles." In *Ablution, Initiation, and Baptism: Late Antiquity, Early Judaism, and Early Christianity*, edited by David Hellholm et al., 505–64. BZNW 176. Berlin: de Gruyter, 2011.

Ysebaert, J. *Greek Baptismal Terminology: Its Origins and Early Development*. Graecitas Christianorum primaeva 1. Nijmegen: Dekker & van de Vegt, 1962.

Embodying the Female Body Politic

Pro-Papal Reception of Ephesians 5 in the Later Middle Ages

Line Cecilie Engh

IN A SERIES OF articles, Turid Karlsen Seim challenged scholars to recognize how the unification discourse in the household code of Eph 5:22–32 envisions a reconciliation of the dualistic pairs male-head and female-body in terms of the former's appropriation of the latter.[1] As unification discourse intersects with gender discourse, the social ordering of male-husband and female-wife is figured as collapse of twoness in the language of marital/sexual unification while simultaneously upholding gender division and gender hierarchy in the language of patriarchal household ideology:

> [22] Let women be subject to your husbands, as to the Lord.
> [23] Because the husband is the head of the wife, as Christ is the head of the church, the body of which he is the Savior . . . [28] So men should love their wives as their own bodies. He who loves his wife loves himself. [29] For no man ever hated his own flesh, but he nourishes and cherishes it, just as Christ does for the church: [30] because we are members of his body, of his flesh, and of his bones. [31] For this reason a man shall leave his father and mother and be joined to his wife, and they shall be two in

---

1. Seim, "Interfacing House and Church," 53–69; Seim, "Efeserne 5.21–33—tolkning og resepsjon," 28–48; Seim, "The Problem of Men's Headship in Ephesians 5," 167–81.

one flesh. [32] This is a great mystery, but I speak of Christ and the church.[2]

With the quotation from Gen 2:24 the analogies of wife/body-church and husband/head-Christ change direction, emphasizing typological meaning and bending the reception of Eph 5:22–32 towards ecclesiology. As the organic image of the church as a multifunctional body is combined with the hierarchical idea of headship, Seim argues, ecclesiology buys into household ideology. Yet the emphasis of Ephesians 5, she points out, lies not only on supporting (male) headship. More subtly, the passage provides the husband, as the wife's head, the possibility of appropriating her body: "The symbiotic understanding of a union in flesh," Seim writes, "makes it possible for the husband/head also to remain embodied."[3]

The present article uses this central insight to analyse medieval pro-papal reception of Ephesians 5, with its language and imagery of "body" (*corpus*) and "head" (*caput*) in the thick of marriage symbolism and marriage ideology. I argue that the subtleties and ambiguities of Ephesians 5, pointed out by Karlsen Seim, are imported and instated into a context of papal theory and rhetoric. From the position of husband-head, the pope appropriates for himself a body—the female body politic—which ultimately allows him to stand as an embodiment of both Rome and *ecclesia-imperium* in papal power theories of the later Middle Ages.

The article emphasizes the formation of this rhetoric in twelfth-century writing, especially in Bernard of Clairvaux, and its further development in the writing of thologians, canonists, and popes of the thirteenth and the early fourteenth century. This period sees on the one hand the papacy strengthening its position as a result of the Gregorian church reforms, before a gradual decline sets in from the late thirteenth century onwards, and on the other hand the papacy's estrangement from Rome with the popes and the Roman curia taking up residence, more or less temporarily, outside Rome (e.g., Viterbo, Lyons, and Avignon).[4] Ironically, the papacy's most immediate obstacles to consolidating papal power, both ecclesiastical and temporal, was Rome itself. The more the popes became head of the universal church, the less support they received in Rome and the less ability they

---

2. Biblical quotes follow the Douay-Rheims Bible, with modifications: http://www.drbo.org/ (accessed May 15, 2015).

3. Seim, "Interfacing House and Church," 59.

4. For an overview of the papacy in the Gregorian period and the subsequent development eventually leading to the transferal to Avignon, see Schimmelpfenning, *The Papacy*; Morris, *The Papal Monarchy*; Robinson, *The Papacy, 1073–1198*.

had to govern the city.[5] Disentangling themselves from previous allies in the Roman aristocracy like the Pierleoni and the Frangipani families, on whom earlier popes had relied on to govern, the popes of the post-Gregorian period depended on the internationally staffed curia and cardinalate, making it, theoretically at least, an international rather than just a local institution but at the same time estranging the popes from their own bishopric.

A Body without a Head

In the winter of 1145 the newly elected Pope Eugene III was driven into exile. Papal control over Rome was at the verge of collapse following urban uprisings in 1143 and 1144, when the Commune of Rome had challenged papal jurisdiction and, proclaiming the revival of the Roman senate, established itself in the Conti fortress on the ancient ruins on the Capitoline Hill.[6] Anti-papalism and revival of Antiquity joined hands in the communal movement, focalized on Rome as seat of secular authority, "the seat of the empire, the fountain of liberty, the mistress of the world" (*sedes imperii, fons libertatis, mundi domina*),[7] over against papal theocracy.[8] Faced with rebellious Romans, Pope Eugene III quietly slipped away, relocating himself and the curia in the relative calm at Viterbo north of Rome. Enraged, Pope Eugene's mentor and former abbot, the formidable Bernard of Clairvaux wrote a letter addressed to "the nobles, the leading citizens, and all the people of Rome."[9] As with most of Bernard's writing, the letter is rhetorically polished and vividly imagistic. Embedded in the figurative language are, I suggest, some highly significant implications regarding Rome, church, and papal authority, intertextually drawing on concepts of head and body from Ephesians 5.

5. Schimmelpfenning, *The Papacy*, 148–49, with reference to the *Annales Romani*, suggests that high medieval popes seldom could govern the city in its entirety, never mind the Papal States.

6. On the Roman commune, see Benson, "Political Renovatio," 339–59.

7. John of Sailsbury, *Historia pontificalis* 31, cited in Benson, "Political Renovatio," 345.

8. Papal theocracy, like the Commune, based its legitimacy on models of Roman Antiquity; on *imitatio imperii* in the Roman Middle Ages, see Dupré Theseider, *L'idea imperiale di Roma nella tradizione del Medioevo*. On papal liturgy as *imitatio imperii*, see Twyman, *Papal Ceremonial*.

9. Bernard of Clairvaux, *Ep.* 243 (PL 182:437D): "Nobilibus, et optimatibus, atque universo populo Romano." I substantially modify the translations in James. All other translations are mine, unless otherwise stated.

Bernard protests at the Romans' treatment of the pope, lamenting the pain inflicted on the church of Rome by an image of a body politic suffering a headache. Underpinning the conceptual framework of the image is the body-head dyad of Ephesians 5: "For the pain is in the head [*in capite*], and so [affects] even the tiniest and the remotest part of the body [*corporis*]."[10] With exquisite monastic humility he represents himself as "tiny" and "remote," adding: "Even me. This great pain affects even me, although I am the tiniest of all; because what affects the head, cannot but affect the whole body, whose member I am."[11] Drawing on 1 Cor 12:12, and thus blending together images of body-head-body members,[12] Bernard subtly promotes himself, as body part, to the position of a "tongue" that cries out its warning: "When the head suffers [*dolente capite*], does not the tongue cry out [*clamat lingua*] on behalf of all the members that the head is in pain, and do they not all confess by means of the tongue that the head is theirs and the pain too?"[13] The rhetorical pitch of the passage is enhanced by more biblical allusions as Bernard continues on the head-body theme, blending himself into the figure of the wailing body-church: "Suffer me, therefore, I beseech you, suffer me to weep a little for my pain [Job 10:20]; and not only I, but the whole Church. Is not her voice heard over the whole world: My head pains me, my head pains me [2 Kings 4:19]!"[14] With the image of the church universal lamenting the "pain in my head" (*caput meo doleo*), Bernard squarely places the Roman church in the position as "head" of the church.

Escalating his tone, Bernard now launches his attack addressing the Romans directly:

> Why do you offend the King of the earth and the Lord of the heavens with such intolerable and irrational ravings? With what nerve do you sacrilegiously attack the sacred and apostolic see, which is singularly exalted by divine and royal privileges, trying

10. Bernard of Clairvaux, *Ep.* 243.2 (PL 182:438C): "Dolor nempe in capite est, ac per hoc minime alienus ne a minimis quidem vel extremis quibusque corporis partibus."

11. Ibid.: "Nec a me ergo. Pervenit profecto usque ad me, quamvis omnium minimum, dolor maximus iste, quia maximus est; et quia cum sit capitis, non potest non esse et corporis, cujus membrum sum ego."

12. 1 Cor 12:12: "Sicut enim corpus unum est, et membra habet multa, omnia autem membra corporis cum sint multa, unum tamen corpus sunt."

13. Bernard of Clairvaux, *Ep.* 243.2 (PL 182:438CD): "Numquid non dolente capite clamat lingua pro omnibus corporis membris, in capite se dolere, et omnia per ipsam suum caput, suumque capitis fatentur incommodum?"

14. Bernard of Clairvaux, *Ep.* 243.2 (PL 182:438D): "Dimittite proinde, quaeso, dimittite, ut plangam paululum apud vos dolorem meum; nec meum tantum, sed et totius Ecclesiae. Nonne ipsius vox est hodie per universum mundum: Caput meum doleo, caput meum doleo?"

to destroy its honour which you instead should be defending singlehandedly and indiscriminately? O foolish Romans! Devoid of judgment and ignorant of right and wrong, you dare to disgrace your head and the head of all [*caput vestrum atque omnium*] for whom you ought rather, if necessary, sacrifice your own necks. Your fathers subjected the world to the City; you hasten to make the City ridiculous to the world. Behold! You have driven Peter's heir from Peter's see and from the city; at your hands cardinals and bishops, ministers of the Lord, have been despoiled of all their goods and houses. O stupid and injudicious people! O wayward dove without a heart! Was he not your head, were he not your eyes? What is Rome now but a body without a head [*capite truncum corpus*]?[15]

A significant re-identification of headship has taken place. It is no longer the Roman church, but the pope who holds the position as head—and not just of the Romans but of "everyone" (*caput vestrum atque omnium*). As he hurls insults at them, Bernard accuses the Romans of offending both celestial and terrestrial order, both "divine and royal privileges" (*divinis regalibusque privilegiis*). He seems to insinuate that the challenge to papal authority implies not one but two wrongs. Is Bernard here asserting papal supremacy in both spiritual and temporal affairs?

Exactly what we may infer from Bernard's allusion to the pope's dual authority—in the reference to "divine and royal privileges"—does not seem clear. Some have seen Bernard as a precursor in papal claims to universal authority—in the sense of full jurisdiction in secular and ecclesiastical matters.[16] But we should not unhesitatingly assume that Bernard is forwarding

15. Bernard of Clairvaux, *Ep.* 243.3 (PL 182:439AB): "Cur Regem terrae, cur Dominum coeli, furore tam intolerabili, quam irrationabili in vos pariter provocatis, dum sacram et apostolicam sedem, divinis regalibusque privilegiis singulariter sublimatam, ausu sacrilego incessere, suoque minuere honore contenditis, quam vel soli contra omnes, si oportuisset, defendere debuistis? Sic fatui Romani; non judicantes, neque quod honestum est discernentes, caput vestrum atque omnium, quod in vobis est, deturpatis, pro quo magis nec vestris ipsis cervicibus parcendum a vobis foret, si necessitas exegisset? Patres vestri Urbi orbem subjugaverunt: vos Urbem properatis orbi facere fabulam. En Petri haeres Petri sede et urbe a vobis expulsus est: en rebus et domibus suis, vestris manibus spoliati sunt cardinales atque episcopi ministri Domini. O popule stulte et insipiens, o columba seducta non habens cor! Nonne ille caput, et illi oculi tui erant? Quid ergo nunc Roma, nisi sine capite truncum corpus."

16. Most assertive in this respect are Ullmann, *The Growth of Papal Government*, 429; and Wilks, *Sovereignty*, 164, 169, and 412. For an opposite position, see Gray, "The Problem of Papal Power," 10–11; and Kennan, "The 'De Consideratione' of St. Bernard," 73–115. Bernard's position on the papacy has been confusingly construed by scholars variously as, in Kennan's phrasing, ibid., 73, "gregorian, anti-gregorian, hierarchical, egalitarian, proto-protestant, or any one of a variety of other hues." The question of his

universal claims for the papacy in the present letter. His references to "divine and royal privileges" are certainly contextual and they regard quite specifically the government of Rome. Temporal authority on a reduced scale had of course been long assumed in papal circles, at least since the time of the (genuine) Donation of Pepin and the (forged) Donation of Constantine in the eighth century, but regarded specifically the Papal States and especially the coronation of the emperor by the hand of the pope.[17] The framework for the current denunciation, furthermore, is firmly established in the letter's prior passage, identifying the body politic in question as the church. Bernard is in all probability asserting nothing more and nothing less than the pope's power in the church, his episcopal primacy, exegetically anchored in the Petrine commission (especially in readings of Matthew 16) and maintained by the Roman church since Pope Leo I (440–61).[18]

Instead of entering into the tormented question of what Bernard's papal theory really was, I wish to draw attention to the entailments and inferences in his image of the pope as "head"—"the head of the Romans and the head of all"—and of Rome without the pope as "a body without a head." First, the figure of the pope as *caput*: In Ephesians the analogy between head/husband-Christ is clear: "the husband is the head of the wife, as Christ is the head of the church." If understood in a context of wider, episcopal claims to church authority by virtue of bishops as representatives of Christ, the assertion of pope as *caput* is not really very startling. In this sense, the bishop of Rome was the "head" of the church of Rome just as the bishop of, say, Milan was the head of the church of Milan. But Bernard does make distinctions regarding the episcopal see of Rome: it is "singularly exalted" and, most importantly, it is not only "your head" (i.e. head of the Romans) but "the head of all." In other words, Bernard positions the pope in Christ's place as head of the universal church. Secondly, assumptions of headship are directly linked to Rome. Rome's unique position is immediately emphasized in terms of subjection and conquest, bearing allusions to Rome's former military prowess: "Your fathers subjected the world to the City." Of course, notions of Christian

---

own views aside, it is beyond doubt that reception of his texts, especially *Csi*—his tract on the papal office written to Eugene in the years from 1145 to 1153—shaped later visions of papal monarchy.

17. On this political development, see Schimmelpfennig, *The Papacy*, 79–80, 83–87; for a critical assessment of the Donation of Constantine, giving a later dating, see Fried, *"Donation of Constantine" and "Constitutum Constantini."*

18. Recent scholarship has questioned Ullmann's classical thesis in *Growth of Papal Government* that standard exegesis of Matt 16:18–19; Luke 22:32; and John 21:15–17 maintained papal primacy before the twelfth century, see Froehlich, "Saint Peter, Papal Primacy, and the Exegetical Tradition," 3–43; see also Sessa, *The Formation of Papal Authority.*

Rome superseding and replacing ancient Rome were part of a commonplace rhetoric, employed in both ecclesiastical and imperial circles in the twelfth century.[19] But in Bernard's letter a quite particular connection, a metaphorical cross mapping, appears between the ancient epithet *caput mundi* and the papal interpretation of *caput ecclesiae*, so that the triad Rome-pope-head tightens and juxtaposes with the position of Christ.

When and how does the pope become "head"? When are popes assigned the role of Christ-husband in relation to the subordinate church-wife? The idea of the church as "body of Christ" was frequently expounded on in early medieval ecclesiology, but there were no stable understandings of where the effective headship of this body resided. Pre-Gregorian texts that discussed the matter, especially the fifth-century Gelasian letter and the ninth-century Pseudo-Isidorian collection of (partially forged) papal decretals, were open to different strands of interpretation, which modern scholarship has divided into "episcopal" and "papal" positions: the former emphasizing episcopal co-equality, the latter papal *principatus* in ecclesiastical government.[20] It has been noted by scholars that the Gregorian program restated (or perhaps reinvented) papal claims to *principatus* and *primatus* with unprecedented vigour.[21] Yet while the Gregorians did occasionally emphasize Rome's primacy in terms of headship, they did not adopt a language of head-body to make systematic assertions about the pope or papal power. In fact, no mention of head and body is made in the *Dictatus papae*, that great manifest of papal authority, with temporal as well as spiritual claims. In Pseudo-Isidore, which was particularly influential with the Gregorians, there are allusions to *ecclesia romana* as *caput*, but the texts of the collection stop short of declaring the pope *caput*.[22] Generally, the Pseudo-Isidorian decretals connect the theme of *ecclesia romana caput ecclesiarum* with notions

19. For example, the poem *Par tibi, Roma, nihil*, see Krautheimer, *Roma: Profilo di una città*, 251–52. For imperial examples, see Houben, "La componente romana nell' istituzione imperiale," 32.

20. See Gray, "The Problem of Papal Power," 4. Both the "papal" and the "episcopal" positions in the Carolingian period may be seen as counter-positions to defend bishops against their metropolitans and secular overlords. See Robinson, "Reform and the Church, 1073–1122," 316.

21. Purging earlier canonical collections of their "episcopal bias"; see Gray, "The Problem of Papal Power," 4.

22. See decretal attr. to Calixtus I in *Collectio Decretalium* (PL 130:130CD): "Non decet enim a capite membra dissidere, sed juxta sacrae Scripturae testimonium omnia membra caput sequantur. Nulli vero dubium est, quod apostolica Ecclesia mater sit omnium Ecclesiarum a cujus vos regulis nullatenus convenit deviare. Et sicut Filius venit facere voluntatem Patris, sic et vos voluntatem vestrae impleatis matris, quae est Ecclesia, cujus caput, ut praedictum est, Romana existit Ecclesia."

of Peter's primacy,[23] a theme which echoes prior exegesis.[24] In keeping with this line, some eleventh-century Gregorians exalted the Roman church in the image of head and body. So Peter Damian (d. 1072), rebuking the church of Milan for its resistance to church reform, declared that the Roman church is "head of the whole Christian religion" (*caput totius christianae religionis*), while Pope Gregory VII spoke of other churches as *membra* of Rome.[25]

Bernard's exegetical shift from Rome (or *ecclesia romana*) as "head" to pope as "head" is slight but significant, and seems to be the first or among the first of its kind.[26] Another early example of the image of pope as *caput* in the exegetical context of Ephesians 5 may be found in Bernard's contemporary Bishop Anselm of Havelberg (d. 1158), who fused it with the theme of pope not only as *vice Petri* but even *vice Christi*:

> The Apostle says: the head of the Church is Christ and the head of Christ is God [Eph 5:23; 1 Cor 11:3]. But Christ the head of the Church, ascending to heaven, commissioned Peter the prince of the Apostles to be his representative [*vice*] on earth. Peter, following Christ's footsteps into martyrdom, ordered Clement to be his vicar [*vicarium*], and thus Roman pontiffs have followed, in succeeding order, as representatives of Christ [*vice Christi*]; they are head of the Church on earth [*caput Ecclesiae in terris*] as Christ is head of the Church in heaven.[27]

23. See decretal attr. to Pius I (PL 130:111D): "Hanc sanctam sedem apostolicam omnium Ecclesiarum caput esse praecepit, ipso dicente principi apostolorum Petro: Tu es Petrus . . . [etc.]"; and decretal attr. to Marcellus (PL 130: 218CD): "Ab illo enim primo instructi estis, ideo non oportet vos proprium derelinquere Patrem, et alteros sequi, ipse enim caput est totius Ecclesiae, cui ait Dominus: Tu es Petrus [etc.]"

24. See Leo I, *Sermo LXXXII: In natali apostolorum Petri et Pauli* (PL 54:422–23): "Isti [i.e. Peter and Paul] sunt qui te ad hanc gloriam provexerunt, ut gens sancta, populus electus, civitas sacerdotalis et regia, per sacram beati Petri sedem caput orbis effecta." See also Gregory I, *Expositio in Psalmos Poenitentiales*; PL 79: 611B: "ut caput omnium Ecclesiarum Romanam Ecclesiam sibi vindicet, et in domina gentium terrenae jus potestatis usurpet. Quod omnino ille fieri prohibuit, qui hanc beato Petro apostolo specialiter commisit, dicens: *Tibi dabo Ecclesiam meam* [Matth. XVI, 18]."

25. Peter Damian, *Opusculum quintum* (PL 145:89BC): "privilegium Romanae Ecclesiae non incongrue comparaverim, quia dum haec una per cathedram beati Petri totius Christianae religionis caput effecta, cunctis in orbe terrarum principetur Ecclesiis"; Gregory VII, *Registrum: lib, 4, ep.*16 (PL 148:470A): "membris ejus, videlicet caeteris Ecclesiis."

26. See Robinson, "Church and Papacy," 253–55, esp. 255.

27. Anselm of Havelberg, *Episcopi dialogi* 3.12 (PL 188:1225AB): "Apostolus dicit: *Caput Ecclesiae Christus, caput autem Christi Deus* [Ephes. V, 23; I Cor. XI, 3]. Sed caput Ecclesiae Christus, ascendens in altum, vicem suam in terris Petro apostolorum principi commisit. Petrus ad martyrium vestigia Christi sequens, Clementem sibi vicarium subrogavit, et sic Romani pontifices per ordinem consequenter vice Christi substituti,

Thus the image of *papa-caput* that emerged distinctly in the mid-twelfth century parallels the development of the theme of the pope as *vicarius Christi*, a theme which will be pursued further below.

A Widow without a Bridegroom

There are more entailments inherent in the image of pope as *caput* to surface in the letter of Bernard. The dyads from Ephesians 5, head/husband-Christ and body/wife-church, exegetically embraced yet another dual pair, namely, bride and bridegroom. The primary exegetical reference for the latter pair is the Song of Songs, a text which, in the tradition from Origen, Ambrose of Milan, Jerome, and Gregory the Great, was read spiritually, i.e. in a non-literal sense, as expressing the relationship between Christ and the church or, secondarily, Christ and the saintly soul.[28] Because of the longstanding interpretation which read the bride of the Song of Songs as the church, readings of Ephesians 5 absorbed bridal imagery from the Song of Songs. This was so entrenched in medieval exegesis that by the twelfth century the two couples, *caput et corpus* and *sponsa et sponsus*, had merged together, as is testified the in glosses to Eph 5:32 in *Glossa ordinaria*:

> For this is a great mystery [*sacramentum*], referring to the copulation and the mixing of bodies between husband and wife [*viro . . . et uxore*] according to their natural sex, adding: But I speak of Christ, etc., according to which the words, they are no longer two but one flesh, are applied to Christ and Church, and likewise they are called bridegroom and bride and thus also head and body [*et quomodo sponsus et sponsa dicuntur, sic caput et corpus*]. Whether they are called head and body or bridegroom and bride it means they are one [*Sive ergo caput et corpus, sive sponsus et sponsa, unum intelligite*]. For the two shall be one person, just like head and body and just like bride and bridegroom [*ex capite et corpore, ex sponso et sponsa*].[29]

---

caput Ecclesiae sunt in terris, cujus Ecclesiae caput Christus est in coelis."

28. On medieval exegesis of the Song of Songs with emphasis on hermeneutical levels, see Matter, *The Voice of My Beloved*.

29. *Glossa Ordinaria*, *Epistola ad Ephesios V* (PL 114:599AB), where the text is erroneously ascribed to Walafrid Strabo: "*Sacramentum hoc magnum. Ne aliquis putaret in viro esse et uxore, secundum utriusque naturalis sexus copulationem, corporalemque mixtionem, addit: Ego dico in Christo, etc., secundum hoc ergo quod in Christo et Ecclesia, accipitur quod dictum est: Non jam duo, sed una caro sunt, et quomodo sponsus et sponsa dicuntur, sic caput et corpus. Sive ergo dicatur caput et corpus, sive sponsus et sponsa, unum intelligite. Fit enim ex duobus quasi una quaedam persona, scilicet ex capite et corpore, ex sponso et sponsa.*"

We should keep in mind, however, that the "wife" (*uxor*) and "husband" (*vir*) of Ephesians 5 are not conceptually identical to the "bride" (*sponsa*) and "bridegroom" (*sponsus*) of the Song of Songs, even if their references were the same: Christ and church. Indeed, the Latin term *sponsa-sponsus*, deceptively related to the English word *spouse* and the French *épouse-époux*, did not indicate marriage but rather betrothal (*sponsalia*), i.e. a fiancé(e).[30] Thereby emphasis of bridal imagery was laid on liminality and tensions of interplay between anticipation and realization, desire and fulfilment, presence and absence, "now" but "not yet."[31] Not only are the references and metaphorical entailments inherent in the Song of Songs' *sponsa-sponsus* different from the Ephesians' *vir-uxor*, the discursive framework is different too. The Song of Songs was fixed solidly, if somewhat paradoxically, within asceticism and monasticism with its prevalent themes of celibacy, virginity, mysticism, and eschatology, whereas the letter to the Ephesians was emerging in the twelfth century as principal prooftext for the new doctrine of marriage as a sacrament.[32] Nevertheless, the two discourses not only met but intersected in the Gregorian reform period and its aftermath since both priestly celibacy and lay marriage were seen to reflect the union of Christ and church.[33]

In Bernard's letter to the Romans, the bride appears in the guise of a related female figure, namely the widow:

> Open your eyes, you miserable people, and see the desolation that is even now upon you. How the finest colour has changed in brief time [Lam 4:1]: the mistress of the world and the prince of the provinces has become a widow [*vidua domina gentium, princeps provinciarum*] [Lam 1:1].[34]

At first glance, the bridal subtext seems muffled, if present at all. The clue lies in Lamentations, cited by Bernard, where Jerusalem is personified as a widow. The decisive intertextual affirmation, linking together Rome,

30. Reynolds, *Marriage in the Western Church*, 315.

31. See Turner, *Eros and Allegory*, 85.

32. See, e.g., Reynolds, "Marrying and Its Documentation in Pre-Modern Europe: Consent, Celebration, and Property," 9; on Augustine's treatment, picked up by twelfth-century exegetes, see Reynolds, *Marriage in the Western Church*, 310.

33. On the significance of marriage symbolism on the development of marriage theology in the twelfth and thirteenth century, see d'Avray, *Medieval Marriage*; on bridal imagery and celibacy, see Engh, *Performing the Bride*.

34. Bernard of Clairvaux, *Ep.* 243.3 (PL 182:439BC): "Aperi, gens misera, aperi oculos tuos, et vide desolationem tuam jamjamque imminentem. Quomodo in brevi mutatus est color optimus [Thren. IV. 1], facta est quasi vidua domina gentium, princeps provinciarum [Thren. I. 1]?"

widowed Jerusalem, and bridal imagery, arrives in the following passage where Bernard, still scolding the Romans, queries: "If you persist, are you not rushing towards your downfall? Come back, come back, O Sunamite, come back to your senses [Song 6:11]."[35] The Sunamite (or Sulamite) is no other than the bride of the Song of Songs, who becomes firmly identified as Rome: "widow" (*vidua*) now, once "mistress of the world" (*domina gentium*). The identification is reinforced grammatically. As Bernard speaks to the Romans, he no longer addresses them in the plural (*vos*) but in the singular (*tu*), creating a firmer identification with the figure of the widow who is also the bride.

In complete consistency with Ephesians 5, the body-wife (Rome), bereaved of her head-husband (pope), is a widow. Like personified Jerusalem weeping at the destruction of the Temple (Lamentations), personified Rome mourns her affliction and loss of prestige at the loss of the pope, represented as widowhood. In Bernard's letter the metaphorical framework establishes not only the typological connection between the violation of the Temple of Jerusalem and the violation of the church of Rome in the person of the pope, it even offers added meaning in the emphasis on the grieving female (wife/body-Rome) in relation to the departed male (husband/head-pope). Images of Rome's widowhood convey extreme need or lack by the social connotations of widowhood while simultaneously evoking the potentially upsetting and destructive forces of latent anger and despair.[36] Widowed Rome takes forceful advantage of the tensions between scenarios of prior and (perhaps prospective) splendour and present degradation, channelling potential for political action towards the focal point of the image: the lack or loss of the male protagonist, namely the pope, and the reasons for his absence.

The rich potential of the image of Rome-as-widow was to capture fourteenth-century imaginations, when it became linked to the papacy's absence from Rome during the Avignon period. In the pontificate of Benedict XII (1334–42), Petrarch composed a metric epistle on the "new Babylonian captivity" in which Rome sits personified as weeping matron amid the ruins of her honour, imploring the return of her negligent spouse, the pope.[37] Shortly after, in Rome, the ill-starred revolutionary leader Cola di Rienzo commissioned a series of mural depictions of political allegories at

35. Bernard of Clairvaux, *Ep.* 243.4 (PL 182:439C): "Numquid non prope interitum es, si persistis? Revertere, revertere, Sunamitis, revertere ad cor tuum."

36. See Baskins, "Trecento Rome," 203–6.

37. On Petrarch's poem, see O'Rourke Boyle, *Petrarch's Genius*, 77, 95. The imagery had been introduced into Italian poetry in the by Jacopone da Todi who portrayed the church as abandoned, widowed matron, lamenting the bereavement of her true sons and bewailing her bastards, who earned her the epithet of "whore"; see ibid., 77.

the façade of the Senator's palace on the Capitoline Hill, now lost, which included Rome personified: represented as a mourning widow on board a sinking ship, praying for delivery (dated 1344).[38] Likewise, in the *Dittamondo* by Fazio degli Uberti, a Dantesque reiteration of history and politics in mid-fourteenth-century Italy, Rome is personified as a disheveled and sad old woman dressed as a widow.[39] The topos of Rome as widow could do effective rhetorical work also for supporters of the emperor, not just the pope. Thus, Dante in *The Divine Comedy* famously portrayed Rome as widowed by the emperor, Albert of Austria: "Come, see your Rome who, widowed and alone, / weeps bitterly; both day and night, she moans: / My Caesar, why are you not at my side?"[40]

Christian Rome, by its identification with Jerusalem, could thus be blended into female relational roles, widow, bride, and matron, emphasizing her relation with the *paterfamilias*, variably understood as pope or emperor. Like the *caput* metaphor, Bernard's depiction of widowed Rome, while grounded on traditional exegesis, anticipated its subsequent upsurge in political rhetoric of the later middle ages. But the final exegetical step in order to complete the imagery, namely explicitly identifying the pope as bridegroom, is a pass that Bernard neither makes here, nor elsewhere.[41] But it will be made—resolutely, definitely, and irrevocably—at the turn of the century by Pope Innocent III (1198–1216).

Once established, the notion of the pope as head developed in two directions, spurred on by its metaphorical entailments. Firstly, bridal imagery was absorbed into the power language drawn from Ephesians 5, with the pope, as head of the church, in the position—Christ's position—of bridegroom. Secondly, the pope-husband/bridegroom/head appropriates the body of his wife/bride, providing the pope with a body by which he

38. Baskins, "Trecento Rome," 201.

39. Fazio degli Uberti, *Il dittamondo*, 1:11; 36: "Vidi il suo volto, ch' era pien di pianto, / vidi la vesta sua rotta e disfatta, / e raso e guasto il suo vedovo manto." For references to fourteenth- and fifteenth-century manuscript illustrations of *Il dittamondo* showing Roma as widow, see Maddalo, *In figura Roma*, 115–21.

40. Dante, *Purg.* 6.112–14: "Vieni a veder la tua Roma che piagne / vedova e sola, e dì e notte chiama: Cesare mio, perché non m'accompagne?"

41. Bernard uses *amicus sponsus* and *paranymphus sponsae*, but never *sponsus* for the pope. In the impressive list of papal qualities that Bernard supplied at the end of the fourth book in "On Consideration" (*Csi*) to Pope Eugene—amidst designations such as "defender of the faith," "leader of the Christians," "father of kings," "light of the earth," "vicar of Christ," and "the Lord's anointed"—there is no reference to "head" or "headship" (*caput*), nor to the collocated image of "husband" (*vir*) or "bridegroom" (*sponsus*). Rather the pope is identified with particular parts of the head, like the "eyes of the blind" and the "tongue of the mute" just as he is not the bridegroom, but rather the "friend of the bridegroom" and the "attendant of the bride." *Csi* 4.23 (PL 182: 788AB).

can position himself as head of the body politic, thus becoming a corporeal representation of both Rome and the Roman church and, ultimately, the universal church itself.

Ubi Papa, ibi Roma

Arriving in 1207 at Viterbo where Pope Innocent III and the curia were in temporary residence, William of Andres, a monk from Flanders, declared: "I arrived at Viterbo and found myself in Rome!"[42] While the monk's exclamation might be perceived in terms of metonymical association, it is part of a much broader rhetorical development. Emerging decisively in the twelfth and thirteenth century, the assimilation of *ecclesia romana* and pope paralleled the definition of pope as *caput* of the body politic, and—I argue—intersected with that definition.

The notion of the pope as an embodiment of the Roman church and Rome was not just a case of elaborated metaphorical panegyric but a canonical principle of considerable juridico-administrative significance. Its development must be sought within a specific context and frame of reference, a tradition dating back to the fifth century known as *limina apostolorum*, obliging bishops of the Roman ecclesiastical province (from the Apennines to Sicily) an annual visit in Rome.[43] A relation—centralized and hierarchical—was thus forged between the bishop of Rome and the bishops of the provinces. From the time of Gregory I (590–604), this visit to Rome was fixed on the feast of Saints Peter and Paul (June 29) and the bishops were required to carry out a visit *ad limina* ("on the thresholds") of their tombs. Thereby a weighty conceptual and religious identification between the *sedes apostolica* and the *limina apostolorum* was established. Meanwhile, the obligation to undertake a visit to Rome was enforced by the ceremony of the consignment of the pallium to archbishops at the hands of the pope.[44] As the visit *ad limina* developed as canonical institution in the eleventh and twelfth centuries, the reform popes extended the obligation to almost the

42. *Willelmi chronica Andrensis* (MGH SS, 24, 737): "Viterbium tandem deveni et ibidem Romam inveni."

43. On this and the following, see Maccarrone, "*Ubi est papa*"; Paravicini-Bagliani, *The Pope's Body*, 60–63; Kantorowitz, *The King's Two Bodies*, 204–5.

44. On the importance of the revived office of archbishop, which could be filled only by the pope's bestowal of the pallium, see Angenendt, "*Princeps imperii—Princeps apostolorum.*"

whole church, reflecting the emphasized position of Rome and the papacy in the Gregorian church.[45]

Sometime after the mid-twelfth century, the long-standing association of the *ad limina* visit with Peter and Paul's tombs began to change direction as the visit to the tombs was overshadowed and gradually replaced by a visit to the Roman curia and the pope. In his commentary to Gratian's *Decretals*, written 1157–59, the canonist Rufinus of Bologna repeats the obligation to undertake an annual visit to Rome, emphasizing the visit to the pope but making no mention of *ad limina* or the tombs.[46] A further step is taken by Huguccio of Pisa, in his comments on the canonical visit *ad limina* in *Summa super decreto* (1187–91). Significantly, Huguccio's work is written in the aftermath of a period during which the papacy was unable to control Rome and the Papal states, resulting in spells of exile and a long series of antipopes.[47] Noting the frequent absence of the popes from Rome, Huguccio states that the visit *ad limina* was to the curia "wherever it may be" (*ubicumque sit*):[48] in other words, wherever the pope was.

The identification between *limina apostolorum* and the pope became evermore explicit in the thirteenth century as the ties between Rome and its bishop further disintegrated. In 1244 Pope Innocent IV had to leave Rome for the usual reasons: political instability, fear of revolt, etc. Heading north, the pope settled with the curia in Lyons. From here Innocent IV called a general council in 1245, thus interrupting the century-long tradition of Lateran councils. This, clearly, was quite another matter than the popes' absence from Rome, however frequent or prolonged. Rather it appeared an abandonment and translocation of the Roman see to Lyons.[49] Indeed, in the papal court Lyons became referred to as "another Rome" (*Roma altera*).[50] Thus Pope Innocent IV, following Huguccio, rephrased *limina apostolorum* as meaning "wherever the pope is" (*ubi papa est*).[51] But the final step, where

45. See *Decretum Gratiani* D. 93 c. 4 (PL 187:434–35): "Unde Anacletus et Zacharias Papa: Singulis annis apostolorum limina visitent episcopi, qui ordinationibus apostolicis subjacent." On the extended obligation, see Maccarrone, "*Ubi est papa*," 372–73.

46. On Rufinus's *Summa*, see Maccarrone, "*Ubi est papa*," 374.

47. Papal inability to control Rome was acute under Alexander III (1159–81) and his immediate successors. Not until the pontificate of Clement III (1187–91) did the pope reside regularly again in Rome.

48. Huguccio, *Summa super decreto*, following Maccarrone's transcription of Pal. lat. 626 fol. 89rb and Barb. lat. 272, fol. 53rb in "*Ubi est papa*," 376n29.

49. See Maccarrone, "*Ubi est papa*," 376–77.

50. Niccolò of Calvi, cited in Paravicini-Bagliani, *The Pope's Body*, 61.

51. Innocent IV, *Decretalium, lib.* 2, *tit.*24, *cap.* 4, fol. 284: "[Apostolorum] scilicet Petri et Pauli. Apostolorum autem limina ibi esse intelliguntur, ubi papa est."

the pope's identification as *limina* is carried over onto a more abstract identification of the pope as Rome, was taken a few years later by Henry of Susa, commonly called Hostiensis (d. 1271), who coined the celebrated dictum: "Rome is wherever the pope is" (*ubi papa, ibi Roma*).

Hostienis, a university teacher and decretalist turned cardinal, synthesized the principles from Innocent IV and Huguccio, explaining that *limina apostolorum* is the pope himself: "And it says the apostles [*apostolorum*], namely, Peter and Paul, that is, the Roman curia: for where the pope is, there Rome is. From this it is clear that it should be understood that where the pope is, there also the apostles are."[52] Eliminating the spatial, literal reality of the tombs, Hostiensis, like his master Innocent IV, focalized on an extended reality—doctrinal and liturgical—of the "threshold," *limina apostolorum*, embodied in the pope, wherever he may be. Rome, identified as the apostolic see, is where the pope is.[53] So Rome was not necessarily in Rome, even when the liturgy firmly anchored it there, as in the ceremony of the pallium. In his synthesis of canon law, *Summa aurea* (1253), Hostiensis comments on this ceremony, traditionally held at the high altar of St. Peter's Basilica in Rome, located over Peter's tomb, where the pallium was conferred on archbishops. Giving the formula with which to concede the pallium, including the mention of Peter's body (*de corporis beati Petri*), he states that this might just as well take place elsewhere, "because it is not where Rome is that there is the pope, but the contrary" (*quia non ubi Roma est, ibi papa est, sed econverso*).[54] Here he bases his argument on a phrasing in Gratian (d. ca. 1150), taken out of its context: "for it is not the place that sanctifies the man, but the man that sanctifies the place."[55] Dramatizing Hostiensis's bold statements, the fourteenth-century jurist Baldus de Ubaldis declared: "Rome is where the pope is, even were he secluded in a peasant's hut."[56] By this canonical principle, capable of transforming ancient liturgical practice,

---

52. Hostiensis, *In secundum decretalium librum commentaria*, on X, 2, 24, 4, cited in Maccarrone, "*Ubi est papa*," 378: "et dic Apostolorum, scilicet Petri et Pauli, id est Curiam romanam: nam ibi papa ubi Roma. Et ex hoc patet, quod ubi Papa sit, ibi et Apostoli esse intelliguntur."

53. Cf. Hostiensis, *In secundum decretalium librum commentaria*, on X, 5, 20, 4, cited in Maccarrone, "*Ubi est papa*," 378: "[Apud sedem apostolicam]: hoc est in Curia Romana ibicumque sit, quia ubi papa ibi Roma."

54. Hostiensis, *Summa aurea* (on X) lib. 1, 8, 3, c. 135.

55. Loc. cit: "locus enim non sanctificat hominem, sed homo locum." Cf. *Decretum Gratiani*, D. 40 c. 12 (PL 187:218A): "non locus sanctificat hominem, sed homo locum." Gratian in turn borrows the phrasing from Pseudo-Chrysosomus, in discussing the legitimacy of sacerdotes.

56. Baldus, on D.1, 18, 1, n26, fol. 44, cited in Kantorovitz, *The King's Two Bodies*, 205n35: "ubi papa, ibi Roma, etiam si esset in quodam tugurio rusticano reclusus."

Hostiensis and his successors in effect transferred the point of reference of the papal institution from the city of Rome to the person of the pope.

Rome—the *limina apostolorum*, the city of Peter and Paul, the new Jerusalem—had become the body of the pope. Once dislocated, this symbolic site, positioned as the pope's physical whereabouts, i.e. his body, accumulated also other holy cities and spaces. Thus for Baldus, writing in the wake of the popes' transferal to Avignon, "where the pope is, there is Rome, Jerusalem, Mount Zion; there is the common homeland."[57]

Kantorowicz has pointed out that the formula *ubi papa ibi Roma* had ancient and imperial connotations in the saying "Rome is where the emperor is."[58] But it never seemed to achieve the significance—juridically, politically, symbolically—that it came to have in papal usage. Indeed, Hostiensis's transferal of Rome onto the pope's person would eventually serve to justify the papal residency at Avignon.[59] Naturally, the political context—with twelfth-, thirteenth-, and fourteenth-century popes residing more or less stably outside Rome, whether in Viterbo, Lyons, or Avignon—provides an important element in this development. Nevertheless the repositioning of *limina apostolorum*—from the tombs to the curia—is conspicuous in that it is the pope himself who becomes the target of the visit. One may ask: Does this position the pope as object of veneration? Or does this reflect, instead, a bureaucratization in the post-Gregorian church, with the pope as administrative focal point? Whichever way one assumes to approach such questions, it is essential to recognize the complexities in medieval representation and concepts of translation of authority. More and more, the papal office (but not the man that filled the office) came to carry representational functions both liturgically and devotionally. In a sense, we may even say that the papal *persona* became an embodied metaphor, a living allegory, a corporeal representation.

Huguccio's concept of the pope's embodiment of the *limina apostolorum* is anchored by canonists in the devotional concept *reverentia*:[60] "Bishops," states Johannes Teutonicus in the *Glossa ordinaria* from 1215 (reworked

57. Baldus, c. 4 X 2, 24, l, n11, fol. 249, cited in Kantorovitz, *The King's Two Bodies*, 205n35: "ubi est papa, ibi est Roma, Hierusalem et Mons Sion, ibi et est communis patria."

58. Kantorowicz gives Herodian of Antioch's *History of the Roman Empire*, 1.6.5 as originator of the maxim. The expression was current also in medieval imperial circles, viz. Frederick II: "ibi sit Alemanie curia, ubi persona nostra et principes imperii nostri consistunt," cit. in *The King's Two Bodies*, 204n34. Cf. sermon attr. to Ambrose on the sacramental presence of Christ in baptism, *Sermo XXXVIII* (PL 17:679D): "Ubique enim nunc Christus, ibi quoque Jordanis est."

59. See Paravicini-Bagliani, *The Pope's Body*, 62, and below.

60. On *reverentia* in the *ad limina*, see Maccarrone, "*Ubi est papa*," 373–76.

by Bartholomew of Brescia after 1245) "owe reverence [*reverentiam*] to the pope; therefore they should make a visit to the curia every single year."[61] In the thirteenth century there emerged evermore explicit assumptions that the pope gave visibility to Christ, that he provided a living image of Christ on earth. In chronicles and in ceremony, the pope's physical, visible, and corporeal presence was orchestrated to emphasize christomimesis. The olive branches of the papal *adventus* procession recalling Christ's entry in Jerusalem, the display of the eucharistic host—Christ's flesh—preceding the pope at the coronation ceremony, and even the announcement of the election of a new pope (*annuntio vobis gaudium magnum*) echoing Paul's announcement of Christ (Acts 17:3), all symbolically pointed to Christ's visible presence, or re-manifestation, in the pope.[62]

Paralleling this development, the canonist principle of *ubi papa ibi Roma* was pushed further still. During the bitter conflict between emperor Louis IV and Pope John XXII, which culminated in 1328 with the emperor invading Rome, Louis declared the pope deposed, claiming that the pope's abandonment of Rome for Avignon was a breach with the Petrine commission.[63] The canonist Alvarus Pelagius (d. 1350) came to John's rescue, accusing the emperor of heresy by invoking Hostiensis while extending the implications of the pope's embodiment of Rome ever further. Alvarus announced that it was heresy and against holy scripture to say that the pope loses his jurisdiction when he is not in Rome:

> [F]or wherever the pope is, there is the church of Rome and the apostolic see and the head of the church, for Peter signifies the church . . . Likewise the church, being the mystical body of Christ [*corpus Christi mysticum*] and the totality of all Catholics . . . is not closed in by city walls: it is there where the head is, that is, the pope [*ibi est, ubi est caput, scilicet papa*] . . . And a place

61. *Glossa ordinaria*, cited from Maccarrone, "*Ubi est papa*," 376: "Episcopi . . . reverentiam debent, ut singularis annis curiam visitent."

62. On *adventus*, see Twyman, *Papal Ceremonial*; on Christly visibility, see Paravicini-Bagliani, *The Pope's Body*, 65–66.

63. Louis of Bavaria, *Constitutio super residentia ponteficis*, 438 (MGH Const. 6,1, 362): "ut sic populus electus et civitas sacerdotalis et imperialis per sacram beati Petri sedem capud totius orbis vocaretur effectu . . . Si vero talis summus pontifex contra prescriptam formam se absentare presumpserit et a clero populoque Romano tertio monitus infra terminum eidem per dictum clerum et populum a moderandum ad urbem Romanam celeriter non redierit, ibidem ut premittitur continue moraturus, ipso iure pontificatus sui honore et dignitate presentis constitutionis auctoritate volumus fore privatum, decernentes ad alterius summi pontificis electionem procedi debere, acsi per mortem ipsius naturalem de alio electionem fieri immineret." On this, see also Wood, *Clement VI*, 45.

does not sanctify men nor does Rome sanctify the pope, but rather the man sanctifies a place and the pope sanctifies Rome.[64]

So the pope is "head" (*caput*) but also embodied because the body "is where the head is." Yet this body is expressly not just Rome; it is "not closed in by city walls" [*non est ambitus murorum*]. With Alvarus, *ubi papa ibi Roma* has in effect become *ubi papa ibi ecclesia*. The pope incorporates the entire church, that is, the *corpus mysticum* of Christ. While Peter—by signifying the church (*Petrus ecclesiam significat*)—remains crucial to undergird the imagery of the papal head with the extended, massive body of the whole ecclesiastical community, the ties between Peter and Rome are loosened. Neither the thresholds of the saints nor the apostles' tombs sanctify the pope; on the contrary, it is the pope who sanctifies Rome. Indeed, turning previous exegesis of the Petrine commission and Rome's primacy on its head, Alvarus suggests that the pope's position as head of the church is not dependent upon the Roman church. Rather the preeminence of the Roman church depends on it being the see of the pope.[65]

Marrying the *corpus mysticum*

The conceptual base of *ubi papa ibi Roma* proposes not one but two metonymic displacements: firstly, an identification of the Roman church with the pope, and, secondly, an identification of the pope with the Roman church, based on a juridical and liturgical identification of *sedes apostolica* as *limina apostolorum*. In other words, it envisions a total absorption of Rome and the Roman church into the person of the pope.[66] From here, the step—taken by Alvarus—towards understanding the pope as the incarnation of the universal church follows from the entailments and the impetus in the imagery as it blends with the emergent theories of pope as *vicarius Christi*.[67]

64. Alvarus Pelagius, *Collirium*, cited in Maccarrone, "*Ubi est papa*," 381: "Quod est contra sacram scripturam, quia ubicumque est papa, ibi est ecclesia Romana et sedes apostolica et caput ecclesie, quia Petrus ecclesiam significat . . . Item ecclesia que est corpus Christi mysticum et que est collectio catholicorum . . . non est ambitus murorum: ibi est, ubi est caput, scilicet papa . . . Et locus non sanctificat homines nec Roma papam, sed homo locum et papa urbem Romanam."

65. See discussion in Wilks, *Sovereignty*, 400–407, esp. 402; cf. Saak, *High Way to Heaven*, 82–83.

66. Paravicini-Bagliani, *The Pope's Body*, 62.

67. On the history and implications of the papal title *vicarius Christi*, see Maccarrone, "*Vicarius Christi*."

But just how might such a thing be envisioned? How might the pope be understood to embody and incarnate the church? I suggest that a primary vehicle for establishing and negotiating, indeed, for imagining, explaining, and thinking about such an appropriation was by means of the marriage between bride/wife/body-church and bridegroom/husband/head-pope, provided by the crossing of Ephesians 5 with the Song of Songs.

It was by his marriage to the Roman church that each individual pope was able to gain possession of the Petrine see, and thereby Christ's commission of power.[68] This idea—simple and far-reaching—was sonorously introduced by Innocent III in a sermon called "He who has the bride" (*Qui habet sponsam*) held in St. Peter's basilica in Rome on February 22 in 1199 at the first anniversary of his election. Innocent's marriage symbolism is significant not only in that it establishes the pope as bridegroom, but in that it uses marriage to anchor papal power, that is, the "fullness of power" (*plenitudo potestatis*).

In this carefully orchestrated sermon Innocent gradually sneaks himself into the imagery. He begins traditionally enough, with the image of Christ as bridegroom and church as bride, assuming for himself the role of "friend of the bridegroom" (*amicus sponsi*) who stands gleefully by to peek at the couple. Before long, however, Innocent solidly situates himself in the position of bridegroom. At each hermeneutical turn in the sermon, he repeats the leading pericope, "he who has the bride, is the bridegroom" (John 3:29), giving the rhetorical effect of a spiral quasi-judicial argument. Producing a string of biblical allusions to the primacy of Peter (among them, predictably, Matthew 16; John 21; and Luke 22), Innocent declares:

> Therefore, he who has the bride is the bridegroom. Or am *I* not the bridegroom, and each of you the friend of the bridegroom? Certainly [I am] the bridegroom, since I have a bride [who is] noble, wealthy, and exalted; beautiful, chaste, and gracious; the most holy Roman church, who—as the Lord orders—is the mother and mistress of all the faithful.[69]

So he who has the bride is the bridegroom, and the bride is the church and he who has her, is Innocent. The audacity of Innocent's image is remarkable. While episcopal elections had been spoken of in terms of marriage

68. Cf. Wilks, *Sovereignty*, 362.

69. Innocent III, *Qui habet sponsam* (PL 217:662CD): "Ergo *qui habet sponsam, sponsus est.* An non ego sponsus sum, et quilibet vestrum amicus sponsi? Utique. Sponsus, quia habeo nobilem, divitem, et sublimem, decoram, castam, gratiosam, sacrosanctam, Romanam Ecclesiam: quae, disponente Deo, cunctorum fidelium mater est et magistra."

by reformers in the eleventh and twelfth century, bishops—not even if they were popes—had not attributed to their brides the traits of the church universal, as "mother and mistress" of all the faithful.[70] Addressing his audience which, apart from the cardinals and the Roman clergy, must have included visiting bishops and various legates,[71] Innocent not only declares himself bridegroom but demotes the assisting bishops and dignitaries to the position of "friends" (*amicus sponsi*), while hurling at them the full weight of Roman primacy. Indulging in a celebratory flourish to exalt his bride—the Roman church—the pope, as her bridegroom, invests himself with the attributes of the fullness of power (*plenitudo potestatis*):

> Therefore, he who has the bride is the bridegroom. But this bride did not marry empty-handed, but presented to me a dowry precious beyond price; fullness of spiritual [authority] and breadth of temporal [authority], a magnitude and multitude of both. For while others have been called to partake in the responsibility [for the church] [*in partem sollicitudinis*], Peter alone assumed the fullness of power [*in plenitudinem potestatis*]. As the sign of the spiritual [gifts] [*pro sacerdotio*] she brought me the mitre, as the sign of the temporal [gifts] [*pro regno*] she gave me the crown—the mitre for the priestly, the crown for the royal, constituting me as the vicar [*vicarium*] of him on whose garments and on whose thigh is written King of Kings and Lord of Lords [Rev 19:16], an eternal priest, according to the order of Melchisedech [Ps 109:4].[72]

Here, then, is Innocent's point: As bridegroom to the church of Rome, he assumes a Christlike position with respect to other bishops and rulers. Evoking Christ's dual function as both priest and king, the pope lays claim to dual authority: both *sacerdotium* and *regnum*. In marrying *ecclesia romana*,

---

70. On the radicalness of Innocent's departure, see Doran, "Innocent III and the Uses of Spiritual Marriage," 107–8; on Gregorian reformers' use of bridal imagery to establish episcopal authority, see McLaughlin, *Sex, Gender, and Episcopal Authority*.

71. On the audience of the sermon, see Doran, "Spiritual Marriage," 105.

72. Innocent III, *Qui habet sponsam* (PL 217:665AB): "Ergo *qui habet sponsam, sponsus est*. Haec autem sponsa non nupsit vacua, sed dotem mihi tribuit absque pretio pretiosam, spiritualium videlicet plenitudinem et latitudinem temporalium, magnitudinem et multitudinem utrorumque. Nam caeteri vocati sunt in partem sollicitudinis, solus autem Petrus assumptus est in plenitudinem potestatis. In signum spiritualium contulit mihi mitram, in signum temporalium dedit mihi coronam; mitram pro sacerdotio, coronam pro regno, illius me constituens vicarium, qui habet in vestimento et in femore suo scriptum «Rex regum et Dominus dominantium [Apoc. XIX]: sacerdos in aeternum, secundum ordinem Melchisedech [Psal. CIX].»

Innocent became *one* with her, transforming him from a son into a father, from a position of subservience to dominance:

> A wondrous thing, that I who promised celibacy have con-
> tracted marriage. But this union does not hinder celibacy, nor
> does the fertility of this union take away the chastity of virginity
> . . . Surely, when I entered the contract, the son led the mother
> into marriage; when I concluded the contract, the father had the
> daughter as wife.[73]

In a strongly patriarchal and patrilineal culture, fatherhood is a weighty symbol of power—or more precisely a weighty symbol of the pope's primacy in the church. Here, in these complicated incestuous family relations, we find the full display of Gregorian reform rhetoric. The pope, positioned as bridegroom for the church, occupies a gendered space whereby he may as-sert authority over princes and other bishops, who are repositioned as sons, and also over mother church, who is repositioned as wife and daughter. By the underlying household imagery, therefore, reconfigurations of celibacy as fecundity secure the pope's procreative role as *paterfamilias*.

With Innocent III the term *plenitudo potestatis* became a technical term to define papal primacy.[74] In a chapter called "On the primacy of the Roman pontiff" in the treatise *On the Mystery of the Sacred Altar*, Innocent defines Peter as "head" (*caput*) of all other bishops, firmly equating head-ship with *plenitudo potestatis*:

> For Cephas in one language is translated *Peter*, in another
> language *head*. And just like the head possesses fullness of the
> senses while the other members participate in its fullness, so
> also other priests are called to partake in responsibility [*in par-
> tem sollicitudinis*] but only the highest pontiff [*summus pontifex*]
> assumes the fullness of power [*in plenitudinem potestatis*].[75]

73. Innocent III, *Qui habet sponsam* (PL 217:662–63): "Mira res, qui coelibatum promisi, contraxi conjugium, sed istud conjugium non impedit coelibatum, nec fecun-ditas hujus conjugis tollit virginitatis castitatem . . . Certe cum ego contraherem, filius ducebat matrem in conjugem: ubi vero contraxi, pater habuit filiam in uxorem."

74. On the term *plenitudo potestatis*, see McCready, "Papal Plenitudo Potestatis."

75. Innocent III, *De sacro altaris mystrio*, 1.8 (PL 217:778–79): "Licet enim Cephas secundum unam linguam interpretetur Petrus, secundum alteram tamen exponitur caput. Nam sicut caput habet plenitudinem sensuum, caetera vero membra partem recipiunt plenitudinis; ita caeteri sacerdotes vocati sunt in partem sollicitudinis, sed summus pontifex assumptus est in plenitudinem potestatis." An almost identical phras-ing, replacing *membra* for *corpus*, is in Innocent III's Sermon on the Feast day of pope Gregory I, *Sermo XIII* (PL 217: 517B).

Repeating the widespread spiritual etymology that took *Cephas* to mean "head," Innocent underscores the uniqueness of the one among the many, Peter among the apostles, the pope among the bishops.[76] Other bishops partake in caring for the church (*in partem sollicitudinis*) by participating, as members or body parts, in the fullness of the head, but only the head—that is, Peter and Peter's successors, the popes, who are given here the ancient epithet *summus pontifex*—possesses the fullness of power (*in plenitudiem potestatis*).

When marriage symbolism, headship, and *plenitudo potestatis* are blended together by pro-papal exegetes and canonists, the striking result is that the pope assumes the position of both head and body—both Christ and church universal.

After Innocent III, this metaphorical network expands ulteriorly, with "bride and bridegroom" absorbing concepts of "head and body" and "husband and wife" from Ephesians 5, thereby further reinforcing the power language of the marriage metaphor. This is exactly what we find in Boniface VIII bull from 1302, *Unam sanctam*: the two dyads head-body and bridegroom-bride are deliberately crossed to undergird the papacy's claims to universal authority in both spiritual and temporal matters:[77]

> Urged by faith, we are obliged to believe and to maintain that the Church is one, holy, catholic, and also apostolic. We believe in her firmly and we confess with simplicity that outside of her there is neither salvation nor the remission of sins, as the bridegroom in Song of Songs [Song 6:8] proclaims: One is my dove, my perfect one. She is the only one, the chosen of her who bore her, and she represents one sole mystical body [*unum corpus mysticum*] whose head is Christ . . . Therefore, of the one and only Church there is one body and one head, not two heads like a monster; that is, Christ and the Vicar of Christ, Peter and the successor of Peter, since the Lord speaking to Peter Himself said: Feed my sheep [John 21:17].[78]

76. See Froehlich, "Saint Peter, Papal Primacy, and the Exegetical Tradition," 5–6.

77. On the historical context of the bull in light of the conflict between Pope Boniface VIII and King Philip the Fair of France, see Schimmelpfennig, *The Papacy*, 195–97.

78. Boniface VIII, *Unam sanctam*; *Extravag. commun.* 1.8, 1245: "Unam sanctam ecclesiam catholicam et ipsam apostolicam urgente fide credere cogimur et tenere, nosque hanc firmiter credimus et simpliciter confitemur, extra quam nec salus est, nec remissio peccatorum, sponso in Canticis proclamante: Una est columba mea, perfecta mea. Una est matris suae electa genetrici suae [Cant. 6:9]; quae unum corpus mysticum repraesentat, cuius caput Christus . . . Igitur ecclesiae unius et unicae unum corpus, unum caput, non duo capita, quasi monstrum, Christus videlicet et Christi vicarius Petrus, Petrique successor, dicente Domino ipsi Petro: Pasce oves meas [John 21:17.]"

Here the bride (from the Song of Songs) is explicitly the body politic (from Ephesians 5): the "one sole mystical body" (*unum corpus mysticum*), whose head is Christ and the pope (*Christus videlicet et Christi vicarius Petrus, Petrique successor*). Boniface refers disparagingly to a two-headed monster, an argument that had already been advanced by Matthew of Aquasparta (d. 1302) against imperial claims to dual headship—represented by both pope/*sacerdotium* and emperor/*regnum*.[79] The bull ends with the famous—or infamous depending on one's point of view—affirmation of papal supremacy: "Furthermore, we declare, we proclaim, we define that it is absolutely necessary for salvation that every human creature be subject to the Roman Pontiff."[80]

In this discourse of unabridged power the pope's claims no longer merely regard the church of Rome—they regard the universal church. By extension, the pope as a corporeal representation is no longer limited to the Roman church (and Rome) but is extended to the whole church. Thus pope Boniface's supporter Giles of Rome, declared around 1300 that: "The supreme pontiff directs the summit of the Church and can be called [the embodiment of] the Church."[81] At the same time, with Boniface and Giles, the church becomes decisively interpreted as the mystical body (*corpus mysticum*) of Christ: meaning the universal body of Christians.[82] Thus Remigio de' Girolami (d. 1319) insisted that all Christians constitute a single body without blemish or defect, governed by a single head.[83] Indeed, the terms "empire" and "church" came to be used as synonymous expressions: *Eccle-*

(trans. Medieval Sourcebook).

79. Matthew of Aquasparta, *Sermo de potestate papae*, 187: "in uno corpore etiam unum caput, non duo capita, quia totum esset monstruosum." Matthew and others considered that the Vicar of Christ alone can be called the rightful temporal ruler of this corpus. To offer the emperor as an additional and equally exalted head was a fiendish attempt to create a two-headed monster. See also Remigio de' Girolami, *Contra falsos Ecclesiae Professores*, and discussion in Chroust, "Body Politic," 432–33.

80. Boniface VIII, *Unam sanctam. Extravag. commun.* 1.8, 1246: "Porro subesse Romano Pontifici omni humanae creaturae declaramus, dicimus, definimus et pronunciamus omnino esse de necessitate salutis." (Using translation provided by Medieval Sourcebook.)

81. Giles of Rome, *De ecclesiastica potestate*, 3.12 (trans. Dyson, 369–67): "Summus Pontifex, qui tenet apicem Ecclesie et qui potest dici Ecclesia"; on Boniface and Giles, see Dyson trans., xi–xxxii.

82. Kantorovitz, *The King's Two Bodies*, 195–96, notes that this meaning begins to develop only in the twelfth century: *corpus mysticum*, in Carolingian writing, refers "not at all to the body of the Church, nor to the oneness and unity of Christian society, but to the consecrated host."

83. Remigio de' Girolami, *Contra Falsos Ecclesiae Professores*, eighth and ninth argument, ref. in Croust, "Body Politic," 432.

sia, for these writers *is* empire, *is* the *imperium*.[84] In this context we may acknowledge the full meaning and impact of Augustinus of Ancona's bold proclamations of papal supremacy in his work *Summa de potestate ecclesiastica* which he wrote for Pope John XXII early in the 1320s: "only the pope is the bridegroom of the church" (*solus papa sit sponsus ecclesie*), and, immediately after, "only the pope is the head of all the church" (*solus papa sit caput totius ecclesie*).[85]

For theorists of papal power in the late thirteenth and early fourteenth century, the unity between Christ-head and body-church carried underlying assumptions of a "personality" that is intangible and invisible but which at the same time embraces terrestrial society.[86] Since this society requires a visible representation, argued Pope Innocent IV, Christ left behind a vicar, a corporeal manifestation of himself.[87] Thus, for Alexander of S. Elpidio (d. 1326), who like Augustinus was writing for John XXII, the vicariate of Christ is to be found in the visible, human personification—the living embodiment—of the mystical, immaterial personality of the *Ecclesia*, who is Christ, which was set up in Peter and his successors:

> Since his corporeal presence was about to be withdrawn his followers, it was necessary that the direction of the universal Church was given to one who could govern the Church in his place [*loco et vice sui*]. This was Peter, so to Peter and all his successors were given the commission of government.[88]

---

84. Croust, "Body Politic," 432, notes that already in the ninth century, with the Carolingian *reformatio imperii*, the terms "world," "empire," "mankind," "church," and "Christendom" began to be used as synonymous expressions. On the pope as *verus imperator*. see Wilks, *Sovereignty*, 153.

85. Augustinus of Ancona, *Summa de potestate ecclesiastica* 19.1 and 19.2.

86. On this, see Wilks, *Sovereignty*, 354–55.

87. Innocent IV, *Decretalium, lib.* 2, *tit.* 27, *cap.* 27, fol. 317; cit. in Wilks, *Sovreignity*, 355n1: "Eadem ratione et vicarius eius potest hoc: nam non videretur discretus Dominus fuisse, ut cum reverentia eius loquar, nisi unicum post se talem vicarium reliquisset qui haec omnia posset: fuit autem iste vicarius eius Petrus, *Matth.*, 16, ultra medium, et idem dicendum est de successoribus Petri, cum eadem absurditas sequeretur si post mortem Petri humanam naturam a se creatam sine regimine unius personae reliquisset."

88. Alexander of S. Elpidio, *De ecclesiastica potestate*, 2.1; cit. in Wilks, *Sovereignty*, 355: "Nam quia suam corporalem praesentiam subtracturus erat a suis fidelibus, expediens erat ut alcui uni committeret Ecclesiae universale regimen qui Ecclesiam regeret loco et vice sui. Hic autem fuit Petrus et in Petro commissum est regimen omnibus successoribus."

The holder of this vicariate is at the same time the image of Christ and earthly society, the living embodiment of both Christ and *Ecclesia*,[89] claimed Augustinus, paraphrasing yet again the canonist maxim *ubi papa ibi Roma*: "where Christ is represented, there is represented the pope [*ubi repraesentatus est Christus, ibi repreaesentatus est papa*], who is the vicar of Christ."[90] All there is left is the pope: a head absorbing the body politic, absorbing the *corpus mysticum*: a husband-bridegroom appropriating his wife-daughter-mother-bride, thus making male embodiment possible.

The historical irony is that although the papacy produced an elaborate imagistic ideology of power unparalleled since the days of imperial Rome, the ability of the papacy to control the activities of the European monarchs was in steady decline during the course of the thirteenth and fourteenth centuries. As Michael Wilks drily remarked: "The less the popes could achieve in the world of fact, the more far reaching were the claims of their supporters, . . . relieved of the necessity for maintaining some sort of relationship between theory and practice."[91] However, the popes, papal theorists, and decretalists of the later middle ages had fashioned a perduring ideological structure for society. Notions of a sacred household, while not altogether new, provided a reinforced model of representing power. Not just papal power but also secular and especially royal power came to be represented in terms of household imagery provided by Ephesians 5 and the Song of Songs. In this sense, imagery of marriage and household did not lose its impact on Western European culture and society with the protestant reformation, but was rather reallocated to the sphere of secular power and domestic household ideology and its accompanying institutional structures.

89. But papal writers emphasize that this is only so in his official capacity—not in a private or personal capacity, see Wilks, *Sovereignty*, 368. The crux of Paravicini-Bagliani's argument is that as the pope came to be understood as the incarnation of the universal church, the physical and human aspect of his person—principally his body and his death—were surrounded and subjected to evermore "rigorous ritual and symbolic analysis and control" (*The Pope's Body*, 236). From the second half of the eleventh century, papal ceremonials came to focus in new, emphatic ways on the individual pope's mortality, such as the rite of flax burning and the enthronement on the *sedes stercoraria*, along with the development of the topos of "Peter's years" ("you'll never see Peter's years"), pointing towards the brevity of the pontifical reigns after Peter, reminding the pope of his physical mortality; see ibid., 6–15, 29–45. In the thirteenth century, the theme of the pope's mortality became more insistent with the appearance of a new topos, i.e. the nudity of the pope's corpse, an image of his loss of power over the church at death; see ibid, 122–32, 238–39.

90. Augustinus of Ancona, *Summa de potestate ecclesiastica* 8.1; cit. in Wilks, *Sovereignty*, 355–56: "ubi repraesentatus est Christus, ibi repreaesentatus est papa, qui est vicarius Christi."

91. Wilks, *Sovereignty*, 151.

Conclusions

As Turid Karlsen Seim argued, male appropriation of femaleness in Ephesians 5 envisioned unity, not duality; it envisioned hierarchical rather than harmonious ordering and subsumption rather than exclusion.[92] In pro-papal reception of Ephesians 5 in the later middle ages this is turned into a full-fledged vision of political authority and power. The female body, whether imagined as Rome or church, serves the male head—conceived of more abstractly as divinely sanctioned authority over the body politic and its individual members—by giving the former access to embody the totality of Christ, head and body. Like in monastic devotion where the (female) body was ideally ordered under and into the (male) spirit, pro-papal exegesis displayed a prevalently hierarchical, rather than dichotomous understanding of the relations male-female and body-spirit.[93] With this discursive impetus towards oneness (absorption, reconciliation, appropriation), differentiation is undercut as the inferior (female, body) is subsumed and absorbed into the superior (male, spirit). In the later middle ages, devotional and clerical writers envisioned Christ as part female (fleshly/human-body), part male (spiritual/divine-head), his two natures conjoined as bride and bridegroom.[94] Thus the salvific reconciliation of spirit and flesh, signalized by Christ's incarnation, and envisioned in terms of gender unification and nuptial imagery, provided underlying assumptions of gender that worked to establish and reinforce both the identification of pope as earthly manifestation of Christ and the identification of pope as simultaneously head and body.

92. Seim, "Kjærlighet, kropp og kjønn," 28, and Seim, "Interfacing House and Church," 54–55.

93. On gender in monastic devotion as hierarchical, not dichotomous, see Engh, *Performing the Bride*.

94. On this, see Bynum, *Fragmentation and Redemption*.

Abbreviations

Csi   *De consideratione*

Ep.   *Epistola*

MGH Const.   *Monumenta Germaniae Historicae: Constitutiones et acta publica imperatorum et regum*

MGH SS   *Monumenta Germaniae Historicae: Scriptores*

PL   *Patrologia Latina*. Edited by Jacques-Paul Migne. 221 vols. Paris: 1841–1866.

Bibliography

Primary sources

Alexander of S. Elpidio. *De ecclesiastica potestate*. In *Biblioteca Maxima Pontificia*, edited by J. T. Rocaberti, 2:1–40. Rome, 1698.

Alvarus Pelagius. *Collirium adverus hereses*. In *Unbekannte kirchenpolitische Streitschriften aus der Zeit Ludwigs des Bayern, 1327–54*, edited by R. Scholtz, 2:491–514. Rome, 1914.

Ambrose (attr.). *Sermones sancto Ambrosio hactenus ascripti: Sermones de diversis: Sermo XXXVIII. De gratia baptismi*. In PL 17:679–80.

Annales Romani. Edited by Georg Heinrich Pertz. In MGH SS, 5:468–80. Hanover, 1844.

Anselm of Havelberg. *Episcopi dialogi*. In PL 188:1139–248.

Augustinus of Ancona. *Summa de potestate ecclesiastica*. Edited by Paulus de Bergamo. Venice, 1487.

Bernard of Clairvaux. *De consideratione ad Eugenium papam*. In PL 182:727–808. ET: *Five Books on Consideration: Advice to a Pope*. Translated by John D. Anderson and Elizabeth T. Kennan. Cistercian Father Series 37. Kalamazoo, MI: Cistercian, 1976.

———. *Epistola 243*. In PL 182: 437–40. ET: *Letter 319*. In *The Letters of Saint Bernard of Clairvaux*, edited and translated by Bruno S. James, 391–94. Chicago: Regnery, 1953.

Boniface VIII. *Unam sanctam*. In *Corpus Iuris Canonici, Extravagantes communes* 1.8, edited by Emil Friedberg, 2:1245–46. Decretalium Collectiones. Graz: Akademische Druck- U. Verlagsanstalt, 1959. ET: taken from a doctoral dissertation written in the Dept. of Philosophy at the Catholic University of America, and published by CUA Press in 1927. Online at Medieval Sourcebook: Fordham University. http://legacy.fordham.edu/Halsall/source/B8-unam.asp.

Dante Alighieri. *La divina commedia*. Edited by Giorgio Petrocchi. Milan: Mondadori, 1966–67; 2nd ed., Florence: Le Lettere, 1994. ET: *The Divine Comedy by Dante Alighieri*. Translated by Allen Mandelbaum. New York: Random House, 1980–84. http://www.worldofdante.org/index.html.

Fazio degli Uberti. *Il dittamondo*. Biblioteca Scelta di Opere Italiane Antiche e Moderne 176. Milan: Silvestri, 1826.

Giles of Rome. *De ecclesiastica potestate*. ET: *Giles of Rome's On Ecclesiastical Power: A Medieval Theory of World Government*. Edited and translated by R. W. Dyson. New York: Columbia University Press, 2004.

Glossa Ordinaria: Epistola ad Ephesios. In PL 114:587–602.

Gratian. *Decretum Gratiani: Concordia discordantium canonum*. In PL 187:27–1870.

Gregory I. *Expositio in Psalmos Poenitentiales*. In PL 79:549–658.

Gregory VII. *Registrum: Liber IV, Ep. 16: Ad clericos romanenses*. In PL 148:69–70

Hostiensis. *In secundum decretalium librum commentaria*. Venice: 1581. Reprint, Torino: Bottega d'Erasmo, 1965.

Hostiensis. *Summa aurea*. Cologne: Zetzner, 1612.

Huguccio of Pisa. *Summa super decreto*. In *De excommunicatione vitiata apud glossatores*, edited by Josephus Zeliauskas, 1140–1350. Institutum historicum juris canonici: studia et textus historiae juris canonici 4. Zurich: Pas, 1967.

Innocent III. *De sacro altaris mystrio*. In PL 217:773–916.

———. *Sermones de diversis: Sermo III. In consecratione pontificis: Qui habet sponsam*. In PL 217:659–66. ET by Corinne J. Vause and Frank C. Gardiner, in *Pope Innocent III: Between Man and God: Six Sermons on the Priestly Office*, 32–40. Washington DC: The Catholic University of America Press, 2004.

———. *Sermones de Sanctis. Sermo XIII. In festo d. Gregorii papae*. In PL 217:513–21.

Innocent IV. *Apparatus in quinque libros decretalium*. Frankfurt: 1570. Reprint, Frankfurt: Minerva, 1968.

Leo I. *Sermones in praecipuis totius anni festivitatibus: Sermo LXXXII: In natali apostolorum Petri et Pauli*. In PL 54:422–27.

Louis of Bavaria. *Acta Regni*, 438: *Constitutio super residentia ponteficis*. Edited by Jakob Schwalm. In MGH Const., 6/1:361–362. Hanover, 1914–27.

Matthew of Aquasparta. Sermo de potestate papae. Appendix in Sermones de S. Fransisco de S. Antonio et de S. Clara. Edited by Gedeon Gàl, 177–190. Florence: Quaracchi, 1962.

Peter Damian. *Opusculum quintum: Actus mediolani, de privilegio romanae ecclesiae, ad Hildebrandum s. r. e. cardinalem archidiaconum*. In PL 145:89–98.

Pseudo-Isidore. *Collectio Decretalium*. In PL 130:7–1177.

Remigio de' Girolami. *Contra falsos Ecclesiae Professores*. Edited by F. Tamburini. Utrumque Ius 6. Rome: Univ. Lateran, 1981.

Willelmi chronica Andrensis. Edited by Ioh. Heller. In MGH SS, *Annales aevi Suevici*, 24:684–773. Hanover: 1879.

Secondary sources

Angenendt, Arnold. "*Princeps imperii—Princeps apostolorum*: Rom zwischen Universalismus und Gentilismus." In *Roma—caput et fons: Zwei Vortrdäge über das päpstliche Rom zwischen Altertum und Mittelalter*, edited by A. Angenendt and R. Schieffer, 7–44. Opladen: Westdeutscher, 1989.

Baskins, Cristelle L. "Trecento Rome: The Poetics and Politics of Widowhood." In *Widowhood and Visual Culture in Early Modern Europe*, edited by Allison Levy, 197–209. Aldershot, UK: Ashgate, 2003.

Benson, Robert L. "Political Renovatio: Two Models from Roman Antiquity." In *Renaissance and Renewal in the Twelfth Century*, edited by R. L. Benson and G. Constable, 339–59. Cambridge: Harvard University Press, 1982.

Bynum, Caroline Walker. *Fragmentation and Redemption: Essays on Gender and the Human Body in Medieval Religion*. New York: Zone, 1992.

Chroust, Anton-Hermann. "The Corporate Idea and the Body Politic in the Middle Ages." *Review of Politics* 9 (1947) 423–52.

D'Avray, David L. *Medieval Marriage: Symbolism and Society*. Oxford: Oxford University Press, 2005.

Doran, John. "Innocent III and the Uses of Spiritual Marriage." In *Pope, Church, and City: Essays in Honour of Brenda M. Bolton*, edited by F. Andrews et al., 101–14. Medieval Mediterranean: Peoples, Economies, and Cultures, 400–1500, vol. 56. Leiden: Brill, 2004.

Dupré Theseider, Eugenio. *L'idea imperiale di Roma nella tradizione del Medioevo*. Milan: Istituto per gli Studi di Politica Internazionale, 1942.

Engh, Line Cecilie. *Gendered Identities in Bernard of Clairvaux's "Sermons on the Song of Songs": Performing the Bride*. Europa Sacra 15. Turnhout: Brepols, 2014.

Fried, Johannes. *"Donation of Constantine" and "Constitutum Constantini": The Misinterpretation of a Fiction and Its Original Meaning*. Millennium Studies 3. Berlin: de Gruyter, 2007.

Froehlich, Karlfried. "Saint Peter, Papal Primacy, and the Exegetical Tradition, 1150–1300." In *The Religious Roles of the Papacy: Ideals and Realities, 1150–1300*, edited by Christopher Ryan, 3–43. Papers in Mediaeval Studies 8. Toronto: Pontifical Institute of Mediaeval Studies, 1989.

Gray, J. W. "The Problem of Papal Power in the Ecclesiology of St. Bernard." *Transactions of the Royal Historical Society* 24 (1974) 1–17.

Houben, Hubert. "La componente romana nell' istituzione imperiale da Ottone I a Federico II." In *Roma antica nel Medioevo: Mito, rappresentazioni, sopravvivenze nella "Respublica Christiana" dei secoli IX-XIII*, 27–47. Milan: V. & P. Università, 2001.

Kantorowitz, Ernst H. *The King's Two Bodies: A Study in Mediaeval Political Theology*. Princeton: Princeton University Press, 1957.

Kennan, Elizabeth. "The 'De Consideratione' of St. Bernard of Clairvaux and the Papacy in the Mid-Twelfth Century: A Review of Scholarship." *Traditio* 23 (1967) 73–115.

Krautheimer, Richard. *Roma: Profilo di una città, 312–1308*. Rome: Elefante, 1981.

Maccarrone, Michele. *"Ubi est papa."* In *Aus Kirche und Reich: Studien zu Theologie, Politik und Recht im Mittelalter: Festschrift für Friedrich Kempf*, edited by H. Mordek, 371–82. Sigmaringen: Thorbecke, 1983.

Maccarrone, Michele. *"Vicarius Christi": Storia del titolo papale*. Rome: Lateranum, 1952.

Maddalo, Sylvia. *In figura Roma: Immagini di Roma nel libro medioevale*. Rome: Viella, 1990.

Matter, E. Ann. *The Voice of My Beloved: The Song of Songs in Western Medieval Christianity*. Philadelphia: University of Pennsylvania Press, 1990.

McCready, William D. "Papal Plenitudo Potestatis and the Source of Temporal Authority in Late Medieval Papal Hierocratic Theory." *Speculum* 48 (1973) 654–74.

McLaughlin, Megan. *Sex, Gender, and Episcopal Authority in an Age of Reform, 1000–1122*. Cambridge: Cambridge University Press, 2010.

Morris, Colin. *The Papal Monarchy: The Western Church from 1050–1250*. Oxford: Clarendon, 1989.

O'Rourke Boyle, Marjorie. *Petrarch's Genius: Pentimento and Prophecy*. Berkeley: University of California Press, 1991.

Paravicini-Bagliani, Agostino. *The Pope's Body*. Translated by David S. Peterson. Chicago: Chicago University Press, 2000.

Reynolds, Philip L. *Marriage in the Western Church: The Christianization of Marriage during the Patristic and Early Medieval Period*. Vigilae Christianae Supplements 24. Leiden: Brill, 2001.

———. "Marrying and Its Documentation in Pre-Modern Europe: Consent, Celebration, and Property." In *To Have and to Hold: Marrying and Its Documentation in Western Europe, 1400–1600*, edited by Philip L. Reynolds and John Witte, 1–42. Cambridge: Cambridge University Press, 2007.

Robinson, I. S. "Church and Papacy." In *The Cambridge History of Medieval Political Thought, c. 350—c. 1450*, edited by J. H. Burns, 252–305. Cambridge: Cambridge University Press, 1988.

———. *The Papacy, 1073–1198: Continuity and Innovation*. Cambridge: Cambridge University Press, 1990.

———. "Reform and the Church, 1073–1122." In *The New Cambridge Medieval History*, edited by David Luscombe and Jonathan Riley-Smith, 4:268–334. Cambridge: Cambridge University Press, 2004.

Saak, Eric L. *High Way to Heaven: The Augustinian Platform between Reform and Reformation, 1292–1524*. Brill: Leiden, 2002.

Schimmelpfenning, Bernhard. *The Papacy*. Translated by James Sievert. New York: Columbia University Press, 1992.

Seim, Turid Karlsen. "A Superior Minority? The Problem of Men's Headship in Ephesians 5." In *Mighty Minorities? Minorities in Early Christianity—Positions and Strategies. Essays in Honour of Jacob Jervell*, edited by David Hellholm et al., 167–81. Oslo: Scandinavian University Press, 1995.

———. "Interfacing House and Church: Converting Household Codes to Church Order." In *Text, Image, and Christians in the Graeco-Roman World: A Festschrift in Honor of David Lee Balch*, edited by A. Cissé Niang and Carolyn Osiek, 53–69. Princeton Theological Monograph Series 176. Eugene, OR: Pick-wick Publications, 2012.

———. "Kjærlighet, kropp og kjønn: Efeserne 5.21–33—tolkning og resepsjon." In *Eros och agape: Barmhärtighet, kärlek och mystik i den tidliga kyrkan: Föreläsninger hållna vid Nordiska patristikermötet i Lund 16–19 augusti 2006, Patristica Nordica VII*, edited by H. Rydell Johnsén and P. Rönnegård, 28–48. Skellefteå: Artos & Norma, 2009.

Sessa, Kristina. *The Formation of Papal Authority in Late Antique Italy: Roman Bishops and the Domestic Sphere*. Cambridge: Cambridge University Press, 2012.

Turner, Denys. *Eros and Allegory: Medieval Exegesis of the Song of Songs*. Kalamazoo, MI: Cistercian, 1995.

Twyman, Susan. *Papal Ceremonial in the Twelfth Century*. London: Boydell, 2002.

Ullmann, Walter. *The Growth of Papal Government in the Middle Ages: A Study in the Ideological Relation of Clerical to Lay Power*. London: Methuen, 1962.

Wilks, Michael. *The Problem of Sovereignty in the Later Middle Ages: The Papal Monarchy with Augustinus Triumphus and the Publicists*. Cambridge Studies in Medieval Life and Thought, new ser. 9. Cambridge: Cambridge University Press, 1963.

Wood, Diana. *Clement VI: The Pontificate and Ideas of an Avignon Pope*. Cambridge Studies in Medieval Life and Thought, 4th ser. 13. Cambridge: Cambridge University Press, 1989.

PART III

Contested Dynamics of Community

——————— 11 ———————

Opportunities and Limits for Women in Early Christianity[1]

Adela Yarbro Collins

IT IS WITH GREAT pleasure that I dedicate this essay to the honor of Professor Turid Karlsen Seim, colleague and friend. Her book, *The Double Message: Patterns of Gender in Luke–Acts*, is a model of nuanced, critical study of issues related to gender among followers of Jesus and Christ-groups. The title of this article is meant to allude to her groundbreaking work.

Since a comprehensive study of the role of women in such groups during the first two centuries would go beyond the space allotted to this essay, I will focus on the phenomenon of women's prophecy. After some brief remarks about prophecy and who prophesied in antiquity, I will treat Paul's remarks on this topic in his Jewish context. I will also look at the role of women in the so-called Montanist movement of the second century. In the middle section, I will try to show that the phenomenon of prophecy did not die out between Paul and the movement involving New Prophecy (later called Montanists). A question to be addressed in the section on the latter movement is its connection with the letters of Paul. Professor Seim has provided an exemplary model on an analogous topic, the relation of the New Prophecy to the works attributed to John that eventually became canonical.[2]

1. I am grateful to Olivia Stewart and Marco Frenschkowski for reading a draft of this essay and for their helpful comments and suggestions.

2. Seim, "Johannine Echoes."

197

What Is Prophecy and Who Were Prophets?

"Prophecy" may be defined as "human transmission of allegedly divine messages." It belongs to the broader category of "divination," that is, consultation of deities to discern their will and seek guidance for human behavior. Prophets typically "act as direct mouthpieces of gods whose messages they communicate."[3] Some were professional prophets, others non-prophets who were sometimes ecstatic, and others lay prophets.[4] The most typical kind of prophetic expression is the oracle, usually oral but sometimes also written.[5] At least some prophets are portrayed as receiving divine oracles in a state of altered consciousness, which may be described as being in a "trance" or "possessed" by a god.[6] Female prophets were active in the ancient Near East and appear in the Hebrew Bible.[7] Since speaking in tongues is an ecstatic phenomenon, it is closely related to the ecstatic type of prophecy.

Jewish Prophecy in Paul's Time

Since Paul was a Jew, it is important to consider what experience of prophets and prophecy Paul might have had before he came to believe that Jesus was the Messiah. In the view of David Aune, "prophecy was alive and well during the Second Temple period."[8] According to the first century CE Jewish exegete and philosopher Philo, "The mind is evicted at the arrival of the divine Spirit, but when that departs the mind returns to its tenancy."[9] The first century CE Jewish historian and apologist Josephus does not comment on the details of the phenomenon of prophecy: "when the divine spirit had moved [David], he began to prophesy."[10] Actual prophets in Paul's lifetime include John the Baptist, Theudas, and an unnamed Egyptian Jew.[11] All

---

3. Nissinen, *Prophets and Prophecy*, 1.

4. Stökl, "Female Prophets," 47–49. Some professional prophets were court prophets (Blenkinsopp, *History*, 54–55).

5. Aune, *Prophecy*, 19; Blenkinsopp, *History*, 20.

6. Aune, *Prophecy*, 19; Blenkinsopp, *History*, 36–38; Wilson, "Prophecy and Ecstasy"; Nissinen, "Prophetic Madness."

7. Stökl, "Female Prophets"; Williamson, "Prophetesses."

8. Aune, "Prophecy," 1101. See also Aune, *Prophecy*, 16–19, 103–88. For an argument that, for most Jews of the Hellenistic and early Roman periods, prophecy had ended, see Frenschkowski, *Offenbarung und Epiphanie*, 1:108–246.

9. Philo, *Who is the Heir of Divine Things* 265, Colson, *Philo*, 4.419. Cited by Aune, "Prophecy," 1101. See also Nasrallah, *"Ecstasy of Folly,"* 36–44.

10. Josephus *Antiquities* 6.166 (Aune's translation, 1101).

11. See Aune, "Prophecy," 1099–100, and the primary and secondary sources he

prophecy in the Second Temple period was considered to be inspired, but it is not always as clear as with Philo how this inspiration relates to the human mind of the prophet.

Paul and Women Prophets

One of the oldest texts that speak about the phenomenon of prophecy in the movement associated with the name of Jesus is what we know as Paul's first letter to the Corinthians. This letter attests the practice of prophesying among the members of the community Paul founded in Corinth.

In his discussion of spiritual gifts and the body of Christ, Paul makes the following remark, "You then are the body of Christ and individually members of it, whom God has appointed (to various roles) in the church: first apostles, second prophets, third teachers, etc." (1 Cor 12:27–28).[12] This list could be interpreted either as chronological or in order of importance. That the latter is the case is made clear by the exhortation to "strive for the greater gifts" (1 Cor 12:31). Although the main thrust of Paul's overall argument here is intended to highlight mutuality and interdependence, it is clear that he presupposes a hierarchy of roles. Chapter 12 as a whole makes clear that, for Paul, the activity of prophesying is one of the higher gifts, granted by the divine spirit acting to fulfill the will of God. The importance of prophecy is then explicitly treated in 1 Cor 14:1–25.[13]

These discussions seem to be significant for understanding Paul's treatment of men and especially women praying and prophesying in 1 Cor 11:2–16. At the end of this passage, Paul comments, "Even if someone is disposed to be contentious, (let such a person recognize that) we have no such custom, and the assemblies of God also do not" (1 Cor 11:16). This concluding statement makes clear that the whole preceding treatment of praying and prophesying presupposes that these activities take place in communal meetings. Later on Paul instructs the community that, when they come together, "let everything happen with the goal of building up (the community and its members)" (1 Cor 14:26). Further, "Let two or three prophets speak, and let the others" (14:29). This communal setting indicates that to speak as a prophet is to exercise authority and leadership in the community of a kind second only to those of the apostles.

cites. He designates all three of these as "eschatological prophets."

12. All translations from the NT are my own.

13. On 1 Corinthians 12–14 as a rhetorical unit in which Paul deals with issues of identity, authority, and epistemology, see Nasrallah, *"Ecstasy of Folly,"* 61–94.

First Corinthians 14:29 is interesting because it subjects prophecy to evaluation. The NRSV translates the Greek phrase οἱ ἄλλοι διακρινέτωσαν as "let the others weigh what is said;" the translator of Hans Conzelmann's commentary as "the others should test what is said"; and Joseph A. Fitzmyer SJ as "the rest should evaluate (what is said)."[14] The verb is related to the noun used in 1 Cor 12:10, "to another (is given the gift of) prophecy, to another (the gift of) distinguishing of spirits." This means deciding whether someone prophesying did so by a holy spirit or by a demon.[15] Such discernment is, in effect, the process of distinguishing between true and false prophecy.[16]

In any case, it is clear that in 1 Cor 11:2–16 Paul does not raise any question at all about the authority and legitimacy of women engaging in the activity of prophecy. Among the gifts discussed in chapters 12 and 14, prophecy is one of the most obviously "spiritual," in the sense of manifesting the power of the spirit in and through a human being.[17] Thus it would be "quenching the spirit" to oppose the exercise of such a gift (1 Thess 5:19).[18] Nevertheless, Paul sets limits on the activity of both men and women in prophesying. These limits, however, combine constraints with the ongoing acceptance of the legitimacy of the activity. Women must cover their heads; men must not. These practical instructions, furthermore, are undergirded by appeal to an interpretation of Genesis 1–2 that establishes a clear hierarchy from God to Christ to human men to human women. Here we have a striking example of a "double message."[19]

Prophecy and Women as Prophets after Paul and before the New Prophecy

First Corinthians was written in the early 50s of the Common Era. The Gospel of Mark, written in the late 60s at the earliest, attests to the opinion

14. Conzelmann, *1 Corinthians*, 240; cf. 245: "prophecy is to be 'examined,'" Fitzmyer, *First Corinthians*, 524, 526.

15. Cf. 1 Cor 12:3; 10:20–22. See also Aune, *Prophecy*, 220–22.

16. Cf. 1 Thess 5:20–22.

17. As Nasrallah points out, in 1 Cor 13:8–9 Paul qualifies the gift of prophecy as having an end in the future and as only partial in the present time (*"Ecstasy of Folly,"* 87–90).

18. In the same context, Paul instructs the Thessalonians, "Do not reject prophecy disdainfully" (1 Thess 5:20). See Aune, *Prophecy*, 190–91, 219–20.

19. Seim's term (*Double Message*); see the first paragraph of this essay above. For a reconstruction of the self-understanding and practices of the women prophets in Corinth, see Wire, *Corinthian Women Prophets*.

among the people of Jerusalem that John the Baptist was a prophet (Mark 11:32; so also Matt 14:5; 21:26, 46; Luke 20:6). Matthew, written after 70 CE, attests to followers of Jesus prophesying in his name (Matt 7:22). The evangelist, however, indicates that the gift of prophecy means nothing for those who fail to do the will of God (7:21, 23).[20] More positively, the Matthean Jesus promises the twelve disciples that, "The one who receives a prophet (hospitably), because he is a prophet, will receive the reward of a prophet" (10:41). He also recognizes John the Baptist as a prophet and more than a prophet (11:9–10; so also Luke 7:26). The evangelist portrays the crowds in Jerusalem hailing Jesus as "the prophet from Nazareth of Galilee" (Matt 21:11).[21] He also has Jesus say to the scribes and Pharisees, "I (will) send you prophets . . . and some of them you will whip in your synagogues and persecute from city to city" (23:34; compare Luke 11:49). Neither Mark nor Matthew, however, attests to women prophesying. Matthew does provide a criterion for discerning false prophets, who are apparently itinerant. The criterion is metaphorical: false prophets are like bad trees that bear bad fruit, "so you will recognize them by their bad fruit" (Matt 7:20).

The Gospel of Luke and the Acts of the Apostles, in contrast to Mark and Matthew, give more evidence of the activity of prophets, including female prophets. The Gospel of Luke is often dated to 80–85 CE.[22] Most think that Acts was composed immediately after Luke, but others date it later.[23] In the speech of the angel Gabriel to Zechariah, he reveals that the son to be granted to him "will be filled with (the) holy spirit from the womb of his mother" (Luke 1:15). This signifies that the child "will be called a prophet of the Most High" (1:76).[24] While Elizabeth, Zechariah's wife, was pregnant with this child, her relative Mary visits and greets her. "When Elizabeth heard the greeting of Mary, the child in her womb sprang up, and Elizabeth was filled with (the) holy spirit and proclaimed in a loud voice, 'Blessed are you among women, and blessed is the fruit of your womb'" (1:41–42). The evangelist does not use language of prophecy here, but the portrayal and its context suggest that Elizabeth's cry is prophetic. As Fitzmyer put it, "This 'filling' of Elizabeth (with the holy Spirit) is the source of her inspiration. Because of it she understands Mary's condition."[25]

20. Cf. Aune, *Prophecy*, 222–24. See also his discussion of 1 John 4:1–3 (ibid., 224–25).

21. On "The Prophetic Role of Jesus" and "The Prophecies of Jesus," see ibid., 153–88.

22. E.g., Fitzmyer, *Luke*, 57.

23. E.g., Pervo, *Acts*, 5.

24. Fitzmyer, *Luke*, 229, 326.

25. Ibid., 363.

After Zechariah and Elizabeth's child is born, the father obeys Gabriel and names him "John." His tongue is then loosened and he, like Elizabeth, is filled with (the) holy spirit. In this case, the evangelist is explicit about the result, "and (Zechariah) prophesied, saying etc." (1:67). Zechariah becomes "a mouth-piece of God," and "The emphasis on prophecy will reappear in the hymn to be uttered, as Zechariah declares his son to be a prophet of the Most High" (1:76).[26]

Mary's speech in response to Elizabeth's greeting foreshadows indirectly the significance of her child, Jesus. After his birth two outsiders, a man and a woman, do so more explicitly (Luke 2:25–38). The scene is the temple in Jerusalem. In the case of the man, Simeon, as we saw with Elizabeth, language of prophecy is not used. The evangelist states, however, that, "(the) holy spirit was upon him." The content of Simeon's speech and the context make clear that what he says is prophecy: Jesus is "the Messiah of the Lord" (2:26). He will bring "(the Lord's) salvation," which consists of "light for revelation to the Gentiles, and glory for (the Lord's) people, Israel" (2:30, 32).

More information is given about the woman. Her name is Anna (Hannah), she is explicitly called "a prophet,"[27] and her father's name and tribe are stated (2:36). She is eighty-four years of age, was married as a young virgin, lived with her husband for seven years, and then as a (celibate) widow until the day of her encounter with Jesus (2:36–37). She was holy, remaining always in the temple, serving (God) by fasting and praying (2:37–38). The report ends with her speaking about Jesus "to all who were waiting for the redemption of Jerusalem" (2:38). The context implies that, as a prophet, she knew who Jesus was and what he would accomplish.

As Turid Karlsen Seim puts it, "The prophetic activity in the infancy narrative shows that Luke apparently does not operate with the concept of a period 'without prophets.' But the question remains as to whether the prophets in Luke 1–3 primarily represent a continuation of earlier Jewish prophecy or a preliminary/early expression of the eschatological breakthrough."[28] In any case, those who prophesy in Luke 1–3, including Simeon and Anna, are presented as Jews. In Anna's case, she is a prophet, a Jew, and a widow.

---

26. Ibid., 382.

27. I do not translate the feminine form of the word "prophet" in Greek (προφῆτις) with "prophetess" because the latter term may be taken to imply a lesser status for female prophets. Another reason is that it is not commonly used.

28. Seim, *Double Message*, 177. See her footnote 37 (pp. 177–78) for a discussion of scholarship on this question. On a "period without prophets," see 168–69.

The connections of her portrayal with other widows who appear later in the narrative indicate her exemplary character.[29]

If Richard Pervo is right in arguing that Acts was written in 115 CE, this text shows a continuity of interest and perhaps practice of prophetic activity among followers of Jesus from the first to the second century.[30] The account of Pentecost in Acts 2 is key to understanding prophecy in Acts, even though the narrative focuses on speaking in tongues. Indeed, the context suggests that prophecy and glossolalia are closely related.[31] In Acts 2 the author interprets the latter phenomenon differently from Paul. For Paul, speech in tongues is unintelligible to other human beings and must be interpreted.[32] In Acts those speaking in tongues speak languages unknown to themselves but understood by those who know those languages.[33] The important thing for the purpose of this essay, however, is that those who had gathered "in the same place" were "all filled with (the) holy spirit." The reference to "all" implies that those filled with the Spirit were not just the newly reconstituted group of twelve apostles but also a number of female disciples, Mary the mother of Jesus, and his siblings.[34] This interpretation is supported by Peter's citation of Joel 2:28–32. He links the pouring out of the divine spirit, which has just occurred, with the fulfillment of the prophecy that, "your sons and daughters will prophesy" and that both the male and the female servants of God will prophesy (Acts 2:17–18).[35]

In Philippi, Paul and Silas encounter a female slave who has "a spirit of prophecy" (πνεῦμα πύθωνα) (Acts 16:16).[36] The author of Acts states immediately that she earned a lot of money for her owners by prophesying (μαντευομένη). This association of prophecy with money implicitly defines the slave's activity as false prophecy. The distinction between true prophecy

29. Seim, *Double Message*, 244–48. Frenschkowski sees Luke 1–2 as a constructed framework into which the story of Jesus' birth could be integrated. If there had been an unbroken presence of the prophetic spirit among Jews, Acts 2 would have been unnecessary (personal communication).

30. On prophecy in Acts, see also Aune, *Prophecy*, 262–70.

31. The two phenomena are also linked in Acts 19:6.

32. 1 Cor 12:10, 30; 14:2, 4–23, 27–28.

33. Acts 2:5–11. Verses 6, 8, and 11 may imply that all the followers of Jesus spoke the same (spiritual, heavenly) language yet those present each understood them all to be speaking in the particular auditor's own language.

34. Pervo, *Acts*, 40 and 46–47 note i.

35. Seim, *Double Message*, 164–71. The term translated "servants" actually refers to "slaves."

36. The Greek phrase associates the slave with the oracle of Apollo at Delphi. Πύθων is the name of the serpent or dragon Python, who had possession of the oracle at Delphi before he was slain by Apollo.

practiced by the followers of Jesus from the magic practiced by outsiders is evident in the different terms chosen by the author of Acts for each of these activities and even more so by the translation in the New Revised Standard Version ("a spirit of divination" and "fortune telling"). This dichotomy was established earlier in the book of Acts. In the account of Simon of Samaria, he is characterized as a practitioner of magic (μαγεύων in 8:9 and μαγεία in 8:11). The signs and miracles (σημεῖα καὶ δυνάμεις) performed by Philip impressed him (8:6–7, 13). He associated the power to perform them with the gift of the Holy Spirit, so he offered Peter and John money so that he also might have the power to endow people with the Spirit (vv. 14–19). Peter's firm rejection of this offer distinguishes the signs and miracles performed by the Spirit from the practice of magic.[37] This attitude foreshadows or perhaps has influenced one of the criteria for distinguishing true and false prophecy in the *Shepherd of Hermas*, which will be discussed below.

When Paul arrives in Ephesus, he finds some apparently male "disciples" there (Acts 19:1; cf. v. 7). These have received only the baptism of John. In response to Paul's teaching, they receive baptism "in the name of the Lord Jesus" (19:5). When Paul subsequently lays his hands upon them, "the Holy Spirit came upon them and they began to speak in tongues and to prophesy" (19:6).

During the journey to Jerusalem that leads to his arrest, Paul and his companions stop in Caesarea and stay at the house of "Philip the evangelist, who was one of the seven" (Acts 21:8). The title "evangelist" occurs in Eph 4:11, where it is not defined. In 2 Timothy 4 it is defined as one who "proclaims the word" persistently and "corrects, rebukes, and encourages" the faithful by patient teaching.[38] Although the phrase "the seven" does not occur in Acts 6:1–6, the statement here probably means that Philip was one of the group appointed in that passage since the name "Philip" occurs in the list given there.[39] Similarly, although the term "evangelist" does not occur in chapter 8, Philip is portrayed in the two accounts there as one who proclaimed the gospel to the people of Samaria and to the Ethiopian eunuch.[40]

Philip is also said to have four virgin daughters who prophesied (Acts 21:9). The characterization of these women as Philip's "daughters" may be an allusion to the prophecy of Joel in 2:17.[41] Eusebius, bishop of Caesarea in

37. Garrett, *The Demise of the Devil*, 70, 145n42.

38. 2 Tim 4:2, 5.

39. Cf. Fitzmyer, *Acts*, 688–89; Pervo, *Acts*, 534, 536.

40. For an interesting "prosopographical sketch" of Philip in the context of Hellenistic Jewish Christianity, see von Dobbeler, *Der Evangelist Philippus*.

41. Karlsen Seim, *Double Message*, 180.

Palestine, quotes information from Polycrates and a dialogue of Gaius with Proclus about these four female prophets. Polycrates or Eusebius or both seem to have confused Philip the apostle with Philip the evangelist and one of the seven.[42] According to Eusebius's quotation from Polycrates, Philip had two daughters "who grew old as virgins" and were buried at Hierapolis with their father. A third daughter "lived in the Holy Spirit and rests in Ephesus."[43] The dialogue agrees more closely with Acts 21:9, "After him the four daughters of Philip who were prophets were at Hierapolis in Asia. Their grave is there and so is their father's."[44] These quotations show that the four prophesying daughters of Philip were remembered in the fourth century. They also provide evidence that they ended their lives at an advanced age in Asia Minor.[45] There were several ancient cities called "Hierapolis," one of which was in Phrygia.

According to Richard Pervo, Luke makes use of a source in Acts 21, which he characterizes as "a letter regarding the collection." The reference to Philip and his prophesying daughters belongs to the source.[46] By incorporating it, Luke has preserved valuable information and a model for later female prophets. In the chapter in its present form, Luke has probably added the dramatic passage about the prophecy of Agabus (21:10–14).[47] The situation here is similar to that of Luke 2:25–38, where a female prophet, Anna, is mentioned, but the only prophecies cited are attributed to Simeon.[48]

The book of Revelation, probably written around 96 CE, provides evidence that prophecy was alive and well among followers of Jesus toward the end of the first century CE.[49] John, the author of the book of Revelation, im-

---

42. Eusebius, *Eccl. Hist.* 3.31.2. Cf. Mark 3:18; Matt 10:3; Luke 6:14; Acts 1:13 with Acts 21:8. See also Frenschkowski, "Philippus."

43. Eusebius, *Eccl. Hist.* 3.31.3; Lake, 1.271.

44. Ibid., 3.31.4; 1.271. I have changed Lake's "prophetesses" to "prophets." See note 27 above.

45. Seim, *Double Message*, 181.

46. Pervo, *Acts*, 534.

47. Ibid. Agabus performs a prophetic symbolic action, taking Paul's belt and binding his hands and feet with it and then declaring, "Thus says the Holy Spirit, 'The man to whom this belt belongs the Jews in Jerusalem will bind in this way and deliver him into the hands of Gentiles'" (Acts 21:11).

48. Ibid., 536–37; cf. Seim, *Double Message*, 182–83. Concerning Agabus and other prophets, see also Acts 11:27–30. In this passage Agabus is said to have "indicated by the spirit" that there would be a great famine throughout the inhabited world. The narrator adds, "which occurred during the reign of Claudius" (41–54 CE). Here we have a case of a prophecy and its fulfillment. Other (male) prophets and teachers are mentioned in 13:1–3; 15:32 (Judas and Silas).

49. On the date of Revelation, see Yarbro Collins, *Crisis and Catharsis*, 54–83.

plies that he is a prophet, although he does not claim to be one directly. The angel who showed John the things he reports refers to himself as, "the fellow slave of you and of your brothers the prophets" (22:9). If John's "brothers" are prophets, he seems to be one as well. Furthermore, the author of the work declares, "I John am the one who hears and sees these things" (22:8). "These things," the content of the work, are defined several times as "prophecy" (1:3; 22:7, 10, 18, 19). This designation also implies that John is a prophet. Finally, after John has eaten the little scroll held by the mighty angel, voices from heaven declare to him, "You must prophesy again about peoples and nations and tongues and many kings" (10:11). John also communicates the revelation that there will be two prophets like Elijah and Moses who will prophesy in the imminent future (11:3–13).[50]

Most importantly for our purposes, John speaks about a female prophet active in the community of Thyatira (Rev 2:20).[51] He denies her the name "prophet" by saying, "who calls herself a prophet." He also disagrees with her teaching, which apparently condoned the eating of meat sacrificed to idols. Whether this was an absolute acceptance of the practice or only under certain circumstances may be concealed by the polemical formulation. He accuses her of teaching "(Christ's) servants (slaves)" to commit sexual immorality (πορνεῦσαι). This could be a metaphor for participating in practices that had the appearance of idolatry, or it could refer to practices related to marriage rejected by John.[52] He does not use her real name but refers to her with the nickname "Jezebel," the Phoenician princess made notorious by the first and second books of Kings. He issues a threat in the name of Christ if she does not repent (2:21–23). One can, however, read between the lines and infer that she was recognized as an authoritative prophet in her city. John reveals this by saying, "I hold against you that you permit" her, presumably, to exercise authority as a prophet. Gudrun Guttenberger has argued that Thyatira had been John's home base, the center of his activity in western Asia Minor. This hypothesis explains, among other things, why John is so incensed about the people there accepting a prophet whose teaching differed significantly from his own.[53]

Witulski dates it to the reign of Hadrian (117–138) in *Johannesoffenbarung* and *Kaiserkult in Kleinasien*. On prophecy in Revelation, see Aune, *Prophecy*, 274–88.

50. I infer this imminence from Rev 1:1; 22:7, 10, 12, 20.

51. I do not translate προφῆτις with "prophetess" for the reasons stated above in note 27. On the conflict between John and "Jezebel," see Aune, *Prophecy*, 218–19.

52. Compare Meier's interpretation of πορνεία in Matt 19:9; *Vision of Matthew*, 248–57.

53. Guttenberger, "Johannes von Thyateira," 173–76, 185–87.

Finally, an important point needs to be made about John the prophet, the author of the book of Revelation. He is presented indirectly as a prophet. His prophetic activity involves more, however, than that of the other prophets we have discussed so far. He speaks oracles, sometimes explicitly attributed to God as, for example, in Rev 1:8. He also sees visions in which revelation is communicated to him. All these things, what he has seen and heard (22:8), he has written down in an authoritative book (1:1–3; 22:10, 18–20).[54] These features, along with his frequent and extensive allusions to the writing prophets of Israel, suggest that he presents himself as a prophet like them.

The letter we know as Paul's first epistle to Timothy was written in the first half of the second century.[55] In 1:18, the Pastoral Paul says that he is entrusting instruction to Timothy "in accordance with the prophecies made earlier about" him (1 Tim 1:18). These "prophecies" may relate to the occasion mentioned in 4:14, "Do not neglect the gift that is in you, which was given to you through prophecy with the laying on of the hands of the elders as a group." The laying on of hands signifies a transfer of power related to commissioning to a particular task or role in the community.[56] This passage is similar to Acts 13:1–3, which states that, "the Holy Spirit said, 'Set aside for me Barnabas and Saul for the work to which I have called them.'" The reference is to a situation of communal worship in which a prophet communicated the words of the Holy Spirit. The response to this oracle was, "Then, after fasting and praying, they laid their hands upon (Barnabas and Saul), and (the latter two) departed." In light of this passage, 1 Tim 4:14 signifies a situation of communal worship in which a prophet communicated the decision of the Holy Spirit that Timothy be appointed to leadership in the reading (of Scripture), exhorting, and teaching (4:13, 16).[57]

It is not clear whether the situation described actually happened while Paul and Timothy were alive. It is evident, however, that the Pastor presents prophecy as an authoritative phenomenon and as an appropriate way to choose leaders. He is careful, though, to emphasize the qualifications such leaders must have. These include, for example, faith and a good conscience (1:19), being married once, temperate, self-controlled, respectable, hospitable, and skillful in teaching (3:2). If prophecy was not actually practiced in the social setting of the author, it was at least highly respected. Since, however, the author instructs women "to learn in silence in complete subordination"

54. For a discussion of John's social identity, see Yarbro Collins, *Crisis and Catharsis*, 34–50.

55. Herzer, "Juden—Christen—Gnostiker," 161, 165, 167.

56. The apostles lay their hands upon the seven in connection with their appointment to a particular activity (Acts 6:6).

57. Dibelius and Conzelmann, *Pastoral Epistles*, 70–71.

and forbids women "to teach . . . and to have power over men," it is unlikely that he would have recognized women prophets (2:11–12).

The *Didache*, that is, the *Teaching of the Twelve Apostles* was composed, with the use of older sources, around 110 or 120 CE probably in Syria.[58] In the section on the thanksgiving meal, the author instructs the audience to "permit the prophets to give thanks (or hold the eucharist) as often as they wish" (10:7). Later he exhorts the audience to "act towards the apostles and prophets as the gospel decrees" (11:3).[59] These two (apparently equivalent) types of leader are itinerant. The audience is charged to welcome them "as the Lord" (11:4). Such leaders may stay one or two days, but any who stays three days "is a false prophet" (11:5). "If (an apostle) asks for money, he is a false prophet" (11:6).[60] The audience is further exhorted not to "test or condemn a prophet speaking in the Spirit. For every sin will be forgiven, but not this sin" (11:7).[61] "The false prophet and the prophet will both be known by their conduct." The true prophet "conducts himself like the Lord" (11:8). Only a false prophet would order a meal in the Spirit and eat of it. False also is the prophet who teaches the truth but does not practice what he teaches (11:9–10). Other regulations follow.

Like the Gospel of Matthew, the *Didache* proposes that prophets and false prophets be distinguished by their behavior. The later work gives more detail than the Matthean metaphor of good and bad trees bearing good and bad fruit. The instructions regarding how many days a prophet may stay in a community, asking for money, and eating of a meal ordered in the spirit are quite concrete and clear. Somewhat more general is the principle of practicing what one teaches. Quite general is the teaching that a true prophet is like the Lord in his behavior.

After a section on hospitality in general, follows instruction concerning how to treat a true prophet who would like "to settle down with you." Such a prophet deserves his food, as does a true teacher, "like the worker" (13:1–2).[62] The first portions of the wine vat, the threshing floor, cattle, and sheep go to the prophets, "for they are your high priests" (13:3). The communities addressed by this work apparently had both charismatic leaders, like apostles, prophets, and teachers, and more institutional leaders, such as

58. Niederwimmer, *Didache*, 53–54. On prophets in the *Didache*, see Aune, *Prophecy*, 208–9, 225–26.

59. Translation from Ehrman, *Apostolic Fathers*, 1:435. Cf. Mark 6:7–13; Matt 10:1–15; Luke 9:1–6.

60. A similar point is made in *Didache* 11:12; on this verse, see Aune, *Prophecy*, 310.

61. Cf. Mark 3:28–30; Matt 12:31–32; Luke 12:10.

62. Ehrman, *Apostolic Fathers*, 1:437–39. Cf. Matt 10:10.

bishops (or overseers) and deacons (or servers). They are urged to elect the latter type of leaders for themselves, "For these also conduct the ministry of the prophets and teachers among you" (15:1).[63] No female prophets are attested, but at the same time nothing is said to exclude them.

The *Shepherd of Hermas* was written in central Italy, probably Rome, over a period of time from the end of the first century until the mid-second century.[64] The eleventh *Mandate* or *Commandment* of *Hermas* is "invaluable witness to the ongoing importance of prophecy in at least some churches in the early second century . . . the chapter is testimony to (the) vitality (of early Christian prophecy) and the ongoing search for viable criteria (for discerning true and false prophets)."[65] The Shepherd tells Hermas that only the double-minded are led astray by false prophets (*Mandate* 11:1). The double-minded treat them like soothsayers, bringing questions concerning what will happen to them in the future and paying them money for their prophecies (11:2, 12). Such a prophet sometimes says true things, "for the devil fills him with his own spirit so that he might be able to break down some of the just" (11:3).[66] The Shepherd also gives guidelines for discerning a (true) prophet, one who has "the divine spirit." Hermas can discern such a prophet "by his way of life."[67] He is "meek, gentle, humble . . . and he never gives an answer to anyone when asked, nor does he speak in private. The holy spirit does not speak when the person wants to speak, but when God wants him to speak" (11:7–8).[68] He goes on, "When, then, the person who has the divine spirit comes into a gathering of upright men . . . and a petition comes to God from the upright men who are gathered together, then the angel of the prophetic spirit lying upon that person fills him; and once he is filled that one speaks in the holy spirit to the congregation, just as the Lord desires" (11:9).[69]

The criterion for discerning true and false prophets by observing their "way of life" is similar to that of Matthew and some of those of the *Didache*. New in *Hermas* is the private versus communal criterion, and the issue of

---

63. Ehrman, *Apostolic Fathers*, 1:441.

64. Osiek, *Shepherd of Hermas*, 18–20; Ehrman opts for a period from 110 to 140 CE; *Apostolic Fathers*, 2:169. On prophecy in *Hermas*, see Aune, *Prophecy*, 299–310.

65. Osiek, *Shepherd of Hermas*, 140–41; see also Aune, *Prophecy*, 226–28.

66. Translation from Osiek, *Shepherd of Hermas*, 139.

67. According to Osiek, this criterion "places this discussion firmly within the early Christian tradition of discernment of prophecy," since the criterion appears in other texts from Matt 7:15–23 to the *Acts of Thomas* 79 (*Shepherd of Hermas*, 143–44 and n32). On the *Acts of Thomas* 79, see Aune, *Prophecy*, 228–29.

68. Translation from Ehrman, *Apostolic Fathers*, 2:287.

69. Translation from ibid., 2:287–89.

payment is discussed in more detail than in the *Didache*. The gift of prophecy is either not present or invalidated by practices involving individual consultation and payment. Its proper function is communal, perhaps in a gathering for worship.

There is no explicit mention of female prophets in *Hermas*. In *Mandate* 11, however, a more gender-neutral term (human being) is used for the prophet (ἄνθρωπος), whereas the gender-specific term, men (ἄνδρες), is used for the rest of those who gather in the assembly. The neutral term may be used to allow for the possibility of female prophets.[70]

The letter attributed to Paul's fellow missionary, Barnabas, was probably written during the reign of the emperor Hadrian around 130. The majority view is that it was written in Alexandria.[71] Prophets and prophecy are mentioned frequently in this work, but in most cases the reference is to the writing prophets of Israel. Chapter 16, however, adds a further dimension. It begins with polemic against the Jewish understanding of the temple in Jerusalem. In support of his criticism, the author cites Isa 61:1. After alluding to the destruction of the temple and Hadrian's plan to rebuild it (and to dedicate it to Zeus), the author asks whether "a temple of God still exists" (16:6). In light of Dan 9:24, the answer is affirmative. He then goes on to argue that God dwells "in us," that is, in those who have become a new creation, received forgiveness of sins, and hoped in the name. He then elaborates on how God dwells in us, stating among other things how "he himself (is) prophesying in us . . . For the one who longs to be saved looks not merely to a person but to the one who dwells and speaks in him . . . This is a spiritual temple built for the Lord" (16:8–10).[72] The author here seems to allude to the activity of prophets in his community and interprets this phenomenon as evidence of God's presence in it. No mention is made of female prophets, but there is no polemic against such.

The majority of scholars date the *Martyrdom of Polycarp* to the 150s.[73] In this work, the figure of Polycarp is highly idealized. One important aspect of his portrait is his activity as a prophet.[74] When Polycarp heard that

70. Osiek finds this usage "puzzling" (*Shepherd of Hermas*, 144).

71. Ehrman, *Apostolic Fathers*, 2:7–8. On prophecy in *Barnabas*, see Aune, *Prophecy*, 343–44.

72. Translation from Ehrman, *Apostolic Fathers*, 2:73–75.

73. With the exception of chapter 22 and possibly 21, which are taken as later additions; Ehrman, *Apostolic Fathers*, 1:361–62. Moss, however, argues for the first half of the third century in "Dating of Polycarp." If the work was written in the second century, it was probably composed in western Asia Minor. If it was written later, it is difficult to determine the place of composition.

74. On Polycarp as a prophet, see Aune, *Prophecy*, 196, 402 n27.

he was to be arrested, he wanted to stay in the city (Smyrna), but others persuaded him to go to a small country house. "Three days before he was arrested, while praying, he had a vision and saw his pillow being consumed by fire. Then he turned to those with him and said, 'I must be burned alive'" (5.1–2).[75] Later, when the people discovered that a lion could not be released on him, "they decided to call out in unison for (Philip, the Asiarch) to burn Polycarp alive. For the vision that had been revealed about the pillow had to be fulfilled: for he had seen it burning while he prayed. And when he turned he said prophetically to the faithful who were with him, 'I must be burned alive'" (12:3).[76] Polycarp's vision is a brief one, like those of Amos.[77] In both cases, the vision is presented as something the prophet experienced yet it is someone else who writes it down (Amos 1:1). The visionary element is common to the *Martyrdom of Polycarp* and the book of Revelation, but it is far more elaborate in the latter.

After the account of Polycarp's death, the narrator states that he had been "an apostolic and prophetic teacher . . . For every word that came forth from his mouth was fulfilled and will be fulfilled" (16:2).[78] This passage implies that the prophecy regarding the manner of his death was not the only one communicated by the bishop of Smyrna. The portrayal of Polycarp in this work manifests a great respect for prophecy, although this gift is explicitly attributed only to a particular leader who is also a bishop and teacher.

Although Justin Martyr presents his work, *Dialogue with Trypho the Jew*, as an account of a discussion he had with Trypho in 135 CE, it was probably written about 160 CE in Rome.[79] After a discussion of the reign of Christ for a thousand years, Justin states, "For the prophetical gifts remain with us, even to the present time. And hence you ought to understand that [the gifts] formerly among your nation have been transferred to us" (82).[80] He goes on to say that, just as there were false prophets at the same time as the holy prophets of Israel, so in his own time there are false prophets. The Lord (Jesus) predicted that false prophets would arise and warned against them, so that "if you know certain amongst us to be of this sort, do not for their sakes blaspheme the Scriptures and Christ" (ibid.). These remarks show that prophecy was widespread among "the friends of Christ" in the

---

75. Translation from Ehrman, *Apostolic Fathers*, 1:373.
76. Ibid., 1:385.
77. Amos 7:1–3, 4–6, 7–9; 8:1–3; 9:1–4.
78. Ehrman, *Apostolic Fathers*, 1:391.
79. Chadwick, *Early Church*, 75.
80. Translation by Roberts and Donaldson, *ANF*, 1:240.

mid-second century.[81] It is not clear whether Justin refers only to (prophet-ic) writers, like the author of Revelation, or to prophets who delivered their oracles orally in local communities. What he says does not seem to rule out the latter type.

The *Ascension of Isaiah* is a work with both Jewish and Christian fea-tures that has a complicated literary history.[82] It was written (or compiled) in the second half of the second century; the place of writing is unknown.[83] Some scholars, however, date it to the first half of that century. It is osten-sibly about the prophet Isaiah and "many of the faithful" who also became prophets and lived with him "on the mountains and in the hills."[84] This group of prophets was opposed by a group of false prophets led by Belchira and Ahaziah.[85] Some interpreters have seen the description of this situa-tion as a reflection of the actual situation of the author and his community: they were prophets who were opposed by people they considered to be false prophets. It is difficult, however, to connect the literary description with evidence for any particular social group in the second century.

An important phenomenon in this work is "the ascension to heaven" (2.9). The ascension of Isaiah to heaven and his return is described in detail in chapters 6–11. A summary of it occurs earlier in the work:

> And [Hezekiah, king of Judah] delivered to [Manasseh his son] the recorded words that Sebna, the scribe, had written and that which Isaiah the son of Amoz had given to [Hezekiah] together with the prophets, that they might write down and store with [Hezekiah] what [Isaiah] himself had seen in the king's house concerning the judgment of the angels and the destruction of this world, concerning the garments of the righteous, and con-cerning the going forth, the transformation, the persecution, and the ascension of the Beloved (Christ).[86]

The type of experience Isaiah had is specified to some degree in another passage:

> And while [Isaiah] was speaking by the Holy Spirit in the hear-ing of all, he [suddenly] became silent and his consciousness was taken from him, and he saw no [more] the men who were

81. The term "friends of Christ" occurs in chapter 8 (*ANF*, 1:198).

82. Müller, "The Ascension of Isaiah," 603–5.

83. Ibid.

84. *Ascension of Isaiah* 2.7–11; Müller, "The Ascension of Isaiah," 606–7.

85. *Asc. Isa.* 2.12—3.12; Müller, 607–8.

86. *Asc. Isa.* 1.5; translation (slightly modified) from Müller, 605–6. All brackets and parentheses are mine.

standing before him: his eyes were open, but his mouth was silent and the consciousness of his body was taken from him; but his breath was [still] in him, for he saw a vision. And the angel who was sent to make him behold it belonged neither to this firmament nor to the angels of the glory of this world but had come from the seventh heaven. And the people standing around, with the exception of the circle of prophets, did (not) think that the holy Isaiah had been taken up.[87]

The extensive vision or ascent in this work may be a speculative exegesis and expansion of the vision the prophet recounts in Isaiah 6. As in the book of Revelation, a figure identified as a prophet is portrayed as one who receives extensive visual revelation, as well as the auditory kind. Furthermore, Paul claims that he ascended to the third heaven in 2 Cor 12:1–10. An ascent was also attributed to Theodotus, the first financial officer of the New Prophecy.[88] Eusebius's anonymous source made the following claim:

> So also general report says that a certain Theodotus, that remarkable man, the first steward as it were of their alleged prophecy, was sometimes taken up and raised to Heaven, when he fell into a trance and trusted himself to the spirit of deceit, but was hurled down and died miserably. They say, at least, that this happened thus.[89]

The story repeated here may be a polemical elaboration of a report that Theodotus experienced ascents analogous to those of Paul and the character Isaiah in the *Ascension of Isaiah*.

Like Justin Martyr, Irenaeus, a native of Asia Minor who eventually became bishop of Lyons, also commented on prophecy during his time, the second half of the second century. Eusebius, writing in the fourth century, gives some information about the context in which Irenaeus wrote. In book five of his *Ecclesiastical History*, Eusebius describes a persecution that arose under the emperor Antoninus Verus (Marcus Aurelius) in the seventeenth year of his reign (177 CE).[90] Around the same time, according to Eusebius:

> The party of Montanus, and Alcibiades, and Theodotus of Phrygia began first to engender among many their views concerning prophecy (for the many wonderful works of the grace of God

87. *Asc. Isa.* 6.10–14; translation (modified) from Müller, 611. All brackets and parentheses are original except "[Isaiah]," which is mine.

88. Trevett, *Montanism*, 87; see also 48, 159.

89. Eusebius, *Eccl. Hist.* 5.16.14; Lake, *Eusebius*, 1.479. Cf. Heine, *Montanist Oracles and Testimonia*, 19.

90. Eusebius, *Eccl. Hist.* 5.preface.1.

that were still being wrought up to that time in various churches produced the belief among many that they also were prophets), and when dissension arose about the persons mentioned the brethren in Gaul again formulated their own judgment, pious and most orthodox, concerning them (5.3.4).[91]

This judgment was committed to writing in letters that "the brethren in Gaul" sent to "the brethren in Asia and Phrygia, and also for Eleutherus, who was then bishop of the Romans" (ibid.). At that time, Eusebius says, Irenaeus was a presbyter in Lyons (in Gaul) and was commissioned to take the letter to the bishop of Rome (*Eccl. Hist.* 5.4.1–2).

The bishop of Lyons, Pothinus, died in prison in that persecution (5.1.29–31). Irenaeus became his successor (5.5.8). During the peace that followed, Irenaeus wrote his best known work, *Refutation and Overthrow of Knowledge falsely so-called* (5.7.1), often referred to with the shorter title, *Against Heresies* (written around 180 CE). He seems to refer in the following quotation to some opponents of the movement Eusebius connects with Montanus and others.

> (Since the gospel has four forms,) all who destroy the form of the Gospel are vain, unlearned, and also audacious; those, [I mean,] who represent the aspects of the Gospel as being either more in number . . . or fewer . . . Others . . . (reduce the number of the Gospels), that they may nullify the gift of the Spirit, which in the latter times has been, by the good pleasure of the Father, poured out upon the human race, (and) do not admit that *aspect* (of the fourfold Gospel) presented by John's Gospel, in which the Lord promised that He would send the Paraclete (John 14:16 etc.); but set aside at once both the Gospel and the prophetic Spirit (3.11.9).[92]

The leaders of the movement connected with Montanus spoke about their "new prophecy" as a fulfillment of the promise of Jesus to send the Paraclete after his resurrection.[93] Thus, the statement of Irenaeus is not, as the parenthetical addition (omitted above) in the translation in the *Ante-Nicene Fathers* implies, criticizing the Montanists but rather their over-zealous opponents.[94] Irenaeus emerges as a defender of the "new prophecy" as a surge in the presence of a gift that has been given to the followers of Jesus since the beginning. This conclusion fits with the remark of Henry Chadwick,

91. Translation (modified) by Lake, 1:443.

92. Translation (modified) by Roberts and Donaldson, *ANF*, 1:429.

93. See the discussion in Seim, "Johannine Echoes," 348–57, esp. 356–57.

94. Ibid., 351–52.

"Irenaeus is the last writer who can still think of himself as belonging to the eschatological age of miracle and revelation."[95]

In another passage, Irenaeus attacks certain claims regarding prophecy.[96] The context is an attack on a certain Mark, a Valentinian teacher whom Irenaeus labels a "heretic" (1.13.1). Irenaeus opines, "It appears probable enough that this man possesses a demon as his familiar spirit, by means of whom he is able to prophesy" and to enable his disciples to prophesy as well.[97] He goes on to say that Mark "devotes himself especially to women," particularly to those who are "well-bred" and wealthy.

Irenaeus recounts a story according to which Mark encourages a certain woman to prophesy. When she replies, "I have never at any time prophesied, nor do I know how to prophesy," Mark tells her, "Open your mouth, speak whatever occurs to you, and you will prophesy."[98] When the woman then thinks herself a prophet, she rewards Mark with both her wealth and her person.[99]

As John rejects the prophet Jezebel, Irenaeus rejects the women who prophesied as followers of Mark, a man he considered to be a heretic. These passages do not necessarily imply that John and Irenaeus rejected female prophets in principle. They do show, however, an emerging tendency on the part of some to direct polemic against movements they consider unacceptable by focusing on the role of women and maligning them.

The New Prophecy[100]

One of the difficulties in studying this movement is that much of the information we have about it comes from its opponents, including the oracles of the new prophets.[101] The question of the authenticity of their reports is an issue. Some evidence comes directly from those involved in the form

---

95. Chadwick, *Early Church*, 53.

96. Irenaeus *Against Heresies* 1.13. For a Greek text, German translation, source analysis, and historical assessment, see Förster, *Kult, Lehre, und Gemeindeleben*, 91–126.

97. 1.13.3; translation from Roberts and Donaldson, *ANF*, 1:334.

98. Ibid.

99. Ibid.; trans. Roberts and Donaldson, 1:335.

100. I am grateful to Olivia Stewart for making her seminar paper "Montanism/New Prophecy" (2011) available to me. It was helpful in orienting myself to studies on this movement.

101. On the oracles, see Groh, "Utterance and Exegesis," 76, 78–86, 90–92; Trevett, *Montanism*, 80–86, 163–70; Heine, *Montanist Oracles and Testimonia*, 1–9.

of inscriptions.[102] A problem here is deciding which inscriptions were produced by supporters of the New Prophecy. Tertullian is also an important witness.[103] He does not, however, "represent the earliest phase of the movement," was not acquainted personally with the founding figures, and we must take into account that his evidence is shaped by his own ideological and rhetorical emphases.[104]

It is likely that the movement in question began in the mid-160s CE.[105] I call it "new prophecy" because its adherents were not called *Montanoi* (Montanists) until the fourth century. Cyril, bishop of Jerusalem, used this term. He also called them "Cataphrygians," that is, "those who are like the Phrygians."[106] In the same century, Jerome's statement that Montanus was "castrated and emasculated" may not indicate, as some have suggested, that he was a priest of Cybele (the Galli of Phrygia) before becoming Christian.[107] Jerome may simply make explicit what was implied by the pejorative name "Cataphrygians." Didymus the Blind of Alexandria referred to "the error of the Montanists (Μοντανιστῶν ἡ πλάνη)."[108] Members of the movement seem to have called it simply "prophecy" or the "new prophecy."

Eusebius quotes an anonymous source written against the phenomenon. This Anonymous writes, "When I was recently in Ancyra of Galatia, I learned that the church in that place was deafened by the noise of, not as they say, this new prophecy, but rather, as will be shown, (this new) false prophecy" (*Eccl. Hist.* 5.16.4).[109] Eusebius also quotes Serapion on the same topic, who was bishop of Antioch from about 190–211 CE. He refers to "the so-called new prophecy" (*Eccl. Hist.* 5.19.2).[110] Clement of Alexandria,

102. Tabbernee, *Montanist Inscriptions*; Trevett, *Montanism*, 198–214.

103. Trevett, *Montanism*, 72–73; Nasrallah, *"Ecstasy of Folly,"* 100.

104. Cf. Marjanen, "Montanism," 188; Groh, "Utterance and Exegesis," 89.

105. Seim, "Johannine Echoes," 346. Powell prefers a date of 172 ("Tertullianists and Cataphrygians," 41). For discussion see Trevett, *Montanism*, 26–45; she argues for the 160s.

106. Cyril of Jerusalem, *Catechetical Letters* 16.8; see the translation by Gifford in *Nicene and Post-Nicene Fathers*, 7:117. Cf. Eusebius *Eccl. Hist.* 5.25.6–7 (ἡ κατὰ Φρύγας γνώμη); 5.16.1 and 5.18.1 (ἡ λεγομένη κατὰ Φρύγας αἵρεσις).

107. Jerome, *Letters* 41.4; cited by Marjanen, who cites W. H. C. Frend as inferring the Gallic priesthood of Montanus ("Montanism," 189 and n14). For an English translation of the letter, see *Nicene and Post-Nicene Fathers*, 6:55–56.

108. Didymus, *De trinitate* 3.41; cited by Powell, "Tertullianists and Cataphrygians," 40 n39. For a range of names used by outsiders to describe the movement over the centuries, see Trevett, *Montanism*, 2.

109. My translation; for the Greek text and another translation, see Lake, *Eusebius*, 1.472–73.

110. Ἡ ἐπικαλουμένη νέα προφητεία. Text and translation from ibid., 1:493.

who died in about 215 CE, writes, "The Phrygians . . . now call those who do not apply themselves to the new prophecy 'natural people'" (*psychikoi*) (*Stromata = Miscellanies* 4.13).[111]

Of great importance and interest for our purposes is that two of the three leading prophets at the beginning of the movement were women: Priscilla and Maximilla. The third was a man named Montanus. Eusebius uses another source, written by Apollonius forty years after Montanus began to prophesy.[112] Apollonius says that Priscilla and Maximilla "left their husbands the moment they were filled with the spirit."[113] This remark calls to mind the apocryphal acts, which depict women converted by an apostle leaving their fiancés or husbands and adopting a life of sexual continence. The Acts of Paul is one of these, written in the second half of the second century. In chapter three, called the "Acts of Paul and Thecla," Paul's opening sermon contains beatitudes blessing those "who have kept the flesh pure," "the continent," and "the bodies of the virgins." Thecla hears Paul's speech and from that moment onward refuses even to speak to her fiancé Thamyris.[114] The Acts of Andrew also date from the second half of the second century. The ancient Latin version contained a narrative about how a proconsul's wife, who happens to be named Maximilla, "has resolved upon continence, which arouses the wrath of her husband against the apostle."[115] The Acts of John may have been composed in the first half of the third century, but they contain older material.[116] In one of the older parts of this work, the story of Drusiana and Andronicus is told. Drusiana is converted, devotes herself to sexual continence, and thus refuses to have further relations with her husband, Andronicus. He puts her in a large tomb, giving her the choice whether to return to relations with him or die. She chooses death and is delivered by a miracle. In the meantime, Andronicus is converted and devotes himself to chastity also. They live from then on as brother and sister.[117]

---

111. Translation (modified) from *Ante-Nicene Fathers*, 2:426.

112. Heine, *Montanist Oracles and Testimonia*, 22–27 (section 24). See section 12 regarding the date when Apollonius wrote (pp. 24–25). This testimonium is taken from Eusebius, *Eccl. Hist.* 5.18.

113. Heine, *Montanist Oracles and Testimonia*, 22–23 (section 3). Marjanen takes this information as reliable and infers that either they divorced their husbands or their husbands divorced them ("Montanism," 189). Another possibility is that Montanus annulled their marriages; see Trevett, *Montanism*, 109–10.

114. Schneemelcher and Kasser, "The Acts of Paul," 239–40.

115. Schneemelcher, "Texts," 122. See also the more detailed account, 129–32.

116. Schäferdieck, "The Acts of John," 166–67.

117. Ibid., 178–79.

The tradition that the prophets Maximilla and Priscilla left their husbands also calls to mind Philo's discussion of Moses in his role as prophet:

> But first he had to be clean, as in soul so also in body, to have no dealings with any passion, purifying himself from all the calls of mortal nature, food and drink and intercourse with women. This last he had disdained for many a day, almost from the time when, possessed by the spirit, he entered on his work as a prophet, since he held it to be fitting to hold himself always in readiness to receive the oracular messages.[118]

Given that asceticism was valued highly in some circles in the second century, it may be that ascetic practices involving sexual continence seemed especially appropriate for prophets.

After mentioning that "these first female prophets" had left their husbands, Apollonius asks, "Did they not lie, then, when they called Priscilla a virgin?"[119] The acclamation of Priscilla as a virgin, however, was not necessarily intended in the sense of being intact, of never having had sexual relations. It could have been used to praise her consistent sexual continence after separating from her husband.[120]

There is evidence that the New Prophets claimed to stand in a succession of prophets.[121] Eusebius states that the Anonymous he quotes includes "a catalogue of those who have been prophets of the New Covenant, and among them numbers a certain Ammia and Quadratus."[122] Ammia was a female prophet recognized by both catholics and New Prophets.[123] She was from the city of Philadelphia in the region of Lydia in western Asia Minor.[124] It became part of the Roman province of Asia in the second century BCE.[125] It was not far from the region of Phrygia, the cradle and center of the New Prophecy. The Anonymous gives evidence in his polemic against them that the New Prophets considered themselves to stand in a succession

---

118. Philo, *On the Life of Moses* 2.68–69; translation from Colson, *Philo*, 6.483.

119. Heine, *Montanist Oracles and Testimonia*, 22–23 (section 24.3).

120. Cf. Marjanen, "Montanism," 189.

121. As Trevett has pointed out (*Montanism*, 33), Josephus attests to the notion of a "succession of the prophets" in the history of his people; Josephus, *Against Apion* 1.8 §41; translation from Thackeray, *Josephus*, 1.179.

122. Eusebius, *Eccl. Hist.* 5.17.2; translation (modified) from Lake, *Eusebius*, 1.485.

123. Trevett, *Montanism*, 34. I follow Trevett in using the term "catholic" to refer to the writers who opposed the New Prophecy, the Gnostics, and others and labeled them as "heretics." Quadratus was also cited by Eusebius as a prophet; *Eccl. Hist.* 3.37.1; Lake, 1.287; Trevett, *Montanism*, 34.

124. Eusebius, *Eccl. Hist.* 5.17.3.

125. Calder et al., "Asia," 189.

including Agabus, Judas, Silas, and the daughters of Philip.[126] He explicitly refers to "the women around Montanus" as claiming to succeed Ammia and Quadratus.[127]

It is likely that Paul and his letters influenced the New Prophets.[128] An oracle attributed to Maximilla states, "I am driven away like a wolf from the sheep. I am not a wolf, I am word ($\dot{\rho}\tilde{\eta}\mu\alpha$) and spirit and power."[129] The first part of this oracle echoes John 10:12. The second part alludes to 1 Cor 2:4, where Paul states, "And my word ($\lambda\dot{o}\gamma o\varsigma$) and my proclamation (were not expressed) in persuasive words of wisdom but with a demonstration of spirit and power."[130] Maximilla here does not merely claim to be a legitimate prophet on the basis of Paul's acceptance of female prophets in Corinth in 1 Corinthians 11. Rather she claims to be a vessel of divine power just as Paul was.[131]

This claim was not widely accepted. Instead opposition to the New Prophets emerged from various catholic circles, although the former had a good deal of support in Carthage, including the otherwise catholic Tertullian. The New Prophecy also had at least qualified support from the Christians in Gaul, including Irenaeus, as suggested above.[132] Several reasons have been identified for the emergence of opposition. One issue is what Dennis Groh referred to as the "scandalous immediacy" of the revelations received by the New Prophets. For example, they claimed that God the Father spoke through them without intermediaries. For some, this was a scandalous bypassing of Christ.[133] It appears, however, that they interpreted their prophecy as a fulfillment of the promises of Jesus in the Gospel of John to send the Paraclete (the Holy Spirit) after his departure. In this way they

126. Regarding these prophets, see the discussion of Acts above.

127. Eusebius, *Eccl. Hist.* 5.17.4; my translation.

128. The interpretation of Paul was a major factor in the debate between "Montanists" and their opponents in the fourth century. See Trevett, *Montanism*, 131–32; Heine, *Montanist Oracles and Testimonia*, testimony #89, "Debate of a Montanist and an Orthodox Christian," 112–27.

129. Quoted by Eusebius from this anonymous source; *Eccl. Hist.* 5.16.17; translation from Lake, *Eusebius*, 1:481. Heine regards this oracle as authentic; *Montanist Oracles and Testimonia*, 2–3 (oracle 5).

130. Or "but in proofs involving spirit and power."

131. On the allusion to 1 Cor 2:4 in this oracle, see Groh, "Utterance and Exegesis," 78–79. For another (set of) allusion(s) to Paul on the part of Maximilla, see Trevett, *Montanism*, 164.

132. On the attitude of Eleutherus, bishop in Rome from 174–189 CE, who received a letter from Gaul brought by Irenaeus, see Trevett, *Montanism*, 56. On early supporters of the New Prophecy, see Marjanen, "Montanism," 192–93.

133. Groh, "Utterance and Exegesis," 90–91.

legitimated the novelty of their Prophecy.[134] In any case, they could have appealed to Acts 13:1–2, where the narrator refers to prophets in Antioch and then says, "While they were serving the Lord (in worship) and fasting, the Holy Spirit said, 'Appoint for me Barnabas and Saul to the work for which I have called them.'"

Another disputed point was what types of ecstasy are legitimate and which are not.[135] Philo defined four kinds of ecstasy, the latter two being of most interest here. His prototypical example of the third type comes from the story of God's creation of Eve from a rib of Adam. In this account, "God 'cast,' [Moses] says, 'an ecstasy on Adam and he slept' (Gen. ii. 21). Here by ecstasy he means passivity and tranquility of mind. For sleep of mind is waking of sense, since waking of the understanding is inaction of sense."[136] He seems to be making the (allegorical) point that "sense perception must be shunted off in order for clarity of mind to be achieved, even if the result paradoxically appears to be madness, strange behavior, or disconnection from one's environment."[137] As noted above in the section on Jewish prophecy, the fourth type is one in which the human mind is replaced by the divine spirit. It is clear that Philo presents the fourth type as the highest and best.[138]

One of the oracles of Montanus suggests that he used the passage about the sleep cast on Adam as a prototype of his own ecstasy and thus to legitimate it.[139] The author of the anti-Phrygian source used by Epiphanius could not deny that Adam experienced ecstasy, since the term is explicitly used in the Greek version of Genesis.[140] He defined Adam's experience, however, as an "ecstasy of sleep" and not an "ecstasy of wits and judgment." This ecstasy of sleep is not the kind Philo discussed. Rather, it was "a kind of divine anesthetic administered out of God's love for Adam, so that he would not feel pain."[141] Besides this unique event, the author of the Anti-Phrygian source

---

134. Marjanen, "Montanism," 198–99; Seim, "Johannine Echoes," 356–57.

135. Marjanen, "Montanism," 197; cf. Aune, *Prophecy*, 19–21.

136. Philo, *Who Is the Heir* 257; translation from Colson, *Philo*, 4:415.

137. Nasrallah, *"Ecstasy of Folly,"* 40.

138. Philo, *Who Is the Heir* 265; trans. Colson, 4:19; for discussion see Nasrallah, *"Ecstasy of Folly,"* 40–44.

139. Heine, *Montanist Oracles and Testimonia*, 3 (oracle #3). The oracle is cited and discussed, along with the Anti-Phyrgian source and Tertullian, by Groh ("Utterance and Exegesis," 84–87).

140. The term "Anti-Phrygian source" comes from Nasrallah, *"Ecstasy of Folly,"* 4, 155–96. This source is reconstructed from Epiphanius, *Panarion haer. (Medicine Box for curing heresies)* 48. Groh dates this source to about 200 CE ("Utterance and Exegesis," 80). Nasrallah defines it as *Panarion* 48.1.4–13.8 and also dates it to the late second or early third century (*"Ecstasy of Folly,"* 167).

141. Nasrallah, *"Ecstasy of Folly,"* 48, discussing Epiphanius, *Medicine Box*, 48.6.3.

admits only two definitions of ecstasy: amazement and madness. He thus implies that the ecstasy of the New Prophets is madness, "an ecstasy of folly."[142]

Another tactic of the opponents of the New Prophecy was to claim that the Prophets were inspired by Satan or demons rather than by the Spirit of God. As noted above in the section on Paul, he spoke, virtually in one breath, of "prophecy" and "distinguishing of spirits" (1 Cor 12:10). Paul, however, set the bar rather low: "No one speaking in a spirit of God says, 'Let Jesus be cursed,' and no one can say 'Jesus is Lord' except in a holy spirit" (12:3). By that criterion, the New Prophets qualify as speaking in a holy spirit.

The author of the anonymous source used by Eusebius, however, states that, because of his "unbounded lust" for leadership, Montanus "gave access to himself to the adversary," that is, to Satan. Under the influence of Satan, or a demon or spirit sent by him, Montanus prophesied in a way not in keeping with "the tradition and succession of the church from the beginning."[143] The same writer states that the devil "raised up two more women [Priscilla and Maximilla] and filled them with the bastard spirit so that they spoke madly and improperly and strangely, like Montanus."[144] As noted above, it would be hard to make such a case on the basis of 1 Corinthians. 1 Timothy, however, may have emboldened the critics of the Montanists: "Now the Spirit says explicitly that in later times some will fall away from the faith, giving heed to spirits that lead (them) astray and to teachings of demons" (1 Tim 4:1).

The accusation of demonic possession led to attempts to examine, test, and refute the spirits by means of which *the female* New Prophets prophesied.[145] Such attempts seem to have been efforts to exorcise those spirits. The anonymous writer quoted by Eusebius says that "eminent men and bishops" tried to refute "the spirit that speaks through Maximilla."[146] Trevett describes this process as "war: male against female; prophet against prophet; cleric

Cf. Heine, *Montanist Oracles and Testimonia*, 37.

142. Nasrallah, *"Ecstasy of Folly,"* 48–50. See also Marjanen, "Montanism," 196–97; Trevett, *Montanism*, 86–89.

143. Eusebius, *Eccl. Hist.* 5.16.7; translation from Lake, *Eusebius*, 1:475. Cf. the translations by Marjanen, "Montanism," 196; and Heine, *Montanist Oracles and Testimonia*, 15–17.

144. Eusebius, *Eccl. Hist.* 5.16.9; Lake, *Eusebius*, 1:477.

145. Trevett notes that there is no evidence that the catholics attempted to exorcise an allegedly demonic spirit from a male New Prophet; *Montanism,* 156.

146. Eusebius, *Eccl. Hist.* 5.16.16; Lake, *Eusebius*, 1:481. See also the reference to this event by Apollonius, cited by Eusebius, *Eccl. Hist.* 5.18.13; Heine, *Montanist Oracles and Testimonia*, 24–25. As noted above, Apollonius wrote "forty years after Montanus took it upon himself to prophesy," that is, between about 196 to 212 CE; Trevett, *Montanism*, 30–31.

against laywoman."[147] She is right to say that in this and similar cases, "Exorcism here should be seen not least as an attempt at social control."[148] In the case of Maximilla, the attempt failed because of the support of her allies.[149]

An accusation lodged against another female prophet, Priscilla, is that she accepted gifts and money. After declaring that calling Priscilla a virgin is a lie, Apollonius goes on: "Does not all Scripture seem to you to forbid a prophet from receiving gifts and money? Therefore when I see that the prophetess [presumably Priscilla] has received gold and silver and expensive clothes, how should I refrain from blaming her?"[150] In a related passage, Apollonius cites sayings of the Lord in support of his view, "For the Lord said, 'Procure for yourselves neither gold nor silver nor two coats.'"[151]

In response to such criticism it may be said first of all that the *Didache* prohibited prophets from *asking* for money, especially "in the Spirit" (11:6, 12). Secondly, the *Shepherd of Hermas* forbade prophets from taking money for private consultations (*Mandate* 11.2, 12). Another point is that Paul accepted money from the Philippians (Phil 4:10–20). He also wrote, "The Lord ordered those who proclaim the gospel to have their livelihood from the gospel" (1 Cor 9:14). The Lukan Jesus told the seventy, "Stay in that house eating and drinking what they have, for the worker is worthy of his remuneration" (Luke 10:7). As we have seen, the *Didache* expanded this teaching by instructing the audience, not only to provide hospitality to prophets and apostles, but also to give the true prophets who settled among them the first portions of the wine vat, the threshing floor, cattle, and sheep, "for they are your high priests" (*Didache* 11:3–5; 13:3). So it may be that Priscilla and other New Prophets accepted free-will offerings from their supporters. Such a practice is of course open to abuse, but it is difficult to tell whether Apollonius' reports are accurate or exaggerated.[152]

It seems then that the early leaders of the New Prophecy were no different from the catholics in their beliefs and teachings.[153] Tensions seem to have arisen over discipline and Scripture. The points of disagreement with regard to discipline were fasting, marriage versus sexual continence, and the withholding of forgiveness. The New Prophets advocated prolonging

---

147. Trevett, *Montanism*, 156.

148. Ibid., 157.

149. Cf. Marjanen, "Montanism," 199.

150. Eusebius, *Eccl. Hist.* 5.18.4; Lake, *Eusebius*, 1:487–89.

151. Ibid., 5.18.7; Lake, *Eusebius*, 1:489. Apollonius alludes to Matt 10:9–10 (Lake's translation modified). Cf. Heine, *Montanist Oracles and Testimonia*, 25.

152. Cf. Trevett, *Montanism*, 48–49, 153–54, 155.

153. Ibid., 155; Marjanen, "Montanism," 194–95.

certain fixed times for Christian fasting and introduced two weeks of dry fasting, during which "succulent foods, wine, and juicy fruits" were to be avoided. The problems seem to have been innovation and making the new practices obligatory, thus "calling into question catholic clergy's discretion" in making the rules. Finally, it may have been off-putting that this allegedly pseudo-prophetic group exercised a discipline stricter than that of the catholics.[154]

With regard to sexual practices, the New Prophets seem to have favored celibacy over marriage, which of course was Paul's position.[155] Furthermore, they "outlawed" second marriages from the beginning of the movement.[156] So what Paul had presented as a personal preference became, in the discipline of the New Prophecy, "a ruling of the Paraclete."[157] Here again the problem was making a previously optional practice obligatory in a way that seemed to challenge the authority of the catholic clergy.

With regard to forgiveness, the New Prophets tended toward rigor. As Christine Trevett has put it, "It seems that the earliest church of the Prophecy and its confessors/martyrs possessed the power of the keys but that their tendency (in line with the Spirit's instructions?) was to bind."[158] There were differences of opinion in the late second century on whether those who lapsed during persecution should be forgiven or not. Such disagreement led to schism in the fourth century after the persecution of Diocletian.[159]

With regard to Scripture, the issue was interpretation. The New Prophets and the catholics appealed to the same writings but understood their significance differently. On the one hand, the New Prophets, judging from Tertullian's view, argued that the Paraclete "*illuminated and interpreted* Scripture." On the other, the catholics doubted that "*any* prophets who postdated the apostles" could be recognized.[160] In an important sense, it was the New Prophets who were conservative, and the catholics who were innovating on this point. To a great extent, the works growing in pre-eminence, the letters of Paul, the Gospels, and the book of Revelation, were prophetic and apocalyptic in character. The New Prophets read them as such and updated

154. Trevett, *Montanism*, 108–9.

155. 1 Cor 7:7. But the Paul of 1 Timothy virtually required marriage; see Yarbro Collins, "The Female Body," 157–58, 160, 163–64. On the tendency toward celibacy among the New Prophets and in their environment, see Trevett, *Montanism*, 111–12.

156. Trevett, *Montanism*, 113.

157. Ibid., 114.

158. Ibid., 118.

159. On the conflict between the Donatists and the catholics, see Shaw, *Sacred Violence*. Cf. Trevett, *Montanism*, 116–19.

160. Trevett, *Montanism*, 133.

and applied them. The catholics, in contrast, used them to defend order and authority. As Christine Trevett has suggested, the catholics "feared the possible triumph of a view of those texts that could resurrect an already partly buried history. In short, [they] feared a prophetic-apocalyptic tradition deemed now not to meet the needs of the Christian in the world as it was."[161]

It seems then that the catholics did not oppose women prophets because they were women but attacked the female prophets as particularly threatening targets in a larger project.[162] In the debate over the New Prophecy two Christian sub-cultures came into conflict. The catholics emphasized apostolic succession in the sense that later, legitimate leaders preserved the deposit of faith as the legacy of the apostles. That body of tradition played a role in their project of creating a third category of humanity in the world: a new, Christian culture.[163] Writers like Justin Martyr, Clement of Alexandria, Origen, and Augustine took and adapted the best from their cultural environment. They were also interested in demonstrating to outsiders that Christian faith and practice were reasonable and honorable. These goals were associated with respectable behavior, for example, that women conform to cultural norms formulated by elite men. In their view, order and hierarchical authority would facilitate the achievement of these goals.

The New Prophecy, in contrast, emphasized the apostolic and prophetic succession as an ongoing manifestation of spiritual gifts.[164] It was in that context that they adapted the traditions of prophecy and apocalypticism. Their ideas and way of life seem related to passages like Rom 12:2, "Do not be conformed to this world (or age), but be transformed by the renewal of your minds, so that you may approve what is the will of God, what is good and pleasing and perfect"; John 17:14, "I have given them your word, and the world hates them because they are not of the world, just as I am not of the world"; Rev 18:4, "Come out from her, my people, so that you may not be associated with her sins and not receive any of her plagues." They were not interested in assimilation, adaptation, or apologetics. They aspired to be conformed to the divine world and to live a disciplined life in accordance with a high moral standard.

161. Ibid., 135. I have slightly altered her wording.

162. Ibid., 196.

163. Buell, *Making Christians* and *Why This New Race*; and for the later period, Cameron, *Christianity and the Rhetoric of Empire*.

164. On the tensions regarding apostolic and prophetic succession, see Trevett, *Montanism*, 136–37.

Conclusion

As we have seen, prophecy, including women prophets, was prominent during the first and early second century in the movement that called upon the name of Jesus, as attested by Paul's first letter to the Corinthians, the Gospels, the book of Revelation, and canonical Acts. Some second-century texts attest to the continuing practice of prophecy and the social role of Christian prophets, although the activity of women prophets is not evident, texts such as the *Didache*, the *Shepherd of Hermas*, the *Epistle of Barnabas*, and Justin Martyr's *Dialogue with Trypho*. Although the author of the book of Revelation and Irenaeus criticize certain female prophets, either because of their teaching or association with men deemed to be heretics, they do not condemn the activity of women prophets in principle.

The movement of the New Prophecy, which emerged in the 160s, changes this pattern dramatically. Highly gifted and influential women prophets burst on the scene along with male prophets, such as Montanus. In the early responses to this movement, its opponents are not able to point to intrinsically heretical teachings, only to innovations that are unacceptable to them. A new criterion for discerning false prophecy emerges in this debate, namely, that ecstasy itself becomes a sign that the possessing spirit is not of God but of Satan. This happens in spite of the long association of ecstasy with Israelite and early Christian prophecy.

Bibliography

Aune, David E. "Prophecy." In *Dictionary of Early Judaism*, edited by John J. Collins and Daniel C. Harlow, 1099–101. Grand Rapids: Eerdmans, 2010.

———. *Prophecy in Early Christianity and the Ancient Mediterranean World*. Grand Rapids: Eerdmans, 1983.

Blenkinsopp, Joseph. *A History of Prophecy in Israel*. Rev. ed. Louisville: Westminster John Knox, 1983.

Buell, Denise Kimber. *Making Christians: Clement of Alexandria and the Rhetoric of Legitimacy*. Princeton: Princeton University Press, 1999.

———. *Why This New Race: Ethnic Reasoning in Early Christianity*. New York: Columbia University Press, 2005.

Calder, William M., et al. "Asia, Roman Province." In *The Oxford Classical Dictionary*, edited by Simon Hornblower and Antony Spawforth, 189–90. 3rd ed. New York: Oxford University Press, 1999.

Cameron, Averil. *Christianity and the Rhetoric of Empire: The Development of Christian Discourse*. Berkeley: University of California Press, 1991.

Chadwick, Henry. *The Early Church*. Baltimore: Penguin, 1967.

Clement of Alexandria. *The Stromata, or Miscellanies*. Translated by Alexander Roberts, James Donaldson, and W. L. Alexander. In *The Ante-Nicene Fathers: The Fathers of the Second Century. Hermas, Tatian, Athenagoras, Theophilus, and Clement of Alexandria (entire)*, 2:299–568. Grand Rapids: Eerdmans, 1986.

Conzelmann, Hans. *1 Corinthians: A Commentary on the First Epistle to the Corinthians*. Translated by James Leitch. Hermeneia. Philadelphia: Fortress, 1975.

Cyril of Jerusalem. *Catechetical Lectures*. Translated by Edward H. Gifford. *Nicene and Post-Nicene Fathers of the Christian Church*, edited by Philip Schaff and Henry Wace, 7:1–157. 1890–1900. Reprint, Grand Rapids: Eerdmans, 1983.

Dibelius, Martin, and Hans Conzelmann. *The Pastoral Epistles*. Translated by Philip Buttolph and Adela Yarbro. Hermeneia. Philadelphia: Fortress, 1972.

Dobbeler, Axel von. *Der Evangelist Philippus in der Geschichte des Urchristentums: Eine prosopographische Skizze*. Texte und Arbeiten zum neutestamentlichen Zeitalter 30. Tübingen: Franke, 2000.

Ehrman, Bart D. *The Apostolic Fathers*. 2 vols. LCL 24–25. Cambridge: Harvard University Press, 2003.

Eusebius. *The Ecclesiastical History*. 2 vols. Translated by Kirsopp Lake. LCL. Cambridge: Harvard University Press, 1926.

Fitzmyer, Joseph A. *The Acts of the Apostles: A New Translation with Introduction and Commentary*. AB 31. New York: Doubleday, 1998.

———. *First Corinthians: A New Translation with Introduction and Commentary*. AB 32. New Haven: Yale University Press, 2008.

———. *The Gospel according to Luke I–IX*. AB 28. Garden City, NY: Doubleday, 1981.

Förster, Niclas. *Kult, Lehre, und Gemeindeleben einer valentinianischen Gnostikergruppe: Sammlung der Quelle und Kommentar*. WUNT 114. Tübingen: Mohr Siebeck, 1999.

Frenschkowski, Marco. *Offenbarung und Epiphanie*. 2 vols. WUNT 2/79–80. Tübingen: Mohr Siebeck, 1995–1997.

———. "Philippus." In *Biographisch-Bibliographisches Kirchenlexikon*, edited by Friedrich Wilhelm Bautz and Traugott Bautz, 507–10. 1st ed., 1970. Hamm in Westfalen: Bautz, 2013.

Garrett, Susan R. *The Demise of the Devil: Magic and the Demonic in Luke's Writings*. Minneapolis: Fortress, 1989.

Groh, Dennis E. "Utterance and Exegesis: Biblical Interpretation in the Montanist Crisis." In *The Living Text: Essays in Honor of Ernest W. Saunders*, edited by Dennis E. Groh and Robert Jewett, 73–95. Lanham, MD: University Press of America, 1985.

Guttenberger, Gudrun. "Johannes von Thyateira: Zur Perspective des Sehers." In *Studien zur Johannesoffenbarung und ihrer Auslegung: Festschrift für Otto Böcher zum 70. Geburtstag*, edited by Friedrich Wilhelm Horn and Michael Wolter, 160–88. Neukirchen-Vluyn: Neukirchener, 2005.

Heine, Ronald E. *The Montanist Oracles and Testimonia*. Patristic Monograph Series 14. Macon, GA: Mercer University Press, 1989.

Herzer, Jens. "Juden—Christen—Gnostiker: Zur Gegnerproblematik der Pastoralbriefe." *Berliner Theologische Zeitschrift* 25 (2008) 143–68.

Irenaeus. *Against Heresies*. Translated by Alexander Roberts and James Donaldson. *The Ante-Nicene Fathers: The Apostolic Fathers—Justin Martyr—Irenaeus*, edited by Roberts and Donaldson, 1:309–567. American Edition edited by A. Cleveland Cox. Grand Rapids: Eerdmans, 1985.

Jerome. *Letters*. Translated by W. H. Fremantle. *Nicene and Post-Nicene Fathers of the Christian Church*. Second Series. Volume 6, *The Principal Works of Jerome*, edited by Philip Schaff and Henry Wace, 1–295. Grand Rapids: Eerdmans, 1983, reprint of 1890–1900 edition.

Josephus. *Against Apion*. In *Josephus*, translated by H. St. J. Thackeray, 1:161–411. LCL. 1926. Reprint, Cambridge: Harvard University Press, 1976.

Justin Martyr. *Dialogue with Trypho*. Translated by Alexander Roberts and James Donaldson. In *The Ante-Nicene Fathers: The Apostolic Fathers—Justin Martyr—Irenaeus*, edited by Roberts and Donaldson (American Edition edited by A. Cleveland Cox), 1:194–270. Grand Rapids: Eerdmans, 1985.

Liddell, Henry G., Robert Scott, and Henry S. Jones. *A Greek-English Lexicon*. Oxford: Clarendon, 1940.

Marjanen, Antti. "Montanism: Egalitarian, Ecstatic 'New Prophecy.'" In *A Companion to Second Century "Heretics,"* edited by Antti Marjanen and Petri Luomanen, 185–212. Vigiliae Christianae Supplements 76. Leiden: Brill, 2005.

Meier, John P. *The Vision of Matthew: Christ, Church, and Morality in the First Gospel*. Theological Inquiries. New York: Paulist, 1979.

Moss, Candida R. "On the Dating of Polycarp: Rethinking the Place of the *Martyrdom of Polycarp* in the History of Christianity." *Early Christianity* 1.4 (2010) 539–74.

Müller, C. Detlef G. "The Ascension of Isaiah." Translated by R. McL. Wilson. In *New Testament Apocrypha*, edited by Wilhelm Schneemelcher, 2:603–20. Louisville: Westminster John Knox, 1992. (German edition 1989.)

Nasrallah, Laura Salah. *"An Ecstasy of Folly": Prophecy and Authority in Early Christianity*. Harvard Theological Studies 52. Cambridge: Harvard University Press, 2003.

Niederwinner, Kurt. *The Didache: A Commentary*. Translated by Linda M. Maloney. Hermeneia. Minneapolis: Fortress, 1998.

Nissinen, Marti. *Prophets and Prophecy in the Ancient Near East*. Writings from the Ancient World 12. Atlanta: SBL, 2003.

———. "Prophetic Madness: Prophecy and Ecstasy in the Ancient Near East and in Greece." In *Raising up a Faithful Exegete: Essays in Honor of Richard D. Nelson*, edited by K. L. Noll and Brooks Schramm, 3–29. Winona Lake, IN: Eisenbrauns, 2010.

Osiek, Carolyn. *Shepherd of Hermas: A Commentary*. Hermeneia. Minneapolis: Fortress, 1999.

Pervo, Richard I. *Acts: A Commentary*. Hermeneia. Minneapolis: Fortress, 2009.

Philo. *On the Life of Moses*. Translated by F. C. Colson. In *Philo*, 6:273–595. LCL. 1935. Reprint, Cambridge: Harvard University Press, 1984.

———. *Who Is the Heir of Divine Things*. Translated by F. C. Colson. In *Philo*, 4:284–447. LCL. 1932. Reprint, Cambridge: Harvard University Press, 1968.

Powell, Douglas. "Tertullianists and Cataphrygians." *Vigiliae Christianae* 29 (1975) 33–54.

Schäferdieck, Knut. "The Acts of John." Translated by R. McL. Wilson. In *New Testament Apocrypha*, edited by Wilhelm Schneemelcher, 2:152–209. Louisville: Westminster John Knox, 1992. (German edition 1989.)

Schneemelcher, Wilhelm. "Texts." In Jean-Marc Prieur and Wilhelm Schneemelcher, "The Acts of Andrew," 118–51. In *New Testament Apocrypha*, edited by Wilhelm Schneemelcher, 2:101–51. Translated by R. McL. Wilson. Louisville: Westminster John Knox, 1992. (German edition 1989.)

Schneemelcher, Wilhelm, and Rodolphe Kasser. "The Acts of Paul." Translated by R. McL. Wilson. In *New Testament Apocrypha*, edited by Wilhelm Schneemelcher, 2:213–70. Louisville: Westminster John Knox, 1992. (German edition 1989.)

Seim, Turid Karlsen. *The Double Message: Patterns of Gender in Luke–Acts*. T. & T. Clark Academic Paperbacks. Edinburgh: T. & T. Clark, 1994.

———. "Johannine Echoes in Early Montanism." In *The Legacy of John: Second-Century Reception of the Fourth Gospel*, edited by Tuomas Rasimus, 345–64. Novum Testamentum Supplements 132. Leiden: Brill, 2010.

Shaw, Brent D. *Sacred Violence: African Christians and Sectarian Hatred in the Age of Augustine*. Cambridge: Cambridge University Press, 2011.

Stökl, Jonathan. "Female Prophets in the Ancient Near East." In *Prophecy and Prophets in the Ancient Near East: Proceeding of the Oxford Old Testament Seminar*, edited by John Day, 47–61. Library of Hebrew Bible/Old Testament Studies 53. London: T. & T. Clark, 2010.

Tabbernee, William. *Montanist Inscriptions and Testimonia: Epigraphic Sources Illustrating the History of Montanism*. Patristic Monograph 16. Macon, GA: Mercer University Press, 1997.

Trevett, Christine. *Montanism: Gender, Authority, and the New Prophecy*. Cambridge: Cambridge University Press, 1996.

Williamson, Hugh. "Prophetesses in the Hebrew Bible." In *Prophecy and Prophets in the Ancient Israel: Proceedings of the Oxford Old Testament Seminar*, edited by John Day, 65–80. Library of Hebrew Bible/Old Testament Studies 531. New York: T. & T. Clark, 2010.

Wilson, Robert R. "Prophecy and Ecstasy: A Reexamination." *JBL* 98 (1979) 321–37.

Wire, Antoinette Clark. *The Corinthian Women Prophets: A Reconstruction through Paul's Rhetoric*. 1990. Reprint, Eugene, OR: Wipf & Stock, 2003.

Witulski, Thomas. *Johannesoffenbarung und Kaiser Hadrian: Studien zur Datierung der neutestamentlichen Apokalypse*. FRLANT 221. Göttingen: Vandenhoeck & Ruprecht, 2007.

———. *Kaiserkult in Kleinasien: die Entwicklung der kultisch-religiösen Kaiserverehrung in der römischen Provinz Asia von Augustus bis Antoninus Pius*. Novum Testamentum et orbis antiquus: Studien zur Umwelt des Neuen Testaments 63. Göttingen: Vandenhoeck & Ruprecht, 2007.

Yarbro Collins, Adela. *Crisis and Catharsis: The Power of the Apocalypse*. Philadelphia: Westminster, 1984.

———. "The Female Body as Social Space in 1 Timothy." *NTS* 57 (2011) 155–75.

———. "Paul's Disability: The Thorn in His Flesh." In *Disability Studies and Biblical Literature*, edited by Candida R. Moss and Jeremy Schipper, 165–83. New York: Palgrave Macmillan, 2011.

12

Emotional Bonds and Roles of the Priestesses of Vesta

KATARIINA MUSTAKALLIO

IN ROME THERE WERE few public offices open to female citizens. Women were strictly excluded from public management of the state, but in public religion there were some priesthoods in which women could take part and in which they could act in public.[1] The most respected of these were the virgin priestesses of Vesta, *Virgines Vestalis*. *Vesta Mater* was the goddess of the hearth of the city, a peaceful symbol of civil life;[2] she was worshipped in Roman households as a domestic guardian of the family. Moreover, the legendary past of the city of Rome was closely connected to the cult. According to Roman historians, the very founders of Rome, Romulus and Remus, were born to the Vestal Virgin Rhea Silvia. A holy virgin gave birth to the divine twins and thus to the holy city of Rome.[3]

In this article I will consider the religious identity and the emotional ties of the Vestal Virgins with their original families as they are described in Roman literary tradition and based on a discussion concerning their role.[4]

1. There is ample the epigraphic evidence of imperial priestesses; see Hemelrijk, *Priestesses of the Imperial Cult*, 138. The picture of Republican priestesses is much less clear.

2. The peaceful figure of Vesta has been seen as the opposite of Vulcan, a sacred masculine force who possessed a warlike character and the power of fire and destruction; see Dumézil, *Fêtes romaines*, 65–66.

3. Liv.1.3.11; Dion. Hal., *Ant. rom.*1.76.4; Plut., *Vit. Rom.* 3.2–3. On the central role of the blazing hearth in various versions concerning the legendary history of Rome, see, Dion. Hal., *Ant. rom.* 4.2.2–3, Ov., *Fast.* 6.626–36; Wiseman, *Remus*, 58; cf. Mustakallio, *Founding the City*, 207.

4. Beard, *The Sexual Status*, 12–27, Scheid, *Religious Roles*, 377, Takács, *Vestal Virgins* 2008, 81–89; see also Parker, *Why Were the Vestal Virgins*, 563–601; Wildfang, *Rome's Vestal Virgins*; Bätz, *Sacrae virgines*.

In this article however, the aim is not to picture the role of the Vestal Virgins at abstract level, but to study the emotional bonds of the Vestal Virgins, how their special identity was created by means of rituals, legal and sacral privileges and obligations, and how their social bonds and emotional ties with their original families were regarded.

We will begin with the legendary background of the Vestal Virgins, then we will consider the life course of a Vestal, their sacral capacities and obligations, and finally we will analyse their emotional ties and their social networks through a number of case studies.

The Origins: Who Were the Vestal Virgins?

According to Plutarch and Livy, the order of the Vestal Virgins was founded by the legendary King Numa Pompilius, who was the Founding Father of the Roman Religion.[5] First four, and later six, virgins acted at the same time in the cult. Ritual service took up a long period of their lives—thirty years; meanwhile they were required to maintain strict ritual and sexual purity and live under the control of the *Pontifex Maximus*.[6] The strictness of this obligation however, varied over time.[7]

Roman authors state that the Vestal Virgins were usually chosen from among the daughters of senatorial families by the *Pontifex Maximus*. Rose argued as early as 1926 that Vestal Virgins were originally daughters of the early kings and that they served the cult before their marriage;[8] when we consider the story of Rhea Silvia, who, according to Roman historians, was a daughter of King Numitor, the case for the daughter-status of the Vestal Virgin seems clear. The period of serving the cult mentioned in this connection was five years.[9] The role of a daughter is dominant even later, as well as their special status outside marriage. Their importance to their original family emerges from different sources that we will discuss further.

In many studies the ritual of choosing a Vestal Virgin has been related to the Roman wedding ceremonies. The dress of a Vestal Virgin resembled that of the Roman brides, *nuptae*; their hairstyle, with *sex crines*,

5. Livy 1.20.3–4; Plut. *Vit. Num.* 1.20.3.

6. According to Livy (1.3.11) and Plutarch (*Vit. Rom.* 3.2–3) "perpetual virginity" was required of them; cf. Dion. Hal., *Ant. rom.* 1.76.3–4.

7. See, e.g., Suet., *Dom.* 8.3–4.

8. Rose, *de Virginibus,* 446–48.

9. For the five years period see Dion. Hal., *Ant. rom.* 1.76.3–4; the five year term was probably a later invention from the fourth or early third century, see the lustral cycle, Astin, *The Censorship,* 174–87, Liou-Gille, *Le "lustrum,"* 573–602.

was a peculiar one and they also wore long robes and hair-bands as married women did.[10] Nevertheless, other important priestesses, like *Flaminica Dialis*, wife of a priest of Jupiter, wore robes resembling that of a bride. This brings us to the suggestion that the veil was not necessarily the dress of a bride but a more common feature to the "old fashioned" or "early" female dress, or later considered to be so.[11]

In Roman religious rituals the celebrants of a cult were usually divided into different groups according to their age, gender or social order—young girls separated from the married women, adolescents separated from the adult male citizens. The role of the Vestals might reveal some important features of the cult itself. It was supposed that Vestal Virgins were considered to play several roles—a *puella* when just elected to the priesthood, then *nupta*, and finally *matrona*. From this point of view, we may argue that the priestesses represented different age groups or stages of the course of life of a Roman woman.[12]

When young girls were taken into the order they evidently had the role of daughters. When they had learned their duties and became performers of the rituals themselves—and later on—teachers of the ceremonies—their sacral role changed. This three-part religious role system is evident when we turn to the Roman authors. Plutarch, who lived in the first century AD, defined it clearly: "during the first decade they are to learn their duties, during the second to perform the duties and during the third to teach others these duties."[13]

Fortunately, there is a detailed document concerning the selection process and the qualities required of a candidate. Aulus Gellius, who lived c. AD 130–180, wrote a whole chapter in his *Noctae Atticae* considering the selection of the Vestal Virgins. First of all the chosen one had to live under her father's *potestas*. Both her parents had to be alive; this meant that she was not

---

10. For *Capta*, see Gell., *Noct. Att.* 1.12L; Plut., *Vit. Num.* 9.5. considers the reason for choosing virgins as priestesses and points out two possible explanations: 1) the nature of fire was considered to be pure (*katharos*) and incorrupt (*aphtharnos*) so it was entrusted to chaste (*akeratos*) and undefiled (*amiantos*) persons; or 2) he interprets it as unfruitful (*akarpos*) and barren (*agonos*) and associates it with virginity (*parthenia*). According to Plutarch (*Vit. Num.* 9.5–6), at Delphi and Athens the perpetual fire was cared for by widows, past the age of marriage. For the matronal role of the Vestals Virgins, see Mustakallio, *Sex Vestae Sacerdotes*, 74.

11. La Follette, *The Costume*, 54–58.

12. Even if I agree with Holt N. Parker, when he says that Vestal's "unique legal status frees her from all family ties so that she can incarnate the collective" (Parker, *Why Were the Vestal Virgins*, 563), I still emphasise that the life course of a Vestal followed the life course of an Roman Matron and she had special ties with her family all her life.

13. Plut., *Vit. Num.* 10.1.

orphaned on either side (*patrimi matrimi*). This was a typical requirement for candidates to religious offices in general, not only Vestal Virgins.[14]

The body of a Vestal Virgin had to be perfect, as did her hearing and speech. Only a perfect six to ten year old girl of noble blood was suitable for the Goddess. Furthermore, according to Gellius, close connection of her family with other sacral duties was an obstacle; if there were priests or priestesses in her family dedicated to other cults, she was excluded. Several religious offices in the same family could possibly produce bad luck.[15]

In Roman religion the maintenance of the order between gods and humans, *pax deorum*, was a central issue. According to Roman authors this order was obtained by strict control of the Senate and higher priests and their *collegia*. The mixing of different categories was regarded as portentous.[16] This attitude to all existing things, positions, time and place, was a peculiar feature of Roman religious thinking. A Vestal had to be pure, uncontaminated, unmixed, untouched by death or sexual intercourse, without any stigma of illness or handicap. She was a representative of the Roman people before the gods. As Holt N. Parker puts it: "Her unique legal status frees her from all family ties so that she can incarnate the collective."[17]

Ritual Tasks

I have already argued that the order of Vestal Virgins was divided into three groups with different religious obligations and tasks—young pupils, grown-up priestesses and older teachers. Each of these stages took ten years, so their ritual office was thirty years in all. After that they were free to leave the order and marry, which, Plutarch reports, happened very seldom.[18]

According to Roman writers the participation of the younger generation, girls and boys, was needed in many religious rituals of the Roman people. Dionysius of Halicarnassus tells that they were important particularly in female cults in which men were excluded. That was also the case in the cult of Vesta. Children, probably sons and daughters of their sisters and

---

14. Servius in his commentaries on Vergilius's *Georgica* confines the term *patrimi et matrimi* to children born of parents who had been married by the religious ceremony *confarreatio*, and it only applied to such children so long as their parents were alive; see Serv.*ad Verg. geog.* 31.; cf. Paul. Fest., 66.23 s.v. *Flaminia*; Dion. Hal., *Ant. rom.* 2.22.

15. Aul. Gel. 1.12L, cites here the jurist Labeo Antistius (died AD 10 or 11).

16. For the portentous signs in Rome, see, e.g., Bloch, *Prodigi e divinazione*, 98–109.

17. Parker, *Vestal Virgins*, 563.

18. Plut., *Vit. Num.* 10.1.

brothers, assisted Vestal Virgins in their ritual tasks. This emphasised the relations between siblings and strengthened emotional ties in the family.[19]

We may assume that younger members of the order of Vestals learned their religious duties by helping older priestesses during the rituals. Vestal Virgins formed a kind of family with different generations, and older Vestals taking care of younger ones. The hierarchical order of the *Virgines Vestalis* was evident. All their important ceremonies were conducted by the *Virgo Vestalis Maxima*, the chief priestess of the Vestals.[20]

Traditionally the ritual tasks of the Vestal Virgins have been compared with early Roman household management. Naturally, their main task was connected with the cult of Vesta and the preparation of *mola salsa*—the sacred grain mixed with salt—used in public sacrifices, especially the purification rites.[21] Their religious activities were focused on tending of the "undying fire" (*ignis inextinctus*) and taking care of it in the circular temple of Vesta.[22]

They also participated in several fertility and purification rituals during the religious year.[23] Beginning with the traditional start of the religious year in March, the Vestal Virgins participated in the rituals of *Juno Lucina* and *Matronalia* on the first of March, both matronal cults, and they performed a *supplicatio* to Vesta and to the *Penates Publici*.[24] On the first of May, and again at the beginning of December, they celebrated the cult of *Bona Dea*, the Good Goddess, whose shrine was connected with the Virgins Claudia or Licinia.[25] These rituals, which were celebrated with the wives of the highest magistrates, were strictly forbidden to the male sex. This

19. Dion. Hal., *Ant. Rom* 22.1–2 points out *kanephoroi* and *arrhephoroi* compared with *tutulatae*, *cadmili* with *camilli*; cf. Cic., *de har.*23. See also Mustakallio, *Roman Funerals*, 183.

20. For *Fordicidia*, see, Ov., *Fast.* 4.637–642, Paul. Fest., 74L (*Fordicidis*); Varro, *Ling.* 6.15 on *Fordicidia*; Dessau, *Inscriptiones Latinae Selectae* 4932; "A typical inscription says of a mid-third century Chief Vestal (*Virgo Vestalis maxima*) that the state felt daily the effects of her chastity (*disciplina*) and exactitude in fulfilling the sacred rites," see Hardy, *The Priestess*, 40–55.

21. Ov., *Fast.* 6.249, see also Serv., *auct. Ecl.* 8.82, Varro, *Ling.* 6.17.

22. Ov., *Fast.*6.297., Plut., *Vit. Num.* 11.1.

23. For a more detailed analysis see Wildfang, *The Vestals*, 223–56. Wildfang, *Rome's Vestal virgins* stresses that the cult practices of the Vestals were not about fertility but purification. This separation between fertility and purification is artificial in my view, because they were interwoven in Roman religious thinking, see Mustakallio, *Sive deus sive dea*, 44–49.

24. Ov., *Fast.* 3.417–18.

25. Ov., *Fast.* 5.147–58, Macr., *Sat.*1.12.21, Cic., *Dom.* 136; *Har.Resp.* 35; Plut., *Quaest. Rom.* 20.

celebration has been compared with the Orphic rites in Greece and probably formed a strong emotional bond between the Vestals and other ladies of the noble families of Rome.[26]

The most important sacred duties of course, were for the celebration of *Vestalia* in June. During this festival they cleaned the house of Vesta. Ovid tells us this was the moment when Roman matrons walked barefoot in the forum to participate in the celebrations in the Temple. This emphasises the closeness of the Vestals with other Matrons.[27]

Privileged or Isolated?

When recounting Roman peculiarities in his *Attic Nights*, Aulus Gellius compares two opposing figures of the legendary history of Rome. One is the foster mother of Romulus and Remus, Acca Larentia, and the other is a Vestal, Gaia Taracia. For these two very different figures, a prostitute Larentia and a holy virgin Gaia Taracia, Gellius finds a common ground in the honours they received from the Roman people. Acca Larentia was honoured by the people after her death because of her generosity, while Gaia Taracia obtained her privileges while she was still alive. [28]

Here we find a typical Roman feature, a story of how the Vestals got their peculiar privileges: these privileges were given first to a certain famous person, not to a whole priesthood. Taracia was the first Vestal to have the right of giving testimony according to the Horatian Law. She was the only woman given the right to call witnesses. She is also mentioned as the first Vestal who obtained the right to leave the priesthood and marry after the age of forty. The reason for all these privileges was that she had given the Campus Tiberinus (Campus Martius) to the Roman people. According to Pliny, a statue was also decreed in honour of Gaia Taracia.[29]

The juridical position of the Vestals in general was peculiar. They had the right to make their own testaments and conduct their other business affairs without a guardian, unlike other Roman women who lived all their lives under the *tutela*.[30] When considering their privileges, Plutarch com-

26. Plut., *Vit. Caes.* 9; see also Cic., *Har. Resp.* 37. For the shrine of Bona Dea see Brouwer, *Bona Dea*, 181–82, and for the Vestal Virgins and Bona Dea in general, see Staples, *From Good Goddess*, 13–52.

27. Ov., *Fast.* 6.3.10, 395–98.

28. Aul.Gel. 7.7.

29. Aul.Gel. 7.7.1–4; Plin., *Nat.Hist.* 34.25.

30. For the position of women in Roman society and family, see, e.g., Dixon, *The Roman Mother*; Treggiari, *Roman Marriages*; Gardner, *Women in Roman Law*.

pares them with Roman matrons, especially those with three children who were liberated from tutelage (*ius liberorum*) by Augustus.[31] Moreover, according to Livy the state paid them a stipend for their services, so they were financially independent.[32]

They had many privileges, but at the same time, they were separated from normal society. These privileges in fact indicated their isolation: they were removed from their own families, and from their father's *potestas*. This isolation is evident even in Roman law. The right of inheritance was one of the basic rights of Roman citizens, men and women alike. Aulus Gellius mentions that Labeo wrote in his commentaries on the Twelve Tables that "A Vestal Virgin is neither heir to an intestate person, nor is anyone her heir if she dies intestate, but her estate passes to the public treasury."[33] So they were the natural heirs of no-one, because they had lost their familial status and ties, and for the same reasons they did not have natural heirs themselves.

The Vestals' birth family might have been somehow responsible for financing the cult, together with the state. If this is so then the Vestals should have also been dependent on their family's financial situation even after their *co-optatio* and inauguration. On the other hand, as we know, the law prevented them to having the right to inherit from their relatives; economic relations between the Vestal and her birth family seem to have been broke off.[34]

This isolation and separation from family bonds becomes even clearer when we consider the festivals of the cult of the forefathers, *Parentalia*, one of the most important religious festivals of Roman families. During the celebrations families, led by the *Pater familias*, made offerings to their ancestors; Vestal Virgins, in contrast, made sacrifices to the deceased Vestal Tarpeia.[35]

Living under Control

Even the topographical situation of the house of the Vestals was a peculiar one. The *Atrium Vestae* was in the centre of the forum—not a normal place for a residence. It was situated in a place where they could be watched and controlled by the *Pontifex Maximus*.

31. Of the *tutela mulierum perpetua*, see Gai., *Inst.* 1.145; Plut., *Vit. Num.* 10.3; Dixon, *The Roman Mother*, 85.

32. Liv., 1.20.3.

33. Aul.Gel. 1.12L.

34. Aul.Gel. 1.12.18.For the relationship between the Vestals and their clients, see Sihvonen, *Fictores and the Cult of Vesta*, 121–132.

35. On the celebration of the *Parentalia,* see Ov., *Fast.* 2.429–452.

The central shrine of the cult itself was not a proper *templum*; it was never properly inaugurated (*certis verbis*). According to Plutarch, its round form represented a primitive house of the kings of Rome and it was situated near the old palace of the kings in the *Forum Romanum*, the *Regia*.[36]

The remains of the Early Republican buildings still exist in the Forum. There were two rooms, one in the near the temple and another on the east side, near the house of the *Pontifex Maximus*. The Republican *Aedes Vestae* east-west oriented house consisted of a large room, possibly an atrium, on the north side, and six or seven small rooms on the south side that opened to a larger room.[37] On the east side there are still some remains of a building, perhaps used as a storeroom or a room for servants.[38] On the eastern side there is a thick wall that separates the house of the Pontifex Maximus from the buildings of the Vestal Virgins, probably the same as that mentioned by Dio Cassius.[39]

The changes of the imperial building programme were drastic. Between the great fire of Rome, in AD 64, and the reign of Galba (AD 68), the area was totally rebuilt. The first phase consisted of the construction of the atrium in the middle and of small rooms around it. During the imperial period the house of the Vestals was rebuilt several times, going from a modest house to a magnificent palace with a cortile of several floors. This indicates that in this time the social position of the Vestal Virgins, and the idea of the cult itself, underwent great changes.[40]

The House of the Vestals was built for the Vestal Virgins to practice their religious duties without any interruption. The memory of the major Vestal Virgins (*virgo vestalis maxima*) served as a role model for them, and was also before them every day: The whole garden of the house of the Vestals was decorated with the busts and statues of famous Vestal foremothers. Furthermore, there is evidence of some Vestals who were considered so important to society that they were honoured by the erection of statues, even at public expense.[41]

The Roman Forum and other public areas were ideal places for honorary statues to keep alive the memory of important statesmen: but in the *Forum Romanum* there were some statues of female heroines too, for example

36. Plut., *Vit. Num.* 14.1; Liv. 1.3.11.

37. Van Deman, *The Atrium Vestae*, 12–13; Carettoni, *La Ricostruzione del Tempio di Vesta,*, 219–24; De Spirito, *Vesta, Templum*, 130, Coarelli, *Roma*, 96–97.

38. Coarelli, *Roma*, 96.

39. Dio Cass. 54.27.4.

40. Tac., *Ann.* 14.4.1, mentions the disastrous great fire of Rome; Tac., *Hist.*1.43, mentions the new building activities.

41. Coarelli, *Roma*, 99.

the equestrian statue of legendary Cloelia, a young heroine who had bravely saved the younger generation of Romans during the attack of King Porsenna. [42] There was also a statue of Cornelia, the mother of the Gracchi, erected in the public colonnade of Metellus.[43] There is also one legendary Vestal whose statue was set in a public place. Pliny tells us that a decree was passed by the senate to erect a statue to Vestal Virgin Taracia or Fufetia to be placed wherever she wished.[44] There is some even later evidence of statues of the Vestals found outside their house in the Forum Romanum.[45]

Emotional Bonds of the Vestal Virgins: Claudia, Fabia, Fonteia, and Junia Torquata

Even if the priestesses lived separated from their families, they were not isolated from their families or the public life of the *res publica*. In Roman literary sources we have several instances when the close relationships with the family emerge. In fact it is possible that it was easier to keep good relations with Vestal Virgins than with other family members because they did not quarrel over the inheritance with their sisters and brothers. To their parents they were valuable because of their high status. As Judith Hallett has already shown in 1984, especially the relationship between fathers and daughters was often close in Roman culture. The close relationship between siblings was also evident.[46]

Concerning a close relationship between a Vestal and her father (or brother) we have a story from the first half of the second century BC of the Vestal Claudia who helped her father Appius Claudius (Consul 143 BC) to celebrate a triumph against the wishes of a tribune. When a tribune tried to pull Claudius from his carriage, Claudia threw herself into her father's arms, thus interposing her Vestal sanctity between Claudius and the tribune, and helping her father to finish the triumph.[47] This highlights the peculiar posi-

---

42. Liv. 2.13; Plin., *Nat. Hist.* 34.28.See also Aul. Gell. 7.7.1.

43. It represented Cornelia in a sitting position, and it was well-known because there were no straps on her shoes, according to Plin., *Nat. Hist.* 34.31.

44. Plin., *Nat. Hist.* 34.25.

45. See, e.g., Coarelli, *Roma*, 96–99.

46. Hallett, *Fathers and Daughters*, 151–52.

47. See, e.g., Cic. *Cael.*14.34, Suet. *Tib.* 2.5; Dio Cass. fr. 74.2; Val. Max. 5.4.6; Oros. 5.4.7. According to Bauman, *Women and Politics*, 47, "now it (the sanctity of a Vestal Virgin) was being given an extended meaning, it was being used as a constitutional, or would-be constitutional, weapon in the game of politics." There was another famous Claudia, Claudia Quinta, to whom the cult of Magna Mater was related. Sometimes these two Claudias were mixed, especially in later tradition; see Scheid, *Claudia the*

tion of the Vestal Virgin. At the same time, it shows the strong will of an upper class lady to use her position as a highly respected priestess in public in order to strengthen her family's status in society.[48]

We have several instances where the close relationship between the members of the family of a Vestal, is emphasised. Cicero's wife Terentia had a half-sister named Fabia who was a Vestal Virgin, a daughter of a patrician named Fabius. In 73 a *Vestal Fabia* was accused of unchaste behaviour with Catiline (the later conspirator) but was acquitted. Nevertheless, we know that in 64 BC Cicero managed to attack Catiline without incriminating his sister-in law.[49] Later the position of a half-sister as a Vestal helped Cicero's wife Terentia during her turbulent years. She found refuge in the house of Vestals in the emergency, so Fabia or her fellow Vestals must have protected her.[50]

For Cicero the important role and highly esteemed status of Vestal Virgins in Roman society was very familiar. In his speech *pro Fonteio* he uses the dramatic figure of a Vestal sister of the accused Fonteius by making her to plead for her brother. Cicero successfully uses the motif of the love of a sister in his speech and puts Vestal Fonteia weeping for her brother in the temple of Vesta so that the fire is in danger of being extinguished. He emphasises a Vestal Virgin needs the comfort and the protection of her brother because she is alone in the world, without the male protection of a father, husband, or son.[51]

In this context, the relationship with the brother is described as essential for the well being of a Vestal Virgin. We have another story from the time of Tiberius in which a Vestal Virgin is active in the same kind of situation. As Tacitus recounts it, in the case of Silanus the appeal of his sister, Junia Torquata, was crucial. The brother Silanus was condemned to exile and he was allowed to retire to Cyhmus instead of the island of Gyarus which was a bleak and uninhabited island. This happened according to the wishes of his sister Torquata. In this context Junia Torquata is described as "a Vestal of old-world holiness." So the appeal of a Vestal Virgin was crucial; it was effective even during the tyrannical power of Tiberius.[52]

Vestal Virgin, 23–33.

48. In this occasion Suet. Tib. 2.5 mentions that App. Claudius Pulcher was Claudia's brother, other sources calls him her father.

49. Cic., *Cat.* 3.9.; Asc., *Corn.* 91, Plut., *Cat. Min.* 19.3, see Treggiari, *Terentia,* 30–40.

50. Treggiari, *Terentia,* 61.

51. Cic., *pro Font.* 46.13; 47.7.

52. Tac., *Ann.*3.69.

Conclusion

During the Late Republic and the Early Principate the popularity of the Vestal order diminished and the new emperor Augustus had to find other ways to persuade Roman families to give their daughters to the order. Nevertheless, even then the priestesses were highly respected. During this period, Vestal Virgins even gained a new role and influence in society. They acted as mediators in political and domestic crises of statesmen, and after Augustus they were even given new ritual occupations in imperial cults.[53] Imperial ladies like Livia, Octavia, and the sisters of Caligula were all honoured by giving them Vestal privileges.[54] This shows the peculiar position of the Vestal Virgins and their social ties with other noble Ladies.

The Vestal Virgins were highly respected in the Roman tradition and their role was important even in the private matters of their original families. Due to their special social position near the centre of power they had the possibility of influence, even in politics, and to benefit their original families. Their emotional bonds and close relationship with their original families were perhaps even stronger than with their sisters who had their own families.

The stories of the Vestal Virgins show us their close relationships with their families. The story of the Vestal Fonteia weeping for her brother in the temple of Vesta includes dramatic hyperbole and exaggeration, but the powerful emotional rhetoric of the author convinces the reader to believe that this kind of relationship and the emotional bond between a Vestal Virgin and her family was credible in this context. These stories show us that even if the Vestal Virgins grew up with the priesthood and lived apart from their families for the major part of their lives, emotionally they were not separated from them. Vestal Virgins represented a valuable resource for their families and the help they provided for them was anxiously admitted in situations of danger.

53. Plut., *Vita Cic.* 20.2–3; Suet., *Claud.* 1.2; Dio Cass. 60.5.2; *Virgo Maxima* Vibia as a mediator between the Emperor Claudius and Messalina, Tac., *Ann.* 11.32.5–6.

54. Tac., *Ann.* 4.16.6; Stein and Petersen, *Prosopographia*, 319; see Bauman, *Women and Politics*, 125 and 157.

Bibliography

Astin, Alan. "The Censorship of the Roman Republic: Frequency and Regularity." *Historia* 31 (1982) 174–87.

Bätz, Alexander. *Sacrae virgines: Studien zum religiösen und gesellschaftlichen Status der Vestalinnen*. Paderborn: Schöningh, 2012.

Bauman, Richard. *Women and Politics in Ancient Rome*. London: Routledge, 1992.

Beard, Mary. "The Sexual Status of Vestal Virgins." *JRS* 70 (1980) 12–27.

Bloch, Marc. *Prodigi e divinazione nel mondo antico*. Rome: Newton Compton, 1974.

Brouwer, Hendrik. *Bona Dea: The Sources and a Description of the Cult*. Études préliminaires aux religions orientales dans l'Empire romain 110. Leiden: Brill, 1989.

Cantarella, Eva. *I Supplici Capitali in Grecia e Roma*. Milan: Feltrinelli, 1991.

Carettoni, Alessandro. "La Ricostruzione del Tempio di Vesta." *Capitolium* 2 (1926–1927) 219–24.

Coarelli, Filippo. *Roma: Guide archeologiche Mondadori*. Milan: Mondadori, 1997.

Dixon, Suzanne. *The Roman Mother*. London: Routledge, 1990.

Dumézil, Georges. *Fêtes romaines d'été et d'automne*. Paris: Gallimard, 1975.

La Follette, Laetitia, "The Costume of the Roman Bride." In *The World of Roman Costume*, edited by Judith Lynn Segesta and Larissa Bonfante, 54–64. Wisconsin Studies in Classics. Madison: University of Wisconsin Press, 2001.

Liou-Gille, Bernadette. "Le 'lustrum': périodicité et durée." *Latomus* 60 (2001) 573–602.

Gardner, Jane F. *Women in Roman Law and Society*. London: Routledge, 1986.

Hallett, Judith P. *Fathers and Daughters in Roman Society: Women and the Elite Family*. Princeton: Princeton University Press, 1984.

Hardy, Edward R. "The Priestess in the Greco-Roman World." In *Why Not? Priesthood and the Ministry of Women*, edited by Michael Bruce and G. E. Duffield, 40–55. New York: Marcham Manor, 1972.

Hemelrijk Emily A. "Priestesses of the Imperial Cult in the Latin West: Titles and Function." *L'Antiquité Classique* (2005) 137–40.

Mustakallio, Katariina. "Founding the City, Creating Identity." In *Reclaiming the City: Innovation, Culture, Experience*, edited by Marjaana Niemi and Ville Vuolanto, 204–13. Studia Fennica Historica 6. Helsinki: Finnish Literature Society, 2003.

———. "Roman Funerals: Identity, Gender and Participation." In *Hoping for Continuity: Childhood, Education and Death in Antiquity and the Middle Ages*, edited by Katarina Mustakallio et al., 179–90. Acta Instituti Romani Finlandiae 33. Rome: Institutum Romanum Finlandiae, 2005.

———. "Sex Vestae Sacerdotes—What Did They Represent?" In *Utriusque Linguae Peritus, Studia in Honorem Toivo Viljamaa*, edited by Jyri Vaahtera and Raija Vainio, 73–80. Annales Universitatis Turkuensis, ser. B, tom. 219, Humaniora. Turku: Turun Yliopisto, 1997.

———. *Sive deus sive dea: La presenza della religion nello sviluppo della società romana*. Pisa: ETS, 2013.

Parker, Holt N. "Why Were the Vestal Virgins? Or the Chastity of Women and the Safety of the Roman State." *American Journal of Philology* 125 (2004) 563–601.

Rose, H. J. "de Virginibus vestalibus." *Mnemosyne* 54 (1926) 440–48.

Scheid, John. "Claudia the Vestal Virgin." In *Roman Women*, edited by Augusto Fraschetti. Translated by Lydia Lappin. Chicago: University of Chicago Press, 2001.

———. "The Religious Roles of Roman Women." In *A History of Women in the West*, edited by Pauline Schmitt Pantel, 1:377–408. Cambridge, MA: Belknap, 1993.

Sihvonen, Outi. "*Fictores* and the Cult of Vesta." In *Religious Participation in the Ancient and Medieval Societies, Rituals Interaction and Identity*, edited by Sari Katajala-Peltomaa and Ville Vuolanto, 121–32. Acta IRF 41. Rome: Institutum Romanum Finlandiae, 2013.

Spirito, G. De. "Vesta, Templum." In *Lexicon Topographicum Urbis Romae*, edited by Eva Margareta Steinby, vol. 5:n.p. Rome: Quasar 1999.

Staples, Ariadne. *From Good Goddess to Vestal Virgins: Sex and Category in Roman Religion*. London: Routledge, 1998.

Stein, Arthur, and Leiva Petersen. *Prosopographia Imperii Romani*. Part IV. 2nd ed. Berlin, 1952–1966.

Takács, Sarolta A. *Vestal Virgins, Sibyls, and Matrons: Women in Roman Religion*. Austin: University of Texas Press, 2008.

Treggiari, Susan. *Roman Marriages. Iusti coniuges from the Time of Cicero to the Time of Ulpian*. Oxford: Oxford University Press, 1991.

———. *Terentia, Tullia and Publilia: The Women of Cicero's Family*. Women of Antiquity. London: Routledge, 2007.

Van Deman, Esther Boise. *The Atrium Vestae*. Carnegie Institution of Washington 108. Washington, DC: Carnegie Institution of Washington, 1909.

Wildfang, Robin. L. *Rome's Vestal Virgins: A Study of Rome's Vestal Priestesses in the Late Republic and Early Empire*. London: Routledge, 2006.

———. "The Vestals and Annual Public Rites." *Classica et Mediaevalia* 52 (2001) 223–56.

Wiseman, Timothy P. *Remus: A Roman Myth*. Cambridge: Cambridge University Press, 1995.

13

Impedimentum sexus

The Cultic Impediment
of Female Humanity

KARI ELISABETH BØRRESEN

From Man–centred Axiom
to Ecumenical Obstacle

IN 1983, JOHN XXIII's Encyclical *Pacem in Terris* was addressed to all
Catholic Bishops, Clergy, and Faithful, including all Men of Good Will,
with the androcentric greeting: "Venerable Brethren and Dearest Sons."
Nevertheless, contemporary society is also described from a gender perspective: "Secondly, the part that women are now playing in political life is
everywhere evident. This is a development that is perhaps of swifter growth
among Christian nations, but it is also happening extensively, if more slowly, among nations that are heirs to different traditions and with a different
culture. Women are gaining an increasing awareness of their human dignity
(*suae humanae dignitatis*). Far from accepting a purely passive role or to be
regarded as a kind of instrument (*patiantur se vel pro re quadam inanima
vel pro instrumento quodam haberi*), they are demanding in domestic and in
public life the rights and duties which belong to them as human persons."
(I, 41). It is important to observe that the perennial gender hierarchy of
Christian marriage is suddenly relinquished, whereas women's gender-
specific exclusion from priesthood is not explicitly stated, but just taken for
granted:

Human beings have also the right to choose for themselves the kind of life which appeals to them: to found a family, in the founding of which man and woman enjoy equal rights and duties, or to embrace the priesthood or the religious life. (*Insuper hominibus iure integrum est vitae genus eligere, quod praeoptent: adeoque aut sibi condere familiam, in qua condenda vir et mulier paribus fruantur iuribus et officiis, aut sacerdotium vel religiosae vitae disciplinam capessere.*)" (I, 15)

Until the II Vatican Council (1962–65), only a few Catholic bishops and theologians questioned women's subordinate position in the Church. In this context, the admission of 18 female conciliar auditors during the third session (1964), joined by five others during the fourth session (1965), was important. These 23 women were leaders of female religious orders or leaders/members of Catholic lay or women's organisations, and therefore already selected or approved by Vatican authorities. Nevertheless, they managed to gain some influence on conciliar reform.[1]

It is necessary to recall that the Catholic feminist pioneer Gertrud Heinzelmann, a Swiss jurist and member of St. Joan's International Alliance, in 1962 sent a protest-petition to the conciliar preparatory commission, where she perspicaciously denounced women's inferior status in the Church, with focus on the cultic impediment of female humanity.[2] After Vatican II, Catholic feminist theology was initiated in Europe, where the German medievalist Elisabeth Gössmann and I are pioneers.[3] From the 1970s onward, European and North-American colleagues followed, among them several Catholic nuns.[4]

As a result of ecumenical revival, Roman-Catholic dialogue with Protestant denominations started soon after the Council. Here, women's

---

1. McEnroy, *Guests in their Own House*; Goldie, *From a Roman Window*; Valerio, *Madri del Concilio*; Perroni et al., *"Tantum Aurora est"*; Perroni and Legrand, *Avendo qualcosa da dire.*

2. Heinzelmann, *Wir schweigen nicht länger.* Heinzelmann, *Die geheiligte Diskriminierungen.*

3. Gössmann, *Metaphysik und Heilsgeschichte*, from 1964 has a chapter on Alexander of Hales's gender models; Gössmann, *Geburtsfehler: weiblich*; Børresen, *Subordination et Equivalence*, is from 1968; cf. outline of my research in Militello, *Donna e Teologia*, 131–42; Alexandre, "La place des femmes," 24–46; Ruether, *Women and Redemption*, 158–61, 305–6.

4. Influential Catholic feminist theologians in Europe: Catharina J. M. H. Halkes (died 2004), Anne Jensen (died 2008), Ursula King, Cettina Militello, Marinella Perroni, Helen Schüngel-Straumann, and Adriana Valerio. In the US: Anne E. Carr (died 2008), Margaret A. Farley, Elizabeth A. Johnson, Rosemary Radford Ruether, Sandra M. Schneiders, and Elisabeth Schüssler Fiorenza.

equivalence with men in society was commonly recognised, but when women obtained cultic capability in the Lutheran, Presbyterian and Anglican Churches, the persistent Catholic and Orthodox exclusion of women from priestly and episcopal ordination became the strongest obstacle to Christian unity.

In fact, although the age-old gender asymmetry of marriage disappeared from the updated *Codex Iuris Canonici* (1983),[5] gender-specific male priesthood is preserved in canon 1024, which literally repeats canon 689, §1 of the *Codex Iuris Canonici* (1917): "*Sacram ordinationem valide recicipt solus vir baptizatus* (only a baptized man can receive valid ordination.)"

As a member of the *Lutheran-Roman Catholic Commission on Unity* (1995–2006), Turid Karlsen Seim proposed to exclude this divisive topic from the agenda. Otherwise, the *Lutheran World Federation* could not pursue its ecumenical dialogue with the *Pontifical Council for Promoting Christian Unity*. In consequence, the Commission's Study Document on *The Apostolicity of the Church* states: "The Commission agreed from the beginning not to take up a point of serious difference between Lutherans and Catholics, namely, the ordination of women to the pastoral ministry and their appointment to the episcopal office. The Lutheran members of the Commission emphasize, however, that when the text speaks of 'ministry' they have in mind men as well as women as office bearers."[6]

Feminist Revolution and Androcentric Collapse

In order to understand the obstinate Vatican ban on female ordination, it is necessary to analyse the historical elaboration of Christian gender models. Since the 1960s, Roman and Orthodox Catholicism have been increasingly challenged by the epistemological revolution of modern feminism, in which women and men are defined to have equal value, *qua* male or female human beings. This collapse of global androcentrism is more fundamental than the previous upheavals of geocentrism (Copernicus) and anthropocentrism (Darwin). In fact, traditional doctrine and symbolism were structured in Christian Antiquity, when women's biological and socio-cultural inferiority was axiomatic. According to traditional doctrine, functional gender hierarchy is established by God in creation and remains normative for human existence on earth. Redemptive gender equivalence belongs to the order of salvation, and will only be realised by eschatological recreation.[7]

5. Reidick, *Die hierarchische Struktur der Ehe*.

6. *Apostolicity of the Church*, 11.

7. Børresen, *Subordination and Equivalence*.

According to Christian doctrine, fully human status is defined as being created in God's image. Based on interacting concepts of God and God-like humanity this prerogative was gradually attributed to women already from creation, thereby back-dating redemptive equivalence to be normative also in this world. It follows that the Roman Catholic *magisterium* is now confronted with the impossible task of explaining why God-like women cannot be Christ-like priests.

Doctrinal Formation of Human God–likeness

In actual feminist perspective, it is essential to recognize how the inclusion of female humanity in creational *imago Dei* was realised through historically shifting, inculturated exegesis of core biblical texts (Gen 1:26–27; 2:7, 18–24; 1 Cor 11:7; and Gal 3:28). This doctrinal process, which was realised from Early Christianity to the twentieth century, can be summarily outlined in three stages: from manlike Godhead and God-like maleness, via meta-sexual Godhead and asexual *imago Dei*, to holistic God-likeness describing God with both female and male metaphors.[8]

The initial stage of God-like maleness corresponds to an andromorphic concept of God, where the human prototype is male, so that Adam is created in God's image. Based on literal exegesis of biblical texts (Gen 1:26–27a; 2:7; 1 Cor 11:7), only men are creationally God-like. Nevertheless, women can achieve this privilege by "becoming male" through redemptive incorporation into Christ (Rom 8:29; Col 3:10–11; Eph 4:13; *Gos. Thom.* 114). This first doctrinal stage was valid into the fifth century and persisted in medieval Canon Law (*Decreti* secunda pars, causa XXXIII, 5,13,17,19). Here, women's lack of creational *imago Dei* was invoked in order to justify the bio-social subordination and cultic incapability of human females, precisely termed *impedimentum sexus*.[9]

The following stage of asexual God-likeness corresponds to a meta-sexual concept of God, structured from the third to the fifth century by Greek and Latin Church Fathers. Based on Platonic anthropology, they redefined human *imago Dei* in terms of sexless quality, linked to the incorporeal and immortal soul. Also referring to Stoic ethics, in which even females and slaves have reason and virtue, these "feminist" Church Fathers could

8. This process is analyzed, from Genesis to the twentieth century, in Børresen, *The Image of God*.

9. Macy, "The Ordination of Women," 481–597; Idem, *The Hidden History of Women's Ordination*; Martin, "The Ordination of Women," 31–175; Minnis, "De impedimento sexus," 109–39; Raming, "The Priestly Office of Women" 3–305.

attribute asexual God-likeness to women already from creation, despite the monotheistic axiom of non-God-like femaleness.[10] In consequence, the androcentric paradigm of one God, creating two different sexes with gender-specific functions and roles, remained unaffected.[11]

This means that female humanity is created to serve men's procreation of offspring, as clearly expressed by Augustine: "I do not see in what sense woman was made a helper for man, if not for the sake of bearing children (*ad quod adiutorium facta sit mulier, si pariendi causa subtrahitur*)" (*De Genesi ad litteram* 9,5). Therefore, spiritually God-like women could only anticipate their genderless, eschatological equivalence through ascetic defeminisation, as virgins and widows.[12] It is essential to observe that the Patristic concept of sexless *imago Dei* became dominant in medieval theology and remained standard in Catholic doctrine until Vatican II, whereas asexual God-likeness is still upheld in Orthodox doctrine.

The current stage of inclusive God-likeness, where both women and men are created in God's image, *qua* human males or females, was initiated by Northern European Church Mothers, from the twelfth to the fifteenth century.[13] These Matristic authors had internalised that all human beings are created in God's image, but they did not invoke the earlier ideas of women "becoming male" in Christ or receiving sexless *imago Dei*. Nevertheless, they perspicaciously understood the correlated interaction between concepts of God and God-like humanity. Consequently, the German abbess Hildegard von Bingen (died 1179, declared *Doctor Ecclesiae* 2012) and the English anchoress Julian of Norwich (died after 1416) sought to provide a divine model of female *imago Dei* by describing the Godhead with female metaphors. In Hildegard's *Scivias*, God's revelatory Wisdom (*Sapientia*) appears as a female figure. In Julian's *Showings*, "Christ our Mother" refers not only to Christ's incarnate, human nature, but extends to God's pre-existent Son as Second Person of the Trinity.

It is important to observe that Renaissance and Baroque "femmes savantes" represent a regression to the Patristic stage, when they invoke women's sexless *imago Dei* in order to claim women's right to education. Likewise, French salon-feminism affirms the Cartesian adage: "L'esprit n'a

10. Børresen, "Patristics," in *From Patristics to Matristics*, 15–89.

11. Børresen, *Christian and Islamic Gender Models in Formative Traditions*; Børresen and Prinzivalli, *Le Donne nello Sguardo degli Antichi Autori Cristiani*.

12. Clark, *Ascetic Piety and Women's Faith*; Elm, *Virgins of God*.

13. Børresen, "Mothers of the Church," in Børresen and Vogt, *Women's Studies of the Christian and Islamic Traditions*,245–314; Børresen, "Matristics," in *From Patristics to Matristics*, 145–272; Børresen and Valerio, *Frauen und Bibel im Mittelalter*; Børresen, "Matristics," in *Encyclopedia of Ancient Christianity*, 730–735.

point de sexe." Mary Wollstonecraft (died 1792) invokes women's God-like rationality to obtain equal education for both sexes. She argues that this is necessary to ensure the socio-political equality of men and women.

In order to realise the radically new goal of equal civil rights for women and men, nineteenth-century Protestant feminists rediscover the Matristic interaction between womanlike Godhead and God-like women, In consequence, they describe God with female metaphors. Although she ignored the medieval Church Mothers, the Norwegian Aasta Hansteen was a pioneer with *Kvinden skabt i Guds Billede* (Woman created in God's image, 1878), soon followed by the North-American Elizabeth Cady Stanton and her collaborators in *The Woman's Bible* (1895, 1898). Precisely because all Christian institutions invoked God's creational gender hierarchy against women's socio-political rights, these activists responded with theological argumentation.

In fact, their holistic *imago Dei* was accepted in early twentieth-century Protestant theology, more resulting from modernist critique of traditional Platonised anthropology than from feminist motifs. Apparently unaware that this new inculturation is inconsistent with classical androcentric typology, inclusive human God-likeness was also endorsed in Catholic theology after Vatican II.

Updated *Imago Dei* and Outdated Typology

It is essential to recall that both Catholic and Orthodox doctrine preserve the Early Christian typology of Adam-Christ and Eve-Church (Rom 5:14; Eph 5:32), which was structured in the second and third centuries, that is in the first doctrinal stage before women were attributed asexual God-likeness already from creation. The resulting incoherence between updated holistic *imago Dei* and outdated androcentric typology is manifest in John Paul II's Apostolic Letter *Mulieris dignitatem* (1988). Referring to women's "feminine genius" and Mariotypic "dignity," he invokes the traditional categories of motherhood or virginity as models of female existence.[14] Euphemistically concealed by so-called "complementarity," this apologetic discourse repeats the 18th-century ideal of sexual polarity, advanced by Rousseau and Kant against feminist claims of women's socio-political equality with men. The

14. Børresen, "Analyse critique de *Mulieris dignitatem*"; Vogt, "Catholicisme et Islam: Une rhétorique apologétique commune," in Børresen and Vogt, *Women's Studies of the Christian and Islamic Traditions*, 343–65. Børresen, "Jean-Paul II et les femmes," 57–69.

pontifical aim is to bolster traditional division of gender roles in society and Church, with special focus on women's cultic incapability.

Likewise, Cardinal Joseph Ratzinger's letter to all Catholic bishops on "The Collaboration of Men and Women in the Church and in the World," issued by the *Congregation for the Doctrine of the Faith* (2004), seeks to protect the premodern paradigm of functional gender division against modern feminism. Therefore, the letter refutes the feminist distinction between biological sex and socio-cultural gender, misinterpreted as sexual antagonism, in which women fight to obtain traditional male rights and roles (I, 2–3). His apologetic wording "collaborazione attiva" (I, 4) is quite misleading since this document does not concern the properly feminist ideal of functional collaboration by women and men in all fields of human existence. The same misunderstanding is pontificated in Benedict XVI's Christmas discourse to the Roman *Curia* (2012). Here, women's rightful claim to share all functions and roles with men in Church and society is condemned as so-called gender philosophy, based on denial of God-willed sexual difference.

Consequently, the Vatican is eager to promote a so-called New Catholic feminism, inspired by the spiritual gender-play of Hans Urs von Balthasar and his convert Adrienne von Speyr.[15] Based on Balthasar's so-called Petrine and Marian principles, the premodern paradigm of functional gender division is here transposed from the creational order and redefined as a God-willed sexual ontology, anchored in the order of salvation.[16] This inverted version of the Church Fathers' attribution of sexless *imago Dei* to women already from creation, has recently been invoked to defend the male priesthood as a Christ-like and therefore gender-specific sex role.

Scholastic Arguments for Male Priesthood

In historical perspective, it is essential to remember that when Scholastic theologians introduced the *quaestio* of women's ordination, more as an intellectual exercise than responding to concrete challenges, their argumentation was logically coherent. Medieval doctrine conformed to the uncontested androcentrism of Church and society. Canon Law justified the cultic impediment of human femaleness by women's lack of creational *imago Dei*, based on persistent literal exegesis of New Testament texts (1 Cor 11:7, 14:34; 1 Tim 2:9–14).[17] Scholastic Commentaries on Peter Lombard's

15. Beattie, *New Catholic Feminism*.

16. Perroni, "A proposito del principio mariano-petrino," 93–116. Perroni, "Principio Mariano-Principio Petrino, 547–53; Zorzi, *Al di là del "genio femminile."*

17. Børresen, "The Ordination of Women," in *From Patristics to Matristics*, 278–87.

Libri Sententiarum (IV, dist. 24–25) present several interpretations. Peter Lombard did not treat this topic, which is also omitted by the Franciscan Alexander of Hales and the Dominican Albertus Magnus. According to the Dominican Thomas Aquinas' Commentary (IV, dist. 25, quaest. 2, art. 1–2, collected in the *Supplementum* of his *Summa Theologica* (quaest. 39), only men can be ordained. Since the female sex is created in a state of subjection, women are unable to signify Christ's male eminence and authority. Consequently, human females are incapable of representing Christ in sacramental priesthood (*Supplementum* 39,1). This *impedimentum sexus* is clearly demonstrated when Thomas explains that the God-given inferiority of human females makes women's ordination both unlawful and invalid, whereas the socio-economic servitude of serfs makes ordination illegal, but not invalid (*Supplementum* 39,3). This example was not only theoretical, because some socially mobile serfs did bribe bishops to ordain them. Being released from serfdom and with canonical dispensation, they could function as priests.

In fact, Thomas adopted Aristotle's androcentric socio-biology, where human females are misbegotten, undeveloped males (*De generatione animalium* (737a, 767a-b, 775a). Consequently, Thomas defined women as a *mas occasionatus* (*Summa Theologica* I, 99,2, ad 2; *Supplementum* 52,1, ad 2). Like other Scholastic theologians, Thomas Aquinas affirmed women's asexual *imago Dei*. Nevertheless, he partly refers to the literal interpretation of Gen 1:26–27a and 1 Cor 11:7, transmitted through texts from the 4th-century, so-called Ambrosiaster. These were often attributed to Ambrose or Augustine by eighth- to twelfth-century monastic exegetes. Therefore, Thomas repeats Ambrosiaster's combination of theocentrism and androcentrism: "But as regards a secondary point (*aliquid secundarium*), the image of God exists in man (*vir*) in a way that is not found in woman (*mulier*). In fact, man is the beginning and end of woman (*principium mulieris et finis*), as God is the beginning and end of all creation (*principium et finis totius creaturae*)." (*Summa Theologica*, I, 93,4).

The Franciscan Bonaventura's argumentation against women's ordination clearly demonstrates the logical connection between androcentric Adam-Christ typology and non-God-like femaleness. He invokes 1 Cor 11:7 in the literal sense of men's exclusive God-likeness, *qua* human males. This indispensable requirement for priestly ordination, both *de iure* and *de facto*, follows from men's creational precedence. Consequently, subordinate females are unable to represent Christ the *Mediator*, who was incarnated in perfect maleness:

Børresen, "Christianesimo e diritti umani delle donne: l'impedimentum sexus," 261–71.

It is impossible to be ordained without possessing God's image, because this sacrament makes man (*homo*) somehow divine by sharing divine power. Only the male (*vir*) is the image of God by virtue of his sex (*ratione sexus*), according to I Cor 11:7. In consequence, woman (*mulier*) can in no manner be ordained. The reason for this is not so much the Church' decision (*ex institutione Ecclesiae*) as the non-congruity of priesthood with the female sex. In this sacrament the person ordained (*persona, quae ordinatur*), signifies Christ the Mediator. Because this Mediator existed only in the male sex (*virilis sexus*), he can be signified only by the male sex. In consequence, only men have the possibility to receive priestly ordination, since they alone can naturally represent and actually carry the sign of the Mediator by receiving the sacramental character. (*Ideo possiblitas suscipiendi ordines solum viris competit, qui soli possunt naturaliter repraesentare et secundum characteris susceptionem actu signum huius ferre*). This proposition (*propositio*) is more probable (*probabilior*) and can be proved by many sainted authorities." (IV dist. 25, art. 2, quaest. 1).

Therefore, Bonaventura's main rationale for women's *impedimentum sexus* in his Commentary to Peter Lombard is based on the Early Christian typology of Christ as new Adam, who is incarnated as *vir perfectus* (Rom 5:12; Eph 4:13). In consequence, non-God-like human females cannot function as priests in *persona Christi*.

The Franciscan Johannes Duns Scotus' innovative argumentation anticipates the current defence of women's cultic incapability. Invoking divine androcentricity, he explains that this *impedimentum sexus* is caused by the Church's obedience to Christ's command. According to his Commentary:

one should not hold that this is decided by the Church, but that it comes from Christ. The Church would not presume to deprive the entire female sex, without any guilt on its part, of an act which might licitly pertain to it, being directed toward the salvation of woman and of others in the Church through her. For this would seem to be an extreme injustice both toward the entire sex and toward a few specific persons. If by divine law the ecclesiastical Order could licitly be fitting to woman, it could be both for their salvation and that of others through them (*quod non est tenendum tamquam praecise per Ecclesiam determinatum, sed habetur a Christo. Non enim Ecclesia praesumpsisset totum sexum muliebrum privasse sine culpa sua, actu, qui posset sibi licite competere, qui esset ordinatus a salutem mulieris et aliorum in Ecclesia per eam, quia hoc esse videretur maximae injustitiae, non solum in toto sexu, sed etiam in paucis personis; nunc autem si de lege divina licite posset competere mulieri ordo Ecclesiasticus, posset esse ad salutem at earum et aliorum per eas).* What the Apostle says in 1 Tim 2:12: 'I do not permit a woman to teach', speaking of public doctrine in the Church, he does not say on his own authority; but 'I do not permit', because Christ does not permit." (IV, dist 25, quaest, 2, in *Opus Oxonense*, Opera omnia XIX, 140, cf. IV, dist. 25, art, 2, quaest. 1 in *Reportata Parisiensis*, Opera omnia XXIV, 369–70).

An Open Question: Women Priests?

The growing Catholic debate on women's ordination started soon after Vatican II and was tolerated as an open question until John Paul II's firm veto in 1994. It is of note that several learned Jesuits were in favour of women priests. According to Pierre Teilhard de Chardin (died 1955): "Il m'a semblé que, dans l'Église actuelle, il y a trois pierres périssables dangereusement engagées dans les fondations: la première est un gouvernement qui exclut la démocratie; la deuxième est un sacerdoce qui exclut et minimise la femme; la troisième est une révélation qui exclut, pour l'avenir, la Prophétie."[18] In 1965, Jean Daniélou affirmed that there was "no basic theological objection to the possibility of women priests." When nominated a cardinal in 1969, he precised that: "Il faudrait examiner où sont les vraies raisons qui font que l'Église n'a jamais envisagé le sacerdoce des femmes."[19]

In 1969, Haye van der Meer presented a pioneering historical and theological study on this *quaestio disputata.*[20] Since the 1970s several solid investigations of women's ministry in ancient Christianity followed suit.[21]

At the Catholic bishops' synod on *The Ministerial Priesthood and Justice in the World*, held in Rome 1971, Cardinal George Bernard Flahiff, an erudite medievalist and archbishop of Winnipeg, intervened on behalf of the Canadian bishops' conference: "The question which I raise today is that of the possibility of a role for women in the ministry, or better, in the ministries of the Church."[22] As a result, in 1973 Paul VI nominated a *Pon-*

---

18. Quoted in Boudignon, *Pierre Teilhard de Chardin*, 177.

19. Danielou is referred to and then cited in note 12 of the official commentary to *Inter insigniores*, in Swidler and Swidler, eds., *Women Priests*, 320, 335.

20. Van der Meer, *Women Priests in the Catholic Church?*

21. Gryson, *The Ministry of Women in the Early Church*; Eisen, *Women Officeholders in Early Christianity*; Madigan and Osiek, *Ordained Women in the Early Church.*

22. Flahiff's intervention in "Women Appeal to the Pastors of the Church."

tifical Commission for the Study of Woman's Role in Society and Church.[23] Composed by 15 women (many representing Catholic women's organisations) and 11 men (five prelates, three priests and four lay men), the female members were classified as "non scientifiques" or not trained in theology. The Commission became a fiasco, mainly because of its secret mandate, which was quickly published by so-called indiscretion. The task was limited to investigate women's gender-specific, so-called complementary functions, with ensuing prohibition to treat women's ordination. In 1975, six female members refused to endorse the Commission's final report and prepared a minority note, which was excluded from the Commission dossier submitted to Paul VI. Unfortunately, they feared to "cause scandal" by public dissent. Therefore, this unedifying procedure remained concealed until 1987, when the minority group finally published their elaborate note together with useful material from WUCWO (*World Union of Catholic Women's Organizations*).[24]

The Doctrine of the Faith

Administered by the Congregation for the Doctrine of the Faith, the Pontifical Biblical Commission was in 1975 asked to study whether women can be ordained priests. In 1976, the Commission unanimously (17 members) concluded that the New Testament does not resolve this question in a clear way. Therefore, 12 exegetes (against 5) found that scriptural grounds alone are not enough to exclude the possibility of ordaining women. It follows that Christ's plan would not be transgressed by permitting the ordination of women (12 against 5). Not published by the Vatican, this important document was soon known by so-called indiscretion.[25] In fact, the Commission's elaborate report makes it clear that Catholic priesthood and a fortiori women priests are anachronistic themes in New Testament context.

Nevertheless, in 1976 the *Congregation for the Doctrine of the Faith* issued its Declaration *Inter insigniores* against the ordination of women. Faced by an increasing Catholic debate and the ecumenical challenge of women ministers in Protestant denominations, the Declaration seeks to explain the traditional position of the Church: "As we are dealing with a debate which classical theology scarcely touched upon, the current argumentation

23. Van Lunen-Chenu, "La Commission pontificale de la femme," 879–91

24. Bellosillo et al., "The WUCWO Council and the Declaration *Inter insigniores*; Donders, "La voix tenace des femmes."

25. "Biblical Commission Report. Can Women be Priests?," in Swidler and Swidler, eds., *Women Priests*, 338–46.

runs the risk of neglecting essential elements" (Proemium). The Document is presented in six parts, starting with the Church's constant tradition of not ordaining women (I). Claiming that women priests were only found in heretical sects in the first centuries, the *Inter insigniores* recalls the fourth-century Epiphanius of Salamis' refutation of various heresies, *Panarion*. Among others, he lists the Montanist movement with the women prophetesses Priscilla and Maximilla (48) and the related Quintillianists, founded by Quintilla (49). The Declaration refers to their female bishops and presbyters (49,2,2–3,3). Also condemned is a group of women in Arabia who performed a sort of Eucharistic liturgy in honour of Mary, called Collyridians (78,23,2; 79,3,1–4,1) (referred to in n. 7). This last text argues that Mary should have functioned as a priest in the New Testament, if God has ordained that women should offer sacrifice or have any canonical function in the Church. She was not even entrusted with the administration of baptism, for Christ could have been baptised by his mother, rather than by John. The classical premise of only male Apostles is already found in the third-century *Didascalia* (15,3,6) and the fourth-century *Constitutiones Apostolorum* (III, 6,1–2), where Christ's female disciples are excluded from apostolic ministry. His mother is not mentioned in these texts, since Mary's apostolicity was not discussed in Early Christian sources. Instead, several Church Fathers call Mary of Magdala *Apostola Apostolorum* (John 20:1–18), and this tradition was inherited by the medieval Church.[26] *Didascalia* (15,3,9) also affirms female cultic incapability in the sense that women cannot confer baptism, arguing that Jesus was not baptised by his mother, Mary, but by John the Baptist. *Constitutiones Apostolorum* (III, 9,1–4) combines this theme with male priesthood, by invoking 1 Cor 11:3 (referred to in n. 8). The Declaration admits that scholastic arguments of women's bio-social inferiority are now obsolete, but Bonaventura's androcentric typology and Duns Scotus' invocation of Christ's will not to ordain women remain crucial. These tests are not cited, but referred to (in n. 9). Nevertheless, apologetically selected excerpts are cited in the official commentary to *Inter insigniores*.[27] Using Gospel texts to explain the attitude of Christ (II), the Declaration echoes the minority vote of the *Pontifical Biblical Commission*: "In order to reach the ultimate meaning of the mission of Jesus and the ultimate meaning of

---

26. Saxer, *Le culte de Marie Madeleine*; Taschl-Erber, "Eva wird Apostel!," 161–96. Eadem, "Apostolin und Sünderin," 41–64.

27. The Declaration with notes, in Swidler and Swidler, eds., *Women Priests*, 37–49. The official Commentary to the Declaration, in ibid., 319–37. Helman, *Women and the Vatican*, presents a useful survey and selection of Vatican Documents from the 1960s to the 2000s, but she does not include accompanying notes, which are necessary to verify the argumentation and sources invoked.

Scripture, a purely historical exegesis of the texts cannot suffice. But it must be recognised that we have here a number of converging indications that make all the more remarkable that Jesus did not entrust the apostolic charge to women. Even his Mother, who was so closely associated with the mystery of her Son, was not invested with the apostolic ministry." In order to demonstrate that Mary was not an Apostle, the Declaration cites from Innocent III's letter in 1210 to the bishops of Palencia and Burgos (quoted in Gregory IX's *Decretales*). They were ordered to restrict the power of Spanish abbesses, who blessed the nuns and heard their confessions, read the Gospel, and even preached in public, as in the Cistercian monastery *Las Huelgas*. Alluding to Peter in Matt 16:19, the pope argued that: "although the Blessed Virgin Mary surpassed in dignity and in excellence all the Apostles, it was not to her but to them that the Lord entrusted the keys to the kingdom of heaven" (referred to in n. 11).

With reference to the Book of Acts and the Pauline Letters (III), the Declaration insists that the attitude of Jesus and the Apostles constitutes the Church's *norma perpetua* (IV). The Declaration proceeds to explain this doctrine in the light of the mystery of Christ: "it seems useful and opportune to illustrate this norm by showing the profound fittingness (*convenientia*) that theological reflection discovers between the proper nature of the sacrament of Order, with its specific reference to the mystery of Christ, and the fact that only men have been called to receive priestly ordination. It is not a question here of bringing forward a demonstrative argument, but of clarifying this teaching by the analogy of faith (*analogia fidei*)." (V). To affirm that the priest represents Christ, by acting *in persona Christi*, the Declaration cites third-century Cyprian: "*sacerdos vice Christi vere fungitur*" (Epistula 63,14, with n. 15). Thomas Aquinas' argument that the priest takes the role of Christ in celebrating the Eucharist, to the point of being his very image, when he pronounces the words of consecration, is also invoked: "*sacerdos gerit imaginem Christi, in cuius persona at virtute verba pronunciat ad consecrandum*" (*Summa Theologica* III, 83,1, cited in n. 17). This doctrine is not controversial as such (cf. *Lumen Gentium* III, 28,1; *Presbyterorum ordinis* I, 3, cited in n. 16). Nonetheless, the crucial question and primary scope of *Inter insigniores* is to explain why female human beings are incapable of representing Christ as priests and functioning *in persona Christi*. Therefore, the Declaration continues to cite from Thomas Aquinas, who emphasizes that: "The sacrament, being a sign, demands that the rites performed in the conferring of a sacrament must not only produce the sacramental reality, but also signify it. (*Quia cum sacramentum sit signum in eis quae in sacramento aguntur, requiritur non solum res, sed significatio rei.*" (IV, dist. 25, quaest 2, art, 1, also cited in n. 18). In the same text, Thomas affirms that:

"Now, the female sex cannot signify any superiority of rank, for woman is in a state of subjection (*status subiectionis*). Therefore, she cannot receive the sacrament of Order." Apologetically, this piece is not cited in the Declaration, although it precisely demonstrates Thomas' axiomatic rationale for women's cultic *impedimentum sexus*. The Scholastic argument that only male priests can represent Christ *ex naturali similitudine*, is again illustrated by citing Thomas: "Sacramental signs represent what they signify by natural resemblance" (IV, dist. 25, quaest. 2, art. 2, and referred to in n. 19). According to Vatican logic, it follows that: "when Christ's role in the Eucharist is to be expressed sacramentally, there would not be this 'natural resemblance' which must exist between Christ and his minister if the role of Christ was not taken by a man (*vir*). In such a case, it would be difficult to see in the minister the image of Christ. For Christ was and remains a man (*secus difficile in eodem ministro imago Christi perspiceretur; siquidem Christus ipse fuit et permanet vir*)." After discussing some recent theological objections to this Christological rationale, the Declaration concludes by a section on the ministerial priesthood illustrated by the mystery of the Church (VI). Again trying to answer new questions with outdated solutions, it is noteworthy that *Inter insigniores* is quite elaborate and sober in tone, especially when compared to subsequent magisterial decisions. For example, women who feel God's call to be priests are not condemned: "Women who express a desire for the ministerial priesthood are doubtlessly motivated by the desire to serve Christ and the Church. And it is not surprising that, at this time when they are becoming more aware of the discriminations to which they have been subjected in society (*olim discrimina se passas esse in civitate*), they should desire the priesthood itself. But it must not be forgotten that the priesthood does not form part of the rights of the individual, but stems from the economy of the mystery of Christ and the Church." Concerning this formulation, I note that women's discrimination in the Church is apologetically omitted. The Declaration correctly states that to be ordained priest or bishop is not a human right. Instead, the invocation of divine androcentrism in order to exclude women priests remains a fundamental challenge.

Increasing Catholic Dissent

Consequently, *Inter insigniores* provoked a great number of theological studies, mainly focused or the document's doctrine and canonical authority. The leading theologian and Jesuit Karl Rahner (died 1984) soon published a critical analysis. He remained in favour of women's ordination and against enforced celibacy for secular priests.[28] I find it impossible to mention the many solid contributions to the growing Catholic debate on women's or-dination here, but it can be useful to list some of the few representative works promoting Vatican doctrine.[29] As an example of the open-minded atmosphere until John Paul II's intervention in 1994, I recall that together with the Dominican Hervé Legrand I participated as speaker at the Catho-lic, Anglican, and Orthodox congress on *Donna e Ministero*.[30] This inter-national event in 1989 was organised by the theological faculty in Palermo and presided by the archbishop, Cardinal Salvatore Pappalardo. He looked somewhat "preoccupato" when the only adversary of women priests was a bearded Orthodox prelate from Romania, whereas the spirited French pioneer of Orthodox feminist theology, Elisabeth Behr-Sigel (died 2005), argued for the ordination of women.[31]

Pontifical Intervention

The Apostolic Letter by John Paul II, *Ordinatio sacerdotalis* (1994), was is-sued shortly after the first ordination of women priests in the Church of England. This magisterial document repeats *Inter insigniores* by stating that the Church is not authorised to ordain women because Christ selected only male Apostles (1). Referring to his Apostolic Letter *Mulieris dignitatem* (1988), where women are described as Mariotypic, John Paul II invokes Christ's non-ordination of his mother to corroborate the cultic impediment of female humanity (2). This argument is quite anachronistic, given that classical Mariology is constructed between the third and fifth centuries. Inversely, it is pertinent to recall the popular veneration of Mary as priest or bishop, which had medieval roots and became widespread from the sixteenth century, even in clerical preaching. Consequently, in 1913 the Holy Office forbade to portray Mary with priestly vestments.[32] The combined argument that Mary was not an Apostle and therefore not ordained is reformulated in

28. Rahner, "Priestertum der Frau?," 291–301. In many of the interviews Rahner gave, he defended women's ordination and optional celibacy for priests, cf. "Interviews," collected in *Sämtliche Werke*, vol. 31.

29. Hauke, *Women in the Priesthood?*; Müller, *Der Empfänger des Weihesakra-ments*; Butler, *The Catholic Priesthood and Women*; Piola, *Donna e sacerdozio*. Paradoxi-cally, Piola's accurate documentation of historical sources and recent theological debate results to be counter-productive for defending the ban on women's ordination.

30. Militello, *Donna e Ministero*; Legrand, "Tradition perpetua servata?," 1–23; Bør-resen, "The Ordination of Women," 275–87.

31. Behr-Sigel and Ware, *The Ordination of Women in the Orthodox Church*.

32. Laurentin, *Marie, l'Église et le sacerdoce*. Prohibition in AAS VIII, 1913, 146.

Mariocentric terms, since she: "neither accepted the function proper to the Apostles nor the ministerial priesthood (*munus non accepit Apostolorum proprium, neque sacerdotium ministeriale*" (3). I note that the more active term *accepit* is here changed to "received" in the official English translation. Otherwise, it is important to observe that the 20th-century deduction from male Apostles to male priests is not found in medieval authors.[33] John Paul II concludes:

> Although the teaching that priestly ordination is to be reserved to men alone has been preserved by the constant and universal tradition of the Church and firmly taught by the magisterium in its more recent documents, at the present time in diverse places it is nonetheless considered still open to debate, or the Church's judgment that women are not to be admitted to ordination is considered to have a merely disciplinary force. Wherefore, in order that all doubt shall be removed regarding a matter of great importance, which pertains to the Church's divine constitution itself, in virtue of my ministry of confirming the brethren (cf. Luke 22:32) I declare that the Church has no authority whatso-ever to confer priestly ordination on women and that this judg-ment is to be definitively held (*definitive tenendam*) by all the Church's faithful (4).

When this papal veto did not silence the theological and pastoral debate, Cardinal Joseph Ratzinger, then prefect of the *Congregation for the Doctrine of Faith*, issued a *Responsio* (1995), where he certifies that: "This teaching requires definitive assent (*assensum definitivum*), since founded on the writ-ten Word of God, and from the beginning constantly preserved and applied in the Tradition of the Church, it has been set forth infallibly by the ordinary and universal Magisterium (*ab ordinario et universali magisterio infallibili-ter proposita sit*)." With this Response to a constructed doubt (*propositum dubium*), the future Benedict XVI (2005–2013) insists that the Roman Pon-tiff: "has handed on this same teaching by a formal declaration, explicitly stating what is to be held always, everywhere, and by all, as belonging to the deposit of faith (*depositum fidei*)." Nevertheless, in a commentary without signature, the cardinal specifies: "In this case, an act of the ordinary papal

---

33. In her autobiography, *Geburtsfehler: weiblich*, 411, the erudite medievalist Elisa-beth Gössmann states that she has not found Christ's election of twelve male Apostles as argument against women priests in the medieval tradition. Consequently, she notes that the vast collection of ancient, patristic, medieval, sixteenth- and twentieth-cen-tury sources in Müller, *Der Empfänger des Weihesakraments*, 512, and the index for "Zwölferkreis," in addition to New Testament texts, only refers to Vatican documents and a few theologians from the twentieth century.

magisterium, in itself not infallible, witnesses to the infallibility of the teaching of a doctrine already possessed by the Church."

Lacking *Consensus Fidelium*

These magisterial documents demonstrate the Vatican deadlock of upholding traditional conclusions despite superseded premises. In consequence, the widespread Catholic dissent was strengthened by the pontifical attempt to stop the theological critique. Since 1994/1995 the number of solid studies on women's *impedimentum sexus* has constantly increased. The focus is both on the canonical authority and the doctrinal content of John Paul II's formal declaration against women's ordination.[34] Unfortunately, assent to the ban on female priests functions as an indispensable test of doctrinal obedience in Vatican nominations of bishops and approval of professors in theology, according to national concordats even in state universities (cf. Austria and Germany).

From Cultic Impediment to Cultic Perversity

In the recent context of clerical paedophilia, the *Congregation for the Doctrine of the Faith* published adjusted norms for dealing with serious crimes against the Church's faith, sacraments or moral, *Normae de gravioribus delictis* (2010). The purpose was to update John Paul II's Apostolic Letter *Sacramentorum sanctitatis tutela* (2001), which guarantees that this Congregation has the canonical jurisdiction of such crimes. The document was soon specified by the Congregation's *Epistula* to all Catholic bishops (2001), conforming to the Church's traditional exemption of ecclesiastical personnel from secular jurisdiction. This policy started when Christianity became the official religion of the Roman Empire, and was enforced by Gregory VII's theocratic reform (reigned 1073–85). In 1559, Paul IV proclaimed that the clergy's sexual abuses were to be judged and punished by the papal *Sanctum Officium*, founded in 1542. This rule was repeated in Pius XI's Decree *Crimen sollicitationis* (1922), updated by the *Sanctum Officium* in 1962. Renamed *Congregatio pro Doctrina Fidei* in 1965, its canonical jurisdiction remains unchanged. This historical context explains why the Vatican is so reluctant to allow civil authorities to investigate, judge and punish clerical paedophilia, but partly yields to secular pressure.

---

34. Pertinent examples are: Byrne, *Woman at the Altar*; Gross, *Frauenordination*; Demel, *Frauen und kirchliches Amt*.

According to *Codex Iuris Canonici* (1983), the following offenses are punished by automatic excommunication (*excommunicatio latae sententiae*): Apostasy, heresy or schism (canon 1346), profanation of the Eucharist (canon 1367), a priest absolving an accomplice in breaking the Sixth Commandment (canon 977 and 1378 §1), a priest breaking the silence of confession (canon 1388 §1) and provoked abortion (canon 1398). It is important to emphasise that although the *Normae* of 2010 define clerical paedophilia as *delictum gravius*, the perpetrator is not automatically excommunicated, but so-called adequately punished, *iustis poenis puniatur* (canon 1395 §2), or *pro gravitate criminis* (*Normae* I, art. 6, §2).

When published in 2010 the *Normae de gravioribus delictis* provoked scandal in the media because the so-called attempted ordination of women was also defined as a *delictum gravius* against the sacrament of Order (I, art. 5). In fact, not listed in canon 1378, this crime was already punished by automatic excommunication in a *Decretum generale* of the *Congregation for the Doctrine of the Faith* (2007). Nevertheless, the real scandal of not only comparing female ordination with clerical paedophilia, but also punishing it more strongly, seems to have escaped both commentators and journalists. Citing the Decree from 2007, these *Normae* make clear "that both the one who attempts to confer sacred ordination on a woman, and she who attempts to receive sacred ordination, incurs in a *latae sententiae* excommunication reserved to the Apostolic See." This means that human femaleness is recently transformed from the canonical impediment of women's subjection to an impediment of moral perversity.

The New Bishop of Rome

I observe that Francis I, in his Apostolic Exhortation *Evangelii Gaudium* (2013) repeats John Paul II's discourse on women's gender-specific "feminine genius," although with more focus on their indispensable contribution to society and Church: "I think, for example, of the special concern which women show to others, which finds a particular, even if not exclusive, expression in motherhood. I readily acknowledge that many women share pastoral responsibilities with priests, helping to guide people, families and groups and offering new contributions to theological reflection. But we need to create still broader opportunities for a more incisive presence in the Church." (Chapter Two, II, n. 103). Unfortunately, the new bishop of Rome also repeats women's axiomatic exclusion from sacramental priesthood and even accentuates the typological argument of Christ's incarnate maleness:

The reservation of priesthood to males, as a sign of Christ the Spouse who gives himself in the Eucharist, is not a question open to discussion, but it can prove especially divisive if sacramental power is too closely identified with power in general. It must be remembered that when we speak of the sacramental power, 'we are in the realm of function, not that of dignity or holiness'. The ministerial priesthood is one means employed by Jesus for the service of his people, yet our great dignity derives from baptism, which is accessible to all. The configuration of the priest to Christ the head—namely, as the principal source of grace—does not imply an exaltation which would set him above others. In the Church, functions 'do not favour the superiority of some vis-à-vis the others'. Indeed, a woman, Mary, is more important than the bishops." (ibid., n. 104)

I note that Francis here cites John Paul II's Apostolic Exhortation *Christifideles laici* (XV, 51, 1988) with its citation of *Inter insigniores* (VI, in ibid. note 190), but he does not refer to *Ordinatio sacerdotalis*. Likewise, Francis' apologetic rhetoric seeks to avoid the fundamental challenge of twentieth-century Vatican Christology, namely that women's *impedimentum sexus* is aggravated when Christ's perfect maleness is now enhanced by typological gender ontology. The basic objection is that Christ's incarnation becomes less inclusive than it was in Patristic theology, which focused on *homo factus est* in the sense of humanity's holistic redemption.

Vatican Overhauling of Feminist Nuns

In the context of Francis' eventual efforts to reform the Roman *Curia*, I observe with dismay that he leaves cardinal (since 2014) Gerhard Ludwig Müller, prefect (since 2012) of the *Congregation for the Doctrine of the Faith*, undisturbed to censure the North American *Leadership Conference of Women Religious* (LCWR). This organisation enrolls the Mother Superiors of about 80% of nuns in the United States. In 2009, the Congregation started a so-called "Apostolic visitation" of the LCWR, with focus on doctrinal control. In 2012, his predecessor, Cardinal William Joseph Levada, issued a *Doctrinal Assessment*, denouncing the LCWR for theological errors and the promotion of "certain radical feminist themes incompatible with the Catholic faith." The document also recalls that the LCWR has never corrected its public refusal (1977) to accept the teaching of *Inter insigniores*. The archbishop of Seattle, James Peter Sartain, was nominated to head a doctrinal overhauling of these subversive nuns on behalf of the Vatican.

Already in 2011, Elisabeth A. Johnson (Fordham University, New York) was denounced by the United States Conference of Catholic Bishops for deviation from the Church's normative magisterium. In 2012, the *Congregation* declared that Margaret A. Farley (Yale University, New Haven, CT) did not follow the *Catechism of the Catholic Church* (1992). Both are nuns and leading feminist theologians, who were strongly defended by the Catholic Theological Society of America.[35] In 2014, the LCWR's nomination of Elizabeth A. Johnson to receive its Outstanding Leadership Award has especially angered Cardinal Müller. Therefore, they were accused of grave disobedience. Nevertheless, on April 16, 2015, the Vatican published a *Joint Final Report on the Implementation of the Doctrinal Assessment of the Leadership Conference of Women Religious and Mandate of the Congregation for the Doctrine of the Faith*, signed by archbishop Sartain and the LCWR. Endorsed by cardinal Müller, this document precises that the LCWR is "under the ultimate direction of the Apostolic See." Consequently, its publications "will be reviewed by competent theologians." Also, LCWR speakers must have "due regard for the Church's faith" and "a revised process for the selection of the *Outstanding Leadership Award* recipient has been articulated." The reason to end archbishop Sartain's investigation two years ahead of schedule is probably Francis I's visit to the United States in September 2015.

Conclusion

The Catholic and Orthodox Churches, which represent the majority of Christendom, are fundamentally shaken by the feminist collapse of androcentrism.[36] Their Christology, Ecclesiology, and Mariology were structured in Late Antiquity, in terms of androcentric inculturation. This historical fact can explain why the Vatican insists on fighting an already lost battle against the cultic collaboration of women and men. An obvious obstacle is the clerical fear of losing a comforting "sacred canopy." Inversely, liturgical ceremonies make conscious women feel suffocated by the man-centred display of officiating priests and bishops. On these occasions, I recall the

35. Their condemned books are: Farley, *Just Love: A Framework for Christian Sexual Ethics*; Johnson, *Quest for the Living God*. See Gaillardetz, *When the Magisterium Intervenes*; Zubía Guinea, "Errores doctrinales o pluralismo teologico?," 119–32.

36. Important surveys of this urgent challenge are: Schneiders, *Beyond Patching*; Moingt, *Faire bouger l'Église catholique*; Küng, *Can We Save the Catholic Church?* The courageous Jesuit Moingt also contributes with a succinct "Préface" to Amandier and Chablis, *Le Déni*, 9–18. Their excellent analysis of the current Vatican deadlock is a fine example of *haute vulgarisation*, accurately documented without heavy scientific apparatus.

refreshing irony of Erasmus of Rotterdam's *Colloquium Abbatis et Eruditae* (1524). Here, the ingenuous abbot is warned by the learned lady: "If you are not careful, we will soon preside in your theological schools and preach in your temples. We will occupy your mitres. (*Quod nisi caueritis vos, res eo tandem euadet, vt not praesideamus in scholis theologicis, vt concionemur in templis. Occupabimus mitras vestras*)."[37] I also remember that a salon feminist and theologian at La Sorbonne University in Paris, François Poullain de la Barre, in *De l'égalité des deux sexes* (1673) affirmed that he found no reason to forbid women's ordination.

In this perspective, it is inspiring to invoke two holy women who were recently praised by the Roman Catholic Church. Thérèse de Lisieux was canonised in 1925 by Pius XI, who in 1932 refused to declare her a *Doctor Ecclesiae*. In 1923, he had equally refused this honour to Teresa de Avila, because of her female sex: "*obstat sexus*." Nevertheless, both Teresa and Caterina da Siena became Doctors of the Church in 1970, followed by Thérèse in 1997. During the Pontifical Mass in Rome, a part of her pertinent text from 1896 was recited: "Sans doute, ces trois privilèges sont bien ma vocation, Carmélite, Épouse et Mère, cependant je sens en moi d'autres vocations, je me sens la vocation de Guerrier, de Prêtre, d'Apôtre, de Docteur, de Martyr" . . . Omitted was: "Je sens en moi la vocation de Prêtre, avec quel amour, ô Jesus, je te porterais dans mes mains lorsque à ma voix, tu descendrais du Ciel."[38] Thérèse explicitly refers to her vocation of priestly function in the Eucharist, although mixed with the traditional symbolism where Christ is polygamous Bridegroom of numerous consecrated virgins. More theologically succinct, the Carmelite and philosopher Edith Stein, who was canonised by John Paul II in 1998 and declared Co-Patroness of Europe (together with Birgitta of Sweden and Caterina da Siena) in 1999, affirmed already in 1932 that she did not see any dogmatic reason that could forbid the Church to ordain women: "Dogmatisch scheint mir nichts im Wege zu stehen, was es der Kirche verbieten können, eine solche bislang unerhörte Neuerung (Priestertum der Frau) durchzuführen. Ob es praktisch sich empfehlen würde, dass lässt mancherlei Gründe für und wider zu."[39] Facing this topic long before women were ordained in any Christian Church or denomination, Edith Stein is an admirable pioneer of feminist theology. In the *communio sanctorum*, she takes part in the inclusive inculturation of Catholic tradition.

37. *Colloquia*, 403–8.

38. Ms. B, in Six, ed., *Thérèse de Lisieux par elle-même*, 3:70.

39. *Die Frau: Ihre Aufgabe nach Natur und Grade*, in Gelber and Leuven, eds., *Edith Steins Werke*, Band V, Louvain, Freiburg im Breisgau: Editions Neuwelarts, Herder, 1959, 43.

This process was first elaborated by the ancient Church Fathers' attribution of asexual God-likeness to women already from creation. When the medieval Church Mothers described God with female metaphors in order to provide a divine model of women's *imago Dei* as female human beings, they prepared the way for the 20th-century holistic definition of God-like humanity, *qua* male or female. At this current dogmatic stage, the traditional typological symbolism which is based on female subordination can no longer be used to preserve the priesthood as a gender-specific male function. The recent Vatican invocation of Christ as the Church's Bridegroom in order to construct an ontological gender-play, in defence of divisive sexual complementarity and female *impedimentum sexus*, is both inapplicable and alien to viable Catholic *sana doctrina*. Only when expressed in terms of both women's and men's gendered experience does theology become a fully human God-language.[40]

Magisterial Documents

published in Acta Apostolicae Sedis = AAS, Città del Vaticano

Littera Encyclica *Pacem in Terris* (April 20, 1963), in AAS 55, 1963, 257–304.

Declaratio *Inter insigniores* (October 15, 1976), in AAS 69, 1977, 98–116.

Epistola Apostolica *Mulieris dignitatem* (August 15, 1988), in AAS 80, 1988, 1653–1729.

Adhortatio Apostolica *Christifideles laici* (December 30, 1988), in AAS 81, 1989, 393–521.

Epistola Apostolica *Ordinatio sacerdo*talis (May 22, 1994), in AAS 86, 1994, 545–48.

Responsio ad propositum dubium (October 28, 1995), in AAS 87, 1114.

Littera Apostolica *Sacramentorum sanctitatis tutela* (April 30, 2001), in AAS 93, 2001, 737–39.

Epistula *De delictis gravioribus* (May 18, 2001), in AAS 93, 2001, 785–78.

Epistula de mutuis relationibus inter viros et mulieres. Lettera ai Vescovi della Chiesa Cattolica sulla collaborazione dell'uomo e della donna nella Chiesa e nel mondo (May 31, 2004, Italian original), in AAS 96, 2004, 671–67.

Decretum generale de delicto attentatae sacrae ordinationis mulieris (December 19, 2007), in AAS 100, 2008, 403.

Normae de gravioribus delictis (May 21, 2010), in AAS 102, 2010, 419–31.

Allocutio: *Dum Summus Pontifex Natalicia Omina Romanae Curiae offert* (December 21, 2012, in Italian), in AAS 105, 2013, 47–54.

40. Børresen, "Sexual difference in Christian Doctrine and Symbolism: Historical Impact and Feminist Critique," in Schmiedel and Matarazzo, Jr., eds. *Dynamics of Difference: Christianity and Alterity*, 161–171. "Male-Centred Christology and Female Cultic Incapability: Women's Impedimentum Sexus," in Dunn and Mayer, eds, *Shaping Identity from the Roman Empire to Byzantium. Studies Inspired by Pauline Allen*, 478–501.

Adhortatio Apostolica *Evangelii Gaudium* (November 24, 2013, Spanish original). *Apostolic Exhortation Evangelii Gaudium* (Official English translation), Città del Vaticano: Vatican Press, 2013.

Commentary to *Inter insigniores* (Italian original), in *Osservatore Romano*, Città del Vaticano, 28–1–1977. English translation in *Women Priests. A Catholic Commentary on the Vatican Declaration*, edited by Leonard Swidler and Arlene Swidler, 319–37, New York, Ramsey, Toronto: Paulist Press, 1977.

Commentary to *Responsio* (Italian original), in *Osservatore Romano*, 19–11–1995. English translation in *Origins* XXV, 24, 1995, 403–5.

Bibliography

Alexandre, Monique. "La place des femmes dans le Christianisme ancien: Bilan des études récentes." In *Les Pères de l'Église et les femmes*, edited by Pascal Delage, 24–46. Rochefort: Histoire et culture, 2003.

Amandier, Maud, and Alice Chablis. *Le Déni: Enquête sur l'Église et l'Égalité des Sexes*. Montrouge: Bayard, 2014.

The Apostolicity of the Church: Study Document of the Lutheran-Roman Catholic Commission on Unity. Minneapolis: Lutheran University Press, 2006.

Beattie, Tina. *New Catholic Feminism: Theology and Theory*. London: Routledge, 2006.

Behr-Sigel, Elisabeth, and Kallistos Ware. *The Ordination of Women in the Orthodox Church*. Geneva: World Council of Churches, 2000.

Bellosillo, Maria del Pilar, et al. "The WUCWO Council and the Declaration *Inter insigniores*. The Pontifical Study Commission on Women in Church and Society." *Pro Mundi Vita Bulletin* 108.1 (1987) 10–21.

Børresen, Kari Elisabeth. "Cristianesimo e diritti umani delle donne: impedimentum sexus." In *Le donne cristiane e il sacerdozio. Dalle origini allâ età contemporanea*, edited by Dinora Corsi, 261–71. Rome: Viella, 2004.

———. *From Patristics to Matristics. Selected Articles on Christian Gender Models*. Rome: Herder, 2002.

———. "Jean-Paul II et les femmes." *Lumière et Vie* 52 (2003) 57–69.

———. "Male-Centred Christology and Female Cultic Incapability: Women's Impedimentum Sexus." In *Shaping Identity from the Roman Empire to Byzantium. Studies Inspired by Pauline Allen*, edited by Geoffrey D. Dunn and Wendy Mayer, Supplements to Vigiliae Christianae, Vol. 132, 478–501. Leiden, Boston: Brill, 2015.

———. "Matristics." In *Encyclopedia of Ancient Christianity*, edited by Angelo Di Berardino et al., 2:730–35. Downers Grove, IL: InterVarsity, 2014.

———. "Sexual difference in Christian Doctrine and Symbolism: Historical Impact and Feminist Critique." In *Dynamics of Difference: Christianity and Alterity. A Festschrift for Werner Jeanrond*, edited by Ulrich Schmiedel and James M. Matarazzo, Jr., 161–171. London: Bloomsbury T&T Clark, 2015.

———. *Subordination and Equivalence: The Nature and Role of Woman in Augustine and Thomas Aquinas. A Reprint of a Pioneering Classic*. Kampen: Kok Pharos, 1995. Updated English edition of French original: *Subordination et Equivalence*. Oslo, Paris 1968.

Børresen, Kari Elisabeth, ed. *Christian and Islamic Gender Models in Formative Traditions*. Studi e Testi TardoAntichi 2. Rome: Herder, 2004.

————. *The Image of God. Gender Models in Judaeo-Christian Tradition.* Minneapolis: Fortress, 1995.

Børresen, Kari Elisabeth, and Emanuela Prinzivalli, eds. *Le Donne nello Sguardo degli Antichi Autori Cristiani.* La Bibbia e le Donne 5/1. Trapani: Il Pozzo di Giacobbe, 2013.

Børresen, Kari Elisabeth, and Adriana Valerio, eds. *Frauen und Bibel im Mittelalter. Rezeption und Interpretation.* Die Bibel und die Frauen 6/2. Stuttgart: Kohlhammer, 2013.

Børresen, Kari Elisabeth, and Kari Vogt. *Women's Studies of the Christian and Islamic Traditions.* Dordrecht: Kluwer Academic, 1993.

Boudignon, Patrice. *Pierre Teilhard de Chardin: Sa vie, son oeuvre, sa réflexion.* Paris: Cerf, 2008.

Butler, Sara. *The Catholic Priesthood and Women: A Guide to the Teaching of the Church.* Chicago: Hillenbrand, 2007.

Byrne, Lavinia. *Woman at the Altar. The Ordination of Women in the Roman Catholic Church.* New York: Continuum, 1995.

Clark, Elizabeth A. *Ascetic Piety and Women's Faith. Essays on Late Ancient Christianity.* Studies in Women and Religion 20. Lewiston, NY: Mellen, 1986.

Demel, Sabine. *Frauen und kirchliches Amt: Von Ende eines Tabus in der katholischen Kirche.* Freiburg: Herder, 2004.

Donders, Dirkje. "La 'voix tenace des femmes.'" ThD diss., Faculté de théologie, Université catholique, Nijmegen, 1997.

Eisen, Ute. *Women Officeholders in Early Christianity: Epigraphical and Literary Studies.* Collegeville, MN: Liturgical, 2000. (German original 1996.)

Elm, Susanna. *"Virgins of God": The Making of Asceticism in Late Antiquity.* Oxford: Oxford University Press, 1994.

Erasmus of Rotterdam. *Colloquia.* In *Desiderii Erasmi Opera Omnia* I, 3, edited by Léon E. Halkin et al., 403–8. Amsterdam: 1972.

Farley, Margaret A. *Just Love: A Framework for Christian Sexual Ethics.* New York: Continuum, 2006.

Flahiff, George Bernard. "Women Appeal to the Pastors of the Church." *Pro Mundi Vita Bulletin* 108.1 (1987) 7–10.

Gaillardetz, Richard R., ed. *When the Magisterium Intervenes: The Magisterium and Theologians in Today's Church: Includes a Case Study on the Doctrinal Investigation of Elizabeth A. Johnson.* Collegeville, MN: Glazier, 2012.

Gelber, Lucy, and Romaeus Leuven, eds. *Edith Steins Werke.* Vol. 5. Freiburg: Herder, 1959.

Goldie, Rosemary. *From a Roman Window: Five Decades. The World, the Church and the Catholic Laity.* Victoria, Australia: HarperCollins Religious, 1998.

Gössmann, Elisabeth. *Metaphysik und Heilgeschichte: Eine theologische Untersuchung der Summa Halensis.* Munich: Hueber, 1964.

————. *Geburtsfehler: Weiblich. Lebenserinnerungen einer katholischen Theologin.* Munich: Iudicium, 2003.

Gross, Walter, ed. *Frauenordination: Stand der Diskussion in der katholischen Kirche.* Munich: Wewel, 1996.

Gryson, Roger. *The Ministry of Women in the Early Church.* Collegeville, MN: Liturgical Press, 1976. (French original 1972.)

Hauke, Manfred. *Women in the Priesthood? A Systematic Analysis in the Light of the Order of Creation and Redemption.* San Francisco: Ignatius, 1998.

Heinzelmann, Gertrud. *Wir schweigen nicht länger: Frauen äusseren sich zum II. Vatikanischen Konzil.* Zurich: Interfeminas, 1964.

———. *Die geheiligte Diskriminierungen.* Bonstetten: Interfeminas, 1986.

Helman, Ivy A. *Women and the Vatican: An Exploration of Official Documents.* Maryknoll, NY: Orbis, 2012.

Johnson, Elizabeth A. *Quest for the Living God: Mapping Frontiers in Theology of God.* New York: Continuum, 2007.

Küng, Hans. *Can We Save the Catholic Church?* London: HarperCollins, 2013.

Laurentin, René. *Marie, l'Église et le sacerdoce.* Étude théologique. Paris: Nouvelles éditions latines, 1953.

Legrand, Hervé. "Traditio perpetua servata? The non-ordination of Women: Tradition or simply Historical Fact?" *One in Christ* 29 (1993) 1–23.

Lunen-Chenu, Marie-Thérèse van. "La Commission pontificale de la femme, une occasion manquee." *Études* 344 (1976) 879–91.

Macy, Gary. "The Ordination of Women in the Early Middle Ages." *Theological Studies* 61 (2000) 481–597.

Madigan, Kevin, and Carolyn Osiek, eds. *Ordained Women in the Early Church: A Documentary History.* Baltimore: John Hopkins University Press, 2005.

Martin, John Hilary. "The Ordination of Women and the Theologians in the Middle Ages." In *A History of Women and Ordination*, edited by Bernard Cooke and Gary Macy, 1:31–175. Lanham, MD: Scarecrow, 2002.

McEnroy, Carmel Elizabeth. *Guests in their Own House: The Women of Vatican II.* New York: Crossroad, 1996.

Meer, Haye van der. *Women Priests in the Catholic Church? A Theological Historical Investigation.* Philadelphia: Temple University Press, 1973. (German original 1969).

Militello, Cettina, ed. *Donna e Ministero. Un dibattito ecumenico.* Rome: Dehoniane, 1991.

———. *Donna e teologia: Bilancio di un secolo.* Bologna: Dehoniane, 2004.

Minnis, Alastair J. "*De impedimento sexus*: Women's Bodies and Medieval Impediments to Female Ordination." In *Medieval Theology and the Natural Body*, edited by Peter Biller and Alastair J. Minnis, 109–39. York: York Medieval, 1997.

Moingt, Joseph. *Faire bouger l'Église catholique.* Paris: Desclée de Brouwer, 2012.

Müller, Gerhard Ludwig, ed. *Der Empfänger des Weihesakraments. Quellen zur Lehre und Praxis der Kirche, nur Männern das Weihesakraments zu spenden.* Würzburg: Echter, 1999.

Perroni, Marinella. "A proposito del principio mariano-petrino: per una metodologia della elaborazione-communicazione della fede che rispetti il dato biblico." In *La fede e la sua communicazione. Il Vangelo, la Chiesa e la cultura*, edited by Piero Ciardella and Silvano Maggiani, 93–116. Bologna: Dehoniane, 2006.

———. "Principio Mariano-Principio Petrino: Quaestio disputanda?" *Marianum* 72 (2010) 547–53.

Perroni, Marinella, and Hervé Legrand, eds. *Avendo qualcosa da dire: Teologhe e teologi rileggono il Vaticano II.* Milan: Paoline, 2014.

Perroni, Marinella, Alberto Melloni, and Serena Noceti, eds. *"Tantum aurora est": Donne e Concilio Vaticano II.* Berlin: Lit, 2012.

Piola, Alberto. *Donna e sacerdozio. Indagine storico-teologica degli aspetti antropologici dell'ordinazione delle donne.* Studia Tauriniensia 18. Cantalupa (Torino): Effatà, 2006.

Rahner, Karl. "Priestertum der Frau?" *Stimmen der Zeit* 15 (1977) 291–301.

———. "Interviews." In *Sämtliche Werke*, 31:2–451. Freiburg: Herder, 2007.

Raming, Ida. "The Priestly Office of Women: God's Gift to a Renewed Church." In *A History of Women and Ordination*, edited by Cooke and Macy, 2:3–305. Lanham, MD: Scarecrow, 2004. (German original 1973.)

Reidick, Gertrude. *Die hierarchische Struktur der Ehe.* Münchener Theologische Studien III, Kanonische Abtellung 3. Munich: EOS, 1953.

Ruether, Rosemary Radford. *Women and Redemption: A Theological History.* 2nd ed. Minneapolis: Fortress, 2012.

Saxer, Victor. *Le culte de Marie Madeleine en Occident des origines à la fin du moyen âge 1–2.* Paris: Clavreuil, 1959.

Schneiders, Sandra M. *Beyond Patching: Faith and Feminism in the Catholic Church.* Mahwah, NJ: Paulist, 2004.

Six, Jean-François, ed. *Thérèse de Lisieux par elle-même.* 3 vols. Paris: Grasset, Desclée de Brouwer, 1997.

Swidler, Leonard, and Arlene Swidler, eds. *Women Priests: A Catholic Commentary on the Vatican Delaration.* New York: Paulist, 1977.

Taschl-Erber, Andrea. "Eva wird Apostel! Rezeptionslinien des Osterapostolats Marias von Magdala in lateinischen Patristik." In *Geschlechterverhältnisse und Macht: Lebensformen in der Zeit des frühen Christentums*, edited by Irmtraud Fischer and Christoph Heil, 161–96. Exegese in unserer Zeit 21. Münster: Lit, 2010.

———. "Apostolin und Sünderin: Mittelalterliche Rezeptionen Marias von Magdala." In *Frauen und Bibel im Mittelalter. Rezeption und Interpretation*, edited by Kari Elisabeth Børresen and Adriana Valerio, 41–64. Stuttgart: Kohlhammer, 2013.

Valerio, Adriana. *Madri del Concilio: Ventitre donne al Vaticano II.* Rome: Carocci, 2012.

Zorzi, Benedetta Selene. *Al di là del "genio femminile": Donne e genere nella storia della teologia cristiana.* Rome: Carocci, 2014.

Zubía Guinea, Marta. "Errores doctrinales o pluralismo teológico?" *Journal of the European Society of Women in Theological Research* 21 (2013) 119–32.

─────────── 14 ───────────

The Dialogue between Catholics and Lutherans

Its Development and Prospects

André Birmelé

Translated from French to English
by Sarah Hinlicky Wilson

THE SIXTEENTH-CENTURY REFORMATION DIVIDED the Western Church into mutually antagonistic ecclesial families. This event was not a mere accident of history but the religious dimension of a profound alteration within Western civilization, starting already during the Renaissance, which touched all aspects of life in Europe. Martin Luther and John Calvin were contemporaries of Christopher Columbus and Magellan, of Leonardo da Vinci and Michelangelo, of King Francis I of France and Holy Roman Emperor Charles V. On this continent that was in such a state of upheaval, theological and ecclesial controversies fused with economic, social, ethnic, and more generally political issues. They contributed to a major religious crisis that had serious and long-lasting consequences for the Church and for all of Western society. Thus there appeared a stream of currents of reform, each of which separated from the Roman Church without leading to one single distinct movement. Despite their common intentions, these diverse ecclesial families (Lutheran, Reformed, Anglican, Zwinglian, Anabaptist, etc.) ended up opposed to one another and even today remain quite distinct.

After the failure of several attempts at conciliation, the rejection of the Roman Church by these Reformation Churches was expressed theologically in the form of doctrinal condemnations in confessional writings or symbolical books, responding also to the anathemas that the Council of Trent would eventually pronounce against them. The relations between Rome and these reforming movements in the centuries ahead would be marked by hostility corresponding to the reciprocal doctrinal condemnations, which signified excommunication. It would be necessary to wait until the second part of the twentieth century for a real dialogue to be taken up between these separated families; and such was officially mandated on the Catholic side by the Second Vatican Council. Today after fifty years of labor, one can better comprehend the issues of the sixteenth century as well as the reasons and prospects for contemporary rapprochement.

We would like in these pages to pay homage in particular to Professor Turid Karlsen Seim. She has been and still is an actor and witness engaged in the search for unity. In the work of the Faith and Order Commission of the WCC, of which she has been one of the vice-presidents for many years, she has always been driven by the desire for a challenging theological dialogue, knowing that only tenacious and careful work can and will permit a real mutual recognition between confessional families as authentic expressions of the one Church of Jesus Christ. We will limit ourselves in these pages to a particular concern of Turid Karlsen Seim, namely her decisive contribution to the international dialogue between Roman Catholics and Lutherans. For many years a member of the board of the Lutheran Foundation for Interconfessional Research, which supports the Institute for Ecumenical Research in Strasbourg, itself connected to the Lutheran World Federation (LWF), Turid Karlsen Seim was directly involved in the Joint Declaration on the Doctrine of Justification (JDDJ), signed in 1999 by the Vatican and the LWF. Thereafter she became a member of the dialogue commission between these two confessional families, a responsibility that she exercises up to the present day.

The limitation of our subject matter here is justified by the fact that the dialogue between Lutherans and Catholics is by far the most advanced. It has been able to manage the signing of a fundamental accord on justification by faith, as mentioned above. This accord fundamentally changes the dimensions of the problem. In effect, by this signing, the two families agree on their common foundation. Future dialogue must be carried out from the starting point of a fundamental consensus, and no longer—as was the case during the nearly five hundred years proceeding—from a situation of division and mutual condemnation. Not every matter has been resolved, for all that, but the situation is radically new and offers prospects hitherto unimagined. Article 43 of the JDDJ underlines that it is necessary at present to draw out the consequences of this accord in the domain of ecclesiology and ethics in order to reach a genuine mutual recognition within the diversity. The task we stand before is great and requires time to unfold.

In recent years, we have had numerous occasions to work with Turid Karlsen Seim. The reflection that we offer below aspires to be only a little indication of our recognition of her ecclesial and ecumenical work.

After having in the first part reported on certain new orientations that the agreement on justification has opened up, we will in the second part specify the ecclesiological challenge that it is our task to undertake in the future dialogue.

The Context and New Pathways

Our intention is not to return here to the history and contents of the JDDJ. We have had occasion to do so in other settings.[1] We want in this contribution to emphasize the theological and methodological choices that allowed us to reach that agreement. They contain the decisive breakthroughs and represent the background upon which were written the consensus upon the particular issues of the problematic of justification. These choices open up new and fundamental ecumenical steps forward. Here will we identify three of them.

1.1.

Based on the progress of historical and exegetical scholarship, modern ecumenical efforts have highlighted that many of the divergences during the Reformation can be explained on the basis of a rupture in the **systems of thought and language**. That fact, often pointed out by researchers in the past thirty years, is today largely admitted also by the Churches themselves. It has been confirmed officially by a commission established by Pope John Paul II himself during one of his trips to Germany in 1981. That group, which brought together the most eminent Catholic and Protestant specialists, was able to show that the conflict of the sixteenth century was not based so much on foundational beliefs as on different manners of articulating faith and reality, on different philosophical and anthropological options that nevertheless intended to bear witness to the same Gospel.[2]

Over against a scholastic theology that applied the categories of classical Aristotelian metaphysics in defining the human being in and of itself in a more substantialist manner, the Reformation offered a new approach: it

---

1. Birmelé, *La communion ecclésiale.*

2. Cf. the conclusions of this commission: Lehmann and Pannenberg, eds., *Thee Condemnations of the Reformation Era: Do They Still Divide?*

would only understand the human person and speak of it as a being before God (*coram Deo*). This approach was founded on a dynamic understanding of the creative word of God that brings about a new situation. The understanding of life is thus relational. The Reformation no longer defined the human person in and of itself. The life of a believer is that of a child. It exists only in the face-to-face encounter with the Father. The Father and the child participate in a new reality of which neither of the two is the sole owner. The fundamental notions of sin, faith, grace, and salvation are understood in a relational manner. Sin is not so much a particular moral fault that can be expiated or satisfied by a surplus of grace as it is the description of a more fundamental situation: the human person is centered on himself, thinks himself able to live by and for himself, and because of this fact is in a state of rupture from God and others. Moral faults are only the consequence of this state. Grace is not so much a characteristic of the state of the believer as that the person discovers her identity outside herself by entering into a new relation to God who, consequently, determines all the moments of her new life. The death and resurrection of Jesus Christ are not in the first place an expiation but an entrance of Christ into death in order to conquer it and establish a new communion that unites believers to God beyond all ruptures caused by sin and death. For the same reason, the very idea of progression in a "state of grace" makes hardly any sense, unless it is evident that all the life of the child will be a witness, recognizing the new situation.

This approach, which the Reformation developed on the basis of new perceptions stemming from exegesis of the Holy Scriptures, was not understood by the Roman Church. Against the view of the Catholic side on acts as definitive of the believing person, the Reformation side emphasized the new being freely offered to the believer as the prerequisite, determining every subsequent act.

The Reformation thus marked the eruption in the West of another anthropology and set to work on it with new philosophical tools. It took the German Catholic theologian O. H. Pesch to prove this. He demonstrated it in his study of 1967, dedicated to a comparison of Luther and St. Thomas Aquinas, where he spoke of an "existential" Lutheran approach (we would prefer the term "relational") replacing the Thomistic "sapiential" approach.[3]

Re-read from this perspective, the reciprocal condemnations of the sixteenth century demand a reinterpretation and can be attributed, in certain cases, to mere misunderstandings. The most typical example is the definition of the notion of "faith." Following in the scholastic line, Roman

---

3. Pesch, *Theologie der Rechtfertigung bei Martin Luther und Thomas von Aquin.*

theology understood by this term the fact of not doubting a revealed truth that had been formulated into dogma. It was evident that such "faith" was not by itself sufficient to qualify a person as a Christian. It was necessary to complete it with works of love (*fides caritate formata*). But Luther, taking up the definitions of St. Paul, defined "faith" as the trusting and living relation that unites the believer to his Lord, a daily relationship nourished by prayer, Bible reading, and community life. Luther distinguished faith from belief in the truth of texts and dogmas. To believe signifies being a child of God. This new situation is a gift. It does not result from a human work nor is it completed by works of love, even if these are indeed a necessary consequence of faith. It is evident that, on the basis of its conception of faith, the Council of Trent could only condemn the idea of salvation by "faith alone," just as the Reformation could not but refuse the Roman approach. Despite using the same terms, the two parties were not speaking the same language. Nevertheless, O. H. Pesch has demonstrated that, by retranslating the one party's categories of thought into those of the other, the ultimate intentions of both parties can be shown to be present analogously in the other. Cardinal Willebrands, president of the Pontifical Secretariat for Unity, was one of the first to underline this fact in his presentation at the assembly of the LWF in Evian in 1969.[4]

Not all the problems can be explained away by calling them misunderstandings. Even if the classical reduction of the problem to a conflict between "salvation by faith" and "salvation by works" is only a caricature, the different philosophical and anthropological approaches still reflect different theological choices. It is undeniable that the more Catholic approach to salvation and grace as a description of the state of the believer and of her progressive evolution under the action of the Holy Spirit is not the same as that of the Reformation, for which grace is participation in the righteousness of God and something for which the person can never prepare herself. In the Catholic understanding, the person touched by grace is rendered capable of cooperating with the divine Spirit in order to progress in her state by multiplying by her meritorious works which are the fruits of this grace, an approach that the Reformation refused vehemently.

The commission of experts established by John Paul II decided that those theological differences are important. The two approaches can nevertheless both be founded upon serious biblical research. Additionally, the two theological options encounter one another today in the heart of both Catholicism and Lutheranism without being mutually exclusive. The commission underlines in its conclusions that for these two approaches, salvation is

4. The acts of this assembly: Grosc, ed., *Sent into the World*, particularly 54–55.

the work of the exclusive gift of God, who by the death and resurrection of Christ accepts human persons freely, declares them to be children of God, and makes them capable of a new life. The dialogue should not therefore occupy itself with a vain effort at uniformization. The JDDJ does not eliminate either of these approaches but shows on the contrary when, how, and under what conditions they can correspond to one another and express the reality of the saving work of God for the benefit of humankind.

1.2.

The observation made above about different anthropological and philosophical choices sends us back to the second aspect of ecumenical methodology put in place by the Joint Declaration, the distinction between **the truth** and **the expression of that truth**. The commission of experts asserted that, in the case of the understanding of salvation, Catholic and Lutheran theological expressions witness to the same reality, which refuses to be itself imprisoned in a single theological formula.

This distinction between the contents of a truth and the doctrinal forms that recognize it in the history of the Church was emphasized by Pope John XXIII. In his celebrated discourse at the opening of the Council, he proposed, on October 11, 1962, to distinguish between "revealed truth," intangible and immutable, and the diverse "formulations" that the Church was called to receive over the course of the centuries: "The substance of the ancient doctrine of the deposit of faith is one thing, and the way in which it is presented is another."[5] In affirming that the historical continuity of the Church resides in the substance of the statement and not in the historical formulations thereof, and by this fact that the historical formulations of the truth are open to dialogue, the pope inaugurated a new epoch. The bishop of Rome proposed to the Council a hermeneutical option that would bring about an evolution in the fundamental attitude of the Catholic Church that had no real historic antecedent: a new understanding of itself and of its teaching such that there was a transition from an attitude of monologue to an attitude of dialogue, while still preserving the traditional fundamentals of Catholicism. In affirming the immutable character of the truth, of which the Church is the treasury, yet distinguishing "the truths contained in our venerable doctrine" from the forms that it had taken in history, John XXIII nevertheless made the critique of certain of these forms possible. The conciliar minority wanted to avoid this orientation and the Roman authorities would search on their part for ways of relativizing the impact of these re-

5. "Pope John's Opening Speech to the Council," 710–19, esp. 715.

marks. But the pope had indeed put forward a new manner of dealing with the teaching of the Catholic Church, and a majority of the council fathers were ready to follow him.

The distinction between the "message" on the one hand and the "doctrine" on the other is also maintained in the Reformation Churches. In a key section, the Leuenberg Agreement (LA), which established full communion between Lutherans and Reformed in Europe,[6] speaks of "the message of justification as the message of the free grace of God." This message is the Gospel, which proclaims Jesus Christ as the salvation of the world in fulfillment of the promise made to the people of the old covenant (LA 7). In the next paragraph, the LA adds: "[t]he Reformers expressed the true understanding of the Gospel in the doctrine of justification." To highlight the *message* of justification is at the same time to distinguish it from an insistence on any particular doctrine or theory. The doctrine of justification is the necessary explanation and the theological form of the message of justification. But only the latter of the two is the *articulus stantis et cadentis ecclesiae*. The message of the free grace of God is not the prisoner of a single doctrinal expression. Other doctrinal formulations could also be authentic expressions of the same message. The understanding of the reformers is a "true understanding," but that does not mean it is the only one. This agreement leads to a declaration of full communion between Churches with "different confessional positions" (LA 29). It does not affirm that the preaching and understanding of the sacraments at present will be identical in each of the traditions participating in this Agreement. The relevance of the Agreement is another one: it affirms that even in its differences, the other tradition practices—with its own piety and with its particular theological accents— true worship through word and sacrament, the means of grace by which God offers salvation. In other words, the one message of salvation is authentically offered through the particular languages of the sister Churches.

Thus the distinction between the inalterable message of the Gospel and the languages chosen by the different ecclesial families had already been established, more than 40 years ago, by the leaders and theologians of the Churches in their earliest dialogues. It is a fundamental distinction for contemporary ecumenical dialogue.

This distinction between the truth and different expressions of it clearly recalls another pair well-known in the history of philosophy, namely "form" and "substance." It would be tempting to use these terms here. Nevertheless a certain prudence is called for, in view of the widely divergent interpretations that these notions have generated in history. It seems more judicious

6. *Agreement between Reformation Churches in Europe (Leuenberg Agreement).*

to speak of a truth of the faith and its different formulations, of a content and its expression in the language(s) of Churches in history. This assessment is an important fruit of the history of contemporary ecumenism, the past centuries having been marked precisely by the fact that each ecclesial family insisted on the exclusive character of its language, which alone was thought to be capable of recognizing the truth of the faith.

This old approach was replaced for the first time in the bilateral dialogues among Reformation Churches, especially in the dialogues between the Lutheran, Reformed, Methodist, and Anglican traditions, which established in many places ecclesial communion between their Churches. But this distinction between fundamental truth and ecclesial languages was absolutely vital for the process and methodology that led to the signing of the JDDJ. The Catholic Church itself also entered into this process. In appropriating the JDDJ, the Roman Church has for the first time in the history of dialogue between the Western Churches consented to say that the same fundamental conviction can be rendered in other languages and with other formulations than its own. This fact is perhaps the major breakthrough of the JDDJ, a fact too rarely emphasized.

1.3.

On the basis of the methodological choices discussed here, it is possible to reach a **differentiated consensus** in the understanding of salvation. The JDDJ understands the consensus as being the relation that exists between two accounts that do not separate the Churches insofar as they are different accounts of the same fundamental truth. The consensus is by definition in itself "differentiated," which is to say capable of distinguishing and accepting the differences. The nonuniformity is not a deficit but the characteristic of the very life of all ecclesial communion, of all *koinonia* among believers, which is in turn the image of the *koinonia* that is God the Trinity. This proposition is not really new, for such a conception of consensus had been developed for many long years in the heart of the ecumenical movement. Without this approach, no agreement allowing for ecclesial communion would have been possible among Lutherans, Reformed, Anglicans, Methodists, etc.

It is appropriate to distinguish between the various levels regarding each particular doctrinal affirmation: the one of fundamental truth and the other of expositions of this truth. The fundamental truth demands an understanding and a common affirmation; the exposition of this truth by contrast occurs under the form of words, of modes of thought, and of theological choices that express a legitimate diversity that is not at all to be deplored. A monolithic understanding of consensus blocks all dialogue, requiring, in effect, (1) that one of the partners abandon their concepts and adopt those of the other instead, or (2) that the two partners elaborate together a compromise that would not conform to either of the two. "Differentiated" consensus by contrast seeks to discover the theological intention behind a doctrinal affirmation and endeavors to see if there is a correspondence at the level of the fundamental truth that the different expositions seek to express, each in their own history and particular context.

For a particular doctrinal question, the search for a differentiated consensus demands a double approach: (1) an agreement on what is to be lifted up of the fundamental truth that calls for a common affirmation regarding the controversial question and (2) a clarification of the particular expressions, which remain different but whose legitimately different character needs to be specified and verified so that it is no longer possible to call into question the fundamental common affirmation. Thus it leads to "unity in reconciled diversity."

2. A Process Transferable to Ecclesiology?

This ecumenical method has, in the JDDJ, been applied to the understanding of salvation. The question which presents itself now is the following: is it possible to transfer this process to ecclesiology? To envisage a differentiated consensus in ecclesiology would signify that diverse ecclesiological approaches and different expressions of the manner of being of the Church could express one and the same fundamental understanding of the ecclesial mystery that confesses the faith. This question is put to the Lutheran and Roman Catholic traditions in different ways.

2.1. The response of the Reformation Churches is positive.

What is important for the understanding of justification counts all the more so for the Church. This conviction is the logical consequence of the fundamental ecclesiogical understanding proposed by the Reformation Churches.

   a. Following the Augsburg Confession, the Lutheran tradition defines the Church as the community of believers "among whom the Gospel is purely preached and the holy sacraments are administered according to the Gospel."[7] The insistence on the authentic celebration of the

7. "Confessio Augustana," 7.

word and sacraments as the definition of the Church is not accidental. It is the ecclesiological translation of the priority that the Reformation Churches accord to the saving work of God. By the cross and resurrection of Jesus Christ, God has reconciled and still reconciles the world; God offers salvation to human beings. The human being is not saved on the basis of his works; he is not what he does, but he does what he is. God having conferred a new identity upon him, he lives in the present in conformity with his inalienable adoption by God and endeavors to make the world also a place better conformed to the will of its creator.

It is by the word and sacraments that this salvation is offered to the human being. It is offered individually so that each person might benefit from the grace of God, but this gift to each particular person always takes place in community, in the Church. The elements that declare the person a child of God are the same elements as those that found and give life to the Church. During the celebration of the word and the sacraments, the believer participates individually and communally in the communion that is of God. The same word of life, the Gospel, comes under the oral form of preaching or under the visible sacramental form of the word. It goes out to the human being to be received in faith. The reality of the word precedes preaching and the sacraments. It is only in them that we can discern and receive the word with certitude.

There is thus a fundamental interdependence between the Church on the one hand and the word and sacrament on the other. The community is the Church on the basis of the action that is accomplished within it. The Church is not only a consequence or an appendix to the event of salvation; it is the location of the advent of grace. In the celebration of the word and sacrament, Christ is present, he justifies, he saves those whom he seizes in faith, and he assembles them into a *koinonia*, the Church. The Church is a fundamental fact of the event of justification; it is more than the simple sum of believers; it is the communion where Christ is present and acts in the Spirit.

This insistence on justification, which does not designate a mere doctrine or a theological abstraction but the event of salvation itself, has a double consequence for the ecclesiology of the Reformation Churches which is often affirmed:

– The same connection between justification and the Church does not allow us to make the Church the author of the justification of the believer. The Church must rather, just like the believers who compose it, be justified itself. It is certainly a sign and instrument of

God and of his reign and it proclaims the word and celebrates the sacraments, but God himself and God alone sustains faith and bestows grace. The Church cannot at any moment become the source or author of human salvation. All understanding of the Church as the "prolongation" of Christ, every notion of the sacramental mediation of the Church upon which the presence of Christ depends, every sacrificial understanding of the eucharistic sacrament are seen to be infringements upon the sole sovereignty of God. The Church hears, preaches, confesses, celebrates, witnesses, sings, and feasts. It is the steward of the mysteries of God (1 Cor 4:1). But it is God who makes it so and he alone performs the act of salvation in and through the Church. The proper action of the Church is fundamentally receptive, characterized by the created passivity of faith. Its life and action are always transparent to the sole work of God.

– The second consequence is the classical affirmation of Lutheranism that the message of salvation is the article on which the Church stands or falls. Salvation in Christ is the key that permits one to read the Holy Scripture aright and is the norm of all ecclesial life. All aspects of the life of the Church should constantly be read, interpreted, and reformed in the light of this one message. It is exactly this point that makes Lutherans insist, as in §18 of the JDDJ, on the relevance of the doctrine of justification for all ecclesial life, an affirmation that the Catholic partner could not make its own.

b. This connection between the Church and salvation is decisive for understanding the unity of the Church. The communion in the celebration of the word and sacraments is—and all churches are in accord on this point—the necessary condition for the full and authentic unity of the Church. Reformation theology goes one step further in affirming that this condition is also sufficient. In effect, the permanence of the Church is not assured by an ecclesial structure but only by the authentic celebration of the word and sacraments.

It thus logically follows that as long as there exists, between different ecclesial communities, a consensus as to the authentic celebration of the word and sacraments, the unity of the Church is a fact, for these communities have a part in the one true Church of Jesus Christ which surpasses all times and places. This approach to unity does not recognize criteria or prerequisites other than those that are constitutive for the Church.

This unity is not intangible or exclusively spiritual but is handed on by a concretely lived ecclesial communion. This itself is understood as "communion in word and sacrament." It "includes the mutual recognition of ordination and the freedom to provide for intercelebration."[8] This understanding of the Church allows the Reformation Churches to take a step further than was possible after the JDDJ. They apply also to ecclesiology the fact that one and the same reality may be translated by different languages. What counts for justification also counts for the Church, the foundation of the Church not being anything other than the work of God in view of the salvation of human beings. The Church, a communion of believers, is itself the object of faith. Its concrete form is nevertheless historically plural, and its life is conditioned by history and specific situations, expressing theologically different accents and choices, bearing the mark of human beings whom God has called into his service. The concrete form of the Church is not an object of faith in the sense of the form of its worship or piety, its ecclesiastical discipline, ministries, structures, organizations, or indeed any of the historical formulations of faith or witness to the faith rendered by words and actions.

Despite this, the form is not without importance for the salvation of human beings. Like any human work, it is placed under the promise of God, who wants to be served by this form as an instrument of his grace. This distinction—but not separation—between the Church as the object of faith on the one hand, and the visible community as a social reality on the other, could be misinterpreted to means that the one side is the true Church and the other side is false. The distinction rather has to do with the foundation and the origin of the Church, which is the work of God, and the form of the Church that bears witness to that foundation, the work of humans.

This conviction is not only that of the dialogue between Lutherans and Reformed, but it also characterizes the declarations signed between the churches of the Anglican communion with others. The agreement between the Anglican Churches of Great Britain and Ireland, and the Lutheran and Reformed Churches of France, are evidence of that. The basic agreement (see below) is expressed through a confession of faith that recalls the common understanding of the authority of Scripture and the creeds of the ancient Church, salvation in Christ, the Church as the communion of believers that God has founded, created, and recreated by the word and sacraments, the common understanding of baptism and the Eucharist, the common mission of Christians, the necessity of a ministry of pastoral oversight, and

---

8. *Leuenberg Agreement* 29 and 33.

eschatological hope. Despite the significant differences in the understanding of episcopal ministry in historic succession, the declaration
declares communion in word and sacrament, the mutual recognition
of the Churches, and the recognition of the ministry in the work of
each of these traditions. The Anglicans insist certainly on the fact that
the full visibility of unity has not yet been acquired. In their eyes it is
not yet possible to practice a common ministry of pastoral oversight
as was possible in the case of the Porvoo Agreement between the Scandinavian and Baltic Lutheran Churches and the Anglican Churches
in the British Isles.[9] It remains the fact, however, that the Church of
Christ is translated by legitimately different ecclesial expressions.

The conviction of each of the partners that the one truth of the
Gospel can be rendered by diverse languages and translated by diverse
theological and spiritual traditions finds its ecclesiological extension
here. The different confessional families that fully recognize each other
and who live at present in communion are, in fact, the translation of
this conviction. It is important to recall that the different confessional
families that are a part of this understanding of differentiated consensus do not only lift up the fact of linguistic translation but express very
clearly the legitimate different theological (and particularly ecclesiology) accents.

2.2 A Step the Roman Catholic Church Cannot Take.

A Lutheran theologian will observe that the Catholic Church is not in a
position to take the same step and draw the immediate ecclesiological
consequences of the signing of the JDDJ. In trying to understand this, one
will discover that such Catholic prudence is explained simply by a different
understanding of the Church.

a) At the level of ecclesiology, Catholic theology does not distinguish
between the foundation and the legitimate different languages in the same
manner as the Reformation Churches. One can certainly name numerous
convergences, such as the insistence on the tight connection between salvation and the Church, the understanding of the Church as a communion of
believers, the decisive place of the preaching of the word and the celebration
of the sacraments, etc., facts that every Catholic theologian highlights. But
the fact remains that the ecclesiological approach of the Reformation appears to be reductionistic in the eyes of Catholic ecclesiology.

9. Texts in: *Anglican-Lutheran Agreements. Regional and International Agreements
1972–2002.*

Ecumenical research at the end of the 1980s came to the conclusion that, in the domain of ecclesiology, there did indeed exist a common denominator that summed up the specific differences. Cardinal Kasper had been asking since 1980—he was at the time a professor of theology at Tübingen—if "the holiness of the Church itself is at this point its own which permits it to act in a holy and sanctifying manner upon its members? Or rather does the Church not have this holiness only under the form of a promise or of a quality?"[10] In other words, can the Church, not at its own initiative but in its being sanctified by God, accomplish acts of which it is the author, sanctifying its members in view of their salvation? The matter at stake does not concern the fact of the instrumentality of the Church in the transmission of salvation but the nature of this instrumentality: is the Church sanctified in such a way that it becomes itself a sanctifying subject? On the Catholic side, the response is in the affirmative, in the sense that the Second Vatican Council affirmed the "sacramentality" of the Church in service of the mediation of Christ, which the Church makes efficaciously present. For their part, the Reformation Churches conceive of the Church as a sign and instrument of God and his reign. But every ecclesial act should, as we have already mentioned, be fully transparent to the sole work of God. The question of the nature of the instrumentality of the Church in the saving work of God recaps the differences that subsist between the Catholic Church and the Reformation Churches. The difference lies not so much in the instrumentality of the Church as in the nature of that instrumentality.

The international Lutheran-Catholic dialogue which in 1994 successfully completed the document "The Church and Justification" highlighted the agreement inherent in the understanding of the Church as the communion of believers, the communion called to transmit the word and sacrament and to offer itself in service of the saving work of God. The Church is the place where, according to the divine will, the Gospel is proclaimed and the sacraments are administered, which is to say where faith is awoken and nourished. The divergence that remains is over the understanding of the Church as a "sacrament of salvation." Insofar as it has to do simply with affirming that the Church is the instrument of salvation, Lutherans can accept this language, even if they fear that such discourse will only obscure the difference between Christ the head and the Church which is his body. Catholics counter that this fear is groundless and that the introduction of the term serves precisely to underline the christocentric character of the Church.[11] Despite the common concern, the two understandings of

---

10. Kasper, "Gegebene Einheit," 5–7, and 53, 54.
11. *Church and Justification: Lutheran-Roman Catholic Joint Commission*, par. 120.

the Church remain different and the international dialogue elucidates it in trying to clarify what certain Catholic authors mean when they speak of the sacraments as the "self-realization" or "self-accomplishment" of the Church,[12] an approach that is difficult for Lutherans to accept.

b) It is not a question here of entering into the details of this divergence in the understanding of the Church. It suffices to observe that this difference leads necessarily to different approaches to the understanding of unity and the necessary conditions for it. Vatican II cites three dimensions required for unity: the profession of one single faith, the common celebration of worship, and the government of the Church by the pope and bishops who are the successors to the apostles.[13] The episcopal ministry is not only an element of unity alongside the two others, but the bishops define simultaneously the two other dimensions "as teachers for doctrine, priests for sacred worship, and ministers for governing."[14] This has to do in fact with a vision of unity based on a conception of "episcopal communion" where "the individual bishops represent each his own Church, but all of them together and with the Pope represent the entire Church in the bond of peace, love and unity."[15] And it is here that, in the name of the understanding of the mystery of the Church, the indelible connection between the Eucharist and the ecclesial ministry in the fullness that is, for Vatican II, the episcopate arises within Catholic theology. The accent is placed not so much on what the tradition called the "power to consecrate" as on the sacramental celebration of the mystery of Christ that is the eucharistic communion, a celebration that understands the preaching of the Gospel, the sacramental reality of the Church and the ministry of Christ who is preacher, shepherd, and priest. It has to do with a unique reality that cannot be deconstructed into its diverse particular elements. This approach largely shared within Catholic theology does not correspond directly to the Reformation vision of unity as discussed in the previous section.

It is for this reason evident that Catholics cannot appropriate the ecclesiological conclusions that the Reformation Churches deduce from the agreement on the understanding of salvation.

---

12. Even if the document avoids citing particular authors, one will think here of Rahner (*Kirche und Sakrament*, 67), Semmelroth (*L'Eglise sacrement de la Rédemption*), or the postconciliar publications of Congar ("L'Eglise, sacrement universel du salut") and the numerous authors cited in: *Die Sakramentalität der Kirche in der oekumenischen Diskussion*.

13. *Unitatis Redintegratio* 2.

14. *Lumen Gentium* 20.

15. Ibid., 23.

c) In order to avoid all misunderstandings, the Catholic Church clarified some months after the signing of the JDDJ that there was not for the moment any question of considering that a Church that was not in full communion with the bishop of Rome could be considered a Church in the full sense of the word. In August 2000, Cardinal Ratzinger published the declaration *Dominus Iesus* (DI) on the unicity and salvific universality of Jesus Christ and the Church in the name of the Congregation for the Doctrine of the Faith. This explanation certainly has the relation to the other religions as its main topic. However, it also contains a judgment concerning the ecclesiality of the non-Catholic Christian Church (§§16 & 17). The text specified that there is only one true Church, which is led by the bishop of Rome, who is the successor of Peter, and the bishops who are in communion with him. With the exception of the Orthodox, other Christian communities could not be understood as Church. Thus the question of the possibility of a differentiated consensus in ecclesiology as a logical consequence of the differentiated consensus in soteriology seems to have received a definitive negative response and one without appeal.

The publication of the Roman declaration *Dominus Iesus* has been quite negatively received by the Reformation traditions. Calling into question any idea of the real ecclesiality of the Churches stemming from the Reformation, this document had necessarily to be understood not only as a response to the remaining open questions in the JDDJ but as a relativization of it and a refusal of the practical model of unity practiced among the Reformation Churches.

2.3. Where to Go from Here?

No ecumenist, regardless of her Church of origin, can be satisfied with this declaration (DI). It cannot be allowed to have the last word. But it does have the advantage of demonstrating where the problem stands at present. It thus defines the task that is before us: to clarify and say with the greatest precision possible how and under which conditions the Roman Catholic Church is prepared to recognize another community as a full and authentic expression of the one Church of Christ that surpasses all times and places and which is not limited to a particular identity, even if it is the Roman Catholic one. *Dominus Iesus* indicates that the Catholic Church is very conscious of the high stakes surrounding every new step along the path toward unity. It thus responds at the present by seeming to shut its doors.

The international Lutheran-Catholic dialogue which was taken up again after the signing of the JDDJ has been marked by a realization of this problematic. The commission, of which Turid Karlsen Seim is at present a member, has successfully completed in the last decade two major texts: one on *The Apostolicity of the Church*[16] and the other titled *From Conflict to Communion.*[17] The second text, concerned with preparing for a common commemoration of the 500th anniversary of the Reformation in 2017, hardly takes up ecclesiological issues. It is markedly different from the first one, which is a detailed and exhaustive (460 paragraphs!) study of ecclesiological issues and more particularly of questions touching on the ministry.

    The Apostolicity of the Church conclusions are remarkable. There exists a real rapprochement between Lutherans and Catholics concerning apostolicity and apostolic succession. The apostolic tradition is always connected to a personal transmission of the Gospel through the ages. The mission entrusted by Christ and taken up by the apostles is always a personal succession inside a particular tradition. Within the Church diverse forms of this succession are at work, such as the communion of the bishops which can rightfully claim to be a divine institution (*Apostolicity* 76). Apostolicity, succession, and communion are to be seen in a tight and inalienable connection. "Thus fidelity to the apostolic Gospel has priority in the interplay of *traditio, successio* and *communio.* The internal order of those three aspects of apostolic succession is of great significance" (*Apostolicity* 291). The document goes on to say that the present unilateral recognition of the Catholic ministry by Lutherans should be accompanied by a Catholic recognition of the Lutheran ministry. "The Roman Catholic Church recognizes a priestly ministry and true sacraments, by apostolic succession, in certain Churches even though the bishops of these Churches are not in communion with the bishops with Peters successor at their head" (ibid., 291). But Catholics do not for all that propose a Roman recognition of the Lutheran ministry. They do not deduce there from any real possibility of sharing in a differentiated consensus regarding ecclesiology that affirms that the other Churches can themselves be authentic expressions of the one Church of Jesus Christ. The text of *Apostolicity* is remarkable, for it shows how one can surpass the issues that were hitherto thought to be insurmountable. It is nevertheless frustrating, for one ends up going in circles. All advances are immediately countered by a new problematic that follows on its heels and forbids any real progress on the path toward unity. One seems to be confronted with a checklist, which it is necessary to tackle point by point on every issue. The

16. *The Apostolicity of the Church: Study of the Lutheran-Roman Catholic Commission on Unity.*

17. *From Conflict to Communion: Lutheran-Catholic Common Commemoration of the Reformation in 2017.*

list seems interminable and it is scarcely possible that one will arrive one day at the goal.

The question posed is that of the method to be used. Among the Reformation Churches the method has led to an agreement on the word and sacraments as well as on the ministry and has permitted them to enter into communion. The consensus in terms of a common understanding of the Gospel among these churches leads to a "conciliary" situation, where various forms of being church are considered legitimate. That is not the case in the dialogue with Rome. This conclusion is not in any sense polemical. The responsible representatives from Rome explicitly underscore that a differentiated consensus, which is practiced among the Protestant churches, by no means corresponds to their basic understanding of the church. The international dialogue to which Turid Karlsen Seim belongs as Lutheran member is very conscious about these difficulties. After the text "From Conflict to Communion" the dialogue now poses the question differently. It tries to find new ways towards the community of churches based on the understanding of baptism. This way has begun and we may only hope that new doors will open up in this new round of dialogue.

Bibliography

Agreement between Reformation Churches in Europe (Leuenberg Agreement). Revised text. Leipzig: Evangelische Verlagsanstalt, 2013.

Anglican-Lutheran Agreements: Regional and International Agreements 1972–2002. Edited by The Anglican Consultative Council and the Lutheran World Federation. LWF Documentation 49/2004.

The Apostolicity of the Church. Study of the Lutheran-Roman Catholic Commission on Unity. Lutheran World Federation and the Pontifical Council for Promoting Christian Unity. Minneapolis: Lutheran University Press, 2006.

Birmelé, André. *La communion ecclésiale: Progrès œcuméniques et enjeux méthodologiques.* Paris: Cerf 2000.

Church and Justification: Lutheran-Roman Catholic Joint Commission. Geneva: Lutheran World Federation, 1994.

"Confessio Augustana." In *The Book of Concord: The Confessions of the Evangelical Lutheran Church.* Edited by Robert Kolb and Timothy J. Wengert. Minneapolis: Fortress, 2000.

Congar, Yves. "L'Eglise, sacrement universel du salut." In *Cette Eglise que j'aime,* 41–63. Paris: Cerf, 1968.

From Conflict to Communion. Lutheran-Catholic Common Commemoration of the Reformation in 2017. Report of the Lutheran-Roman Catholic Commission on Unity. Leipzig-Paderborn, 2013. Verlag: Paderborn, Bonifatius und Leipzig, Evangelische Verlagsanstalt.

Lumen Gentium. The Vatican. www.vatican.va/archive/hist_councils/ii_vatican_council/index.htm. (accessed Oct. 14, 2014)

Grosc, Lavern K, ed. *Sent into the World: The Proceedings of the Fifth Assembly of the Lutheran World Federation.* Mineapolis: Augsburg, 1972.

Kasper, Walter. "Gegebene Einheit—bestehende Schranken—gelebte Gemeinschaft." In *KNA: Ökumenische Information* 52 (1980).

Lehmann, Karl, and Wolfhart Pannenberg, eds. *Thee Condemnations of the Reformation Era: Do They Still Divide?* Mineapolis, Fortress, 1990.

Pesch, O. H. *Theologie der Rechtfertigung bei Martin Luther und Thomas von Aquin. Versuch eines systematisch theologischen Dialogs.* Mainz: Günewald, 1967.

"Pope John's Opening Speech to the Council." In *The Documents of Vatican II*, edited by Walter M. Abbott, 710–19. London: Kindle Edition, 1967.

Rahner, Karl. *Kirche und Sakrament.* Fribourg: Herder, 1960.

Die Sakramentalität der Kirche in der oekumenischen Diskussion: Referate und Diskussion eines Symposions anlässlich des 25jährigen Bestehens des Johann-Adam-Möhler-Instituts. Edited by Johann-Adam-Möhler-Institut. Paderborn: Bonifatius-Druckerei, 1983.

Semmelroth, Otto. *L'Eglise sacrement de la Rédemption.* Paris: Saint Paul, 1962.

Unitatis Redintegratio. The Vatican. www.vatican.va/archive/hist_councils/ii_vatican_council/index.htm. (accessed Oct. 22, 2014)

15

The Unity of Life

The Statement on Unity from
the 10th WCC Assembly Busan, 2013

Olav Fykse Tveit

A New Formula for Unity?

WHAT IS UNITY? WHAT is the unity of the church? How can the goal of the ecumenical movement best be defined?

The search for formulations of what the visible unity of the church should look like has been central to the modern ecumenical movement. Different descriptions and different experiences have been offered to describe the history of divisions, the dividing forces and the destructive realities of division among the churches. Accordingly, different definitions of the unity we are seeking have been developed as the quest to overcome the divisions has proceeded.

Quite often we see that models for church unity significantly reflect the basic ecclesiology of those who propose them. Thus, we can see what has contributed to unity in different historical, confessional, denominational or contextual circumstances.

A description of unity also may be some combinations of such consequences of ecclesiology, with certain modifications that have been elaborated by professional ecumenists or by processes of dialogue. To some degree, these models or visions of unity are possible to combine or accept as one shared platform for unity.

Ecumenical bilateral dialogues often search for way to find common ground and combine these models into a common vision and into practicable agreements, e.g. of eucharistic hospitality or sharing, or sharing or exchanging ordained ministries. In ecumenical multilateral dialogues and processes like those going on in the framework of the World Council of Churches, we attempt to find new concepts based on new configurations. This has particularly been the brand mark of the work of Faith and Order, and significant texts have been developed as the result of this process.

Another context of multilateral definitions of or widely shared visions for the unity of the church has been the making of "unity statements" presented to and approved in the Assemblies of the WCC, the widest and most representative meetings in the modern ecumenical movement. These statements have become landmarks in the joint work for visible church unity, defining dimensions of what goals should be pursued and what are the most significant characteristics of a multilateral, open quest for unity. Even if they do not represent one model of unity, they are based within the context of conciliar ecumenism, combining the search for unity in church fellowship and unity in common witness. As multilateral texts, they reflect or combine other discussions on the unity of the church and the ecumenical movement.

The 10th Assembly of the WCC in Busan, Republic of Korea, November 2013, issued a statement on unity.[1] It is the purpose of this article to describe and analyze this statement, "God's Gift and Call to Unity—and Our Commitment." This will be done by 1) giving a short description of the profile and scope of some of the former WCC Assemblies' statements of this kind, particularly reflecting on the contexts (in time and place) in which they were made; 2) describing the process that led to the final decision in the Assembly, particularly discussing what was unique to this process; 3) concluding with the Busan statement. Definitely, the latest unity statement does not attempt to rewrite what has already been said in former statements. Neither is to be seen as an alternative to them, to replace them, as the Busan text refers to them with clear affirmation. It is built on the former statements, but it refers to them without repeating them. Still, the ambition was to say something new, to say something more and something else.

The observation that any statement about unity is shaped in the theological and cultural context in which it is formulated should not be disturbing if we are able to see it and identify both the relevance for what is said in its context and to be open to critical evaluations from other perspectives.

---

1. The text has sixteen numbered paragraphs, and I will refer to those numbers here. The text is published in several publications, i.e., "God's Gift and Call to Unity—and Our Commitment," *Ecumenical Review* 65 (2013) 453–58. It is also published in *Encountering the God of Life: Official Report of the 10th Assembly*, ed. Erlinda N. Senturias and Theodore A. Gill Jr. (Geneva: World Council of Churches, 2014) 37–41. Also available at oikoumene.org, PRC_01_1_ADOPTED_Unity_Statement.

This statement from Busan has its context in time and space in this phase of the ecumenical movement. Even though I was among those who facilitated and accompanied the process, from the beginning until the final decision in the Assembly, I have been aware of some of the challenges and limitations of this text. In this article, I will present both some of the positive contributions of this text as well as analytical comments I have regarding its specificity as shaped by this particular time in the history of the WCC.

This statement expresses the framework of the work regarding the unity of the church in a different way than it has been done before. There are several dimensions with this statement that can be seen as "new," and I will present them in this article. I shall do my best to analyse how this statement may be received and used in churches and dialogues as a new inspiration and empowerment in regard to the ongoing quest to create and embody expressions of unity. More than merely voicing definitions of unity, the quest is to be able to express it and live it. That this text requires a process of reception is perhaps its most significant new feature. It is a text that calls for a new shared recognition of how disunity hurts us, and even more, how it destroys the life God has created us for. More than that, it gives us glimpses of the reality that unity is a gift realized in the institutionalized expressions of it, but also far beyond that, sometimes it may even be found in spite of or actually in contradiction to the forms of unity we might have been imagining. This is a text that calls for reactions from Christians at every level, not only from ecumenical officers or in the words formally adopted by official bodies of the churches.

Statements on Unity

The ten Assemblies of the WCC from 1948 to 2013 have most often agreed on a statement on unity. These statements have a significant status in the WCC, and beyond it in the ecumenical movement. They express the vision of the unity we are seeking, and how we might respond to God's call. These statements demonstrate the evolution of the ecumenical movement in that they build upon previous statements, offering new insights or ways of approaching the commitment to the full visible unity of the Church. Shifts in the ecumenical landscape are reflected in these unity statements, just as the ongoing harvest of the ecumenical movement are brought to bear in their approaches.

In these statements, particular attention has been given to ecclesiological divisions and challenges. They were, in a very real and intentional

way, responses to the primary purpose of the World Council of Churches'
fellowship:

> to call one another to visible unity in one faith and in one Eu-
> charistic fellowship, expressed in worship and common life in
> Christ, through witness and service to the world and to advance
> towards that unity in order that the world may believe.[2]

In 1948, the first Assembly in Amsterdam asserted, "We intend to stay together." These statements are responses to that conviction and promise.

The commissions of Faith and Order[3] have usually had an influential
role in the preparation of these texts. Turid Karlsen Seim served as a del-
egate to the 7th Assembly (Canberra, 1991). Later she was a member of the
Standing Commission and vice-moderator of Faith and Order. As an active
participant in the drafting of Faith and Order texts in the period between
the 8th Assembly (Harare,1998) and the 9th Assembly (Porto Alegre, 2006),
she is thus one who knows well the process of producing and agreeing on
these statements. Her commitment to bring together a classical theological
discourse and a contextual theological reflection in the ecumenical texts
corresponds to the major concerns and overall profile of the Busan unity
statement.

The statement for the Busan Assembly was developed following a decision made by the Central Committee of the WCC in 2011 which asked the
General Secretary to appoint a drafting group to develop a unity statement
for the 10th Assembly. The group was duly appointed and it was moderated
by the former moderator of Faith and Order, Dame Mary Tanner of the
Church of England.

The former statements have presented different profiles and have conveyed significant dimensions of unity. It is impossible to review all of these
statements in detail, but a focus on those from New Delhi, Canberra and
Porto Alegre may be particularly illustrative of the development of thought
and format.

At New Delhi (1961), the assembly statement on unity focused on the
understanding that Christians in each place are united to all Christians in
every place, and are further united to all Christians through time. In other
words, we may understand that the unity of the Church, expressed both locally and globally, unites us to the witness of the faithful through time. The

2. The Constitution and Rules of the World Council of Churches as amended by
the 9th Assembly, Porto Alegre, Brazil 2006; III: Purposes and Functions.

3. Until the WCC Central Committee meeting in July 2014 there were for many
years both a Plenary Commission and a Standing Commission, the latter doing most of
the ongoing work of study projects and having the mandate to publish texts.

famous, albeit lengthy, essence of the text was captured in the memorable words:

> We believe that the unity which is both God's will and his gift to his Church is being made visible as all in each place who are baptised in Jesus Christ and confess him as Lord and Saviour are brought by the Holy Spirit into one fully committed fellowship, holding the one apostolic faith, preaching the one gospel, breaking the one bread, joining in common prayer, and having a corporate life reaching out in witness and service to all and who at the same time are united with the whole Christian fellowship in all places and all ages in such wise that ministry and members are accepted by all, and that all can act and speak together as occasion requires for the tasks to which God calls his people.[4]

The statement posited that unity can be understood only as a costly unity; the response to the call to unity means abandoning some forms of church life and embracing others.

It is essential to note that the Orthodox representatives at the Third Assembly could not find themselves reflected in the New Delhi formulation of unity and issued their own refutation. A fundamental area of disagreement was the inference of denominationalism; the ecclesiology of the Orthodox Church could not allow for a denominational understanding in which the Orthodox confession is seen as just one confession among many others.[5]

The Canberra statement (1991), *The Unity of the Church as Koinonia: Gift and Calling,* like the Busan statement, was influenced by the theme of its assembly; in the case of Canberra, the theme was "Come Holy Spirit renew the whole creation." In part, the Canberra statement reads:

> The purpose of God according to Holy Scripture is to gather the whole creation under the Lordship of Christ Jesus, in whom, by the power of the Holy Spirit, all are brought into communion with God.[6]

The Canberra statement contributes significantly to the understanding of unity. In its understanding of koinonia it gives centrality to diversity in all its dimensions. At the same time, it offers insight into what we may understand as the limits of diversity. The Canberra statement offers something else to the legacy of unity statements: a direct challenge to the churches in terms of

---

4. "Reports of Sections: Unity," 116–34.

5. See Mateus, "At the Core of the Ecumenical Vision: An Overview of World Council of Churches' Statements on Unity 1948–2006."

6. "The Unity of the Church as Koinonia: Gift and Calling," 172.

living into the vision of mutual recognition of baptism and ministries and the call to work together in areas of justice and peace. We can see echoes of both of these developments in the Busan statement.

The Porto Alegre statement (2006), *Called to be the One Church*, was a more sharply defined ecclesiological text. It built upon the foundations of catholicity and koinonia, and in its list of questions to the churches, it evoked a spirit of mutual accountability. The Porto Alegre statement coincided with another Faith and Order process, the publication of the text *The Nature and Mission of the Church*, a step along the way towards a consensus text in ecclesiology. In one sense, the statement and the text offered a consistent and cohesive message about developments within the ecumenical movement on ecclesiology. On the other hand, issuing both at the same time complicated and thereby compromised reception by the churches of each.

There is much more that could be said about these three statements, and indeed the whole history of assembly statements on unity. What is important to establish is that the Busan statement is firmly in the theological trajectory of these milestones in discussion of the question of the full visible unity of the church. Busan's four-part structure, moving from experience to scripture, to ecumenical harvest and on to commitment, builds on similar themes found throughout the history of the World Council of Churches. But, as has already been asserted, the Busan statement brings new and exciting dimensions to these reflections on the unity we seek.

Unity of Life–Life in Unity

The statement from Busan focuses on the unity of the church as being inextricably related to the unity of world, both the unity of creation and the unity of humanity. Inspired by the theme of the 10th Assembly, "God of life, lead us to justice and peace," the statement situates itself in the scriptural narrative of creation. Referring to Genesis 1 and Ephesians 1, alluding to John 1, a strong connection is established to trinitarian theology and the doctrine of creation.

Thus, the statement conveys the perspective that unity is an expression of the purpose of the Creator God. The deepest meaning of life is evidenced in relationships of unity; life is only life in fellowship. This relational understanding of unity most clearly contains in itself a recognition that unity is something dynamic, ever changing, ever evolving. Diversity is likewise an inherent quality of the gift of creation, a characteristic of the gift of relationship. Unity can be understood only as the manifestation of God's creative and re-creative reconciling activity in the world and within the human community.

Life's dimensions are even more nuanced than reconciled diversity, however. Within the dynamic of creation there are signs of hope and signs of despair. This, too, is part of the story of creation. The statement from Busan acknowledges this dichotomy, offering a realistic and self-critical perspective. An articulation of the qualities of the unity with which we are gifted and to which we are called must avoid the temptation of utopian idealism; the yearning for unity must have the capacity to hold within itself the dawn from on high and the groans of creation.

The unity of the church cannot be seen apart from participation in the ongoing creation of God. The church also experiences the reconciling love of God in all its diversity and seeks to be a sign of God's will for the sake of the world. And just as humanity celebrates when divisions are overcome, or laments when differences keep communities apart, so the church seeks to be a place of healing and wholeness and cannot but repent that the people of God may not yet share together at one Eucharistic table.

A vision of unity must not ignore how justice and peace ought to be nurtured or restored to find proper expression in the life of creation. The unity of the church, when it is visible and real, expresses the signs of the kingdom of God, breaking into this world with its qualities of justice and peace and love. The Busan statement proposes a vision in which justice and peace are preconditions of the unity of the Church, of humanity, of creation. The unity that is the will of the God of Life demands life in its fullness, uncompromized by injustice or detriments to peace.

Unity in Its Context

A contextual dimension to the unity statement is reflected in its structure and content, and moreover in the very process that led to its composition. Those charged with the responsibility for drafting the statement had to ask not only why the imperative to unity, but also where, in their experiences, disunity hurts the most. The text is grounded in a breadth and balance of real contextual encounter, spiritual insight and harvested wisdom. The diversity of voices behind the words of the Busan statement led to a text that says something new about unity because it moves in a direct and concrete way beyond the questions of ecclesiology and doctrine to considerations that are not only existential, but also at the heart of moral discourse.

The composition of the drafting group included women and men from many different confessional backgrounds, ecumenical experiences, geographical and cultural contexts, ages and socio-political perspectives.[7] The people in the group, in expanding from a strictly Faith and Order based study, were intentionally selected under the conviction that the very persons charged with writing the text needed to be part of the overall methodology. That is to say, it was not only important that the text adopt a contextual theological approach in order to convey an understanding of unity, but the combination of voices and the process of building consensus within that group should be a living example of the vision of the statement itself.

The drafting group was initially divided about taking such a contextual approach. Some felt that it was only possible to begin the text with a scriptural analysis and then move into questions of experience. Others believed that if the text was to speak of the interconnectedness of the unity of the church, humanity and all of creation, it needed to speak directly and in the first place to what defines those areas of life. Eventually, through discussion, all became convinced that it was necessary to begin the statement with the lived reality of the human condition so that the text could be best owned by its audience. The importance of self-recognition in the statement from the very beginning was asserted. The language of "we" was not to be only a rhetorical device or intended as a message from the writers, but an indicator of the inclusivity of the statement.

Thus the text seeks to speak authentically about experience:

> We give thanks for the diversity of human cultures, for the wonder of knowledge and discovery, for communities being rebuilt and enemies reconciled, for people being healed and populations fed. We rejoice when people of different faiths work together for justice and peace. These are signs of hope and new beginnings. But we grieve that there are also places where God's children cry out. Social and economic injustice, poverty and famine, greed and war ravage our world. There is violence and terrorism and the threat of war, particularly nuclear war. Many

7. The members of the Unity Statement Drafting Committee were Bishop Dr Geevarghese Mor Coorilos, moderator of the WCC Commission on World Mission and Evangelism; Rev. Dr Susan Durber, member of the Faith and Order Standing Commission; H.E. Metropolitan Gennadios of Sassima, vice moderator of WCC Central Committee; Ms Alice Fabian, United Congregational Church of Southern Africa; Rev. Dr Joseph Freitag, Roman Catholic Church (appointed by the Pontifical Council for Promoting Christian Unity); Rev. Dr Cyril Hovarun, Moscow Patriarchate; Rev. Dr Yeong Mee Lee, Presbyterian Church in the Republic of Korea; Bishop Mark MacDonald, National Indigenous Bishop of the Anglican Church of Canada (elected at Busan as WCC president for North America); Bishop Ambrose Moyo, Evangelical Lutheran Church in Zimbabwe; and myself as WCC General Secretary; we were moderated by Dame Mary Tanner, then WCC president for Europe, and served by the secretary Ms Natasha Klukach.

suffer from HIV and AIDS and other epidemics; peoples are displaced and their lands dispossessed. Many women are victims of violence, inequality and trafficking. Some men also suffer abuse. There are those who are marginalized and excluded. We are all in danger of being alienated from our cultures and disconnected from earth. Creation has been misused and we face threats to the balance of life, a growing ecological crisis and the effects of climate change. These are signs of our disordered relations with God, with one another and with creation, and they dishonour God's gift of life.[8]

All are placed within struggle as well as hope. The text, in this sense, is interactive and dynamic. Challenge and reflection are urged upon the reader; self-reflection and self-identification are implicit features of a contextual approach to unity.

Unity as an Expression of Humility

Deep realism thus characterizes the description of the world and the unity we seek. It may be said that this is in itself not very unique. But in moving the reflections on unity into the reality of daily struggle, of life under threat, of life in and between the churches, an attitude of humility is elicited. The vision of unity should not be viewed as a goal of perfection; there is no room for triumphalism in a vision that is as comprehensive in its analysis as it is in its objective.

The church, as the body of Christ, embodies Jesus' uniting, reconciling, and self-sacrificial love to the world on the cross. At the heart of God's own life of communion is forever a cross and forever resurrection—a reality that is revealed to us and through us. We wait and pray with eager longing for God to renew the whole creation (Rom. 8:19–21). God is always there ahead of us in our pilgrimage, always surprising us, calling us to repentance, forgiving us our failures, and offering us the gift of new life. [9]

This is a statement that posits the urgency of the need for fullness of life, for all, together. The WCC has much to offer in such an approach. Insofar as there is an intentional realism in the description of life's conditions, there is a valuable harvest of the fruits of the ecumenical movement. The work

---

8. "God's Gift and Call to Unity—and Our Commitment," par. 2.

9. Ibid., par. 8.

of Faith and Order in the legacy of *Baptism, Eucharist and Ministry*, for example, is thoroughly evident in the text's analysis of the Church:

> As foretaste God gives to the Church gracious gifts: the Word, testified to in Holy Scripture to which we are invited to respond in faith in the power of the Holy Spirit; baptism in which we are made a new creation in Christ; the Eucharist, the fullest expression of communion with God and with one another, which builds up the fellowship and from which we are sent out in mission; an apostolic ministry to draw out and nurture the gifts of all the faithful and to lead the mission of the Church.[10]

The Busan statement likewise positions itself in full consistency with the new convergence text, *The Church: Towards a Common Vision* in its particularly helpful distinction between unity and uniformity and the gifts and limits of ecclesial diversity. The missiological dimensions of the ecumenical harvest are indebted to the work of the Commission on World Mission and Evangelism in its own new statement, *Together Towards Life: Mission and Evangelism in Changing Landscapes.*

But neither the depiction of the pain of disunity, nor the ecumenical contribution is limited to ecclesiological or doctrinal questions. The work for visible unity demands new dynamics. "Divisions and marginalization on the basis of ethnicity, race, gender, disability, power, status, caste and other forms of discrimination also obscure the Church's witness to unity."[11] Therefore, what we can say about unity may be inspired and strengthened by experiences and reflections on what we at the WCC know from our work in diakonia; ecumenical solidarity and service as a measure of interconnectedness. We similarly may look to a great many programmes of the WCC that offer evidence of what a just and faithful community may bring: divisions of race, gender, power structures and ethnicity can be challenged and overcome. The work of the Decade to Overcome Violence and the document *An Ecumenical Call to Just Peace*, stemming from the work of the International Ecumenical Peace Convocation in 2011, are but two examples.

The objective of unity is not and cannot be limited to one problem or perspective. Ultimately, the gift of the World Council of Churches is the ability to draw together issues of doctrine and ecclesiology with the issues of justice and peace to offer a comprehensive and faithful offering to the Church, to humanity, to creation. It does so in a spirit of humility, understanding that it is only through the God of life that the gift and calling of unity may be realized.

10. Ibid., par. 10.
11. Ibid., par. 11.

The Affirmation of Disunity
and the Missing Perspectives

Whenever we speak of context and whenever we speak of the pains of division there is a risk of excluding someone's experience. The text sought from its very conception to be a document in which everyone might, in some way, find herself or himself present. The difficulty of this undertaking became acutely evident during the Busan Assembly itself.

At the first hearing session on the unity statement, some delegates questioned why sexual orientation was not named specifically as a type of discrimination, prompted by the experience in their own contexts of painful experiences of marginalization. This led to counterarguments by those who were of the belief that homosexuality was not condonable and thus should be excluded from any mention within the text. Subsequent written submissions to the sub-committee tasked with revisions of the statement echoed these two distinct perspectives. Both sides of the disputed issue threatened rejection of the document on the basis of their convictions.

It is ironic that a statement on unity prompted some of the most heated discussions present in the Busan Assembly. In fact, this underscored the valuable place of the WCC in offering safe ecumenical space for conversation and the relevance of Faith and Order's work on Moral Discernment in the Churches. Nevertheless, the uncompromising opinions on the issue inspired much soul-searching on the part of those with the responsibility of revision. It seemed at points that the statement might fail to receive the approval of the assembly over this one point.

Within the revision sub-committee, the same two perspectives were reflected. On one hand, some saw no problem in acknowledging that discrimination occurs on the basis of sexual orientation while never implying a judgement on the issue either way. On the other hand, there were those who were convinced that the very mention of sexual orientation would be a cultural, moral and doctrinal affront. There was conversation about whether it might be possible to say, at least, that the churches are conflicted over the issue. But what seemed self-evident to some, and easy to acknowledge, was seen by others as an imposed burden in contexts where the issue was simply not acknowledged or discussed.

The sub-committee ultimately brought to the assembly a compromise formulation. The phrase "and other forms of discrimination" was added and deemed to be inclusive of all interpretations of marginalization, even beyond those named and specifically the disputed question of sexual orientation. Not surprisingly, there were those who were dissatisfied with this solution. At the point of testing for consensus on approval of the entire text, at least one church requested to record formal disagreement with the omission of sexual orientation from the list of named discriminatory experiences. Notwithstanding this dissent, consensus was reached and the text was formally adopted by the Busan Assembly.

The experience in Busan of trying to find a formulation which could speak to the needs of all present was about far more than the places where disunity hurts in society or in the churches. Certainly, the issue of human sexuality and, even beyond that, theological anthropology must be seen as a critical matter for our time in the ecumenical movement. Safe space and appropriate methodology should be found to facilitate conversation. But the issue points to something even bigger than that, the question of our common life together. The struggle to make visible the unity we seek goes beyond opinion and definitions. The pain of disunity can be experienced in the very ways we try to emulate the qualities and values of the kingdom of God. Once more, this is evidence that the only approach to the question of unity is an attitude of humility as we seek to understand the other and to offer, as churches, an aspiration for unity speaking to all of humanity and creation.

Making a New Commitment

A statement such as this one cannot stand by itself; its words and aspirations only make sense if they lead to a response from the reader.

The question of response is really a question about ecumenical reception. What is clear from this text, and its more holistic treatment of the question of unity, is that it is a very different kind of reception that is called for. The test of the efficacy of the text is measured not so much in documents and agreements which may be inspired by this call to unity, but in *action*.

The Busan unity statement opens with the perspective of what may nurture unity among us. It is not without doctrinal importance and relevance, but it also speaks to a broader question of how we are or might live united as the Church, as humanity, as part of the whole of creation. It is about our common life and what we may do to break down divisions of every kind. These are strong and comprehensive commitments:

> In faithfulness to this, our common calling, we will seek together the full visible unity of the one, holy, catholic and apostolic church when we shall express our unity around the one table of the Lord. In pursuing the unity of the church we will open ourselves to receive the gifts of each other's traditions, and offer our gifts to one another. We will learn to commemorate together

the martyrs who witnessed to our common faith. We will continue theological conversations, giving attention to new voices
and different methods of approach. We will seek to live out the
consequences of our theological agreements. We will intensify
our work for justice, peace, and the healing of creation, and address together the complex challenges of contemporary social,
economic, and moral issues. We will work for more just, par-
ticipatory, and inclusive ways of living together. We will make
common cause for the well-being of humanity and creation with
those of other faith communities. We will hold each other accountable for fulfilling these commitments.[12]

The Pilgrimage of Justice and Peace that the World Council of Churches
embraced following the Busan Assembly may well be the testing ground
for the premise and promise of the unity statement. A pilgrimage involves
a journey made together. It is a journey that involves bringing with us the
qualities of God's kingdom even as we search further for those signs from
the God of Life. It is not a programmatic strategy of itself, but an attitude
and an orientation for the ecumenical movement. Like the unity statement,
it unites the historic strands of ecumenical engagement; unity and mission
with the call for justice and peace.

In concrete terms the Pilgrimage of Justice and Peace will place particular emphasis on four areas: life-affirming economy, climate change, just
peace, and human rights. In these areas, the concerns of justice and peace
will be addressed in a way inspired by the unity statement. The pilgrimage
intends to bring people together: the churches and people of good will all
have a place in moving together and taking common action. How we work
and walk together, as one, matters as much as our aspirations. Our common
life, the way we emulate the vision of unity, has direct impact on our ability
to be a witness in the world. To be a credible sign of the will of the God
of Life, there must be inclusivity, mutual commitment and accountability,
humility, repentance when we fail in the search for unity, exchange of the
gifts of our different traditions and walks of life. We must never forget that
we are called "to gather up all things in Christ, 'things in heaven and things
on earth.' (Eph 1:9–10)"[13]

12. Ibid., par. 15.
13. Ibid., par. 13.

Unity in Prayer

In the long passage cited above (paragraph 15), the unity statement details the commitments agreed upon by the churches of the WCC fellowship. It ends in a very deliberate way, drawing together the essence of the statement into what must be the very first response to the document:

> Above all, we will pray without ceasing for the unity for which Jesus prayed (John 17): a unity of faith, love and compassion that Jesus Christ brought through his ministry; a unity like the unity Christ shares with the Father; a unity enfolded in the communion of the life and love of the Triune God. Here, we receive the mandate for the Church's vocation for unity in mission and service.[14]

There is no more significant expression of life than prayer, if we understand life to be held in relationship to God. Prayer involves every dimension of our being. We pray for unity because Jesus himself prayed for unity, reminding ourselves that it is not we who create unity, but rather it is a gift and calling from God.

> O God of life,
>
> lead us to justice and peace,
>
> that suffering people may discover hope;
>
> the scarred world find healing;
>
> and divided churches become visibly one,
>
> through the one who prayed for us,
>
> and in whom we are one Body,
>
> your Son, Jesus Christ,
>
> who with you and the Holy Spirit,
>
> is worthy to be praised, one God,
>
> now and forever. Amen.[15]

In being, in a sense, the very first response and commitment we undertake as readers of the unity statement, we soon realize that it is not only that we pray, but that we pray together. Our prayer must be where we begin in

14. Ibid., par. 15.
15. Ibid., par. 16.

pilgrimage, and it must be our guide and reference at every point along the way: "God of Life: lead us to justice and peace."

Bibliography

Baptism, Eucharist and Ministry, Faith and Order Paper No. 111 (Geneva: WCC Publications, 1982).

"Called to Be the One Church" in *God in Your Grace...: Official Report of the Ninth Assembly of the World Council of Churches*, ed. Luis N. Rivera-Pagán (Geneva: WCC Publications, 2007), 244.

"The Constitution and Rules of the World Council of Churches as amended by the 9th Assembly." Porto Alegre, Brazil, 2006.

"An Ecumenical Call to Just Peace" in *Just Peace Companion*, 2d ed. (Geneva: WCC Publications, 2012), 1–13.

"God's Gift and Call to Unity—and Our Commitment." *Ecumenical Review* 65 (2013) 453–58.

Mateus, Odair P. "At the Core of the Ecumenical Vision: An Overview of World Council of Churches' Statements on Unity 1948–2006." World Council of Churches, publication pending.

The Nature and Mission of the Church: A Stage on the Way to a Common Statement, Faith and Order Paper No. 198 (Geneva: WCC Publications, 2005).

"Reports of Sections: Unity." In *The New Delhi Report*, edited by W. A. Visser 't Hooft, 116–134. London: SCM, 1962.

"The Unity of the Church as Koinonia: Gift and Calling." In *Signs of the Spirit: Official Report—Seventh Assembly*, edited by M. Kinnamon, 172. Geneva: World Council of Churches, 1991.

————— 16 —————

Diaconal Ministry in
the Diaconal Church

Reflections on the Interrelationship between
Ministerial Theology and Ecclesiology

STEPHANIE DIETRICH

Introduction

MANY ECUMENICAL DIALOGUES DURING the last centuries have achieved
far-reaching agreements on core aspects of Christian doctrine. Ecumenical
agreements, like the Porvoo Common Statement between churches belonging to the Anglican and the Lutheran tradition in Northern Europe (1992),
or the Joint Declaration on the Doctrine on Justification (1999), between
the Lutheran and the Roman Catholic tradition, show a basic theological
agreement on core doctrinal issues between different denominational traditions. Nevertheless, when it comes to *ministerial* theology, i.e. the concrete
understanding and practice of ordained ministries, there are still profound
differences between the traditions. This concerns all forms of ordained ministries, but especially the *diaconal ministry* or so called *diaconate*, which will
be the main subject for this article.

In 1982, the ecumenical statement *Baptism, Eucharist and Ministry*,
noted:

> In many churches there is today considerable uncertainty about
> the need, the rationale, the status and the functions of deacons
> ... Today, there is a strong tendency in many churches to restore

the diaconate as an ordained ministry with its own dignity and meant to be exercised for life.[1]

The BEM document viewed the question of the understanding of the diaconate mainly to be a question of church order and the organization of ordained ministry, not to the understanding of *diakonia* in general, or diaconal ecclesiology. Nevertheless, the questions raised in 1982 in the framework of the World Council of Churches' Faith and Order Commission are still relevant today and have influenced most of the debate on the diaconate ever since.

While *diakonia* in the framework of an ecumenical theological discourse is dealt with as a matter of social ethics, and mostly related to Inter-Church-Aid, the *diaconate*, i.e. *diaconal ministry*, is discussed as a doctrinal matter, within the framework of Faith and Order, as rightly pointed out by Kjell Nordstokke.[2] Thus, this article seeks to contribute in overcoming the strict distinction between *diakonia* as social work, humble service and Inter-Church-Aid on the one hand, and *diaconal ministry* as merely a question of ministerial orders and dogmatics on the other hand. This will be done by emphasizing that ministries and ministerial structures of the Church need to mirror and correspond with the Church's identity as diaconal Church, and vice versa.

In the author's opinion, the understanding of ordained ministries in the Church needs to be discussed on the background of the Church's identity. The ministries of the Church can only be understood and shaped in an adequate way if they are developed and described as signs and instruments of what the Christian Church is. Thus, this article focuses on the diaconate in its relation to a diaconal ecclesiology. Much attention in the theological and ecumenical discourse has been given to episcopal and pastoral ministry, while diaconal ministry has often not received the attention it deserves. Institutional and conceptual change in relation to the diaconate and diaconal ministry might be used as an opportunity to explore new forms of ecclesial self-understanding and common mission. Thus, the diaconate and diaconal ministry can be considered as an ecumenical opportunity both within and between the Churches.[3] This article attempts to show in which

1 World Council of Churches, *Baptism, Eucharist and Ministry*, 24–25.

2 Nordstokke, "Diakonia and Diaconate in the World Council of Churches."

3. This was underlined within the context of the Anglican-Lutheran dialogue, which resulted in the so-called Hanover Report, *The Diaconate as Ecumenical Opportunity*. The report stated that the diaconate should not be understood as a problem, but rather as an opportunity to overcome utilitarian approaches to ecclesiology and ministerial theology. According to the Hanover Report, the diaconate makes visible the fundamental integrity of all ordained ministries as a key to understanding the identity of the Church as being sent to the world, placed in the world through living out and

way ministerial theology, especially diaconal ministry, can be understood and developed on the background of a diaconal ecclesiology.

The author's hypothesis is that differences within ministerial theology need to be explored both through biblical, historical, contextual and ecclesiological studies and studies on power imbalances and gender discrepancies, in order to achieve a more agreed approach towards the understanding *and* practice of the diaconate. However, this article cannot cover all these approaches, and addresses mainly the ecclesiological framework for the understanding of the diaconate. Coming from a Norwegian, Lutheran background, the author tries to outline the core aspects of the understanding of the diaconal Church and diaconal ministry in a Norwegian Lutheran context. This will be exemplified by discussing the relationship between the understanding of the ministry of the deacon and a theological and ecclesiological understanding of *diakonia*, mainly within a Church of Norway context. Within the author's context, Church of Norway, there has been a long lasting discussion on the understanding of diaconal ministry. The discussion is shaped by both internal Norwegian disagreements[4] on ministerial theology and a Lutheran self-understanding. At the same time the understanding has been influenced by ecumenical and international agreements and developments.

Furthermore, the author will take into account parts of the ecumenical discourse on diaconal ministry within the Porvoo Communion context. The main sources for the discussion here are selected ecumenical documents

---

communicating the gospel in a holistic way.

4. Turid Karlsen Seim, as a member of the Committee on ordained ministry which prepared the background paper for Church of Norway (CoN) General Synod in 2001 (Kirkerådet, *Embetet i Den norske kirke*), played a decisive role in pointing to the ecumenical dimension and implications in the development of the understanding of the diaconate in CoN. Her inputs played an important role in leading the Synod to decide on further deliberations concerning the threefold ministry, instead of following the former approaches to consider only the presbyteral ministry as ordained ministry within CoN. While the majority of the Committee argued for an understanding of the diaconate "outside the ministerium ecclesiasticum," as a "realization of the commandment of love" and "a consequence of the justifying faith" (*Embetet*, 107; my translation), a minority in the Committee (Karlsen Seim and Tjernæs) disagreed and asked for further work on the issue. They underlined: "The question is if- and eventually how- we can consider a permanent and caritative diaconate as a part of the ordained ministry instituted by God, as a steward of the means of grace from which the Church gets its power of life" (*Embetet*, 107; my trans.). Karlsen Seim and Tjernæs also emphasized that *diakonia* does not need to be understood in a consecutive way, and that introducing the diaconate as a function of the ordained ministry of the church should not mean confusing the distinction between Gospel and Law. The Synod decided that Church of Norway should look for "new ways to think about the diaconate" (Synod decision, *Embetet*), hereby following Karlsen Seim's and Tjernæs's recommendation.

related to the Porvoo agreement context (mainly Anglican Churches in Great Britain and Ireland and Lutheran Churches in Nordic and Baltic countries), developed during the last two decades.

The author will first look at terminological clarifications, since the different terminologies deserve close attention and contribute to the clarification of the discussion. Secondly, the author will focus on theological assumptions describing diaconal ecclesiology and focusing on the Christological foundation of *diakonia*. Furthermore, the "diaconate of all baptized" and specific challenges within Lutheran theology will be discussed as a background for considerations on ecumenical developments within the understanding of the diaconate. These reflections will form the background for the discussion of the specific situation within Church of Norway concerning the development of the diaconate as an ordained ministry and the concluding remarks, emphasizing the un-negotiable relatedness of ecclesiology and ministerial theology.

Terminological Clarifications

Terminologically, the terms diaconal ministry, deacon's ministry and diaconate are overlapping, describing a personally exercised service or ministry within a church framework. When discussing ministerial theology and questions that have emerged within Faith and Order, one often uses the term diaconate or diaconal ministry. Thus, all the three terms are used in this article, as they are all used in a corresponding manner in the ecumenical discourse. The *diaconate* is closely related to the term *diakonia*. The *Dictionary of the Ecumenical Movement* defines *diakonia* as "the 'responsible service of the gospel by deeds and by words performed by Christians in response to the needs of people', (and) is rooted in and modelled on Christ's service and teachings."[5] Terminological and semantic differences become relevant when discussing the understanding of *diakonia* and the *diaconate*. A terminological problem might also reveal substantial differences in the understanding of what it means to be church, to communicate the gospel and to practice *diakonia*, understood as service for humankind and the whole creation.

The understanding of *diakonia* as Christian social service is dominating, especially within churches shaped by the Reformation era, like the Protestant churches. Nevertheless, different Christian traditions do not share a unique understanding of *diakonia*. Some traditions, like the European Protestant tradition, have used it frequently, especially during the last 200

5. White, "Diakonia."

years, against the background of what may be called a "diaconal revival," as a term for the Church's or Christian social action or involvement in our societies. Others, like the Anglican or Roman Catholic traditions are not as used to this connotation of *diakonia* and would prefer terms like *caritas* in the Roman Catholic tradition, or they associate *diakonia* mostly with the deacon's ministry as a first stage on the way to priesthood, as in the Anglican and Roman Catholic traditions, with mere liturgical functions. Social service within an Anglican tradition is usually not called *diakonia*. Within the Orthodox tradition, *diakonia* has been characterized as "liturgy after the liturgy,"[6] thus indicating that the Church's social action and responsibility cannot be separated from its worship and celebration of the Eucharist. Still, *diakonia* is not a widespread terminology in the Orthodox context. Based on such a varying understanding of *diakonia*, also the understanding of *diaconal ministry* is shaped differently in different Church traditions.

In the New Testament, diakonia and the deacon's ministry have a broad range of connotations.[7] John N. Collins criticized the narrow interpretation of these terms as related to mere humble service through providing a semantic and linguistic interpretation of *diak*-words in a survey of Greek literature, papyri and inscriptions for the period 400 BC to around 400 AC. He showed that this interpretation, to a large degree influenced by the German theological New Testament dictionary of Gerhard Kittel,[8] led to the misunderstanding that *diakonia* and the *deacon's ministry* were mainly about humble and lowly service to the needy. Collins underlined that these terms, both in the New Testament and its surrounding Hellenistic context, had a much broader connotation, and often related to being a messenger with an authoritative message, as a go-between minister carrying out an authoritative task. Collins' interpretations are highly discussed, both amongst New Testament scholars

---

6. Bria, "Liturgy after the Liturgy."

7. *Diakonia* is associated with central aspects of the church's identity as service, outreach, humility, concern for human needs. While there is no ecumenical consensus on the nature and form of the diaconate and diaconal ministry, there seems to be a reinvigoration of diakonia within many churches caused by a strong consciousness that the church has a mission in today's world. The renewed emphasis on diakonia has been heightened by a fresh exegetical look on its New Testament use, showing that diakonia in the New Testament does not primarily mean waiting at the table and humble service, but far more needs to be related to the mission of the church as the church's outreaching ministry. There has been an ongoing discussion on the understanding of diakonia based on the interpretation of the terms *diakonia, diakonein* and *diakonos* on the New Testament and the New Testament context, mainly inspired by the Australian theologian John Collins. See Collins, *Diakonia: Reinterpreting the Ancient Sources.*

8. Beyer, "*diakoneo, diakonia, diakonos.*"

and among scholars in the field of *diakonia* research and education.[9] Notwithstanding the results of this discussion on biblical interpretation and semantics, Collins' findings on the broad connotation of the *diak*-words in the New Testament have encouraged theologians to explore in which way one may have a fresh look at *diakonia* and *diaconal ministry*. Collins' research contributed thus to a fundamental reform within the understanding of *diakonia* and the *diaconate*. He highlighted the fact that a former understanding of *diakonia* and the *diaconate* as mere humble service was very much based on the narrow interpretation of *diakonia* which shaped the diaconal movement in the eighteenth and nineteenth centuries in Central Europe and its respective historical context, and not by a biblical understanding.

In the author's opinion, it should be underlined that today's understanding of *diakonia* cannot only be based on a narrow interpretation of the semantic connotation of the *diak*-words in the New Testament, but has to be interpreted much broader, in light of biblical theology in general, and in particular in the light of modern multidisciplinary and hermeneutical studies. Based on a biblical and epistemological interpretation, and taking into account the development of the Church's involvement in social service throughout history, one should take a fresh look at the understanding of *diakonia*. The mission and ministry of the church should be based on a holistic view on a New Testament perspective on Christian social service as determinative for the ministry and ministries of the church.

The author wants to argue that the starting point for discussing diaconal ministry, its understanding and its function, should be the diaconal mission and ministry of the church. Diaconal ministry is important for the understanding of what the nature of the Church is, not simply *functionally* and as a matter of practical theology, but *ecclesiologically*, concerning the nature and identity of the Church. Vice versa, the Church's diaconal identity forms the understanding for and shapes diaconal ministry. Therefore, it is necessary to elaborate on the understanding of the church as a diaconal church firstly before discussing diaconal ministry.

The Diaconal Church

The Lutheran World Federation published in 2009 the report *Diakonia in Context,* where the specific link between ecclesiology and *diakonia* is emphasized: "Diakonia . . . is related to the congregation's ethos and structures. In other words, it is both an expression of what the Church is by its very nature,

9. See Dunderberg, "Vermittlung statt karitativer Tätigkeit?," 177. See also Hentschel, *Diakonie im Neuen Testament.*

and what is manifested in its daily life, plans and projects."[10] *Diakonia*, as Christian social action, both individually and corporately, both in the name of the church and unofficially, is about the serving identity of the church and the church's presence in civil society. This includes becoming agents for the transformation of worldly structures and institutions. The church's *diakonia* serves as a practical expression of God's redeeming love in concrete acts of justice, reconciliation and healing. Therefore, this practice of *diakonia* belongs to the identity of the church and participates in the communication of the Gospel. When speaking ecclesiologically, understanding *diakonia* as one of the marks of the church has fundamental consequences for the self-understanding of the church and the development of ecclesiologies which are relevant in a theological context today.

The necessary correspondence between the *practice* and the *origin* of the church has been emphasized within the framework of European protestant churches (CPCE: Community of Protestant Churches in Europe). According to their main study document on ecclesiology, *The Church of Jesus Christ*, witness and service should be held together in a way that shows that they both belong to the identity of the church. "Since the church as community of people sanctified by God is holy, the ecclesial practice of witnessing must be measured by how far it corresponds to this in its praxis of proclamation and celebration of the sacraments an in service to people."[11] The study also points to the fact that the Reformers within different protestant churches from the right beginning during the Reformation era, understood Christian life and Christian service as marks of the Church, though related to the second table of Commandments. As marks of the Christian life they correspond and are interrelated to the marks of the true Church (i.e. word and sacrament), even though they are not identical with them.

> The Christian life comprises the entire living witness of all believers. It extends beyond the realm of the visible church into the whole everyday life of Christians and therefore far into the life of society. Of course, it also includes keeping the Commandments of the first table: witnessing to the gospel by word and sacrament. In this way, the visible church takes shape within the Christian life. In this respect the Christian life is itself fundamental for the concrete shape of the church.[12]

The understanding of diaconal ministry can only be developed in close relation to the understanding of the church as a diaconal church. Therefore, an

10. Lutheran World Federation, *Diakonia in Context*, 29.

11. Bünker and Friedrich, eds., *The Church of Jesus Christ*, 121.

12. Ibid., 115.

understanding and practice of *diakonia* closely linked to the church, and an understanding of the church which need to fully include *diakonia* in its self-understanding needs to be developed; *diakonia* understood as a constitutive part of being church. In order to develop a diaconal ecclesiology, specific attention should be given to a Christological foundation of diaconal ministry.

A Christological Foundation of the Diaconate

A Christological basis is widely accepted for the understanding of diaconal ministry. Therefore, it is important to outline some of the basic aspects within Christology, which should be kept in mind when discussing the diaconate. As T.Pädam underlines:

> The ministry of the deacon in the interpretation of the churches is always related to Jesus Christ and to his ministry: this ministry has catechetical, liturgical and caritative responsibilities; it participates in the Church's prophetic *diakonia* and all-round care for those in need.[13]

All of the church's members have, in baptism, been consecrated to ministry for Christ and their fellow human beings. The church's *diakonia* is a call to ministry that has its foundation in Christ's office as representative of the Father to the world, to serve. Christ's own call to ministry for the world and the call to the baptized to serve are inseparable. Therefore, to be a servant does not primarily imply selfless humility, but a call to ministry as Christ's coworker and follower.

Within the Church's tradition, Jesus Christ himself is understood and believed as the basis for the church in its worship and witness and service. According to Mark, 10:45, Christ is *diakonos*, servant, as an agent and image of the one who sent him, mediating the Father's will to the world. When practicing *diakonia*, the church does so as an agent of Christ's salvation. At the same time, Christ's own way to communicate the gospel becomes the core aspect of the understanding of *diaonal ministry*. According to the New Testament Gospel stories, Jesus did not only tell people he met what they ought to do and what was right, or preach to them, but took care of them in a holistic way, healing their diseases, offering forgiveness and inclusion into his fellowship, turning traditional values in society upside down and having table fellowship with sinners. Healing the sick and showing solidarity with the weak were integrated parts of Jesus' life and Messianic service. Therefore, the church needs to take a fresh look at how it understands its

---

13 Pädam "The Diaconate."

communication of the gospel. In a protestant context, this Christological basis for the understanding of *diakonia* is described as follows: "In dealing with us . . . Jesus Christ also at the same time grants us insights into what he alone can and will do and into what we can and ought to do. Thus the experience of Christ is always also the experience of the freedom and responsibility of faith."[14]

The church is not just that which passes on the means of grace, in a mere functional manner, the church itself is constituted by the means of grace and would not exist without them. The church is primarily a *receiver* of God's grace. In other words: The church is not the giver of the means of grace, but passes on the means of grace. In the same way, the church's diaconal actions are not the church's "merit," but through the church and its servants, Christ is present as the one who sympathizes with and stands beside those who need it and suffers with them. The church, according to its ecclesiological self-understanding "dressed in Christ" (cf. Col 3:12–17), as "Christ's body" (1 Cor 12:27), is present in people's lives. In the final analysis, it is not the church or people who act, but Christ himself through his body, the church. Thus, understanding *diakonia* as a non-negotiable aspect of the identity of the Church and Christian life does not contradict the basic Lutheran understanding of salvation by grace alone, but is an aspect or mark of the Church.

In a Protestant tradition, emphasis is given to the people of God and the local congregation gathering around the Word and Sacraments as the decisive and constitutive element of the Church. In this connection, there is an emphasis on everybody's responsibility to follow their consciousness, read the Bible, gather in community and live out their lives as Christians and act according to God's will, in mutual service for each other and all humankind. It is therefore important to reflect on this "responsibility of all the baptized," also related to the specific service of Church ministers, when discussing diaconal ministry.

The Diaconate of All the Baptized

In a Lutheran tradition, there has been a strong emphasis on the priesthood of all the baptized. According to Luther, "priest," in the original and strict sense of the Word, is Christ alone. Christians are priests only by sharing in Christ in faith, according to the logic of the 1. Pet 2:9. Christians become priests not through ordination, but through a new birth, the spiritual birth of baptism. Accordingly, we are all consecrated priests through baptism.

14. Bünker and Friedrich, eds., *The Church of Jesus Christ*, 108.

The difference between a pastor and a Christian who is not a pastor is a difference of office. All Christians are priests, but not all Christians are pastors.

In the same way, one can distinguish between the diaconal ministry of all the baptized and the church's ordained diaconal ministry. Similar to the priest's administration of the sacraments, the ministry of deacons is carried by Christ's commissioning and call, where people become "Christ for their neighbor." This goes for all the baptized who take part in the priesthood of all believers, at the same time as some are called to this task as a special ministry and function—who carry out this task and their call as representatives and servants for Christ. It is meaningful to speak of a "diaconate of all believers"[15], all the Christian's diaconal responsibility in the world, which makes up the foundation for "the special diaconate," an ordained diaconal ministry.

Even so, the question whether diaconal ministry should be a part of the Church's ordained orders, is not easily answered for many Churches belonging to the Protestant tradition. The reason for this lies both in a skeptical attitude towards hierarchical ministerial clerical structures, discussions on the relation between word and deed, Gospel and Law, and on the identity of the Church. Especially Lutheran theology, with its strong emphasis on salvation by grace alone, has struggled with the integration of *diakonia* in its dogmatic principles, being afraid of confusing the Reformation "*sola*"-principles through an emphasis on good deeds as an integrated part of a Christian life.

Challenges within Lutheran Theology

Within Lutheranism there has been a strong tradition to emphasize that the Church is present "wherever the gospel is preached in its truth and purity and the sacraments are administered according to the gospel" (Augsburg Confession §7).[16] Ecumenical and ecclesiological debates within Lutheran theological discourse during the last decenniums have emphasized the importance of avoiding a reductionistic reading of §7. This article should be read in the context of §§4–6, emphasizing that Christians are justified by

15. See Kirkemøtet 2004: KM 8.2./04, 21.

16. This understanding dominated the majority position in the Report from the Commission on ministry (*Embetet*) in CoN, as described in footnote 4. "This includes that *diakonia* is understood as a fruit of faith. Therefore, *diakonia* is understood as consecutive, not constitutive, i.e. as a consequence of the gospel. Including *diakonia*, according to this understanding, in the structure of the ordained ministry (understood as the ministry which creates faith with the means of grace), means according to the understanding of the Committee's majority a danger in making *diakonia* necessary for faith, and thus mixing up Gospel and Law." (*Embetet*, 107; my translation).

faith and through this empowered to act rightly as participants in God's mission and sending, in service to the world.

The separation between justification and sanctification, which after the Reformation era resulted in an *ordo salutis* thinking within Lutheran orthodoxy, was not intended by Luther himself, who clearly linked the forensic and the ontological understanding of justification and salvation in his writings. Good works within Luther's theology are neither instruments of salvation, giving merit before God, nor a necessary consequence of salvation, as in the pietist revivalist tradition. Good works are seen as a visible and necessary expression of the new life in Christ given in faith, as the Augsburg Confession §6 underlines:

> Also they teach that this faith is bound to bring forth good fruits, and that it is necessary to do good works commanded by God, because of God's will, but that we should not rely on those works to merit justification before God.

Analyzing the latest documents from the Lutheran World Federation, one can see a move from interpreting the Church's *diakonia* as a possible *consequence* of the Church's interaction with the world towards integrating it into its ecclesiology as a *mark* of the Church in continuation from the Early Church and throughout history until today. Speaking in reformatory terms, the Word and sacraments are not mere vehicles for *favor Dei*, in a forensic sense, but also vehicles for *donum Dei*, ontologically transforming the Christians and shaping their lives. This development within Lutheran theology also contributes to integrate *diakonia* as a necessary part of the Church's life, without overloading it theologically or making it a means of Christianizing the world. Concerning the concept of *diakonia* "as a theological imperative," Kjell Nordstokke underlines that

> it's hermeneutical strength lies in its ability to relate the identity of the church to its mission, of integrating different perspectives and connecting to central Christological motifs. This has contributed to a better understanding of the holistic nature of mission, and of renewing the reflection of how to be relevant in the world when responding to today's challenges.[17]

This specific Lutheran challenges concerning the understanding of ordained ministries have also played an important role within the Norwegian discussion. Within Church of Norway, in the Committee's Report to the General Synod 2001 on the understanding of ordained ministry, the minority

17. Nordstokke, *Liberating Diakonia*, 27.

position (Karlsen Seim and Tjernæs) gave a short outline why such a traditional understanding of *diakonia* and the diaconate should be revised:

> The minority of the committee wants to underline that *diakonia* not only should be understood as the Church's care for people in need, but bears witness of life that offers itself for others, as God's voice in the world. As Jesus, the incarnated Word, did, God's reign is brought close through word and deed, and through this communication faith is created when God's charity is expressed through care for spirit, body and soul.[18]

The inputs given to the General Synod then, together with an ecumenical awakening within Church of Norway in general and a growing consciousness about the necessity of *diakonia* as an expression of the Church's being present in and for the societies within confessional bodies like the Lutheran World Federation, formed the background for all further work on the diaconate and *diakonia* within Church of Norway.

Within the context of Church of Norway, the definition of *diakonia* as "Gospel in action" in the *Plan for diakonia* (2007) reflects this move in the understanding of Lutheran theology. *Diakonia* as Christian social service is not a mere consequence of the preaching of the Gospel and the administration of the sacraments, but *diakonia* witnesses about and participates in the sharing and communicating of the Gospel. This implies consequences for the understanding of diaconal ministry, since ministerial structures should reflect the church's self-understanding and needs.

Ecumenical Developments within the Understanding of the Diaconate

In the Western church, the diaconate always existed as a grade of ordination, but only in a stunted form as a transitional stage to the presbyterate. It had already lost its function as an independent ministry before the end of the first millennium. In some western churches, the diaconate as permanent diaconate has been revived. In the Roman Catholic Church, the Second Vatican Council used a formulation from the Early Church and says that they receive the laying–on hands "not for the priesthood but for a ministry of service (*non ad sacerdotium sed ad ministerium*)" (LG 29). This led to a rediscovery of the ordained diaconal ministry in the Roman Catholic Church as a quite "open" ministry, employed in various services in the church. For

---

18. Kirkerådet, *Embetet*, 107; my trans.

several years, the diaconal ministry has been a topic of theological research and discussion, also in Roman Catholic and Anglican churches.[19]

The Faith and Order Commission of the World Council of Churches has focused on the nature of the ordained ministry and its role for many decades. Without going into depth concerning all the publications on this issue, one should mention that Faith and Order already in 1963/1964 at the Montreal Conference located the discussion on the understanding of ordained ministry within its work on ecclesiology. It was then recognized that *diakonia* belongs to the whole life of the Church and is concretely expressed and embodied in a particular ministry, which can serve as a sign of what the Church essentially is. This was followed up in the BEM study from 1982, where the ecumenically sensitive question of the ordained ministry is approached via "the calling of the whole people of God." One could therefore say that BEM was breaking the ground for the understanding of ordained ministry as deeply grounded in the nature and mission of the Church. This approach has since then dominated both multilateral and bilateral dialogues, including the Porvoo Common Statement (Porvoo) from 1993.[20] Since the Nordic Lutheran churches and the Anglican churches are in communion through the Porvoo agreement, specific notice should be given to the ongoing processes within this context. One may note that the need for a distinctive diaconate is being recognized and worked on increasingly. The Porvoo Joint Declaration, which all signatory-churches signed, commits the churches "to work towards a common understanding of diaconal ministry."[21] Since its first signing, a number of consultations have been arranged, discussing the understanding and development of the diaconate in the Porvoo communion.

The *Hanover report* underlined its understanding of diaconal ministry by saying: "Diaconal ministers are called to be agents of the church in interpreting and meeting needs, hopes and concerns within church and society" (48). Irrespective of which area of work diaconal ministers are involved in, diaconal ministry is carried out based on Christian faith. Thus, diaconal ministers and the Church stand in a relation of mutual accountability. Through their work, diaconal ministers interpret the needs, hopes and concerns of the people to the Church, and they operate and mediate at the same time the service of the church to the world.

---

19. Cf. Church of England, *For Such a Time as This*.

20. For an overview of the ongoing work on the understanding of the diaconate in the Porvoo Communion, see Pädam, "The Diaconate," 2014.

21. *The Porvoo Common Statement*, 85b (vii).

Many of the diaconal ministries within the churches shaped by the Reformation era arose in response to specific needs in different contexts and societies. Therefore, one might say that the dominant factor in the diversity of diaconal ministries has been the various needs, which they have sought to meet, and the historical contexts in which they arose and which shaped their character. The church at various times needed different forms of diaconal ministry. Diaconal ministry managed to a large degree to adapt and transform itself according to the needs of the changing times.

One of the challenges concerning a renewed understanding of *the diaconate* is the fear for clericalization and institutionalization. This might also be one of the reasons, why the threefold ministry has not been an attractive choice for many in Lutheran churches. There is a fear that *diakonia* might lose its identity which lies in its focus on *caritas* and *justitia* in church and society.

From a Lutheran point of view, one might ask in how far the transitional diaconate as practiced in the Anglican churches really deals with *diakonia* in the broad sense, as the church's ministry in the world. Does diaconal ministry in the Anglican Churches actually relate to *diakonia* and a diaconal understanding of the Church, or which understanding of *diakonia* is the basis for its diaconal ministry? On the other hand, one might ask in which ways the Lutheran diaconal ministry and the different areas of diaconal work the church is involved in, are carried by a self-understanding as the *church's* ministries.

The Deacon's Ministry in the Latest Decisions within the Church of Norway

In the context of the Church of Norway, *diakonia* embraces "everybody's *diakonia*" ("the diaconate of all believers"), congregational *diakonia* (including the deacon's ministry), institutional *diakonia* and international *diakonia*. The diaconal revival in Germany in the 19th century inspired church leaders in Norway to establish diaconal institutions very much alike the institutions we know from Wichern, Fliedner and Löhe. These institutions focused on caritative work and education, especially within social sciences and nursing. Over the years, this also contributed to the rise of a specific congregational *diakonia* which is based on both diaconal ministers' and volunteer work. After World War II, the church reform movement focused on a differentiation of ministries within the church. This also brought about a new emphasis on diaconal work in the church's governing structures. It involved the establishing of positions for congregational deacons and an extended work on the understanding of diaconal ministry. Until the reformation time, the ministerial structure which was developed was a mono-presbyteral system, while the Church's social service was gradually transferred to the state and municipial authorities.[22]

As already mentioned the understanding of *diakonia* in Norway and in the Nordic countries has been strongly related to the diaconal revival in Central Europe in the nineteenth century. According to that tradition, *diakonia* is mostly understood as the church's social work and care for the needy. *Diakonia* was understood as duty of every Christian. Following Christ's example, it is seen as an obligation for every Christian to help other people who are suffering, ill or in need. For many years, the understanding of *diakonia* was mainly based on stories like the parable of the Good Samaritan and understood as humble service for people in need.

This understanding was very much influenced by the "Mutterhaus-tradition" coming from Germany. The ideal was that people through their service should offer themselves by serving the others. The whole idea of *diakonia* as humble service was thought to be the understanding of *diakonia* deriving directly from the New Testament. As mentioned above, there has been a move in the understanding of *diakonia* in recent years.[23] This move is reflected in different ways in the understanding of *diakonia*. Church of Norway decided in 2007 on a new *Plan for diakonia*. The plan has its main focus on diaconal work practised on a congregational level, but it also relates to institutional and international *diakonia*.

The General Synod approved the following definition of *diakonia*:

> *Diakonia* is the caring ministry of the Church. It is the Gospel in action and is expressed through loving your neighbour, creating inclusive communities, caring for creation and struggling for justice.[24]

There are several aspects in this new understanding of *diakonia* which need to be underlined. The fundamental move from a Lutheran perspective is that *diakonia* is understood as a part of being church. It is not an appendix to being the church, which according to Confessio Augustana VII is constituted through the preaching of the gospel and the administration of the sacraments. By defining *diakonia* as the acting out of the Gospel, *diakonia* itself participates in the proclamation of the Gospel. Three aspects of this definition of *diakonia* should be considered:

22. For more information about the development in Norway, cf. Fanuelsen, "A Distinct and Independent Ministry."

23. See paragraph on terminological clarifications.

24. Church of Norway, *Plan for Diakonia*, 2007.

First: The communication of the Gospel is not only proclamation by words, but also by deeds and humankind's whole way of living. The church is only church if it is a diaconal church. This has been an important move in ecclesiology, since this approach seeks to bring together the Church's liturgical life and the Church's and Christians' life in civil society. *Diakonia* as the acting out of the Gospel refers to Jesus' proclamation of the Gospel through words and deeds. The imparting of the gospel happens through the proclaimed Word, and the Word's proclamation, the liberating message about Jesus Christ, is brought to life both with and without words. Care for the whole person is thus a part of the church's nature, and not an "optional arrangement."

Secondly, the new definition of *diakonia* reveals a move from the subject-object relation to a relation of mutuality and empowerment. Serving each other in a diaconal way does not mean that one person or institution is the giver, while the other one is the receiver. The new definition of *diakonia* is inspired by the understanding of humankind as a fellowship and community of people who rely on each other. For *diakonia* as social service, this includes the basic realization that all those involved in the act of *diakonia* are actors in interdependency, and not mere subjects or objects or helpers or recipients of help.

Thirdly, the new understanding of *diakonia* shows a broadened perspective on how *diakonia* is understood today. It is not only humble service and caretaking of those who are in need, but includes a focus on community and inclusiveness, and a broader, pro-active role as engaging in issues of justice and care for creation, as part of the church's diaconal engagement. This also includes a move from the focus on the individual in need to a wider focus on community and care for the whole creation. *Diakonia* implies an empowerment of the people to cope with their lives and an encouragement to get involved in the struggle of humankind and the whole creation. As Johannes Degen underlines: "The former diaconal ethos of care has come to an end. The former 'for' needs to be transformed to a 'together-with' culture in care relations. A new conception of diaconal care needs to understand itself as a means of assistance towards a self-governed life."[25]

After decades of deliberation and discussion, the Church of Norway General Synod made a decision in April 2011 on its understanding of the diaconate. The decision clearly shows a development in the understanding of the diaconate since 2001. At the same time, there is still some unclarity. The Synod decision reads as follows (author's translation):

25. Degen, *Freiheit und Profil*, 37; my translation.

1. The ministry of the deacon is an independent and necessary ministry within the framework of the fellowship of ministries of the Church of Norway.

2. The ministry of the deacon is based on an independent theological foundation and is primarily understood as a caring ministry.

3. The ministry of the deacon presupposes consecration/ordination. The Synod supports the Bishops' Conference's recommendation that the consecrated/ordained deacon should wear a stole in the liturgy, and has asked for the subject of the introduction of the stole to be brought to the Synod for decision as soon as possible.

4. Consecration/ordination in the Church of Norway is a consecration/ ordination to a specific ministry. Moving from one ministry to another implies a new consecration/ordination to the new ministry.

In addition, the Synod asked that the number of positions for deacons be increased, and that steps be taken to ensure that every congregation has access to "diaconal competence" within 2015.

By emphasizing that the ministry is independent, the Synod wanted to highlight that the diaconate is not to be understood as an introductory ministry to the presbyterate, but that it is a distinct and permanent ministry with its own identity. The Synod also distanced itself from a threefold understanding of ordained ministry. At the same time, it is underlined that the diaconate is an important and un-negotiable ministry in Church of Norway. When saying that it is a "caring ministry," the Synod refers to the main tasks and duties of diaconal ministry according to the Church regulations, underlining that the deacon's ministry firstly is related to care or social ministry, and not to liturgical ministry, even if the deacons within Church of Norway have a number of liturgical functions, like intercession during Sunday worship or celebration of the Eucharist in relation to certain diaconally defined circumstances.

Concerning terminology, the Synod decided that consecration to diaconal ministry, as all other consecrations to specific ministries, should be termed "vigsling," which means consecration, *not* "ordination." The term "ordination" should, according to the Synod's decision, be reserved for consecration to the priesthood, due to so called "historical reasons." In this way, the Synod tried on the one hand to avoid a threefold ordained structure of ministry, but on the other hand emphasize that there are several consecrated ministries in the church which are separate and have their own distinct identity.

The decision might be seen as wise from a pragmatic view, since it seems to eliminate the division lines and thus theological and professional disagreements between the different ministries. On the other hand this decision results in terminological, and thus also theological, ambiguities, which makes it difficult to translate and transfer the Church of Norway decisions precisely and in an ecumenically accountable manner. The decision emphasizes the distinctiveness and necessity of the diaconate for Church of Norway, based on the Church's diaconal self-understanding, but leaves open in which way the connectedness of all the consecrated/ordained ministries should be understood and what are the implications concerning interchangeability of ministries between churches who are in communion.

Conclusion

Diakonia and the diaconal ministry are not optional for the church, nor is the foundation of *diakonia* and diaconal ministry in the mission and ministry of the church optional for the actors of *diakonia*. Especially in the Lutheran context, *diakonia* has sometimes had a tendency to be isolated from the official church, and vice versa. Therefore, the challenge lies in finding an identity of *diakonia* which places diaconal work in the framework of the mission and ministry of the church and through this to enrich both the diaconal work and the church's proclamation of the Gospel in its different forms.

The move in the understanding of *diakonia* can be seen together with a move in the understanding of ecclesiology in general and diaconal ministry in particular. Through their structures of ministry, churches elucidate their self-understanding as diaconal churches, where diaconal activities are an interrelated, necessary and obvious part of the churches' mission. Diaconal ministry, both of ordained and non-ordained people, the church's bridge-building and serving attitude and action, contribute towards making the church's holistic care for human beings visible and creating plausibility for the church. Diaconal ministry acts as a bridge and connection point by making visible the fact that the church in fact has a holistic care for people. This includes also struggle for justice and pro-active work.

The ongoing work on the understanding of diaconal ministry has made it obvious that outer structures of church organization and theological discussions on the understanding of ordained ministry should be closely interrelated with the self-understanding of the Church as a whole.

Faith in the triune God—Creator who meets us in everything that is created and challenges humankind to take care of creation; Savior, who in solidarity with the suffering, suffers with and for all people and frees them to a new life; and the Life Giver, the Spirit, who carries and nurtures humankind and renews the congregation by blowing life into it—all these dimensions of faith in God make up the framework or the understanding of the identity of the church as a diaconal church in the world. *Diakonia* is anchored in belief in creation, salvation and renewal; it is anchored in the world and in the congregation. Thus, it is important to emphasize a trinitarian approach to the understanding of *diakonia* in order to reflect its broad meaning. The church's self-understanding as a diaconal church is, according to the Study "The Church of Jesus Christ," rooted in the commission to all Christians to serve: "In being directed not only to members of the church but to all people in need, the diaconate of Christians corresponds to the universality of salvation."[26]

The starting point for the understanding of diaconal ministry lies in God's mission that is given to the church, followed by the specific task the church is faced with in the world.

Irrespective of the different forms and structures diaconal ministry has taken throughout history, the diaconate needs to define itself with a starting point in the mission and ministry of the church. At the same time, the mission and ministry of the church need to be redefined and adapted according to the concrete circumstances, needs, and conditions in its specific context. Diaconal ministry might therefore play a specific role in the act of bridge building and communicating the Gospel to the world, in our societies, with and without words.

Bibliography

Beyer, Hermann Wolfgang. "*diakoneo, diakonia, diakonos.*" In *Theologisches Wörterbuch zum Neuen Testament*, edited by Gerhard Kittel, 2:81–93. Stuttgart: Kohlhammer, 1935.

Bispemøtet, Den norske kirke. *BM 03/10: Diakontjenesten i Kirkens tjenestemønster.* Oslo, 2010.

Boettcher, Reinhard, ed. *The Diaconal Ministry in the Mission of the Church.* LWF Studies 1/2006. Geneva, 2006.

Bria, Ion. "The Liturgy after the Liturgy." *International Review of Mission* 67, no. 265 (1978) 86–90.

Bünker, Michael, and Martin Friedrich, eds. *Die Kirche Jesu Christi: Der reformatorische Beitrag zum ökumenischen Dialog über die kirchliche Einheit / The Church of Jesus Christ: The Contribution of the Reformation towards Ecumenical Dialogue on Church Unity.* Leuenberger Dokumente Nr.1. (1. Auflage 1995). Leipzig: Evangelische, 2012.

---

26. Bünker and Friedrich, eds., *The Church of Jesus Christ.*

Brodd, Sven-Erik. "The Deacon in the Church of Sweden." In *The Ministry of the Deacon*, edited by Gunnel Borgegård and Christine Hall, 1:97–140. Uppsala: Nordic Ecumenical Council, 1999.

Church of England. *For Such a Time as Shis: A Renewed Diaconate in the Church of England. A report to the General Synod of the Church of England of a Working Party of the House of Bishops*. GS 1407. London: Church House, 2001.

Collins, John N. *Diakonia: Reinterpreting the Ancient Sources*. New York: Oxford University Press, 1990.

Degen, Johannes. *Freiheit und Profil: Wandlungen der Hilfekultur—Plädoyer für eine zukunftsfähige Diakonie*. Leiten-Lenken-Gestalten: Theologie und Ökonomie 13. Gütersloh, Gütersloher, 2003.

Dietrich, Stephanie. "Diakonie in den nordischen Ländern- Praxis und Akteure." In *Dem ganzen Menschen dienen. Praxis und Verständnis von Diakonie in der lutherischen Gemeinschaft*, 63–74. Dokumentation 54. Genf: Lutherischer Weltbund, 2009.

———. "Diakontjenesten I Den norske kirke i et økumenisk perspektiv." In *Diakoni—en kritisk lesebok*, edited by Kai Ingolf Johannessen et al., 45–68. Trondheim: Tapir, 2009.

———. "Diakontjenesten i et økumenisk perspektiv." In *Diakonen—kall og profesjon*, edited by Stephanie Dietrich et al., 127–51. Trondheim: Tapir 2011.

Dunderberg, Ismo. "Vermittlung statt karitativer Tätigkeit? Überlegungen zu John N. Collins' Interpretation von diakonia." In *Diakonische Konturen im Neuen Testament*, edited by Volker Herrmann and Heinz Schmidt, 171–83. DWI-INFO Sonderausgabe 9. Heidelberg: DWI, 2007.

Embetet i Den norske kirke (2001). Innstilling fra en arbeidsgruppe nedsatt av Kirkerådet. (transl.: Report from a working group installed by the Church Council)(Sak KM 10/01). Church of Norway, National Council.

Fanuelsen, Olav. "A Distinct and Independent Ministry—The Deacon's Ministry in Church of Norway: Answers and Questions on the General Synod's Decision." In *International Journal for the Study of the Christian Church* 13 (2013) 312–26.

Hanover Report of the Anglican-Lutheran International Commission: The Diaconate as an Ecumenical Opportunity. Published for the Anglican Consultative Council and the Lutheran World Federation. London: Anglican Communion, 1996.

Hentschel, Annie. *Diakonie im Neuen Testament*, Tübingen: Mohr Siebeck, 2007.

Joint Declaration on the Doctrine of Justification. Lutheran World Federation, Roman Catholic Church. Grand Rapids: Eerdmans, 2000.

Kirkerådet. Den norske kirke *Embetet i Den norske kirke*. Innstilling fra en arbeidsgruppe nedsatt av Kirkerådet. Oslo: Church of Norway, National Council, 2001.

Kirkerådet. Den norske kirke KM 9/11 *Diakontjenesten i kirkens tjenestemønster*. Oslo, Kirkerådet. Oslo, 2011.

Kirkemøtet. Den norske kirke KM 08/04 *Diakonal tjeneste i Den norske kirke*. Oslo, Kirkerådet. Oslo, 2004.

Kirkerådet. *Church of Norway Plan for Diakonia*. Church of Norway, National Council: Oslo, 2009.

Lutheran World Federation. *Diakonia in Context: Transformation, Reconciliation, Empowerment*. Geneva: Lutheran World Federation, 2009.

The Mission and Ministry of the Whole Church. Biblical, theological and contemporary perspectives. The Faith and Order Advisory Group of the Church of England, GS Misc 854, The Archbishops' Council. London: Archbishops' Council, 2007.

Nordstokke, Kjell. "Diakonia and Diaconate in the World Council of Churches." In *International Journal for the Study of the Christian Church* 13, no. 4 (2013) 286–99.

Nordstokke, Kjell. *Liberating diakonia*. Trondheim: Tapir, 2011.

Pädam, Tiit. *Ordination of Deacons in the Churches of the Porvoo Communion: A Comparative Investigation in Ecclesiology*. Tallinn: Kirjastus TP, 2011.

Pädam, Tiit. "The Diaconate after the Signing of the Porvoo Declaration: An Overview of Methods and Hermeneutics." *International Journal for the Study of the Christian Church* 13 (2014) 300–311.

Pohjolainen, Terttu. "The Deacon in the Evangelical Lutheran Church in Finland." In *The Ministry of the Deacon*, edited by Gunnel Borgegård and Christine Hall, 1:141–80. Uppsala: Nordic Ecumenical Council, 1999.

The Porvoo Common Statement. Conversations between the British and Irish Anglican Churches and The Nordic and Baltic Churches. Text agreed at the fourth plenary meeting, held at Järvenpää, Finland, 9–13 October 1992. Council for Christian Unity Occasional Papers 3, London: Council for Christian Unity, 1992.

"Porvoo Consultation on the Diaconate London 25–27 January 2006." Edited by Matti Repo. In *Reseptio* 1 (2006) 73–157.

Rogerson, Barry. "The Diaconate." In *Community—Unity Communion: Essays in Honour of Mary Tanner*, edited by Colin Podmore, 204–15. London: Church House, 1999.

White, Teresa Joan. "Diakonia." In *Dictionary of the Ecumenical Movement*, edited by Nicholas Lossky, Jose Miguez Bonino, and John Pobee, 1–7. Geneva: World Council of Churches, 2002.

World Council of Churches. *Baptism, Eucharist and Ministry*. Faith and Order Paper No.111. Geneva: World Council of Churches, 1982.

World Council of Churches. *Baptism, Eucharist & Ministry 1982–1990, Report on the Process and Responses*. Faith and Order Paper No. 149. Geneva: World Council of Churches, 1992.

PART IV

Patterns of Ambiguity

Placing Men in *The Double Message* of Luke's Gospel

Halvor Moxnes

In her *The Double Message*, Turid Karlsen Seim poses a question that summarizes what the book is about: "in the architecture of the Lukan text, how is a place given to women?"[1] The expression "place given to women," brings to mind a popular phrase, "a woman's place," which indicated an inferior place, often one of domesticity ("a woman's place is in the kitchen"), and one that was taken for granted, as given. For the longest time this was also the way biblical texts were read, as historical texts that at the same time carried moral authority to prescribe "a woman's place" in the present. But Seim's use of the terminology of building: "in the architecture of the Lukan text," suggests that this is a man-made construction. Her phrase implies that in Luke's gospel there was a conscious ideology behind the place that was "given" to women.

A Place for Men?

My question, as a follow up to Seim's study, is what place does Luke give to men and how does he construct masculinity in the world that he describes? This is the kind of questions that masculinity studies now raise; since it is recognized that in literary texts, modern as well as ancient, images of both men and women are constructed. Their places are carefully given to them, by authors and not least by readers; the texts present portraits and ideals,

---

1. Seim, *Double Message*, 127. I would like to thank Turid Karlsen Seim for many years of collaboration, inspiration, and friendship in the New Testament group at the University of Oslo. With energy and vision she changed our academic and social life into a gender-inclusive environment.

not historical facts. This understanding was not so clearly understood when Seim wrote her study in the late 1980s; this was before the impact of masculinity studies on New Testament research. However, *The Double Message* points towards the future. Seim's study does not primarily raise an historical question: "What was the role of women?"; it is a study of literary constructions. Her study was also unusual for its time by focusing on the ambiguities of the place given to women, as it is indicated by the title of her study. Feminist studies that had started in the 1960s and 1970s had to wrest the images and constructions of women out of the male presuppositions that were taken for granted in studies of the narratives and discourses in the gospels. Seim's study continues that tradition, but although based on women's studies, it is also pointing toward a wider gender inclusive perspective. With her comparison between women and men, Seim has pointed to how gender in Luke–Acts is constructed, and I want to follow up on this insight by investigating the place given to men.

One of the aspects of change since Seim wrote her study, more than twenty years ago, is the beginning of studies of masculinity/masculinities. Many of them were inspired by feminist studies, for instance in literary and classical studies, and some were also initiated by women scholars.[2] The first masculinity studies were taken up in literary studies and in sociology, and it is an indication of how young this approach is in New Testament studies that the first collection of essays, *New Testament Maculinities,* appeared only in 2003.[3] In a recent article on "Feminist criticism," based on works on Luke–Acts after the publication of her book, Seim also briefly discusses the new studies of masculinity.[4] She recognizes that it is obvious that "construction of feminity/ies and masculinity/ies somehow are mutually dependent, and that how the mutual dependence and interplay between men and women are conceived should be investigated."[5] Seim is skeptical, however, if feminist criticism should shift its focus to studies of masculinity, and says: "Given the homosocial interest in the new male, the focus on masculinity may be another, more subtle way to marginalize women, another guise of

2. Thus, studies of masculinities had a different origin than the men's movement, that also started at about the same time, with the aim to strengthen manhood and manly power felt to be threatened by a feminist culture.

3. Moore and Anderson, eds., *New Testament Masculinities.* The book contains essays that cover most of the books in the New Testament; for an overview of masculinity studies in the New Testament and a broad range bibliography, see Moore, "'O Man, Who Art Thou . . . ?'"

4. Seim, "Feminist Criticism." Thanks to Marianne Bjelland Kartzow who made me aware of this passage in Seim's article.

5. Ibid., 47.

seeing men as more important than women and paying attention to women primarily for how their presence in texts may contribute to the understanding of masculinity."[6]

I think Seim's criticism is more valid with respect to various "men's movements" in recent years, that represent a "homosocial interest in the new male," e.g., with groups like Promise Keepers or Robert Bly's book *Iron John: A Book about Men.*[7] There is no doubt that the feminist movement and particularly the growth of equal rights as official policies in many countries, have resulted in some vocal reactions and reactionary movements from (small) groups of men. But this does not seem to be the motivation for academic studies of masculinities, many of them undertaken by feminist men and women.

Models for Masculinities: Hegemonic Masculinity

The main context for New Testament and Early Christian masculinity studies are studies of masculinities in the classical and ancient Mediterranean world,[8] and theoretical perspectives and models from studies in sociology and literature. The study of masculinities in antiquity was greatly influenced by Michel Foucault's *History of Sexuality* (French originals 1976–1984), and in general by Foucault's introduction of *discourse* as the main term to establish knowledge. "Gender," "sexuality," and "subject," Foucault emphasized, are not objective categories, they are produced through our discourse through the way we speak of them. His perspective changed the way sexuality was studied. Foucault argued that "sexuality" was a term within modern discourses, and that the discourses in antiquity dealt with "desire" and "pleasure." He emphasized that the subject, that is, male individual shaped his own life; for this exercise Foucault used the term *askesis,* with the meaning "an exercise of oneself in the activity of thought."[9] The term is of course related to *asceticism* as an activity in Early Christianity, but indicates an active engagement in shaping one's life instead of the negative aspect often associated with asceticism.[10] Feminist scholars criticized Foucault for concentrating on a small group of elite free men, so that other groups, especially women, but also non-elite men and slaves, were not included in

6. Ibid.

7. See, e.g., Messner, *Politics of Masculinities.*

8. See Anderson with Moore and Kim, "Masculinity Studies: A Classified Bibliography."

9. Foucault, *The Use of Pleasure,* 9.

10. Moxnes, "Asceticism and Christian Identity."

his discussion. However, despite this criticism, some feminist scholars have also found Foucault's perspectives inspiring.[11] And the focus on men within a group of other men, for instance in the study of sexual relations between men in Roman society, have turned out to be a fruitful approach to studies of men in general.[12]This influence from classical studies have also meant that studies of masculinities in New Testament and Early Christianity have their context in the Greco-Roman world, and that the Jewish context represents a sub-set of this world. For instance, in the study of presentations of Jesus in the New Testament, the context is broadened from mainly Jewish traditions to Greco-Roman literature and history. An example of that is Colleen M. Conway's study *Behold the Man*, with the subtitle *Jesus and Greco-Roman Masculinity*.[13]

Conway's study illustrates another use of context, and that is the use of theoretical models for the study of masculinities. Conway employs the model of "hegemonic masculinity," developed by the sociologist Robert (later Raewyn) W. Connell.[14] Connell's theory is that masculinities in a society are structured hierarchically with masculinity as dominant, i.e. "hegemonic." It is associated with the elite and with power, so that it dominates other forms of masculinities that are considered subordinate, along a sliding scale. This is a model that has been very influential not only in sociological studies, but also in historical ones. Conway's study of the masculinity of Jesus is a case in point, comparing the descriptions of Jesus in various writings of the New Testament to the ideals of masculinity among the elite in Greco-Roman societies.

Other studies in *New Testament Masculinities* also use the model of hegemonic masculinity, with slightly other words, like "imperial masculinity" or "masculinity in the ancient Mediterranean world." This model is used by Mary Rose D'Angelo, who has written two important studies of masculinity in Luke–Acts, based on a comparison with "imperial masculinity."[15] She holds that Luke and his addressee, Theophilus, are men who belong to the elite, and she suggests that the same is the case for the readers or hearers of his writings. The ideal for an elite Roman male, D'Angelo claims, was to "'know how to preside over the household' . . . in which the women, children, and slaves follow the direction and example of the male head of the

11. See Cameron, "Redrawing the Map."

12. See Williams, *Roman Homosexuality*.

13. Conway, *Behold the Man*.

14. Connell, *Masculinities*; and Connell and Messerschmidt, "Hegemonic Masculinity: Rethinking the Concept."

15. D'Angelo, "The *ANER* question in Luke–Acts"; and D'Angelo, "Knowing How to Preside."

household."[16] Thus, D'Angelo presents a picture of the gospel and Acts as "an exchange between elite males, between noble, initiated patron and literate, sophisticated narrator."

It is here that I see a problem; I think that D'Angelo is emphasizing too much the function of the initial addresses to Theophilus, so that it overshadows the narratives and discourses in the texts themselves. The men presented in the narratives in the Gospels are for the most part *not* elite persons; most of the subjects in the narratives as well as the addressees of Jesus' discourses belong to the "common people" leading "everyday lives." This suggests that we ought to look at models in which constructions of masculinities are played out in relationships at the same level, not primarily within hierarchical relations.

Alternative Models: Between Men

One such model was suggested by George L. Mosse in *The Image of Man: The Creation of Modern Masculinity*. Mosse traced changes in the ideas of masculinity in the development of modernity in the eighteenth and early nineteenth centuries, and he established the categories "stereotype" and "countertype." He studied how the "ideal man" was contrasted with his counterpart, through relations between men, *not* between men and women. This perspective reflects the literature of its time, at least that written by men. A very influential study along the same lines was *Between Men* by Eve Kosofksy Sedgwick. It is a study of homosocial relations between men in seventeenth-century English literature and of how these relationships affect women. Sedgwick builds on Lévi-Strauss's description of culture as a transaction between men concerning the possession of women. But Sedgwick's study does not confirm traditional masculine roles; she explores the complexities of literary presentations of men and masculinity and introduces a reading of English literature that destabilizes gender and secure relations between genders. She explores how, even when women are involved in relationships between men, in this literature the main relations of desire or competition are between men. Thus, her books are early examples of queer studies;[17] they break down binary opposites between genders and, in *Between Men*, they destabilize fixed masculine roles.

I propose that we find similar destabilizing elements in Luke's presentations of men and masculinity in his gospel. There seems to be a parallel to such homosocial relations in seventeenth-century English literature in

16. D'Angelo, "Knowing How to Preside," 287.

17. See an introduction to queer theory in Turner, *A Genealogy of Queer Theory*.

the competition between men to gain honour and avoid shame in literature from ancient societies, including writings in the New Testament. Many of the issues of male honour are directly related to a man's control of women under his responsibility: wife, daughters, sisters, but are basically a matter of competition between men, to protect and gain honour and to avoid shame.

Both studies of early modern literature and of writings from antiquity seem to confirm Seim's criticism, that they are "seeing men as more important than women and paying attention to women primarily for how their presence in texts may contribute to the understanding of masculinity." These studies reflect the discourses in the literature they are studying, and the way these discourses construct masculinity, and in this way they may reveal that these texts are not written from a modern perspective in which the main relations are between women and men, based on equality. The issue that may be underlying Seim's criticism is that such studies may be used as normative, that is, that constructions of masculine superiority may be used to establish a historical situation, or even as arguments for male superiority today. To the best of my knowledge, however, masculinity studies are aware that they deal with discourses and not with historical "facts," and most also show a critical awareness that ancient models should not be transferred to modern societies. Moreover, Sedgwick's and other queer studies destabilize hegemonic or stereotypical masculinities in a way that challenges also traditional male roles. However, gender and queer studies that explore the theoretical constructions of gender may pose challenges to women's studies that are based on a more political approach to relations between women and men and that are concerned with equal rights issues.

Challenging Male Roles and Locations in Luke

Granted that Luke has a masculine focus in his gospel, I suggest that the text nevertheless destabilizes the masculine role. One of the ways that Luke does that, and that I will explore, is through the "place" that Luke gives to men in his gospel, in the "architecture" of his text, which I consider as the ideal structure that Luke wants to build. I am not asking an historical question of Luke as an historical source for men's roles in Palestine at the time of Jesus, but rather how he presents the role of men and masculinity in the movement shaped by Jesus. To ask about the "place" that Luke constructs for men is similar to the way in which Joel Green asks about the "world of Luke." In *The Theology of the Gospel of Luke* Green finds that in "the world of Luke's Gospel," "world" has three different meanings. [18] First, it is the world

18. See Green, *Theology of the Gospel of Luke*, 1–22.

in historical terms, the social, cultural, and religious situations that were known to author and addressees (but not to modern readers). Second, it is this world as it is (selectively) described by Luke; and finally, it is "the world" as Luke wants it to be or to become, shaped by the story he tells. It is "male place" in this third meaning that I will explore, how Luke will shape man and his location in the Jesus community.

The format of a brief essay does not allow for a full discussion of all the relevant material in Luke's gospel, nor is it possible to include material from Acts of the Apostles. I have chosen to focus on a small part of Luke's discourse, on the way he speaks of "leaving" home etc. and of "following" Jesus.[19] I will see these terms as categories in space rather than time, and therefore I will make a little twist to Seim's question "What is the place given to men," and rephrase it as "How does Luke construct gender by using place?" The importance of place in Luke's gospel can be understood in light of studies of place by the Marxist philosopher Henri Lefebvre and the social anthropologist David Harvey.[20] Among the perspectives they apply to spatial practices, two are particularly useful for this study. One is called the "appropriation and use of space," which we may think of as the work on farms, in fishing and in households at the level of village life in Galilee. The other perspective is "domination and control of space," or what we might call politics.[21] Political activity was associated with the elite, the rulers, be they vassal kings like the Herods in Palestine or Roman rulers, who through taxes, forced labour etc. dominated local spaces. These material practices were underpinned by "representations of space," that is the ideologies that made these practices legitimate. Ideology was at work on the local village level, it was expressed in ideals and expectations that differed according to gender, status, and age. The ideology at the political, elite level legitimated practices of taxation, social control, and demands of obedience.

In the first part of Luke's gospel Jesus addresses men at the household and village level. In the final part of the gospel the story moves to Jerusalem, the location of the elite and the political power that now clearly dominates the scene. The importance of household and village as places for support, sustenance, and identity is obvious in Luke's gospel, reflecting its setting in the ancient Mediterranean world. References to households and villages in narratives, discourses, and parables in the gospel reflected a location from

---

19. See an extended discussion of this question in Moxnes, "Where is 'Following Jesus'?"

20. Harvey, *Condition of Postmodernity.*

21. Ibid., 219–22.

which to experience life, and in which life and identity were shaped. In modern terms, we would say that they represented the first socialization.[22]

This situation makes it plausible that in his discourse on masculinity Luke takes as his starting point that men in his narrative or men who are his addressees have their primary location in the household and village scene. One of the plots in the gospel is based on the history of men who leave or are asked by Jesus to leave this place in order to "follow" Jesus. This implies to enter into a space in which they have left behind their primary male location. Thus, this discourse shares the characteristics of pilgrimage or rites de passage.[23] The subjects go through three phases: originally based in a secure location (the household), the addressees are dislocated, and they enter into a new location that is open, not fixed or permanent. This is a pattern that is repeated several times in Luke, most characteristic at incisive moments in the narrative, first by the calling of the first disciples, 5:1–11, and second in the beginning of the important "travel narrative" (9:51–19:27), 9:57–62. In addition this pattern is repeated in abbreviated forms several times, 9:23; 10:1–12; 14:25–27, 33; 18:28–29. This discourse based on the pattern of "leaving" and "following" is typically directed at men or has men as their subjects. Those who follow or who are called to follow are described as experiencing a spatial dislocation from their stable place and being transformed, in the same way as the pilgrim portrayed by Richard Valantasis, "by the experience of not having a stable home or by the encounter with holy places and people."[24]

As Seim observes, women who are in the company of Jesus, remain in their houses, or, if they are accompanying Jesus and the male disciples, are not described as "following" but as "providing for them/him" (8:1–3).[25] It is only at the end, that the women who watched Jesus being crucified, are described as those "who had followed him from Galilee," 23:49. So we are here dealing with a typically male discourse, addressed to men who are in their male location.

But there was not just one male location; it was differentiated based on age and responsibility.[26] There is an interesting difference between the stories of the calling of the first disciples in Luke compared to those of Mark and Matthew. In Mark 1:16–20 and Matt 4:18–22 there are two call stories; in the second story James and John are in a boat, fishing with their father.

22. Moxnes, *Putting Jesus in His Place*, 43–45.

23. See Valantasis, "Power in Asceticism," 805–9.

24. Ibid., 809.

25. Seim, *Double Message*, 57–81.

26. Destro and Pesce, "Fathers and Householders," 216–25.

The story portrays the father as the householder and in charge of the boat. The two sons belong to the younger generation, still living in the household of their father; and they leave a situation in which they have responsibilities towards their father and an obligation of obedience.[27] In Luke's Gospel the setting is different, Peter is the owner of a boat (5:3), and James and John are not in the boat together with their father, but partners with Peter in his boat (5:10). Thus, they are not leaving their father, but, together with Peter, they "left everything and followed him (Jesus)" (5:11). This story gives the impression that at least Peter as owner of a boat was a householder himself, with the responsibility for the material support of his household and of their social standing in the village. Thus, to leave everything to follow Jesus meant a drastic leaving of his responsibilities towards wife, children, other dependents in the household. It meant to leave behind a male location of responsibility and a transition to a little defined "following" of Jesus, a man who himself was in no position of responsibility and who had no household of his own.

This same situation is repeated at the beginning of Luke's special combination of narratives of stories and speeches in the "travel narrative." It is more than a description of a geographical journey; the travel becomes a preparation for the disciples (and hearers/readers) to follow Jesus on his way to Jerusalem. Thus, the calls to follow Jesus in 9:57–62 form a parallel to the call of the disciples in 5:1–11. Both discourses are built on the patterns of: a) being in a fixed place, b) choosing displacement, and c) following Jesus. In the brief exchanges in 9:57–62 the addressees are men, who are asked to leave their location of male responsibility, but who are not able or willing to leave that place. However, it is uncertain what the first man actually did; he says to Jesus that he will follow him "wherever you go," but is warned by Jesus that "Foxes have holes, and birds in the air have nests, but the son of man has nowhere to lay his head" (9:57–58). Here Luke emphasizes the "no place" of Jesus. Permanent dwellings were the signs of civilized life, even animals had them. A dislocation from a fixed place was therefore a loss not only of status, but of social identity. The philosopher Edward S. Casey has discussed what being without a place may mean. He says that being *unplaced*, to face the very image of a no-place-at all creates deep anxiety: "we feel not so much displaced as *without place*."[28]

How threatening the idea of losing one's place was, becomes apparent in the next narrative, of the man whom Jesus called "follow me" (9:59), but who said "Let me first go and bury my father." Whether this was the first or

27. Cf. Späth, *Männlichkeit und Weiblichkeit bei Tacitus,* 121–57.
28. Casey, *Getting Back into Place,* x.

the second burial, it was an absolute filial responsibility, and a step in his own transition to take over the male responsibility as a householder. To leave that responsibility was to negate his own role as a son and a man. Therefore Jesus' words "Leave the dead to bury their own dead," would throw the son into a no-place, although with a task "but as for you, go and proclaim the kingdom of God." The man in the last scene, 9:61–62, who also volunteer to follow Jesus, but who asks to say farewell to the people of his house, receives the same absolute demand from Jesus: it is a matter of the kingdom of God. In all these scenes Jesus' call demands that the location and responsibility of male identity are left behind. And even more frightening, in the "following" of Jesus with the task of proclaiming the kingdom of God, there is no permanent location and no fixed male role for the followers. Like the task for Peter and the first disciples that they should be "catching people" (5:10), there was a new responsibility, but phrased in vague, symbolic terms that did not immediately represent a known male role. This is in contrast to the description of the women who "served/provided," that is, they continued with their traditional, household role.

To grasp how frightening this "leaving" and "following" might have sounded for men who heard Luke's discourse, we may consider the way the Pastoral letters, at about the same time, made the male role of the house-holder the model and ideal for the leader of the Christian community.[29] There the stability and responsibility of the householder was the requirement for the role as community leader (1 Tim 3:1–5; Tit 1:5–9).

In several instances Luke seems to be explicitly addressing male followers when the parallel texts in Mark and Matthew leave the gender of the addressees open. There is one passage in which Peter uses the discourse of "leave" and "follow" to describe the situation for him and his fellow disciples: "Look, we have *left* our homes and *followed* you." To which Jesus responds: "there is no one who has left house or *wife* or brothers or parents or children, for the sake of the kingdom of God, who will not get back very much more in this age, and in the age to come eternal life" (18:28–29). The significant difference compared to Mark 10:29 and Matt 19:29 is that Luke has added *wife*. This appears not to be accidental, because Luke does the same in 14:25–26, by adding *wife* to the family members one must "hate" to become Jesus' disciple (cf. Matt 10:37). These texts add another dimension to the implications of leaving "male place" to those in 9:57–62. By leaving wife, or by non-marrying male disciples opted out of the responsibility to secure continuation of the family in the male line; they discontinued the system of patriarchy upon which society was built.[30]

29. Glancy, "Masculinity in the Pastoral Epistles."

30. However, in Luke 20:34–36, a text in which Luke appears to encourage

There seems to be no coincidence that Luke's discourses on "leaving" and "following" are directed towards men; these terms are used about men in their specific male locations and responsibilities. In the first part of the gospel men are portrayed in their male places in the household and village, in their locations as responsible for the material support of the household, or in familial and filial responsibilities within the household as a social group. Fathers/parents, wives and children are all part of the household in which the men belong, as dependents or as having the right of respect and obedience, but it is the male disciple who is in focus for Luke's concern. And it is the "new" location, that of "following Jesus" that takes first priority. The primary concern in these texts is therefore not the relations between men and women in the fellowship around Jesus (cf. 8:1–3), but the challenges for would-be followers of Jesus in relation to the male places they were asked to leave.

The greatest challenge appears to be that there was no fixed place to enter for those who followed Jesus. Jesus speaks of himself as being in "no place," without a permanent abode that could provide identity and security. Therefore Jesus himself becomes a "place" to follow: into insecurity, into itinerancy and into suffering.[31] But since the call to "leave" and "follow" was addressed at men, Luke makes to follow Jesus into this "no-place" the masculine ideal, and the itinerancy in the travel narrative represents this new place. If we start with the household as the central place of male identity in a peasant community, the call to leave it results in a construction of masculinity that is very different from that D'Angelo presents, that Luke follows the Roman male ideal "to know how to preside over the household."[32] Thus, I contend that Luke presents a challenge to the traditional male ideal, not only of the Roman elite, but also of peasant village communities.

The first part of Luke's gospel takes place in Galilee, along the road, and interacts with the local scene and a male role where the matter is use and appropriation of space, and the responsibilities involved in the household and village. The travel narrative is concerned with shaping the life of those who encounter Jesus into "following" him on the road to Jerusalem, a place that is identified with Jesus' suffering and death. Thus, Jerusalem is characterized as a place of power.

Entering into Jerusalem, Jesus and the disciples enter this place of domination and control, and it becomes clear that Jesus is coming up against a dominant power structure. Here another aspect of place in Lefebvre's

---

 asceticism, he uses a terminology that includes both men and women; they "neither marry nor are given in marriage," Seim, *Double Message*, 214–16.

31. See how Stewart in *Gathered around Jesus* explores Jesus as a "place" in Mark's Gospel.

32. D'Angelo, "Knowing How to Preside," 287.

model becomes visible:[33] Jerusalem with the temple authorities represented an authority that claimed domination and control of space; at this Easter with the added presence of the Roman prefect Pilate and Herod Antipas, the tetrarch of Galilee.

However, not only does Luke portray a transformation of the lives of followers of Jesus, also the role of Jerusalem is transformed in his narrative.[34] Upon entering Jerusalem Jesus is presented as introducing the hope of a new form of power over place: the Kingdom of God (19:11), and Jerusalem is threatened by destruction because it rejects Jesus (19:41–44). The kingdom of God as a spatial category represents a different form of power than that of the temple authorities, and the Roman forms of rule and domination. In the midst of Jerusalem that is described as a place of terror with the arrest, humiliation and crucifixion of Jesus, Jesus proclaims the hope of a new realm, the kingdom of God.

The main scene for this proclamation is the Passover meal Jesus has with his disciples (22:14–23), in which the hope of the kingdom is brought near (22:15–18), and with Jesus' words "do this in remembrance of me" is made into a performative text. Luke combines the meal with a long farewell speech from Jesus (22:24–38); the central part of which is concerned with what type of power structure this kingdom represents. It is represented as a kingdom that comes from God, it was transferred to Jesus, who now has authority over kingdom space and over the seats of authority and judgment, and who confers upon his disciples these seats (22:28–30). But this kingdom and the authority structures are compared to, and presented as alternatives to the kingdoms of "this world" (22:24–27). With a reference to power structures of the Greco-Roman world of Luke, the kings and "those with authority" are described as using power and claiming subservience; falsely, we understand. The alternative is not to make away with power and authority,[35] but to introduce true authority and greatness. Jesus introduces himself as the ideal: as one who serves. This is the masculine ideal that is held up before the disciples: the young man and the one who acts as a servant (22:26–27).

Gender Shift or Challenged Masculinity?

Once more Luke introduces an alternative form of masculinity, this time in the area of political power over others, wielding dominion and control, as a criticism of the competition to be regarded "as the greatest" (22:24).

33. Harvey, *Condition of Postmodernity*, 222.

34. Moxnes, "Landscape and Spaciality," 103.

35. Seim, *Double Message*, 84–85.

Clearly Luke wants to shape a masculinity that conforms to the kingdom of God, as a landscape imagined by Jesus. It is interesting, as Seim observed, that the term *diakonein* is used as an ideal for exercising power; a term that Luke elsewhere uses of women and slaves (4:39; 8:3; 10:40; 17:8). Seim finds that when service in this text becomes an ideal, women's "seemingly conventional life in service receives a new dignity in the new context." [36] Seim notices a "gender shift" that takes place when "the service function becomes a vital trait in the role of a ruler . . . From serving women to ruler who are to be like those who serve. The reversal of the dignity of the roles coincides with a masculinisation . . ." Even if women in this way become ideals of "the people of God" and of the leaders of this people, leadership is in Luke still restricted to men. And Seim therefore concludes: "The idealisation and the matching rhetoric of service do, however, legitimate a masculinisation and means in practice that the women who served are excluded from the actual positions of leadership."[37]

Seim has undertaken a comparative analysis of "serve" used of women and men in different contexts; on that basis her thesis that Luke's use of "serve" represents a masculinization of the term seems justified. But I will suggest that another reading is also possible, and that is reading "serve" used as a male ideal in its context in Luke 22:24–30, challenging the male roles of kings and powerful men (22:25). In this context, a male ideal of "serving" represented a demasculinisation of powerful (hegemonic) masculine roles. Jerome H. Neyrey makes a similar argument in his study of masculinity in Matthew's Gospel.[38] In general, Neyrey argues that Matthew portrays Jesus as conforming to the male code of honour in the Roman world. However, Neyrey recognizes that in some instances Matthew's Jesus challenges the code of honour in the political world. One of his examples is the parallel text to Luke 22:24–27 in Matthew 20:25–28; the disciples are urged to identify with the roles as servant and slave in contrasts to rulers and "great men." They were asked to take positions which were regarded as shameful by other men, but Matthew presents them as honourable in the eyes of God and of Jesus. Likewise in Luke, by presenting himself as "one who serves" (22:27), Jesus gives dignity to the male role of those who follow him in service, and thereby encourages them to disregard the shame incurred in the eyes of powerful men. The immediate context is one of comparison and competition between men. In the following story of Jesus' suffering and crucifixion, Jesus is placed in a position of shame, but he is still in command of his

---

36. This and the following quote from ibid., 86.

37. Seim, *Double Message*, 88.

38. Neyrey "Jesus, Gender and the Gospel of Matthew," 63–66.

kingdom, granted him by God (23:42). It is this paradoxical juxtaposition of shame "in this world" and honour and power in the eyes of God that characterizes Jesus' male role, and that is also reflected in that of those men who accepted the call to follow him.

The result is that Luke presents a new masculinity and a new place for men, at a distance from the male location in the household and with a strong warning of traditional masculinity in leader positions.

Feminist and masculinity studies in the New Testament and Early Christianity have many similarities and shared perspectives. But my discussion of the discourse on male followers in Luke compared to *The Double Message* by Turid Karlsen Seim's has also showed some differences. Feminist studies of the Gospels have had a major interest in the relation between women and men in the Jesus movement. Masculinity studies on the other hand have focused more on Jesus and on men in the Jesus-movement in relation to masculinity of the Greco-Roman world. That has been my interest here: I have asked about what place Luke gives to men and how he constructs masculinity in the world of Jesus followers that he wants to shape. In that respect a homosocial perspective may give some new insights, since it helps us see the men who followed Jesus in Luke's Gospel in relation to their role as men in their society and in relation to the masculinity of contemporary writings.

Bibliography

Anderson, Janice C., with S. D. Moore and S. H. Kim. "Masculinity Studies: A Classified Bibliography." In *New Testament Masculinities*, edited by Stephen D. Moore and Janice C. Anderson, 29–33. Semeia Studies 45. Atlanta: SBL, 2003.

Cameron, Averil. "Redrawing the Map: Early Christian Territory after Foucault." *Journal of Roman Studies* 76 (1986) 266–71.

Casey, Edward S. *Getting Back into Place: Toward a Renewed Understanding of the Placeworld.* Studies in Continental Thought. Bloomington: Indiana University Press, 1993.

Connell, Robert W. *Masculinities*. Cambridge: Polity, 1995.

Connell, Raewyn, and J. W. Messerschmidt. "Hegemonic Masculinity: Rethinking the Concept." *Gender and Society* 19 (2005) 829–59.

Conway, Colleen M. *Behold the Man: Jesus and Greco-Roman Masculinity*. Oxford: Oxford University Press, 2008.

D'Angelo, Mary Rose. "The *ANER* question in Luke–Acts: Imperial Masculinity and the Deployment of Women in the Early Second Century." In *A Feminist Companion to Luke,* edited by Amy-Jill Levine, 44–69. Feminist Companions to the New Testament. Sheffield: Sheffield University Press, 2002.

———. "'Knowing How to Preside Over His Own Household': Imperial Masculinity and Christian Asceticism in the Pastorals, *Hermas*, and Luke–Acts." In *New*

Testament Masculinities, edited by Stephen D. Moore and Janice C. Anderson, 265–95. Semeia Studies 45. Atlanta: SBL, 2003.

Destro, Adriana, and Mauro Pesce. "Fathers and Householders in the Jesus Movement: The Perspective in the Gospel of Luke." *Biblical Interpretation* 11 (203) 211–38.

Foucault, Michel. *The Use of Pleasure.* Vol. 2 of *The History of Sexuality.* New York: Vintage, 1985.

Glancy, Jennifer A. "Protocols of Masculinity in the Pastoral Epistles." In *New Testament Masculinities,* edited by Stephen D. Moore and Janice C. Anderson, 235–64. Semeia Studies 45. Atlanta: SBL, 2003.

Green, Joel B. *The Theology of the Gospel of Luke.* New Testament Theology. Cambridge: Cambridge University Press, 1995.

Harvey, David. *The Condition of Postmodernity.* Oxford: Blackwell, 1989.

Messner, Michael A. *Politics of Masculinities: Men in Movements.* Thousand Oaks, CA: Sage, 1997.

Moore, Stephen D., and Janice C. Anderson, eds. *New Testament Masculinities.* Semeia Studies 45. Atlanta: SBL, 2003.

Moore, Stephan D. "'O Man, Who Art Thou . . . ?' Masculinty Studies and New Testament Studies." In *New Testament Masculinities,* edited by Stephen D. Moore and Janice C. Anderson, 1–22. Semeia Studies 45. Atlanta: SBL, 2003.

Mosse, George L. *The Image of Man: The Creation of Modern Masculinity.* Oxford: Oxford University Press, 1996.

Moxnes, Halvor "Asceticism and Christian Identity in Antiquity: A Dialogue with Foucault and Paul." *JSNT* 26 (2003) 3–29.

———. "Landscape and Spaciality: Placing Jesus." In *Understanding the Social World of the New Testament,* edited by Dietmar Neufeld and Richard E. DeMaris, 90–106. Oxford: Routledge, 2010.

———. *Putting Jesus in His Place: A Radical Vision of Household and Kingdom,* Louisville: Westminster John Knox, 2003.

———. "Where Is 'Following Jesus'? Masculinity and Place in Luke's Gospel." In *In Other Words: Essays on Social Science Methods and the New Testament in Honor of Jerome H. Neyrey,* edited by Anselm C. Hagedorn et al., 155–70. Social World of Biblical Antiquity 2/1. Sheffield: Sheffield Phoenix, 2007.

Neyrey, Jerome H. "Jesus, Gender and the Gospel of Matthew." In *New Testament Masculinities,* edited by Stephen D. Moore and Janice C. Anderson, 43–66. Semeia Studies 45. Atlanta: SBL, 2003.

Sedgwick, Eve Kosofsky. *Between Men: English Literature and Male Homosocial Desire.* New York: Columbia University Press, 1985.

Seim, Turid Karlsen. *The Double Message of Luke's Gospel: Patterns of Gender in Luke–Acts.* Edinburgh: T. & T. Clark, 1994.

———. "Feminist Criticism." In *Methods for Luke,* edited by Joel B. Green, 42–73. Cambridge: Cambridge University Press, 2010.

Späth, Thomas. *Männlichkeit und Weiblichkeit bei Tacitus: Zur Konstruktion der Geschlecter in der römischen Keiserzeit.* Frankfurt: Campus, 1994.

Stewart, Eric C. *Gathered around Jesus: An Alternative Spatial Practice in the Gospel of Mark.* Matrix. Eugene, OR: Cascade, 2009.

Turner, William B. *A Genealogy of Queer Theory.* Philadelphia: Temple University Press, 2000.

Valantasis, Richard. "Constructions of Power in Asceticism." *JAAR* 63 (1995) 775–821.

Williams, Craig A. *Roman Homosexuality: Ideologies of Masculinity in Classical Antiquity.* New York: Oxford University Press, 1998.

18

Two Mothers: Veturia and Mary;
Two Sons: Coriolanus and Jesus[1]

David L. Balch

The two mothers have significant similarities; the two sons are radical contrasts. The lengthy speech in public by Veturia,[2] a Roman woman but narrated by an ancient Greek historian, is one of the most remarkable that I know in Greek or Latin literature; the speech by Mary, the Magnificat, is the only one by a woman in Luke–Acts in which we actually read/hear what she says, also a speech announcing key themes for Luke–Acts that Greeks and/ or Romans would have grasped immediately.[3] I narrate the story of Veturia and her son, Coriolanus, in parallel with the story of Mary and her son,

---

1. Seim, *The Double Message*, contributed significantly to women's studies; I celebrate her redactional reading of Luke by giving a complementary history of religions reading.

2. Analogous speeches happen only twice in Luke–Acts, once when the prophet (προφῆτις) Anna, a widow who had worshipped in the temple for decades, fasting and praying night and day, "came and began to praise God and to speak about the child to all (πᾶσιν) who were looking for the redemption of Jerusalem" (Luke 2:36–38; cf. 1:42–45). However, we hear none of the words Anna spoke "to all" (male and female). Compare Plutarch's story of the "wise and far-famed" Eumetis, some of whose "conundrums have found their way [from Greece] to Egypt; her statesman's mind and an amiable character . . . has influence with her father, so that his government of the citizens has become milder and more popular" (*Dinner of the Seven Sages* 148B–E, cited by Osiek and Balch, *Families in the New Testament World*, 129 n. 113). But Plutarch gives us not one of Eumetis' internationally famous riddles! Instead he informs us (*Advice to Bride and Groom* 142D; trans. Babbitt in LCL) that Phidias sculpted a tortise next to his Aphrodite at Elis to indicate that silence becomes "womankind keeping at home and keeping silence." Mary's Magnificat, on the other hand, gives us her words, a short parallel to Vetruia's speech.

3. This remains true whatever the ultimate origin of the Magnificat. See, e.g., Brown, *The Birth of the Messiah*, 355–66, 642–55.

Jesus, as a contribution to women's studies of the gospel of Luke pioneered so insightfully by Turid Karlsen Seim.

In an earlier article I outlined four stories of Roman political friendship[4]; in this article I give a close reading of the final one of those four, which involves reading Luke–Acts in light of Dionysius of Halicarnassus.[5] Livy's shorter Latin version (2.33–40, at chap. 40[6]) of the story of Veturia, her speech, and of Coriolanus is well known. Dionysius' more elaborate Greek version is not; therefore, I give extensive quotations.

1. Coriolanus[7] (Dionysius, *Ant. rom.*, book 8)

The lengthy public speech and supplication by Veturia is understandable only in light of and in contrast to the exploits and values of her son; therefore, I also narrate his character in the story. Gaius Marcius, surnamed Coriolanus, "became the most illustrious man of his age" (Dionysius, *Ant. rom.* 6.94.2, trans. Cary in LCL), so Dionysius begins the story. Nevertheless, this proud Roman warrior falls from eminence because he hates the poor and humble. The Coriolanus story fills two of Dionysius' books (*Ant. rom.* 6.92–8.62), taking vastly disproportionate space within his history of archaic Rome. Schultze characterizes it as "virtually Dionysius' history in miniature, having an episode of every important type except a major battle."[8] Dionysius, *Ant. rom.*, book 7, narrates the conflict between the proud aristocrat Coriolanus and the poor humble plebeians. At the end of book 7, the plebeians

4. Balch, "Political Friendship in the Historian Dionysius of Halicarnassus, *Roman Antiquities*," 123–45, republished in Balch, *Contested Ethnicities and Images*, chap. 6.

5. Dionysius wrote twenty books of *Roman Antiquities* in the final decade BCE, a model one century later for Josephus, *Jewish Antiquities*, also in twenty books. For further discussion of Dionysius's intellectual, social and political context, see Wiater, *The Ideology of Classicism: Language, History, and Identity in Dionysius of Halicarnassus*, reviewed by Balch, *Contested Ethnicities and Images*, chap. 19.

6. "Then the married women . . . prevailed with them that both Veturia, an aged woman, and Volumnia . . . should go to the camp of the enemy; and that, since the swords of the men could not defend the City, the women should defend it with their prayers and tears . . . There was no envy of the fame the women had earned, on the part of the men of Rome—so free was life in those days from disparagement of another's glory—and to preserve its memory the temple of Fortuna Muliebris was built and dedicated" (Livy 2.40.1–2, 11–12; trans. Foster in LCL).

7. See Shakespeare, *Coriolanus* (1608), and Bertolt Brecht, *Coriolan* (written between 1951 and 1953), analyzed by Reynolds, "Shakespeare's *Coriolanus* and Brecht's *Coriolan*."

8. Schultze, "Dionysius of Halicarnassus as a Historian: An Investigation of his Aims and Methods in the *Antiquitates Romanae*," 216.

persuade the senate to create the new office of tribunes, who put Coriolanus on trial, and the populace vote to banish him from Rome forever.[9]

Dionysius, *Ant. rom.*, book 8, opens with Coriolanus resenting his misfortune and wanting "to avenge himself on his enemies" (τιμωρίαν παρὰ τῶν ἐχθρῶν, *Ant. rom.* 8.1.2; all following references are to book 8, unless noted otherwise). Instead of reconciling with the plebeians in Rome, Coriolanus goes to his former military enemies, the Volscians,[10] whose territory lay in the mountains to the southeast of Rome, and whose language was closely related to Oscan and Umbrian, more distantly to Latin. He goes to the leading aristocrat among the Volscians, Tullus Attius, confesses himself "unfortunate and humbled" (ἀτυχοῦντας καὶ τεταπεινωμένους, 1.5), "forsaken, exiled, and abased" (νῦν ἔρημος καὶ ἄπολις καὶ ταπεινός), bearing in mind that the "fortunes of men are subject to change." Coriolanus offers his services, but the alternative is to "grant me the speediest death by sacrificing the suppliant (ἱκέτην; see Fig. 18.1) with your own hand and at your own hearth; 1.6).[11] Tullus "gave him his hand and raises (ἀναστήσας) him from the hearth . . . declaring that he looked upon even this as no small honor" (2.1; compare 54.1 below).

9. Balch, "Political Friendship," now in *Contested Ethnicities and Images*, chap. 6, #3.

10. He had earned his cognomen, Coriolanus, after taking the Volscian town of the Corioli (Livy 2.33.4–5)!

11. Compare supplication by a military enemy in the *Iliad*, 24.478–79, and in the *Aeneid* 3.599–607 (cited nn. 24–25 below). See Büchsel, "ἱκετηρία," 296–97. Liddell and Scott, *A Greek-English Lexicon*, s.v. "ἱκεσία" and "ἱκετεία," with many texts. On Hebrews 5:7 see Attridge, *The Epistle to the Hebrews*, 149–50; Siebert "Supplicatio," 955; Freyburger, "La supplicatio d'action de graces sous le Haut-Empire," 1418–39; Freyburger, "Supplication grecque et supplication romaine," 501–25; Halkin, *La supplication d'action de graces chez les Romains*; Brilliant, *Gesture and Rank in Roman Art*; Gabelmann, *Antike Audienz- und Tribunalszenen*; Naiden, *Ancient Supplication*, figs. 2.1–9.

Figure 18.1. Miniature fresco dating to final decades of 1st century BCE, between second and third style, La Villa della Farnesina, triclinio C, Rome, now in the National Roman Museum, Palazzo Massimo alle Terme. This was a sumptuous residence of the Augustan age in Trastevere, perhaps owned by Marcus Vipsanius Agrippa (see Gabelmann 152, n. 611; Sanzi Di Mino 9), author of Augustus' victory at Actium. Mols and Moormann have a plan of the villa (their Fig. 4) and reproduce this fresco (Fig. 42; also in Gabelmann, Tafel 17, and Sanzi Di Mino, Figs. 59–67), in which a judge is seated on a platform. ("In one [of the 9 scenes painted parallel to each other] the judge is certainly feminine" [Bragantini, 47].) I observe that the two persons bowing down before the judge in this figure are in the position of suppliants (see section 4 below). Photo by David L. Balch with the kind permission of the Soprintendenza Speciale per i beni Culturali di Roma.

The two decide to begin a war against the Romans, but first they must find a pious and just ground for war, "since the gods take a hand in all actions, and especially in those relating to war" (2.2). If the Romans are first to violate the existing treaty between the two nations, the Volscians will seem to be waging a pious and just war (2.3). The two create a scenario in which the city of Rome ejects only Volscian visitors, who have journeyed there to watch the spectacles; they then seem indignant to have been the only strangers expelled (4.2). All the Volscians gather in a single assembly (4.3) and decide to go to war; Tullus gets them to summon (καλεῖν) Marcius to ask how the power of Rome might be overthrown (5.1). He gives a speech to defend (ἀπολογεῖσθαι) his own recent biography (5.2–8.6).

The original constitution of the Romans was a mixture of monarchy and aristocracy, he claims; but "the poorest and idlest of the citizens, bad men, were trying to overthrow the aristocracy" (5.4), to establish a government by the worst elements instead of the best men (5.5). The "working class and vagabonds" (οἱ θῆτες καὶ ἀνέστιοι), plotting against the possessions of others, were about to prevail over good and just men (6.2; compare his later speech, 30.4–31.4, and contrast his mother's account, 50–51). Coriolanus was tried by the mob, and condemned by only two votes (6.3, also 24.3; cp. 7.64.6 and 7.65.1). He then "felt that the rest of my life would not be worth living unless I took revenge upon them" (εἰ μὴ λάβοιμι παρ' αὐτῶν δίκας; 6.4). "What kind of man should I be" (τίς ἂν εἴην ἀνήρ) otherwise (7.1)? "I could not count as a real man (οὐδ'ἐν ἀνδρὸς μοίρᾳ θείην) anyone who feels neither anger against those who make war upon him nor affection for those who seek his preservation. And I regard as my fatherland, not that state which has renounced me, but the one of which I, as an alien (ἀλλότριος), have become a citizen" (7.1). He hopes that there will be a great and sudden change (μεταβολήν, 7.2). Coriolanus then advises the Volscians on a "pious and just pretext (πρόφασις) for war" (8.1).

In Dionysius' narrative, Coriolanus never wavers from his "hatred" of the poor plebeian citizens (see 7.21.1; 7.34.2–5).[12] Indeed, Coriolanus' trial had been "the first summoning of a patrician before the tribunal of the plebeians . . . From this beginning the people rose to great power, while the aristocracy lost much of its ancient dignity . . . by sharing (κοινωσαμένη) with all the citizens the other privileges that . . . had been the special prerogatives of the patricians . . . , some because of necessity and against their will, others through foresight and wisdom" (7.65.1). Coriolanus never accommodated. Rather than reconcile himself to this political and social change in the structure of the Roman state, through supplication Coriolanus sought instead reconciliation with his former military enemies, and they willingly employed this great general against Rome. Coriolanus preferred hostile, aristocratic foreigners to the local poor; he valued economic class, not ethnicity.

---

12. Plutarch develops this character trait. Pelling, "Dionysius, Plutarch, and Shakespeare," 403: "[W]herever [Plutarch's] Coriolanus turns, he now finds, or moulds, people like himself: the Volscians . . . It is this universal aggressiveness, irascibility, and pride which creates a world in which Coriolanus' own passions can wreak such shattering consequences." Pelling, "Dionysius, Plutarch, and Shakespeare," 406: "In [Plutarch's] Coriolanus . . . the hero does not interact with his countrymen, he clashes and confronts; he does not speak with them or even (Menenius-like) speak their own language; he shouts at them and past them; he feels himself misunderstood and rejected by people who ought to be in his debt; he is a lone figure facing an alien world."

However, as leader of the Volscians in dialogue with the Romans, Coriolanus invents new arguments, which are more persuasive than his desire for vengeance, arguments that oppose his own former function as an imperial, expansionist Roman general. They send ambassadors to Rome, offering friendship, "if they received back the lands and the cities that had been taken from them by the Romans"—that is, by Coriolanus. Otherwise there would be no peace, "since the injured party is always by nature (φύσει) an enemy to the aggressor" (9.3). The Romans give a colonial response: the Volscians "made a present to us of these places, . . . having been deprived of them by war . . . [If] you demand them back, you are doing wrong in coveting the possessions of others" (10.2).

Tullus then invades the territory of the Latins, Marcius of the Romans (12.1), capturing many free persons, slaves, oxen, corn, and iron tools. Coriolanus' tactics conform to his consistent aristocratic values: he sets fire to many country houses (αὐλὰς), especially to farms of the plebeians, not to those of the patricians, "in order to increase the suspicion of the plebeians against the patricians and to keep the sedition (τὸ στασιάζον) alive in the state" (12.2–3). He succeeds: "the poor clamoured against the rich (κατεβόων μὲν τῶν πλουσίων οἱ πένητες; 12.4). And "the patricians reproached the populace with having driven from the state a man who was a great warrior, energetic, and full of noble pride" (14.3).

Given the political chaos in Rome, the Volscians attack and destroy many Latin and Roman cities (chaps. 14–21 and 36), even Lavinium, "the first city built by the Trojans who landed in Italy with Aeneas, and the one from which the Romans derive their origin" (31.1)! The Volscians now admire Coriolanus for his "good fortune" (τῆς τύχης αὐτὸν ἐμακάριζον ἅπαντα; 17.2), as he reduced the Romans "to a helplessness that was abject and anything but manly" (εἰς ταπεινὴν καὶ ἄνανδρον; 17.3)! In this story, reversals of fortune do happen. Some Romans in their turn throw away their arms and become suppliants; Coriolanus does not put them to death (17.6; compare 1.6). He himself remains a great warrior, often being the first to mount enemy walls (17.5; 20.1; 29.5).

Finally, he marches on Rome (22.1), and here in the narrative, we encounter many speeches, as in Acts. The Romans send five of the oldest members of the senate, all ex-consuls and close friends of Coriolanus, to sue for reconciliation and friendship (22.4), one of whom, Marcus Minucius, gives a speech (chaps. 23–28, ten pages of Greek). Minucius asks a question we have heard before, "what sort of man you are" (ὅστις ἔφυς; 23.2; cp. 5.3; 7.1). He has not shown any moderation (οὐδὲ μετριάζεις) in exacting punishment (23.2). He hates not only the plebeians, but all the women and children; hating the guilty, he does not spare the innocent or his friends. He destroys the sepulchers of his ancestors and the altars of the gods, which is not just (24).

Minucius asks Coriolanus to be reconciled to his country. "While your power is greatest and Heaven (τὸ θεῖον) still assists you to act with moderation and husband your good fortune, bearing in mind that all things are subject to change (μεταβολὰς) . . . All things that wax too great, when they reach the peak of eminence, incur the displeasure of the gods and are brought to naught again. And this is the fate that comes especially to stubborn and haughty (μεγάλαυχα) spirits and those that overstep the bounds of human nature (τοὺς ὅρους ἐκβαίνοντα τῆς ἀνθρωπίνης φύσεως; 25.3; compare 1.5–6). He should give up his anger, his hatred toward them, his evil passion (πονηρὸν ἔρωτα) for overthrowing the power of Rome, which is impossible (26.1). If he fails, the Volscians will reproach him (27.3); if he succeeds, he will be called the slayer of his mother, the murderer of his children, the assassin of his wife, the evil genius of his country (28.3).

Coriolanus, of course, replies (chaps. 29–35, twelve pages of Greek).[13] He is still a friend to Minucius, who did not turn away from him after his banishment, "as if I were no longer able either to serve my friends or to hurt my enemies" (29.1). "But to the rest of the Romans I am as hostile as I can be and am at war with them, and I shall never cease to hate them" (29.2). We learn that when young, Coriolanus had fought against Roman kings, who tried to restore their power against the aristocrats (29.4); he is then, I conclude, not opposed to all social change, only to aristocrats losing their exclusive power. As earlier, he again argues, "you senators admit, I take it, that you are governed by the baser element . . . , in which the better element is governed by the worse? (31.2; compare 6.2) With his political principles, if he returns to Rome, he will be a sacrifical victim (σφάγιόν με; 32.1).

In Rome fortune had upset expectations (32.4). "Who would not praise me on hearing that when I found my friends from whom I had the right to expect kindness, to be my enemies, and my foes, by whom I should have been put to death (see 2.1), to be my friends, instead of hating those who hate me, and loving those who love me, I took the opposite view!" (32.5; again 34.1 and 50.3)

---

13. For the central function of opposing speeches in Dionysius, see Walker, *The Genuine Teachers of this Art: Rhetorical Education in Antiquity*, 270. Walker characterizes the speeches in Dionysius as rhetorical confrontation (275), "a series of materially situated speech acts whose cumulative effect eventually tips the balance and occasions a major shift . . . in civil institutions" (277). "Political wisdom and the successful evolution of the Roman state required the disruption of consensus, the play of opposing arguments, people capable of making those arguments effectively, and people capable of hearing them intelligently, in difficult as well as in easy times" (279).

Then he considers "the gods' treatment of me, who at present assist him in every enterprise (33.1; contrast 50.3 below). If he had undertaken an impious war against his country, the gods would have opposed him, but he enjoys the favoring breeze of Fortune (33.2). He is a pious man. What if he changes (μεταβάλωμαι) his course, attempting to increase (αὔξειν) Rome's power and to humble (ταπεινὰ ποιεῖν) the Volscians? (33.3) Will he not incur "the dire wrath of Heaven, which avenges the injured, and just as by the help of the gods I from a low estate have become great, shall I not in turn from a great be brought again to a low estate, and my sufferings become lessons to the rest of the world?" (ὥσπερ ἐκ ταπεινοῦ μέγας διὰ τοὺς θεοὺς ἐγενόμην, οὕτως αὖθις ἐκ μεγάλου ταπεινὸς γενήσομαι, καὶ τἀμὰ παθήματα παιδεύματα γενήσεται τοῖς ἄλλοις; 33.3).

Those who call themselves his friends seem ignorant of the most common facts: "a friend or an enemy is not determined either by the lineaments of a face or by the giving or a name, but both are made manifest by their services and by their deeds (ταῖς χρείαις καὶ τοῖς ἔργοις); and we all love those who do us good and hate those who do us harm." This "has been enacted from the beginning of time by the universal Nature" (ὑπὸ τῆς κοινῆς φύσεως ἐξ ἅπαντος τοῦ χρόνου) for all creatures (34.1). This is the common judgment of all mankind (παρὰ τὴν κοινὴν ἁπάντων ἀνθρώπων; 34.3). Coriolanus is doing what is just, advantageous, honorable, and holy in the eyes of the gods, who are pleased with what he does (34.3).

As for moderation (περὶ δὲ τῆς μετριότητος), Romans should apply to the Volscian soldiers, who decide on peace and war (35.1). He does feel compassion (ἐλεῶν) for their wives and children. "If the Romans will return to the Volscians the land they have taken from them and the cities they hold, first recalling their colonists, and if they will enter into a league of perpetual friendship with them and give them equal rights of citizenship[14] . . . , I will put an end to the war" (35.2).

As for justice, "how fine a thing it is for everyone to enjoy his own possessions and to live in peace, how important to have no enemy and no crisis to fear, but how disgraceful it is for a people by clinging to the possessions of others, to expose themselves to an unnecessary war . . . (35.3) The Romans should blame not Marcius, but their own folly . . . They will hazard their all by their continued fondness for the possessions of others" (35.4).

Coriolanus then dismisses the conference, giving the Romans thirty days to respond, during which time he conquered seven Latin cities and returned toward Rome. But the Romans would pass no friendly vote. "For the

14. Rome extending citizenship became a possibility in the first, not the fifth century BCE (see n. 53).

Romans always made it a great point never to do anything at the dictation of an enemy or to yield to fear of him, but when once their adversaries had made peace and acknowledged themselves as their subjects (ὑπηκόους), to gratify (χαρίζεσθαί) them and concede anything in reason that they asked." And this proud spirit the commonwealth has continued to preserve down to our own time . . . ." (36.4) Further negotiations by the pontifs, the augurs and others failed, so that the Romans gave up all hope of reconciliation (38.3).

2. Valeria and Veturia (Dionysius, *Ant. rom.* book 8)

Their wives (αἱ δὲ γυναῖκες αὐτῶν), seeing the danger, abandoned their houses (οἴκοι) and ran to the shrines of the gods, lamenting and throwing themselves at the feet of the statues (τῶν ξοάνων), especially in the Temple of Jupiter Capitolinus (39.1). Valeria, sister of Publicola, one of the men who freed the commonwealth from the kings, moved by some divine inspiration (θείῳ τινὶ παραστήματι κινηθεῖσα), comforted the women and told them that there was only one hope of safety (μίαν εἶναι σωτηρίας ἐλπίδα, 39.2). A woman then asked, "What can we women do to save our country, when the men have given it up for lost? What strength (ἰσχύς) so great do we weak and miserable women (τὰς ἀσθενεῖς καὶ ταλαιπώρους) possess?" Valeria replied, a strength not for weapons, for Nature excused us from this, but for good will and speech (εὐνοίας καὶ λόγου, 39.3).

Valeria proposes, wearing their shabby garb, going to the house of Veturia, mother of Marcius, placing their children at her feet, and entreating her with tears to go the enemies' camp to become the suppliant (ἱκέτιν) of her son (39.4). He may feel compassion, while a mother grovels at his feet. They pray to the gods to invest their plea with persuasion and charm, and go to Valeria's house.

Volumnia, Coriolanus' wife, sees them coming and asks, "What is it you want, women (γυναῖκες),[15] that so many of you have come to a household that is distressed and in humiliation (ταπεινήν)? (40.1) Valeria then gives the speech (40.2–5) to Veturia that she had outlined earlier to the women, observing that they and their children "have become suppliants (νήπια ταῦτα καταπεφεύγαμεν ἱκέτιδες)) to you, Veturia" (40.2, also 40.3 and 43.4), and suggesting that "not only will you yourself most likely gain immortal glory (ἀθάνατον κλέος) for having rescued your country from so great a danger and terror, but you will be the cause to us also of some honour (τιμῆς) in the eyes of our husbands for having ourselves put an end to a war which they had

---

15. This vocative occurs several times in the story (also 42.1, 2; 47.3). Contrast the typical vocatives in Acts, e.g., 7:1, Ἄνδρες ἀδελφοὶ καὶ πατέρες.

been unable to stop; and we shall show ourselves to be the true descendants of those women who by their own intercession put an end to the war that had arisen between Romulus and the Sabines . . ." (40.4, referring to the story narrated in *Ant. rom.* 2.45–46). "It is a glorious venture, Veturia, to recover your son, to free your native land, to save your countrywomen, and to leave to posterity an imperishable reputation for virtue (κλέος ἀρετῆς ἀθάνατον). Grant us this favour (χάριν) willingly . . ." (40.5).

Valeria embraces Veturia's knees (43.2), and finally, Vetruia agrees, despite Coriolanus' "hatred of his whole family" (μεμίσηκε τὴν οἰκίαν ὅλην) when he left Rome, despite seeing them mourning, abased (ταπεινάς; 41.2). Valeria recounts Coriolanus' parting prayer to the gods, his leaving the city where there was "no longer any room for good men," his suggestion that Volumnia take another husband, and his description of his children as orphans and forsaken (ὀρφανοὶ καὶ ἔρημοι; 41.4). Since then he has treated them as strangers (ἀλλοτρίους), not writing or sending news (41.5).[16] Intriguingly, the other women supplicate Veturia to become a suppliant to her son, and after Valeria embraces her knees, she agrees.

Veturia asked the women to instruct her (διδάσκετέ με) with words[17] that she should address to her son. "To be merciful and compassionate to the plebeians, from whom he received neither mercy nor compassion (οὔτ' ἐλέου μετέσχεν οὔτε συμπαθείας)? (42.1). "What courage can I pluck up to ask my son to love those who have ruined him (τὰ μὲν ἀπολέσαντα φιλεῖν) and to injure those who have preserved him? These are not the words of a sane mother to her son . . ." (42.2). Would not the other women permit us miserable women to lie abased (ταπεινὰς) as we have been cast down by Fortune . . . ? (42.2)

Nevertheless, Veturia yields and promises to perform the mission (πρεσβείαν) in behalf of her country, invoking the gods for the accomplishment of their hopes, and informs the consuls (43.2). The senators make many speeches concerning this exodus of the women (περὶ τῆς ἐξόδου τῶν γυναικῶν), but permit it (43.3).

Coriolanus was astonished at the daring of the women (ἐθαύμασε τῆς τόλμης τὰς γυναῖκας) coming with their children into an enemy camp, not showing regard for the modesty becoming to free-born and virtuous women, which forbids them to be seen by men who are strangers . . ." (44.2). He goes to meet his mother, laying aside the axes and lowering the rods

16. Pelling, "Dionysius, Plutarch, and Shakespeare," 395–96, compares and contrasts Dionysius and Plutarch's accounts of Coriolanus abandoning his mother and family.

17. For women counseling women, see Osiek, *Families in the New Testament World*, 167–73.

that are customarily carried before generals (44.3). His mother wore rent garments of mourning and her eyes melted in tears. Coriolanus himself was "carried away by his emotions into human kindness (ὑπὸ τῶν παθῶν ἐπὶ τὸ ἀνθρώπινον; 45.1). He caresses his mother, greets his wife, and draws his children to him. "You have acted the part of a good wife, Volumnia, in living with my mother and not abandoning her in her solitude (ἐρημίαν), and to me you have thereby done the dearest of all favours" (45.2).

Veturia states that "she would speak out in the presence of all," and after preparations, Coriolanus asks his mother to speak (τὴν μητέρα λέγειν; 45.2–3) before him and the Volscians, and she does (chaps. 46 and 48–53, eleven pages of Greek). She places Coriolanus' wife, his children, and the other women around her, and weeps, rousing great compassion (ἔλεον; 46.1). She asks him not to let these women suffer evil at his hands; they have cared for his family when they were left desolate, no longer of any account (ἔρημοι καὶ τὸ μηθέν; 46.3).

Marcius interrupts her, saying that he has promised the gods and the Volsians that he would not betray them (47.1). If the Romans will restore their land to the Volscians, he will end the war. She should persuade the Romans "to cease their unjust fondness for the possessions of others and to be content if they are permitted to keep what is their own" (47.3). "And of you, mother, I, who am your son, beg in my turn that you will not urge me to wicked and unjust actions." But "taking your place at my side, as is right, you will make the land where I dwell your fatherland, and your home the house I have acquired, and that you will enjoy my honours and share in my glory, looking upon my friends and enemies as your own" (47.4).[18] Without her the pains in his inmost being (σπλάγχνοις) render his life bitter, so he invites her to share all he possesses (47.5).

Veturia resumes her speech to "her dear and only son" (τὸν ἀγαπητὸν καὶ μόνον υἱὸν), denying that she encourages him to shameful and wicked actions (48.1). Rather, he should withdraw from the war only with the consent of the Volscians, winning them over by persuasion and exhortation (48.3); she suggests instructive maxims (παιδεύματα), such as, "any peace is preferable to any war" (48.4). If the Volscians refuse, he could resign publicly. He has given the Volscians many fine returns, surpassing the kindnesses received from them (49.2).

She refers to the unjust hatred he bears toward his country, denying that Rome was healthy when it banished him (49.4). Others such as king Tarquinius have had this experience, but bore their exile with moderation.

18. Cf. Ruth 1:16–17. However, Naomi and Ruth are without resources, while Coriolanus is inviting his mother into honor and wealth.

He has suffered grievously, but has he not taken sufficient revenge? He has turned their best land into a sheep walk and reduced them to scarcity. "But you carry your mad and wild resentment (τὴν ἀγριαίνουσαν καὶ μαινομένην ὀργὴν) even to the point of enslaving them and razing their city" (50.1). Coriolanus even dismissed the Roman envoys.

"For my part, I cannot commend these harsh and overbearing claims, which overstep the bounds of human nature (τὴν θνητὴν φύσιν ἐκβεβηκότα), when I observe that a refuge for all men and the means of securing forgiveness for their offences one against another (παραιτήσεις . . . ἐξαμαρτάνωσι περὶ ἀλλήλους) have been devised in the form of suppliant boughs and prayers (ἱκετηρίας καὶ λιτάς), by which all anger is softened and instead of hating one's enemy one pities him (ἀντὶ τοῦ μισεῖν τὸν ἐχθρὸν ἐλεεῖ); and when I observe also that those who act arrogantly and treat with insolence the prayers of suppliants (λιτὰς ἱκετῶν ὑβρίσαντας) all incur the indignation of the gods and in the end come to a miserable state. For the gods themselves, who in the first place instituted and delivered to us these customs, are disposed to forgive (συγγνώμονες) the offences of men and are easily reconciled (εὐδιάλλακτοι) . . . Unless you think it fitting, Marcius, that the anger of the gods should be mortal, but that of men immortal! You will be doing, then what is just and becoming both to yourself and to your country, if you forgive (ἀφεὶς) her her offences, seeing that she is repentant (μετανοούσῃ) and ready to be reconciled and to restore to you now everything that she took away from you before" (50.3–4).

But if he is irreconcilable to his country, she asks this favor for herself, to whom he owes body and soul (52.1). She begs him not to make war on his country. Since she was a widow, she was mother, father, nurse, sister and everything dearest to him (51.3). He has, however, made her the most wretched of mothers, undertaking wars upon wars (51.4). And when he took up the life of a statesman, she has enjoyed no pleasure on his account. His opposition to the plebeians in behalf of the aristocrats[19] filled her with fear, knowing that divine vengeance opposes prominent men. She proved a true prophet (μάντις ἀληθής), and he was overpowered by the ill-will of fellow citizens, which snatched (ἀνήρπασεν) him away from his country, leaving her, his wife and children desolate (ἔρημον; 52.1). In return, she asks him to be reconciled to his fellow citizens, and to cease his implacable anger (χόλον; 52.2).

She can then live her life happy, and it will bring her everlasting fame (εὔκλειαν ἀθάνατον; 52.3). And if there is a place that receives human souls, it will not be that subterranean and gloomy place where the unhappy

19. Contrast Coriolanus's own account (chaps. 5–6; 12; and 30.4—31.4).

dwell, nor the Plain of Letho, but the pure ether high up in the heavens, where those sprung from the gods dwell, enjoying a happy and blessed life (εὐδαίμονα καὶ μακάριον βίον). Her soul will then relate his piety and acts of kindness, and she will ask the gods to requite him (52.4).

However, if he dishonors his mother, she will kill herself, leaving a grievous curse and furies to be her avengers (53.2). She prays to "the gods who guard the empire of the Romans." "Though it was fitting that he should rule all others, by his mother he should be ruled" (ὑπὸ δὲ τῆς μητρὸς ἄρχεσθαι). He should now honor her and give her back their common country. "And if it is right and lawful for a mother to grovel at the feet of her son, even to this and every other posture and office of humility (ταπεινὸν σχῆμα[20] καὶ λειτούργημα) will I submit in order to save my country (53.3–4).[21]

She throws herself on the ground and kisses his feet; the women cry, so that the Volscians had to turn away. Marcius leaps up and raises his mother from the ground (ἀνίστησιν αὐτήν; compare 2.1 above). He announces, "Yours is the victory, mother . . . Though you have saved your country, you have ruined me, your dutiful and affectionate son" (τὸν εὐσεβῆ καὶ φιλόστοργον υἱὸν; 54.1).

---

20. Compare the *kenosis* hymn, Phil 2:7–8. Bertram, "ὕψος, ὑψόω," 607, compares Isa 52:13.

21. A note on the term "humility" that Veturia has just used: the humble (οἱ ταπεινοί, *Ant. rom.* 6.76.2) and the proud (οἱ ὑπερήφανοι; 6.72.3) are economic terms, both in Dionysius and in Luke, which correspond to Jesus blessing the poor (μακάριοι οἱ πτωχοί; Luke 6:20b), those who have nothing, and cursing the rich (οὐαὶ ὑμῖν τοῖς πλουσίοις; Luke 6:24a). However, as Dionysius moves from books 7 to 8, from the conflict between the poor "humble" plebeians with the rich "proud" aristocrats, the contrast humble/proud fades. In book 8 two of the formerly "proud" have been humbled, Coriolanus himself (8.1.5, 6) and Veturia (8.53.4, quoted just above), both of whom become suppliants, Coriolanus to Tullus Attius and Vetruia to her son. Both Coriolanus and his mother have become economically poor: Veturia reports that Coriolanus "went out of the house [in Rome] alone, . . . without a servant, without means (ἄπορος), and without taking from his own stores, wretched man, even a day's supply of food" (8.41.5). And Valeria, also as suppliant (40.2, 3; 43.4) "wearing this squalid and shabby garb" (8.39.4) goes to the house of Veturia, who in turn goes to her son, Coriolanus, in "rent garments of mourning" (45.1; 46.2), stating that he left them desolate and no longer of any account" (ἔρημοι καὶ τὸ μηθέν; 46.3). Coriolanus asks his mother to cease avenging herself on him by such garb (47.5). "Humble" suppliants recognize those to whom they appeal as having power a) to accomplish their immediate death b) or to "raise them up" to membership in the community. In book 8 those in polar relation to "the humble" are not specified as "the proud," but as ones who have the power to become their patrons, to effect their death or life. In book 8 the word "humble" does not lose its reference to those who are poor economically, but it takes on the additional connotation of one who is a suppliant, as in the text cited above (53.4) and also in 8.1.5, 6, a meaning which informs the designation "humble" in Mary's Magnificat (Luke 1:48a and 52b).

The family retires to his tent, and through the rest of the day, he consults with them (σκοπούμενος σὺν αὐταῖς). The decisions they reached (τὰ δόξαντα αὐτοῖς; 54.2) were that Coriolanus should lead his army away, give an account of his services to the Volscians, ask them to admit their enemies into friendship, and come to a fair and just agreement. If they refuse, he should resign his command, even though an unreasoning mob might put Marcius to death (54.4). The women return to Rome, and Marcius asks the Volscians to forgive him and to remember the benefits they received from him (54.5).

This completes the story, although there is a fascinating sequel (as in Livy 2.40.12). Before the arrival (παρουσίαν) of the women in Rome, the men go out to meet them (55.1). The senate gives the women an "eternal remembrance" (μνήμην αἰώνιον) by establishing a Temple to Fortuna Muliebris (Τύχης γυναικῶν; 55.2–3) on the spot where they interceded for their country, at the fourth milestone of the *via Latina*.[22] Valeria, the woman who had proposed the embassy, performed the initial sacrifices (55.3). Our author argues against those who "think that the gods are neither pleased with the honours they receive from men nor displeased with impious and unjust actions" (56.1). As proof Dionysius narrates two epiphanies of the goddess, both confirmed by a voice that spoke words in Latin (56.2–3).[23] The women cause a second statue to be sculpted, and establish it as a custom that no woman who had been married a second time should crown this statue with garlands or touch it (56.4; cp. 45.2). Alternative views of women's role in Roman society have a social and ritual location, the Temple of the Fortune of Women.

3. Contested Values in Dionysius' Narrative

Who is a woman? Are women simply weak, or do they have strength, and if so, what is that strength? Does female modesty mean staying at home, raising the children, and never being seen by male strangers? Should a woman marry more than once? Even though their men are surprised, do women dare to go out of the city as ambassadors and negotiate at a conference with male enemies?[24] Might women too seek glory and honor, for example, by putting an end to wars? Might women give speeches in public, arguing

22. Graf, "Fortuna," 505–9, esp. 507. Eder, "Coriolanus, Marcius C.," 804. Patterson, "Via Latina," 141, with figs. I, 38, 67; III, 190; and V, 83. Villard and Rausa, "Tyche/Fortuna," 8/1, 115–25, 125–40; and 8/2, 85–89, 90–109.

23. Cf. Acts 2:2–4, 8–11, 17.

24. *1 Clem.* 55.3–6 gives examples of the humble Judith and Esther.

successfully against their opponents? In this narrative the woman/mother Vetruia argues publicly against a man/her son that the gods are easily reconciled, and that human anger likewise should be mortal, not immortal. Do appropriate methods of persuasion include supplication, "humbling" themselves[25] as suppliants, with the possibility of being "raised up" to victory?

Who is a man? Until his mother argues otherwise at the end of the story, Coriolanus insists that a man loves those who love him and hates those who hate him, that one's own city or ethnic group (or family?) is not the highest value. This is not an individualistic judgment: Coriolanus' actions show that he is utterly unwilling to love those outside the aristocracy, the upper economic and political class, a tighter bond than ethnicity. He never once values the needs of the poor, the lower social and political class in his own city, Rome, not even at the conclusion of the story. He loves his mother, never the Roman poor.

What is justice? Is justice to enjoy one's own possessions and live in peace? After a war, is it just to claim the possessions of the defeated? Is it just before the gods to go to war on the basis of a pretext that the other nation offended first? Is it just in a war to destroy the sepulchers of one's own ancestors and/or the altars of the enemy's gods? When one experiences change from a low estate to high and becomes great, does this prove that the present course of action is just before the gods? Having sworn to be loyal to one army, is it unjust to negotiate with the enemy?

What pleases the gods? Who is pious? Are the gods especially concerned with war? Are the gods displeased when humans reach a peak of eminence, so that they crush proud spirits who overstep the bounds of nature? When fortune favors a person, can s/he conclude that the gods are pleased and support their actions, also concluding, therefore, that it would displease the gods to change direction? Does it please the gods to be worshipped in temples, that their statues are reverenced—although this is assumed, not doubted, in the story? Do the gods help humans to accomplish their hopes? Do the gods invest human speech with persuasion and charm? Are the gods disposed to forgive human errors? Are they easily reconciled? Or are the gods neither pleased with the honors they receive from humans nor displeased with impious and unjust actions? Might humans live in the pure ether high up in the heavens, enjoying a happy and blessed life with the gods?

The ancient historian Dionysius narrates these stories of Valeria and Veturia, the foundation legends of the Temple to Fortuna Muliebris (Τύχης γυναικῶν) in Rome, repeatedly narrated and celebrated by the women

---

25. See the discussion by Schottroff, *Lydia's Impatient Sisters,* 43–46, of Briggs, "Can an Enslaved God Liberate?," 137–53. Compare the important article by Harrison, "The Imitation of the 'Great Man' in Antiquity," 213–54,

priests who served their goddess. Did these legends have practical, social consequences? The legends do call into question Roman gender stereotypes, although even in this case Valeria argues to Veturia, "you will be the cause to us also of some honour in the eyes of our husbands for having ourselves put an end to a war which they had been unable to stop; and we shall show ourselves to be the true descendants of those women who by their own intercession put an end to the war that had arisen between Romulus and the Sabines . . . ." (8.40.4). This is ironic, of course: the wives are doing something that their husbands could not accomplish, but they still seek honor from their men (compare Livy's short account, n. 6 above), rather close to Luke's ironic portrayal of gender as Prof. Seim has interpreted that gospel.

4. Supplication

4.1. Dionysius of Halicarnassus

Supplication plays a central role in Dionysius' stories of Veturia and Coriolanus. To understand those stories and to raise questions for the parallel stories of Mary and Jesus, I investigate this ritual and its social/religious meaning. In our story, Coriolanus goes to the leading aristocrat among Rome's enemies, Tullus Attius, confesses himself "unfortunate and humbled" (ἀτυχοῦντας καὶ τεταπεινωμένους, 8.1.5), "forsaken, exiled, and abased" (νῦν ἔρημος καὶ ἄπολις καὶ ταπεινὸς), recalling that the "fortunes of men are subject to change." Coriolanus becomes a suppliant (ἱκέτην, 8.1.6), and Tullus does not kill him, but "raises (ἀναστήσας) him from the hearth" (8.2.1).

Second, after Coriolanus becomes a successful general among his former enemies, now fighting the Romans, his former friends, his new friends admire Coriolanus for his "good fortune" (8.17.2), because he reduced the Romans "to a helplessness that was abject and anything but manly" (εἰς ταπεινὴν καὶ ἄνανδρον, 8.17.3). Some Romans in their turn become suppliants of Coriolanus, and he does not put them to death (8.17.6).

Third, Valeria and other Roman women become suppliants to Veturia, asking that she go the enemies' camp and become the suppliant (ἱκέτιν) of her son (8.39.4; also 40.2, 3, and 43.4); he may feel compassion, while a mother grovels at his feet. After Valeria embraces Veturia's knees (43.2), she agrees and, after giving a speech, does grovel at the feet of her son, a posture and office of humility (ταπεινὸν σχῆμα καὶ λειτούργημα), to which she submits in order to save her country (8.53.4). She throws herself on the ground and kisses his feet. Marcius leaps up and raises his mother from the ground (ἀνίστησιν αὐτὴν), announcing, "you have saved your country, . . . but ruined your . . . son" (8.54.1).

4.2. Greek and Latin Supplication

The acts of supplication narrated by Dionysius fit a pattern explicated by Freyburger,[26] who gives three famous Greek examples and two Roman ones; I narrate one major Greek and one Latin example, plus smaller examples in Greek and Latin of supplication rejected. At the conclusion of the *Iliad*, Priam, king of Troy, goes to Achilles, clasps his knees and kisses the hands that had killed his many sons (24.478–79). He brings a huge ransom and asks Achilles to pity him, who is more piteous (ἐλεεινότερός) even than Achilles' father (504). He reaches out his hand to the man who killed his son (506), Hector, and clasps Achilles' feet. Their moaning and weeping fill the house. Achilles sprang from his seat, and raised the old man by his hand (χειρὸς ἀνίστη), pitying his gray head (515). No profit springs from lament, "for so have the gods spun the thread for wretched mortals, that they should live among sorrows, and they themselves are without care" (525–26). Priam is his suppliant (ἱκέτην, 570). The danger is that Achillles' anger will slay Priam, "and so transgress the charge of Zeus" (586). They share a meal (601–30) and sleep before Achillles gives Priam the dead body of his son (*Iliad* XXIV.508–674, trans. Murray in LCL[27]).

Freyburger also gives a Greek example of supplication rejected: Iphigenia speaks, "How oft unto my father's beard I strained Mine hands, and clung unto my father's knees, Crying, O Father . . . , I am dying by thy hand!" (Euripides, *Iphigenia in Taurica* 362–63, 368, trans. Way in LCL) Agamemnon (would have) killed/sacrificed her, in some versions thwarted by Artemis. In the other example from the Iliad (see n. 27), this same Agamemnon is the one who dishonors Achilles, generating the successful supplication of Zeus by his mother, Thetis.

Freyburger's two famous Latin examples are from Virgil's *Aeneid*, As the Trojans sail up the Cyclopes' coast toward the Italian bay of Tarantum, "on a sudden out of the woods comes forth the strange shape of an unknown man, outworn with uttermost hunger, and of piteous guise, and towards

26. Freyburger, "Supplication grecque et supplication romaine," with plates V–X; and Brilliant, *Gesture and Rank in Roman Art,* with, e.g., figs. 1.4–7, 9–10, 14; 2.60–63, 90, 108; 3.12, 45, 47–50, 69–70, 112–13, 118–19, 131–36; also chap. 17: "submission," and an appendix: "manus." See fig. 1 above.

27. The other Greek examples: Thetis supplicates Zeus (*Iliad* 1.500–525; see 8.371–72), and Odysseus supplicates Arete and king Alcinous (*Odyssey* 7.133–81).

the beach stretches suppliant hands (*supplexque manus*). We gaze at him. Ghastly in his squalor, with unshorn beard, and garb fastened with thorns, he was yet in all else a Greek, and had once been sent to Troy in his country's arms . . ." (3.590–95, trans. Fairclough in LCL). With tears and prayers, he says, "'I own that I warred against the gods of Ilium. For that, if my guilt hath done so much wrong, strew me piecemeal over the waves or plunge me in the vast sea. If I die, it will be a boon to have died at the hands of men!' He ceased, and clung to our knees, clasping them and groveling there" (3.599–607). Aeneas' father, Anchises, gives the Greek his right hand (610); he loses his fear, and tells of his evil fortune in the Cyclops' cave.[28]

Freyburger also gives a Latin example of supplication refused. Turnus, vanquished by Aeneas in combat (*Aeneid* 12.920 ff.), asks for grace, stretching forth his hands (12.936–38). But Aeneas sees Turnus wearing the young Pallas' belt, whom Aeneas had loved, and he buries his sword in him (12.950), the final event of the *Aeneid*.[29]

4.3. Comparisons and Conclusions

This is not the place for a complete study of supplication; I give only a few conclusions. The rite of touching the knees belongs to the Indo-European community (Greece, Rome, Persia) and has a juridical/religious value, a ritual not found in Egypt or in the Bible (Freyburger 509, 522, 524, and his Fig. 5). Touching the chin is also important, and in a Roman context, touching the right hand (Livy 25.16.13; Freyburger, 525). Roman suppliants present open hands, palms to the sky (Livy 3.50.5).

> The knees of a human being also possess a sort of religious sanctity in the usage of the nations. Suppliants (*supplices*) touch the knees and stretch out their hands towards them and pray at them as at altars . . . There is a religious sanctity belong to other parts also, for instance in the right hand . . . It was a custom with the Greeks in early days to touch the chin in entreaty. (Pliny, *Nat. Hist.* 11.250–51, trans. Rackham in LCL, cited by Freyburger, 504)

However, scholars do not know whether the ideology itself is Indo-European; there is no etymological connection between ἱκέτης and *supplex* (Freyburger, 515, 524).

---

28. The other famous Latin example is of Aeneas's envoy, Ilioneus, supplicating king Latinus (*Aeneid* 7.236–66). Latinus grants the request by offering his right hand (7.266).

29. The closing supplications in the *Iliad* and the *Aeneid* are striking contrasts.

Greek and Roman religious conceptions differ. Zeus is the protector of suppliants, but Jupiter is not (Freyburger 522, 525, n. 186). Not Jupiter, but Roman *fides* protects a suppliant. Nevertheless, some scholars conclude that the suppliant has a right of protection related to a supreme deity, an unwritten law (524).[30] Ancient Greeks did, but Romans did not recognize the right of asylum; the first Roman king Romulus giving asylum is a late legend (515, n. 127; 523).

In Greece supplication evokes the sentiment of αἰδώς (honor, respect), and the suppliant becomes a member of the community; in Rome it evokes rather *fides* (loyalty, protection, security; Freyburger, 521–23). In Rome the suppliant capitulates/devotes (*deditio*) his person and all his goods, a voluntary act in which a person or a city humbly placed its protection in another; the suppliant becomes a client, not an equal (523, 525). Freyburger (525) concludes that a suppliant in Greece is given immediate protection, while a suppliant in Rome is granted lengthy faithfulness.

Freyburger does not emphasize it, but when the suppliant humbles him- or herself, the radical alternative is either a) death[31] or b) being "raised up" (ἀνίστημι) from the ground/hearth.[32] In a Roman context, this includes the giving of the right hand.[33]

5. Mary

5.1. Mary in Luke–Acts

I have narrated the story in Dionysius, *Ant. rom.*, book 8, because Valeria and Veturia have significant roles in the plot, and because Veturia's speech and supplication have analogies to Mary's speech (and supplication?) in Luke 1. The root ταπειν- is fundamental to this story; it has psychological overtones, but for both males and females, it denotes primarily social, political, and economic status. As an upper class woman, Veturia is willing

---

30. Nilsson, *Greek Popular Religion*, 77–78. Dionysius, a Greek author, represents a Roman woman, Veturia, insisting that those who "act arrogantly and treat with insolence the prayers of suppliants all incur the indignation of the gods and in the end come to a miserable state" (*Ant. rom.* 8.50.3).

31. Dionysius, *Ant. rom.* 8.1.6; 17.6; Homer, *Iliad* 24.586; Euripides, *Iphigenia in Taurica* 362–63, 368; Virgil, *Aeneid* 3.590–95; 12.950–52, the final words of the *Aeneid*. Cf. Paul's *kenosis* hymn: ἐταπείνωσεν ἑαυτὸν γενόμενος ὑπήκοος μεέχρι θανάτου (Phil 2:8ab).

32. Dionysius, *Ant. rom.* 8.2.1; 8.17.6; 8.54.1; see 8.39.1, 4; 8.40.2, 3; Homer, *Iliad* 24.515; *Odyssey* 7.162–63, 168. Cf. again the *kenosis* hymn (Phil 2:9a).

33. Virgil, *Aeneid* 3.610; 7.266; Livy 25.16.3.

to humble herself (see nn. 21 and 32 above), hoping to be "raised up" and honored for saving her country, Rome. Fortune/the gods may humble a person, but Veturia chooses to humble herself, to fall at the feet of her son in supplication.

Might we compare and contrast the humility of this upper class woman in Rome, Veturia, with the humility of Mary, an economically lower class woman from a provincial village in Galilee? As Valeria was "moved by some divine inspiration" to suggest that weak women as suppliants go to Veturia, asking that she in turn become a suppliant to her son, so also Elizabeth was filled with the Holy Spirit and cried, "Blessed are you [Mary] among women, and blessed is the fruit of your womb" (Luke 1:41–42). Mary believes what was spoken to her by the Lord, chanting:

> My soul magnifies the Lord, and my spirit rejoices in God my Savior, for he has looked with favor on the humility of his slave woman (ἐπὶ τὴν ταπείνωσιν τῆς δούλης αὐτοῦ). Surely, from now on all generations will call me blessed (μακαριοῦσίν με), for the Mighty One has done great things for me, and holy is his name. His mercy (τὸ ἔλεος αὐτοῦ) is for those who fear him from generation to generation. He has shown great strength (κράτος) with his arm; he has scattered the proud (ὑπερηφάνους) in the thoughts of their hearts. He has brought down the powerful (δυνάστας) from their thrones (ἀπὸ θρόνων), and lifted up the lowly (ὕψωσεν ταπεινούς); he has filled the hungry (πεινῶντας) with good things, and sent the rich (πλουτοῦντας) away empty. He has helped his servant Israel, in remembrance of his mercy (μνησθῆναι ἐλέους), according to the promise he made to our ancestors, to Abraham and to his descendants forever (εἰς τὸν αἰῶνα; Luke 1:46b–55, NRSV modified).

In Mary's hymn the opposite of humble is proud (ὑπερήφανος), a term that is not prominent in Dionysius, *Ant. rom.*, book 8, although it was key in book 7,[34] which I will summarize in a few sentences in order to illuminate the contrast proud/humble. Decius, who had persuaded the senate to pass a decree for the trial of Coriolanus, accused him of trying to dissolve the bonds between the senate and the people, which are unlawful to loose as long as the city is inhabited (7.44.1). "Giving to the liberty of the poor (πενήτων) the name of insolence, and to equality that of tyranny, he [Marcius] advised you to deprive us of them" (7.44.2). But a "multitude of poor men, when deprived of the necessities of life" (πένητες ἄνθρωποι τῆς ἀναγκαίου

---

34. For more detail from book 7, see Balch, "Political Friendship," now in *Contested Ethnicities and Images*, chap. 6, #3.

τροφῆς ἀποκλειόμενοι), will either leave the city and perish or, calling on the divinities to witness their sufferings, attack those who keep the price of corn high, no longer regarding them as friends (7.44.3–4). He advises Coriolanus to descend from his haughtiness (ὑπερηφάνων), to assume the humble and piteous demeanor (σχῆμα ταπεινὸν καὶ ἐλεεινόν) of one who has erred (ἡμαρτηκότος) and is asking pardon (7.45.4). Even the senator Manius Valerius advises Marcius/Coriolanus to change his way of life to an humble deportment (σχῆμα ταπεινὸν[35] μεταλαβεῖν, 7.54.5). Coriolanus never agreed, but an upper class woman, his mother, Veturia, was willing to humble herself as a suppliant, which we saw above (8.53.3–4). The senate, therefore, gives the women an "eternal remembrance" by establishing of a Temple to Fortuna Muliebris (55.3) on the spot where they interceded for their country. As the women had hoped, by "humbling" themselves in supplication (see n. 21 above), they gained honor (8.40.4) and remembrance.

Is this not also true of Mary of Nazareth? Gerd Theissen[36] observes, "primitive Christian ethics often consists of making the values and norms of the upper class accessible to all. One could speak of a 'democratization' of an ancient aristocratic ethic . . . ." This brings the "radicalization of demands . . . when ordinary people . . . take over not only the substance of norms but also the aristocratic self-confidence which is associated with them: the claim to do things better than others." Mary sang of herself as God's humble slave woman (Luke 1:48a), not politically correct language in the twenty-first century, but in the first century CE, she was indeed honored, remembered (Luke 1:48b), and lifted up/exalted (Luke 1:52b; compare Acts 2:32–33a and Phil 2:9a of Jesus).

I will interpret Mary, the mother of Jesus, largely following Prof. Seim (the numbers in parentheses refer to *The Double Message*). Seim (15) gives a significant list of man–woman parallels in Luke. In some texts specific persons of the larger male-female groups are mentioned (Luke 8:1–3; 24:9–11; and Acts 1:13–14). After listing the Eleven (males) by name (Acts 1:13), the text continues, "all these were constantly devoting themselves to prayer, together with certain women, including Mary the mother of Jesus, as well as his brothers" (Acts 1:14; at the end of this section, I will return to 1:14).

---

35. Compare Paul's Phil 2:7e–8a: σχήματι . . . ὡς ἄνθρωπος ἐταπείνωσεν ἑαυτὸν. Walker, *The Genuine Teachers of this Art: Rhetorical Education in Antiquity*, 279, quotes Dionysius, *Ant. rom.* 7.45.4, "Drag yourself down, wretched man [Coriolanus], from that overbearing, tyrannical haughtiness to an attitude more populist, and make yourself at last like other people." Walker comments, "This would seem to be the heart of Dionysius' political-philosophical lesson in the *Roman Antiquities*." Walker's interpretation of the heart of Dionysius's rhetoric is very close to Luke's Magnificat as well as to the *kenosis* hymn in Philippians.

36. Theissen, *The Religion of the Earliest Churches*, 82, 116.

The distinction between men and women renders the women visible, but the "corollary of women becoming visible seems to be an inclusiveness still tasting of segregation" (19).

There is a later reference to Mary: "a woman in the crowd raised her voice and said to him, 'Blessed is the womb that bore you and the breasts that nursed you!' But he said, 'Blessed rather are those who hear the word of God and obey it!'" (Luke 11:27–28). Similarly, when Jesus' mother and brothers could not reach him because of the crowd, Jesus affirms, "My mother and my brothers are those who hear the word of God and do it" (8:21). The macarism of 11:27 focuses on the maternal functions of the female body: womb and breasts, but Jesus corrects this in 11:28: "Mary is blessed, not because she is Jesus' biological mother, but because she hears the word of God and keeps it" (Seim 114, referring back to 8:21). This recalls previous observations about Mary, her response to the Annunciation, "let it be with me according to your word" (1:38). And when the shepherds reported the angels' words that they would find a Savior, the Messiah, the Lord, lying in a manger, "Mary treasured all these words and pondered them in her heart" (2:19). Still a third time in the infancy narrative, after Passover when she found her twelve-year old questioning teaching in the Temple, "his mother treasured all these things in her heart" (2:51).

> Other traits in the narratives of Jesus' infancy and birth in Luke emphasize likewise that Mary is to be understood as the exemplary disciple, a Christian prototype, ἡ δούλη κυρίου. Even if full discipleship is not possible at this early preparatory stage in the gospel, Mary is a disciple *in nuce* through her listening obedience and her openness towards the future explanation and fulfillment. But Mary's obedience is not portrayed merely in passive terms: she expresses active acceptance and positive response (1:38), and further she proclaims God's wonderous acts with prophetic authority (1:46–55; Seim 115).

Seim (136, 144, 166, 169) repeatedly emphasizes the importance of Joel 3:1–5 (LXX) in Peter's inaugural sermon (quoted Acts 2:17–21), drawing a clear conclusion: "for the promise by Joel to be fulfilled, women too must indeed prophesy" (166).[37] On the few occasions when Luke employs δοῦλος/δούλη of the relation of humans to God, it is always connected with

---

37. "[U]niversalism is combined with the outpouring of the Spirit, while also implying the crossing of other socio-religious barriers. The Spirit overcomes the gulf between those who are near and those who are far off (cf. Peter's summary at 2.39), and also the gulf between woman and man and between slave and free, in other words, the antitheses which the baptismal formula at Gal 3:26–28 proclaim as having been overcome in Christ." (Seim, *Double Message*, 170)

the Spirit. Mary is the prototype of the Lord's slave in her obedience to the Spirit; by the Spirit she becomes pregnant, "and she is also given prophetic power" (Seim 175). The women prophesying on Pentecost have their fore-runners in Mary, Elizabeth and Anna (Seim 176). The Spirit enables them to interpret what is happening to them. Anna is specifically called προφῆτις, the only woman so named in the New Testament (Seim 179).

I return to Acts 1:14: why is Mary, the mother of Jesus, mentioned there, as a disciple or a prophet? Seim notes (22) that the mention of "women" in this verse is not necessarily enhancing. After σὺν γυναιξὶν D adds καὶ τέκνοις, which weakens the implicit reference to the women from Galilee (Luke 8:1–3; 23:55—24:10). Here Martin Hengel, by asking a related question, makes a clarifying suggestion.[38] Hengel observes that in the New Testament, short lists of names often implies order in rank, including those lists in which Mary Magdalene is named first, e.g., Mark 15:40–41 and 47; Matt 28:1; Luke 8:2–3; 24:10, with an explanation of why this is not the case in John 19:25.[39] Hengel rejects (251) the suggestion that she is so impor-tant because Jesus healed her; rather the early church writers named her ἰσαπόστολος. She was so important, even in relation to women related to the Jesus, because she was the first one to whom Jesus appeared (Matt 28:9–10 and John 20:11–19), which are not secondary texts (Hengel 251–52, 256).

Acts 1:13 names the Eleven males who were leaders of the early church in Jerusalem, and Acts 1:14 is parallel,[40] mentioning not simply family or church members, but the women who were influential leaders of that earli-est church.[41] Among the 500 of 1 Cor 15:6 there were certainly women, and

---

38. Hengel, "Maria Magdalena und die Frauen als Zeugen," 243–56.

39. Ibid., 248–50. Contrast Koch, *Geschichte des Urchristenbtums*, 541–45.

40. An additional reason that 1:14 is parallel to 1:13 is that it mentions Jesus' "brothers," also leaders of the church, e.g., James (Acts 12:17; 15:13; 21:18, although Luke never notes that this James is Jesus' brother).

41. Dionysius portrays Veturia speaking in a crisis when the society's highest value, Rome itself, is at stake. Rutledge, "Commemorating Women," 173–85 (with bibliog-raphy, esp. Milnor, *Gender*), in *Ancient Rome as a Museum*, observes that "[Roman] women take on a male identity" when they are involved in "the preservation of the state from both war and plague" (181). However, this destabilized gender categories (Rutledge 180, 185). The case of women apostles in earliest Jerusalem church is par-tially analogous. When imperial Rome threatened the group's primary value, faith in the living Jesus Christ, by crucifying him, women—moved by the Spirit—spoke and led, witnessing to Jesus' resurrection from the dead. Jesus' resurrection appearances to Mary Magdalene (first to her, before Jesus' appearance to Peter) and to Junia destabi-lized gender categories.

See also Lewis, *Ecstatic Religion* (1989), chap. 3: spirit possession provides espe-cially married women "(acting consciously or unconsciously) with an opportunity to pursue their interests and demands in a context of male dominance" (71). Lieu, "The

Junia of Rom 16:7 was also an early "apostle"[42] to whom Jesus appeared, which would have given these women authority and influence in the Jerusalem church, even though Luke has made their leadership virtually invisible in Acts 1. Luke 8:1–3 is a close parallel: Jesus goes through Galilean cities and villages, "and the twelve were with him, as well as certain women who had been cured of evil spirits and infirmities: Mary, called Magdalene, from whom seven demons had gone out . . ." Mary Magdalene is prominent, as Hengel argues, because of Jesus' resurrection appearance to her, which is no longer visible in Luke–Acts. Seim's summary (254) refers to "Acts reduction of women to invisibility in favour of the activity of the leading men." Manuscript D further robs these women of their role as influential leaders by adding "and children," making them no longer leaders but simply family members. However, the only adequate explanation of their leadership role in the early Jerusalem church is that Jesus appeared to them, giving them authority.

"Mary, the mother of Jesus" (Acts 1:14) was also a leader in that early Jerusalem church, not because of Jesus' resurrection appearance to her, but for a variety of other reasons that have already been given above, e.g. she "believed what was spoken to her by the Lord" (Luke 1:45), whereas Zachariah the male priest "did not believe my words" (ἀνθ᾽ ὧν οὐκ ἐπίστευσας τοῖς λόγοις μου, 1:20). This female/male contrast in the opening chapter is matched by a similar contrast in the concluding chapter: Mary Magdalene and the other women hear and announce the word (Luke 24:6–10), in contrast to the male apostles who do ""not believe" (ἠπίστουν, 24:11). Seim characterizes these contrasts as ironic: the official male leaders do not believe, but the female followers are paradigms,[43] contrasts that frame the gospel by an *inclusio*.

Besides the influential leadership of these women, almost invisible in Acts, another conclusion follows. Her spirit moves Mary to rejoice in God her Savior, to prophesy that the Lord "exalts the humble" (ὕψωσεν ταπεινούς; Luke 1:52b), and this has indeed happened to the Lord's humble slave woman, Mary (τὴν ταπείνωσιν τῆς δούλης αὐτοῦ; Luke 1:48). The economically

---

'Attraction of Women' in/to Early Judaism and Christianity," also cites (93 n. 47) Lewis, but questions his anthropological conclusions, which however persuade me: aristocratic males in patriarchal (most human) societies control access to the traditional gods/goddesses; marginal groups (most women, the poor [male and female], and excluded ethnic groups), often gain direct access to the divine through ecstatic religion.

I note also that post-Pauline, third generation Christian writers began reestablishing patriarchy utilizing Aristotelian household codes: see Balch, *Let Wives be Submissive* (a title that quotes 1 Pet 3:1).

42. Epp, *Junia*.

43. For this gender irony, cf. the citations of Livy 2.40.1–2, 11–12 (n. 6 above) and Dionysius, *Ant. rom.* 8.39.3 and 8.40.4, both cited above.

lower class, humble woman from a village in Galilee has been raised by God to an influential role in the urban church in Jerusalem (Acts 1:14). Mary is parallel to Veturia; both women humbled themselves, were "raised up," honored, and are eternally remembered.

5.2. The Magnificat:
Mary Suppplicating God for the Humble and Hungry

Not only Veturia, but Mary too is a suppliant,[44] not for her country, but to God for the poor and humble like herself. Mary's Magnificat has many contacts with the social and religious ritual of supplication embedded in the Greek and Latin narratives outlined above. Both Veturia and Mary become "blessed" (Luke 1:45).[45] Both Veturia and Mary rejoice in "salvation" (Luke 1:47).[46] Most strikingly, both women are "humble" (Luke 1:48, 52b; see n. 21 above).[47] Both women experience everlasting fame (Luke 1:48b).[48] In both narratives "mercy/pity" is key (Luke 1:50).[49] In both narratives, the deity humbles the proud, the rich, removing them from high office (Luke 1:51b,

44. Figure 18.1. Turia's husband, Quintus Lucretius Vespillo, gave a *laudatio* at her funeral (7 or 6 BCE) and had it inscribed on her tomb on large marble slabs (*Corpus Inscriptionum Latinarum* 6.41062). See Josiah Osgood, *Turia: A Roman Woman's Civil War* (Women in Antiquity; Oxford: Oxford University, 2014), 5, 153, 155. He praises her for influencing Caesar Augustus to restore him as a citizen in 42 BCE, and continues, "You then confronted his colleague Marcus Lepidus, who was in charge in Rome, about my reinstatement. Prostrate on the ground before his feet, not only were you lifted up you were also dragged and carried off like a slave. Your body was covered with bruises, but most strenuously you kept reminding him about Caesar's edict ...." (Osgood's translation, p. 163, of Turia's supplication; see his discussion, pp. 56-64.) Turia's supplication is a contemporary, partial analogy to both Dionysius' narrative of Veturia's and to Luke's narrative of Mary's supplications.

45. Dionysius, *Ant. rom.* 8.52.4; see 8.17.2 of Coriolanus, temporarily changed from humble to great and blessed.

46. Dionysius, *Ant. rom.* 8.39.3; 40.5; 54.1.

47. Dionysius, *Ant. rom.* 8.40.1; 41.2; 42.2; 53.4; Coriolanus too is humbled: 8.1.5, 6, and becomes a suppliant.

48. Dionysius, *Ant. rom.* 8.52.3; 55.3.

49. Dionysius, *Ant. rom.* 8.42.1; 46.1; 50.3; Homer, *Iliad* 24.505.

52a),[50] and/or the reverse: a powerful arm lifts up the humble (Luke 1:51a, 52b).[51] The experience of "hunger" by the poor is central (Luke 1:53a).[52]

Some Greek and Roman hearers/readers would have recognized this cluster of terms and associated it with supplication. An author like Luke, concerned with the theological history of Israel and living in Greco-Roman culture, could make these associations. This is clear from an analogy in Heb 5:7, "in the days of his flesh, Jesus offered up prayers and supplications (ἱκετηρίας), with loud cries and tears, to the one who was able to save him from death, and he was heard because of his reverent submission."

It was not only possible to imagine Jesus and Mary as suppliants; the cluster of terms in the Magnificat is odd, e.g. what have "the hungry" to do with "the proud"? But in the context of a narrative like that of Coriolanus and Veturia, the combination makes narrative sense. Mary's Magnificat appeals to the God of Israel, who made promises to Abraham and his descendants (Luke 1:55), in behalf of the poor and humble like herself, not to a God who has no cares.[53] Luke–Acts was written between cultures, affirming the God of Israel fulfilling promises, while employing selected vocabulary and values of Greco-Roman cultures.

Further, Dionysius narrated a legend set five centuries earlier[54]; he has not written a unique modern novel with highly individual characters. Earlier in Dionysius' narrative, the senator Manius Valerius observes that "we are not the only people, nor the first, among whom poverty has raised sedition against wealth, and lowliness against eminence (πενία πρὸς πλοῦτον ἐστασίασε καὶ ταπεινότης πρὸς ἐπιφάνειαν), but that *in nearly all states*, both great and small, the lower class is generally hostile to the upper . . ." (6.54.1, my emphasis). Dionysius' story has typical elements. There is tension between rich and poor; the high price of corn and hunger are related. Further,

---

50. Dionysius, *Ant. rom.* 8.25.3; 33.3; 52.1; "ταπεινός," in *TDNT*, 8–10, cites Isa 1:25; 2:11; 5:14–15; 10:33; 11:4; 49:13; 61:1–2; 66:2; Ps 17:28; 74:8; 87:16; 112:4–7; 114:6; 118:71, 67, 75, 107; Judith 9:11.

51. Dionysius, *Ant. rom.* 8.2.1; 8.54.1; see 8.40.2–3; Homer, *Iliad* 24.515; *Odyssey* 7.162–63, 168.

52. Dionysius, *Ant. rom.* 7.44.3–4; see Balch, "Political Friendship," in *Contested Ethnicities and Images*, chap. 6, #3, for further instances.

53. See Dionysius, *Ant. rom.* 8.52.1; 56.1; Homer, *Iliad* 24.525–26.

54. Conflict between the patricians and plebeians began with the first secession (494–493 BCE), but Dionysius narrates that earlier conflict in light of the problems of the present, that is, of the events of the year 133 BCE and the tribunate of Ti. Sempronius Gracchus. Dionysius intends to give typical examples for statesmen and citizens. Both points are argued by von Ungern-Sternberg, "The Formation of the 'Annalistic Tradition': the Example of the Decemvirate," 77–104. See chap. 4 in Balch, *Contested Ethnicities and Images*.

the cultural anthropologist Lewis observes (see n. 41) that in male-domi-
nated societies (rather numerous in ancient and modern times), the spirit
moves women to speak and act in their own interests, another typical element. Since Dionysius' narrative involves these typical elements, one would
not necessarily have to have known his particular narrative to recognize
the cluster of terms combined in the Magnificat, although in Rome itself
and in Roman colonies such as Philippi and Corinth, some version of the
Coriolanus/Veturia story would have been known.

I dislike gender stereotypes, but there are some in this story. The male
Coriolanus believes in hard reciprocity: you give only what you get. The
female Veturia believes rather that the gods are forgiving, and that humans
would do well to be more like the gods, more open to reconciliation. Luke's
theology stressing God's forgiveness that promotes reconciliation between
ethnic groups (Luke 24:47) is close to the female Veturia's theology, distant
from Coriolanus' thoughts on the gods. Luke differs from both in that the
core theological value is not the Roman state.

As a Christian author addressing Christian readers for a moment,
I add a caution. When we in the First World psychologize, that is, when
we suppress the economic meaning of these terms and make the central
concern whether we ourselves feel proud or humble, we reverse the meaning of Mary's Magnificat. Mary may simply be a paradigm, encomiastically
praising the God who exalted her, a humble, economically poor woman;
God is then a Savior who analogously will raise other humble, economically
poor persons. If the humble Mary is parallel to the humble suppliant Veturia
and is also supplicating God for other poor and humble persons, as Veturia
supplicated her son for the humble women of Rome, the force is stronger. In
either case, as paradigm or as suppliant, Mary prays for those living on the
streets of our urban centers and also for those in the Two-Thirds World who
live in poverty, which we in the First World might take into account when
we repeat her words in prayer.

6. Jesus

This section could be long, but I will be brief. Jesus' life and words are an
extreme contrast to Coriolanus, as we see in the contrasting terms proud/
humble (ὑπερήφανος/ταπεινός), equivalent to the contrast rich/poor, in both
biographies. Greek and Roman hearers/readers of Luke would have been
aware of this contrast, as we may see in the earlier biography of the Roman
general Coriolanus by the Greek Dionysius (late first century BCE) and in
the biography by Plutarch contemporary with Luke–Acts (late first or early

second century CE). The similar mothers did not generate similar sons. I give only three or four examples. Jesus pronounced, "Blessed are you who are poor (μακάριοι οἱ πτωχοί)," and "Woe to you who are rich" (πλὴν οὐαὶ ὑμῖν τοῖς πλουσίοις; Luke 6:20b and 24a). Jesus tells a parable of slaves

> waiting for their master to return from the wedding banquet, so that they may open the door for him as soon as he comes and knocks. Blessed are those slaves (μακάριοι οἱ δοῦλοι) whom the master finds alert when he comes; truly I tell you, he will fasten his belt and have them sit down (ἀνακλινεῖ [recline]) to eat, and he will come and serve them (διακονήσει αὐτοῖς, Luke 12:36–37, NRSV modified).

A master serving slaves at a symposium/convivium—probably not for Coriolanus. The parable of the wedding banquet in Luke 14:7–11[55] similarly turns the social/economic world upside down. Here I quote only the final saying, "For all those who exalt themselves will be humbled; and those who exalt themselves will be humbled" (πᾶς ὁ ὑψῶν ἑαυτὸν ταπεινωθήσεται, καὶ ὁ ταπεινῶν ἑαυτὸν ὑψωθήσεται, 14:11).

At the Last Supper, immediately after the words of institution, "a dispute also arose among them as to which one of them was to be regarded as the greatest" (22:24). The redactor of Luke has taken an incident that occurred in Mark (10:35–45; see 9:33–37) when Jesus was on the road from Galilee to Jerusalem and purposefully placed it in the passion story itself at the conclusion of the Last Supper. As in the parable quoted above, here too Jesus pronounces, "For who is greater, the one who is at (ἀνακείμενος, who reclines at) the table or the one who serves (ὁ διακονῶν)? Is it not the one at (ὁ ἀνακείμενος, reclining at) the table? But I am among you as one who serves" (εἰμι ὡς ὁ διακονῶν, 22:27, NRSV modified).

When Peter preaches the sermon that inaugurates the church, he proclaims Jesus whom God did "not abandon in Hades" (Acts 2:27a and 31b, quoting Ps 15[LXX 16]:10). Rather Peter exults, "this Jesus God raised up (ἀνέστησεν ὁ θεός)[56] . . . Being therefore exalted (ὑψωθείς[57]) at the right hand of God . . ." (Acts 2:32a, 33a). Unlike Luke 1:48a, 52b, and Phil 2:8a, Luke chooses not to write ταπεινός of Jesus, but records instead Peter's claim from Psalms that God did not abandon Jesus in Hades. As Veturia and Mary humbled themselves and were raised up, exalted, so too Jesus, not Coriolanus, served as a slave at the Last Supper, and God raised him up and exalted the son of Mary to God's right hand.

---

55. Braun, *Feasting and social rhetoric in Luke 14*.

56. Compare n. 32 above.

57. The *kenosis* hymn (Phil 2:9a) has "highly exalted" (ὑπερύψωσεν).

7. A Hermeneutic for Social/Political Life

In these narratives of Veturia and Coriolanus, Mary and Jesus, Lazarus and the rich man, the proud rich are contrasted with the humble poor. Decius, a poor plebeian, advises Coriolanus, "the most illustrious man of his age" (Dionysius, *Ant. rom.* 6.94.2), to descend from his haughtiness (ὑπερηφάνων), to assume the humble demeanor (σχῆμα ταπεινὸν) of one who has erred (7.45.4), which the Roman general rejects. The people vote against him, and Coriolanus goes into exile, humbled (8.1.5). Coriolanus' mother, Veturia is also an aristocrat but unlike her son; she does assume the posture of humility (ταπεινὸν σχῆμα; 8.53.3) in order to save Rome. She gains immortal glory, an eternal remembrance (8.40.4; 55.2). Both Coriolanus and Veturia are aristocrats presented with the possibility of humbling themselves in a crisis for a purpose. The mother chooses to humble herself; the son refuses.

Since both the Magnificat in Luke and the *kenosis* hymn in Philippians employ the basic contrast between those who are "humble" and those who are "exalted," I briefly observe structural analogies to the narratives of Coriolanus and Veturia. In Phil 2:6 "Jesus rather than the emperor deserves the honorific *isa theo*."[58] From that divine status, unlike Coriolanus but like Veturia, Jesus took the form of a slave (2:7b); he "humbled himself" (ἐταπείνωσεν ἑαυτὸν, Phil 2:8a). Similarly in the Magnificat, God exalts the humble (ὕψωσεν ταπεινούς, 1.52b) slave woman (τὴν ταπείνωσιν τῆς δούλης αὐτου, 48a) Mary, but scatters the proud (ὑπερηφάνους) and sends the rich (πλουτοῦντας) away empty (Luke 2:51b, 53b). The rich man (πλούσιος) who ignored the poor finds himself in Hades, while the angels carry the poor (πτωχὸς) man named Lazarus to Abraham (Luke 16:19–23). Finally, at Pentecost Peter declares that God pours out God's Spirit on God's slaves (ἐπὶ τοὺς δούλους μου καὶ ἐπὶ τὰς δούλας μου), both men and women (Acts 2:18), who shall be saved (2:21), in contrast to the rulers (Acts 3:17; 4:5, 8, 23, 26–27). God "raised"[59] (2:24a) Jesus, not abandoning him to Hades (2:27a, 31), but rather places him on David's throne (ἐπὶ τὸν θρόνον αὐτοῦ, 2:30), exalting (ὑψωθείς) him to the right hand of God (2:33).

---

58. Heen, "Phil 2:6–11 and Resistance to Local Timocratic Rule: *Isa theo* and the Cult of the Emperor in the East," 139, based on his doctoral dissertation at Columbia (1997). Paul too originally had an aristocratic origin and upbringing, which he lost permanently when he began to proclaim the gospel to Gentiles; *after* his conversion, he chose to learn the slavish, humiliating (2 Cor 11.7) trade of a tentmaker. See Hock, "The Problem of Paul's Social Class," 7–18. Cf. Harrison, "The Imitation of the 'Great Man' in Antiquity: Paul's Inversion of a Cultural Icon," 213–54.

59. See n. 32.

In these narratives those called on to humble themselves are the upper class rich; the poor/humble Mary and Lazarus are exalted. Nietzsche[60] misperceived Christianity as a religion of slaves, unless one interprets that to mean a religion of slaves calling for the rich to humble themselves and be in solidarity (κοινωνία, *Ant. rom.* 6.36.1; 79.3; 80.4; and 7.65.1) with the poor, trusting that God, as the prophets proclaim (Luke 1:54–55; Acts 2:30–33), will exalt the humble poor.[61]

Bibliography

Ancient Authors

Dionysius of Halicarnassus. *Roman Antiquities*. Translated by E. Cary. LCL. Cambridge: Harvard University Press, 1945 and 1962, 1950 and 1986, vols. 4–5.

Euripides. *Iphigenia in Taurica*. Translated by A. S. Way. LCL. Cambridge: Harvard University Press, 1916 and 1958.

Homer. *Iliad*. 2 vols. Translated by A. T. Murray and W. F. Watt. LCL. Cambridge: Harvard University Press, 1999.

Livy. *History of Rome*. Vol. 1. Translated by B. O. Foster. LCL. Cambridge: Harvard University Press, 1925 and 1988.

Novum Testamentum Graece. Edited by Nestle-Aland et al. 28th rev. ed. Stuttgart: German Bible Society, 2012.

Pliny. *Natural History*. Vol. 3. Translated by H. Rackham. LCL. Cambridge: Harvard University Press, 1940 and 1983.

Plutarch. "Advice to Bride and Groom" (*Mor.* 138 B–146A) and "The Dinner of the Seven Wise Men" (*Mor.* 146B–164D). Translated by F. C. Babbitt In Plutarch's *Moralia*, vol. 2. LCL. Cambridge: Harvard University Press, 1962.

Plutarch. *Coriolanus*. Translated by B. Perrin. LCL. New York: Putnam, 1916.

Virgil. *Aeneid*. Translated by H. R. Fairclough. LCL. New rev. ed. Cambridge: Harvard University Press, 1986.

60. Nietzsche, "On the Genealogy of Morality," #7 & 8, Pearson and Large, eds., *The Nietzsche Reader*, 394–95: "[T]he slaves' revolt in morality begins with the Jews: a revolt which has two thousand years of history behind it . . . This Jesus of Nazareth, as the embodiment of the gospel of love, this 'redeemer' bringing salvation and victory to the poor, the sick, to sinners—was he not seduction . . . to just those very *Jewish* values . . . ?" (italics in original); Nietzsche, "The Greek State": "[W]e must learn to identify as a cruel-sounding truth the fact that *slavery belongs to the essence of a culture*" (*The Nietzsche Reader*, 90; italics in original). See Figal, "Nietzsche, Friedrich," 171–74. My essay above argues, however, that key values in the Magnificat and the *kenosis* hymn are Greco-Roman (see n. 35). Dionysius is a Greek writing on Roman origins.

61. I thank my friend F. E. Brenk, SJ, for critical suggestions, which does not mean, of course, that he becomes responsible for my theses.

Modern Authors

Attridge, Harold W. *The Epistle to the Hebrews*. Hermeneia. Philadelphia: Fortress, 1989.

Balch, David L. *Contested Ethnicities and Images: Studies in Acts and Art*. WUNT 345. Tübingen: Mohr Siebeck, 2015.

———. *Let Wives be Submissive: The Domestic Code in 1 Peter*. SBLMS 26. Chico, CA: Scholars, 1981.

———. "Political Friendship in the Historian Dionysius of Halicarnassus, *Roman Antiquities*." In *Greco-Roman Perspectives on Friendship*, edited by John T. Fitzgerald, 123–45. Resources for Biblical Study 34. Atlanta: Scholars, 1997. Republished in Balch, *Contested Ethnicities and Images*, chap. 6.

Bragantini, I. "Triclinio C." in *La Villa della Farnesina: in Palazzo Massimo alle Terme*, edited by M. R. Sanzi Di Mino, 46–55, with Figs. 50–67. Soprintendenza archeologica di Roma. Milan: Electa, 1998.

Brenk, F. E. Review of *Prüfstein der Gemüter: Untersuchungen zu den ethischen Vorstellungen in den Parallelbiographien Plutarchs am Beispiel des Coriolan*, by B. Ahlrichs. *Gnomon* 79 (2007) 751–53.

Briggs, Sheila. "Can an Enslaved God Liberate? Hermeneutical Reflections on Philippians 2:6–11." *Semeia* 47 (1989) 137–53.

Brilliant, Richard. *Gesture and Rank in Roman Art: The Use of Gestures to Denote Status in Roman Sculpture and Coinage*. Memoirs of the Connecticut Academy of Arts & Sciences 14. New Haven: The Academy, 1963, with 479 Figs.

Braun, Willi. *Feasting and Social Rhetoric in Luke 14*. SNTSMS 85. Cambridge: Cambridge University, 1995.

Brown, Raymond E. *The Birth of the Messiah: A Commentary on the Infancy Narratives in the Gospels of Matthew and Luke*. New updated ed. New York: Doubleday, 1993.

Büchsel, F. "ἱκετηρία." In *TDNT*, edited by G. Kittel and G. Friedrich, translated by G. W. Bromiley, 3:296–97. Grand Rapids: Eerdmans, 1985.

Eder, W. "Coriolanus, Marcius C." *Brill's New Pauly* 3 (2003) 804.

Epp, Eldon J. *Junia: The First Woman Apostle*. Minneapolis: Fortress, 2005.

Figal, G. "Nietzsche, Friedrich." In *Religion Past and Present: Encyclopedia of Theology and Religion*, edited by Hans Dieter Betz et al., 9:171–74. Boston: Brill, 2011.

Freyburger, Gerard. "La supplicatio d'action de graces sous le Haut-Empire." In *ANRW* 16/2: *Principat* (1978) 1418–39.

———. "Supplication grecque et supplication romaine." *Latomus* 47 (1988) 501–25, with plates V–X, containing figs. 1–8.

Gabelmann, Hanns. *Antike Audienz- und Tribunalszenen*. Darmstadt: Wissenschaftliche Buchgesellschaft, 1984.

Graf, F. "Fortuna." In *Brill's New Pauly* 5 (2004) 505–9.

Halkin, Leon. *La supplication d'action de graces chez les Romains*. Paris: Les Belles lettres, 1953.

Harrison, J. R. "The Imitation of the 'Great Man' in Antiquity: Paul's Inversion of a Cultural Icon." In *Christian Origins and Greco-Roman Culture: Social and Literary Contexts for the New Testament*, edited by Stanley E. Porter and A. W. Pitts, 213–54. Texts and Editions for New Testament Study 9. Leiden: Brill, 2013.

Heen, Erik M. "Phil 2:6–11 and Resistance to Local Timocratic Rule: *Isa theo* and the Cult of the Emperor in the East." In *Paul and the Roman Imperial Order*, edited by Richard A. Horsley, 125–53. Harrisburg, PA: Trinity, 2004.

Hengel, Martin "Maria Magdalena und die Frauen als Zeugen." In *Abraham unser Vater: Festschrift für Otto Michel*, edited by O. Betz, M. Hengel, and P. Schmidt, 243–56. Leiden: Brill, 1963.

Heschel, Susannah. *The Aryan Jesus: Christian Theologians and the Bible in Nazi Germany*. Princeton: Princeton University, 2008.

Hock, Ronald F. "The Problem of Paul's Social Class: Further Reflections." In *Paul's World*, edited by Stanley E. Porter, 7–18. Pauline Studies 4. Leiden: Brill, 2000.

Koch, Dietrich-Alex. "Exkurs 4: Verdrängt Maria Magdalena—die eigentliche Empfängerin der ersten Erscheinung der Auferstandenen?" In *Geschichte des Urchristenbtums: Ein Lehrbuch*, 541–45. Göttingen: Vandenhoeck & Ruprecht, 2013.

Lewis, I. M. *Ecstatic Religion: An Anthropological Study of Spirit Possession and Shamanism*. 2nd ed. London: Routledge, 1989.

Liddell, H. G., and R. Scott, revised H. S. Jones and R. McKenzie. *A Greek-English Lexicon*. Oxford: Clarendon, 1996, s.v. ἱκεσία and ἱκετεία.

Lieu, Judith. "The 'Attraction of Women in/to Early Judaism and Christianity: Gender and the Politics of Conversion." In *Neither Jew nor Greek? Constructing Early Christianity*, 83–99. London: T. & T. Clark, 2002. Originally published in JSNT 72 (1998) 5–22.

Milnor, Kristina. *Gender, Domesticity, and the Age of Augustus: Inventing Private Life*. Oxford: Oxford University, 2005.

Mols, S. T. A. M., and E. M. Moormann. *La villa della farnesina: le pitture*. Milan: Electa, 2008, 2012.

Naiden, F. S. *Ancient Supplication*. Oxford: Oxford University, 2006.

Nilsson, M. P. *Greek Popular Religion*. New York: Harper, 1961.

Osiek, Carolyn, and David L. Balch. *Families in the New Testament World: Households and House Churches*. Family, Religion, and Culture. Louisville: Westminster John Knox, 1997.

Patterson, J. R. "Via Latina." In *Lexicon Topographicum Urbis Romae*, ed. E.M. Steinby 5 (1999): 141, with Figs. I, 38, 67; III, 190; and V, 83. Rome: Quasar, 1993.

Pearson, Keith Ansell, and Duncan Large, eds. *The Nietzsche Reader*. Oxford: Blackwell, 2006.

Pelling, C. "The Shaping of Coriolanus: Dionysius, Plutarch and Shakespeare." In *Plutarch and History: Eighteen Studies*, 387–411. London: Duckworth, 2002.

Reynolds, B. "'What Is the City but the People?': Transversal Performance and Radical Politics in Shakespeare's *Coriolanus* and Brecht's *Coriolan*." In *Shakespeare without Class: Misappropriations of Cultural Capital*, edited by D. Hedrick and B. Reynolds, 107–33. New York: Palgrave, 2000.

Russell, D. A. "Plutarch's Life of Coriolanus." *JRS* 53 (1963) 21–28.

Rutledge, S. H. *Ancient Rome as a Museum: Power, Identity, and the Culture of Collecting*. Oxford Studies in Ancient Culture and Representation. Oxford: Oxford University, 2012.

Sanzi Di Mino, M. R., ed., with articles by I. Bragantini, A. M. Dolciotti, and M. R. Sanzi Di Mino. *La Villa della Farnesina: in Palazzo Massimo alle Terme*. Soprintendenza archeologica di Roma. Milan: Electa, 1998.

Schottroff, Luisa. *Lydia's Impatient Sisters: A Feminist Social History of Early Christianity*. Translated by Barbara and Martin Rumscheidt. Louisville: Westminster John Knox, 1995.

Schultze, Clemence Elizabeth. "Dionysius of Halicarnassus as a Historian: An Investigation of His Aims and Methods in the *Antiquitates Romanae*." PhD diss., Oxford University, 1980.

Seim, Turid Karlsen. *The Double Message: Patterns of Gender in Luke–Acts*. Nashville: Abingdon, 1994.

Siebert, A. V. "Supplicatio." In *Brill's New Pauly* 13 (2008) 955.

"ταπεινός." In *TDNT*, edited by G. Kittel and G. Friedrich, translated by G. W. Bromiley, 8:1–26. Grand Rapids: Eerdmans, 1985.[62]

Theissen, Gerd. *The Religion of the Earliest Churches: Creating a Symbolic World*. Translated by John Bowden. Minneapolis: Fortress, 1999.

Ungern-Sternberg, J. von. "The Formation of the 'Annalistic Tradition': the Example of the Decemvirate." In *Social Struggles in Archaic Rome*, edited by K. A. Raaflaub, 77–104. Berkeley: University of California, 1986. Also in an expanded and updated edition: Oxford: Blackwell, 2005, pp. 75–97.

"ὕψος, ὑψόω." In *TDNT*, edited by G. Kittel and G. Friedrich, translated by G. W. Bromiley, 8:602–20. Grand Rapids: Eerdmans, 1985.[63]

Villard, L., and F. Rausa. "Tyche/Fortuna." In *Lexicon Iconographicum Mythologiae Classicae*, 8/1:115–25, 125–40; and 8/2:85–89, 90–109. Zurich: Artemis, 1981.

Walker, Jeffrey. *The Genuine Teachers of this Art: Rhetorical Education in Antiquity*. Studies in Rhetoric/Communication. Columbia: University of South Carolina Press, 2011.

Wiater, Nicolas. *The Ideology of Classicism: Language, History, and Identity in Dionysius of Halicarnassus*. Untersuchungen zur antiken Literatur und Geschichte 105. Berlin: de Gruyter, 2011.

---

62. I refuse to pollute my manuscript by naming the Nazi who wrote this article. See Heschel, *The Aryan Jesus*, e.g., chap. 2 on "the Institute for the Study and Eradication of Jewish Influence on German Church Life, 1939–1942."

63. This author too was a Nazi, so I do not print his name. See Heschel, *The Aryan Jesus*, 162–63, 174–75, 242–43, 275–76.

19

Seeds of Violence or Buds of Peace?

Faith Resources for Creating a New Peace Consciousness and Culture

Ursula King

In recent years increasing attention has been given to the potential connections between religion and violence, especially since the growth of international terrorism. A whole new field of studies on religion and violence has come into existence.[1] Violent incidents have occurred within very different religions and cultures, so that the question arises of how far religious teachings and practices fuel violent action. Some argue that increasing global violence has nothing to do with religion, but is caused by political and economic factors, whereas others take the view that religion is part of the problem of violence, therefore religion must also be part of finding a solution for overcoming violence.

Some years ago, I remember taking part in debating a motion at an international conference that "interreligious unity and peace are impossible," since religions divide people more than unite them, due to their different truth claims, their different ways of life, their support of ethnic and religious antagonisms, and also due to some of their teachings which can promote hatred, conflict, even violence and war. Scholars have particularly pointed to the intransigence of monotheistic religions where the outsiders, the "others," are often seen as being in error; they are therefore *either* excluded by

---

1. See de Vries, *Religion and Violence: Philosophical Perspectives from Kant to Derrida*; Murphy, ed., *The Blackwell Companion to Religion and Violence*; Juergensmeyer et al., *The Oxford Handbook of Religion and Violence*. Some parts of this essay draw on earlier discussions in King, "Reflections on Peace, Women, and the World Faiths."

force *or* included by force, through conversion. If there exists a phenomenon of religious violence, we have to analyse it in detail, examine and explain its causes, find its perpetrators and victims, but we also need to enquire what resources religions possess for overcoming violence and transforming violent into non-violent behaviour. Given the growing militarisation around the world, the ever more refined technological possibilities of destroying lives, property and the environment, the increasing occurrence of numerous regional conflicts and wars, the growing nuclear capability to extinguish life on earth, peace is no longer an optional alternative to violence, but it takes on the character of an urgent imperative, an absolute necessity, if humanity and the planet are to have a viable future at all.

Before I explore how a contemporary engagement with the world's faiths can make an important, in fact essential, contribution to creating peace, I will first examine the legitimation of violence in religion, then look at seeds for peace-making in different faiths, followed by reflections on women's commitment to, and work for, the creation of peace.

Seeds of Violence

More than ten years ago the eminent British historian Eric Hobsbawm (1917–2012) argued in the British newspaper *The Guardian* that the past 100 years have changed the nature of war, that the world as a whole has not been at peace since 1914, is not at peace now, and that the prospect of peace in the twenty-first century is remote. The twentieth century has been called the most murderous century in history: an estimated 187 million people have died in the numerous terrible wars since 1914. That is the equivalent of more than 10% of the world's population in 1913. Interstate wars used to dominate in the past, but international wars have now declined whereas the number of conflicts within state frontiers has risen sharply and the burden of war has increasingly shifted from armed forces to civilians. Hobsbawm writes that only 5% of those who died during World War I were civilians whereas this figure increased to 66% during World War II; it is estimated that 80–90% of those affected by war today are civilians.[2] According to another source,[3] of the 101 conflicts that occurred between 1989–1996, only six were interstate wars and all the others were territorial, tribal intra-state wars. Moreover, 80% of the countries that are at war, train children as soldiers. How can we ever achieve peace?

2. Hobsbawm, "War and Peace," *The Guardian,* 23 February 2002. The statistics are taken from Hobsbawm's article.

3. Worldwatch pamphlet, *Small Arms, Big Impacts*, 34.

To quote from Brian Wicker's article on "War" in *The Oxford Companion to Christian Thought*: "the more organized society becomes the more complex its wars, which naturally follow the cultural, religious, political, and technological conditions of the time. Nowadays these conditions make war potentially suicidal for humanity. Christians in the past have only interpreted war. But today the point is to prevent it."[4] In other words, peace is simply no longer an option; it is an *imperative*.

At present numerous individuals, groups and institutions are working to overcome and abolish war. Yet how often has the cry "Never again war!" been uttered without any effect. More than ever before do we desperately need a new peace consciousness and culture in the contemporary world. The attainment of greater peace, of conflict resolution in non-violent rather than violent ways, will only be possible if we put our mind and heart to it—if we will want to make it happen. And that will require tremendous effort and much work. Much rethinking, in fact, which involves a development of both new ideas and practices. Is it not disturbing that Christian theology knows a well-developed theory of just war, but it has no fully articulated theology of peace? Where to find seeds for making peace?

Initially it seems that the different religions create more hatred, conflict and violence than bring peace. How many battles, persecutions and wars are not due to religious factors and fanaticism, not only on September 11th, but throughout all of history? Think of the many ethnic and religious antagonisms which fuel nationalism and breed violence—antagonisms rooted in rival claims to exclusive truth and to the superiority of one faith and culture over another. We can think of the crusades, the wars of religion in Europe, the pogroms, the persecutions, the teachings on holy and just war to remind ourselves that religions provide one of the sources for conflict, bloodshed and wars. Not only today, but throughout history, religions have helped people to conceive the very idea of war in their minds and have encouraged them to wage war; religious leaders go on blessing and sanctifying war, even though such warring is in blatant contradiction to a universalist ethic about the sisterhood and brotherhood of all people. How many political leaders appeal even today to religious beliefs and sacred symbols to rally the support of their people and encourage them to participate in state-organized violence. Even Stalin in an atheistic communist state appealed during the World War II to the Orthodox Church to rally the whole population into supporting the Soviet war effort.

If we need a new peace culture, what can religions contribute to it? For many contemporary peace activists religions may seem irrelevant or more

---

4. Wicker, "War," 746; and Wicker, "Pacifism," 508–9.

of a hindrance than a help. Yet the different faiths continue to provide many ethical and spiritual explanations of human existence and a vision of what ought to be; they offer systems of beliefs and practices which nourish and strengthen life and can help to build up the human community. The question then is: how do religions relate to the existence of violence and hatred? How do they explain the origin of violence and legitimate its use, especially in organised forms of war?

Throughout history people have sought meaning by seeking explanations through either *mythos* or *logos,* through the use of stories or through rational explanations. Religious explanations exist at widely varying levels and can range from myths, legends and folklore to highly developed metaphysical speculations. However, religious explanations are by and large of a different kind than those of scientific rational discourse. We must therefore be aware of two difficulties when drawing on the sources of religion: first, we often strive for different kinds of explanation than religious sources can provide; secondly, we often seek answers to particular problems today which are without exact precedents in earlier ages. We have to acknowledge these difficulties and cannot expect to find in ancient religious teachings fully developed answers to our contemporary problems of global violence. Yet we can find many *seeds* or *resources* in the teachings of the world's faiths which can make an important contribution to our present-day thinking about developing a more effective peace consciousness and culture.

The religious diagnosis of the human condition includes numerous myths and stories to explain the origin of evil, suffering, conflicts and aggression. The existing plurality of competing, even contradictory, religious worldviews with their absolute, mutually exclusive truth claims are a genuine source of profound tensions which can lead to violence and war. One of the most extreme forms of violence which human beings inflict on each other is the deliberate killing of other fellow beings, especially in war. Some argue that religion is only superficially responsible for this, and that the real reason for any military aggression is the difference in political and economic power and the competitive struggle for chronically scarce resources. But there can be little doubt that religions have played a very significant role in war, and religious justifications for violent actions have been legion. Far from abolishing wars, religions have integrated them into their symbolic universe by ritualising and even absolutising war. The Christian pacifist John Ferguson wrote an insightful study on *War and Peace in the World's Religions* wherein he came to the conclusion that while Christianity and Buddhism have been the most clearly pacifist religions in their origins and essence, both have been deeply involved with militarism from an early stage in their history. By contrast, Zoroastrianism, Islam and Shinto have been clearly militarist in their origins and essence, and yet they have also produced figures of reconciliation and peace. He writes of Christianity: "The historical association of the Christian faith with nations of commercial enterprise, imperialistic expansion and technological advancement has meant that Christian peoples, although their faith is one of the most pacific in its origins, have a record of military activity second to none."[5]

The Dominican Roger Ruston has argued that in a sense war itself is a religious phenomenon which feeds on the symbols of existing religions. This is due to the religious words and emotions connected with the supreme value of blood sacrifice, and there exists "a deep confusion between the goals of the nation at war and the purposes of God." He writes:

> War itself has a kinship with religion in what it demands of people and the way it heightens religious feelings. It does something to people which churches are always supposed to be trying to do: to promote selflessness and courage, to take people out of themselves and their own little designs and make them live for something greater . . . It gives them an absolute, a totally demanding cause which relativises even life itself. People experience what has been accurately called 'the false transcendence of violence.'[6]

Ruston also argues that while Christian teaching originally introduced a desacralisation of war into human history, the wars of the twentieth century have progressively brought about a new *re-sacralisation* of war through the rise of nationalist passions and new absolutes.

A well-known example of the close association of religion and war is the Islamic notion of *jihad,* often identified with the idea of a holy war. However, the original meaning of *jihad* is "striving"; the word is used to describe human effort and striving for the way of God. Eventually four types of *jihad* were distinguished, performed with the human heart, tongue, hands and the sword. The first kind of *jihad* refers to the personal fight against evil, whereas the *jihad* of tongue and hands can be that of preaching and persuasion, of the support of what is right and the correction of what is wrong. The fourth *jihad* means war against unbelievers and enemies of the faith, and this meaning has become widely dominant. It is almost universally agreed that *jihad* is a collective obligation and not an individual one; the Qur'an explicitly states that not all believers should actively engage in war. There is also a tradition of interpreting *jihad* in a spiritual sense, especially among Sufis who understand it as the purification and conquest of the self. So there

---

5. Ferguson, *War and Peace in the World's Religions,* 122.

6. Roger Ruston, *War of Religions, Religion of War,* 1993, 5 & 6.

is a movement away from the lesser *jihad* to the greater *jihad* where the inner conquest is considered to be a greater struggle than the conquest of external enemies. The Muslim Ahmadiyya movement sees the test of *jihad* in the willingness to suffer, not in the practice of warfare; its very essence is the active concern for the oppressed.

Among Christians there have been three different historical responses to war, radical pacifism until Christianity became a state religion, the formulation of the just-war theory, taken over from Cicero and articulated by St Ambrose, St Augustine and St Thomas of Aquinas, the idea of the crusade which emerged during the Middle Ages and was much influenced by the Hebrew concept of a holy war. The New Testament, so obviously more oriented towards peace than war, has been used as a justification for all three Christian responses to war—pacifism, just-war and crusade. No major Christian Church or denomination has been consistently pacifist and Christian pacifism has been largely confined to small groups such as the Quakers, Anabaptists, Mennonites, Brethren and Jehovah's Witnesses. Pacifists within the churches have in times of war been barely tolerated by their fellow Christians. Conscientious objection or the refusal to give military service is treated by the larger contemporary churches as a matter of individual conscience rather than as a fundamental issue of the Christian community.[7]

The Hebrew Bible, which became the Old Testament for Christians, celebrates in many stories the works of a warrior God and his holy war against the enemies of his people, proclaiming God's kingship and sovereignty over the whole world. This is a world where history is a struggle and where the coming of peace is promised for messianic times, an eschatological hope to be realised in the future. It has been said that

> An attentive reading of the Old Testament reveals that . . . no other activity or condition occurs more often than violence. More than six hundred passages deal explicitly with peoples, kings or other individuals attacking and killing others; about one thousand texts speak of God's wrath which often punishes people with death and annihilation; and there are over a hundred instances in which God is said to order the killing of people.[8]

However, our contemporary experience and acts of violence are quite different in character from the violent actions of ancient Near Eastern peoples described in the Bible. Biblical texts, as well as those from the scriptures

---

7. See Gill, *Theology and Social Structure,* 37; and also Wicker's article on "Pacifism."

8. Hendrickx, *A Time for Peace,* 39.

of other religions, have to be interpreted within their specific historical and cultural contexts so different from our own. Religious institutions have often constrained tendencies to violence through the emergence of the ideal of social justice and through preaching universal values.

Traditionally the participation in certain religious rites has helped individuals to develop not only courage in general, but also the special kind of courage needed to commit violent acts. From this point of view the religious blessings bestowed on warriors and armies through the ages have been of the greatest significance in fostering the psychological acceptance of what appears as the legitimate use of violent force in war. Equally important is the perception of the enemy as the "demonic other"—the "alien" outside the boundaries of one's own social and religious group, the enemy of God, the representative of a false doctrine, the agent of most hideous crimes. Bruce Lincoln speaks of the "lethal redefinition" of the victim by the killer and the community that passes judgement upon the other as something less than human—a monster, beast, animal, even rotting matter such as "garbage" and "trash." Verbal abuse regularly accompanies such redefinition which establishes that the effecting of death of such an individual (or of whole groups of people) is a permissible, even worthy act. But the same author also perceptively points to the final paradox of this pattern of violence: whilst one must dehumanise one's enemies in order to employ violence against them, one must at the same time dehumanise oneself to become an instrument of slaughter, eradicating such tendencies as guilt, fear and compassion.[9]

Such perceptions of the "demonic other" had fewer implications when armed conflicts could be contained locally or nationally. Tendencies toward conflict and aggression have been seen as part of human nature, as part of the mysterious and inexplicable existence of evil within and without, and thus the use of organised force and violence in war has been reckoned to be almost inevitable.

This brief account shows that the different religious traditions have provided a great store of mythical and metaphysical explanations to account for the origin and existence of evil in its different forms, for the violent conflicts and struggles that beset human beings and societies. At the same time religious institutions have been implicated in aggression and conflicts through legitimising state violence and wars, especially in societies where the religious and political elites are drawn from the same class and share identical interests. While many other ideological factors than religious ones may be important in modern warfare, certain political leaders still continue to appeal to religious beliefs and images to rally support and create a

9. See Lincoln, "War and Warriors: An Overview," 9679–83.

consensus among their people for a war effort. The close associations of religion with war in past and present is one of the strongest proofs for showing
that religion buttresses the existing social order. Yet there has always existed
a tension in religion between giving this support whilst also providing a
prophetic critique that challenges the existing order through a vision of a
higher morality, a greater unity and universal values which transcend the
boundaries of one's own group. What are some of these alternatives which
may foster greater harmony and cooperation among humankind? Where
are the much needed seeds for peace, even when they still remain primarily
in buds? How can we draw on religious resources to promote peace-making?

Religious Resources for Peace-making

Besides the numerous seeds for violence, the human community also possesses an extraordinarily rich religious heritage on peace. This represents a
tremendous resource for developing the art of peace-making—if we only
practised what we preach. The world's religions possess countless seeds for
nurturing attitudes of peace, seeds which we can make grow to flourish if we
tend them with love and care and learn about each other's faiths and traditions. The soteriological vision of all religions, the promise of final salvation
and release, implies a transcendent vision of unity, harmony and wellbeing
that is grounded in a profound hope for peace. This vision should empower
us not only to desire peace as an eschatological goal, but to work ardently for
and achieve genuine peace in our global world today.

But what is peace? Too often our understanding of peace is too fragmentary, more defined by the absence of war than by a more positive content. This is too meagre and uninspiring a vision, for most religions know of
the *fullness of peace* as something that permeates all of life and transforms
it in a profound sense. Peace can be seen as external to the human being,
as something created by socio-economic and political conditions, by human groups and institutions. Yet, most importantly, peace is also an inner
state of the human spirit that can be cultivated and nurtured; here especially the spiritual teachings of different faiths have much to contribute. For
contemporary peace work and peace education we need a holistic vision of
peace which embraces both our inner and outer life, the state we experience
personally within ourselves together with the state of the world we live in.

In the development of peace studies and peace education perhaps not
enough attention is given to these spiritual resources of the world faiths for
learning how to work for more peace. The religious and spiritual resources
for peace-making are so large and varied that they deserve the closest study.

But much of this still remains to be undertaken since little of this heritage is widely known.[10] The human community is extraordinarily rich in spiritual resources which include a vast religious heritage on peace that represents a tremendous reservoir for the art of peace-making.

Religious visions of peace imply profound personal and social transformations which include questions of equity and justice as well as inner harmony and compassion. The striving for peace is today strongly associated with the notion of nonviolence, a term which only came into general English usage in the early twentieth century through its association with Gandhi and his non-violent approach to resolving conflicts.[11] The idea of non-violence—*ahimsa*—stems primarily from the religious traditions of India, although injunctions against taking human life can virtually be found in every religious tradition. Like nonviolence, pacifism is also a modern word and an idea defined as "the advocacy of peace at any price."[12] But the idea of peace can be documented from ancient times, and many examples of peace-making by different individuals and groups of the past could be cited.

Peace is truly *the* major issue today. Humanity's yearning for peace is greater than ever before, yet we seem to live in a permanent state of war and violence. Since 9/11, the twenty-first century search for peace and the overcoming of violent military attacks are primarily associated with combating world terrorism, whereas in the second half of the twentieth century working for peace mainly meant fighting communism and averting the danger of nuclear war. While the fear of the latter may have receded for some time, the immense threat of nuclear contamination has now come to the fore again since the recent earthquake in Japan with its impact on a major nuclear power station.

Seeking, finding, and making peace is widely connected with meditation and prayer practices. For example, since ancient times Hindu prayers have included the invocation "*om, shanti, shanti, shanti*," the thrice-repeated prayer for peace which invokes tranquillity, quiet, calmness of mind, and absence of passions. In both Hinduism and Buddhism it is important for the individual to be at peace, but the practice of peace has social implications

10. A useful starting point is Gordon and Grob, *Education for Peace. Testimonies from World Religions.* A helpful collection from just one religious tradition is found in Chappell, *Buddhist Peacework: Creating Cultures of Peace.* Many other examples exist, but a comprehensive survey goes beyond the scope of this article.

11. The *Oxford English Dictionary Supplement* (OED) has no entry on non-violence, but lists the first usage of "non-violent" for 1924 in a book associated with Gandhi.

12. The *OED Supplement* lists the first usage of "pacifism" in a French speech of 1901.

too. The Buddhist tradition teaches an important meditation on loving kindness (*metta*) which begins with kindness and concern for oneself, followed by developing loving kindness first towards a friend, then towards a person one is indifferent to, then towards someone one feels an antipathy against, and finally one's feelings should expand slowly to include all persons in the world and all beings throughout the whole of space and time.

This meditation practice is based on the belief in the interdependence of all sentient beings in the universe, a state of harmony which is not simply given, but has to be attained and worked for. To strive for loving kindness implies that human beings transform their hate into love, and abstain from any desire to commit acts of violence. To be truly nonviolent is to adopt the mode of love over that of power, and thereby live in the spirit of joy and light. There are numerous rules that regulate social behaviour in the Buddhist precepts and scriptures. The call for peace is nothing short of a call for the transformation of the world. Buddhism teaches that if we desire peace to be realized in the world, we must first find it within. It is indicative that a Thai journal published by Buddhist activists is called *Seeds of Peace*.

The Hebrew Bible contains many stories of wars, yet some of the great deliverances, such as that of the Israelites from Egypt, were achieved without violence, and the idea of peace runs throughout the Hebrew scriptures where the word peace—*shalom*—is found 249 times. It comes from a root meaning "wholeness" and thus is richer in meaning than our word "peace." *Shalom* is also very prominent in the Rabbinic tradition where it stands for truth, justice and peace. It is said that the Torah was given to make peace in the world and one of God's names is peace. *Shalom* refers to both spiritual and material conditions. Famous is the passage from the prophet Isaiah 2:2–4 describing how the Lord will gather all nations together in peace when peoples "will hammer their swords into ploughshares, their spears into sickles," and "nation will not lift sword against nation, there will be no more training for war."

The images used by Isaiah to describe peace were interpreted by later traditions as being of three kinds: the peace of the river, of the bird and of the cauldron. The fullest image is that of the river (referring to Is. 66:12), a state of being and a dynamic movement which carries with it the prosperity and love between peoples and with the Lord. The image of peace as a flying bird (Is. 31:5) is the peace which is obtained by preparing for war, by maintaining an armed force to keep off, intimidate and destroy the enemy in order to protect and save the people. The Lord watches over his people like the bird spreading its wings to protect its young. One has to be vigilant because evil is near—this is a diminished *shalom* indeed. An even more desperate and diminished kind of peace is that associated with the image of the cauldron (Is. 26:11–12), a fragile peace full of anguish where divine power is poured out to the detriment of the enemy like a boiling cauldron and where one has to save one's skin and possessions. Discussing these three kinds of peace Armand Abecassis maintains

> There is the peace that comes when violence, injustice and trouble are happening to someone else; there is the peace that comes from the power to intimidate and prevent others from harming us; finally there is *Shalom* imaged in the river that unites, enriches and fulfils the whole human race. Peace that is just the absence of war, or the peace that exists in a cemetery are not the *Shalom* that comes into being when men and women strive to love each other and to see in every human person a reflection of the infinitely loving and life-giving God.[13]

For the ancient Hebrews peace was a social concept; it applied to harmonious relationships within the family, local society and between nations. The greeting "*shalom*," used since the time of the Judges and King David, expressed the positive aim of encouraging cooperation. Related to the Hebrew "*shalom*" is the Arabic "*salaam*," the greeting "peace be with you," which has been used as a salutation and blessing among Muslims since the time of the Qur'an. "*Salaam*" again means more than our "peace"; it extends to contentment, good health, prosperity, security, fullness of life. Contrary to the western view which associates Islam with military power, Muslims understand Islam to be the religion of peace, for the Qur'an sees peace as the will of Allah whom it describes as "the King, the Holy, the Peaceable." Peace is a transcendent gift, but it is also present in personal relations and it is part of wise statesmanship. Historical examples from the time of the Prophet and later show that Islam has often been a considerable instrument of peace in different parts of the world.

Christians too, in spite of their violent history and theory of just war, have a strong tradition of peace grounded in the *Sermon on the Mount*: "Blessed are the peacemakers, for they shall be called sons of God" (Matt 5:9). Jesus's parting message to John was, "Peace I leave with you, my peace I give you, not as the world gives it" (John 14:27). Christian pacifists have been inspired by Jesus's own example and what one might call the *bias to peace* in the Christian gospel. The church applied the title "Prince of Peace," first used for the Davidic king in the Hebrew Bible, to Jesus, and the Christian liturgy often repeats the word "The peace of the Lord be always with you." The contemporary Christian peace movement uses the Bible as a

---

13. See Abecassis, "Three Kinds of Peace: Shalom-Shelomot." The quotation is from the English edition entitled *Violence and Peace,* 14.

teacher of peace, drawing particularly on Jesus's saying "love your enemies" (Mt. 5:44; Lk. 6:27) and on the Sermon on the Mount. Its insights have been directly applied to practical matters in the discussion of military politics by German peace campaigners, whose call for peace based on a new politics of the Sermon of the Mount raised widespread debate.[14] This debate was influential in the abolition of the communist regime in former East Germany, and in the movement for the reunification of Germany. Here we have an example of using Christian religious ideas as a resource for contemporary peace thinking and action, just as Gandhi drew on the resources of the Indian tradition in developing his practice of nonviolent action in situations of conflict, or the Muslim Abdul Ghaffar Khan from Afghanistan practised nonviolent resistance based on the Qur'an. In fact, we know of quite a few religiously inspired peacemakers: Gandhi, Martin Luther King, Desmond Tutu, Helder Camara and Oscar Romero, the Dalai Lama and Aung San Suu Kyi of Myanmar.

These pilgrims of peace who draw on the religious peace heritage of their own religious tradition show us that peace has to be willed and aimed for, that it can be attained through the transformation of one's mind and heart as well as one's actions. Working for peace can help us find contentment, equanimity and wellbeing. At its fullest and richest, peace is linked to the idea of perfection, of wholeness, of divine presence and the power of spirit—peace in that ultimate sense is considered a gift, a fruit of the spirit itself.

While most of us feel completely impotent with regard to international power politics, there is much we all can do to bring about a change of heart. The peace and ecological movement, the women's movement with its deep commitment toward acting and educating for peace, the many liberation movements to bring about social justice and eradicate debilitating poverty from our globe—all have a spiritual dimension and immense transformative potential for achieving "the art of living in peace" in the human community. Education for peace is promoted at many levels, from schools and universities devoted to peace to prayers for peace. There has been a World Conference on Religion and Peace in existence for many years, and there is an annual week of Prayer for World Peace supported by people from different faiths and groups.

So much can be done to promote peace at local, regional and international levels, and yet much more remains to be accomplished to eradicate violent conflicts from the earth. Peace is no longer simply an option, it has

---

14. One example of this is Franz Alt's influential book, *Frieden ist möglich*, of which well over 100,000 copies were sold in Germany.

become an urgent necessity that impels us to transcend collective violence and war among societies, tribal groups and states to create a new peace consciousness and culture in the world.

We have to learn how to relate peacefully to diversity and pluralism with their inherent tensions. We have to learn how to cope with the tremendous complexity of ourselves and the human community at the threshold of a new age. If we search deeply enough within the past, and within ourselves, we can find tremendous resources for change and renewal—resources for developing our interiority, awareness, sensibility, imagination and vision. The seeds of wisdom, knowledge and experience present in the great religious and philosophical traditions of our globe—all of which contain deep patterns of wholeness and harmony—can help us to discover a new action-oriented spirituality that can find and forge a new way ahead, a new harmonious way of being for the whole of humankind. This way does not exist as ready-made; it has to be created and presents a tremendous task that requires sincere dedication and will power as well as large human and material resources, and the creation of new organisations.

Efforts at Peace-making by Women and Other Groups

Women from different faiths and cultures are more in dialogue with each other than ever before; they are working together in new ways in many different fields. This is also true in the area of peace-making. Women have long been associated with peace-making, and countless women are active peace campaigners today. Peace was an important feminist issue right from the beginning of the modern women's movement and many women of faith, involved in campaigning for more peace in the world, have drawn on the seeds of peace present in their faith traditions.

Women's work for peace did not begin with modern feminism but has a long history. The first Women's Peace League in Europe was founded in 1854, but it is less well known than the Women's International League for Peace and Freedom (WILPF) which developed out of an International Women's Congress against World War I that took place in The Hague, the Netherlands, in 1915, although the name WILPF was not chosen until 1919. One of its founders, and its first president, was the sociologist and leader of women's suffrage, Jane Addams, the first American woman to be awarded the Nobel Peace Prize in 1931. The WILPF still exists today and is the oldest women's peace organisation.

Much later, from 1981 onwards, the Greenham Common Women's Peace Camp became internationally known for its protest at the siting of nuclear weapons at a Royal Air Force base in the south of England. The women remained at the site from 1981–2000; at the height of their campaign more than 30.000 women were present, and their vigorous campaign caught the imagination of people around the globe. There exists a large literature on women's involvement with countering violence and war by working for peace at local, regional and international levels. [15] Many remarkable organisational efforts exist today of which I can only briefly mention two. "Women in Black. For Justice. Against War" (WIB) is an international network that began in Israel in 1988 but now has active groups in many cities of the world. "Women in Black" was originally inspired by earlier movements of women demonstrating on the streets to create a public space for women to be heard, particularly Black Sash in South Africa, and the Madres de la Plaza de Mayo, seeking the "disappeared" in the political repression in Argentina. But WIB also shares a genealogy with women's groups who explicitly refuse violence, militarism and war, such as the much older Women's International League for Peace and Freedom, and the more recent Greenham Common Women's Camp in England. The WIB London group meets every Wednesday evening to hold their weekly one-hour silent vigil for peace with justice near Trafalgar Square, in front of the statue for Edith Cavell, the British nurse who was shot by the Germans in Brussels during the First World War. "Women in Black" are now found in many different countries and continents.[16]

Another women's group of special interest is the "Nobel Women's Initiative" established in 2006 by Nobel Peace Laureates Jody Williams, Shirin Ebadi, Wangari Maathai, Rigoberta Menchu Tum, Betty Williams and Mairead Corrigan-Maguire to bring together their extraordinary experiences in a united effort for peace with justice and equality.

The American Quaker and peace-maker Elise Boulding (1920–2010) worked for many years toward creating a new culture of peace to replace the violent culture of war. She promoted workshops on alternative visions of the future where participants learnt to imagine a world without war or weapons, a world that is peaceful, so as to become empowered to change the situation around them. Only if we take the peace imperative absolutely seriously can we survive as a global community. Since the violent events of 9/11 that shook the world, this has become more urgent than ever.

15. I have written at greater length on this in my book *Women and Spirituality*; see the section on "Power, peace, non-violence and ecology," 199–211. See also the resources on the worldwide web on "Peace, Conflicts and International Women's Human Rights" and "Women's Peace Organisations."

16. See http://womeninblack.org/old/es/history.

Today, at a crucial turning point in history, women feel a very special responsibility for the continuity of life on earth, for the lives of their children and all future generations to come, as also for the life of the whole Earth. This is visible in many women's movements, and especially in the contemporary ecofeminist movement. In their demonstrations for peace, women often use innovative visionary action such as threading webs, lighting candles, planting tombstones, making puppets of mourning and rage. Such symbolic gestures based on hope and faith are meant to indicate a change of orientation and values. But how effective will these be in solving the world's troubles? Are they merely the dreams of powerless passive resisters, or are they potent signs of prophets whose vision will shape a different world for tomorrow?

Current levels of violence and wars of destruction may easily feed a profound pessimism. But there exist also many signs of hope that encourage changes of direction and new ventures, giving us grounds for believing that it is still possible to make our world a more peaceful place. Elise Boulding has argued that peace-making is an evolutionary capacity in the human species, that we possess the capacity to develop a peaceful social order, but that it will only be created with great effort. She describes this evolutionary transformation as

> consisting of a growing awareness that we live on a tiny planet, and that technology and power alone cannot ensure peace and justice on that planet, nor control or eliminate violence and war. The dimension of human caring has entered the public domain, and the need to understand the Other, the different, is beginning to be acknowledged as a condition for human problem-solving.[17]

A new vision of peace is integral to many other contemporary statements and documents, some of which draw explicitly on religious ideas. Robert Muller (1923–2010), Under-Secretary-General of the United Nations for forty years, called already long ago for a "new genesis" within humanity, based on a "global spirituality."[18] He suggested we need to develop a new set of commandments that must include "You shall never kill a human brother or sister, not even in the name of a nation"; in fact, he speaks of "the right not to kill and not to be killed, not even in the name of a nation."[19]

17. Boulding, "Peace Making as an Evolutionary Capacity"; and Boulding, "Learning Peace," 317–29.

18. Muller, *New Genesis*.

19. Muller, *The Birth of a Global Civilization*, 136, 78.

Some perceptive contemporaries are wondering whether humans as a species can really evolve the capacity for true peace-making, not the kind of peace achieved at the end of a war or as an intermittent period between wars, but peace as a *new form of life*. That would be a new wholeness whereby peace would become an imperative that would make all war immoral. As long ago as 1982 Muller argued that

> there is even more reason to eradicate armaments from this planet than there was to eradicate smallpox. All conceivable files and proposals for disarmament are ready. They have been painstakingly worked out over the last three decades. All depends on the will of peoples and nations, especially the big nations who bear the main responsibility in this matter. [20]

Another powerful testimony to the search for greater peace are the efforts of the German theologian Hans Küng. In 1991 he published his book *Global Responsibility: In Search of a New World Ethic*,[21] which concluded with a powerful appeal to peace, often quoted since:

> No human life together without a world ethic for the nations; no peace among the nations without peace among the religions; no peace among the religions without dialogue among the religions.[22]

Küng's efforts were decisive in creating the *Declaration Toward a Global Ethic*[23] promulgated by the Parliament of the World's Religions in Chicago in 1993. This document expresses a strong commitment to a culture of nonviolence and respect for life, summed up in the categorical statement "There is no survival for humanity without global peace!"[24]

This commitment was reiterated in the principles of the more recently published document *The Earth Charter*, developed through an international consultation process and approved at UNESCO Headquarters in Paris in March 2000. It is a declaration of fundamental principles for building a just, sustainable, and peaceful global society in the twentieth century, drawing its inspiration among others from "the wisdom of the world's great religions and philosophical traditions." Again, its call for action includes the promotion of "a culture of tolerance, nonviolence and peace" (IV.16) and it

---

20. Muller, *New Genesis*, 104.

21. Küng, *Global Responsibility*.

22. Ibid., 138.

23. Küng and Kuschel, *A Global Ethic. The Declaration of the Parliament of the World's Religions*.

24. Ibid., 25.

underlines the need for "sustainability education" (IV.14b) and "the importance of moral and spirituality education for sustainable living" (IV.14d).
The Earth Charter calls all people to "Recognize that peace is the wholeness
created by right relationships with oneself, other persons, other cultures,
other life, Earth, and the larger whole of which all are a part" (IV.16f). This
is a profoundly spiritual statement which could provide an inspiring motto
for peace education, drawing on all religious and secular sources available to
us to meet the greatest challenge humankind has ever met: to create a new
peace culture on earth.[25]

Many different religious groups have commented on *The Earth Charter*
as has a group of women, brought together in Boston in 1997 to comment
on one of its drafts.[26] Elise Boulding was one of its leading participants. She
called the Charter "a new kind of peace proclamation," requiring a stagger-
ing amount of consciousness change, a "new tool" in working "for a more
inclusive kind of peace."[27] She also referred to "the spiritually grounded
ecofeminist movement" that articulated "new visions of the planet as a community of interconnected species and new awareness of the evolutionary
potential of this community."[28]

To create such an earth community with a new peace consciousness
and culture represents one of the greatest priorities and hopes for our future. To achieve these goals, interreligious encounter and dialogue are essential. It is through such encounter that we can learn to meet each other
honestly, openly, with sensitivity and respect. It is in such encounter that we
learn to listen to each other and experience both the pain of difference, the
different histories, the different identities, the different beliefs and practices
that divide us, but we can also learn where there are points of contact and
agreement, and the possibility of common tasks.

Genuine dialogue is an exercise in communication and mediation; it
is the process whereby we can discover and weave together our differences
in a more meaningful way. We then become enriched by the dynamics of
diversity, for dialogue based on the respect for differences, not the search for
syncretism, a dialogue which recognizes our spiritual interdependence and
creates a wider sense of "we," a larger circle of community whose strongest
bonds are those of fellowship and love.

25. For more information on the Earth Charter contact Earth Charter International Secretariat c/o Earth Council, PO Box 319–6100 San José, Costa Rica. E-mail
info@earthcharter.org; website: http://www.earthcharter.org

26. See *Women's Views on the Earth Charter*. Boston Research Center for the 21st
Century, November, 1997.

27. Ibid., 32.

28. Ibid., 8.

Love is relational in creating bonds between people. It brings forth strong connections between individuals, groups, and communities. Reflecting on the transformative power of love, Teilhard de Chardin wrote: "Love is the free and imaginative outpouring of the spirit over all unexplored paths."[29] This statement anchors love in the dynamic action of the Spirit while implying that there still exist many unexplored paths of love that human beings can discover and follow. This is our great task today—a task that many women are deeply involved with at a practical level.

We need to awaken more of these love energies to stir and transform the people on our planet. For this, the old ways of understanding and practising love are no longer enough. While making use of all the resources of knowledge and wisdom available to us, we also have to push the boundaries of our understanding of love further.

To develop and strengthen the bonds of human fellowship requires the powers of reconciliation, compassion and love, for which all religion possess a wealth of resources, if they but put them into practice. To create a just and peaceful coexistence beyond discrimination and violence in the pluralistic world we live in, we have to harness the powers of love and cooperation. That also requires education, dialogue, awareness, and transformation.

Conclusion

We are not short of seeds, of seminal ideas, to create more cooperation and harmony in our suffering, war-torn and threatened world. But how can we sow those seeds, make them grow, and reap their harvest?

Slowly a global vision is emerging in every discipline and field of human activity, a more integral perspective whereby humanity is seen as intrinsically one, and closely interdependent both materially and spiritually. A global perspective requires that we help and support each other rather than destructively compete against each other. To develop and strengthen such a global vision in individuals and nations we need to spend time, thought and money on fostering global peace education.

The nature of war and violence has radically changed in today's world; to work for the abolition of war means more than ever that violence, strife, and hatred have to be addressed in all their ramifications. We have to find non-violent conflict resolutions and peaceful, non-violent ways of dealing with religious, ethnic, social, economic, and political differences. In order to create a new *peace culture* in the world, we need above all to develop a new *peace consciousness* among the world's citizens. This is a very challenging

29. Teilhard de Chardin, *The Future of Man*, 55.

practical task, but one that is intrinsically connected to spiritual and ethical values. That is why the resources of the world faiths, and a spiritual outlook on life, are indispensable ingredients for developing peace education, peace action, and the growth of a peace consciousness and culture. We also need political negotiations, and new peace instruments for non-violent conflict resolutions, as well as a stronger United Nations-related global authority to control and settle armed disputes. Ultimately this requires profound attitudinal, economic and political changes—in fact it calls for a radical *civilisational change* in the contemporary world.

Current levels of violence and wars of destruction might easily feed a profound pessimism, but there are also many signs of hope, encouraging changes of direction and new ventures which inspire a more optimistic approach, and the belief that it is still possible to make our world a more peaceful place. A new vision of peace is integral to many contemporary statements and documents; some of these draw explicitly or implicitly on religious and spiritual ideas. If we have the real strength of faith and the will to unite as one human family, we can hope to find all the spiritual power and help needed to respond to the great challenge of creating peace and justice on earth.

I end my reflections by quoting from a song by Miriam Therese Winter entitled "Circle of Love." Her words praise the remarkable power of love that can unite us into a larger circle of community, into a greater "we." They also express the profound truth that we humans must not only bear this hope as a large vision, but take on the responsibility for making this great ideal come true:

> The circle of love
>
> is repeatedly broken
>
> because of the sin
>
> of exclusion.
>
> We create separate circles:
>
> The inner circle
>
> and the outer circle,
>
> the circle of power
>
> and the circle of despair,
>
> the circle of privilege
>
> and the circle of deprivation.
>
> We carefully define our circles,
>
> at work

or at worship,

with family

and with friends . . .

[set blank line]

The circle of love

is broken,

whenever we cannot see eye to eye,

whenever we cannot link hand to hand,

whenever we cannot live heart to heart

and affirm our differences.

Before we can pray,

before we can dream,

before we can witness

to justice and peace,

we must be a single circle,

a single, unbroken circle.

Let us build this circle of love.[30]

Bibliography

Abecassis, Armand. "Three Kinds of Peace: Shalom-Shelomot." In *SIDIC* (Service International de Documentation Judéo-Chrétienne, Rome) 21, no. 1 (1988) 11–14.

Alt, Franz. *Frieden ist möglich. Die Politik der Bergpredigt.* Bielefeld: Bertelsmann, 1983.

Boulding, Elise. "Peace Making as an Evolutionary Capacity: Reflections on the Work of Teilhard de Chardin, Martin Buber and Jane Addams." Cyclostyled lecture: Dartmouth College, 1981.

———. "Learning Peace." In *The Quest for Peace: Transcending Collective Violence and War among Societies, Cultures and States,* edited by Raimo Väyrynen et al., 317–29. London: Sage, 1987.

Chappell, David W., ed., *Buddhist Peacework: Creating Cultures of Peace.* Boston: Wisdom 1999.

De Vries, Hent. *Religion and Violence: Philosophical Perspectives from Kant to Derrida.* Baltimore: John Hopkins University Press, 2002.

Ferguson, John. *War and Peace in the World's Religions.* London: Sheldon, 1977.

Gill, Robin. *Theology and Social Structure.* London: Mowbrays, 1977.

Gordon, Harrison, and Leonard Grob, eds. *Education for Peace: Testimonies from World Religions.* Maryknoll, NY: Orbis, 1988.

30. Winter, *Woman Prayer, Woman Song,* 185–86.

Hastings, Adrian, et al., eds. *The Oxford Companion to Christian Thought*. Oxford: Oxford University Press, 2000.

Hendrickx, Herman. *A Time for Peace. Reflections on the Meaning of Peace and Violence in the Bible*. London: SPCK, 1988. First published in the Philippines as *Peace, Anyone?* Quezon City: Clarentian, 1986.

Hobsbawm, Eric. "War and Peace." *The Guardian*, 23 February 2002.

Juergensmeyer, Mark, et al. *The Oxford Handbook of Religion and Violence*. Oxford: Oxford University Press, 2013.

King, Ursula. *Women and Spirituality. Voices of Protest and Promise*. 2nd ed. Houndmills, Basingstoke, UK: Macmillan, 1993.

————. "Reflections on Peace, Women, and the World Faiths." *Dialogue and Alliance* 25 1 (2011) 8–18.

Küng, Hans. *Global Responsibility. In Search of a New World Ethic*. London: SCM, 1991.

Küng, Hans, and Karl-Josef Kuschel. *A Global Ethic: The Declaration of the Parliament of the World's Religions*. London: SCM, 1993.

Lincoln, Bruce. "War and Warriors: An Overview." In *The Encyclopedia of Religion*, edited by Lindsay Jones, 14:9679–83. 2nd ed. Chicago: Macmillan Reference, 2005.

Muller, Robert. *New Genesis: Shaping a Global Spirituality*. New York: Doubleday, 1982.

————. *The Birth of a Global Civilization: With Proposals for a New Political System for Planet Earth*. Anacortes, WA: World Happiness and Cooperation, 1991.

Murphy, Andrew, ed. *The Blackwell Companion to Religion and Violence*. Oxford: Wiley-Blackwell, 2011.

Ruston, Roger. *War of Religions, Religion of War*. Manchester: Blackfriars, 1993.

Teilhard de Chardin, Pierre. *The Future of Man*. London: Collins, 1965.

Wicker, Brian. "Pacifism." In *The Oxford Companion to Christian Thought*, edited by Adrian Hastings et al., 508–9. Oxford: Oxford University Press, 2000.

————. "War." In *The Oxford Companion to Christian Thought*, edited by Adrian Hastings et al., 746–48. Oxford: Oxford University Press, 2000.

Winter, Miriam Therese. *Woman Prayer, Woman Song: Resources for Ritual*. Oak Park, IL: Meyer-Stone, 1987.

Worldwatch. *Small Arms, Big Impacts: The Next Challenge of Disarmament*. Quoted in *Abolishing War: Dialogue with Peace Scholars Elise Boulding and Randall Forsberg* (Boston Research Center for the 21st Century, November 1998) 34.

Websites

http://www.earthcharter.org
http://womeninblack.org/old/es/history

———————— 20 ————————

Reproductive Capital
and Slave Surrogacy

Thinking about/with/
beyond Hagar[1]

Marianne Bjelland Kartzow

Surrogacy is not new: It goes back to the Old Testament and Hagar, who
carried a child—Ishmael—for Abraham and Sarah. What is new is the
improved medical technology which makes it more likely for you to
attain your goal of parenthood.

HAGAR CENTER (HTTP://WWW.HAGARCENTER.ORG
/SURROGACY.SHTML)

IN THE RECENT DEBATE of reproductive health the story of Hagar as surrogate mother has become increasingly popular. This article will address
some of the interesting and challenging possible overlaps between biblical
texts and this debate.

How can the recent language, concepts and ideas that are introduced
related to reproduction and fertility contribute to nuance the understanding
of ancient texts? If the nativity scene in Luke's gospel is read through the
lenses of the present day discourse of surrogacy and parenthood, it may

1. This article is written in gratitude to Turid Karlsen Seim, for her inspiration,
courage, and creativity.

be argued that Jesus had two fathers and God used Mary as a surrogate mother.[2] Insights, dilemmas, and ethical questions from the recent debate may bring new knowledge—or at least new questions—to the discussion on gender, slavery, and the body in early Christian discourse. In this article I will look at early Christian texts in light of this debate, showing how the concepts of mother and father have always been complex and negotiable and how "patchwork families" are no new invention.[3]

Issues of fertility, surrogacy and reproduction in our fast changing world relate to global discourses of wealth and poverty, medical technology, and gender.[4] It gives new possibilities, but also creates new hierarchies.[5] Critics argue that *the recent disconnection of parenthood to bodily processes is threatening for family life and dangerous for future generations.*[6] But how new is this disconnection? How are "mother" and "father" constructed in ancient texts, as biological, socio-juridical and religious categories?[7]

I am interesting in understanding the role of reproduction in early Christianity, in a context where the ideal of motherhood for (free) woman and fatherhood for (free) men was under pressure. As far as we know neither Jesus nor Paul were fathers. Eunuchs or barren women populate early Christian literature (see Acts 8:26–40; Gal 4:27).[8] Although stigmatized in the Jewish scripture, Jewish wisdom literature from the first century CE blessed barren and childless women, as the New Testament did: "Blessed are the barren, and the wombs that never bore, and the breast that never gave suck," says Jesus according to Luke (Luke 23:29) and in the Gospel of Thomas (*Gos. Thom.* 79).[9] With this flexibility, in what ways did the reproductive body produce meaning? To use the distinction of Vander Stichele and Penner: What did they think *about* the reproductive body and how did they think *with* it and *beyond* it?[10]

---

2. Jacob, "Surrogacy as a Performance of Violent Love."

3. Harders, "Roman Patchwork Families: Surrogate Parenting, Socialization, and the Shaping of Tradition."

4. Inhorn and Van Balen, eds., *Infertility around the Globe: New Thinking on Childlessness, Gender, and Reproductive Technologies.*

5. Bergstrøm, "Surrugati lager hierarki mellom ulike typer morsroller."

6. See some of the very many web pages listed at http://www.morfarbarn.no/viktige-linker. Their quotation of the day (21 March 2014) is: "BIOLOGY, CHILDREN and BIBLE give the same answer: Marriage is for one man and one woman. All children have their God-given right to their own parents."

7. Nzegwu, "Cultural Epistemologies of Motherhood."

8. Moxnes, *Putting Jesus in His Place*, 92–95.

9. Seim, *The Double Message*, 205–6

10. Vander Stichele and Penner, *Contextualizing Gender in Early Christian*

My interest is not to draw a distinct line between reproductive terminology as used either metaphorical, rhetorically, or as describing bodily processes. Instead I try to distinguish between different concepts of parenthood along a whole set of lines, related to intersections of gender, sexuality, and class (slavery). In my reasoning I lean on recent attempts to use theories of intersectionality in New Testament studies.[11] Intersectional studies have become increasingly influential among gender and race-scholars the last decades.[12] Accordingly, this study can be placed within the discourse of feminist criticism, "not a single, monolithic position but a label that covers a variety of approaches and methodologies; . . . not a particular method of interpretation so much as it is a critical sensibility," as Turid Karlsen Seim phrases it.[13]

There were several practices in the ancient world where the categories mother and father could be disconnected from bodily reproduction. For example: Interpreters suggest that adoption of exposed babies could be a way to cure childlessness.[14] Adoption of adult men to become heirs is well documented,[15] and in early Christian discourse this language could also be used in a theological sense.[16] In addition: The practice that another woman than the birth giving woman nursed a baby could be viewed as a type of motherhood.[17] And last, and the main focus of this article: The master narrative in Genesis on Sarah and Hagar, reinterpreted by Paul in Galatians (4:21–31), shows that female slaves' reproductive capital could destabilize the fixed hierarchy between slave and free. Stories about slave owners who use their slaves for reproduction almost follow a given pattern in the Hebrew Bible: the slave women Bilhah and Zilpah share several features with

---

Discourse, 6–7.

11. See for example Schüssler Fiorenza, "Introduction: Exploring the Intersections of Race, Gender, Status, and Ethnicity in Early Christian Studies"; Kartzow, *Destabilizing the Margins.* See also Kartzow, "Intersectional Studies."

12. For a broader update on this concept, see the theme issue of *Sign* in 2013 and in particular MacKinnon, "Intersectionality as Method: A Note."

13. Seim, "Feminist Criticism," 44.

14. See Glancy, *Slavery in Early Christianity,* 74–77; and Osiek and MacDonald, with Tulloch, *A Woman's Place,* 64–67

15. Harders is not concerned with legal adoption as such, but asks about who socialized and educated sons in times of mortality, divorce and remarriage. She finds a mother, several uncles, and other related male adults in her Roman sources. Daughters or surrogate slave mothers are not discussed in her article. See Harders, "Roman Patchwork Families."

16. See for example Tsang, *From Slaves to Sons.*

17. Se for example the extended list of qualifications required of a nurse by Soranus in his *Gynecology.*

Hagar as they "bear upon the knees" (Gen 30:3) of their female owners. Did childless women who joined early Christian groups use their reproductive slaves to help them become mothers? Or did they find alternative spaces? This complex situation indeed challenges the idea of parenthood as given and fixed, and conceptualizes it as a whole set of possible situations and processes. It seems like reproduction was seen as teamwork.

By use of the Bourdieuan concept of "capital" I will argue that the field of reproduction must be understood not only by looking at reproductive capital as a bodily process, but also include social, juridical and religious matters.[18] I will therefore in the following add to the conventional notion that reproductive capital relates to the body, the concept of social reproductive capital, juridical reproductive capital and religious reproductive capital.

As a biblical scholar with interest in gender and reproduction I draw on recent media debates dealing with medical and ethical issues. I am impressed by and curious towards recent knowledge, and enthusiastic towards the potential for interdisciplinary conversations, but I consider myself a true amateur within these fields.

Recent Trends in Parenthood Concepts and Vocabulary: Reproductive Complexity

Today, a woman in India can be a surrogate mother for a Norwegian couple, with genetic material from USA or South Africa. The discussion on reproductive health is transnational, and the ethical challenges are mixed up with development of advanced medical technology.[19] Occasionally it is argued that these issues were easier in the past: a child had one mother and one father, since they did not know of any technology of IVF (In-Vitro-Fertilization, or Befruchtung im Glas);[20] there were no organ donors, DNA-tests, shared parenthood or surrogacy. The ancient texts presented here, however, show much more variety and flexibility, and thereby disturb this fantasy about the past.

The public debate on IVF and surrogacy is rather diverse, and so is the legal situation around the globe. It seems like national laws and values are challenged by international practice. What is considered acceptable in

18. Bourdieu, "The Forms of Capital."

19. For a recent discussion, see various articles in Barrett and Groes-Green, eds., *Studying Intimate Matters*.

20. *In vitro* is used to refer to any biological procedure that is performed outside the organism it would normally be occurring in, to distinguish it from an *in vivo* procedure, where the tissue remains inside the living organism within which it is normally found.

countries that normally see themselves as comparable vary a lot, for example related to surrogacy and egg donors: South Africa or USA, for example, have well regulated and established, publicly accepted systems for these practices. In Norway, on the other hand, where such practices are illegal, some politicians compare surrogacy with human trafficking,[21] and according to the German federal office, surrogacy is unethical and illegal.[22] This discourse has global, ethical and technical aspects that cannot limit the conversation to national or regional contexts.[23]

As childless women, but also as egg donors and surrogate mothers, women of all sorts are the main actors in the controversial discourse of reproduction.[24] Women tend worldwide to bear the major burden of infertility: they are blamed for the reproductive failing, they experience personal anxiety, frustration, grief, fear and social stigma, and they go through life-threatening medical intervention.[25] Women with bodily reproductive capital run risk through pregnancy and birth, at times in bad conditions for bad payment.[26] Surrogacy is at times compared with prostitution or—at the other side of the scale—categorized alongside other forms of organ donoring[27] or biological work.[28] Feminist are on both sides of this debate, showing how difficult and complex it is to agree on good solutions.[29]

In some countries, childlessness is defined as a medical problem, and the health systems help couples, heterosexual but sometimes also homosexual and singles, who are unable to produce their own offspring. It is at times considered a human right to have children and already in 1994 the phrase "reproductive justice" was coined.[30]

21. http://www.vl.no/samfunn/vg-liberal-take-over-debatt-om-surrogati/.

22. http://www.auswaertiges-amt.de/EN/Infoservice/FAQ/GermanFamilyLaw/Leihmutterschaft.html?nn=479790.

23. According to Andersen the term "surrogacy" was not mentioned in a Norwegian newspaper until 2008, see "Offerposisjonenes paradoks."

24. See the editors' introduction in Inhorn and Balen, *Infertility around the Globe*, 7.

25. See ibid.

26. Naveen calls for "fairtrade surrugacy." See *Den globale baby.*

27. Gupta, "Surrogati er i slekt med organhandel."

28. Bergstrøm, "Surrugati lager hierarki mellom ulike typer morsroller."

29. Thompson, "Fertile Ground: Feminists Theorize Infertility." See also Naveen, *Den globale baby.*

30. The phrase "reproductive justice" describes an intersectional framework drawing attention to how the right to have a child and the right to parent are as important as the right to not have children. Note the recent book series from University of California Press *Reproductive Justice: A New Vision for the 21st Century* and the first book by Rickie Solinger and Loretta Ross, *What is Reproductive Justice?*

In the media debate on surrogacy, Andersen finds three types of parenthood.[31] Motherhood, traditionally connected to pregnancy, birth giving, and breast-feeding, is renegotiated and divided into three stages or qualities, while fatherhood can be both genetic and juridical:

- Genetic mother/father: those whose eggs and seed the child is made by

- Biological mother: That is, the mother who carries the baby and gives birth to it

- Juridical mother/father: That is, the parent/s who have the juridical right of parenthood

According to this classification, a child can have three different mothers and two different fathers. The person/s who initiated the process, who took the decision to "create" the child, has/have the juridical reproductive capital, but not the biological or genetic reproductive capital. He/she/they is/are often called the "intentional parent/s."

I will use these distinctions and ask about different concepts of parenthood in early Christian texts dealing with Hagar. Obviously, in the ancient world genetic and biological motherhood could not be separated. In the following this type of mother- and fatherhood is called bio-genetic. Due to a more complex juridical situation, aspects of social position, economy, and law interact in several ways related to ancient parenthood. In addition, the models used to describe the new Christian identity employed cultural ideas where parents-terminology was common: God was seen as a father, and at times as a mother, and the community was constructed as a family and as children of God.

Childless Couples with Reproductive Slaves: Reproductive Capital Destabilized?

The format of this article will not allow me to go into details in each text about Hagar and reproduction. Rather I borrow and adjust the terminology from the recent debate and try to enlighten the ancient texts and how they construct reproduction.[32]

The system of letting those with bio-genetic reproductive capital have children for those who lack such capital but had juridical and economical

---

31. Andersen, "Offerposisjonenes paradoks," 43.

32. For a discussion of a whole set of New Testament texts on birth and women, see Seim, "Smerte og forløsning."

reproductive capital is not new, although recent medical and technological developments have changed this global exchange dramatically. Today barren women and men, who have socio-juridical reproductive capital, can get their own children, by use of seed donors, egg donors and/or surrogate mothers. These practices are regulated by national laws, but the marked is international, with legal and illegal transactions. Although being controversial and challenging, the recent debate also points at possibilities and strategies among surrogate mothers that somehow destabilize the picture of victim and abuser.[33]

According to Hebrew Bible scholars the most serious and frequent disability for women was infertility.[34] The master narrative in Genesis on Sarai/Sarah and Hagar (Gen 16 and 21) shows that female slaves' reproductive capital could destabilize the fixed hierarchy between slave and free.[35] Stories about slave owners who use their slaves for reproduction are frequent in the Hebrew Bible, for example in the case of the slave women Bilhah, Zilpah and Hagar mentioned in Genesis.

It is the story of Hagar and Sarah that appears in the New Testament, but something has happened to the different parents. With the lens of intertextuality I want to look at these two representations of Hagar and her reproductive network and son, in Genesis and Galatians, in order to conceptualize various ideas about slavery and surrogacy.[36]

Sarai, later named Sarah, who in Genesis forced her Egyptian slave girl Hagar to give her a son by her husband Abram/Abraham (Gen 16:2), intended to let the child be her own, although the text never mention any close relation between Sara and Ishmael. The Jewish historian Josephus who retells the Genesis story, on the other hand, points out that Sarah cherished Ishmael "with an affection no less than if he had been her own son."[37] For him, the intended mother of Ishmael functioned as a real mother too. In Genesis, Hagar was supposed to be the surrogate, impregnated by the husband of Sarah, but even before the boy was born Sarah is not interested in him. "Hagar bore Abram a son," as it is phrased (Gen 16:15). Later Sarah got

---

33. Jacob, "Surrogacy as a Performance of Violent Love" and Naveen, *Den globale baby.*

34. Raphael, *Biblical Corpora.*

35. Reinhartz and Walfish, "Conflict and Coexistance in Jewish Interpretation," 107.

36. See also Kartzow, "Navigating the Womb: Surragacy, Slavery, Fertility—and Biblical Discources."

37. *Ant.* 1.215–19, as discussed in Reinhartz and Walfish, "Conflict and Coexistance in Jewish Interpretation," 103.

her own bio-genetic son Isaac by Abraham and God's intervention and the relationship got even more challenging.

In Galatians 4:21–31 Paul follows this tendency: Ishmael is mentioned as one of Abraham's sons, but only Hagar's child. What happened to the intended mother, the mother who forced the surrogate Hagar to give her a child?

The free woman Sarah, who came up with the idea of letting Hagar give her and Abraham a child, is never a social-juridical mother to Ishmael after he is born, neither in Genesis, nor in Galatians. Hagar started out as a surrogate mother, but already in the pregnancy period the intentional mother withdrew from her motherhood.

In what way is this transformation reflecting ancient practices? Is it echoing the reality, with competition and hostility? Did a child born by a slave woman for her female owner loose its privileges if/when the mistress got her own child/son? Or: was it other reasons why Ishmael did never become a real son of Sarah, as was the intention? For Josephus, however, we may say that Sarah was Ishmael mother, at least partly.

When Paul recalls these mothers and sons in Galatians they must have been familiar characters to the audience. How did they interpret Hagar or Sarah's motherhood? If we follow the argument that barren woman joined the early Christian groups, it is interesting to imagine how they handled their own childlessness. Did barren women who joined the Jesus movement also use their reproductive slaves to help them become mothers or did they find comfort in Jesus' words that blessed the barren or Paul's words "Rejoice, you childless one" (Gal 4:27)?

To understand ancient texts on childless couples and reproductive slaves we have found several categories of parents. The example of Abraham, Sarah and Hagar and their relation to Ishmael, as it is described in Genesis and Galatian 4, represent a very interesting case:

- Bio-genetic.
  - Mother: The slave woman Hagar
  - Father: The free man (slave owner) Abraham
- Social. The intended parents Abraham and Sarah.
  - Mother: The female slave owner Sarah. But social motherhood seems to be transferred from Sarah to Hagar. Thereby Ishmael also lost his "legal" father

- Father: The one who had the intent and who had impregnated the slave woman, Abraham. But Ishmael was never acknowledged fully as son

- Juridical.

    - The role of Ishmael as son is heavily influenced by Sarah's lack of loyalty to her intention, leading her to force her slave Hagar to give her a son by Abraham

In addition to these distinctions, Galatians also operate with two different kinds of motherhood to Ishmael and Isaac: Abraham had two sons, but one of them, that is the son he had by the slave woman Hagar is "born according to the flesh" (κατὰ σάρκα γεγέννηται) while Isaac who he had by Sarah is "born thought the promise" (ἐκ τῆς ἐλευθέρας δι' ἐπαγγελίας). How shall these two types of motherhood be categorized? The two women are both bio-genetic mothers, but only Sarah's motherhood is given a religious privilege, according to Paul in Galatians. Interestingly, the fatherhood, who normally defined a child's juridical and social status, is acknowledged to be the same for the two boys. How can one of the sons of the forefather Abraham, even the firstborn, be born only according to nature? Is this not an insult to Abraham's fatherhood and masculinity?

The reproductive relations involving Hagar, Sarah, Abraham, Ishmael and Isaac, and how they are presented in Genesis and Galatians are really complex and hard to conceptualize. The most stable factor is that Abraham is the bio-genetic father of the two boys. He is also said to name the boys (Gen 16:15 and 21:3), indicating that he acknowledged them both as sons on one level, but only Isaac is said to be circumcised as newborn baby (Gen 21:4). Ishmael, on the other hand, is circumcised together with his father and the other male slaves, those born in the household and those bought for money (Gen 17:10–14 and 23). Abraham's social and juridical fatherhood is granted to Isaac, while his fatherhood to the son he has with the slave woman do not have similar consequences: In Genesis Hagar flees alone with Ishmael (lack of social fatherhood) and in Galatians Ishmael is born only according to flesh and not included in his father's promise as his brother is (lack of religious fatherhood).

Maybe the fact that Genesis mentions that only Isaac is born by a circumcised father and circumcised himself on the eight day explains why he in the writings of Paul is born according to the promise in contrast to his brother?[38] They both were named by Abraham, indicating that he acknowledged them as (socio-biological?) sons, but only Isaac got the sign of

---

38. Thiessen, *Contesting Conversion*.

being a real and proper son and heir (socio-juridical and religious), thought correct circumcision.

It seems as if Abraham's fatherhood to Ishmael is reduced to bio-genetic fatherhood because of the social status of the mother. In this family, proper fatherhood, that is socio-juridical and religious fatherhood, was depended on and required, proper motherhood. Accordingly, Abraham's fatherhood to Ishmael was connected in flesh, but disconnected to social-juridical and religious fatherhood. Sarah's intended motherhood to Ishmael was disconnected in flesh, but intended to be a social-juridical motherhood, although it developed differently.

Conclusion

Pregnancy and birth as bio-genetic reproduction seem to interact with so many other issues in the ancient texts under investigation. If reproductive capital had the potential to destabilize the fixed hierarchy between slave and free, different types of motherhood complicated this picture. For a child such as Ishmael, the socio-juridical-religious reproductive capital of the intentional mother Sarah still never made her his mother, and therefore never made him a legal son of his father Abraham. Ishmael was not born through the promise. The slave woman's son was only born according to the flesh, and did not get access to relations of socio-juridical-religious parenthood.

In this social system, reproduction depended on class and gender. Building on the current way of splitting up mother- and fatherhood (bio-genetic, social, economic-juridical, and religious) I will suggest several subcategories that seem relevant:

When it comes to *bio-genetic reproductive capital*, both slaves and free (Hagar, Sarah and Abraham) could have such reproductive capital, although only freeborn babies could be acknowledged legal fatherhood. The classification *social reproductive capital* is indeed difficult to define, due to a whole set of reasons. What do we man by "social" parenthood? A slave responsible for raising a freeborn child would probably not be considered a mother or father related to the child's position in the society, although she or he could function as the most significant adult for the child, in many other ways (emotional, education, care etc.).[39] It was the father who was responsible by being the *paterfamilias*. A slave child did not have a similar social standing as being someone's property, but obviously, there must have been some adults that cared for them, raised them, and fed them, and gave them some sort of social protection. So, in the texts treated here who were

---

39. Discussed in Kartzow, *Destabilizing the Margins,* 35–36.

the social mother and father of Ishmael and Isaac, intentionally and after they were born?

Economic-juridical reproductive capital represents a mixture of economy, social matters and law. Overall, slaves did not have such reproductive capital, although female slaves could be more worth economically if they were reproductive.[40] Hagar and other slave parents did not have this type of reproductive capital. When it comes to *religious reproductive capital* it is at times hard to separate from the socio-economic-juridical, but often easy to separate from the bio-genetic. In the texts read here we find some rather different examples: The free woman Sarah (but not the slave woman Hagar) gave birth to a son according to promise in Galatians. Sarah had religious reproductive capital, as also Abraham had in relation to his son born by the free woman, according to promise (through proper circumcision).

In many ways this complex picture may touch upon issues known from the current debate of reproductive industry, although the medical technology is a very different one. They did not have surrogacy and IVF as we have, but they had female slaves, owned bodies that could contribute to whatever the owners needed, including the production of children. In this social system the categories mother and father were rather flexible and negotiable, and splitting them up may help us nuance the way we talk about these concepts in New Testament texts.

Reproduction seems to have been a team work, including several men and women. For free persons to get an heir was indeed crucial both economical and juridical, and probably also social and emotional. For slaves the economic interest was that a slave mother increased the fortune of her owner, and she could be manumitted after surviving a given number of childbirths.

In this process of producing offspring and securing reproduction it seems like there was some alternative spaces: there is a certain ambiguity towards reproduction in early Jewish and Christian discourse. The great founding men Jesus and Paul seem to downplay reproduction in terms of biology. Gender bending, eunuchs, barren women and extended families blend with conventional discourses of reproduction, to construct theology and community. In this landscape the reproductive body indeed seems productive to think *about, with* and *beyond.*

---

40. See Kartzow, "Navigating the Womb."

Hagar as Role model?

But what about Hagar? What do we think about her, and how can we think with her and beyond her? She is the mother who survived (at least in the narrative), a destiny not given for all surrogates. She became pregnant for others by force, but ended up taking care of the child herself, since the intentional mother was not interested. Sarah never became Ishmael's mother. She withdrew from her original role as intentional mother.

With this nuanced language of reproductive capital the present usage of Biblical stories become challenging. When Hagar is used to legitimate surrogacy today, the story's many problematic factors are downplayed: Hagar was a slave and she was forced to be impregnated on Sarah's command and by Abraham's seed. She was never asked whether she was willing and no compensation is mentioned. As a slave her reproductive capital was owned by others, and to use her for socio-genetic motherhood was one among several types of surrogacy a slave could be used for.[41]

How can such aspects of surrogacy be related to present-day practices? Although it is argued that surrogate mothers today do it voluntarily and are paid according to contracts, issues of inhumane treatment and lack of insurance for the mothers have reached the international media debate. Cases where the intentional parents withdraw from their contracts, for a variety of reasons, have also been known. Anyway, it seems like the global exchange of surrogacy will grow in the future: Perhaps a model of *fair trade surrogacy* would be worth considering?[42]

When it comes to Hagar as a role model: Perhaps the story of Hagar is more adequate to address the problematic aspects of surrogacy than to legitimate and celebrate the current practice and technology?

Bibliography

Andersen, Unn Conradi. "Offerposisjonenes paradoks: Offentlig debatt om surrogati." *Tidsskrift for samfunnsforskning* 54 (2013) 31–62.

Bergstrøm, Ida Irene. "Surrugati lager hierarki mellom ulike typer morsroller." *Kilden. forskningsradet.no (15.07.2014)*, 2014.

Bourdieu, Pierre. "The Forms of Capital." In *Cultural Theory: An Anthology*, edited by Imre Szema and Timothy Kaposy, 81–93. Malden, MA: Wiley-Blackwell, 2011.

Glancy, Jennifer A. *Slavery in Early Christianity*. Oxford: Oxford University Press, 2002.

Gupta, Ram. "Surrogati er i slekt med organhandel." *Aftenposten.net* (1. mai 2013).

---

41. Glancy talks about slaves as surrogate bodies, see *Slavery in Early Christianity*, 15–16.

42. Naveen, *Den globale baby.*

Harders, Ann-Cathrin. "Roman Patchwork Families: Surrogate Parenting, Socialization, and the Shaping of Tradition." In *Children, Memory, and Family Identity in Roman Culture*, edited by Véronique Dasen and Thomas Späth, 49–72. Oxford: Oxford Univeristy Press, 2010.

Inhorn, Marcia C., and Frank Van Balen, eds. *Infertility around the Globe: New Thinking on Childlessness, Gender, and Reproductive Technologies.* Berkeley: University of California Press, 2002.

Jacob, Sharon. "Surrogacy as a Performance of Violent Love: Reading Luke's Mary alongside Low Caste Surrogate Women in India." Paper presented at the SBL Annual Meeting, Boston, 2008.

Kartzow, Marianne Bjelland. *Destabilizing the Margins: An Intersectional Approach to Early Christian Memory.* Eugene, OR: Pickwick, 2012.

———. "Intersectional Studies." In *The Oxford Encyclopedia of the Bible and Gender Studies.* New York: Oxford University Press, 2014.

———. "Navigating the Womb: Surragacy, Slavery, Fertility—and Biblical Discources." *Journal of Early Christian History* 2 (2012) 38–54.

MacKinnon, Catharine A. "Intersectionality as Method: A Note." *Signs* 38 (2013) 1019–30.

Moxnes, Halvor. *Putting Jesus in His Place: A Radical Vision of Household and Kingdom.* Louisville: Westminster John Knox, 2003.

Naveen, Mala. *Den globale baby: Det norske surrogatieventyret i India.* Oslo: Aschehoug, 2013.

Nzegwu, Nkiru. "Cultural Epistemologies of Motherhood: Refining the Concept of 'Mother.'" *JENdA: A Journal of Culture and African Women Studies* 5 (2004) 1–5.

Osiek, Carolyn, Margaret Y. MacDonald, with Janet H. Tulloch. *A Woman's Place: House Churches in Earliest Christianity.* Minneapolis: Fortress, 2006.

Raphael, Rebecca. *Biblical Corpora: Representations of Disability in Hebrew Biblical Literature.* London: T. & T. Clark, 2008.

Reinhartz, Adele, and Miriam-Simma Walfish. "Conflict and Coexistance in Jewish Interpretation." In *Hagar, Sarah, and Their Children: Jewish, Christian, and Muslim Perspectives*, edited by Phyllis Trible and Letty M. Russell, 101–25. Louisville: Westminster John Knox, 2006.

Schüssler Fiorenza, Elisabeth. "Introduction: Exploring the Intersections of Race, Gender, Status, and Ethnicity in Early Christian Studies." In *Prejudice and Christian Beginnings: Investigating Race, Gender, and Ethnicity in Early Christian Studies*, edited by Laura Nasrallah and Elisabeth Schüssler Fiorenza, 1–23. Minneapolis: Fortress, 2009.

Seim, Turid Karlsen. *The Double Message: Patterns of Gender in Luke–Acts.* Studies of the New Testament and Its World. Edinburgh: T. & T. Clark, 1994.

———. "Feminist Criticism." In *Methods for Luke*, edited by Joel B. Green, 42–73. Cambridge: Cambridge University Press, 2010.

———. "Smerte og forløsning: Nytestamentlige fødselsbilder i spenningen mellom virkelighet og ritualisert utopi." *NTT* 91.2 (1990) 85–99.

Soranus. *Soranus' Gynecology.* Translated by Owsei Temkin. Baltimore: Johns Hopkins University Press, 1991.

Thiessen, Matthew. *Contesting Conversion: Genealogy, Circumcision, and Identity in Ancient Judaism and Christianity.* New York: Oxford University Press, 2011.

Thompson, Charis M. "Fertile Ground: Feminists Theorize Infertility." In *Infertility around the Globe: New Thinking on Childlessness, Gender, and Reproductive Technologies*, edited by Marcia C. Inhorn and Frank Van Balen, 52–78. Berkeley: University of California Press, 2002.

Tsang, Sam. *From Slaves to Sons: A New Rhetoric Analysis on Paul's Slave Metaphors in His Letter to the Galatians*. New York: Lang, 2005.

Vander Stichele, Caroline, and Todd Penner. *Contextualizing Gender in Early Christian Discourse: Thinking Beyond Thecla*. London: T. & T. Clark, 2009.

21

Die präsentisch-immanente Wirkung des Zornes Gottes (Römer 1,21–32)

David Hellholm

English Abstract

Within the refutational subtext, Romans 1:21–32 Paul is deal-ing with the reasons for the necessity of God's justification (3:21—8:39) by means of three indictments of gentiles because of their failure to honor him (v. 21), their exchange of the truth about him (v. 25), and their lack of acknowledgment of him (v. 28a). Therefore God in three corresponding responses handed them over to their homoerotic passions: to the lust of their hearts to impurity (v. 24), further to the degrading of their bod-ies by means of feminine and masculine homoerotic passions (vv. 26–27), and finally to all kinds of violations of the divine order of life in a list of vices (vv. 29–31). At the very end, God's verdict is proclaimed (v. 32). The accusations against Gentiles are followed by corresponding accusations against Jews, and all mankind although for different reasons (2:1–11; 2:12–29 and 3:1–9).

There is a continous *amplification* in the structural com-position of the section beginning with the short passage on the gentiles' impurity, continuing with the much longer passage on their homoerotic passions, and furthermore to the concluding violations of the divine order in life by means of the extensive list of vices and the final divine verdict in v. 32. The sodomy results in a presentic-immanent punishment for males whereas nothing of that kind is stated for females. The punishment is the result of God's wrath, not its prerequisite!

The references to Jewish, Greco-Roman and Iranian sources show that Paul by no means was alone in condemning homoerotic passions in antiquity. In his argumentation against homosexuality, however, he is for the most part using the Jewish moral code and its so called »Heidenspiegel« in order to repudiate accusations against him for his libertinistically perceived Gospel by Jews, Jewish-Christians, and in particular by Judaizers from the east (cf. Galatians, 1 and 2 Corinthians).

The verdict (v. 32) does not only refer to homoerotic men and women but to the entire mankind as the list of vices that directly precedes the divine verdict clearly indicates. This implies that homosexuality cannot be conceived of as the main transgression of God's order of life. Everyone is guilty of equally punishable sins; therefore the righteousness of God has been disclosed in order to save mankind as displayed in the treatment in the *confirmatio*-section 3:21—8:39.

Der makro-strukturelle Aufbau vom *Briefkorpus* (1,8—15,33) des Römerbriefs besteht aus sechs Abteilungen: *Proömium* (1,8–12), *Narratio* (1,13–15), *Propositio* (1,16–17), *Probatio* (1,18–11,36), *Exhortatio* (12,1—15,13) und *Peroratio / Conclusio* (15,14–33).

Der erste Probatio-Teil umfasst die *quaestio infinita/generalis*: Gottes Gerechtigkeit durch den Glauben an Jesus Christus (1,18—8,39) und die *quaestio finita / particularis* (9,1—11,36).[1]

Innerhalb der *Refutatio / Confutatio*: die Notwendigkeit der Gottesgerechtigkeit (1,18—3,20) findet sich ein Argumentationsschritt in Form einer Gerichtsrede mit Anklage gegen die Heiden und deren Ungerechtigkeit (1,18–32); dies als Begründung für Gottes Zorn mit präsentisch-immanenter Wirkung (1,21–32).[2] Dieser Teiltext soll im folgenden näher analysiert werden.

Der Co-text des Probatio-Teils 1,21–32

Kurz zur *Strukturanalyse*. (1) Der Abschnitt beginnt mit einer *Sub-These* in V. 18, die besagt, dass der Zorn Gottes die ganze Menschheit trifft (Ἀποκαλύπτεται γὰρ ὀργὴ Θεοῦ ἀπ'οὐρανοῦ ἐπὶ πᾶσαν ἀσέβειαν καὶ ἀδικίαν ἀνθρώπων). (2) Daraufhin folgt in den VV. 19-20 eine

---

1. Siehe Hellholm, »Theoretische Überlegungen,« 39–45.
2. Ibid., 40–41.

allgemeine oder übergreifende Begründung, die die Ursache für den Zorn Gottes nennt, nämlich die Verweigerung aller Menschen Gott zu ehren. (3) Danach bringt Paulus eine *weitere Begründung* in mehreren Schritten: Zuerst eine vorbereitende Anklage gegen die *Heiden* in 1,21–32, gefolgt von einer umfassenden Hauptanklage zuallererst gegen die ganze Menschheit (2,1–11), danach gegen die *Juden* (2,12–29) und abschließend gegen die Untreue der *Juden* Gottes Bundestreue gegenüber (3,1–8).[3] Abgeschlossen wird der *Refutatio*-Teil durch eine Zusammenfassung: alle Menschen stehen unter dem Gesetz und sind demzufolge alle Sünder (3,9–20). Die Anschuldigung gegen die Heiden ist so aufgebaut, dass drei Anklagen wegen unterschiedlicher *Aktionen* und die darauf folgenden *Reaktionen* Gottes in 1,21–31 geboten werden.[4] Abschließend wird in V. 32 das Urteil Gottes mit einem Urteilsspruch verkündigt: »sie verdienen den Tod« (ἄξιοι θανάτου εἰσίν)![5]

Inhaltsanalyse. In V. 18 beginnt nun die *Refutation*, u.zw. wie schon gesagt mit einer Sub-These: »Der Zorn Gottes«. Durch die Konjunktion γάρ wird an die Hauptthese in 1,16–17 angeknüpft. Aber damit ist die Verbindung nicht alleine hergestellt, denn ausgerechnet mit dem Verb ἀποκαλύπτεται, das in V. 17 die Offenbarung der Gerechtigkeit Gottes im Evangelium angibt (δικαιοσύνη γὰρ θεοῦ ἐν αὐτῷ [sc. ἐν τῷ εὐαγγελίῳ[6]] ἀποκαλύπτεται), fängt dieser Abschnitt direkt an (ἀποκαλύπτεται γὰρ κτλ.). Allerdings nicht, wie zu erwarten ist, mit der Offenbarung der Gerechtigkeit Gottes, sondern überraschenderweise mit der Offenbarung der ὀργή Gottes.[7] Diese Motivierung (γάρ), die mit der Sub-These »Die Offenbarung von *Gottes Zorn* über alle Menschen« anfängt, steht demzufolge in einem

---

3. Siehe Köster, »φύσις κτλ.,« 267: »Wie schon im Grunde R[ömer] 1,18–32 indirekt den Angriff auf den Selbstruhm der Juden *vorbereitet*, so schließt nun R[ömer] 2,1ff ausdrücklich die Juden in das ›alle‹ der dem Gericht verfallenen Menschheit ein« (meine Hervorhebung). Woyke, *Götter,* »*Götzen,*« *Götterbilder,* 443f.: »Allerdings scheint Röm 1,18–32 nur *vorbereitenden* Charakter auf 2,1ff. hin zu haben. Damit konterkariert Paulus das hellenistisch-jüdische Argumentationsmuster, welches nach der Beschreibung von Polytheismus und Idolatrie der Völker bzw. Menschheit, die wahre Gotteserkenntnis und -verehrung des jüdischen Volkes herausstellt (EpArist 139; Philo, SpecLeg 2,166; SapSal 15,1–5; TestNaph 3,2–4; 1Q34 Frgm. 3 Kol. 2; vgl. Gal 2,14)« (meine Hervorhebung). So auch Popkes, »Aufbau,« 499: »Der Abschnitt 1,18–32 bildet also nur einen *Vorspann* zu dem eigentlichen Anliegen des Paulus nämlich den Torafrommen der Heillosigkeit zu überführen.« Ferner Horn, »Götzendiener,« 217.

4. Popkes, »Aufbau,« 492, 496–97, 499. Aufgenommen von Horn, »Götzendiener,« 213–17: Grafik auf S. 213.

5. Vgl. Josephus in Anm. 53; Videvdad 7.52.3. sowie weitere Iranische Texte unten in Anm. 54–55; siehe ferner auch Seneca in Anm. 39.

6. So auch z.B. Schlier, *Der Römerbrief,* 44; Jewett, *Romans,* 142.

7. Vgl. Theobald, »Zorn Gottes,« 68–100; von Bendemann, »›Zorn‹ und ›Zorn Gottes,‹« 179–215.

radikalen Gegensatz zum Hauptthema (VV. 16–17). Man stelle sich die Reaktion der Zuhörer vor,[8] als sie diese »frohe« Botschaft vom Zorne Gottes zu hören bekamen!

Durch die Konjunktion (γάρ) wird angegeben, in welchem Verhältnis die Offenbarung von »Gottes Zorn« zu »Gottes Gerechtigkeit« steht. Paulus will in diesem Abschnitt die Voraussetzung und den Grund für die Offenbarung von Gottes Gerechtigkeit angeben. Mit anderen Worten: hier wird die *Notwendigkeit* der Offenbarung seiner δικαιοσύνη klargestellt.[9] Konkret wird dies in Paulus übergreifenden Begründung sowie in seiner ausführlichen Argumentation im Blick auf die Sub-These entfaltet.

Dass der Zorn Gottes nicht erst im *eschaton* beim Endgericht den Menschen trifft, geht aus der Präsensform ἀποκαλύπτεται hervor.[10] Dass dieser Begriff außerdem noch eine echte eschatologisch-futurale Bedeutung haben kann geht aus anderen Texten wie Röm 2,5.8; 3,5; 5,9; 9,22; 1 Thess 1,10; 5,9 hervor; Die präsentische Bedeutung begegnet aber auch an anderen Stellen bei Paulus wie in Röm 4,15; 12,19; 1 Thess 2,16.

Mit Gottes Zorn ist nicht eine Eigenschaft Gottes, etwa seine Sinnesstimmung, gemeint, sondern die Manifestation seines »Zorngerichts«; also: *genitivus auctoris*!

Die Sub-These mit Begründung und Wirkung: Aktion / Reaktion–Anklage / Verdikt

Die Ungerechtigkeit der *Heiden* (im »Heidenspiegel«) als Begründung für Gottes Zorn mit daraufhin anschließender *präsentisch-immanenter* Wirkung (1,21–32).

(1) Die *erste Anklage* lautet:

> *(21)Denn obwohl sie (sc. die Heiden) Gott erkannt haben, haben sie ihm als Gott nicht Ehre und Dank dargebracht, sondern sie wurden zunichte gemacht in ihren Gedanken und verfinstert*

---

8. Bezüglich der Zuhörer, siehe Hellholm, »Universalität und Partikularität,« 256–58. Paulus von Tarsos weicht wie Hermogenes von Tarsos in seiner Schrift περὶ ἰδεῶν λόγου nicht vor scharfem Tadel und konkreten Vorwürfen zurück; siehe Wooten, *On Types of Style*; hierzu in Bezug auf den Galaterbrief bes. Du Toit, »Galatians ... 1–4«; Du Toit, »Galatians . . . 5–6«.

9. Popkes, »Aufbau,« 490: »Erlösungsbedürftigkeit.«

10. Mit Peterson, *Der Brief an die Römer*, 39: »Der Zorn Gottes ist also nicht bloß etwas Eschatologisches, erst am Jüngsten Tag in Erscheinung Tretendes, sondern etwas, was es jetzt schon gibt, . . .« Gegen Eckstein, »Denn Gottes Zorn wird vom Himmel her offenbar,« 19–35; und Woyke, *Götter*, »Götzen,« *Götterbilder*, 370; Anm. 1, welche beide die präsentische Form ἀποκαλύπτεται futurisch deuten.

wurde ihr unverständiges Herz. (22)Indem sie behaupteten, weise zu sein, wurden sie töricht (23)und haben die Herrlichkeit des unvergänglichen Gottes vertauscht (ἤλλαξαν) mit der Gleichgestalt des Bildes des vergänglichen Menschen und von Vögeln und Vierfüßlern und Kriechtieren.

Hier wird die »allgemeine Begründung« in den VV. 19–20 konkretisiert. Dass diese Konkretisierung auf Heiden zutrifft und nicht auf Juden, ist evident, denn diese haben eben nicht Bilder von Menschen und Tieren als Götter verehrt. Dies passt genau zum jüdischen »Heidenspiegel«![11]

Auf diese Anklage erfolgt die *Reaktion* Gottes, wie Paulus sie in 1,24 darstellt: Διὸ παρέδωκεν αὐτοὺς ὁ θεός. Διό deutet ausdrücklich an, dass es sich um die Reaktion Gottes auf die Anklage wegen des Agierens der Heiden handelt. »Παραδιδόναι meint den Entscheid des Richters«.[12]

Der Richterspruch lautet:

(24)Deshalb hat Gott sie an die Begierden (ἐπιθυμίαι) ihres Herzens in Unreinheit preisgegeben, so dass ihre Leiber durch sich selbst geschändet wurden.

Es handelt sich um eine Auslieferung in Unreinheit in Form sexueller Fehlorientierung.[13] Denn εἰς ἀκαθαρσίαν ist nicht im kultischen Sinne zu verstehen, sondern es handelt sich um Unzucht (vgl. Röm 6,19; Gal 5,19 und TestJos 4,6). Schlier schreibt dazu zutreffend: » . . . die Sexualisierung öffentlichen und privaten Lebens war ein Hauptkennzeichen der verfallenen heidnischen antiken Welt nach jüdischem und christlichem Urteil«.[14] Die Menschen verherrlichen und ehren sich auf diese Weise selbst, anstatt Gott als Schöpfer Ehre zu bringen. Es geht also in diesem ersten »*Aktions-* und *Reaktions*-Verhältnis« im wahren Sinne um »Götzendienst«. Die Infinitivkonstruktion τοῦ ἀτιμάζεσθαι ist konsekutiv zu verstehen: »so dass sie ihre eigenen Leiber durch ihr eigenes tun entehrten«.[15]

(2) Die *zweite* Anklage lautet:

---

11. Siehe Braun, »πλανάω κτλ.,« 244. Belege finden sich vor allem in den Kommentaren von Fitzmyer, siehe Anm. 17 und Jewett, siehe Anm. 6.

12. Lohse, *Der Brief an die Römer*, 89; vgl. 1 Kor 5,5; Horn, »Götzendiener,« 214. Zum terminus technicus der gerichtsprachlichen Formel παρέδωκεν αὐτοὺς ὁ θεός, siehe bes. Popkes, *Christus Traditus*, 82–85. Vgl. 1. Kor 5,5 (παραδοῦναι τὸν τοιοῦτον τῷ σατανᾷ εἰς ὄλεθρον τῆς σαρκός) und dazu Popkes, ibid., 138–140.

13. Siehe z.B. Seneca, *Ep. mor.* 15.95, 20–21. Zu Lukian und Ps.-Lukian siehe zusammenfassend Betz, *Lukian von Samosata*, 199–201.

14. Schlier, *Römerbrief*, 59.

15. So Schlier, ibid., 47, 60.

> (25)*Haben sie doch die Wahrheit Gottes mit der Lüge vertauscht (μετήλλαξαν) und der Schöpfung anstelle des Schöpfers Verehrung und Dienst erwiesen. Gepriesen sei er in alle Ewigkeit. Amen.*

War in der ersten Anklage von Bilderverehrungen die Rede, wird hier in der *zweiten Anklage* die Verdrehung der Wahrheit Gottes zum Ausdruck gebracht und ausdrücklich, wenn auch in allgemeiner Formulierung, vom »Götzendienst« gesprochen: es stehen sich »Gottes Wahrheit« und »menschliche Lüge« gegenüber. Dies ist ein weiterer und *steigernder* Ausdruck des »Götzendienstes«, denn es ist deutlich, dass für Paulus die religiöse Verehrung der Schöpfung als des Schöpfers nicht anderes als »Götzendienst« ist. Wie abscheulich dem Paulus diese Verdrehung anmutet, kommt durch den abrupten Schluss der Anklage zum Ausdruck. Anstelle den Gedankengang fortzuführen, bringt er eine feierliche Benediktion im *jüdischen* Stil: ὅς ἐστιν εὐλογητὸς εἰς τοὺς αἰῶνας, ἀμήν.[16] So wird Gott als Gott geehrt, nicht der Mensch als Gott! Deutlicher könnte Paulus es nicht zum Ausdruck gebracht haben!

Auf diese zweite Anklage folgt auch eine *zweite Reaktion* Gottes, wie wir sie in den VV. 26–27 ausführlich vorfinden: Διὰ τοῦτο παρέδωκεν αὐτοὺς ὁ θεός. Διά hier verstärkt durch τοῦτο, wie vorhin διό allein, deutet ausdrücklich an, dass es sich erneut um die Reaktion Gottes auf die Anklage wegen des Agierens der Heiden handelt.

In ihrer Ausführlichkeit lautet Gottes Urteil:

> (26a)*Darum hat Gott sie schändlichen Leidenschaften (πάθη ἀτιμίας) preisgegeben (παρέδωκεν). (26b)Denn ihre Frauen vertauschten (μετήλλαξαν) den natürlichen Verkehr mit dem widernatürlichen (αἵ τε γὰρ θήλειαι αὐτῶν μετήλλαξαν τὴν φυσικήν χρῆσιν εἰς τὴν παρὰ φύσιν). (27)Ebenso (ὁμοίως τε καί) haben auch die Männer (οἱ ἄρσενες) den natürlichen Verkehr mit der Frau aufgegeben und sind in ihrer Brunst (ὄρεξις) zueinander entbrannt (ἐξεκαύθησαν). Männer trieben mit Männern Schamloses (τὴν ἀσχημοσύνην κατεργάζεσθαι) und erhielten die gebührende Vergeltung (ἀντιμισθία) an sich selbst (ἐν ἑαυτοῖς) für ihre Verwirrung (πλάνη).*

War die erste Reaktion Gottes einigermaßen allgemein und kurz gehalten, wohl aber mit einem »Richterspruch« versehen, ist die *zweite Reaktion* deutlich ausführlicher und vor allem sehr viel konkreter gehalten. Zwar war auch dort von sexueller Fehlorientierung die Rede, hier aber begegnet als Urteil Gottes zuerst seine Preisgebung an »schändlichen Leidenschaften«

---

16. Zu dieser jüdischen Formel, siehe Dahl, »Benediction and Congratulation,« 279–314.

im sexuellen Bereich in allgemeiner Formulierung (V. 26a), auf die sodann zwei Vergegenständlichungen in Bezug auf das Verhältnis von Frauen untereinander (V. 26b) und danach ebenso von Männern untereinander folgen (V. 27). Durch ὁμοίως τε καί wird deutlich, dass es sich bei Frauen um ein lesbisches Verhalten handelt.[17]

Der erste Beleg von lesbischen Beziehungen auf jüdischer Seite ist anscheinend *Ps-Phok.* 192 mit dem Verbot lesbischer Beziehungen nach dem Verbot der männlichen Homosexualität:[18]

(190)Weiche nicht ab von naturgemäßem Lager zu sittenwidriger Wollust (ἐς Κύπριν)—(191)nicht einmal bei Tieren findet Beischlaf unter Männlichen Beifall. (192)Auch sollen Frauen nicht das Beilager von Männern nachahmen (μηδέ τι θηλύτεραι λέχος ἀνδρῶν μιμήσαιντο).

Zahlreiche Belege für die Kritik an lesbischen Beziehungen in der griechisch-römischen Literatur finden sich bei Bernadette Brooten.[19] Aus Platzgründen muss ein Zitat aus M. Valerius Martialis (1.90) genügen.[20] Die Bassa war niemals mit Männern zusammengesehen worden, sondern nur mit Geschlechtsgenossinnen und deshalb als eine Lucretia, die tugendhafte Matrone,[21] bewertet:[22]

Doch du, Bassa warst—welche Schande!—eine Frau die vögelt. Du wagst es, deine Möse mit der einer anderen Frau zusammenzubringen, und den Mann imitiert deine unnatürliche Leidenschaft. Du dachtest dir eine Perversität aus, die dem

17 Siehe Fitzmyer, *Romans*, 287; Brooten, *Love between Women*, 253. Anders Haaker, *Der Brief des Paulus an die Römer*, 53: »Warnung vor Geschlechtsverkehr mit Tieren.« Dagegen Brooten, ibid.

18. Deutsche Übers. in Walter, »Pseudo-Phokylides.« 213; Text, engl. Übers. und Kommentar in van der Horst, *The Sentences of Pseudo-Phocylides*, 100–101, 237–40. Text, engl. Übers. und ausführlicher Kommentar bei Wilson, *The Sentences of Pseudo-Phocylides*, 187 (Übers.), 196–99 (Komm.), 221 (Gr. Text).

19. Brooten, *Love between Women*, 41–57.

20. Ähnlich kritisch Lukian, *Dial. meretr.* 5.289; Vettius Valens, *Anth.* 2.17.66–68; Plautus, *Truc.* 262–63; Ovid, *Metam.* 9.724–48; Seneca d.J., *Ep.* 95.23–24; Phaedrus, *Fab. Aesop.* IV 16; Juvenal, *Sat.* 2.43–50; Maximus von Tyros, *Dial.* 20.9; siehe Brooten, *Love between Women*, 48–49; Strecker / Schnelle, *Neuer Wettstein*, 2/1:32–50.

21. Zu Lucretia, siehe Prescendi, »Weiblichkeitsideale in der römischen Welt,« 221–26: Text und Übers. von Ovid, *Fast.* 2.721–852. Ferner die Beiträge, *ibid.*, »VI. Erotik und Sexualität«; von Hartmann, »Hetären im klassischen Athen«; Dierichs, »Erotik in der Bildenden Kunst der Römischen Welt«; Schneider, »Das Ende der antiken Leiblichkeit«; Zittel, »Hieronymus und Paula,« 377–437.

22. Barié und Schindler, Hgg., *M. Valerius Martialis, Epigramme*, 96–97; vgl. ibid., 7.67 (Tageslauf einer Tribade); weiter Ps.-Lukian, *Erōtes*, 28.

thebanischen Rätsel würdig war: dass es dort Hurerei gibt, wo kein Mann ist (*hic ubi vir non est, ut sit adulterium*).

In dem Abschnitt im Röm über die männliche Homosexualität treten zwei *Hapax legomena* im Neuen Testament auf (ἐκκαίω—»entbrennen« und ὄρεξις—»Begierde«)[23]. Die Exemplifizierung, die Paulus hier bringt, ist insofern höchst adäquat, denn vor allem in der griechischen aber auch in der römischen Welt galt die Homosexualität als akzeptabel und dies besonders bezüglich der sog. »Knabenliebe« (τὸ παιδεραστεῖν).[24] Kritik an der Knabenliebe, die in den hellenistischen Städten vorkommt, findet sich aber nicht nur bei jüdischen Verfassern wie Philon, *Spec. leg.* III 37–39, 42:[25]

> Es hat sich aber in den Städten noch ein anderes . . . Übel eingenistet, die Knabenliebe (τὸ παιδεραστεῖν): während es früher als große Schande galt, auch nur davon zu sprechen, rühmen sich ihrer jetzt nicht nur die, welche sie üben, sondern auch diejenigen, die sich dazu gebrauchen lassen,

oder *Or. Sib.* III 594–600: Ein heiliges Geschlecht wird wiederum kommen:[26]

> [D]och weitaus am meisten von allen Menschen sind eingedenk stets sie des keuschen und heiligen Lagers und sie treiben nicht mit Knaben schamlosen Umgang, wie die Phöniker, Ägypter es machen, sowie die Latiner und das weiträumige Hellas und zahlreiche andere Völker, Perser und Galater und ganz Asien, die überschritten des unsterblichen Gottes Gesetz, das er hat gegeben (παραβάντες ἀθανάτοιο θεοῦ ἁγνὸν νόμον, ὅνπερ ἔθηκεν);

Ferner heißt es in V. 430: in der Zeit der Erlösung gibt es

> bei den elenden Menschen nicht mehr Gewalttat, schändlichen Ehebruch nicht, noch ruchlose Liebe zu Knaben (καὶ παίδων Κύπρις ἄθεσμος).[27]

23. Siehe Bauer und Aland, *Wörterbuch*, 484 bzw. 1175.

24. Cranfield, *The Epistle to the Romans*, 1:127: »The fact that ancient Greek and Roman society not only regarded paederasty with indulgence but was inclined to glorify it as actually superior to heterosexual love is too well known to need to be dwelt on here.«

25. Philo, *Spec. leg.* III 37–39, 42; Text bei Cohn, *Philonis Alexandrini*, 160; Übers. Heinemann, *Philo von Alexandria*, Bd. II, 194–95. Hier wie in anderen zitierten Texten handelt es sich sowohl um passive wie aktive Personen.

26. Text und Übers. bei Kurfeß und Gauger, Hgg., *Sibyllinische Weissagungen*, 100–101. Vgl. auch Geffcken, *Die Oracula Sibyllina*, 78–79.

27. Text und Übers., Kurfeß und Gauger, Hgg., *Sibyllinische Weissagungen*,, 148–49. Siehe ferner die zahlreichen Belegstellen bei Strecker und Schnelle, *Neuer Wettstein*, 2/1:32–50.

Aber auch bei den Griechen, wie z.B. bei Xenophon, *Resp. Lac.* 2,12–14,[28] wird von der gängig praktizierten »Knabenliebe« ablehnend berichtet; der spartanische Lykurgos, der die Bewunderung der Seele eines Knaben bejahte, war allerdings anderer Meinung in Bezug auf die körperliche Annäherung:

> [W]enn aber jemand offenkundig den Körper eines Knaben begehrte, hielt er dies für äußerst schädlich (αἴσχιστον) und bewirkte in Sparta, dass Liebhaber sich um nichts weniger von geliebten Knaben fernhalten als Eltern sich von ihren Kindern und Geschwister sich von ihren Geschwistern in Hinsicht auf den Liebesgenuss fernhalten.

Ein weiteres Beispiel ist bei Polybios, *Hist.*, VIII 11,9–12 zu lesen, der eine Stelle aus den *Philippika* des Historikers Theopompos von Chios bezüglich der Freunde König Philipps II. von Makedonien zitiert:[29]

> Die Freunde Philipps (10)führten zwei oder drei Lustknaben mit sich herum und ließen sich gleichzeitig selbst von anderen in derselben Weise missbrauchen (αὐτοὶ δὲ τὰς αὐτὰς ἐκείνοις χρήσεις ἑτέροις παρείχοντο). (11)Daher muss man sie mit Fug und Recht nicht Freunde, sondern »Freundinnen« nennen, nicht Soldaten, sondern Dirnen, (12)Messerhelden von Natur, zu Männer-Huren entartet (ἀνδροφόνοι γὰρ τὴν φύσιν ὄντες ἀνδρόπορνοι τὸν τρόπον ἦσαν).

Die Akzeptanz der männlichen Homosexualität inklusive Knabenliebe war also ambivalent in der griechisch-römischen Welt wie sogar Platon's Überlegungen im *Symp.* 181a–185e zeigen:[30]

> Es ist nämlich nicht schlechthin einerlei in allen Fällen, . . . , dass es an und für sich weder schön (καλόν) noch schändlich (αἰσχρόν) sei, sondern schön behandelt ist es schön, anders aber schändlich. Schändlich (αἰσχρῶς) nämlich ist es, einem Schlechten (πονηρῷ) und auf schlechte Art (πονηρῶς) gefällig zu werden; schön (καλῶς) aber, einem Guten (χρηστῷ) und auf schöne Art (καλῶς). (183d).

Eine positive Darstellung findet sich aber in *Symp.* 191e:[31]

---

28. Übers. bei Strecker und Schnelle, *Neuer Wettstein*, 2/1:40–41.

29. Übers. bei ibid., 2/1:42.

30. Text und Übers. bei des Places & Méridie und Schleiermacher & Kurz, *Platon. Werke in acht Bänden*, Bd. 3, 247–48.

31. Platon, *Werke*, 3:190–91.

> Welche Weiber aber Abschnitte eines Weibes sind, die küm-
> mern sich nicht viel um die Männer, sondern sind mehr den
> Weibern zugewendet und die Tribaden kommen aus diesem
> Geschlecht; die aber Schnitte eines Mannes sind, suchen das
> Männliche auf und, solange sie noch Knaben sind, lieben sie
> als Schnittstücke des Mannes die Männer, und bei Männern zu
> liegen und sich mit ihnen zu umschlingen ergötzt sie, und dies
> sind die trefflichsten unter den Knaben und heranwachsenden
> Jünglingen, weil sie die männlichsten sind von Natur (φύσει).

Hier findet sich auch die wohl erste Belegstelle in der griechischen
Literatur für weibliche Homoerotik.[32]

Wie aber aus Platon's, *Leg.*, 1, 636c hervorgeht, wenn er über Kinderzeugung schreibt, beurteilt er nunmehr die Homoerotik in ganz anderer
Weise:[33]

> . . . muss man doch bedenken, dass dem weiblichen und dem
> männlichen Geschlecht, wenn sie sich zu gemeinsamer Zeu-
> gung vereinen, die damit verbundene Lust offensichtlich gemäß
> der Natur (κατὰ φύσιν) zugeteilt worden ist, während die
> Vereinigung von Männern mit Männern und von Frauen mit
> Frauen wider die Natur (παρὰ φύσιν) ist . . .

Die Gläubigen, Heiden- wie Judenchristen, in Rom wussten also alle
genau, wovon Paulus redete.

Warum aber behandelt Paulus zuerst die Frauen und ihre lesbischen
Leidenschaften und erst nachher die Männer und ihre homosexuellen
Leidenschaften? Darauf findet man in der Literatur zumindest drei Er-
klärungen: (1) Otto Michel in seinem Kommentar weist auf die Schöp-
fungsgeschichte mit Eva als die zuerst verführte hin.[34] (2) Robert Jewett
erklärt die Reihenfolge unter Verweis auf die griechisch-römische Auffassung, dass das lesbische Verhalten der Frauen noch viel schlimmer als das
männlich-homosexuelle beurteilt wurde, da letzteres viel akzeptabler sei
und in der antiken Literatur weit ausführlicher behandelt wird. In Bezug auf
die »Knabenliebe« unter den Philosophen und in der Oberschicht dürfte
dies zutreffen, aber so nicht für erwachsene Männer;[35] (3) Eduard Lohse
dagegen ist der Auffassung, dass Paulus hier eine *Steigerung* beabsichtigt,

---

32. So Brooten, *Love between Women*, 41.

33. Text und Übers. bei des Places und Schöpsau, *Platon. Werke in acht Bänden*,
8/1:34–37.

34. Michel, *Der Brief an die Römer*, 105. Dagegen Käsemann, *An die Römer*, 44–45;
Cranfield, *The Epistle to the Romans*, 1:125.

35. Jewett, *Romans*, 174ff.

da »das viel schlimmere Treiben der Männer« auf das weniger Schlimme folgt;[36] also das genaue Gegenteil von Jewetts Erklärung der Reihenfolge.

Bei der Befürwortung der einen oder anderen Interpretation sollte man berücksichtigen, erstens dass hier die »Knabenliebe« erstaunlicherweise mit keinem Wort erwähnt wird, sondern ausschließlich von männlichem Fehlverhalten im Einverständnis die Rede ist;[37] zweitens dass es außerdem beachtenswert ist, wie viel ausführlicher die Darstellung der männlichen Homosexualität im Vergleich zum weiblich-lesbischen gestaltet wird;[38] drittens dass ausschließlich bei der Darstellung der Homosexualität der Männer von der immanent-präsentischen Vergeltung oder Strafe gesprochen wird,[39] wenn es heißt:

Die »*Männer . . . erhielten die gebührende Vergeltung / Strafe (ἀντιμισθία) an sich selbst (ἐν ἑαυτοῖς) für ihre Verwirrung (πλάνη)*«.

Aus diesen drei Gründen meine ich, dass Paulus in der Tat eine *Steigerung* beabsichtigt,[40] wie er dies auch an vielen anderen Stellen tut.[41]

Die Differenz zwischen Jewett und Lohse beruht auf zwei verschiedenen methodischen Ansätzen: Jewett interpretiert den Paulustext hauptsächlich aufgrund Parallelmaterials aus griechisch-römischen astrologischen und medizinischen Quellen; also auf einer text-*externen* Basis. Lohse, wenn auch sehr knapp, folgt eher dem Duktus des Textes;[42] also aufgrund einer text-*internen* Analyse. Man sollte auch notieren, wie Jewett den Unterschied in der Darstellung von weiblicher und männlicher Homoerotik

36. Lohse, *Brief an die Römer*, 90. Vgl. unten Anm. 38.

37. Anders Scroggs, *The New Testament and Homosexuality*, 116.

38. Cranfield, *The Epistle to the Romans*, 1:125.

39. Eine presentisch-immanente Wirkung bei Frauen findet sich aber in Seneca, d.J., *Ep. mor.* 15.95.20–21: »In der Lüsternheit aber stehen sie auch hinter Männern nicht zurück: zur Hingabe geboren—die Götter und Göttinnen mögen sie vernichten! (*di illas deaeque male perdant!*)—haben sie eine äußerst widernatürliche Art von Unzucht ersonnen und begatten die Männer. Was also muss man sich wundern, dass der größte Arzt und beste Kenner der Natur (sc. Hippokrates) bei einer unzutreffenden Aussage ertappt wird, weil so viele Frauen gichtkrank und kahlköpfig sind?« Siehe auch Brooten, *Love between Women*, 45.

40. So auch Popkes, »Aufbau,« 497: »Die Darstellung erfolgt in eindrücklicher Steigerung; in den drei παρέδωκεν-Runden fällt die Schilderung des Verfalls immer umfangreicher, die der Verfehlung immer knapper aus . . . Die Steigerung bei der Verfallsschilderung ist bewußtes Stilmittel (v. 24, 26–27, 28b–31).«

41. Zur Steigerung (*amplificatio*), siehe die angeführten Aufsätze von mir oben in Anm. 1 und 8.

42. Popkes, »Aufbau,« 492: »Die traditionsgeschichtliche Betrachtung von Röm 1,18–32 bietet nicht für alle Schwierigkeiten die Lösung . . . [W]ichtiger ist in jedem Fall die paulinische Argumentationslinie selber.«

herunterspielt und die Egalität unterstreicht. Außerdem berücksichtigt er zum größten Teil die jüdischen Voraussetzungen bei Paulus eher beiläufig.

Wenn Paulus von τὴν φυσικὴν χρῆσιν, »dem natürlichen Geschlechtsverkehr« spricht,[43] dann geht er von seinem jüdischen kulturellen Verständnis aus, aber unter Verwendung griechisch-römischer kultureller Begrifflichkeit.[44] Richtig hat Jewett das Vorgehen des Paulus charakterisiert, wenn er schreibt: »Paul is raising a cultural norm to the level of ›natural‹ and thus biological principle, which would probably have to be formulated differently today«.[45]

Man sollte auch notieren, dass Paulus weder hier noch anderswo von Kinderzeugung (παιδοποιία) im Zusammenhang mit der Sexualität spricht,[46] was im Hinblick vor allem, aber nicht ausschließlich, auf seine jüdische Herkunft und Argumentationsweise eher erstaunlich ist.[47] Man vergleiche nur Josephus in seiner Schrift »Gegen Apion«, wo es im Hinblick auf das Ehegesetz heißt:[48]

> Das Gesetz (ὁ νόμος) anerkennt keine sexuellen Beziehungen mit Ausnahme des natürlichen (κατὰ φύσιν) Verkehrs des Mannes mit der Frau in der Absicht Kinder zu erzeugen.

Auch in anderer Hinsicht weicht Paulus in gewissem Grade von traditionell antiken Vorstellungen ab, insofern als er in egalitärer Weise die Homoerotik beider Geschlechter negativ bewertet und somit in etwa gleichstellt (vgl. weiter I Kor 7,4.7). Beim Vergleich zwischen den weiblichen und männlichen Ausführungen, sollte man allerdings, wie Jewett zurecht bemerkt, nicht übersehen, dass in V. 26 ein Moment der patriarchalischen Gesellschaftsordnung noch stehengeblieben ist, wenn Paulus schreibt αἱ θήλειαι αὐτῶν »ihre Frauen« (sic!); von »ihren Männern« ist aber nicht die Rede![49]

Ich habe schon darauf hingewiesen, dass die immanent-präsentische Vergeltung bzw. Strafe nur im Zusammenhang mit den männlichen

---

43. Χρῆσις in dieser Bedeutung findet sich im NT nur hier, siehe Bauer und Aland, *Wörterbuch*, 1766.

44. Jewett, *Romans*, 179.

45. Ibid., 177.

46. Fitzmyer, *First Corinthians*, 276, mit Hinweis u.a. auf Musonius Rufus, *Fragm.* XIII. Deming, *Paul on Marriage*, 51ff., 78–79; Schrage, *Der erste Brief an die Korinther*, 2:65; Zeller, *Der erste Brief an die Korinther*, 238. Vgl. ferner Delling, »Geschlechtsverkehr,« 816–17, 818–21.

47. Könnte dies damit zusammenhängen, dass er wohl selber keine Kinder hatte?

48. Josephus, *Contra Apionem*, II.199.

49. Jewett, *Romans*, 177.

homoerotischen Leidenschaften (ἐπιθυμίαι) erwähnt wird. Wie soll man diesen Sachverhalt erklären? Direkt sagt Paulus es nicht, aber man kann es mit Vorsicht aus antiken Quellen erschließen. Schlier deutet es allerdings nur sehr vage an: »Diese Perversion . . . vollzieht sich innerweltlich schon jetzt am Leib der Heiden«;[50] genauer müsste es heißen: »am Leib der männlichen Heiden«! Deutlicher drückt sich Jewett unter Verweis auf griechisch-hellenistische Quellen (z.B. Hippokrates: δῆσαι) sowie ein Reihe Sekundärliteratur aus, wenn er schreibt: »The ›recompense‹ that homosexual males therefore receive is this soreness (δῆσαι) that they experience ἐν ἑαυτοῖς (›in themselves‹). The ancient sexual logic of this passage helps to explain why Paul employs this phenomenon of male homoeroticism as a prime instance of divine wrath that manifests itself in the act itself«.[51] Beispiele aus einer Reihe antiker Quellen beleuchten diese Interpretation. Im *Sl. Henoch* X, 4–5 findet sich folgende Erklärung für die Strafen im Hades:[52]

»Und die Männer [sc. angeli interpretes] sprachen zu mir: ›Dieser Ort Henoch ist denen bereitet, die Gott verunehren; die Böses tun auf Erden, Unzucht gegen die Natur, das ist Knabenschändung im After [d.h. Anus], sodomitisch, . . . ‹« bzw. im XXXIV, 2: Gott kennt die Bosheit der Menschen und droht ihnen deshalb: »Und die ganze Erde wird zusammenbrechen durch Ungerechtigkeiten und Kränkungen, und unreinen Ehebruch, das ist einer mit dem anderen im After, und alle anderen gottlosen Schlechtigkeiten, die widerwärtig sind auszusprechen, und schlechten Dienst«.

Auch im Zoroastrismus gelten die homoerotischen Leidenschaften in einer Reihe von Avestatexten sowie in Pahlavitexten als schwere Sünde und wird demgemäß schwer bestraft, u.a. mit der *Todesstrafe*,[53] wie vor allem Prods Oktor Skjærvø mit zahlreichen Belegen gezeigt hat,[54] besonders in *Videvdad* (*Vendidad*), die einzig vollständig bewahrte von den 21 Nasks

---

50. Schlier, *Römerbrief*, 62; Lohse, *Brief an die Römer*, 91.

51. Jewett, *Romans*, 179; Dunn, *Romans 1–8*, 65: »the genital act itself.«

52. Übers. Böttrich, »Das slavische Henochbuch,« 856–57, bzw. 937.

53. So aber auch Josephus, *Contra Apionem* II.199: »Es (sc. das Gesetz) verabscheucht, wenn Männer mit Männern schlafen und *bestraft mit dem Tode* wer solches betreibt« (τὴν δὲ πρὸς ἄρρενας ἀρρένων ἐστύγηκε, καὶ θάνατος τοὐπιτίμιον εἴ τις ἐπιχειρήσειεν). Wohl im Anschluss an Lev 18,22 und 20,13. Siehe unten zu V. 32: οἱ τὰ τοιαῦτα πράσσοντες ἄξιοι θανάτου εἰσίν.

54. Skjærvø, »Homosexuality i. in Zoroastrianism,« 440–41. Weitere iranische Texte zum Thema sind u.a. *Dādestān ī Dēnīg*, Fragen 72–77; *Mēnōy ī Xrad*, 35/36.4–5; *Ardā Wirāz Nāmag*, 19: The first punishment of sin that Wirāz encounters in Hell is that of a passive anal intercourse: »I saw a man whose soul entered into his anus and came out of his mouth, as a beam-like snake . . . This is the soul of that wicked man who committed sodomy in the world and allowed a man over himself« (text und trans. in Vahman, *Ardā Wīrāz Nāmag*, 202).

(d.h. Bündel von Schriften): »The information about ›homosexuality‹ contained in this literature is restricted to anal intercourse, as defined in the *Videvdad* (8.32): ›When a man releases his semen in a man or when a man receives the semen of men‹. The action takes place between sexually mature males (*aršan-*), and there is no mention of sexual intercourse between prepubescent boys and adult males . . . or between women . . . According to the myth of the establishment of the lands of Iran in the *Videvdad* (1.11), anal intercourse between men was produced by the Evil Spirit to plague Ahura Mazdā's ninth creation . . . The term used is *narō.vaēpiia*—›male anal intercourse‹ . . .«.[55] »Elsewhere in the Avesta anal intercourse is only mentioned as an instance of sinful behavior that is to be punished. There is a distinction between consensual and non-consensual passive partners«.[56]

Die Ausübung der Homosexualität unter Männern ist nach Paulus ein »sich bereits hier und jetzt vollziehendes Gericht Gottes«.[57] In diesem Zusammenhang muss noch darauf hingewiesen werden, dass diese ausführliche Darstellung als die Bestrafung Gottes hingestellt wird und nicht als die Ursache für eine Bestrafung.[58] Es ist das Resultat des Zornes Gottes und nicht dessen Voraussetzung!

Mit Recht stellen Joseph Fitzmyer und Robert Jewett die Frage, warum Paulus ausgerechnet dieses Beispiel für die Verfallenheit der heidnischen Welt benutzt, da ja die Homoerotik in großem Ausmaß in der griechisch-römischen Welt für »normal« oder zumindest »akzeptabel« galt.[59] Die Antwort geht von zwei gegenseitigen Sachverhalten aus: (1) die Romgemeinden waren überwiegend heidnisch und (2) unter den Mitgliedern befanden sich Herren und deren männlichen Sklaven, die von ihren Herren sexuell ausgenützt und belästigt worden waren und möglicherweise immer noch wurden nachdem sie Christen geworden waren.[60] Es gibt im Römerbrief allerdings keine wahrhaften Anhaltspunkte für eine sexuelle Zügellosigkeit in den Romgemeinden, die zu diesen Ausführungen Anlass gegeben hätten.

55. Skjærvø, »Homosexuality i. in Zoroastrianism,« 440; Der Pahlaviterminus ist »*kun-marz.*«

56. Ibid.

57. Lohse, *Brief an die Römer*, 91. So schon Peterson, *Der Brief an die Römer*, 39 (siehe oben Anm. 10) und Schlier, *Römerbrief*, 62.

58. So auch Käsemann, *An die Römer*, 43; Dunn, *Romans 1–8*, 64; Jewett, *Romans*, 173.

59. Fitzmeyer, *Romans*, 275–76; Jewett, *Romans*, 189ff. Siehe aber die angeführten Texte oben.

60. Siehe die Belegstellen bei Jewett, *Romans*, 180–81; Vgl. Glancy, *Slavery in Early Christianity*, 50–53. Ferner Harrill, *Slaves in the New Testament*, 129–33.

Man muss aber meiner Meinung nach differenzierter vorgehen: (1) Die Romgemeinden bestanden sicherlich überwiegend aus Heidenchristen (1,5; 16,26), aber nach 54, als Nero Claudius Edikt aufgehoben hatte, waren viele Juden und Juden-Christen nach Rom zurückgekehrt, u.a. Priska und Aquila (Röm 16,3),[61] und sie hatten ein noch abschlägigeres Verständnis von Homosexualität als die Heiden bzw. Heidenchristen; (2) Der Hinweis auf das Herren-Sklaven-Verhältnis dürfte zutreffend sein, obwohl die christlichen Quellen größtenteils darüber schweigen.

Es gibt aber noch eine Erklärung, die außerdem eine Rolle gespielt haben dürfte, als Paulus dieses Beispiel für die Verdorbenheit der Heidenwelt anführte. Hier argumentiert er als Jude und damit beugt er gewissermaßen Angriffe seitens der Judenchristen und vor allem der Judaisten vor, sein Evangelium führe zu einer laxen (sexuellen) Lebensweise. Diesen Vorwurf muss er in 3,8ff. und 6,1ff. zurückweisen.[62] Aber schon hier bei der Verwendung des »Heidenspiegels« wehrt er sich zumindest indirekt gegen solche Vorwürfe, und zwar dadurch, dass er den jüdischen Moralkodex aufrechterhält und die Heidenwelt mit dem Zorn Gottes bedroht.[63]

(3) Die *dritte Anklage* lautet:

(28a) *Und weil sie es nicht wert geachtet haben, Gott in der Erkenntnis (ἐπίγνωσις) zu bewahren, . . . «.*

Anders als in den vorherigen Anschuldigungen besteht die Anklage nur aus einer generellen Zusammenfassung ohne Konkretisierung. Ἐπίγνωσις bedeutet Erkenntnis, die in Anerkennung mündet.

Auch auf diese dritte Anklage folgt eine *Reaktion* Gottes (παρέδωκεν αὐτοὺς ὁ θεὸς), wie wir sie in den VV. 28b–31 ausführlich vorfinden. Die Reaktion besteht hier aus zwei Teilen: zuerst zur Auslieferung zu einem allgemeinen korrumpierten Denken (εἰς ἀδόκιμον νοῦν), so dass sie tun, was sich nicht gehört; hier können wir ein Wortspiel mit den Lexemen οὐκ ἐδοκίμασαν—ἀδόκιμον (»nicht wert achten—unbewährt«) beobachten; danach folgt eine *Steigerung* in Form einer Präzisierung bzw. einer ausführlichen

---

61. Hierzu Lampe, *Die stadtrömischen Christen*, 53–65. [Engl. trans., 68–79.]

62. Siehe Vielhauer, *Geschichte der urchristlichen Literatur*, 183–84; Hellholm, »Enthymemic Argumentation,« 142–46; ferner Hellholm, »Vorgeformte Tauftraditionen,« 468: »Im Blick auf die schon eingetretene oder unmittelbar bevorstehende Bedrohung der paulinischen Rechtfertigungsbotschaft durch Vertreter der Synagoge oder durch judaistische Propagandisten argumentiert Paulus in Kap. 6 besonders ausführlich, und angesichts der absurden Anklage des Libertinismus tut er es . . . gewiss schon in 3,8, aber jetzt in Kap. 6 in voller Intensität.«

63. Allerdings war dieser jüdische Moralkodex nicht immer aufrechterhalten, wie die Beispiele bei [Strack] und Billerbeck, *Kommentar zum Neuen Testament aus Talmud und Midrasch*, 3:71–72, bekunden.

Zusammenfassung der bisherigen Argumentation mittels eines überaus umfassenden *Lasterkatalogs:*[64]

> *(29)Sie sind voll (πεπληρωμένους) allerlei Ungerechtigkeit, Schlechtigkeit, Habsucht, Bosheit; voll (μεστούς) von Neid, Mord, Streit, List, Verschlagenheit; Ohrenbläser, (30)Verleumder, Gotteshasser, Gewalttäter, Überhebliche, Prahler; erfinderisch (ἐφευρετάς) im Bösen, den Eltern Ungehorsame, (31)unverständig, unbeständig, lieblos, ohne Erbarmen.*

Durch diesen Lasterkatalog bestätigt sich, dass Paulus hier am krönenden Ende seiner Anklage bzw. des göttlichen Gerichtsurteils gegen die pagane Welt den von Juden erstellten »Heidenspiegel« in seiner Argumentation benutzt.

Zu den Lasterkatalogen bei Paulus (1 Kor 5,10f.; 6,9f.; 2 Kor 12,20; Gal 5,19–21) sowie in den Deuteropaulinen (u.a. Kol 3,5.8; Eph 4,31; 5,3–5) siehe den Artikel »Lasterkatalog / Tugendkataloge« von Hans Dieter Betz.[65] Wert zu notieren ist, dass in den Lasterkatalogen hier und anderswo im Neuen Testament das Thema Homoerotik, mit zwei Ausnahmen, nicht auftaucht. Die einzige zusätzliche Stelle bei Paulus, wo männliche Homosexualität erwähnt und verdammt wird ist 1 Kor 6,9: »Wisst ihr etwa nicht, dass Ungerechte Gottes Reich nicht erben werden? Verfallt keinem Irrtum« (μὴ πλανᾶσθε)[66]. Die Erwähnung der Homosexualität findet sich hier, anders als im Röm 1,26–27, innerhalb eines Lasterkatalogs:[67]

> *(9)Weder Unzüchtige noch Götzenverehrer noch Ehebrecher (μοιχοί) noch Weichlinge (μαλακοί) noch die mit Männern schlafen (ἀρσενοκοῖται), (10)noch Diebe noch Habgierige, nicht Trunkenbolde, nicht Lästerer, nicht Räuber werden das Reich Gottes erben.*

---

64. Zur Stilistik dieses Lasterkatalogs siehe u.a. Peterson, *Brief an die Römer*, 42: (1) Assonanz mittels Dativendungen auf *epiphora*: ἀδικίᾳ, πονηρίᾳ, πλεονεξίᾳ, κακίᾳ; (2) Assonanz durch Vokalwechsel von α zu ο/ου: φθόνου, φόνου, ἔριδος, δόλου; (3) die syntagmatische Reihenfolge: ἐφευρετὰς κακῶν, γονεῦσιν ἀπειθεῖς; (4) συμπλοκή / *complexio* mit *anaphora* und *epiphora*, die z.T. auch eine Paronomasie bilden: ἀσυνέτους, ἀσυνθέτους, ἀστόργους. Vgl. die schwedische Übers. 2000: »tanklösa, trolösa, kärleckslösa, [hjärtlösa]« bzw. die norwegische Übers. (Bokmål) 2008: »uforstandige, upålitelige, ukjærlige [og ubarmhjertige].« Zu den rhetorischen Begriffen, siehe Hellholm, »Universalität und Partikularität,« 263.

65. Betz, »Lasterkataloge/Tugendkataloge,« 89–91.

66. Siehe Braun, »πλανάω κτλ.,« 244.

67. Ob Paulus hier zitiert oder aufgrund Traditionsmaterials selber formuliert ist schwer zu sagen, siehe Fitzmyer, *First Corinthians*, 255.

Eine zweite Stelle findet sich in einem deutero-paulinischen Laster-katalog (1 Tim 1,9–10). Dieser Text baut auf paulinische Lasterkataloge ist aber anscheinend von Verf. selber formuliert wie Jürgen Roloff gezeigt hat.[68]

Zwei Lexeme, die im Neuen Testament sehr selten und deswegen in ihrer Bedeutung umstritten sind, sind μαλακοί (1 Kor 6,9; Matt 11,8// Luk 7,25: ἱμάτια) und ἀρσενοκοῖται (1 Kor 6,9; 1 Tim 1,10).[69] Öfters wird μαλακοί / molles mit »Weichlinge«,[70] oder sogar »Lustknaben«[71] übersetzt. »Weichlinge« ist indessen mehrdeutig, da es entweder passive Knaben bzw. Jünglinge oder passive erwachsene Männer als Partner bezeichnen kann.[72] Für die letztere Bedeutung spricht anscheinend ἀρσενοκοῖται / mas-culorum concubitores in dem Syntagma οὔτε μαλακοὶ οὔτε ἀρσενοκοῖται.[73] Ἀρσενοκοῖται mit »Knabenschänder«[74] zu übersetzen scheint mir auf jeden-fall missverständlich, da das Wort nicht nur mit »Knabenliebe« in Verbind-ung zu setzen ist.[75]

Ist im Lasterkatalog 1 Kor 6,9 die Homosexualität also ein Thema, so können wir jedoch feststellen, dass dies im abschließenden Lasterkatolog im Röm 1,29–31 nicht der Fall ist. Für die Lasterkataloge gilt also, dass ho-mosexuelles Vergehen kein konstitutives Merkmal darstellt.

In V. 32 schließt Paulus seine Gerichtsrede gegen die Heiden mit Urteilsspruch und verstärkender Begründung ab.[76] Die Heiden, die solche Ungerechtigkeiten—die im Lasterkatalog aufgezählten Sünden—ausüben,

68. Jürgen Roloff, *Der erste Brief an Timotheus*, 61, 74–79.

69. Das Lexem findet sich aber außer in anderen christlichen Stellen wie *Polyk.* 5,3 [nach 1 Kor 6,9–10]; Euseb., *praep.* VI 10,25 nur noch in *Or. Sib.* II,73 und in einem anonymen Epigramm, *Anth. Pal.* IX 686; siehe Weiß, *Der erste Korintherbrief*, 153. Kritzer, »Ein ἀρσενοκοίτης ist in den dokumentarischen Papyri bisher nicht belegt,« 231.

70. Conzelmann, *Der erste Brief an die Korinther*, 132; Schrage, *Der erste Brief an die Korinther (1Kor 1,1–6,11)*, 426; Lindemann, *Der erste Korintherbrief*, 133; Zeller, *Der erste Brief an die Korinther*, 210.

71. Wolff, *Der erste Brief des Paulus an die Korinther*, 112.

72. Bauer und Aland, *Wörterbuch*, 991: »Männern oder Jünglingen die sich missbr-auchen ließen.« So auch Zeller, *Der erste Brief an die Korinther*, 217 Anm. 134.

73. Siehe Liddell, Scott, und Jones, *Greek-English Lexicon*, 246: ἀρρενοκοίτης— «sodomite«; dazu auch ausführlich Hoheisel, »Homosexualität,« 339–41; Horn, »Nicht wie die Heiden!,« 301–3.

74. So z.B. Bauer und Aland, *Wörterbuch*, 220; Conzelmann, *Der erste Brief an die Korinther*, 132; Lindemann, *Der erste Korintherbrief*, 133. Für Knabenschänder wird eher παιδεραστής gebraucht.

75. Bauer und Aland, *Wörterbuch*, 220: »jmd., d. m. Männern u. Knaben Unzucht treibt«; Fitzmyer, *First Corinthians*, 257: »[T]he meaning is per se clear . . . and is in no way limited to pederasty«; so auch Zeller, *Der erste Brief an die Korinther*, 210, 217.

76. Michel, *Der Brief an die Römer*, 107: »V. 32 bildet den Abschluß des ganzen

> *(32a)erkennen zwar Gottes Rechtssatzung (δικαίωμα), dass die,*
> *die dergleichen tun, des Todes schuldig sind (ἄξιοι θανάτου εἰσίν),*
> *(32b)tun sie es doch nicht nur selber, sondern zollen auch denen*
> *Beifall, die so handeln.*

Erneut kommt die *Steigerung* durch den unabänderlichen *Richterspruch des Todes* zutage, die alle Menschen betrifft, welche solche Untugenden betreiben, die im Lasterkatalog aufgezählt werden und nicht nur diejenigen, die sich weiblicher bzw. männlicher Homoerotik hingeben oder gutheißen.

Damit ist die *vorbereitende* Anklage gegen die *Heiden* beendet und er kann zur *Hauptanklage* gegen die *Juden* und damit gegen die *ganze Menschheit* (2,1—3,20: Juden wie Heiden) übergehen.[77] Mit Günther Bornkamm können wir folglich feststellen, dass Paulus im Aufbau dieses Teiltextes eine »prophetische List« verwendet, da er »hier auf den Beifall des Juden rechnen kann. Denn dass über die Heiden das Gericht Gottes ergeht, bejaht der Jude [bzw. Judaist –DH] ja viel zu gern. Aber er weiß nicht, was er damit tut, dass er nämlich eben mit diesem Beifall, diesem Richten über die anderen sich selbst das Urteil spricht«.[78] Von nun an geht Paulus von der 3. Pers. pl. zum 2. Pers. sing. über. »Darum, bist du (εἶ) unentschuldbar, o Mensch, wer du auch seist, der du richtest (2,1) . . . ; [2,17] Wenn du dich aber Jude nennst (Εἰ δὲ σὺ Ἰουδαῖος ἐπονομάζῃ) und dich auf das Gesetz verlässt . . . Im Sinne des ›Du bist der Mann!‹, das Nathan dem David auf den Kopf zusagte, oder der plötzlichen Wendung in der Weinbergsparabel Jes 5,1–7 wird hier dem Juden gesagt: ›Διὸ ἀναπολόγητος εἶ, ὦ ἄνθρωπε πᾶς ὁ κρίνων‹«.[79] Unter Verweis auf 2 Sam. 12,1ff., Jes. 5,1ff., und Amos 1–2 weist auch Wiard Popkes darauf hin, dass »Paulus in einer alten prophetischen Tradition (steht). . . . Typisch für diese prophetische Argumentation ist, dass man dem Adressaten zunächst eine juridische Darlegung vorbringt, ihn dabei jedoch von sich selber ablenkt und in Sicherheit wiegt, dann aber das Gottesvolk selber mit Gottes Urteil konfrontiert«.[80]

Abschnitts und klingt wie ein Richterspruch.«

77. Siehe oben Anm. 3.

78. Bornkamm, »Gesetz und Natur. Röm 2,14–16,« 95.

79. Ibid.

80. Popkes, »Aufbau,« 499.

Konkludierende Überlegungen

Bemerkenswert ist, dass nicht nur unter den Juden / Judenchristen / Judaisten die Homoerotik abgelehnt, sondern selbst in der griechisch-römischen Tradition in vielen Fällen beanstandet wurde, was in den Kommentaren leider nicht immer genügend notiert wird.[81] Paulus und die Juden sind demzufolge nicht allein in ihrer negativen Beurteilung der Homoerotik! Selbst bezüglich des Richterspruchs zur Todesstrafe kommen solche Verdikte, wie wir gesehen haben, in anderen antiken Texten auch vor. Es handelt sich im Aufbau des Römerbriefs nicht nur um eine *sachliche*, sondern auch um eine *affektische* Beweisführung für die—wegen der Verschuldung der ganzen Menschheit—notwendige Voraussetzung für die Darlegung der durch Gott bewirkten Gerechtmachung im darauffolgenden *Confirmatio*-Teil (3,21–8,39).

Durch den Übergang hinsichtlich der Anklagen an »Heiden« (1,19ff.), zu denen an »Menschen« (2,1ff.) und schließlich zu denen an Juden / Judenchristen / Judaisten (2,17ff.; σύ !) wird eine Steigerung in der paulinischen Argumentation ersichtlich.[82] Diese *Steigerung* ist genauestens durchdacht: Zuerst die Heiden, dann die Verallgemeinerung auf alle Menschen, die Juden einbegriffen, und schließlich die Zielrichtung auf die Juden, die auf ihre Gesetzestreue bzw. -observanz vertrauen. Wir können deshalb nur wiederholen, was schon zur zweiten Reaktion Gottes geäußert wurde: Hier argumentiert Paulus als Jude und damit beugt er gewissermaßen Angriffen seitens der Judenchristen und vor allem der Judaisten vor, sein Evangelium führe zu einer laxen Lebensweise. Hier allerdings geht es nicht nur um laxe sexuelle Praktiken, sondern *amplifikatorisch* um viel allgemeinere und damit *alle* Lebensgebiete umfassenden Verstöße gegen die göttliche Lebensordnung.

Wenn Paulus im Röm 1,21–32 abschließend das Fazit seiner Ausführungen zum Thema des »Zornes Gottes« in Bezug auf die Heidenwelt zieht, dann kann festgestellt werden, dass eine Reihe anderer ebenso schwer ins Gewicht fallender Verfehlungen als Klimax der Sünden aufgelistet werden, die genauso zu Verdrehung der Wahrheit Gottes führen. Man beachte das Vorkommen der Verbformen ἤλλαξαν in V. 23 (Vertauschung der Herrlichkeit Gottes) und μετήλλαξαν sowohl in V. 25 (Vertauschung der Wahrheit Gottes) als auch in V. 26 (Vertauschung des natürlichen Verkehrs): Vertauschung des natürlichen Verkehrs gehört also nach Paulus engstens zusammen mit der Vertauschung der Herrlichkeit und Wahrheit Gottes.

---

81. Auch bei Horn, »Nicht wie die Heiden!,« 293–95, 301, kommt das griechisch-römisch-hellenistische Material viel zu kurz.

82. Vgl. Wischmeyer, »Römer 2,1–24,« 356–76.

Hinsichtlich der eindeutigen Steigerung in Paulus Argumentationsverfahren gilt absolut und uneingeschränkt: Wer die Homosexualität als Hauptsünde proklamieren will, muss im Hinblick auf die Forderung der Schriftgelehrten und Pharisäer, die Ehebrecherin zu töten (Joh 8,3–11), sich an Jesu Antwort an die Ankläger erinnern: »Wer von euch ohne Sünde ist, der werfe auf sie den ersten Stein«.

Bibliography

Textausgaben–Übersetzungen–Wörterbücher

Ardā Wirāz Nāmag: F. Vahman, *Ardā Wīrāz Nāmag: The Iranian "Divina Commedia."* Scandinavian Institute of Asian Studies Monograph 53. London: Curzon, 1986.

2 Enoch: Ch. Böttrich, "Das slavische Henochbuch." In *JSHRZ* V/7. Gütersloh: Gütersloher Verlagshaus, 1995.

Josephus: H. St. J. Thackeray, *Josephus, The Life / Contra Apionem* (LCL), Cambridge, MA: Harvard University Press 1926 (repr. 1997).

Martialis: P. Barié / W. Schindler (Hgg.), *M. Valerius Martialis, Epigramme. Lateinisch-deutsch* (Sammlung Tusculum), Darmstadt: Wissenschaftliche Buchgesellschaft 1999.

Nestle–Aland. *Novum Testamentum Graece,* 28. revidierte Auflage. Stuttgart 2012.

Oracula Sibyllina: J. Geffcken, *Die Oracula Sibyllina,* Leipzig: Hinrichs, 1902. [Nachdruck, Leipzig: Zentral-Antiquariat der DDR 1967].

Oracula Sibyllina: Kurfeß / J.-D. Gauger (Hgg.), *Sibyllinische Weissagungen. Griechisch-deutsch.* Darmstadt: Wissenschaftliche Buchgesellschaft 1998.

Philo: L. Cohn, *Philonis Alexandrini. Opera Quae Supersunt, Bd. V.* Berlin: de Gruyter 1962.

Philo: I. Heinemann, *Philo von Alexandria. Die Werke in deutscher Übersetzung, Bd. II.* Berlin: de Gruyter 1962.

Platon: E. des Places and L. Méridie / F. Schleiermacher & D. Kurz, *Platon. Werke in acht Bänden. Griechisch und Deutsch, Bd. 3.* Darmstadt: Wissenschaftliche Buchgesellschaft 1974.

Platon: E. des Places and Kl. Schöpsau, *Platon: Werke in acht Bänden. Griechisch und Deutsch, Bd. 8/1.* Darmstadt: Wissenschaftliche Buchgesellschaft 1977.

Ps-Phokylides: P. W. van der Horst. *The Sentences of Pseudo-Phocylides* (SVTP 4). Leiden: Brill 1978.

Ps-Phokylides: N. Walter, »Pseudo-Phokylides." In *JSHRZ IV/3*, Gütersloh: Gütersloher Verlag 1983, 182–216.

Ps-Phokylides: W. T. Wilson, *The Sentences of Pseudo-Phocylides* (CEJL), Berlin: de Gruyter 2005.

Wörterbuch: Walter Bauer, Kurt und Barbara Aland, *Griechisch-deutsches Wörterbuch.* Berlin: de Gruyter, 1988.

Wörterbuch: H. G. Liddell, R. Scott, and H. S. Jones. *A Greek-English Lexicon.* Oxford: Clarendon, 1966.

Sekundärliteratur

Bendemann, R. von. "'Zorn' und 'Zorn Gottes' im Römerbrief." In *Paulus und Johannes: Exegetische Studien zur paulinischen und johanneischen Theologie und Literatur*, edited by D. Sänger and U. Mell, 179–215. WUNT 198. Tübingen: Mohr Siebeck, 2006.

Betz, Hans Dieter. *Lukian von Samosata und das Neue Testament. Religionsgeschichtliche und paränetische Parallelen*. TU 76. Berlin: Akademie Verlag, 1961.

―――. "Lasterkataloge/Tugendkataloge." In *RGG⁴*, 5:89–91.

Bornkamm, G. "Gesetz und Natur. Röm 2,14–16." In *Studien zu Antike und Urchristentum: Gesammelte Aufsätze*, edited by G. Bornkamm, 2:93–118. BEvTh 28. Munich: Kaiser 1963.

Braun, Herbert. "πλανάω κτλ." In *ThWNT*, 6:244. Stuttgart: Kohlhammer 1959.

Brooten, Bernadette. *Love between Women: Early Christian Responses to Female Homoeroticism*. Chicago: University of Chicago Press, 1996.

Conzelmann, Hans. *Der erste Brief an die Korinther*. KEK 5. Göttingen: Vandenhoeck & Ruprecht, 1981.

Cranfield, C. E. B. *The Epistle to the Romans*. Vol. 1. ICC. Edinburgh: T. & T. Clark, 1977.

Dahl, Nils Alstrup. "Benediction and Congratulation." In *Studies in Ephesians*, by Nils Dahl, 279–314. WUNT 131. Tübingen: Mohr Siebeck, 2000.

Delling, G. "Geschlechtsverkehr." In *RAC* 10:812–29. Stuttgart: Hiersemann, 1978.

Deming, W. *Paul on Marriage and Celibacy: The Hellenistic Background of 1 Corinthians 7*. SNTS.MS 83. Cambridge: Cambridge University Press, 1996.

Dierichs, A. "Erotik in der Bildenden Kunst der Römischen Welt." In *Frauenwelten in der Antike: Geschlechterordnung und weibliche Lebenspraxis*, edited by Th. Späth and B. Wagner-Hasel, 394–411. Darmstadt: Wissenschaftliche Buchgesellschaft, 2000.

Dunn, James D. G. *Romans 1–8*. WBC 38A. Dallas: Word, 1988.

Eckstein, H. J. "'Denn Gottes Zorn wird vom Himmel her offenbar werden': Exegetische Erwägungen zu Röm 1,18." In *Der aus Glauben Gerechte wird leben: Beiträge zur Theologie des Neuen Testaments*, by H. J. Eckstein, 19–35. BzVB 5. Münster: Lit 2003.

Fitzmyer, Joseph A. *Romans*. AB 33. New York: Doubleday, 1993.

―――. *First Corinthians*. AB 32. New Haven: Yale University Press, 2008.

Glancy, Jennifer A. *Slavery in Early Christianity*, Minneapolis: Fortress, 2006.

Haaker, Kl. *Der Brief des Paulus an die Römer*. ThHK 6. Leipzig: Evangelische Verlagsanstalt, 1999.

Harrill, J. Albert. *Slaves in the New Testament. Literary, Social, and Moral Dimensions*. Minneapolis: Fortress, 2006.

Hartmann, E. "Hetären im klassischen Athen." In *Frauenwelten in der Antike: Geschlechterordnung und weibliche Lebenspraxis*, edited by Th. Späth and B. Wagner-Hasel, 377–94. Darmstadt: Wissenschaftliche Buchgesellschaft, 2000.

Hellholm, David. "Enthymemic Argumentation in Paul: The Case of Romans 6." In *Paul in His Hellenistic Context*, edited by Troels Engberg-Pedersen, 119–79. Minneapolis: Fortress, 1995.

―――. "Universalität und Partikularität. Die amplifikatorische Struktur von Römer 5,12–21." In *Paulus und Johannes: Exegetische Studien zur paulinischen und johanneischen Theologie und Literatur*, edited by D. Sänger und U. Mell, 217–69. WUNT 198. Tübingen: Mohr Siebeck 2006.

———. "Vorgeformte Tauftraditionen und deren Benutzung in den Paulusbriefen." In *Ablution, Initiation, and Baptism*, edited by David Hellholm et al., 415–95. BZNW 176/1. Berlin: de Gruyter, 2011.

———. "Theoretische Überlegungen zur Gesamtstruktur des Römerbriefs." In *Paulusperspektiven,* edited by M. R. Hoffmann, F. John, and E. E. Popkes, 33–62. BThSt 145. Neukirchen-Vluyn: Neukirchener, 2014.

Hoheisel, K. "Homosexualität." In *RAC* 16:289–364. Stuttgart: Hiersemann, 1994.

Horn, F. W. "Götzendiener, Tempelräuber und Betrüger. Polemik gegen Heiden, Juden und Judenchristen im Römerbrief." In *Polemik in der frühchristlichen Literatur. Texte und Kontexte*, edited by O. Wischmeyer and L. Scornaienchi, 209–32. BZNW 170. Berlin: de Gruyter, 2011.

———. "Nicht wie die Heiden!. Sexualethische Tabuzonen und ihre Bewertungen durch Paulus." In *Anthropologie und Ethik im Frühjudentum und im Neuen Testament*, edited by M. Konradt / E. Schläpfer, 283–307. Tübingen: Mohr Siebeck, 2014.

Jewett, Robert. *Romans*. Hermeneia. Minneapolis: Fortress, 2007.

Käsemann, Ernst. *An die Römer*. HNT 8a. Tübingen: Mohr Siebeck, 1974.

Köster, Helmut. "φύσις κτλ." In *ThWNT* 9:246–71. Stuttgart: Kohlhammer, 1973.

Kritzer, R. E. "Ad 6,9." In *1. Korinther: Papyrologische Kommentare zum Neuen Testament*, edited by P. Arzt-Grabner et al., 231. PKNT 2. Göttingen: Vandenhoeck & Ruprecht, 2006.

Lampe, Peter. *Die stadtrömischen Christen in den ersten beiden Jahrhunderten*. WUNT 2/18. Tübingen: Mohr Siebeck, 2. Aufl. 1989. [Engl. trans. *From Paul to Valentinus: Christians at Rome in the First Two Centuries*. Translated by Michael Steinhauser. Edited by Marshall Johnson. Minneapolis: Fortress, 2003.]

Lindemann, A. *Der erste Korintherbrief*. HNT 9/1. Tübingen: Mohr Siebeck, 2000.

Lohse, Eduard. *Der Brief an die Römer*. KEK 4. Göttingen: Vandenhoeck & Ruprecht, 2003.

Michel, O. *Der Brief an die Römer*. KEK 4. Göttingen: Vandenhoeck & Ruprecht, 1966.

Peterson, E. *Der Brief an die Römer*. Ausgewählte Schriften 6. Würzburg: Echter, 1997.

Popkes, W. *Christus Traditus: Eine Untersuchung zum Begriff der Dahingabe im Neuen Testament*. AThANT 49. Zürich: Zwingli, 1967.

———. "Zum Aufbau und Charakter von Römer 1,18–32." *NTS* 28 (1982) 490–501.

Prescendi, F. "Weiblichkeitsideale in der römischen Welt: Lucretia und die Anfänge der Republik." In *Frauenwelten in der Antike. Geschlechterordnung und weibliche Lebenspraxis,* edited by Th. Späth and B. Wagner-Hasel, 217–227. Darmstadt: Wissenschaftliche Buchgesellschaft, 2000.

Roloff, Jürgen. *Der erste Brief an Timotheus*. EKK 15. Zürich: Benziger, 1988.

Schlier, H. *Der Römerbrief*. HThK 6. Freiburg: Herder, 1977.

Schneider, W. Ch. "Das Ende der antiken Leiblichkeit: Begehren und Enthaltsamkeit bei Ambrosius, Augustin und Maximian." In *Frauenwelten in der Antike. Geschlechterordnung und weibliche Lebenspraxis,* edited by Th. Späth and B. Wagner-Hasel, 412–26. Darmstadt: Wissenschaftliche Buchgesellschaft, 2000.

Schrage, Wolfgang. *Der erste Brief an die Korinther (1Kor 1,1–6,11)*. EKK 7/1. Zürich: Benziger, 1991.

————. *Der erste Brief an die Korinther (1Kor 6,12–11,16)*. EKK 7/2). Solothurn–Düsseldorf: Benziger, 1995.

Scroggs, Robin. *The New Testament and Homosexuality: Contextual Background for Contemporary Debate*. Philadelphia: Fortress, 1983.

Skjærvø, P. O. "Homosexuality i. in Zoroastrianism." In *Encyclopædia Iranica*, 12:440–41. Winona Lake, IN: Eisenbrauns, 2014.

[Strack], H. L., and P. Billerbeck. *Kommentar zum Neuen Testament aus Talmud und Midrasch*. Vol. 3. Munich: Beck, 1926.

Strecker, Georg, and Udo Schnelle. *Neuer Wettstein*. Vol. 2/1. Berlin: de Gruyter, 1996.

Theobald, M. "Zorn Gottes. Ein nicht zu vernachlässigender Aspekt der Theologie des Römerbriefs." In *Studien zum Römerbrief*, by M. Theobald, 68–100. WUNT 136. Tübingen: Mohr Siebeck, 2001.

Vielhauer, Ph. *Geschichte der urchristlichen Literatur: Einleitung in das Neue Testament, die Apokryphen und die Apostolischen Väter*. GLB. Berlin: de Gruyter, 1975.

Weiß, J. *Der erste Korintherbrief*. KEK 5. Göttingen: Vandenhoeck & Ruprecht, 1910 [Nachdruck, 1970.]

Wischmeyer, O. "Römer 2,1–24 als Teil der Gerichtsrede des Paulus gegen die Menschheit." *NTS* 52 (2006) 356–76.

Wolff, Ch. *Der erste Brief des Paulus an die Korinther*. ThHNT 7. Leipzig: Evangelische Verlagsanstalt, 1996.

Woyke, J. *Götter, "Götzen," Götterbilder: Aspekte einer paulinischen "Theologie der Relationen."* BZNW 132. Berlin: de Gruyter, 2005.

Zeller, D. *Der erste Brief an die Korinther*. KEK 5. Göttingen: Vandenhoeck & Ruprecht, 2010.

Zittel, D. "Hieronymus und Paula: Brief an eine Asketin und Mutter." In *Frauenwelten in der Antike. Geschlechterordnung und weibliche Lebenspraxis*, edited by Th. Späth and B. Wagner-Hasel, 426–37. Darmstadt: Wissenschaftliche Buchgesellschaft, 2000.

22

"Saved through childbirth? That's not what the Koran says."

Muslim and Christian Women in Norway Making Meaning of 1 Timothy 2:8–15

Anne Hege Grung

Introduction

THE TEXTS OF THE Bible, the Koran and the Hadith have many dimensions, but to a far extent they have been read and interpreted within their respective religious traditions only. Historically speaking they have been read by an even more limited circle of readers, consisting of literate, educated religious elites. This situation changed through educating the religious masses, through increased literacy and printed copies of the texts. In current times of cyber-activity, migration and inter-religious encounters the canonical scriptures are more exposed than earlier.[1] It is now relatively easy to get access to the canonical scriptures from other traditions than one's own through the web, and there are reflections on how this may alter the distribution of power and authority to interpret these scriptures. The situation generates questions on how this situation influences the perception of other traditions. When the texts are read outside of their context by readers with no or little pre-knowledge of the tradition they are part of, the possibility for misconceptions is present, in particular if the texts in this way is seen as the sole representative of their respective traditions and isolated from their nearest contexts of readers.

---

1. Roald, "European Islamic Gender Discourses," 286–87.

In my PhD dissertation "Gender Justice in Muslim-Christian Readings: Christian and Muslim Women in Norway Making Meaning of Text from the Bible, the Koran and the Hadith" I analyzed how a mixed group of women discussed and interpreted 1 Tim 2:8–15 among other selected texts.[2] Turid Karlsen Seim as my main supervisor has together with me, hour after hour, discussed how one could read and interpret the transcriptions of the conversations at the arranged meetings with the participants. We also performed a co-reading, coming close to an exegesis—not of the canonical texts, but of the sayings of the women participating in my study. Turid Karlsen Seim's extraordinary skills as a reader, which includes an immense curiosity, a sharp gaze for contradictions and openness to the texts filled these hours of work with colors, nuances, frustrations—and laughter.

Through the study I realized that the path to knowledge about other tradition's texts and their interpretations in situ is not primarily going through the texts, but through the text's readers. It is the readers who provide the contextual understanding, who know the subtle elements of the interpretations and the possible conflicting narratives about how the text makes meaning within its home tradition. It is also the readers who know the relative significance of the text, and how it is related to other, possibly diverging texts in the same tradition regarding content. The participants in my study achieved a different view on the contents of the texts from the other religious tradition present through listening to their interpretations, explanations and knowledge about the use of the text. The latter consisted of both formal and informal knowledge. The questions and the criticism of a canonical text coming from what we could call "foreign readers," however, can also become a source of significant insight although of a different kind: it may reveal how a text is perceived from a particular outside. What is it possible to understand from the other position, in which frame is it interpreted, and what is difficult to grasp for the "foreign reader." In the study I refer to here, the hermeneutical situation was complex: The texts came from the Christian and the Islamic traditions, and the readers from various cultural backgrounds and included Sunni—and Shi'a Muslims, as well as Protestant and Catholic Christians. What I will investigate in this contribution is how the group and in particular the Muslim participants interpreted the particular part of 1 Timothy 2 cited in the headline on women being saved through childbirth, including the reasoning given for it in the verses before:

> 13 For Adam was formed first, then Eve; 14 and Adam was
> not deceived, but the woman was deceived and became a

---

2. Grung, *Gender Justice*. The other texts were Sura 4:34 from the Koran, and the Hagar narratives from both traditions.

transgressor. 15 Yet she will be saved through childbearing, provided they continue in faith and love and holiness, with modesty.[3]

Situating the Group Interpretation of 1 Timothy 2: The Premises

The text from 1 Tim was read aloud in the group, together with the other text discussed at the same time, Sura 4:34 from the Koran.[4] In the two organized meetings before, the narratives about Hagar and Ishmael in the desert from Genesis and the Hadith was read and discussed. The discussions following the reading of these narratives was intense, and the particularly intense parts was on Hagar's role and status, and if it was possible to view Hagar as a bad mother.[5] The narrative form of the texts opened up for a narrative reader-response, and as the narratives diverged in the Muslim and Christian tradition just as the status of Hagar is different between the two, it should not be a surprise that the readers in the group had different and sometimes contradictory perspectives. The texts from 1 Tim and Sura 4 both represents a different kind of canonical texts, they could be called prescriptive, or even normative texts. My interest was to find out if the Muslim and the Christian readers at any point developed a shared hermeneutical strategy to make meaning of these texts, well known for their use in constructions of patriarchal structures and engaged in limiting women's space in various ways in both traditions. The readers in the group, despite their different backgrounds, all articulated that it was important for them to be religious believers and feminists. They also claimed that their religious beliefs were significant sources in establishing their feminist identity. Al-

3. New Revised Standard Version (NRSV) of the Bible. The text read and distributed in the group was from the Norwegian Bibelen, 1978 edition in bokmål, The Norwegian Bible Society.

4. Sura 4:34: Men are in charge of women, because Allah hath made the one of them to excel the other, and because they spend of their property (for the support of women). So good women are the obedient, guarding in secret that which Allah hath guarded. As for those from whom ye fear rebellion, admonish them and banish them to beds apart, and scourge them. Then, if they obey you, seek not a way against them. Lo! Allah is ever High Exalted, Great. From The Glorious Qur'an: Text and Explanatory Translation. Muhammad M. Pickthall, and Marmaduke William Pickthall, Tahrike Tarsile Qur'an, 1996 (first edition 1984). The text read and distributed in the group was from the Norwegian version of the Koran Koranen, translated by Einar Berg, Universitetsforlaget, 1980. In the Norwegian version Sura 4:34 is numbered Sura 4:38.

5. Grung, "Hagar as a bad mother."

though they defined 'feminism' in slightly different ways, they clearly shared a strong confidence in the ideal of gender equality as an ethical valid ground position.

Reactions on 1 Timothy 2: Is This Text Really a Part of the New Testament?

It was one of the Christian participants, Maria, with an African-Norwegian background, who stated, "I think this is a typical Old Testament [text] where women should stay in their place and the men in theirs, and women should be subjugated to men."[6] When the others explained that this actually was a text from the New Testament, Maria asked the question "Is this really a part of the New Testament?" It became clear that throughout the discussion so far she had taken for granted that it was an Old Testament text. The question was thus not polemical, but reflected a sincere bewilderment on Maria's part. When the group discussed the Hagar narratives, the Christian readers in the group established a hermeneutical hierarchy between the Old and the New Testament, claiming that the Hagar narrative in Genesis reflected an archaic and misogynic time, that all texts needed to be understood in their historical context, and that the text did not have the same authority as New Testament texts would have. Maria seems to connect the patriarchal reflection in 1 Tim to the earlier evaluation of the Genesis text.

The Christian participants then established a new hermeneutical hierarchical structure when they discussed the text from 1 Tim: That texts allegedly written by the apostle Paul was less authoritative than the narratives about Jesus in the gospels. Inger (Lutheran Christian, Norwegian background) stated the following: ". . . it is not Jesus who says these things, it is Paul, and one has to take Paul with a pinch of salt . . . this is said by Paul, and we can criticize him."[7] She is supported by Eva, also a Lutheran Christian with a Norwegian background: ". . . we must take Paul for what he was; he was not Christ. He . . . did not even know Christ. But of course, he is an apostle, and he has said a lot of nice things . . . here, it seems as if he was having a bad day."[8]

Inger continues to reflect over the text, and she disputed the logics that Adam should rule over Eve because he should have been created first (v. 13). Referring to biology, she states that there is no support in science

6. Grung, *Gender Justice*, 372.

7. Ibid., 280.

8. Ibid., 286.

for the claim that the man was created before the woman. She criticizes the interpretation of the narrative of the fall in 1 Tim to women's disadvantage and questions the legitimacy of basing a permanent gendered hierarchy upon elements in the story. But it is verse 15 that really provokes her, to the extent that she calls the content 'completely unchristian': "Jesus never said anything about being saved through one's childbearing."[9] She asks if the text should be interpreted as if one has to go through suffering to be 'set free' or saved, and that childbearing could represent such a saving kind of suffering. However, she dismisses this as 'not comprehensive' with the Christian gospel.

The interpretative strategy of the Christian participants when they are negotiating with the text from 1 Tim and each other trying to make meaning of its content contains two main elements. The first one is already presented: to distinguish between texts connected to Paul and narratives about Jesus, where alleged Pauline texts are evaluated as less significant.[10] The second element of the strategy is far more radical, and represents an ethical critique of the text where the readers in the group decides that parts of the content of 1 Tim 2:8–15 contains a message they reject as part of a legitimate Christian ethics and soteriology. Oddbjørn Leirvik does under the headline "The ethical critique of the scriptures" address the issue of ethical critique of canonical texts in the Islamic and the Christian traditions in an inter-religious hermeneutical frame.[11] He refers to Elizabeth Schüssler Fiorenza who in 1987 stated that biblical scholars had a political responsibility for the ethical consequences of the biblical text and its meanings. To perform ethical and moral critique of biblical texts is according to her a crucial responsibility, and it is not enough to criticize the interpretations of the texts. Anne-Louise Eriksson suggests in her article "Bibelens autoritet og kvinners erfaringer" ("The authority of the Bible and the experiences of women") that reading a Biblical text should always lead to an experience of life and freedom.[12] If a Biblical text is experienced to convey the opposite message, the text should be dismissed as part of any authoritative Biblical message. Eriksson's point is

9. Ibid., 284.

10. During the study process, my role was strictly defined as a facilitator, and I did not engage in the discussions or contribute with information of any kind. Thus, it was not an element in the discussion that scholars do not regard 1 Tim to be a Pauline letter. One of the participants (Eva) did, however, state that she was not sure whether Paul was the author or had anything to do with the text. She also said that she found it weird that Paul in other texts adviced people to remain unmarried, if he believed that women's way to salvation was through childbirth.

11. Leirvik, "The ethical critique," 340–341.

12. Eriksson, "Bibelens autoritet."

that the experience many women have with the use of Biblical texts in ways that limits their space and possibilities to act is to overrule the significance of the text. This is exactly what the Christian women in the group in my study do: They claim that 1 Tim 2: 8–15 is representing a message that is not only contradicting what they see to be the core message of Jesus, and state that it even contradicts other alleged Paul-sayings, but most importantly, it strongly contradicts their own ethical and moral stances. Eva articulates this: "I don't think that this text has anything to say to us today. It is a kind of text that . . . what did Luther say . . . 'Do not make this my stumbling block.' Get on with it, and step over that rock."[13] Susanne, Lutheran Christian with a Norwegian background says: "I am very close to abandon it totally . . . There is nothing to gain from it for our time . . . For my part they could be erased. Except as historical documents."[14]

Inger makes this statement: "I feel that as a Christian, I have the right to abandon parts of the Bible. I don't have to find an interpretation or a meaning in every single paragraph. So this belongs to the past."[15] Besides establishing a perspective of historical evolutionism, adding the argument that the text is old and therefore represents only a historical, illustrative perspective—which is clearly reducing the authority of the text in this case— Eva uses Luther to argue against the authority of the text. Susanne and Inger use their own interpretative authority without referring to anything or anyone external to justify it. In the discussions not referred here, they discuss the various elements in the texts with their own experiences, views and perspectives, and the conclusion is cited above.

What about the Muslim participants in the group? How did they interpret the text from 1 Tim, and what was their response to their Christian co-readers' abandonment of the Biblical text?

This Is not What the Koran Says

The Koran in the Islamic tradition has a different status than the Bible in the Christian tradition: In Christianity, God's revelation is not the Biblical text but the person of Jesus. In Islam, the Koran is traditionally seen as God's revelation word by word, sound by sound in the Arabic language. This view on the Koran is also reflected in the interpretative work done by the Muslims among the readers in the group. When discussing the meaning of Sura 4:34, together with 1 Tim 2:8–15, the Muslim readers spent much time on

13. Grung, *Gender Justice*, 289.

14. Ibid., 389–390.

15. Ibid., 390.

explaining and working on the concept of qiwama (translated as "in charge of" in the Koranic version that was read). This exegetical work created a new understanding of the text's message. Based on extensive work on the Koranic text and commentaries on the text, the Muslim readers suggested that qiwama first and foremost meant 'support', not 'authority over'.[16] The premise for the Muslim participants was that the Koran originally conveys a message of human equality, including gender equality. Any conflicts between this message and messages from Muslim preachers or practitioners would exist because of false or incorrect interpretation from the interpreters' side according to their theological stance. The Muslim participants spent much time explaining what skills they wanted the Islamic clergy to have: It is not enough to have linguistic, theological, juridical and historic knowledge—the clergy should also have extensive contextual knowledge about the society they interpreted from and the everyday challenges of men and women around them. They wanted women and women's perspectives and experiences to be a more included part of the present interpretative context of the Koran, and situated themselves as authoritative interpreters of the texts, standing firmly within the Islamic tradition.

For the Muslim participants in the group, it was not an option to abandon a particular Koranic text if they struggled with its content. On the contrary, they claimed that only if they respected and cherished the Koran as divine revelation they would be able to see its message of human equality and achieve the necessary authority among Muslims to be agents for transformation of Islamic practice. The Koran itself was seen as their most powerful tool for transformation of the tradition to make it more gender fair, reflecting a complete trust in the Koran on the one side and a critical perspective of the traditional male interpretations of the Koran on the other side.[17]

How was the Muslim readers response on the text from 1 Tim, and how did they respond to the critical interpretation of the text done by their Christian co-readers? Of particular interest is how the Muslim readers reacted to the differences in the interpretative strategy regarding the possibility to abandon a specific Biblical text based on its content.

Aira, Sunni Muslim with a Pakistani-Norwegian background, discussed 1 Timothy verse by verse, and started in this way:

> Concerning the purity of the men before the prayer, this is exactly like our ritual ablution . . . Concerning the women's appearance, this is the same, too, that they should have . . . not

16. Ibid., 305.

17. Ibid., 391.

be too provocative, and the message about wearing a hijab or
decent clothes is something we regard as a Koranic message . . . I
view it very much this way that this is a message that is intended
to create good relations.[18]

Aira's reference point for her interpretation of the New Testament text is the
Koran and her own tradition. This was part of her general interpretative pattern towards the Christian canonical texts during the co-reading process,
she interpreted the Bible through the Koran, so to speak. She looks for similarities, and sometimes she would take the position to defend the authority
and integrity of the Biblical texts against the criticism of her Christian co-
readers. But she did not take this position when giving response to the last
verses of the text from 1 Timothy:

> When it comes to the restriction that women should not be
> teachers, I don't understand it, for this is not consistent with the
> message of the Koran . . . So this is a bit different from the mes-
> sage of the Koran . . . there are many similarities here, but they
> can also be a bit different. And concerning the part that "Adam
> was created first, and then Eve, and he was not deceived, but the
> woman was deceived," this message is different from the Koran
> too. Because the Koran states clearly that they both lost the way
> of God because of Satan's . . . temptation.[19]

Regarding the particular statement on childbirth and salvation, Aira
says: "If we have love for God, we must believe in him, and then we show
love to humans too, and when we submit to God's will, we are saved, and
this has nothing to do with childbirth."[20]

This is the most explicit criticism of the Biblical texts that ever appeared
among the Muslim readers in the group throughout the process. Aira clearly
dismisses the idea that childbirth has anything to do with women's salvation, and she formulates a very inclusive statement about salvation where
she seems to include both Christians and Muslims alike. Her contribution
to the discussion on 1 Tim was picked up by Inger in the further discussion:

> I prefer the Koran on this issue [the narrative of the fall]. And
> then, there is this getting saved through childbirth . . . it can't be
> right. Paul must have misunderstood. Faith, love, holiness—to

---

18. Ibid., 354.
19. Ibid., 354, 355, 356.
20. Ibid., 357.

live in decency, that's all fine. But here it is linked to her behavior
and not to the grace that will set us free.[21]

The divergence between the narrative of the fall in the Bible and in
the Koran concerning the roles of Adam and Eve in the story has caught
the attention by others, such as the pioneer feminist Islamic scholar Riffat
Hassan. In an article from 1987 "Equal Before Allah? Woman-Man Equality
in the Islamic tradition," she stated that the Judeo-Christian Biblical version
of the narrative as well as its further interpretations among Christians had
altered Islamic interpretations of the story in a patriarchal direction.[22] Hassan claims that the alleged Pauline writings of 1 Tim 2 as well as 1 Cor 11
represents patriarchal interpretations of the narrative of the fall in Genesis,
and that these functioned as a strengthening of the negative gendered patterns of blame and guilt found already in the Genesis narrative which was
conveyed to the Muslim interpreters. In the current discourse in Europe
and elsewhere, there is much attention connected to whether an increased
numerical presence of Muslims in many places with a Christian or non-reli-
gious majority will challenge gender equality or gender fairness as a shared
societal aim. The Christian tradition is rarely challenged in public according its gendered practice and lack of gender fair theology and organization.
Kari Børresen has earlier pointed out that the Islamic tradition does not,
different from the Christian tradition historically speaking, connect gender
differences to soteriology (1 Corinthians 11).[23] In Islam, the gender differences are rather connected to the construction of social roles in the Koran
and the Sunna. But currently, public accusations of being a religious tradition subjugating women are mostly targeted towards Islam and Muslims.
Muslim feminists are well aware of this, but few have articulated a returned
challenge of this kind to the Christian tradition, at least publicly. Hassan is,
however, recently criticized by another Muslim feminist, Aysha Hidayatullah. The criticism is based on what Hidayatullah calls Hassans project to
"purify" the Koran from Biblically influenced interpretations.[24] Hidayatullah finds this effort contra-productive regarding a necessary cooperation
between Judaist, Christian and Islamic feminist theology to reveal shared
as well as particular challenges regarding their canonical scriptures. She
states that panels and interfaith meetings including all three religions at the
moment are not able to move sufficiently beyond using Muslim women as
tokens due to a neo-colonial dominant perspective in the present, but she

21. Ibid., 359.
22. Hassan, "Equal Before Allah."
23. Børresen, *Christian and Islamic*, 8.
24. Hidayatullah, "The Qur'anic Rib-ectomy," 151.

insists that any move to a purification of Islam and Islamic sources is not a constructive way forward for Muslims if the aim is to confront religious patriarchy:

> We could opt to achieve a short-term feminist gain for ourselves at the expense of other women, and engage in interpretative maneuvers that confine us to oppositional relationships with the religious Other from whom we separate ourselves through a claim of purity. But what will be gained in the process? In the end, when we use the master's tools, we must ultimately lose to the master, adopting his rigid and arrogant ways as our own.[25]

Aira, and the other Muslim participants in the co-reading, had their main focus on how to transform their own religious tradition into a more gender fair practice—but they did not articulate any need to purify the Islamic sources from Judeo-Christian influence. Neither did they, however, engage with particular challenges within the Christian tradition regarding gender questions connected to the texts. This can be explained by how their Christian co-readers represented their own tradition in the group. Throughout the discussions, the Christian co-readers claimed almost unanimously that their tradition as they knew it practiced gender equality, and that challenges connected to gender justice belonged to the past. There was, however, one significant exception, Maria with an African-Norwegian background, who extended the perspective the immediate interpretative context for the discussions by bringing in her African experiences. Her contributions reminded the others that the Christian tradition is not completely overlapping with Lutheranism as practiced in Norway.

Aira in particular, but also Shirin (Shia Muslim with an Iranian-Norwegian background) used their own tradition explicitly as a framework for their interpretation of the Biblical texts, and when there were differences between the two traditions, they simply stuck to the Islamic version and stated that this was how they viewed it. At some moments, like described above with Inger's response, the Islamic version of texts and interpretations were embraced and envied by the Christian participants. Mostly, however, the Christian participants disclosed that they were critical to the Islamic tradition's view on women, in the same way that they criticized their own texts. So, if the Muslims read the Bible through the eyes of the Koran, one may say that the Christians related to the Islamic texts from the Koran and the Hadith through the Bible. The intertextual interpretation happened in the minds of the readers, and was then brought to the table. The texts met through their readers.

25. Hidayatullah, "The Qur'anic Rib-ectomy," 167.

If we move back to the moment where Aira—at least indirectly—criticized the text from 1 Tim through an Islamic perspective, there is another significant interpretative tool in play. I mentioned the concept of ethical critique of the texts among Christian theologians. In the Islamic tradition, we can find scholars arguing along the same lines, although with a more positive presupposition towards the Koran than her approach to the Bible. Khaled Abou el-Fadl has established the term 'moral enrichment of the text' connected to Islamic hermeneutics.[26] He focuses on the readers' responsibilities to engage her moral universe in the encounter with the text, and finds his primary reasoning behind this in the Koran itself. The message of the text is grasped and conveyed by the reader, and this message should be shaped and reformed through the moral and ethical reflections of the reader.[27] For the Muslim participants in the study, their own moral universe seems to be integrated in their reasoning about the Islamic texts discussed. It is also present when they discuss the Biblical texts.

Abandonment, Criticism, Questioning: Approaches to the Statement "Saved through Childbearing"

For the Christian readers, ethical criticism of this statement connecting salvation and childbirth for women is based on what they find to be a heavy male bias in the Biblical text itself. It contradicts both their ethical stance on gender justice and their perception of Jesus' message in the New Testament. They conclude that this text should be abandoned and stripped of any authority. The Muslim readers are more in the position that they indirectly criticize the text and then question it on the basis of their own tradition. But the connection between child-bearing and salvation for women are rejected by both Muslim and Christian readers. Instead, Inger and Aira both give an explanation of how they view divine salvation. For Inger, divine salvation is connected to divine grace, and any connection to human-made efforts to obtain salvation is obscuring this, including the effort of childbearing. For Aira, love for God and fellow human beings and submitting to God's will is salvation, and she firmly stated that 'this has nothing to do with childbearing'. The two women do not start a discussion on the different concepts of salvation in Lutheranism versus Sunni Islam which they both describe in a precise manner. Their point of connection is that they agree on what divine salvation does not require, namely childbirth. The shared criticism

26. Abou el Fadl, "The place of tolerance in Islam," 15.
27. Ibid.

they articulate on the interpretation of the consequences of the narrative of the fall in 1 Tim 2 may have different sources: Aira with the Muslim version of the narrative, and Inger with a reference to the narratives of Jesus, but they have the same ethical stance. To state that women are saved through childbearing is not gender just statement, it is not even close. And to argue that Eve brought this situation upon all women is a patriarchal hoax. It is not coherent with these women's image of God, neither in the Christian nor in the Islamic tradition, and it is not coherent with their own moral universe(s).

What Is the Added Value of Co-reading Texts as 1 Tim 2: 8–15?

The Muslim readers in the group braced for the discussion on Sura 4:34 which they probably knew would be painful, due to the negative attention this particular sura gets in Norwegian public discourse. This meant that they came well prepared and had searched for different ways to make constructive meaning of the text. They shared their work with their Christian co-readers and gave them valuable insight in their own interpretative tradition, demonstrating that readers from within a religious tradition can change the premises for how outsiders interpret the text without contextual knowledge. The Christian readers in the group did not make any efforts to rescue the more challenging parts of 1 Timothy or to present exegetical work on the text. Their contribution of knowledge from within to their Muslim co-readers was their interpretative strategies which included criticism and abandonment of a text. But what was the contribution from the outside readers in this case?

The contribution from the Muslim readers was obviously their polite criticism, their resistance to what they found to be the problematic content from their own perspective, and an alternative narrative of the fall—the version from the Koran. If the Muslim participants were surprised that the text from 1 Tim 2:8–15 was included in the New Testament, they did not show it. One of the Christian participants, on the other side, was openly surprised. Aira connected to the requirement in verse 9 for women to cover their hair, and aligned it with what she claimed to be the Koranic message for women wearing the hijab. Interestingly enough, the group did not start a discussion on the use of hijab, even if there were articulated different views on this among the Muslims as well as the Christians. But the comment showed a point of identification from Aira's part, and possibly also showed, together with the other similiarities she pointed out between the traditions based on the text from 1 Timothy 2, that the two traditions of Christianity and Islam are historically connected in many ways and share much of the same cultural influences. Through her confirmation and her resistance, Aira uses her own moral universe to make meaning of the text, so that the text represents a possibility to connect the Muslim and Christian readers together. But what does this togetherness consist of, and what could be the significance of it?

Connecting Moral Universes through Co-reading of Canonical Scriptures

All the readers in the group, regardless of their religious and cultural background, were provoked by the text from 1 Tim, as I have shown examples of. This shared provocation generated reflections which displayed parts of the moral universes of the respective readers. Ethical values, in this case identified as gender fairness and the readers responsibility for the interpretation and evaluation of the texts and their social consequences are shared and establishes a common ethical ground. Although the readers showed different interpretative strategies, they also showed a shared agency with regards to the meaning making of the text. This shared agency is not primarily directed towards the text(s). The Christian readers as readers from 'within' decide that the ethical responsible action is to abandon the text from 1 Tim as authoritative. The Muslim readers evaluate it from their perspective of the Koran. But the shared agency is surfacing connected to contextual challenges, and towards acknowledgement of women's right to interpret the texts and to criticize other interpreters—exactly what this group of women is performing. Connecting moral universes between Muslim and Christian women readers would provide exchange of knowledge and disclosure of blind spots; it may provide a space for shared action in a particular context preventing the all too common gap between Muslim and Christian feminists that happens when one or the other party is concentrating on re-establishing a particular religious purity (Cf. Hidayatullah) or engaging in gendered religious identity politics where women of the other tradition is accused of either not being true believers, or not being true feminists. The canonical texts need readers; and the faithful readers from different traditions need each other to obtain access to the contextual web of knowledge connected to the texts.

Bibliography

Abou El Fadl, et al. *The Place of Tolerance in Islam*. Boston: Beacon, 2002.

Bible, Holy. *New Revised Standard Version containing the Old and New Testaments*. Peabody, MA: Hendrickson, 1989.

Børresen, Kari Elisabeth. *Christian and Islamic Gender Models in Formative Traditions*. Studi e testi tardoantichi. Rome: Herder, 2004.

Eriksson, Anne-Louise. "Bibelens autoritet og kvinners erfaringer." In *Feministteologi på norsk*, 85–97. Oslo: Cappelens akademiske, 1999.

Grung, Anne Hege. "Hagar as a Bad Mother, Hagar as an Icon of Faith: The Hagar Narratives from the Islamic and the Christian Traditions Discussed among Muslim and Christian Women in Norway." In *In the Arms of Biblical Women*, edited by John T. Greene and Mishael M. Caspi, 65–78. Piscataway, NJ: Gorgias, 2013.

———. *Gender Justice in Muslim-Christian Readings: Christian and Muslim Women in Norway Making Meaning of Texts from the Bible, the Koran and the Hadith*. Amsterdam: Brill Rodopi, forthcoming 2015.

Hassan, Riffat. "Equal Before Allah? Woman-Man Equality in the Islamic Tradition." *Harvard Divinity Bulletin* 17.2 (1987) 2–14.

Hidayatullah, Aisha. "The Qur'anic Rib-ectomy: Scriptural Purity, Imperial Dangers, and Other Obstacles to the Interfaith Engagement of Feminist Qur'anic Interpretation." In *Women and Interreligious Dialogue*, edited by Catherine Cornille and Jillian Maxey, 150–67. Interreligious Dialogue Series 5. Eugene, OR: Cascade Books, 2013.

Leirvik, Oddbjørn. "Interreligious Hermeneutics and the Ethical Critique of the Scriptures." In *Interreligious Hermeneutics—Between Texts and People*, edited by David Cheetham et al., 333–52. Amsterdam: Brill Rodopi, 2011.

Qur'an, The Glorious: Text and Explanatory Translation. 2nd ed. Muhammad M. Pickthall and Marmaduke William Pickthall. Tahrike Tarsile Qur'an., 1996.

Roald, Anne Sofie. "European Islamic Gender Discourses." In *Interreligious Hermeneutics—Between Texts and People*, edited by David Cheetham et al., 267–88. Amsterdam: Rodopi, 2011.

Bibliography

Turid Karlsen Seim's Monographs,
Edited Volumes, Essays, and Articles
1972–2014

COMPILED BY
SVEIN HELGE BIRKEFLET

1972–1980

"Apostolat og forkynnelse. En studie til Mk 4:1–20." *Dansk teologisk tidsskrift* 35 (1972) 206–22.

"Frihet, likhet—og underordning? Om synet på kvinnen i det Nye testamente." *Kirke og kultur* 77 (1972) 286–95.

"Kvinnen i mannens bilde. Om kvinnen i senjødedommen." *Kirke og kultur* 80 (1975) 539–44.

"Nye veier i lignelsesforskningen." *Norsk teologisk tidsskrift* 78 (1977) 239–58.

"Herre, frels! Vi går under-." Momenter til frelsesforståelsen i den synoptiske evangelielitteratur." *Norsk teologisk tidsskrift* (1979) 161–75.

"Seksualitet og ekteskap, skilsmisse og gjengifte i 1. Kor. 7." *Norsk teologisk tidsskrift* 1980 (1980) 1–20.

1981–1990

"Gudsrikets overraskelse. Parablene om et sennepsfrø og en surdeig." *Norsk teologisk tidsskrift* (1983) 1–18.

"Kvinneblikk på bibeltekster." *Kirke og kultur* 89 (1984) 258–70.

447

"Kirkenes kvinnesyn: En bremsekloss for kristen enhet?" *Kirke og kultur* 91 (1986) 167–77.

"Roles of Women in the Gospel of John." In *Aspects on the Johannine Literature: Papers Presented at a Conference of Scandinavian New Testament Exegetes at Uppsala, June 16–19, 1986*, edited by Lars Hartman and Birger Olsson, 56–73. Coniectanea Biblica, New Testament Series 18. Uppsala: Almqvist & Wiksell, 1987.

"Teologisk utdannelse i ekumenisk perspektiv." *Norsk teologisk tidsskrift* 88 (1987) 31–45.

"I asketisk frihet? Urkirkens enker i nytt lys. Glimt fra en forskningssituasjon." *Norsk teologisk tidsskrift* 89 (1988) 27–45.

"Kvinners rom. Begrensning og muligheter for tidligkristne kvinner i spenningen mellom privat og offentlig sfære." *Nytt om kvinneforskning* 12 (1988) 18–24.

Det doble budskap: Avhengighet og avstand mellom kvinner og menn i Lukas-Acta. Oslo: 1989. (Doctoral Thesis, University of Oslo, 1990. English translation 1990.)

"Ascetic Autonomy: New Perspectives on Single Women in the Early Church." *Studia theologica* 43 (1989) 125–40.

". . . for han har sett til sin tjenerinne": Noen korte mariologiske refleksjoner." *Ung teologi* 22 (1989) 83–85.

"Hustavlen 1 Pet 3.1–7 og dens tradisjonshistoriske sammenheng." *Norsk teologisk tidsskrift* (1990) 101–14.

"Smerte og forløsning: Nytestamentlige fødselsbilder i spenningen mellom virkelighet og ritualisert utopi." *Norsk teologisk tidsskrift* 91 (1990) 85–99.

1991–2000

"De døde—de levendes spørsmål og smerte. Noen paulinske perspektiver." In *Tekst og rite: Vigsel og gravferd som teologisk utfordring. Foredrag fra etterutdanningsuken for prester, kateketer og diakoner Vestre Aker menighetshus, 17.–21. august 1992*, 2–10. Etterutdanning for prester; 1. Oslo: Universitetet i Oslo, Det teologiske fakultet, 1993.

"Den lange veien mot fellesskap: Den femte verdenskonferanse om Faith and Order." *Kirke og kultur* (1993) 425–37.

The Double Message: Patterns of Gender in Luke–Acts. Studies of the New Testament and its World. Edinburgh: T & T Clark, 1994. (Published translation of her doctoral thesis, University of Oslo, 1990. Republished in 2004.)

"The Gospel of Luke." In *Searching the Scriptures*, edited by Elisabeth Schüssler Fiorenza, 2:728–62. New York: Crossroad, 1994.

"Undere og åndelige øvelser: Tekstbetraktninger for 13. s. e. pinse, 1. rekke." In *Prekenen, et kunsthåndverk?*, edited by Geir Hellemo and Nils Jøran Riedl, 69–72. Etterutdanning for prester 1. Oslo: Etterutdanningskomitéen ved Det teologiske fakultet og Det praktisk-teologiske seminar, Universitetet i Oslo, 1994.

"Økumeniske observasjoner." *Norsk teologisk tidsskrift* 95 (1994) 131–51.

Mighty Minorities: Minorities in Early Christianity—Positions and Strategies: Essays in Honour of Jacob Jervell on His 70th Birthday 21 May 1995. Edited by Turid Karlsen Seim et al. Oslo: Scandinavian University Press, 1995. (Also published as issue 1 of *Studia Theologica*, 1995.)

"Døpt med en Ånd til å være ett legeme." In *Ånden blåser dit den vil: Ånd og spiritualitet som almenmenneskelig og økumenisk utfordring*, edited by Geir Hellemo og Nils Jøran Riedl, 55–62. Etterutdanning for prester 2. Oslo: Etterutdanningskomitéen ved Det teologiske fakultet, Det praktisk-teologiske seminar, Universitetet i Oslo, 1995.

"Fortellingen om den barmhjertige samaritan. En utfordring til hatets hermeneutikk." In *Upptäckter i kontexten. Teologiska föreläsningar till minne av Per Frostin*, edited by Sigurd Bergmann and Göran Eidevall, 52–72. Skrifter från Institutet för kontextuell teologi 3. Lund: Institutet för Kontextuell Teologi, 1995.

"Introduction." In *Mighty Minorities: Minorities in Early Christianity—Positions and Strategies: Essays in Honour of Jacob Jervell on His 70th Birthday 21 May 1995*, edited by Turid Karlsen Seim et al. Oslo: Scandinavian University Press, 1995. (Written together with David Hellholm and Halvor Moxnes. Also published in issue 1 of *Studia Theologica*, 1995.)

"Maria Magdalena—en disippel Jesus elsket." In *Maria Magdalenas evangelium: Fire gnostiske skrifter*, edited by Turid Nystøl Rian, 11–29. Emilias grøde. Oslo: Emilia, 1995. (2nd ed., 2002.)

"A Superior Minority? The Problem of Men's Headship in Ephesians 5." In *Mighty Minorities. Minorities in Early Christianity—Positions and Strategies: Essays in Honour of Jacob Jervell on His 70th Birthday 21 May 1995*, edited by Turid Karlsen Seim et al., 167–81. Oslo: Scandinavian University Press, 1995. (Also published in issue 1 of *Studia Theologica*, 1995.)

"Gjennombruddet i Porvoo—hva betyr det for den Norske kirke." *Årbok for Den norske kirke* (1995) 80–83.

"Kirken som communio—en utfordring til den praktiske teologi." *Kirke og kultur* 100 (1995) 227–29.

"Nødvendighet, nytte og tverrfaglighet: Perspektiver fra et profesjonstudium." In *Perspektiver på tvers: Disiplin og tverrfaglighet på det moderne forskningsuniversitet*, edited by Thomas Dahl and Knut H. Sørensen, 45–55. Trondheim: Tapir, 1997.

"Searching for the Silver Coin: A Response to Loretta Dornisch and Barbara Reid." *Biblical Research* 42 (1997) 32–42.

"Kirkens enhet i mangfoldets tid." *Kirke og kultur* 103 (1998) 415–27.

"Å være 'liv laga': Antikke forestillinger om fødsel." *Kirke og kultur* 103 (1998) 565–72.

"Alle vaart livs kilder er i deg." Refleksjoner over liv og død i Det nye testamente." In *Livet etter livet: Mennesket og døden*, edited by Notto R. Thelle, 39–51. Etterutdanning for prester 5. Oslo: Etterutdanningskomitéen ved Det teologiske fakultet og Det praktisk-teologiske seminar, Universitetet i Oslo, 1999.

"Children of the Resurrection: Perspectives on Angelic Asceticism in Luke-Acts." In *Asceticism and the New Testament*, edited by Leif E. Vaage and Vincent L. Wimbush, 115–25. New York: Routledge, 1999.

"Luke-Acts." In *The Oxford Companion to Christian Thought*, edited by Adrian Hastings et al., 397–98. Oxford: Oxford University Press, 2000.

"Parable." In *The Oxford Companion to Christian Thought*, edited by Adrian Hastings et al., 512–14. Oxford: Oxford University Press, 2000.

"Akademisk kultur og akademisk redelighet. Utdrag fra en samtale med Nils A. Dahl." *Norsk Teologisk Tidsskrift* 101 (2000) 90–93. (Written together with Trygve E. Wyller.)

"Approaching Luke: Glimpses of a Gospel." *Currents in Theology and Mission* 27 (2000) 444–52.

"Den Hellige Ånd og vi har besluttet: Tanker om makt og myndighet i kirken." *St. Sunniva* 8 (2000) 10–22.

"Fortolkning og forkynnelse: Det Nye Testamente ved Universitetet i Oslo i det 20. århundre." *Norsk teologisk tidsskrift* 101 (2000) 33–51. (Written together with Halvor Moxnes and Reidar Aasgaard.)

2001–2010

"Abraham, Ancestor or Archetype? A Comparison of Abraham-Language in 4 Maccabees and Luke-Acts." In *Antiquity and Humanity. Essays on Ancient Religion and Philosophy Presented to Hans Dieter Betz on His 70th Birthday*, edited by Adela Yarbro Collins and Margaret M. Mitchell, 27–42. Tübingen: Mohr Siebeck, 2001.

"Udødelig og kjønnsløs? Oppstandelseskroppen i lys av Lukas." In *Kropp og oppstandelse*, edited by Troels Engberg-Pedersen and Invild Sælid Gilhus, 80–98. Oslo: Pax, 2001.

"Den egentlige historien om Jesus. En analyse av Jacob Jervells fagprosa." *Kirke og kultur* (2001) 219–27.

"Conflicting Voices, Irony and Reiteration. An Exploration of the Narrational Structure of Luke 24:1–35 and Its Theological Implications." In *Fair Play: Diversity and Conflicts in Early Christianity. Essays in Honour of Heikki Räisänen*, edited by Christopher Tuckett and Kari Syreeni Ismo Dunderberg, 151–64. Supplements to Novum Testamentum 103. Leiden: Brill, 2002.

"'Sikkerhet for det som håpes': Faith and Order's arbeid med den apostoliske tro (Apostolic Faith-studiet) i et hermeneutisk og ekklesiologisk perspektiv." In *Teologi for kirken: Festskrift til professor dr.theol. Torleiv Austad på 65-årsdagen*, edited by Gunnar Heiene, Svein Olaf Thorbjørnsen, and Jan-Olav Henriksen, 34–46. Oslo: Verbum, 2002.

"Six Bible-Studies to the Gospel of Luke." In *"For the Healing of the World": Assembly Study Book: The Lutheran World Federation, Tenth Assembly, Winnipeg, Canada, 2003*, 45–48, 61–64, 69–71, 77–80, 95–98, and 113–15. Geneva: Lutheran World Federation, 2002.

"The Virgin Mother. Mary and Ascetic Discipleship in Luke." In *A Feminist Companion to Luke*, edited by Amy-Jill Levine and Marianne Blickenstaff, 89–105. Feminist Companions to the New Testament and Early Christian Writings 3. London: Sheffield Academic, 2002.

"Hvem er Abrahams barn? Tekstlige refleksjoner om identitet og hybridisering i hellenistisk jødedom." *Religionsvidenskabeligt Tidsskrift* 40 (2002) 75–84.

"In Heaven as On Earth? Resurrection, Body, Gender and Heavenly Rehearsals in Luke-Acts." In *Christian and Islamic Gender Models in Formative Traditions*, edited by Kari Elisabeth Børresen, 17–41. Studi e Testi TardoAntichi 2. Rome: Herder, 2004.

"Tracking Down the Bishop: A New Testament Exploration." In *Búsquedas y Senales: Estudios en Biblia, Teologia, Historia y Ecumenism. En homenaje a Ricardo Pietrantonio*, edited by Mercedes L. García Bachmann et al., 89–105. Buenos Aires: Lumen, 2004.

"In Living Memory: Reflections on 'Collective Memory' and Patterns of Commemoration in Early Christianity." In *Cracks in the Walls: Essays on Spirituality, Ecumenicity and Ethics. Festschrift for Anna Marie Aagaard on the Occasion of her 70th Birthday*, edited by Else Marie Wiberg Pedersen and Johannes Nissen, 93–106. Frankfurt: Lang, 2005.

"Lærespørsmål—hvem bestemmer? Autoritet og tolkningsmakt i et luthersk perspektiv." In *Den norske kirke—for folk flest: Aktuelle perspektiver på utviklingen av det kirkelig demokrati*, edited by Marit Halvorsen Hougsnæs, 22–30. KA-perspektiv. Oslo: KA Kirkelig arbeidsgiver- og interesseorganisasjon, 2005.

"Reflections on Authority in the Roman Catholic-Lutheran Dialogue." In *One, Holy, Catholic and Apostolic: Eumenical Reflections on the Church*, edited by Tamara Grdzelidze, 109–23. Faith and Order Paper 197. Geneva: WCC, 2005.

"Descent and Divine Paternity in the Gospel of John. Does the Mother Matter?" *New Testament Studies* 51 (2005) 361–75.

"Descent and Divine Paternity in the Gospel of John: Does the Mother Matter?" In *Gender and the Body in the Gospel of John*, edited by Gitte Buch-Hansen et al., 19–22. Working Papers 1. Copenhagen: Biblical Studies Section, University of Copenhagen, 2006.

"'Trudomssamfunn og ymist anna': Teologiske refleksjoner i en kirkelig reformsituasjon." In *Endring og tilhørighet: Statskirkespørsmålet i perspektiv*, edited by Ulla Schmidt, 205–10. KIFO perspektiv. Trondheim: Tapir, 2006.

"The Diaconal Ministry in the Church of Norway: Ecclesiological and Ecumenical Reflections on Recent Developments." *Reseptio* 1 (2006) 115–31.

"I Jesu følge: En kommentar til Halvor Moxnes' 'Hva er kristendom?'" *Norsk teologisk tidsskrift* (2007) 81–86.

Farsmakt og moderskap i antikken. Oslo: Scandinavian Academic, 2009. (Written together with Ingvild Sælid Gilhus and Gunhild Vidén.)

Metamorphoses: Resurrection, Body, and Transformative Practices in Early Christianity. Edited by Turid Karlsen Seim and Jorunn Økland. Ekstasis 1. Berlin: de Gruyter, 2009.

Woman as Subject and Object. Edited by Turid Karlsen Seim and Siri Sande. Acta ad archaeologiam et artium historiam pertinentia 22. Rome: Scienze e lettere, 2009.

"Introduction." In *Metamorphoses: Resurrection, Body and Transformative Practices in Early Christianity*, edited by Turid Karlsen Seim og Jorunn Økland, 1–19. Ekstasis 1. Berlin: de Gruyter, 2009. (Written together with Jorunn Økland.)

"Kjærlighet, kropp og kjønn: Efeserne 5:21–33—tolkning og resepsjon." In *Eros och Agape: Barmhärtighet, kärlek och mystik i den tidiga kyrkan. Föreläsningar hållna vid Nordiska patristikermötet i Lund 16–19 augusti 2006*, edited by Henrik Rydell Johnsén and Per Rönnegård, 28–48. Patristica Nordica 7. Skellefteå: Artos, 2009.

"Paul's Discourse on Desire and Devotion in 1 Corinthians 7." In *Saint Paul and Corinth*, edited by Konstantinos I. Belezos et al., 2:697–708. Athens: Ekdoseis Psichogios, 2009.

"The Resurrected Body in Luke-Acts: The Significance of Space." In *Metamorphoses: Resurrection, Body and Transformative Practices in Early Christianity*, edited by Turid Karlsen Seim and Jorunn Økland, 19–39. Ekstasis 1. Berlin: de Gruyter, 2009.

Private and Public in the Sphere of the Ancient City. Edited by Turid Karlsen Seim and
  Siri Sande. Acta ad archaeologiam et artium historiam pertinentia 23. Rome:
  Scienze e lettere, 2010.
"Feminist Criticism." In *Methods for Luke*, edited by Joel B. Green, 42–73. Cambridge:
  Cambridge University Press, 2010.
"Johannine Echoes in Early Montanism." In *The Legacy of John: Second-Century
  Reception of the Fourth Gospel*, edited by Tuomas Rasimus, 345–64. Supplements
  to Novum Testamentum 132. Leiden: Brill, 2010.
"Luke, Gospel of." In *The Cambridge Dictionary of Christianity*, edited by Daniel Patte,
  740–41. Cambridge: Cambridge University Press, 2010.
"Motherhood and Making of Fathers in Antiquity: Contextualizing Genetics in the
  Gospel of John." In *Women and Gender in Ancient Religions: Interdisciplinary
  Approaches*, edited by Stephen P. Ahearne-Kroll et al., 99–123. Wissenschaftliche
  Untersuchungen zum Neuen Testament 263. Tübingen: Mohr Siebeck, 2010.
"Race and Gender in St. Paul." In *In the Footsteps of St. Paul: An Academic Symposium.
  Papers Presented at the Pauline Symposium, October 11–16, 2008 under the Auspices
  of His All Holiness Ecumenical Patriarch Bartholomew*, edited by Demetrios
  Trakatelles, 181–96. Brookline, MA: Holy Cross Orthodox, 2010.

2011–2014

Inscriptions in Liturgical Spaces. Edited by Turid Karlsen Seim and Kristin Bliksrud
  Aavitsland. Acta ad archaeologiam et artium historiam pertinentia 24. Rome:
  Scienze e lettere, 2011. (With an introduction by the editors.)
"Baptismal Reflections in the Fourth Gospel." In *Ablution, Initiation, and Baptism: Late
  Antiquity, Early Judaism, and Early Christianity*, edited by David Hellholm et al.,
  717–34. Beihefte zur Zeitschrift für die neutestamentliche Wissenschaft und die
  Kunde der älteren Kirche 176/1. Berlin: de Gruyter, 2011.
"Fortolkning, forkynnelse og kjønn: Studiet av Det nye testamente inn i det 21.
  århundre." In *Teologi og modernitet: Universitetsteologien i det 20. hundreåret*,
  89–116. Oslo: Unipub forlag, 2011. (Written together with Halvor Moxnes and
  Reidar Aasgaard.)
"Ordinasjon av kvinner—noen økumeniske betraktninger." In *Hun våget å gå foran.
  Ingrid Bjerkås og kvinners prestetjeneste i Norge*, edited by Bjørg Kjersti Myren and
  Hanne Stenvaag, 274–83. Oslo: Verbum, 2011.
"Beyond the Joint Declaration on the Doctrine of Justification: Recent Developments
  in the Lutheran-Roman Catholic Dialogue." *Centro Pro Unione Bulletin* (2011)
  14–20.
Recycling Rome. Edited by Turid Karlsen Seim and Marina Prusac. Acta ad
  archaeologiam et artium historiam pertinentia 25. Rome: Scienze e lettere, 2012.
  (With a preface by the editors.)
"Frauen und Genderperspektiven im Johannesevangelium." In *Evangelien. Erzählungen
  und Geschichte*, edited by Irmtraud Fischer et al., 206–33. Die Bibel und die
  Frauen. Eine exegetisch-kulturgeschichtliche Enzyklopädie, Hebräische Bibel—
  Neues Testament 2/1. Stuttgart: Kohlhammer, 2012.
"Interfacing House and Church: Converting Household Codes to Church Order." In
  Text, Image and Christians in the Graeco-Roman World: A Festschrift in Honor of

David Lee Balch, edited by Aliou Cissé Niang and Carolyn Osiek, 53–71. Eugene, OR: Pickwick, 2012.

From Site to Sight: The Transformation of Place in Art and Literature. Edited by Turid Karlsen Seim and Victor Plahte Tschudi. Acta ad archaeologiam et artium historiam pertinentia 26. Rome: Scienze e lettere, 2013. (With a preface by the editors.)

"In Transit from Tangibility to Text. Negotiations of Liminality in John 20." In *To Touch or not to Touch? Interdisciplinary Perspectives on the Noli me tangere,* edited by Barbara Baert et al., 39–61. Annua Nuntia Lovaniensia 67. Leuven: Peeters, 2013.

Acta ad archaeologiam et artium historiam pertinentia. Edited by Turid Karlsen Seim. Acta ad archaeologiam et artium historiam pertinentia 27. Rome: Scienze e lettere, 2014.

* 9 7 8 0 2 2 7 1 7 5 9 6 5 *

An environmentally friendly book printed and bound in England by www.printondemand-worldwide.com

PEFC Certified

This product is
from sustainably
managed forests
and controlled
sources

PEFC™

PEFC/16-33-415

www.pefc.org

®

MIX

Paper from
responsible sources

FSC

www.fsc.org

FSC® C004959

This book is made entirely of sustainable materials; FSC paper for the cover and PEFC paper for the text pages.

Reprint of # - C0 - 229/152/25 - PB - Lamination Gloss - Printed on 11-May-16 04:29